CW01301274

RESEARCH HANDBOOK ON CHILD SOLDIERS

RESEARCH HANDBOOKS IN INTERNATIONAL LAW

This highly original series offers a unique appraisal of the state-of-the-art of research and thinking in international law. Taking a thematic approach, each volume, edited by a prominent expert, covers a specific aspect of international law or examines the international legal dimension of a particular strand of the law. A wide range of sub-disciplines in the spheres of both public and private law are considered; from international environmental law to international criminal law, from international economic law to the law of international organisations, and from international commercial law to international human rights law. The *Research Handbooks* comprise carefully commissioned chapters from leading academics as well as those with an emerging reputation. Taking a genuinely international approach to the law, and addressing current and sometimes controversial legal issues, as well as affording a clear substantive analysis of the law, these *Research Handbooks* are designed to inform as well as to contribute to current debates.

Equally useful as reference tools or introductions to specific topics, issues and debates, the *Research Handbooks* will be used by academic researchers, post-graduate students, practising lawyers and lawyers in policy circles.

Titles in this series include:

Research Handbook on UN Sanctions and International Law
Edited by Larissa van den Herik

Research Handbook on Remote Warfare
Edited by Jens David Ohlin

Handbook of Research on International Consumer Law, Second Edition
Edited by Geraint Howells, Iain Ramsay and Thomas Wilhelmsson

Research Handbook on Territorial Disputes in International Law
Edited by Marcelo G. Kohen and Mamadou Hébié

Research Handbook on the Sociology of International Law
Edited by Moshe Hirsch and Andrew Lang

Research Handbook on Human Rights and Investment
Edited by Yannick Radi

Research Handbook on International Water Law
Edited by Stephen C. McCaffrey, Christina Leb and Riley T. Denoon

Research Handbook on International Law and Peace
Edited by Cecilia M. Bailliet and Kjetil Mujezinovic Larsen

Research Handbook on Foreign Direct Investment
Edited by Markus Krajewski and Rhea Tamara Hoffmann

Research Handbook on Feminist Engagement with International Law
Edited by Susan Harris Rimmer and Kate Ogg

Research Handbook on Child Soldiers
Edited by Mark A. Drumbl and Jastine C. Barrett

Research Handbook on Child Soldiers

Edited by

Mark A. Drumbl

Class of 1975 Alumni Professor of Law and Director, Transnational Law Institute, Washington and Lee University, USA

Jastine C. Barrett

Independent Human Rights Consultant and Honorary Researcher, Kent Law School, University of Kent, UK

RESEARCH HANDBOOKS IN INTERNATIONAL LAW

Edward Elgar
PUBLISHING

Cheltenham, UK • Northampton, MA, USA

© The Editors and Contributors severally 2019

All rights reserved. No part of this publication may be reproduced, stored in a retrieval system or transmitted in any form or by any means, electronic, mechanical or photocopying, recording, or otherwise without the prior permission of the publisher.

Published by
Edward Elgar Publishing Limited
The Lypiatts
15 Lansdown Road
Cheltenham
Glos GL50 2JA
UK

Edward Elgar Publishing, Inc.
William Pratt House
9 Dewey Court
Northampton
Massachusetts 01060
USA

Paperback edition 2021

A catalogue record for this book
is available from the British Library

Library of Congress Control Number: 2019945343

This book is available electronically in the Elgaronline
Law subject collection
DOI 10.4337/9781788114486

ISBN 978 1 78811 447 9 (cased)
ISBN 978 1 78811 448 6 (eBook)
ISBN 978 1 78990 332 4 (paperback)

Typeset by Servis Filmsetting Ltd, Stockport, Cheshire

Printed and bound by CPI Group (UK) Ltd, Croydon, CR0 4YY

Contents

List of contributors	viii
Preface and acknowledgements	xiv
List of common abbreviations	xvi
Table of select treaties and other international and regional instruments	xviii

Introduction to the *Research Handbook on Child Soldiers*   1
Mark A. Drumbl and Jastine C. Barrett

PART I   THE CONCEPT AND CONSTRUCTION OF THE CHILD SOLDIER

1. In search of the lost kingdom of childhood   28
   Mohamed Kamara

2. Challenges for the protection of child victims of recruitment and use in an era of complex armed conflicts: the Colombian case   52
   Ana María Jiménez

3. The construction of gender in child soldiering in the Special Court for Sierra Leone   74
   Valerie Oosterveld

4. 'We were controlled, we were not allowed to express our sexuality, our intimacy was suppressed': sexual violence experienced by boys   95
   Omer Aijazi, Evelyn Amony and Erin Baines

5. Getting Tambo out of limbo: exploring alternative legal frameworks that are more sensitive to the agency of children and young people in armed conflict   110
   Karl Hanson and Christelle Molima

6. This Is Belonging: children and British military recruitment   132
   Rhys Crilley

PART II   CONDUCT: AGENCY, CAPACITY AND RESILIENCE

7. Child soldiers in historical and comparative perspective: creating a space for data-driven analysis   150
   David M. Rosen

8. The voiceless child soldiers of Afghanistan   175
   Anicée Van Engeland

9. Weaponizing the weak: the role of children in terrorist groups   195
   Mia Bloom

vi *Research handbook on child soldiers*

10 Retracing the journey of child soldiers and looking for the path to return them home: a report from southern Philippines 217
David N. Almarez, Ajree D. Malawani, Sittie Akima A. Ali, Princess Mae S. Chua and Primitivo C. Ragandang III

11 Children born of conflict-related sexual violence within armed groups: a case study of northern Uganda 240
Myriam Denov

12 Social reintegration following armed conflict in northern Uganda: how former child soldier young mothers use symbolic resources 258
Fiona Shanahan and Angela Veale

PART III ENCOUNTERS WITH THE LAW

13 The regional African legal framework on children: a template for more robust action on children and armed conflict? 279
Godfrey Odongo

14 Minors and miners: accountability beyond child soldiering in the Democratic Republic of Congo 298
Sharanjeet Parmar and Yann Lebrat

15 Crimes committed by child soldiers: an argument for coherence 325
Nikila Kaushik and Steven Freeland

16 Child soldiers in international courtrooms: unqualified perpetrators, erratic witnesses and irreparable victims? 350
Barbora Holá and Thijs B. Bouwknegt

17 Dominic Ongwen on trial: problematizing definitional boundaries and exploring the possibilities of socialization 374
Carse Ramos

18 Child soldiers and asylum – duality or dilemma? 390
Joseph Rikhof

PART IV AFTERWORLD(S)/AFTERWARDS: TRANSITIONAL JUSTICE AND BEYOND

19 Navigating the mystical: child soldiers and reintegration rituals in northern Uganda 409
Jastine C. Barrett

20 Child agency and resistance to discourses within the Paris Principles in rehabilitation and reintegration processes of former child soldiers in northern Uganda 436
Grace Akello

21	Children associated with Boko Haram: disassociation, protection, accountability and reintegration *Stuart Casey-Maslen*	452
22	Do no harm: how reintegration programmes for former child soldiers can cause unintended harm *Michael G. Wessells*	471
23	How to find the 'hidden' girl soldier? Two sets of suggestions arising from Liberia *Leena Vastapuu*	493

PART V EPILOGUE

Beyond 'the child soldier': from a recognition of complexity to an ethics of engagement   513
Nesam McMillan

Index   519

Contributors

Omer Aijazi is a Postdoctoral Fellow at the University of Toronto. His work lies at the intersections of social repair and non-normativity in settings of multiple forms of violence.

Grace Akello, PhD, is currently an Associate Professor and Coordinator of a pioneer Master's of Medical Anthropology Programme in East and Central Africa hosted by Gulu University. She trained in Medical Anthropology at the University of Amsterdam and Leiden University in the Netherlands, where she was a NUFFIC and WOTRO fellow respectively. Since 2012, she has been a Research Fellow at the African Studies Centre in Leiden University. Her main research interests include how people living in complex emergencies and with HIV/AIDS identify, prioritize and manage their health complaints.

Sittie Akima A. Ali is a Doctor of Public Administration candidate at Xavier University (Ateneo de Cagayan) in the Philippines. She is also the Focal Person of the Institute Records and Archives Office and Administrative Officer IV in the Office of the Vice Chancellor for Administration and Finance, Mindanao State University – Iligan Institute of Technology (MSU-IIT), Philippines. She lectures on civic welfare training at MSU-IIT and her research interests include social governance, public policy and administration and gender.

David N. Almarez (Doctor of Management) is the Vice Chancellor for Administration and Finance and Professor of Political Science, Mindanao State University – Iligan Institute of Technology (MSU-IIT) in the Philippines. His research interests include e-Government, democracy and government reform.

Evelyn Amony is a Researcher with the Justice and Reconciliation Project in Gulu, Uganda, an activist and chairperson of the Women's Advocacy Network and author of *I am Evelyn Amony: Reclaiming my Life from the Lord's Resistance Army* (University of Wisconsin Press 2015).

Erin Baines is the Ivan Head South–North Chair at the School of Public Policy and Global Affairs, the University of British Colombia. She is the author of *Vulnerable Bodies: Gender, the UN and the Global Refugee Crisis* (Ashgate 2017) and *Buried in the Heart: Women and Complex Victimhood in Northern Uganda* (Cambridge 2017).

Jastine C. Barrett is a UK-qualified lawyer and independent human rights consultant. She is currently an Honorary Researcher at Kent Law School, the University of Kent. She completed her PhD at the University of Cambridge and also holds an LLM in International Law and International Relations and a BA(Hons) in Languages. Jastine has served as Editor and Managing Editor for *CJICL* and on the management committee of the UK's Solicitors' International Human Rights Group. She is the author of *Child Perpetrators on Trial: Insights from Post-Genocide Rwanda* (Cambridge University Press 2019) and several peer-reviewed articles and book chapters on international human rights law and transitional justice. Her research interests include international human rights and child rights law and transitional justice.

Mia Bloom is Professor of Communication at Georgia State University. She conducts ethnographic field research in Europe, the Middle East and South Asia and speaks eight languages. Her books include *Dying to Kill: The Allure of Suicide Terror* (2005), *Living Together After Ethnic Killing* (with Roy Licklider) (2007) and *Bombshell: Women and Terror* (2011). Bloom's forthcoming book *Small Arms: Children and Terror* examines children in terrorist organizations and will be published with Cornell University Press (2019).

Thijs B. Bouwknegt is a Researcher at the NIOD Institute for War, Holocaust and Genocide Studies and Assistant Professor at the University of Amsterdam and Leiden University. Since 2003, he has attended, monitored and reported on atrocity crime trials at the ICTY, ICTR, SCSL, ICC, ECCC, STL and a variety of national jurisdictions in Africa and Europe.

Stuart Casey-Maslen is Honorary Professor at the University of Pretoria, specializing in humanitarian protection and the use of force under international law. He was the first head of research at the Geneva Academy of International Humanitarian Law and Human Rights in 2012–14. From 1999 to 2010 he was a research consultant for the Geneva International Centre for Humanitarian Demining, addressing mine action in more than 25 countries. In the mid-1990s, he served as researcher for the UN Study on the Impact of Armed Conflict on Children, worked as legal advisor at the International Committee of the Red Cross, and was subsequently the first Coordinator of the NGO Coalition to Stop the Use of Children as Soldiers.

Princess Mae S. Chua is an instructor in the Department of Political Science, Mindanao State University – Iligan Institute of Technology (MSU-IIT), Philippines. Her research interests include gender, human rights and public policy.

Rhys Crilley is a Postdoctoral Research Associate in Global Media and Communication at the Open University, UK. His research explores the intersections of social media and global politics with a specific interest in war and militarism. Rhys has published several journal articles and he is currently working on writing his first monograph on the legitimation of war in social media. He tweets at @rhyscrilley.

Myriam Denov is a Full Professor at McGill University and holds the Canada Research Chair in Youth, Gender and Armed Conflict. Her research interests lie in the areas of children and families affected by war, migration and the intergenerational impact thereof. A specialist in participatory research, she has worked with war-affected children and families in Africa, Asia and the Americas. She has presented expert evidence in court on child soldiers and has advised government and non-governmental organizations on children in armed conflict and girls in armed groups. She has authored and co-authored five books addressing the impact of war on children and was recently inducted into the College of the Royal Society of Canada.

Mark A. Drumbl is the Class of 1975 Alumni Professor of Law at Washington and Lee University, where he also serves as Director of the University's Transnational Law Institute. His research and teaching interests include public international law, global environmental governance, international criminal law, post-conflict justice, and transnational legal process. He has published and lectured widely in these areas. His highly acclaimed book *Reimagining Child Soldiers in International Law and Policy* (OUP 2012) challenges much of conventional wisdom when it comes to preventing child soldiering, meaningfully reintegrating child soldiers and engaging with former child solders as vibrant contributors to post-conflict reconciliation. In 2007, he wrote *Atrocity, Punishment, and International Law* (CUP).

Steven Freeland is Dean of the School of Law and Professor of International Law at Western Sydney University and holds permanent Visiting Professor positions at a number of European and other universities. He has been a Visiting Professional within the Appeals Chamber at the International Criminal Court and a Special Advisor to the Danish Foreign Ministry in matters related to the ICC. He represents the Australian Government at various United Nations Conferences and Committee Meetings and is the Co-Editor of *Annotated Leading Cases of International Criminal Tribunals*, a long-established series of casebooks annotating the jurisprudence of all of the major international courts/tribunals administering international criminal justice.

Karl Hanson is Professor in Public Law and Deputy Director of the Centre for Children's Rights Studies at the University of Geneva (Switzerland). His research and publications deal with theorizing children's rights studies, rights advocacy for children, working children and juvenile justice. He is an editor of the journal *Childhood* and chair of the Children's Rights European Academic Network (CREAN).

Barbora Holá is Senior Researcher at the Netherlands Institute for the Study of Crime and Law Enforcement and Associate Professor at Vrije Universiteit Amsterdam. She is co-director of the Center for International Criminal Justice and co-chair of the European Society of Criminology Group on Atrocity Crimes and Transitional Justice. She has an interdisciplinary focus and studies transitional justice after atrocities, in particular international criminal trials and the punishment of international crimes.

Ana María Jiménez is a human rights lawyer with extensive experience with children and armed conflict in Colombia. She is Professor of International Human Rights Law and International Humanitarian Law at the Santo Tomas University in Colombia. She is the former coordinator of the Coalition against the involvement of boys, girls and youths in the armed conflict in Colombia and co-founder of Quilting for Change (Consultoría Social para el Cambio). For the past 12 years she has advised the Ombudsman's Office, the Colombian Institute for Family Welfare (ICBF) and the Prosecutor's Office in Colombia, as well as different international NGOs on child rights and transitional justice.

Mohamed Kamara teaches French and Francophone literatures and cultures at Washington and Lee University, Virginia. He has published on Léopold Sédar Senghor, Abdelkébir Khatibi, Birago Diop and Yulisa Amadu Maddy, as well as on the teaching of the Francophone African novel and French colonial education. Mohamed is currently working on a book-length study of French colonial education.

Nikila Kaushik is an Australian lawyer specializing in criminal law and international law. She practises in Sydney and has taught at Western Sydney University and the University of New South Wales.

Yann Lebrat is an international development professional specializing in the extractive industries. He is a Senior Manager at CowaterSogema, a development consulting firm, and leads on the company's work in extractives. Yann has implemented donor-funded development programmes throughout sub-Saharan Africa, including in the Democratic Republic of Congo. He is an experienced researcher on the impact of extractives on conflict and communities, having conducted studies on the issue in Somaliland and South Sudan, and having worked as a human rights analyst for mining multinationals.

Ajree D. Malawani is a Political Science PhD candidate at the Universitas Muhammadiyah Yogyakarta (UMY), Indonesia. She is also a Research Assistant at the Jusuf Kaila School of Government, Universitas Muhammadiyah Yogyakarta (UMY), Indonesia. Her main research interests are social governance and policy-making.

Nesam McMillan is a Senior Lecturer in Global Criminology at the University of Melbourne. Her research and teaching focuses on social, legal and political understandings of international crime, international justice and structural injustice. Her work interrogates the ethics and politics of how and what events of harm come to matter in global and local spheres, from a post-colonial and post-structuralist perspective. She was also a Chief Investigator on the 'Minutes of Evidence' project which brought together researchers, educators, government and community agencies and performing artists to spark new modes of engaging with structural and colonial injustice and explore the possibility of structural justice (http://www.minutesofevidence.com.au/).

Christelle Molima holds a degree in law from the Catholic University of Bukavu, Democratic Republic of the Congo (DRC), a specialized Master's in Judicial Careers from the Lumière University Lyon 2, France, and a research Master's in the History of Human Rights from the Pierre Mendès-France University in Grenoble. She is currently undertaking a PhD in Law at the Centre for Children's Rights Studies at the University of Geneva, Switzerland, on the criminal responsibility of child soldiers in the context of their social and community reintegration in eastern DRC.

Godfrey Odongo is a Senior Program Officer with the Human Rights Program at the Wellspring Philanthropic Fund, a US-based private foundation. He has previously served as a regional research expert with Amnesty International's International Secretariat, in a programme advisory role with Save the Children – Sweden, and held research fellowship roles with the Dullar Omar Institute for Constitutional Law, Governance and Human Rights at the University of the Western Cape, South Africa and the Danish Institute for Human Rights in Copenhagen, Denmark. An advocate of the High Court of Kenya, he is the author of several book chapters and peer-reviewed articles on the domestication of international human and children's rights law and norms.

Valerie Oosterveld is a Professor of International Law at the University of Western Ontario Faculty of Law (Western Law) in Canada. Her publications focus on gender issues within international criminal justice. Prior to joining Western Law, she served in the Legal Affairs Bureau of Canada's Department of Foreign Affairs and International Trade, providing legal advice related to the International Criminal Court, the Special Court for Sierra Leone and other transitional justice mechanisms. She holds a JSD and LLM (Columbia), an LLB (Toronto) and a BSocSc (Ottawa).

Sharanjeet Parmar is an international human rights lawyer and President of Glasshouse Initiatives, a development consulting firm. She has served as a war crimes prosecutor with the Special Court for Sierra Leone and lectured on human rights at Harvard Law School. She has over 15 years' experience working across Africa and Asia on children and armed conflict, gender, justice and security issues. She has published numerous articles on international justice, gender equality and sexual violence, as well as on children's rights in situations of armed conflict.

Primitivo C. Ragandang III is a Doctor of Sustainable Development and Assistant Professor in the Department of Political Science, Mindanao State University – Iligan Institute of Technology (MSU-IIT), Philippines. He also coordinates the university's Centre for Human Rights Education. His research interests include peace and conflict and sustainability.

Carse Ramos is Assistant Professor of Sociology at Rhode Island College. She earned her PhD from the Graduate Institute of International and Development Studies in Geneva, where her dissertation focused on Uganda's transitional justice policy and its mechanisms for navigating the overlapping victim-perpetrator spaces occupied by former child conscripts. She has been working and travelling in the Great Lakes Region of Africa since 2008.

Joseph Rikhof is an Adjunct Professor at the Faculty of Common Law of the University of Ottawa where he teaches the course International Criminal Law. His expertise lies in the law related to genocide, war crimes and crimes against humanity, especially as practised at the domestic level and in the context of immigration and refugee law. He has published over 45 articles as well as the books *The Criminal Refugee: The Treatment of Asylum Seekers with a Criminal Background in International and Domestic Law* (2012), *International and Transnational Criminal Law* (co-authored with Robert Currie, 2nd edition, 2013) and *A Theory of Punishable Participation in Universal Crimes* (co-authored with Terje Einarsen, 2018).

David M. Rosen is Professor of Anthropology and Law at Fairleigh Dickinson University. His recent books include *Child Soldiers in the Western Imagination: From Patriots to Victims* (2015) and *Armies of the Young: Child Soldiers in War and Terrorism* (2005). His articles have appeared in numerous scholarly journals, including *American Anthropologist*, *Ethnology*, *Anthropological Quarterly* and the *Connecticut Journal of International Law*. His current research is on Jewish child partisans in Eastern Europe during World War II and the Holocaust.

Fiona Shanahan is a psychologist whose work involves psychosocial interventions to support family and community resilience, with a specific focus on sexual and gender-based violence responses in humanitarian emergencies and protracted conflict. Her research and publications concern the reintegration of women and girls formerly associated with the LRA and their children born of forced marriage in northern Uganda, and psychosocial interventions in humanitarian settings including Sierra Leone and Syria/Lebanon. She is a Humanitarian Protection Adviser with Trócaire, fulfilling a global advisory role which involves supporting Trócaire and local partners' humanitarian programmes in Myanmar, DRC, Syria/Lebanon, Pakistan, South Sudan and Somalia.

Anicée Van Engeland is a senior lecturer at Cranfield University in the United Kingdom. She was a human rights worker and an aid worker before becoming an academic. Her main areas of research and practice are international law and governance with a focus on the Muslim world.

Leena Vastapuu is a Visiting Research Fellow at the Tampere Peace Research Institute. Leena is the author of *Liberia's Women Veterans: War, Roles and Reintegration* (Zed Books 2018), which narrates Liberian civil wars through the eyes of 133 girl war veterans. The book is based on her doctoral dissertation; recently, the Foundation for Foreign Policy Research awarded Leena with the Raimo Väyrynen dissertation prize for the best doctoral dissertation on international politics written in a Finnish university between 2016 and 2018. Leena has studied and/or worked in Liberia, Senegal and Zambia and is the scientific head of the Metal Women project that popularizes her research results through contemporary art.

Angela Veale is Lecturer in Applied Psychology, University College Cork and a child psychotherapist. Her research and publications examine issues related to the post-conflict social reintegration of children and families, children, globalization, 'new migrations' and psychosocial interventions. She was partner to the NORFACE-funded Transnational Child-Raising project between Europe and Africa, and co-director of the Provictimus/Oak Foundation-funded project on the social reintegration of young mothers formerly associated with armed groups in Sierra Leone, Liberia and northern Uganda. She is a former Fulbright Scholar.

Michael G. Wessells is Professor at Columbia University in the Program on Forced Migration and Health. A long-time psychosocial and child protection practitioner, he is former Co-Chair of the IASC Task Force on Mental Health and Psychosocial Support in Emergency Settings. He also served on the Steering Committee that developed the Paris Principles and is the author of *Child Soldiers: From Violence to Protection*. He regularly advises UN agencies, governments and donors on issues of child protection and psychosocial support.

Preface and acknowledgements

This *Research Handbook* aspires to further enrich current conversations about child soldiers. Our goal as editors is to create a space in which to better understand child soldiering so as to more effectively deter the practice, sustainably reintegrate children associated with armed forces or armed groups, as well as promote a vibrant culture of juvenile rights and gender equality. It is fitting that the *Research Handbook* appears in a series dedicated to international law, in that both of us are lawyers, but our aim is to bring law into contact with a multi-disciplinary kaleidoscope of critical approaches about children affected by armed conflict. This *Research Handbook* harnesses thought-provoking contributions from authors on six continents who reflect a broad array of perspectives, methodologies and experiences. We would like to warmly thank our contributors for the enthusiasm, collegial spirit and commitment with which they engaged in this project. As contributors, you all made our journey as editors that much easier. We hope that we have done justice to your brilliant work and built a sum that is a little bit larger than the parts. As for this sum – this *Research Handbook* – we intend that it shall be of interest to academics, practitioners, activists, officials and students from all walks of life concerned with the rights of the child. While this *Research Handbook* sets out how children caught up in violent circumstances experience adversity, loss and pain, we hope it strikes a resonant chord with its emphasis on the capacity, humanity and potentiality of youth.

Many of the chapters herein are informed by interviews or more informal conversations with child soldiers, former child soldiers and people who have worked on behalf of children in conflict. This book would not have been possible without such an intimate sharing of personal experiences, which in the case of child soldiers were often harrowing but frequently inspirational, and we extend our deepest thanks to them. These accounts are carefully anonymized or, in the rare case when not fully anonymized, permissions and consents have been obtained by contributors.

Jastine Barrett wishes to express her gratitude to Kent Law School, which provided the time, space and financial support for her to work on this project whilst she was a postdoctoral researcher. Mark Drumbl similarly thanks his home institution – Washington and Lee University, School of Law – for its positivity and backing, in particular that of the Frances Lewis Law Center. Both of us appreciate the hard work undertaken by Washington and Lee law students in editing and formatting the text: Lauren Sayers, Ryan Johnson, Matt Dare, Carrie Macon, Natey Kinzounza, Courtney Wolf, David Thompson and Brittney Ryers-Hindbaugh. Mark also thanks Terri Byrnes and Franklin Runge for ongoing assistance. We are in addition very appreciative to Edward Elgar Publishing for commissioning this book in the first place, and in particular to Laura Mann, Ben Booth and Alex Pettifer for their encouragement and ongoing support.

While the journey to edit this *Research Handbook* and bring it to fruition has been deeply rewarding, it has not come without some sacrifice. The time spent in the journey has been enlivening, to be sure, but also meant time away from others. And those others, well, without their unconditional support the journey to finish this book would not have been possible. Mark thanks Michelle for her patience, laughter and love over many marvellous years; their sons Paul and Luke for the joy they bring during a childhood through which they are so rapidly bounding; and his parents for the grandparenthood they now are sharing. Mark is indebted to friends near and far for all their input and ideas about children and conflict – for chats, conversations, unique chime and rhyme. From Jastine, a special thanks goes to Paul for his support – moral, emotional and in the form of wine and good holidays – and to Giuseppe and Huxley who, whilst they will never read this book, provided company and amusement throughout the writing and editing process. It might be a little unusual for the editors to thank each other, so we confine ourselves to saying what a truly fun editorial journey this has been for both of us. We started out as international law colleagues, who had met each other just a handful of times, but through this *Research Handbook*, have become firm friends. It is fantastic of course to get this *Research Handbook* out into the public domain, but we will miss our transatlantic Skype calls: perhaps we will just have to find another project to embark on.

Mark A. Drumbl and Jastine C. Barrett

List of common abbreviations

AFRC	Armed Forces Revolutionary Council
AU	African Union
AUC	Autodefensas Unidas de Colombia (United Self-Defense Forces of Columbia)
BiH	Bosnia and Herzegovina
CAC	Children and Armed Conflict
CAR	Central African Republic
CDF	Civil Defence Forces
CRC	United Nations Convention on the Rights of the Child
DDR	Disarmament, demobilization and reintegration
DRC	Democratic Republic of the Congo
ECCC	Extraordinary Chambers in the Courts of Cambodia
ELN	Ejército de Liberación Nacional
FARC	Fuerzas Armadas Revolucionarias de Colombia
FARDC	Forces Armées de la République Démocratique du Congo
FRELIMO	Mozambican Liberation Front (Frente de Libertação de Moçambique)
ICC	International Criminal Court
ICCPR	International Covenant on Civil and Political Rights
ICRC	International Committee of the Red Cross
ICTR	International Criminal Tribunal for Rwanda
ICTY	International Criminal Tribunal for the former Yugoslavia
IDDRS	Integrated Disarmament, Demobilization and Reintegration Standards
IDP	internally displaced person
ISIS	Islamic State of Iraq and Syria
LRA	Lord's Resistance Army
LTTE	Liberation Tigers of Tamil Eelam
LURD	Liberians United for Reconciliation and Democracy
MILF	Moro Islamic Liberation Front
MNLF	Moro National Liberation Front
MODEL	Movement for Democracy in Liberia
NGOs	non-governmental organizations
NPFL	National Patriotic Front of Liberia
NRA	National Resistance Army
OHCHR	Office of the United Nations High Commissioner for Human Rights
OPAC	Optional Protocol to the Convention on the Rights of the Child on the Involvement of Children in Armed Conflict
OTP	Office of the Prosecutor (ICC)
PTSD	post-traumatic stress disorder
RENAMO	Mozambican National Resistance (Resistência Nacional de Moçambique)
RUF	Revolutionary United Front

SCSL	Special Court for Sierra Leone
STL	Special Tribunal for Lebanon
TRC	truth and reconciliation commission
UN	United Nations
UNHCR	United Nations High Commissioner for Refugees
UNICEF	United Nations Children's Fund
UNSC	United Nations Security Council
UNSG	United Nations Secretary-General
UNTAET	UN Transitional Administration in East Timor
UPC	Union des patriotes congolais
UPDF	Uganda People's Defence Forces

Table of select treaties and other international and regional instruments

Accord entre le gouvernement de la République du Sénégal et l'Union Africaine sur la création de chambres africaines extraordinaires au sein des juridictions Sénégalaises (22 August 2012) [EAC Accord]
African Charter on Human and Peoples' Rights (entered into force 21 October 1986), 1520 UNTS 217
African Charter on the Rights and Welfare of the Child (entered into force 29 November 1999), OAU Doc. CAB/LEG/24.9/49
Agreement between the United Nations and the Lebanese Republic on the Establishment of a Special Tribunal for Lebanon (6 February 2007), annex to UNSC Resolution 1757 (30 May 2007) [STL Statute]
Cape Town Principles and Best Practices on the Prevention of Recruitment of Children into the Armed Forces and Demobilization and Social Reintegration of Child Soldiers in Africa (27–30 April 1997) [Cape Town Principles]
Convention Against Torture and Other Cruel, Inhuman or Degrading Treatment or Punishment (entered into force 26 June 1987), 1465 UNTS 85 [CAT]
Convention Concerning the Prohibition and Immediate Action for the Elimination of the Worst Forms of Child Labour (ILO No. 182) (entered into force 19 November 2000), 2133 UNTS 161 [ILO Convention 182]
Convention on the Elimination of All Forms of Discrimination Against Women (entered into force 3 September 1981), 1249 UNTS 13 [CEDAW]
Convention on the Prevention and Punishment of the Crime of Genocide (entered into force 12 January 1951), 78 UNTS 277 [Genocide Convention]
Convention on the Rights of the Child (entered into force 2 September 1990), 1577 UNTS 3 [CRC]
Convention Relating to the Status of Refugees (entered into force 22 April 1954) 189 UNTS 137 [Refugee Convention]
European Convention for the Protection of Human Rights and Fundamental Freedoms, as subsequently amended (entered into force 3 September 1953), 213 UNTS 222 [ECHR]
Geneva Convention Relative to the Protection of Civilian Persons in Time of War (Fourth Geneva Convention) (entered into force 21 October 1950), 75 UNTS 287
International Covenant on Civil and Political Rights (entered into force 23 March 1976), 999 UNTS 171 [ICCPR]
International Covenant on Economic, Social and Cultural Rights (entered into force 3 January 1976), 993 UNTS 3 [ICESCR]
Law on the Establishment of the Extraordinary Chambers in the Courts of Cambodia for the Prosecution of Crimes Committed During the Period of Democratic Kampuchea, with inclusion of amendments (27 October 2004), NS/RKM/1004/006 [ECCC Law]
Optional Protocol to the Convention on the Rights of the Child on the Involvement of

Children in Armed Conflict (entered into force 12 February 2002), 2173 UNTS 222 [OPAC]

Paris Commitments to Protect Children from Unlawful Recruitment or Use by Armed Forces or Armed Groups (February 2007) [Paris Commitments]

Paris Principles: Principles and Guidelines on Children Associated with Armed Forces or Armed Groups (February 2007) [Paris Principles]

Protocol Additional to the Geneva Conventions of 12 August 1949 and Relating to the Protection of Victims of International Armed Conflicts (entered into force 7 December 1978), 1125 UNTS 3 [Additional Protocol I]

Protocol Additional to the Geneva Conventions of 12 August 1949 and Relating to the Protection of Victims of Non-International Armed Conflicts (entered into force 7 December 1978), 1125 UNTS 609 [Additional Protocol II]

Rome Statute of the International Criminal Court (entered into force 1 July 2002), 2187 UNTS 90 [Rome Statute or ICC Statute]

Statute of the Special Court for Sierra Leone, annexed to the Agreement between the United Nations and the Government of Sierra Leone on the Establishment of the Special Court for Sierra Leone (entered into force 10 April 2002), 2178 UNTS 137 [SCSL Statute]

United Nations Standard Minimum Rules for the Administration of Juvenile Justice, adopted by General Assembly Resolution 40/33 of 29 November 1985 [Beijing Rules]

Universal Declaration of Human Rights, UNGA Resolution 217A(III) (10 December 1948) [Universal Declaration]

Vancouver Principles on Peacekeeping and the Prevention of the Recruitment and Use of Child Soldiers (15 November 2017) [Vancouver Principles]

Introduction to the *Research Handbook on Child Soldiers*
Mark A. Drumbl and Jastine C. Barrett*

> I was skinny, weakly, slight; you were strong, tall, broad.
> Franz Kafka, *Letter to Father* (1919)[1]

Throughout history, armed conflict has ensnared children. On occasion such children have been lauded as heroes or, at least, praised for their martial courage in the darkness of desperate times. Increasingly, however, the involvement of children in armed conflict is no longer seen as unbecoming or an anguished last stand but, instead, as flatly impermissible with the affected children projected as afflicted victims. Global consciousness has shifted. The drift of international human rights law, international criminal law and international humanitarian law both reflects and hardens this shift. The relationship of the child with armed conflict has migrated from one informed by ethics, needs and morality to one regulated by law, rules and public policy. The international community is progressively moving towards a position where the conscription, enlistment or use in hostilities of persons under the age of 18 – in particular by armed groups but also increasingly by armed forces – is seen as unlawful.

Many activist and humanitarian groups commit to the cause of ending child soldiering. UNICEF and other United Nations (UN) organs have deeply invested themselves in this mission as well. In 1996, pursuant to a UN General Assembly resolution, Graça Machel of Mozambique submitted a ground-breaking report entitled *Impact of Armed Conflict on Children* (widely known as the Machel Report).[2] The Machel Report firmly put children and violent conflict on the international agenda and has had considerable social constructivist influence. In light of one of its recommendations, for example, the Office of the Special Representative on Children and Armed Conflict was established within the UN system. The UN Security Council, generally fractured, has unified to issue 12 resolutions over the past two decades on children in armed conflict.[3] The focus of law- and policy-makers has further expanded to address the place of children in terrorist groups and to interrogate how counter-terrorist strategies and initiatives should approach such children.

Popular culture, along with the international legal imagination, generates a rather simplified image of the child soldier: stereotypically, a poor, abducted, prepubescent African boy, in dilapidated sandals, barely able to hold his AK-47. This essentialized image nonetheless belies the far greater complexity of *where* children become implicated

---

* Some parts of this Introduction draw from and re-work sections of Drumbl 2019.
[1] Kafka 2018: 15.
[2] Machel 1996.
[3] These are: UN Security Council Resolutions 1261 (1999), 1314 (2000), 1379 (2001), 1460 (2003), 1539 (2004), 1612 (2005), 1882 (2009), 1998 (2011), 2068 (2012), 2143 (2014), 2225 (2015) and 2427 (2018).

1

in armed conflict and *when* (as a matter of age) children become soldiers, as well as *how* and *why* they become involved. Readers may be surprised to learn the following facts: many children soldier outside Africa (and increasingly so); many children fulfil functions that do not involve carrying weapons; most child soldiers worldwide are adolescents rather than young children; the most common path to militarized life is not abduction and kidnapping but for children to come forward with varying degrees of volition and become enlisted; and children may face greater threats from their 'side' than from the 'enemy', including sexual slavery and forced marriage.

In assembling contributions for this *Research Handbook on Child Soldiers*, we as editors have sought to imbue the project with a global scope, disciplinary diversity and innovative angles. We hope to lift the reader beyond customary places and reflexive spaces and increasingly ill-fitting conventionalities.

Although it is estimated that 40 per cent of child soldiers worldwide are girls, the invisibility of the girl soldier from the imagery of child soldiering – and hence from rehabilitative and re-integrative programming – remains deeply disappointing. Many research studies on child soldiers that do approach gender do so as a silo, that is, as a separate dimension. This *Research Handbook* proceeds differently. It holistically incorporates gender throughout the entire text as a core constitutive element of violence, reintegration, identity and transition. In this vein, as Valerie Oosterveld has compellingly noted, the goal is to 'surface' the experiences of girls, and to do so integrally and not in a separate side-bar.[4] This means 'surfacing' the multiple ways in which armed conflict affects girls (and how girls affect armed conflict) – as victims, bystanders, side-standers, perpetrators and leaders – with a view towards promoting cultures of juvenile rights and gender equality. This *Research Handbook*, moreover, also aims to 'surface' the experiences of boys, including as perpetrators but also as victims of wretched sexual violence, thereby presenting boys in the variety of composite roles they may play in armed conflict.

The historicity of child soldiers – of drummer boys and Spartans and Jeanne d'Arc – also means that child soldiering has a deep intertemporal dimension to it. This *Research Handbook* seeks to address this as well, by including contributions that present the *then* as well as the *now*. The experiences of the child soldier are dual in nature: the life of the soldier as lived in the body and soul of the child. These experiences are intertwined – oxymoronically perhaps – but each is fragile in its own way. The soldiering aspect erupts with threats, chaos, brutality, hunger, opportunity, loss and victory. Childhood, too, presents as a moment of contingency. As Franz Kafka remembers, childhood implicitly is a state of vulnerability: the inexorability of smallness in contrast to the unavoidability of the girth of adults, adults who take up all the room, who suck up all the oxygen. Kafka, assuredly, was no child soldier. Growing up as he did in Prague, when he did at the turn of the twentieth century, Kafka did come of age amid periods of distress and violence: wars, the imposition and dissolution of empire, the reality of his Jewishness in a world besotted with anti-Semitism. But, no, Kafka didn't soldier. In his *Letter to Father* he touches nonetheless on childhood. And his childhood was a taut one. It was one of anxiety. Along with masterpiece novels, Kafka wrote over 1,500 letters in the 41 years of his life. He loved writing letters. He was impatient to receive them from others. *Letter to*

---

[4] Oosterveld in this volume.

Father, which he penned at the age of 36, is his longest. It filled over 100 sides of written manuscript pages. Yet Kafka never sent it. Instead, it was published well after his death and after the death – several years later – of his father, to whom the letter was addressed. Hermann Kafka, the father, was by all means a towering – if not omniscient – figure (certainly to Franz). Starting from nothing in a village in Bohemia, Hermann began as a haberdasher and then grew into a commercially successful shopkeeper. His shop, located in the oldest part of Prague's gorgeous Old Town, was a central fixture of Franz's life. Franz's memories, however, were sour. The father was strict and demanding. He was tough. Franz, the eldest and only surviving boy, was not. Franz struggled – as all children do, though Franz struggled a great deal – to be himself, to become himself, to move out of the shadows of the adult, to speak and not only be spoken to. Kafka's letter, then, is as much about him as it is about all children; it is as much about his recollections as it is about all adults when they replay their childhood(s); it is about agency and authority, love and suffocation, abuse and growth, legacies and reincarnations.

One of the goals of this *Research Handbook* is – tracing Kafka's words that opened this introduction – to make the child *less slight*, and the adult *less broad*. Doing so may blunt the might of gerontocracy and lay the groundwork for more humanistic relations among ages and a richer culture of intergenerational equity. Such a recalibration seems all the more necessary in a world in which the future feels so precarious due to the conduct of the adults of today; with legacies of climate change, for example, among other destructive *imperia* foisted upon the young as their inheritance. This, too, is a goal of this *Research Handbook*: to think twice about the forces, and the orthodoxies, that conspire to crowd out the child (and the future) with the needs of the adult (and today). We hope to make the child a greater part of the present.

While most of the contributors to this *Research Handbook* are not lawyers – and one of the sparks catalysing this volume is to bridge disciplinary and professional divides – international law, best practices and transnational policies constitute a central touchstone of the discussion. In order to welcome readers to this thicket and offer some common ground, this introduction sets forth a snapshot of how law, policy and best practices attribute responsibility for child soldiering and approach the allocation of responsibility to child soldiers. This introduction continues with an overview of the contents of this *Research Handbook*. It ends by gesturing towards roads not taken, gaps that arise and journeys that still might be initiated. First, however, three quick successive interventions: first on terminology, then on globality and last on an emancipatory epistemology.

1. A NOTE ON TERMINOLOGY

The 2007 Paris Commitments and Paris Principles, two connected non-binding instruments, cultivated different language than 'child soldier', that is, 'a child associated with an armed force or armed group'.[5] The Paris Principles did so to underscore the variety

---

[5] These Principles and Commitments, endorsed by 108 states, build upon the 1997 Cape Town Principles and Best Practices on the Recruitment of Children into the Armed Forces and on Demobilization and Social Reintegration of Child Soldiers in Africa.

of roles that children may play in armed conflict, namely as more than 'soldiering', and also to recognize the range of actors that may recruit or use them.[6] According to the Paris Principles:

> A child associated with an armed force or armed group' refers to any person below 18 years of age who is or who has been recruited or used by an armed force or armed group in any capacity, including but not limited to children, boys, and girls used as fighters, cooks, porters, messengers, spies or for sexual purposes. It does not only refer to a child who is taking or has taken a direct part in hostilities.

The phrase 'children associated with armed forces and armed groups' is indeed tongue-tying, so UN agencies and international activists have turned to the acronym CAAFAG instead. Yet this, too, is phonetically awkward. It is noteworthy, in a cyclical sense, that the most recent set of political commitments on the topic of children affected by armed conflict, fostered by the Canadian government in 2017, are expressly titled the Vancouver Principles on Peacekeeping and the Prevention of the Recruitment and Use of Child Soldiers.[7] The old phrase, once disfavoured yet still evocative, seems to be regaining some ground.

So the bottom line is this: in this *Research Handbook* we tend to deploy the term 'child soldier' but always understand its meaning to reflect the definition as provided by the Paris Principles.

The lines between the delinquent, criminal, terrorist, extremist and soldier may be gauzy and may be appropriated for ulterior purposes. Language matters. For example: how to narratively imagine 17-year-old Burhan Hassan, a straight-A high schooler who disappeared from Minnesota in 2008 for Somalia to train for recruitment into al-Shabaab only to be killed half a year later?[8] Was Burhan a child terrorist, a child gang member, a child thug, or a child soldier?[9] The 'law on child soldiers' differentiates armed groups (and armed forces) from other groups – thugs, gangs, criminal organizations – and bestows legal personality only on armed groups (and armed forces), meaning that the protective embrace, for example of the Paris Principles, only hugs children associated with groups determined to have the capacity to engage in armed conflict. States may resist the appellation of child 'soldier' to children associated with terrorist groups, citing security concerns. This jeopardizes the rights of those children and triggers potential abuses.[10]

This *Research Handbook* adopts a broad lens and therefore also discusses children not associated with an armed force or armed group whatsoever but otherwise affected by conflict-related violence, as well as children associated with groups discursively character-

---

[6] An armed force refers to the national militaries of a state, whereas an armed group refers to a fighting force that is separate from a state, for example, rebel groups.

[7] As of 12 October 2018, 68 states have endorsed the Vancouver Principles. These Principles strive to prevent child recruitment in the context of peacekeeping operations and mandate peacekeepers to receive clear guidance regarding children associated with armed forces or armed groups.

[8] Many thanks to Hawa Allen for sharing her thoughts on Burhan Hassan; see also Bloom in this volume.

[9] For discussion of comparable tensions within Colombia, see Jiménez in this volume.

[10] For discussion of Omar Khadr and other children, see Rosen in this volume and Casey-Maslen in this volume.

ized as 'terrorist' or 'extremist' rather than 'armed'. Children in 'criminal syndicates' are also present throughout these pages. Recruitment patterns into such syndicates may bear parallels to those operative in the context of 'armed' groups.

The term 'child soldier' may alternately be deployed to signify urgency, exigency and crisis. One recent news report about criminal activity in the Cape Flats areas of Cape Town, South Africa, begins with a mother speaking of her 15-year-old as referring to himself 'as a soldier for the local gang'.[11] A founder of a civil society organization adds: 'Commonly it is understood a child soldier is a youngster with a gun in war and many of us deny child soldiers exist in the Western Cape. But the meaning of child soldier in our societies is very simple and we cannot deny there are youngsters with guns in Cape Town.'[12] A South African academic pleads:

> A child soldier in the Ugandan context has primarily been associated with groups that are directly working to overthrow established state institutions. However, in other contexts, children may also become participants trapped in the violence of armed groups in their own communities, and they are still children at war and we must go beyond conventional notions of who the child soldiers are.[13]

Regardless of nomenclature, the point remains: creative thinking about reintegration and prevention in the context of child soldiering has the potential to catalyse much wider reflections upon the general interactions between children and criminal justice systems.

A final point on terminology: the vast majority of children associated with armed forces or armed groups worldwide are 16- and 17-year-olds who may consider themselves less as children and more as young adults.[14] Obviously there are horrific exceptions of very young children who become militarized against their will, including in terrorist groups, but these remain exceptions. It is important to keep this in mind – both when considering how children join armed groups, but also how they leave armed groups: infantilizing juveniles may not only underestimate their agency but can also have a counterproductive impact on efforts taken to reintegrate them.

2. A NOTE ON GLOBALITY

Child soldiering is a global phenomenon that is much more nuanced than might appear at first blush. It is generically estimated that, in recent decades, between 250,000 and 300,000 children worldwide are associated with armed forces or armed groups. Some observers suggest that these figures, however potentially accurate at one point, have since diminished in terms of quantifying the numbers of children currently serving in armed forces or armed groups.[15] We believe these observers make a good point. Yet children who have once served become former child soldiers who seek to reintegrate into society, and

---

[11] Lepule 2018.
[12] Ibid.
[13] Ibid.
[14] See generally Drumbl 2012.
[15] See Talbert and Wolfendale 2018 ('At least 100,000 people under the age of 18 serve in various capacities in armed groups around the world').

remain a crucial component of studies aimed at youth, militarization and transitional justice. Former child soldiers constitute a central concern of this *Research Handbook*.

What is more, sadly, conflicts wax and wane and, concomitantly, so do the numbers of children affected by armed conflict and the locations where child soldiering occurs. Child soldiers – as with former child soldiers – exist in each of the world's regions. The 2018 Annual Report of the UN Secretary-General on Children and Armed Conflict noted an increase in the number of children affected by armed conflict and the severity of the grave violations in question. Specific mention was made of recruitment and use in the Central African Republic, Somalia, Democratic Republic of the Congo, South Sudan, Syria and Yemen.[16] Reporting in 2018, the Office of the Special Representative of the Secretary-General on Children and Armed Conflict found that progress has been made in terms of releasing children from armed groups in Colombia, the Philippines, Sudan and Mali,[17] but also expressed concerns about abduction and recruitment in Somalia, Nigeria, Libya, Cameroon, Niger, Iraq and Syria.[18] In 2016, it was found that armed groups accounted for 54 out of 63 parties listed for grave violations against children.[19] Armed groups, however relevant, still only form part of the picture. In 2018, the Special Representative noted that:

> More than 50 per cent of armed groups included in the annexes to the annual report of the Secretary-General on children and armed conflict for the recruitment and use of children are active in countries where government forces are also listed, illustrating that the actions of armed groups are influenced by the conduct of government forces.[20]

Myanmar's government, for example, has recruited children through harsh methods. Estimates are that one-quarter of its national armed forces (the Tatmadaw) consists of persons under the age of 18. The Tatmadaw are currently implicated in mass violence perpetrated against Rohingya Muslims.

Persons under the age of 18, moreover, volunteer to join armed forces under special conditions and protections. In the years 2013 to 2015, for example, the United States recruited 49,035 (35,581 males and 13,454 females) 17-year-olds (about 6 per cent of total voluntary enlistments).[21] The United Kingdom is another example of armed forces in which minors are voluntarily enlisted.[22] So, too, is Canada (at the age of 16). France also allows for the voluntary recruitment of under 18s into its armed forces – non-nationals can also be recruited at 17 in the Foreign Legion.[23] In 2017, the number of minors in the German army (the *Bundeswehr*) rose to 2,128 – the highest recorded level – from a previous high-water mark in 2016 of 1,907 (in 2011, the year that mandatory military

---

[16] UN Secretary-General 2018: [6]. See also [7] ('In Nigeria, Boko Haram continued to force civilians, including children, to perpetrate suicide attacks, which led to over half of all the verified child casualties in the country').
[17] UN SRSG for Children and Armed Conflict 2018a.
[18] UN SRSG for Children and Armed Conflict 2018b.
[19] UN SRSG for Children and Armed Conflict 2016: 3.
[20] UN SRSG for Children and Armed Conflict 2018a: [28].
[21] US Department of Defense 2016.
[22] See Crilley in this volume.
[23] See Hanson and Molima in this volume.

Introduction 7

service for males ended, there were only 689).[24] Of the 2,128 recruits in 2017, 448 were women – an eightfold increase since 2011 (when there were 57 female soldiers under 18). In 2017, persons under the age of 18 accounted for 9 per cent of the *Bundeswehr*'s new recruits.[25] In 2014, the UN Committee on the Rights of the Child told Germany that it should raise its recruitment age. The *Bundeswehr* has nonetheless defended its recruitment of 17-year-olds and, like its counterpart in the UK, has turned to online video campaigns in its recruitment drive. In 2017, the German army spent about 35 million euros on recruitment, a figure that one news report identified as double the level of spending in 2011.[26] One recent German juvenile recruit, Marlon, had watched a series of YouTube videos before signing up. As for his mother's consent: well, 'she was happy to give it and is now pleased her once-messy son has become more organized'.[27]

National armed forces and police constabularies, moreover, come into contact with child soldiers who may fight for the 'other side'. How to act in such invidious circumstances? Throughout 2017, authorities in Iraq, Kurdistan and Syria routinely detained and abused children suspected of association with ISIS. The UN Office of the Special Representative specifically criticizes the detention by states of children for alleged association with such armed groups, and, also, the use by these armed groups of children as human bombs.

3. AND A FINAL PREFATORY NOTE ON AN EMANCIPATORY EPISTEMOLOGY

From where do 'we' know what 'we' know about child soldiers? In terms of the development of the law, best practices and policy, two informational sources have dominated: child psychology and trauma studies, on the one hand, and reports published by transnational pressure groups, NGOs, activists and UN agencies, on the other.

Other disciplines and their literatures have not resonated as earnestly with the international legal imagination. Thus, contributions from other fields remain untapped, which is unfortunate since many hail from the Global South. Examples of undervalued contributions include ethnographic participant observation, anthropological studies, qualitative research, survey data and feminist theory. Another is adolescent developmental neurobiology, which focuses on the social category of adolescents as distinct from young children. These literatures articulate a more dynamic account of child soldiers as interacting with, instead of overwhelmed by, their environments. These literatures also tend to align children, adolescents, youth and adults along a broader continuum that is less rigidly stratified by chronological age demarcations and bright-line distinctions tethered to the age of 18 (or any age). This *Research Handbook*, whilst it does not contain contributions from all of these fields, does seek to look beyond the usual disciplinary suspects and engages with multifarious methodological approaches in an attempt to broaden the conversation.

---

[24] The Local 2018.
[25] Alkousaa 2018.
[26] Ibid.
[27] Ibid.

There are three main ways in which individuals under the age of 18 become associated with armed forces or armed groups: (1) they are abducted or conscripted through force or serious threats; (2) they present themselves, whether independently or through recruitment programmes and become enlisted/enrolled; or (3) they are born into forces or groups. It is not always easy to demarcate the first two paths but they are distinguishable and, moreover, should be distinguished. The third path, birth into armed forces or groups, is the most uncommon and also among the most understudied. As editors, we are therefore delighted to be able to include in this *Research Handbook* a cutting-edge chapter by Myriam Denov of interview data from such children, born of war-time rape, in northern Uganda's Lord's Resistance Army.

Most child soldiers are neither abducted nor forcibly recruited.[28] The international legal imagination, nevertheless, heavily emphasizes this path to militarization. Although helping to expose this horrific reality, this emphasis also leads to the under-theorization and under-exploration of youth volunteerism. Significant numbers of children join armed forces or armed groups in the absence of evident coercion and, in fact, exercise some – and at times considerable – initiative and enterprise in this regard. The picture is more far more complex than the international legal imagination acknowledges. To be sure, cases arise where determinations of volunteerism would be specious.[29] Adults may deceive children and trick them into joining. Children may be offered up by family and community members in exchange for money or protection. Children may rashly present themselves for service because of excessive impulsivity. That said, many children, notably older adolescents, come forward intentionally to join armed forces or groups. Assuredly, they are influenced by environmental factors and fierce situational constraints: poverty, insecurity, lack of education, socialization into violence and broken families. We believe it useful to characterize the relationships of children with these factors as ones of push and pull in which children navigate circumscribed spaces. In joining armed forces or groups, children may simply – as best they can in tough circumstances – be negotiating paths of economic advancement, seeking inclusion in occupational networks, and pursuing political or ideological reform. Although assertions of volunteer service made by child soldiers should not be immune from rigorous interrogation, we believe it is wrong summarily to dismiss them. Young people may understand volunteerism within the context of their lives and apply it fairly to themselves.

One theme that weaves throughout this *Research Handbook* is that of recognizing that children's rights approaches oscillate between the protective impulse (children are vulnerable and need to be shielded) and the emancipatory impulse (children have evolving capacities and need to be supported, recognized and encouraged as societal participants). While the emancipatory approach fills many spaces associated with political participation (e.g. to lower the voting age, to permit autonomy in matters of reproductive rights and religious freedoms), the protective impulse tends to fill advocacy spaces regarding the desirability of military life. That said, many children may see their own participation in military life as emancipatory, and it remains crucial not to dismiss or condescend to those with such self-perceptions. One important path forward is to ensure that the best interests

---

[28] Drumbl 2012: 13.
[29] See Van Engeland in this volume.

of the child principle, situated in Article 3 of the UN Convention on the Rights of the Child (CRC), be fully actuated. Respecting best interests means foregrounding the voices of the children themselves. This *Research Handbook* seeks to vivify an ecology in which children are treated with respect, are listened to and not spoken over (or for) and remain included in decisions that affect them, others and everyone. Protective policies predicated upon children being constructed as enfeebled before and during conflict may counterproductively result in children persistently being treated as enfeebled after conflict.

4. RESPONSIBILITY FOR CHILD SOLDIERING: LAW, POLICY AND BEST PRACTICES

When is recruitment of children into armed groups or armed forces unlawful? The CRC provides that states 'shall take all feasible measures to ensure that persons who have not attained the age of fifteen years do not take a direct part in hostilities'.[30] In terms of recruitment, states 'shall refrain from recruiting any person who has not attained the age of fifteen years into their armed forces'.[31]

Many states and transnational activists felt that the CRC protections were inadequate. This led to the entry into force in 2002 of an Optional Protocol to the CRC on the Involvement of Children in Armed Conflict (OPAC).[32] As of 2018, 167 states are parties thereto. Article 1 of OPAC affirms that states 'shall take all feasible measures to ensure that members of their armed forces who have not attained the age of 18 years do not take a direct part in hostilities'. Article 2 mandates that states 'shall ensure that persons who have not attained the age of 18 years are not compulsorily recruited into their armed forces'. Article 3(1) then somewhat nebulously adds:

> States Parties shall raise the minimum age for the voluntary recruitment of persons into their national armed forces from that set out in article 38, paragraph 3, of the [CRC], taking account of the principles contained in that article and recognizing that under the [CRC] persons under the age of 18 years are entitled to special protection.

Article 3(1) mandates states to increase the threshold age for the voluntary recruitment of persons into their national armed forces beyond 15 – ostensibly, then, at the very least to 16. Pursuant to the OPAC, then, 16- and 17-year-olds can be recruited into national armed forces. Their recruitment, however, is subject to strict conditions. It must be 'genuinely voluntary' and 'carried out with the informed consent of the person's parents or legal guardians'; recruits are to be 'fully informed of the duties involved in such military service'; and they must 'provide reliable proof of age prior to acceptance into national military service'.[33]

---

[30] CRC, art. 38(2). See also Additional Protocol I, art. 77(2) and Additional Protocol II, art. 4(3)(c).
[31] CRC, art. 38(3) (adding that 'In recruiting among those persons who have attained the age of fifteen years but who have not attained the age of 18 years, States Parties shall endeavour to give priority to those who are oldest').
[32] For further discussion of the OPAC, see Hanson and Molima in this volume.
[33] OPAC, art. 3(3).

Each state party to the OPAC is required to deposit a binding declaration upon ratification or accession that sets forth its minimum age of voluntary recruitment as determined under national law. Approximately three-quarters of states that have filed declarations list minimum ages of voluntary recruitment of 18 or, in a handful of cases, older. A generalized practice, therefore, is emerging (at least if the metric is to undertake a head-count of states). Among the minority of states that have declared an age lower than 18, most adopt 17.

The OPAC is more restrictive in cases of armed groups. These groups 'should not, under any circumstances, recruit or use in hostilities persons under the age of 18 years'.[34] What is more, pursuant to Article 4(2), states agree to take 'all feasible measures' to criminalize such practices. State responsibility therefore arises, at least in theory.

A number of other instruments – both international and regional – also address the recruitment of children into armed forces or armed groups. The International Labour Organization's Convention No. 182 on the Prohibition and Immediate Action for the Elimination of the Worst Forms of Child Labour defines a child as a person under the age of 18.[35] This convention explicitly links 'forced or compulsory recruitment of children for use in armed conflict' to 'slavery or practices similar to slavery' and obliges ratifying member states to 'take immediate and effective measures to secure the prohibition and elimination' thereof.[36] The African Charter on the Rights and Welfare of the Child, which came into force in November 1999 defines a child as 'every human being below the age of 18 years' and requires parties to 'take all necessary measures to ensure that no child shall take a direct part in hostilities and refrain, in particular, from recruiting any child'.[37]

CRC Article 38(1) requires that states 'undertake to respect and to ensure respect for rules of international humanitarian law applicable to them in armed conflicts which are relevant to the child'. How does international humanitarian law approach children? This is a very complex topic. At its core, international humanitarian law generally requires that children receive 'special protection' and remain the 'object of special respect'.[38] This applies directly to how child fighters ought to be detained and treated upon capture. Operationalizing these protections in the context of armed conflict becomes particularly fraught with regard to the poignant question of whether children can be targeted on the battlefield. Presumptions of protected civilian status and special respect would, at a very minimum, inform rules of engagement.

International criminal law also specifically addresses responsibility for child soldiering. As it currently stands, whether in international or non-international armed conflict, the conscription, enlistment, or use of children under the age of 15 to participate actively in hostilities is a war crime to which individual penal responsibility attaches. Prosecutions have occurred at the Special Court for Sierra Leone (SCSL) and the International

---

[34] OPAC, art. 4(1).
[35] Art. 2.
[36] Arts 1, 3(a).
[37] See also Odongo in this volume.
[38] See, e.g., Additional Protocol I, arts 77(1), 77(3), 77(4) (this last article states that '[i]f arrested, detained or interned for reasons related to the armed conflict, children shall be held in quarters separate from the quarters of adults, except where families are accommodated as family units'); Additional Protocol II, art 4(3).

Criminal Court (ICC).[39] In fact, the ICC issued its very first conviction solely on charges of unlawful recruitment. Thomas Lubanga, a rebel leader in the DRC, was sentenced to 14 years' imprisonment. Jurisprudence from the ICC and SCSL discussed throughout this *Research Handbook* has clarified important aspects of this war crime, along with offences such as forced marriage (as a crime against humanity falling under the category of other inhumane acts), sexual enslavement and sexual violence.[40] Individual criminal responsibility for the illicit recruitment of children is also entering national criminal jurisdictions. As the age of unlawful recruitment inches towards 18, it may also be that the scope of individual criminal responsibility for such recruitment also moves upwards to 18.

5. RESPONSIBILITY OF CHILD SOLDIERS: LAW, POLICY AND BEST PRACTICES

Child soldiers suffer crimes, and child soldiering is a crime, but child soldiers also may commit crimes – including grievous atrocity crimes – against adults as well as children. What are the consequences that arise for child soldiers in such instances? Although criminally prosecuting child soldiers for their alleged involvement in acts of atrocity is technically permissible under international law, hardly any such prosecutions have taken place before international or internationalized penal institutions.[41] Moreover, such a move is increasingly viewed as inappropriate and undesirable.[42]

The constitutive statutes of the International Criminal Tribunal for the former Yugoslavia (ICTY, 1993) and the International Criminal Tribunal for Rwanda (ICTR, 1994) offered no guidance regarding the minimum age of criminal responsibility. The Rome Statute of the International Criminal court has no jurisdiction over any person who is under the age of 18 at the time of the alleged commission of the crime.[43] The Statute of the Special Court for Sierra Leone limited the SCSL's jurisdiction to defendants who were 15 years of age or older at the time of the alleged offence, though incarceration was not a possible sanction for defendants under the age of 18.[44] In any event, the SCSL's first Chief Prosecutor promptly and unequivocally stated that he would never prosecute children under the age of 18, including child soldiers, *inter alia* because they do not bear

---

[39] The International Military Tribunal at Nuremberg prosecuted Baldur von Schirach for *inter alia* his leadership of the *Hitler Jugend*. Von Schirach was acquitted of this charge (though he was convicted of other crimes against humanity and sentenced to a 22-year term). His successor, Artur Axmann, was tried before a De-Nazification court which sentenced him to a prison term of 39 months; in 1958 a West Berlin court fined him for having indoctrinated German youth with Nazi ideology.

[40] The ICC may also award reparations to victims, including children under the age of 18. A reparative order may be made directly against a convicted person, although such individuals are generally impecunious, or may also be effected through a separate trust fund for victims. Rome Statute, art. 75(2).

[41] See Kaushik and Freeland in this volume; Holá and Bouwknegt in this volume.

[42] Paris Principle 8.6 flatly states that '[c]hildren should not be prosecuted by an international court or tribunal'.

[43] Rome Statute, art. 26.

[44] SCSL Statute, arts 7(2), 19(1).

the greatest responsibility.[45] But international institutions can prosecute and incarcerate former child soldiers who committed crimes as adults. Currently, Dominic Ongwen faces prosecution at the ICC in The Hague on many counts of horrific crimes. Ongwen himself was a violently abducted and abused child soldier who came of age in the LRA.[46]

It remains unclear how these tendencies towards non-prosecution of those under 18 map onto national legal practices, in particular, in the case of children associated with 'terrorist' groups or 'violent extremists'. Children may be prosecuted for all sorts of crimes at the national level, including atrocity crimes, and, of course ordinary common crimes. Rwanda, for example, tried and convicted many individuals, who had been children at the time of their crimes, of genocide following the 1994 tragedy that engulfed that country.[47]

National ages of criminal responsibility may be gradated. This means that jurisdictions establish a minimum age of criminal responsibility and a separate age of adult criminal responsibility. Article 40(3)(a) of the CRC requires states to seek to promote the establishment of 'a minimum age below which children shall be presumed not to have the capacity to infringe the penal law' but sets no such age. The Committee on the Rights of the Child, a UN treaty body of independent experts which helps monitor state compliance with the CRC, has concluded that 12 years should be the 'absolute minimum' age of criminal responsibility, and has encouraged states to increase it to a higher age level, commending states that have adopted the age of 14 or 16.[48] The CRC restricts the use of certain sanctions for juveniles. It permits the 'arrest, detention or imprisonment of a child', but requires that these measures 'shall be used only as a . . . last resort and for the shortest appropriate period of time'.[49] It precludes the death penalty and life imprisonment without parole as sentences for children who are convicted of offences. Where children are deprived of liberty, the CRC requires that they 'be separated from adults unless it is considered in the child's best interest not to do so'.[50] The CRC specifies a minimum level of due process protection for children subject to criminal proceedings, which broadly reflects due process guarantees for anyone coming into conflict with the law, but it also encourages the development of enhanced frameworks attuned to their specific needs. The CRC does not favour incarceration, preferring instead rehabilitation and reintegration. That said, the CRC does not bar incarceration.

An entirely separate question, which should not be occluded by conversations regarding the criminal responsibility of minors for international crimes, is the positive role that transitional justice initiatives *other than* criminal trials can play in the rehabilitation, reintegration and recovery of such children, and perhaps better finesse the dual position of such children as victims and perpetrators. Such initiatives include truth commissions,

---

[45] SCSL Public Affairs Office 2002.
[46] See Ramos in this volume.
[47] Barrett 2019.
[48] CRC Committee 2007: [30] and [32]. CRC state parties are required to submit regular reports to the Committee.
[49] CRC, art. 37(b) (also requiring that '[n]o child shall be deprived of his or her liberty unlawfully or arbitrarily'). Turning to international humanitarian law, Article 68 of the 1949 Fourth Geneva Convention precludes imposing the death penalty on 'a protected person who was under eighteen years of age at the time of the offence', as do both of the 1977 Additional Protocols.
[50] CRC, art. 37(c).

ceremonial rituals,[51] art and drama therapy, community service and other processes to rebuild trust among war-affected youth and their afflicted communities. These initiatives may assist in demobilization programmes, encourage durable shifts to civilian life, promote gender equality and dissuade from recidivism. It remains unclear, however, how welcoming the international legal imagination is of the multidimensional involvement of children (as victims, witnesses *and as* perpetrators) in transitional justice institutions.[52] Grace Akello bemoans this reticence in her contribution to this *Research Handbook*.

6. THIS *RESEARCH HANDBOOK*: STRUCTURE AND RATIONALES

This *Research Handbook* contains 23 chapters. Contributors hail from six continents. Contributors approach the subject matter from a great diversity of disciplinary perspectives: literary theory, sociology, ethnography, social work, psychology, political science, criminology, medical anthropology and law. The contributors themselves remain deeply diverse and reflect a wonderful mix of established scholars and emerging voices – as well as practitioners and theoreticians – who, when assembled, present the very latest in research, entrepreneurialism and experiences with state-of-the-art policy implementation. Methodologies, too, are pluralistic: ranging from ground-breaking empirical studies, qualitative research and rich interview data to literary analysis and doctrinal review. Throughout, an emphasis is placed on the many stages of the life-cycle of the child soldiering experience: from recruitment, to the period in which the child is associated with armed forces or armed groups, and then to disarmament, demobilization and – by far the trickiest stage – reintegration.

While a broad swathe of jurisdictional case studies is referenced throughout the chapters, those unfurled with the greatest intensity include Colombia, Sierra Leone, Uganda, the Democratic Republic of the Congo, Nigeria (and the Lake Chad basin), the United Kingdom, the United States, Afghanistan, ISIS (in Iraq and Syria), the Philippines and Liberia. The chapters bind together in that, regardless of origin and methodology, each involves application of academic rigour to conventional wisdom that in some places reinforces, in others unsettles and, in some instances, upends it. Contributors to this edited collection are also diverse in terms of what they recommend, suggest or imply. As editors, our goal was never to present a pointed or monolithically normative volume with all entries singing off the same hymn sheet. Rather, in these pages we hope to bear witness to the kinetic energy that fills the field of child soldier studies. The end product, we feel, is not to be overly manicured and curated but, instead, to stand on its own, assuring the

---

[51] See Barrett in this volume.
[52] See, for example, how the Paris Principles address truth-seeking and reconciliation mechanisms:

> 8.15 All children who take part in these mechanisms, including those who have been associated with armed forces or armed groups should be treated equally as witnesses or as victims.
>
> 8.16 Children's participation in these mechanisms must be voluntary. No provision of services or support should be dependent on their participation in these mechanisms.

autonomy and independence of the author and reader. To be sure, when authors speak to each other and address similar themes, whether in agreement or in dissent, we highlight the cross-pollination through references and other signposts.

As editors, we have constelled this *Research Handbook* around four themes, represented in the following Parts: (I) The Concept and Construction of the Child Soldier; (II) Conduct: Agency, Capacity and Resilience; (III) Encounters with the Law; and (IV) Afterworld(s)/Afterwards: Transitional Justice and Beyond. We have placed the chapters in each 'theme' based on substantive 'fit', but we also have made a conscious effort to include within each theme authors at various career stages, various disciplines, various backgrounds and concerning themselves with various jurisdictions. To be sure, these parts and themes are not hermetically sealed. Plenty of cross-overs and pass-throughs arise. The book ends with an elegant epilogue by Nesam McMillan, who – invoking W.E.B. Du Bois – encourages reflection on what it means to be a 'problem', that is, what it means for the child soldier to see him or herself framed and mirrored by others as problematic. McMillan calls for a granular, humanistic approach to the experiences of militarized children that prioritizes careful and sustained engagement with actual lives and the actual ways in which those lives are lived.

6.1 Part I: The Concept and Construction of the Child Soldier

How are child soldiers conceived and perceived across time, place and narrative method? When does construction become concoction? Constriction? Constellation? What is the place of the subject in the concept? This part weaves together contributions that unspool how the child soldier is imagined. This part is as much about looking (and who looks) as it is about seeing (and who is seen).

Mohamed Kamara opens with a powerful, raw and visceral exposition of the child soldier as constructed in literature – whether fiction or autobiography. Kamara entitles his chapter 'In Search of the Lost Kingdom of Childhood' and peppers his analysis with a broad array of literary and cinematographic references. He focuses on three novels: Ahmadou Kourouma's *Allah Is Not Obliged*, Emmanuel Dongala's *Johnny Mad Dog* and Ishmael Beah's *A Long Way Gone*. Kamara examines how (and why) child soldiers become conceptualized as celebrities. He unpacks the child soldier as a character in popular culture. He does so to nudge the reader to interrogate what is to be learned generally from the stories of celebrity child soldiers since, after all, 'every person comes from somewhere and has a story'. Like McMillan, Kamara also invokes W.E.B. Du Bois, in this case Du Bois' writing about the double consciousness that resounds in *The Souls of Black Folk*, the 'two-ness' of being 'an American, a Negro', which Kamara suggests is relational to the 'oxymoron' of the child soldier. As for agency, well, can children 'make a heaven of hell, after grown-ups have done the opposite'?

Ana María Jiménez follows with a comprehensive account of the effects of legal categorization upon the status of militarized children in Colombia. Her chapter 'Challenges for the Protection of Child Victims of Recruitment and Use in an Era of Complex Armed Conflicts: The Colombian Case' begins with a deft summary of the changing nature of armed conflict, drawing on the history(ies) of conflict in Colombia as an illustration. What is conflict? What is peace? What are the in-betweens? Jiménez follows with a detailed survey of current efforts in Colombia to negotiate and sustain peace through law.

She identifies a great contingency, however: a contingency of conceptualization and construction. Are militarized children in Colombia child soldiers? Are they child criminals? Are they child terrorists? Rebels? Bandits? Agents of the state? Or just children? In the Colombian case, the answers to these questions transcend semantics and nomenclature. They are deeply consequential. Jiménez adroitly exposes how the way the child is classed bears directly upon that child's prospects for reintegration, resocialization and rehabilitation. Jiménez laments how the 'generally shifting nature of armed conflict' fits poorly with law's predilection for categories, templates and flowcharts, leading in her words to 'blind spots'. Her work is all the more topical in light of the opening of investigations in Colombia in 2019 with regard to the mass recruitment of 6,000 children during the decades of conflict.

Chapter 3 is titled 'The Construction of Gender in Child Soldiering in the Special Court for Sierra Leone'. Authored by Valerie Oosterveld, this chapter unearths the gendered nature of violence in Sierra Leone. Oosterveld illustrates how testimony before the Special Court for Sierra Leone (SCSL) revealed how rebel groups targeted both boys and girls. In the case of girls, the SCSL authenticated the vulnerability of girls to sexual violence and the terror of forced marriage (determined to be a crime against humanity). Oosterveld's granular and exacting review of the SCSL's work highlights how judges and prosecutors applied constructions of gender in order to secure crucially important justice goals, notably when it comes to condemning horrific gender-based violence against girls, but also how that very same process led to omissions, elisions, invisibilities and distortions. One example is 'silence on sexual violence directed against boy soldiers'. Essentialized constructions of the child soldier experience, while facilitating criminal convictions for adult abusers and exposing certain kinds of violence, may simultaneously occlude other forms of abuse. Law's light leads to law's shadows. Law reveals as it conceals.

Chapter 4 is also about gender and atrocity. This chapter picks up and advances Oosterveld's charge. It squarely addresses how the international legal imagination overlooks sexual violence against boys. '"We Were Controlled, We Were Not Allowed to Express Our Sexuality, Our Intimacy Was Suppressed": Sexual Violence Experienced by Boys' presents extensive interview data collected by Omer Aijazi, Evelyn Amony and Erin Baines in northern Uganda. This chapter tears the wrapping off the 'conceptual trap of girls and women as victims and boys and men as perpetrators found in second wave feminist legal studies' and resonates with words from what Derrick Bell has, in a different context, called the 'faces at the bottom of the well', that is, those who have never been thought of as having suffered nor have ever been asked about their experiences.[53] It opens with an encounter between Fred, a boy soldier, and Erin Baines, a Canadian academic, acknowledging that, amid her many years of work in northern Uganda, '[t]his was the first time [she had] knowingly spoke[n] to a male survivor of wartime rape'. The remainder of this chapter presents the words of the boys themselves, words about their worlds. These words are tales of counter-narratives: the strict regulation of sexual relations in the Lord's Resistance Army; the 'forged' nature of forced marriage relationships and the pain that was inflicted on both 'wives' and 'husbands'; the choicelessness faced by many boys; powerful women who 'preyed on young boys' and used them for

---

[53] Bell 1992.

sex; and the sexual assault of boys by senior male commanders. Aijazi, Amony and Baines conclude by urging 'legal feminist frameworks' to 'sufficiently make room for boys and men in their advocacy and policy efforts' while also encouraging that another limiting concept be shed, if not shredded, namely 'heteronormative ideals of manhood and masculinity'.

In Chapter 5, Karl Hanson and Christelle Molima highlight disconnects between transnational conceptions of child soldiers and how child soldiers see themselves. They urge that dominant constructions that approach children 'as the helpless objects of well-meaning interventions' be discarded and instead replaced with a framework of 'living rights, social justice and translations' that 'include[s] children and young people's own conceptions of their rights'. In this vein, then, Hanson and Molima wish for the child soldier no longer to be an object that is peered at through outsider adult lenses. Entitled 'Getting Tambo Out of Limbo: Exploring Alternative Legal Frameworks that are More Sensitive to the Agency of Children and Young People in Armed Conflict', this chapter elevates an emancipatory view of children's rights that energetically ensures that child soldiers remain key stakeholders in how they are seen. This means that they have rights to present themselves, be heard, associate, engage and participate. Hanson and Molima link debates over child soldiering and the unlawfulness of recruitment, with a much broader discussion about youth activism and empowerment generally.

Part I concludes with Rhys Crilley's contribution: 'This Is Belonging: Children and British Military Recruitment'. Crilley airs constitutive debates over child soldiers in many ways, notably by challenging assumptions that non-state actors in the Global South embroiled in feral wars accurately reflect the 'problem' of child soldiering. Crilley writes about how an influential Western state, the United Kingdom, through active state practices and deployment of social media, recruits youngsters into military forces from the age of 16. Crilley thereby disrupts the shibboleth as to 'who' constitutes the 'universalized' child soldier. Crilley also exposes what he calls a 'child soldier culture'. Rather than seeing child soldiering as an inevitable outcome of uncontrollable wars, Crilley underscores how the state may deliberately stoke such a culture based on a marketing strategy that invokes the emotions of camaraderie, play and community. On this note, then, Crilley's work contributes to the epistemology of how recruitment happens. Crilley's work may well point to broader patterns at play everywhere, whether in the Global North or Global South, that derive from the push and pull of global capital, loneliness, poverty and the yearning to belong.

6.2 Part II: Conduct: Agency, Capacity and Resilience

How do children end up in fighting forces? What do they do once there? How do they recount their experiences? The contributions in this part tackle tough questions about children's agency, capacity and resilience. These contributions take the form of a series of national case studies, including in several instances ground-breaking interview data collected through extensive fieldwork. Structuring this part in this serial fashion permits a granular appreciation of the divergent experiences of child soldiers and gestures towards the shortcomings of over-generalization and monochromatic assumptions. This part also reveals how accurate understandings of the lives of children while militarized lays the groundwork for their successful 'exits' from militarization, and, thereby, presages some of the conversations about decommissioning, demobilization and reintegration that infuse Part IV of this edited collection.

The first chapter herein explores the role and conduct of children in military forces from a historical perspective, specifically children in the US army during the Revolutionary War and the Civil War. This chapter – Chapter 7 – also examines children in US armed forces and UK armed forces during the First World War. Authored by David Rosen, 'Child Soldiers in Historical and Comparative Perspective: Creating a Space for Data-Driven Analysis' meticulously documents historical patterns of recruitment, youth volunteerism and the effects of national conscription on children in the armed forces. Rosen laments that, when it comes to researching child soldiers, currently the 'language of advocacy' has become adopted as the 'language of inquiry'. For Rosen, this obfuscates accurate portrayals of how and why children become militarized, what they do in those contexts and who is now recruiting them (Rosen maintains that the focus should be on non-state actors). For Rosen, a less didactic account of child soldiers is desirable: practices cannot be eliminated without being accurately understood. Rosen also warns of the dangers of advocacy imagery, notably the construction of the modern child soldier as a faultless passive victim. According to Rosen, the rhetorical puffery of such imagery fuels the unequal treatment of children. He points to the wretched way the US abused child detainees in the 'War on Terror'. Rosen makes a powerful argument that the lack of 'data-driven analysis' that undergirds the faultless passive victim image of child soldiers 'permits the emergence of a counter-narrative, when politically expedient ... of the purposeful and dangerous child terrorist, which becomes deployed when the interests of powerful Western states may be seen as threatened'.

Chapter 8 addresses 'The Voiceless Child Soldiers of Afghanistan'. Anicée Van Engeland argues in favour of contextualization when considering child soldiering, notably, to take account of cultural and traditional factors. She explores the concepts of agency and child soldiers as social navigators and circumscribed actors and applies these theoretical concepts to Afghanistan. Van Engeland concludes that child soldiers in Afghanistan exercise little in terms of what can be called agency. They are 'pawns in a game' who are 'perceived as duty-bearers born into a world of expectations, rather than rights-bearing subjects'. Van Engeland argues that 'the recruitment of child soldiers in Afghanistan is the outcome of a security context that has shaped traditional, religious, cultural and customary behaviours, making it acceptable, if not normal, to recruit children as combatants'. Van Engeland's contribution addresses questions of how to speak of – and how to redress – child soldiering at the extreme ends, where children in her view simply have no 'room to manoeuvre' because of embedded gerontocracy, control, abduction and deprivation.

In Chapter 9, Mia Bloom considers children implicated in acts of terrorism. She principally focuses on ISIS but offers readers an array of comparative insights and impressions from a multiplicity of groups variously determined to be terroristic, extremist or armed in nature. Hence, 'Weaponizing the Weak: The Role of Children in Terrorist Groups' includes references to the Liberation Tigers of Tamil Eelam in Sri Lanka, Maoists in Nepal and armed factions in Sierra Leone, among others. Bloom paints a rather composite picture of children: whereas in some instances the amount of agency exercised is minimal, in other cases it may be notable. She contrasts 'child soldiers' and 'children recruited by militant terrorist organizations'. Bloom's comprehensive chapter notes significant variation among groups in how they approach children, including pointedly in the context of gender and role differentiation, once again suggesting the need for heterogeneity in analysis rather than assumptions about uniformity. Bloom carries the reader through each stage of ISIS' use of children, which she characterizes as 'an institutionalized form of child abuse': recruitment, socialization, desensitization, schooling, selection, training, specialization and stationing. She delves into the conduct of children and adults – what actually happens – at each of these stages. This chapter, in a manner similar to Crilley's, also offers a fascinating vignette into the manipulation of youth through social media, including as it does a detailed discussion of ISIS' deployment of internet resources.

Chapter 10 concerns the Philippines, specifically child soldiers in the Lanao provinces located on Mindanao Island. This chapter presents the fascinating and crucially probative results of a descriptive-qualitative study (personal interviews and focus-group discussions) that, through the voices of Philippine child soldiers, brings to light the factors that influenced them to join the armed struggle by a number of groups (including the Moro Islamic Liberation Front) against the government. This ground-breaking study was conducted by a team of five researchers: David N. Almarez, Ajree D. Malawani, Sittie Akima A. Ali, Princess Mae S. Chua and Primitivo C. Ragandang III. This chapter begins by discussing the history of violence in Mindanao, presents processes of recruitment, explains the training and roles of children, identifies the centrality of *madrasah* education at all stages and finally offers wise recommendations to ensure the reintegration of affected youth (notably educational reform). Throughout, the authors present the day-to-day activities and motivations of their interviewees. What is more, the authors also present accounts of the conduct of children in actual armed conflict, their relationships with each other and their families, as well as their experiences of escape. 'Retracing the Journey of Child Soldiers and Looking for the Path to Return Them Home: A Report from Southern Philippines' is a treasure trove of information, insights and suggestions.

Myriam Denov, in Chapter 11, also shares the highly informative results of extensive fieldwork. Between June 2015 and December 2017, Denov participated in a series of interviews in northern Uganda with 71 children born in captivity (i.e. children born as a result of acts of war-time rape) in the Lord's Resistance Army. The results of these interviews are at once poignant and inspiring. Denov foregrounds the voices of her interlocutors, bringing visibility to this largely invisible set of children. She pushes the epistemic frontiers beyond the women and girls who were victims of repeated acts of sexual violence so as to begin to 'document the realities of their children who were born of conflict-related sexual violence, and in some cases, raised within the LRA'. Denov nimbly preserves the autonomy of these voices but neatly arranges her chapter so that readers learn of the children's perspectives on home, family, identity, belonging and reintegration. Voices speak of the 'bush' as 'home' and elaborate upon the rapport between home and identity and family when one's home is constantly moving and in flux; they talk of trainings to use weapons and of children's relationships with their mothers and fathers in captivity, as well as musing on marginalization and reintegration, including for Denov the 'highly disconcerting' fact that 'participants often identified the state of war and captivity – when violence, upheaval, deprivation and ongoing terror were at its height – as *better* than life during peacetime'. Denov concludes 'Children Born of Conflict-Related Sexual Violence within Armed Groups: A Case Study of Northern Uganda' with some programmatic recommendations tailored to the needs of children born into captivity as a subset of child soldiers.

Chapter 12 is entitled 'Social Reintegration Following Armed Conflict in Northern Uganda: How Former Child Soldier Young Mothers Use Symbolic Resources'. Here, Fiona Shanahan and Angela Veale share results from a qualitative study they conducted with mothers in northern Uganda. These results are presented in some instances as lively transcripts of conversations. Shanahan and Veale illuminate how these mothers deployed symbolic resources, which they understand to mean 'specific cultural elements used intentionally by people to facilitate developmental change'. These include songs, images, prayers and rituals. Shanahan and Veale present the vivacity of such symbolic resources in northern Uganda: folktales; riddles – many riddles – including one of a rooster and a millipede; and jokes. These symbolic resources helped the women 'mediate their sense of self' and also served a pedagogic function for their children. Shanahan and Veale consistently emphasize how their interlocutors signalled the continuities of their civilian and rebel identities, in contrast to conventional wisdom that presents war as discontinuous, as a rupture and as a break – therefore presenting a new perspective on the peace–war–peace transition. Shanahan and Veale unwrap for the reader the coping mechanisms that mothers availed themselves of while in captivity as child soldiers, thereby attesting to the touchstone themes of resilience, capacity and agency – in particular, the idea of 'internal' agency in contexts where the women were unable to bring about change in their 'external circumstances'. Does an individual's action constitute agency if she is unable to effect external change? Shanahan and Veale certainly show this question in a far more refined light.

6.3 Part III: Encounters with the Law

Law is a lurker throughout this edited collection. Part III, however, features contributions that squarely address the encounters that child soldiers have with the law. What are these moments like? Are they smooth, joyful, abrupt, pained – or all of the above? How does the law approach the child? What does the law make of the child who soldiers? How does the law leave that child after having involved the child in its processes? What are the consequences to adults who unlawfully recruit children? While 'law' in this part is understood broadly, the central focus lies with international and regional instruments in the areas of human rights, criminal law and refugee and asylum protection. In terms of institutions, this part primarily considers courts (including the International Criminal Court), although it also actively involves administrative bodies, fact-finding missions and human rights institutions.

In Chapter 13, Godfrey Odongo studies an innovative legal regime: the African Charter on the Rights and Welfare of the Child adopted under the auspices of the African Union. State compliance with this Charter is overseen by an Expert Committee, which issues important reports and conducts fact-finding missions. Odongo details the substantive law of the Charter when it comes to child soldiering, sets out procedures and processes and digs into the content of many of the communications issued by the Expert Committee. He thereby adds fascinating new dimensions to the discussion of 'law': regional instruments, state responsibility, reporting requirements and the power of naming and shaming (instead of criminal sanction) to achieve compliance with agreed-upon standards. 'The

Regional African Legal Framework on Children: A Template for More Robust Action on Children and Armed Conflict?' also includes excerpts from the reports themselves, including ones concerning the Central African Republic and South Sudan, which present a glimpse at the literature of fact-finding and the ability of such reporting to authenticate and narrate incidents not only of child soldiering but other violations, including hazardous child labour. What is more, Odongo draws parallels and contrasts between the African Charter and the CRC as well as the work of their respective monitoring bodies.

The theme of child labour is expanded robustly in Chapter 14, 'Minors and Miners: Accountability Beyond Child Soldiering in the Democratic Republic of Congo'. In this chapter, Sharanjeet Parmar and Yann Lebrat present results from qualitative fieldwork they undertook in conflict-riven gold mining areas in the DRC, which they merge with the content of open source data. They argue that the 'problem' of child soldiering cannot be understood, let alone redressed, without confronting the realities of child labour and economic crimes. Parmar and Lebrat isolate the illicit mining of conflict materials as a key driver of instabilities and illegalities, including child soldiering. In addition to providing a comprehensive *exposé* of mining in the Misisi area of the DRC, including the discomfiting and shady role of Congolese armed forces, Parmar and Lebrat offer an array of reformist recommendations. These include ways in which to improve the efficacy of the UN Security Council on matters of child soldiering, options for judicial accountability and the pursuit of criminal liability for economic crimes (including pillage and corporate responsibility).

In Chapter 15, Nikila Kaushik and Steven Freeland advance the discussion beyond how law can shame or punish states and individuals who may harm children to the very tricky question of the penal responsibility of children themselves when they harm others. This is an encounter with the law, to be sure, but an encounter of a very different nature. How does the law approach the child atrocity perpetrator? How should it? How ought the law to permit someone harmed by a child to seek justice? 'Crimes Committed by Child Soldiers: An Argument for Coherence' provides a detailed summary of international law and practice. Kaushik and Freeland note how the international legal imagination is reluctant – indeed, most hesitant – to prosecute minors before international penal institutions for international crimes. They welcome this reluctance. That said, they wisely flag the unprincipled nature of this reluctance. They rue how the intersection of minors with international courts and tribunals has become a bland jurisdictional move rather than a thoughtful jurisprudential journey. In the end, Kaushik and Freeland urge more reflection and justification. They do so since '[p]reserving integrity in law making is fundamental to ensuring the place of the rule of law' and because '*[a]d hoc* law making is not to be celebrated, even if the results might appear to be sound on their face'.

Barbora Holá and Thijs Bouwknegt lead readers to encounters of a different kind, that is, between children, on the one hand, and the architecture, mechanics and formalities of international courtrooms, on the other. These encounters, regrettably, are neither felicitous nor reinforcing. On the contrary, Holá and Bouwknegt find that they are often 'inappropriate, uncomfortable and uneasy'. Holá and Bouwknegt develop an explorative empirical study that zooms in and out of the courtroom (specifically the ICC and SCSL) to disentangle the child from the procedures. What is to be learned? For starters, children called upon to serve as witnesses – including when testifying against the adults who may have recruited them – often are seen as lacking in credibility. Children who speak of the harms they have endured shrink in size rather than grow in stature. '[A]dversarial adult courtrooms' diminish children to 'fragile and malleable figurants' and 'ghost victims'. In the end, the eclectic title of Chapter 16 captures the mood: 'Child Soldiers in International Courtrooms: Unqualified Perpetrators, Erratic Witnesses and Irreparable Victims?' While beyond the scope of this chapter, this leads to ruminations central to this *Research Handbook* as a whole – one being: how to change the mood? How to refresh this scenario, just because, and add some spice – well, perhaps by opening wide a window to wonder about all the adult 'rules' and to welcome surprising irregularities. That way, when someone – including a child, a teenager – slips up at a trial, messes up, well, that's just a slip: it's not a fall, flail or fail. What about venues other than courts for war-affected youth to build narratives, nurture empowerment and assess obligations?

Chapter 17 is entitled 'Dominic Ongwen on Trial: Problematizing Definitional Boundaries and Exploring the Possibilities of Socialization'. Carse Ramos delivers a sensitive and nuanced depiction of Dominic Ongwen – formerly a Brigadier Commander in northern Uganda's Lord's Resistance Army – who is on trial at the International Criminal Court. Ongwen faces 70 charges of crimes against humanity and war crimes, the most ever brought at the ICC, including gender-based violence. Ongwen also is singular in a different manner, namely, he is accused of crimes that he himself had endured after having been brutally abducted into the LRA as a child. Ongwen came of age in this armed group. The Ongwen trial, then, reflects the encounter of a former child soldier with the solemnity of a courtroom in The Hague and the categorical angularity of the law. How to speak of his childhood? Should it matter? Questions of duress, mitigation, responsibility, justice and deterrence abound. Mostly, however, Ramos encourages us to reflect on the painful realities that victims can become victimizers, the persecuted can persecute and violence can become a tool of survival and self-promotion. She urges the incorporation of a sociological framework to map the encounters of former child soldiers with the prospect of their own penal accountability as adults.

The final piece in this part, 'Child Soldiers and Asylum – Duality or Dilemma?' (Chapter 18), doctrinally examines child soldiers' encounters with refugee law. Joseph Rikhof observes that children in conflict zones putatively may face well-founded fears of persecution, which would entitle them to make asylum claims. Yet, one well-known bar to an otherwise eligible refugee claimant is if there is evidence that the claimant had persecuted others in the past, in other words, has committed serious crimes (including international crimes). In the case of child soldiers, then, how do national jurisdictions respond? Should the child be barred if evidence arises of implication in atrocity crimes? What if the participation therein was compelled – should duress operate as an exception to the bar? Rikhof provides a highly informative survey of the law and practice of a number of states and comes to the conclusion that the current state of affairs remains fragmented. In the end, while recognizing the need to acknowledge that some of these children may have committed serious crimes, Rikhof urges that consideration of humanitarian factors, including the special vulnerability of children and recognition of the stress and duress that encircles such children, 'should make their path to a permanent immigrant status easier than is the case for adults'.

6.4 Part IV: Afterworld(s)/Afterwards: Transitional Justice and Beyond

How do children 'leave' armed forces or armed groups? What is the afterworld of war like? The afterwards? This part examines disarmament, demobilization and reintegration (DDR) of former child combatants.[54] Some mention is also made of reconciliation, perhaps as a fourth stage, further along. Reintegration is tricky: how is it to be measured? Recidivism and re-recruitment: how are these to be avoided? Contributions to this part assess the role of customs, magic, the mystical, therapy, education, civic life and job training in the reintegration process. Contributions also push the conversational frame into the realm of transitional justice, namely, how do collectivities reckon with human rights violations in cases where victims may victimize others in a manner that transcends criminal law (the limitations of which Part III addressed)? And, finally, what are the responsibilities of those, often outsiders, involved in DDR programming?

Jastine Barrett engages with indigenous forms of justice and assesses their role in reintegration, reconciliation and transitional justice initiatives for war-affected youth. Chapter 19, 'Navigating the Mystical: Child Soldiers and Reintegration Rituals in Northern Uganda' provides an overview of the main reintegration rituals used in the Acholi region for LRA returnees. Barrett underscores their mystical elements and then links these to the importance of the spirit world in Acholi cosmology. One fascinating take-away is that indigenous mechanisms may be perceived as both a form of justice and of cleansing. Barrett also provides valuable insights into how indigenous methods 'were seen by' UNICEF and other organizations as compatible or not with their institutional ethos. Her interviews with current and former staff members of such organizations yield crucially important data in this regard. In the case of UNICEF, Barrett concludes that it 'was open to all approaches provided that they did not conflict with child rights, in particular the key principle of the best interests of the child'.

Grace Akello, a medical anthropologist, also reports on her work with LRA returnees in northern Uganda. Akello assesses the limits of 'sensitizing' local communities into a carefully manicured imagery of child soldiers as passive faultless victims. In 'Child Agency and Resistance to Discourses within the Paris Principles in Rehabilitation and Reintegration Processes of Former Child Soldiers in Northern Uganda' (Chapter 20), Akello presents findings from her 12-month-long ethnographic study in Gulu District. This study involved observation of local and emergency aid agencies as they organized workshops to promote awareness about 'the innocence of' rescued LRA child fighters as part of the reintegration process. Akello concludes that one of the 'unintended consequences' of this approach 'was silencing victims of war violence who would have preferred disclosure, reparation and compensation'. Akello underscores how communities did not see the returnees in the way that practitioners didactically presented them, and, as a result, reintegration was not as effective as it otherwise might have been. She identifies high rates of returnees subsequently becoming involved in criminal activities. Akello urges that community perspectives be better taken into account, that a diversification of remedies be pursued in a transitional justice framework, that the Paris Principles be rethought and that a more nuanced view be embedded that recognizes that, in some communities,

---

[54] See Casey-Maslen in this volume: 'Disarmament is the collection, documentation, control and disposal of small arms, ammunition, explosives, and light and heavy weapons of fighters. Demobilization is the formal and controlled discharge of active fighters from armed forces or other armed groups. Reintegration is the process by which former fighters acquire civilian status and gain sustainable employment and income.'

'victims of war violence do not make a clear distinction between acts of violence committed by a child and any other acts of violence'.

Chapter 21 is entitled 'Children Associated with Boko Haram: Disassociation, Protection, Accountability and Reintegration'. Authored by Stuart Casey-Maslen, this chapter delivers a careful assessment of how best to return children abducted into Boko Haram to civilian life. Like Akello, Casey-Maslen questions the usefulness of the Paris Principles, but also the UN's Integrated Disarmament, Demobilization and Reintegration Standards (IDDRS), in dealing with children associated with armed groups. He urges a review of both of these documents. In the Lake Chad Basin, one major impediment to the reintegration of these children is the reality of their ongoing detentions at the hands of governments and security forces. These children, horribly abused by Boko Haram, face more human rights violations upon capture by governmental forces; Casey-Maslen documents these practices. Challenges to the reintegration of these children, however, remain fuelled (perhaps even legitimized) by fear and suspicion. From our perspective as editors, these challenges can be traced to the reality of imagery, namely, to how they are seen. And they are seen in a way similar to how the US sees 'terrorists' captured in Afghanistan, as set out in Rosen's chapter, namely, not as faultless passive victims. Instead, these 'terrorist' children, regardless of how they became recruited, are constructed as baleful, sinister, purposeful and incorrigible – to be feared like snakes in the grass, recalling Shakespeare's evocation of how Henry VI saw Richard, so hungry for the throne, as Richard (then Duke of Gloucester) is set to murder him. Henry exclaims: 'Teeth hadst thou in thy head when thou wast born/To signify thou camest to bite the world'.[55] Accepting the need for age-appropriate accountability for all children, Casey-Maslen offers wise counsel to policy-makers as to how to constructively approach children trapped in the security-fuelled context of operations dubbed as 'counterterrorism'. He also questions the concept of afterworld(s) and afterwards by emphasizing the need to adopt DDR measures while armed conflict is still ongoing.

Michael Wessells also worries – like Akello – about inadvertent effects. He elevates these concerns to a broad scale. In Chapter 22, 'Do No Harm: How Reintegration Programmes for Former Child Soldiers Can Cause Unintended Harm', Wessells writes about practitioner ethics. He argues forcefully that practitioners need to develop greater self-awareness so as to avoid and manage harmful negative externalities. Wessells' chapter therefore links DDR practitioners to all sorts of professionals who, in myopically pursuing their vision of the right thing to do, may hurt others, including the very individuals they intend to help. For Wessells these questions far transcend virtue ethics and good intentions – neither suffice. The goal is mindfulness of effects. Wessells identifies a number of key concerns. One is the excessive targeting of former child soldiers in a fashion that may engender reverse discrimination against them and actual discrimination against children affected by war but who had not been associated with armed forces or armed groups. A second is gender discrimination, namely, the dismissive treatment of girl soldiers. Another is the risk that programmes 'quietly trample children's participation rights'. Yet another is 'the neocolonial imposition of outsider categories' at the expense of local approaches, such as those analysed by Barrett, which may be rooted in cosmology. Wessells, again like

---

[55] Shakespeare 1590: Act V, Scene 6, London, The Tower, 3048–3049.

Akello, also warns about what happens when practitioners avoid holding former child soldiers accountable for their actions. In the end, these behaviour patterns on the part of practitioners may lead to former child soldiers being exposed to risks, such as labelling, re-recruitment and susceptibility to securitization.

Leena Vastapuu concludes this Part with an insightful piece – lyrically written in the first person – about her experiences in Liberia. In 'How to Find the "Hidden" Girl Soldier? Two Sets of Suggestions Arising from Liberia' (Chapter 23), Vastapuu is motivated to 'produce the kind of chapter I would have once yearned to read myself, preferably before embarking for Liberia for the very first time'. In this sense she follows beautifully from Wessells' input on practitioner ethics – and to do no harm – to speak of the ethics of observation. Writing from an autoethnographic perspective, Vastapuu 'describe[s] some of the challenges and successes' that she encountered in her work with and about former girl soldiers in Liberia between 2012 and 2014. She offers two sets of counsel: first to researchers and second to DDR officers. Vastapuu speaks of herself, to be sure, but does so accompanied with extensive lively text about her interlocutors in Liberia, the risks they took to photograph their current lives with cameras, the conversations that ensued and their roles as girls in the armed conflict that had raged throughout the country. Vastapuu addresses what we know about why girls get left behind in terms of DDR and makes suggestions for how to remedy that disturbing gap. She focuses on contradictions within DDR best practices that conspire to underserve women and girls.

7. GAPS AND FUTURE DIRECTIONS

Assembling any edited collection takes on a life of its own. The process generates its own energies and synergies – centrifugal and centripetal. The pneumatics and hydraulics of these movements lead to gaps and surfeits.

One gap we as editors have noted is geographic in nature. This *Research Handbook* does not address child soldiering, or the reintegration of former child soldiers, everywhere. Sri Lanka, although tangentially referenced by Mia Bloom in her chapter, presents as a lacuna. UNICEF estimates over 6,000 cases of child recruitment between 2003 and 2008 by rebels in Sri Lanka. The Liberation Tigers of Tamil Eelam (LTTE) – a secessionist group that fought the Sri Lankan government until its defeat in 2009 – turned extensively to child soldiers and child suicide bombers.[56] Another Asian lacuna is Cambodia. The Khmer Rouge used youthful cadres in the 'killing fields' between 1975 and 1979. In 2018, the Extraordinary Chambers in the Courts of Cambodia convicted two elderly leaders of genocide, as well as charges related inter alia to sexual violence and forced marriage, and have thereby opened a further space to discuss the place of children as victims and victimizers. In the Americas, the involvement of children in narco-trafficking, and their association with groups that ply such trades, is a festering concern that merits closer attention.

As for surfeits? One is Uganda. Seven chapters base themselves in whole or in part upon the (post)conflict in Uganda. We could, moreover, have had even more about Uganda

---

[56] For a vivid recounting of life as an LTTE child soldier in this conflict, see de Soyza 2012.

in this *Research Handbook* but diverted some of those energies to other directions so as to mitigate against this surfeit becoming fulsome. What does this suggest? Why did this happen? Is this reflective of the Africanization of child soldier studies – a tendency that this *Research Handbook* laments and seeks to dilute? In this sense, then, perhaps this *Research Handbook* solidifies the exact tendency that it aims to dissipate. Or is it because jurisdictions that have become subject to international judicialization efforts, such as Uganda, attract more attention? Or is this traceable to the spectacular nature of the Lord's Resistance Army's violence, made viral in the Kony 2012 video? Or the ongoing place of conversations nationally in Uganda over the reintegration of formerly militarized children, which continue in 2019? These possibilities, all conjectures, certainly are not mutually exclusive, so the truth could well be a combination of all of them. That said, as editors we also feel that this surfeit opens a wonderful space for more textured analysis within one jurisdiction of a variety of themes and contrasting perspectives. In this regard, Uganda infuses each of the four sections of this book: concept, conduct, encounters with the law and the afterwards of transitional justice. This permits one contextualized strand in which to unwind the life-cycle of child soldiering.

8. TO CLOSE WITH ANNIVERSARIES

Recent and immediately upcoming years evince many anniversaries when it comes to international treaties and international organizations. A generation has now passed since the excitement of the 1990s, the thawing of the Cold War and what was (then) a heyday of internationalist institutionalism. The International Criminal Court has turned 20 – an age of adulthood (though many say the institution is still in its infancy and finding its sea legs, having only convicted three individuals so far). The CRC turns 30 this year! The Rwandan genocide, which involved children as victims, perpetrators and liberators, took place 25 years ago; later that same year, 1994, the ICTR (now closed, its work 'completed') was established. Throughout all these anniversaries, commemorative (at times celebratory) events are planned and the progress narrative of international law and policy feted. This *Research Handbook* forms part of these patterns of acknowledgement and recognition. But as editors we hope to participate in slightly different ways. We hope to contribute through the lenses of nuance and subtlety, through critical engagement and by respecting the voices of the children themselves. We aspire to render the invisible visible, map the unmapped and chart new directions. Self-awareness is key, a point that Michael Wessells is blunt about: 'Practitioners need to adopt a self-critical stance, demonstrate a willingness to document and discuss openly the negative, unintended consequences of programmatic activities, and incorporate the lessons learned to adjust . . .'.[57] Finally, as editors, we hope to bring an uplifting energy and upbeat cadence that focuses on adversity but also embraces capacities and potentialities and individualities. So, to end with the words of Kafka that initially opened this introduction, now twice repeated, we hope to render the child *less slight* and the adult *less broad*.

---

[57] Wessells in this volume.

REFERENCED WORKS

Alkousaa, R. 2018. 'German Military Turns to Under 18s to Boost Recruitment', *Reuters World News* (24 August)
Barrett, J.C. 2019. *Child Perpetrators on Trial: Insights from Post-Genocide Rwanda* (Cambridge: Cambridge University Press) (forthcoming)
Bell, D. 1992. *Faces at the Bottom of the Well: The Permanence of Racism* (New York: Basic Books)
CRC Committee [Committee on the Rights of the Child] 2007. 'General Comment No. 10: Children's Rights in Juvenile Justice' (UN Doc. CRC/C/GC/10) (25 April)
de Soyza, N. 2012. *Tamil Tigress: My Story as a Child Soldier in Sri Lanka's Bloody Civil War* (Pune: Mehta Publishing House)
Drumbl, M. 2012. *Reimagining Child Soldiers in International Law and Policy* (Oxford: Oxford University Press)
Drumbl, M. 2019. 'Children in Armed Conflict', in J. Todres and S. King (eds), *Oxford Handbook on Children's Rights* (Oxford: Oxford University Press) (forthcoming)
Kafka, F. 2018. *Letter to Father* (translated by K. Reppin) (Prague: Vitalis) (originally written 1919)
Lepule, T. 2018. '"Child Soldiers" are Terrorizing Cape Flats Communities, Says Study', *Weekend Argus* (13 May)
The Local 2018. 'German Army Recruits More Minors than Ever Before' (9 January 2018) [available at: https://www.thelocal.de/20180109/german-army-recruits-more-minors-than-ever-before-report (accessed 26 November 2018)]
Machel, G. 1996. 'Impact of Armed Conflict on Children: Report of the Expert of the Secretary-General Submitted Pursuant to General Assembly Resolution 48/157' (UN Doc. A/51/306) (26 August)
SCSL Public Affairs Office 2002. 'Special Court Prosecutor Says He Will Not Prosecute Children' (press release) (2 November)
Shakespeare, W. 1590. *History of Henry VI, Part III*
Talbert, M. and Wolfendale, J. 2018. 'The Moral Responsibility of Child Soldiers and the Case of Dominic Ongwen' (Stockholm Centre for the Ethics of War and Peace) (6 March) [available at: http://stockholmcentre.org/the-moral-responsibility-of-child-soldiers-and-the-case-of-dominic-ongwen/ (accessed 20 November 2018)]
UN Secretary-General 2018. 'Report of the Secretary-General on Children and Armed Conflict' (UN Doc. A/72/865-S/2018/465) (16 May)
UN SRSG for Children and Armed Conflict 2016. 'Children and Armed Conflict, Report of the Secretary-General: Annual Report Summary' [available at: https://childrenandarmedconflict.un.org/wp-content/uploads/2018/05/Summary-Annual-Report-2016_Children-and-Armed-Conflict.pdf (accessed 28 November 2018)]
UN SRSG for Children and Armed Conflict 2018a. 'Annual Report of the Special Representative of the Secretary-General for Children and Armed Conflict' (UN Doc. A/HRC/37/47) (8 January)
UN SRSG for Children and Armed Conflict 2018b. 'Report of the Special Representative of the Secretary-General for Children and Armed Conflict' (UN Doc. A/73/278) (30 July)
US Department of Defense 2016. 'OPAC Annex 2 – Voluntary Recruits (Accessions) of Persons Under 18', in 'US Third and Fourth Periodic Report on the Children's Protocols, Jan. 22, 2016 (revised Feb. 8, 2016)' [available at: https://www.state.gov/j/drl/rls/c70331.htm (accessed 26 November 2018)]

PART I

THE CONCEPT AND CONSTRUCTION OF THE CHILD SOLDIER

1. In search of the lost kingdom of childhood
Mohamed Kamara

In Ahmadou Kourouma's *Allah Is Not Obliged* (first published in 2000; republished in 2006), the child soldier narrator, Birahima, tells us that child soldiers are 'the most famous celebrities of the late twentieth century'.[1] Indeed, earlier texts like Ken Saro-Wiwa's 1985 *Sozaboy*[2] and Florent Couo-Zotti's *Charly en guerre* (1998) had already broached the topic of the child soldier. However, it was after the publication of Kourouma's novel that we saw a proliferation of books and films on African child soldiers (mimicking, as it were, the explosion of civil strife on the continent since the end of the 1980s). Attesting, perhaps, to the veracity of Birahima's observation is the popularity of Beah's memoirs, *A Long Way Gone* (2007); Iweala's *Beasts of No Nation* (the book [2005] and the movie [2015]); Dongala's *Johnny Mad Dog* (the book [2002, 2005] and movie [2008]); and the novel by Chris Abani, *Song for Night* (2007). Other films include Kim Nguyen's *War Witch* (2012) and two documentaries, Neil Abramson's *Soldier Child* (1998) and Sorious Samura's *Return to Freetown* (2002). Additionally, we have seen since the 1990s the creation of NGOs, international instruments and international institutions and offices relative to the child soldier: War Child (1993), Child Soldiers International (1998), the Optional Protocol to the Convention on the Rights of the Child on the Involvement of Children in Armed Conflict (OPAC), the Special Representative for Children and Armed Conflict (1997) and in 2002, the International Criminal Court (ICC), established by the Rome Statute of 1998, which declared the use of children under 15 in armed conflicts a war crime.

Birahima's statement about child soldiers being celebrities raises some vexing questions pertaining to the how, what and why of the condition of being a child soldier. What is childhood? What does it mean to be a child soldier? How does the definition of childhood (legal or otherwise) square with the child's own perception or understanding of his/her place (and perhaps role) in society? Did the child have a childhood before becoming a soldier?

Each of the three major characters (Birahima, Johnny and Ishmael) to be examined in this chapter is engaged in an odyssey of sorts. Whether the journey undertaken as related in the novel lasts a few days (as in the case of Johnny) or months (as in the case of Birahima) or years (in Ishmael Beah's case), and whether the child-traveller returns home (physically or otherwise) or not doesn't change this fact: the journey has implications for the lifetime of the traveller. What are the child's circumstances before the odyssey? What does s/he do or what gets done to him/her during the odyssey? Does s/he return home and to a family? Are home and family still there and the same post-war? Was there really 'home' or 'family' to start with? What are home and family in the context of society writ

---

[1] Kourouma 2006: 83.
[2] Twenty-one years later, Chimamanda Adichie's *Half of a Yellow Sun* would address the issue of the child soldier in the Biafran War (1967–70), albeit very briefly. Adichie 2006.

large? Does the journey really end? What does the experience of the child say about society as a whole?

Using three first person narratives, Ahmadou Kourouma's *Allah Is Not Obliged*, Emmanuel Dongala's *Johnny Mad Dog* and Ishmael Beah's *A Long Way Gone*, as my primary sources of reference, I will engage these and other questions in the present chapter. In the process, I hope to interrogate the larger question pertaining to agency, victimhood and the human capacity to transcend adversity, focusing specifically on how the child (or child soldier) negotiates the meandering road upon which s/he has been thrust, with no properly functioning compass, if any at all.

1. SYNOPSIS

Allah Is Not Obliged: Kourouma's story is about Birahima, an orphaned boy. After the death of his parents, and in the absence of any blood relative in his native Côte d'Ivoire (other than his grandparents), he is forced to embark on a search for his maternal aunt, who, as custom dictates, should be his new mother. The aunt lives somewhere in war-torn Liberia. A family acquaintance, Yacouba,[3] volunteers, not for unselfish reasons, to accompany the child on his odyssey. Birahima is all too happy to leave behind a known reality marked not only by the suffering and death of his mother and other close relatives, but by a society that has lost its ability to treat its children as children. He prefers an unknown future in Liberia where, Yacouba tells him, 'small-soldiers got every-fucking-thing'.[4] By the time he returns to his home country at the end of the story, Birahima, 'maybe ten, maybe twelve' years of age, has already 'killed lots of guys with an AK-47 (we called it a "kalash") and got fucked-up on kanif and lots of hard drugs'[5] while being abused physically and sexually by his guardians.

Johnny Mad Dog: Emmanuel Dongala's novel is about the eponymous anti-hero, Johnny, also known as Mad Dog.[6] Johnny has been a child soldier for at least three years when the book opens *in medias res* with a militia leader authorizing his fighters to loot anything they want 'for a period of forty-eight hours'.[7] Johnny's account is framed and counterbalanced by that of the more reliable Laokolé who shares his age. This narrative structure adds a complexity to Dongala's story that we don't see in Kourouma's or Beah's. Laokolé is a more rounded character; we have more bio-genealogical information about her than we do about the self-absorbed Johnny who, to boot, is 'drunk with blood and sperm'.[8] In fact, of the 319 pages of narrative, Lao has 174 pages (or 17 chapters) compared to Johnny's 145 pages (or 14 chapters). Lao grows up in a close-knit family of love and care, a family that is destroyed by the war in which Johnny is a willing participant. Lao's circumstances change throughout the story, but her name doesn't, another marker

---

[3] Also known as Tiécoura, or new man, in Malinke: a fitting name, seeing his chameleonic ability to remake himself as the circumstances demand.
[4] Kourouma 2006: 37.
[5] Ibid.: 3.
[6] Johnny goes through many nomenclatural baptisms before settling on Mad Dog.
[7] Dongala 2005: 6.
[8] Ibid.: 240.

of her psychological stability and reliability, even in the midst of a world in constant turmoil.

A Long Way Gone: The only autobiographical novel of the three under study here, Ishmael Beah's memoirs are a harrowing exposé of the causes and consequences of the militarization of children. Before becoming a child soldier, Beah, like so many of his compatriots far removed from the loci of the civil war that started in Sierra Leone in 1991, lived a sheltered life: 'There were all kinds of stories told about the war that made it sound as if it was happening in a faraway and different land.'[9] The sight of internally displaced people in his town brought to the young Ishmael a more urgent and physical reminder that the war was actually taking place in his country. At 12, the war comes to his hometown while he is away for a talent show with friends. Ishmael is barely 13 years old when he joins the ranks of the Sierra Leone army. He would remain a child soldier until his demobilization at the age of 15. By this time, Ishmael had become a drug addict and an efficient killing machine, one for whom 'killing had become as easy as drinking water'.[10]

2. EXITING CHILDHOOD

In Sony PlayStation's *God of War*, as they embark on a journey to find a final resting place for the ashes of the boy's mother, Kratos, a Spartan warrior, prepares his son, Atreus, for what is ahead:

> On our journey, we will be attacked by all manner of creature[s]. To be effective in combat, a *warrior* must not feel for his enemy. Close your heart to their desperation. Close your heart to their suffering. The road ahead is long and unforgiving. No place for *a boy*. You must be a warrior.[11]

Gone are the days when Atreus' mother, Laufey, protected her son from the violent and cynical world of adults, teaching him that 'not everyone is bad'.[12] Atreus thus finds himself transitioning from childhood to adulthood, from a boy to a warrior, with little, if any, psychological or physical preparation.

The advice Kratos gives his son as he ushers him into the new reality is the same advice, in one form or another, given to all child soldiers by those who use them as sidekicks or instruments of war. But Atreus has at least two advantages over the African children I will examine in this chapter: first, he is part giant (from his mother) and part god (from his father). Second, he is being accompanied on his journey by his father who will do everything he can to protect him.

War is the greatest disrupter of societal and personal development. This disruptive effect of war becomes even more pronounced where children are concerned. War, like most seriously traumatizing violence, forces children (combatants or not) to 'grow up' prematurely. With the killing of her father and the maiming of her mother by militia

---

[9] Beah 2007: 5.
[10] Ibid.: 122.
[11] Sony PlayStation 2017.
[12] Ibid.

In search of the lost kingdom of childhood 31

forces, Laokolé suddenly finds herself the one in charge of what is left of her family: 'No, I couldn't cry – Fofo mustn't see me crying. At sixteen, a girl is already a woman. I was now the mother of my mother, and the mother of my brother. I had to go on.'[13] Where the natural reaction for a child in a situation such as the one in which Laokolé finds herself is seeking comfort and reassurance in grown-ups, this is no longer possible. Laokolé applies this logic to her crying brother, almost four years her junior, when she says Fofo 'was almost twelve now, no longer a small child, old enough to help the family'.[14] This topsy-turvy world is no longer a place for a child. To survive, the child has to die, at least temporarily, and then re-emerge as a grown-up.

If this sudden transformation from child to parent/caretaker is dramatic, the transformation from child to soldier must be even more so, potentially carrying with it a more lasting damage to the child. Upon their arrival in Liberia, the vehicle Birahima and Yacouba are travelling in falls into an ambush set up by children fighting for Colonel Papa le Bon, who is described as

> shockingly garbed . . . wearing a white soutane . . . tied at the waist with a leather belt held up by a pair of black leather braces crossed across his back and his chest . . . a cardinal's mitre . . . leaning on a papal staff . . . with a crucifix at the top . . . carrying a bible in his left hand . . . wearing an AK-47 slung over his shoulder.[15]

The Colonel is 'the representative of the NPFL[16] . . . in northern Liberia' and in charge of the 'important trafficking coming in from Guinea'.[17] Birahima and Yacouba, with other travellers, are taken to the rebels' 'fortified camp, a compound with human skulls on stakes all round the border and battle stations protected with sandbags' and manned by child soldiers.[18] The compound is a miniature town, with 'offices too, and an arsenal, a temple, living quarters and a prison'.[19] All who live in the camp, including combatants and non-combatants, are the colonel's captives. He is chief executive, judge and executioner. Here, Birahima is inducted into the child soldier hall of infamy, becoming part of what the boy calls 'Colonel Papa le Bon's racket': 'I was sent to the child soldier barracks where I got a uniform from an old grown-up Para. It was far too big for me, I was swimming in it. After that, in a solemn ritual, Colonel Papa le Bon himself presented me with a kalash and made me a lieutenant.'[20] All this happens within 24 hours of their capture and arrival at the rebel base camp.

As if it is not enough for grown-ups to initiate children into their war, child soldiers, now grown-ups in their own right and left to their own devices, recruit other children. During their pursuit of the beleaguered inhabitants of the city, Johnny, whose own entry into fighting is as matter-of-fact as it is illogical (see below), comes across his girlfriend

---

[13] Dongala 2005: 47.
[14] Ibid.: 4.
[15] Kourouma 2006: 52.
[16] The National Patriotic Front of Liberia, the armed group that started the first Liberian civil war (1989–96).
[17] Kourouma 2006: 59.
[18] Ibid.: 63.
[19] Ibid.
[20] Ibid.: 66.

during one of their raids. Lovelita, though belonging to the tribe against which Johnny and his group are supposedly fighting, is summarily co-opted into Johnny's squad:

> I'd already asked her to put on combat fatigues. There was only one spare pair of boots, which luckily fit her. She put them on, and fastened a wide belt around her waist. I gave her one of the two extra Kalashnikovs we had, and showed her how to fire it . . . she was excited and happy as a child.[21]

From fleeing child-civilian to gun-wielding child soldier, all within minutes.

If, for Laokolé, leaving childhood is primarily a matter of basic survival, for Johnny, it is much more; it is a means of becoming a grown-up and enjoying the privileges that come with that. He exposes this reality as he contemplates his rape of Tanya Toyo, a TV anchor he had met a few years earlier:

> Three years before, when we met at the Malian shop, my biggest dream was that she'd take me in her arms and comfort me like a big sister. Because at the age of twelve you think of a beautiful woman as being like a mother, the only difference being that the beautiful woman is nicer and you can tell secrets to her that you'd never share with your mother. Now I was no longer a kid; at almost sixteen, I was a man. I knew what you could do with a chick, what you *ought* to do with a beautiful chick, even a chick two or three times older than you, like TT.[22]

Children, it is often said, want to grow up fast. War certainly accelerated that desire for Johnny.

Ishmael, for his part, presents a powerful description of his baptism of fire. A short while after their arrival at the makeshift government military camp, Ishmael and other recruits were given Kalashnikovs. Then they received new clothes and shoes:

> I took off my old pants, which contained the rap cassettes. As I was putting on my new army shorts, a soldier took my old pants and threw them into a blazing fire that had been set to burn our old belongings. I ran toward the fire, but the cassettes had already started to melt. Tears formed in my eyes, and my lips shook as I turned away.[23]

To understand Ishmael's reaction to the burning of the music tapes is to appreciate the significance of rap music in the boy's life. Throughout his journey up to this point, rap music had been Ishmael's anchor. In fact, the reason he and his friends left home (Mogbemo) for Mattru Jong was to participate in a talent show involving singing and dancing to rap music. As they flee one attack after another, gradually losing elements of their previous life, rap music (represented in the physical tapes) becomes a saving grace for Ishmael and his friends. Rap music saves their life at least on one occasion. At a village where the small group is mistaken for mercenaries and called 'little devils'[24] (this was before he becomes a soldier), Ishmael has to mime and dance to the 1991 Naughty by Nature song 'OPP' in order to prove they are indeed children, not devils.[25] Clearly, the tapes are the last physical

---

[21] Dongala 2005: 74–5.
[22] Ibid.: 23.
[23] Beah 2007: 110.
[24] Ibid.: 66.
[25] Ibid.: 67.

vestiges of his childhood. With them now gone, and Ishmael clad in his new military accoutrements, the barely 13-year-old boy has finally exited the realm of childhood.

Of the three boys, Ishmael is the one most reluctant to become a soldier. Before he convinced himself of the need to avenge the death of his family in the hands of rebels,[26] his unpreparedness, psychological and physical, for his inevitable participation in combat becomes an emotional weight to be cast aside. After their capture by government soldiers, Ishmael sees:

> four men lying on the ground, their uniforms soaked with blood. One of them lay on his stomach, and his eyes were wide open and still; his insides were spilling onto the ground. I turned away, and my eyes caught the smashed head of another man. Something inside his brain was still pulsating, and he was breathing. I felt nauseated. Everything began to spin around me.[27]

A soldier close to Ishmael tells him he 'will get used to it, everybody eventually does'.[28] Indeed, with the help of drugs and indoctrination, killing becomes second nature to the boys. For kids who had at best only played with a 'toy gun made out of bamboo'[29] before the war, war becomes a shortcut to adulthood and its accompanying paraphernalia. The consequences inherent in this rushed transition could be real and immediate, as shown in this example of Kik, one of Birahima's friends: during one of their attacks, the 'cunning child soldier took a shortcut' and 'stepped on a mine'. Kik was left alone by his squad (his newfangled family) 'dying, in the middle of the afternoon in some fucked-up village, to the tender mercies of the villagers' they had just attacked.[30] No amount of cunning can help him now. In the context of child militarization, the road to adulthood is paved with snares. One way or the other, the child will die.

A major consequence of children's direct participation in conflict is the way the violence transforms them, making them unrecognizable even to their own acquaintances. A good example of this is seen in *Johnny*. Johnny recognizes his girlfriend, Lovelita, in a crowd of fleeing refugees. However, Lovelita doesn't recognize Johnny: 'I must confess she didn't recognize me when she saw me approach. She was afraid, I suppose – she thought I was one of those brutes who wanted to rape her.'[31] Similarly, in their quest for a safe haven from the war, Ishmael and his friends are shunned, called devils and monsters and beaten up by grown-ups they encounter. An old man in an abandoned village (the other villagers had left their homes upon hearing a band of boys was heading their way) reminds them: 'My children, this country has lost its good heart. People don't trust each other anymore. Years ago, you would have been heartily welcomed in this village. I hope that you boys can find safety before this untrustworthiness and fear cause someone to harm you.'[32] They have become victims of the death of trust.

At the end of William Golding's *Lord of the Flies*, Ralph, one of the novel's central characters, 'wept for the end of innocence, the darkness of man's heart, and the fall

---

[26] Ibid.: 124.
[27] Ibid.: 100.
[28] Ibid.
[29] Ibid.: 111.
[30] Kourouma 2006: 90.
[31] Dongala 2005: 73.
[32] Beah 2007: 56.

through the air of the true, wise friend called Piggy'.[33] Golding's 1954 allegorical tale,[34] one of the most popular novels of all time, is a story about a group of pre-adolescent British schoolboys stranded on a Pacific island, after their plane crashed. Far from 'civilization' and the supervision of adults, the boys are on their own. Before long, they begin to resemble the adults of the so-called civilized society they have left behind; splitting up into factions and hunting each other down like wild animals. Ralph's realization of the death of their innocence comes just before their rescue by officers of the British Navy, only to be taken back into civilization and its endless wars. According to Harold Bloom, '[t]hough *Lord of the Flies* is a moral parable in the form of a boys' adventure story', it is much more about war, 'the dreadful gift adults keep presenting to children'.[35] We see a similar reaction to Ralph's from Laokolé. Upon seeing Johnny and his friends driving the truck belonging to her friend's family, Laokolé concludes that Melanie (her friend) has been killed together with her family: 'I wept uncontrollably . . . I'm not sure whether I was crying for my friend or for that boy, whom I didn't even know. I think I was weeping for both of them.'[36] It is all the same, for both the child victim and the child perpetrator. Even the perpetrators are not completely oblivious to their own fall from innocence. After killing a little boy whom they consider an enemy spy and eating some of the bananas he was selling, Johnny describes the reaction of his squad: 'the whole bunch of us burst out howling, unable to contain ourselves . . . for some reason Lovelita's laughter turned into racking sobs. Only Piston, who'd stayed in the car, didn't laugh. He gazed at us with a puzzled air, as if we had suddenly gone mad.'[37]

3. THE OXYMORON

According to both the UN Convention on the Rights of the Child (CRC) (including its Optional Protocol) and the African Charter on the Rights and Welfare of the Child, a child is anyone below the age of 18. Whereas the African Charter sets this age – 18 – as the minimum age for recruitment and participation in armed conflict, the CRC and OPAC adopt lower thresholds: 15 is the minimum age under the CRC for recruitment and participation, whilst the OPAC requires states to raise the age to at least 16 for voluntary recruitment into state armed forces and sets 18 as the minimum age for compulsory recruitment and direct participation. It also prohibits the recruitment or use in hostilities of under-18s by non-state armed groups. The Rome Statute, like the CRC, uses the age of 15 as the benchmark, making the recruitment or use of children under 15 in hostilities a war crime. Despite these legal anomalies, there is widespread agreement amongst humanitarian and

---

[33] Golding 1954: 202.
[34] Golding's novel is a parody of R.M. Ballantyne's *The Coral Island* (1858), a novel that 'presents a romantic vision of three boys who, without the conventions of society, are still able to usefully work together for each other's good and against the savage forces that threaten them. Golding shatters this illusion in *Lord of the Flies*. Without rules and without adult guidance, Golding's boys demonstrate the evil within.' Presley 2017.
[35] Bloom 2008: 1.
[36] Dongala 2005: 55.
[37] Ibid.: 78.

human rights advocates that 18 should be the threshold for the recruitment and use of children in armed conflicts (the 'Straight-18' approach), and efforts are afoot to bring international law in line with this approach. Given this consensus, the terminology child soldier (and all its avatars) is an oxymoron. In all three texts under study, the writers and their characters grapple with the notion of childhood and the confusion that accompanies the treatment and participation of children in armed conflicts.

In *Allah Is Not Obliged*, the first real victim of war Birahima sees is a child soldier called 'Captain Kid'. Kid, like other children, has been used as a decoy against convoys transporting civilians through war zones. Earlier, even before arriving in Liberia, Birahima insists on the difference between 'child soldiers and real soldiers',[38] pointing out, in the process, the nomenclatural anomaly. The physicality of this anomaly becomes evident in his description of the child fighters he encounters and works with, children usually used as expendable props to lure convoys into traps:

> A four-by-four comes out of the forest . . . full of kids, child soldiers, small-soldiers. Kids about this tall . . . as tall as an officer's cane. Child soldiers showing off, their kalashes, their AK-47s, slung over their shoulders, all dressed in . . . parachute gear way too big for them, so the uniforms are falling down round their knees, and they're swimming in them.[39]

Children and their childhood disappearing under the weight of the rules of adult games they did not make.

The *nom de guerre* of one of Johnny's comrades, 'Twin-head' or 'Amphisbaena',[40] captures eloquently the nature of the child soldier. An entity with an unresolved identity, bestriding two separate worlds like an overgrown seedling. We see a similar conundrum in Johnny's confusion regarding Laokolé's unconventional behaviour during their encounter at the end of the book. As noted earlier, circumstances have forced the 16-year old Lao to become and behave like a grown-up, assuming full responsibility for what remains of her family. Not sure what to make of her, Johnny refers to Lao as a 'strange woman, strange girl',[41] recognizing at once her natural childhood and her premature womanhood. Ishmael Beah proclaims a final indictment on the contradictory notion when he reminds participants at a UN conference in New York: 'I have been rehabilitated now, so don't be afraid of me. I am not a soldier anymore; I am a child.'[42]

Even with their own childhood upended by circumstances mostly beyond their control, both Johnny and Lao sometimes forget that they are still children. Ironically, we see in this disconnect (when they talk about other children as if they themselves were grown-ups) that their notion of what constitutes a child cannot be totally erased. At the refugee camp, Laokolé observes: 'All around me were emaciated children with swollen bellies, discolored hair, limbs puffy from edema, faces prematurely aged with malnutrition and hunger. It was hard for me to look at those girls and boys who had been robbed of their childhood.'[43] This is particularly telling in Johnny's case, who, of the three child soldiers, is the farthest

---

[38] Kourouma 2006: 44.
[39] Ibid.: 46–7.
[40] Dongala 2005: 39.
[41] Ibid.: 312.
[42] Beah 2007: 199.
[43] Dongala 2005: 294–5.

removed from childhood (both in terms of age and attitude). Forced, among other things, to negotiate with UN officials[44] and to kill without remorse, Johnny has not forgotten the difference between a child-victim and a soldier-perpetrator. Talking about the little boy his squad has captured and declared an enemy spy, Johnny acknowledges the boy was 'just a kid' though that does not stop him from eliminating him, for, he remarks, 'kids are often used as spies'.[45]

4. REASONS CHILDREN JOIN ARMED FORCES

As Mark Drumbl warns, we should not regard the child soldier phenomenon, as contradictory as it is, 'simply as an anachronism'.[46] All over the world, for as long as we can remember, children have been recruited to fight in wars by state and non-state actors; not that the line separating these two is always clear-cut, especially in failed states where governments change hands the same way a corrupt functionary changes cars.[47]

What makes this oxymoron of the child soldier possible? In other words, why do children become soldiers?

4.1 The Failure of the State

Real-life child soldiers are not the hapless boys in the novels of Ballantyne and Golding who find themselves marooned on a tropical island, left to their own devices, forced to figure out how to govern themselves. The main reason children join armies is because adults want them to and let them, either through force or through the dereliction of their responsibility, voluntary or otherwise, to protect children and their childhood. Acknowledging progress made towards adherence to the Straight-18 standard, Child Soldiers International laments the fact that states 'that still allow child recruitment in law tend to be relatively affluent and democratically controlled'.[48] These same countries, including G7 states,[49] 'capitalise on the social, economic and psychological vulnerabilities of disadvantaged adolescents to meet recruiting targets'.[50] Furthermore, and with particu-

---

[44] Ibid.: 131–3.
[45] Ibid.: 77.
[46] Drumbl 2012: 1.
[47] The distinction between state and non-state became so irrelevant during the Sierra Leone Civil War (1991–2002) that the neologism 'sobel', 'soldier-by-day, rebel-by-night' (Feldman and Arrous 2013: 67), was coined by Sierra Leoneans who could no longer tell state soldier from non-state soldier. While the term 'sobel' may have originated during the civil war in Sierra Leone, the phenomenon of what Ali Mazrui called back in 1973 'the lumpen militariat' or a 'class of semi-organized, rugged, and semi-literate soldiery' (Mazrui 1973: 1) had already presented itself decades back in the late 1960s. In the case of Sierra Leone, Jimmy Kandeh notes that the '"Sobelisation" of the national army, or the transformation of army regulars into brigands and armed robbers, can be traced to the mode of recruitment in the security apparatuses of the state' (Kandeh 1999: 362) that took place between independence in 1961 and the onset of the civil war in 1991.
[48] Child Soldiers International 2018a: 2.
[49] See also Crilley in this volume; Hanson and Molima in this volume.
[50] Crilley (in this volume) provides a comprehensive critique of recruitment practices by the British Army.

lar reference to the issue of Straight-18, the organization notes that the 'reluctance thus far of these powerful states to embrace the Straight-18 standard themselves diminishes their credibility when prescribing that same standard elsewhere, and so frustrates efforts across the world to eliminate the use of child soldiers'.[51] If states deemed respectful of the rule of law still recruit children, it is not difficult to see how easy it is for less democratic states or armed groups to use children in armies.

What is it that makes children a prime target for state and non-state recruiters? Child Soldiers International points out that children are 'more compliant and easier to manipulate'.[52] This question of the malleability of children receives special mention in Hannah Arendt's 1954 essay, 'The Crisis in Education'. Referring particularly to totalitarian regimes in Europe, she asserts:

> The role played by education in all political utopias from ancient times onward shows how natural it seems to start a new world with those who are by birth and nature new . . . For this reason, in Europe, the belief that one must begin with the children if one wishes to produce new conditions has remained principally the monopoly of revolutionary movements of tyrannical cast which, when they came to power, took the children away from their parents and simply indoctrinated them.[53]

Outside this sinister motivation, other reasons emerge.

Both the UN Convention and the African Charter recognize the responsibility of the family and the state to their children. Because children, through no choice of their own, tend to be placed at the front and centre of society's future, the inability or unwillingness of the state to protect the family, and the family the child, always spells doom for the entire society. In its preamble, the CRC is 'convinced that the family, as the fundamental group of society and the natural environment for the growth and well-being of all its members and particularly children, should be afforded the necessary protection and assistance so that it can fully assume its responsibilities within the community'. For its part, the African Charter in its preamble recognizes 'that for the full and harmonious development of his personality, the child should grow up in a family environment in an atmosphere of happiness, love and understanding', and to achieve this 'requires legal protection in conditions of freedom, dignity and security'. The state's basic responsibility then is to ensure the safety of its children, to provide an environment in which they can thrive. In *Johnny Mad Dog*, while talking about her friend, Melanie, Laokolé laments the condition of the child: 'Yet again, our shitty country had killed one of its children . . . What kind of country kills its children in cold blood?'[54] Decrying the failure of the state in regard to the child's development within a family, Laokolé offers her personal story:

> If I'd gone to America, I would have been in college now, since my grades had always been good. But no – at sixteen, I'd had to flee the bullets on the very day I was due to take my baccalaureate exam, and here I was, shipwrecked in the middle of the rain forest, with no father, no mother, no brother. What had I done to deserve this? I cursed my country and its politicians . . .[55]

---

[51] Child Soldiers International 2018a: 5.
[52] Child Soldiers International 2018b.
[53] Arendt 1961: 176–7.
[54] Dongala 2005: 55.
[55] Ibid.: 268.

38 *Research handbook on child soldiers*

Since Lao comes from a loving and caring family, and with both parents now dead thanks to the war, the state here becomes the main culprit for the potential underdevelopment of the child, not having been able to provide the 'conditions of freedom, dignity and security' necessary to her 'full and harmonious development'.

Beyond the failure of the state (but inextricably linked to it), other factors motivate children to take up arms: 'Some children choose to join a military organization as a route out of poverty, for protection, or as a way of making up for the loss of family or a lack of education.'[56]

4.2 The Family Is Gone, Long Live the Family

The family as a biological and social unit is at once an antidote to chaos and an easy target of it. The African family, says Dayo Olopade in *The Bright Continent*, is the original social network, 'one of the oldest non-state networks in Africa'.[57] Expanding on this observation, Olopade notes that the 'first feature of Africa's Family Map is not charity, but solidarity. Family is grounded in positive affiliation – recognizing yourself in those around you'.[58] Society is the aggregate of concentric circles (a network of relations and connections), with the family situated at its core. Preserving the family is indispensable to preserving the future of a people. Blacks survived in America during slavery thanks mainly to their ability to preserve the family, against all odds. The slave masters did everything to damage the integrity of the black family, knowing that if they could do this, their stranglehold on enslaved blacks would be that much firmer. One needs only peruse the slave narratives to get a good sense of this.[59] When the core of society (the family) is infected, the rest of society gets seriously sick. More specifically, when the child no longer feels the 'positive affiliation', no longer recognizes herself in those around her, that child becomes easy prey to outside maleficent forces.

The disintegration of Birahima's family is the single most important catalyst for the child's enlistment. Early on in his story, Birahima gives us a glimpse into his future's possible course: 'Before I went to Liberia, I was a fearless, blameless kid. I slept anywhere I wanted and stole all kinds of stuff to eat. My grandmother used to spend days and days looking for me: that's because I was what they call a street kid.'[60] Something was already broken with Birahima before he ran into armed groups. His father, 'an important farmer and a devout believer who always made sure that maman had enough to eat', passed away when Birahima was still a baby.[61] His mother, whom he 'only ever got to see . . . lying down or crawling around on her arse' though she used to be as 'pretty as a gazelle, as a *gouro* mask' before her excision, died 'after thirty years of shit and stink, of smoke from the

---

[56] Child Soldiers International 2018b.
[57] Olopade 2014: 90.
[58] Ibid.: 70.
[59] Stephen A. Berrey makes a similar case in relation to the black family in Jim Crow Mississippi: 'the black family – including not only parents but additional relatives, neighbors, and other adults in the community – functioned as a critical institution for protecting children from racial violence and for planting the seeds of subversion' (Berrey 2009: 66).
[60] Kourouma 2006: 5.
[61] Ibid.: 24.

hearth and suffering and tears'.[62] In a shocking display of adult and societal irresponsibility, the neighbourhood imam appears to blame the child for his mother's death by telling him he 'had not been kind' to her,[63] creating a feeling of guilt in the child that never leaves him. Birahima's grandmother and stepfather, Balla, take him under their wing. However, even though Birahima loves Balla and spends all his time with him,[64] the grandmother is worried the child is not getting a proper education by hanging out with the pagan Balla: 'She wanted to send me away, far from Balla, because she was afraid I would grow up to become a Bambara kaffir *feticheur*, and not a proper Malinké who performs the five daily prayers.'[65] Consequently, she and the rest of the family decide Birahima should go to his aunt, Mahan, in Liberia, where he 'would have rice and meat with *sauce graine* to eat'.[66] It is during his journey to Liberia, accompanied by a man who feeds him dithyrambic accounts of child soldiers getting everything they want,[67] that Birahima is captured and conscripted.

In the midst of the war that has supporters of the 'Movement for the Democratic Liberation of the People, the MFDLP . . . fighting against the partisans of the Movement for the Total Liberation of the People, the MFTLP',[68] commandos of the MFLDP come to Johnny's neighbourhood to recruit fighters. Johnny and his neighbours argue that there is no real difference between the two parties – 'frankly, it was six of one and half a dozen of the other. Why should we take sides?'[69] Consequently, the recruiters change tactics and tell the audience that the leader of the MFDLP was from their region, 'so his party was automatically' their party, and that 'any man or woman who was against him was a traitor'.[70] The apparent leader of the recruiters, a man Johnny had 'never seen',[71] shows them colour photos of alleged Dogo-Mayi victims of the ruling Mayi-Dogo party. Johnny, like many others, remains sceptical: 'We'd never lived our lives in tribal terms. Besides, wasn't my current girl a Mayi-Dogo? I adored her.'[72] However, when the leader of the group tells them he was a doctor and professor, Johnny, who has 'great respect' for intellectuals, is sold, thus exposing his gullibility: 'I wouldn't hesitate to put my faith in the intellectual. With so much knowledge in their heads, people like that couldn't possibly lie.'[73] Johnny is the first to enlist. He immediately becomes the second-in-command of his assigned group and is placed in charge of recruiting young people in his district and surrounding villages, 'by force, if necessary'.[74] At this time in his life, the teenage Johnny seems to be living by himself.

As noted already, we have scant details about Johnny's prehistory, except that before joining the militia, he was 'a member of the Society of Ambiancers and Persons of

---

[62] Ibid.: 11.
[63] Ibid.: 24.
[64] Ibid.: 22.
[65] Ibid.: 28.
[66] Ibid.: 28.
[67] Ibid.: 37.
[68] Dongala 2005: 83.
[69] Ibid.: 84.
[70] Ibid.
[71] Ibid.: 85.
[72] Ibid.: 86.
[73] Ibid.: 87.
[74] Ibid.: 88.

Elegance, one of the kings of SAPE – those nightclub patrons and arbiters of taste, always dressed in the height of fashion'.[75] We also know that he worked as a day labourer at a local market. We know all of Johnny's names, yet we do not know his real name, and we have no information about his family, except a passing reference to his grandfather and his grandfather's wife.[76] The absence of these biographical details is as telling as the copious information we have about the family of Laokolé, his counter-narrator.

Unlike Birahima and Johnny, Ishmael – the only one to be orphaned by armed fighters – is forced to pick up arms. He is 13 years old. During their seemingly interminable journey to escape the fighting, Ishmael and his friends get confirmation that their families are in a village on their path. Ishmael's elation at the prospect of reuniting with his parents and brothers is short-lived. Just before they enter the village, rebels attack it and kill everyone there, burning the entire village. Ishmael watches, helpless, as the rebels, two of whom looking just 'slightly older than' him, celebrate their carnage by 'laughing and giving each other high fives' and playing 'cards'.[77] Ishmael and his friends have to flee for their own lives from the same group of rebels. After running for hours and walking for days, they are rounded up by government soldiers. Back at their base, the leader of the soldiers, Lieutenant Jabati, tells Ishmael and the villagers that they have the choice to join them in their fight against the rebels or go without rations and leave the village.[78] To discourage them from thinking of escaping, he shows them the bullet-ridden bodies of a man and his son, freshly killed by the rebels as they tried to leave the village. He then proceeds to describe, in gruesome detail, how the rebels kill their victims. He concludes: 'They have lost everything that makes them human. They do not deserve to live. That is why we must kill every single one of them. Think of it as destroying a great evil. It is the highest service you can perform for your country.' 'All of us hated the rebels', Ishmael reports.[79] Ishmael eventually joins the government forces, albeit reluctantly. The night following their first combat training, back in his tent, Ishmael begins to 'visualize scenarios of shooting or stabbing a rebel'. In a re-enactment of what rebels did to his family, he imagines 'capturing several rebels at once, locking them inside a house, sprinkling gasoline on it, and tossing a match'.[80] By and by, Ishmael becomes a cruel and fearless soldier, eventually attaining the 'rank of junior lieutenant', an achievement he celebrates 'with more drugs and war movies'.[81]

Every child is a person, every person comes from somewhere and has a story. Birahima tells us that because child soldiers are 'the most famous celebrities of the late twentieth century. . . . whenever a child soldier dies, we have to say a funeral oration. That means we have to recount how in this great big fucked-up world they came to be a child soldier.'[82] Birahima goes on to provide the biographies of child soldiers, both boys and girls. Every single oration is of a child who has been failed by his or her family, making them prime

---

[75] Dongala 2005: 315.
[76] Ibid.: 236.
[77] Beah 2007: 96.
[78] Ibid.: 106.
[79] Ibid.: 108.
[80] Ibid.: 113.
[81] Ibid.: 125.
[82] Kourouma 2006: 83.

candidates for militarization when the opportunity presents itself. One particularly touching case is that of a girl soldier named Sarah. Given away to a relative by her sailor father after the death of her mother, abandoned by that relative, then exploited, beaten, raped, by others, Sarah, 'pretty as four girls put together', ended up wielding a gun while smoking 'enough hash for ten'.[83] Wounded accidentally by another child soldier and now useless to the cause, she is left alone in the forest at the mercy of 'the army ants and the vultures'.[84] As noted earlier, before becoming a child soldier, Birahima himself was a street kid.

After the monumental failure of state and family, what recourse does the child have? Birahima asks this question during his oration for a boy named Kik: 'when you've got no one left on earth, no father, no mother, no brother, no sister, and you're really young, just a little kid, living in some fucked-up barbaric country where everyone is cutting everyone's throat, what do you do?'[85] In his effort to recruit Ishmael and his friends into his squadron, Lieutenant Jabati tells them: 'Some of you are here because they have killed your parents or families, others because this is a safe place . . . This is your time to revenge the deaths of your families and to make sure more children do not lose their families.'[86] After the family has been destroyed, it has to be rebuilt somehow. In times of conflict, armed groups step in to fill the void, because nature, as the saying goes, abhors a vacuum. A rebel leader in *War Witch* tells his child recruits; 'Respect your guns. They are your new mother and father.'[87] Just after the ambush that lands them in Colonel Papa le Bon's camp, Birahima starts to cry for his aunt while saying he wants to be a 'small-soldier'. A child solder with a machine gun tries to stop him from crying. However, the colonel stops that child: 'Colonel Papa le Bon stopped the kid and came over and patted my head like a proper father. I was happy and proud as a Senegalese wrestling champion . . .'[88] Similarly, for Ishmael, Lieutenant Jabati represents something more than the mastermind of their collective security. He becomes a father figure to him, asking him if he has enough to eat and discussing Shakespeare with him. For children who have lost their parents, gestures of kindness from total strangers can carry great emotional power. It is true that the pact – 'we made a pact that no matter what, we will try and stay together'[89] – that binds fighters together is an artificial one built on fear, and that what ends up becoming their family in situations of conflict is a perverted surrogate of the one they have lost.[90] But this matters little to children in quest of belonging.

To underscore the importance of family (real or surrogate), it suffices to show what happens to Ishmael and one of his friends. After their rehabilitation, Ishmael and his companions have to be repatriated to their families. Since both his parents are dead, an

---

[83] Ibid.: 82.
[84] Ibid.: 86.
[85] Ibid.: 90.
[86] Beah 2007: 106.
[87] Nguyen 2012.
[88] Kourouma 2006: 52.
[89] Beah 2007: 116.
[90] This is evident in Ishmael's fear after the May 1997 AFRC/RUF coup that toppled the elected government of Ahmed Tejan Kabbah: 'I knew I would risk running into my former military friends, who would kill me if I told them I wasn't part of the war anymore.' Months before the coup, Ishmael had been decommissioned and had already gone through rehabilitation and repatriation. Ishmael had no intention of returning to his child soldiering days. Ibid.: 204.

uncle takes Ishmael in. The uncle tells him, 'You are my son. I don't have much, but I will give you a place to sleep, food, and my love.'[91] Things every child needs. In Freetown, Ishmael resumes his schooling; he even travels to New York to talk to the UN about war and children in Sierra Leone. Conversely, a friend of Ishmael's, Mambu, returns to the frontlines because his family refuses to take him back.

4.3 School's Out

In the reference to her interrupted schooling above, Laokolé touches on a recurring theme of war narratives about children: the role of schools and education in the development of the child, or lack thereof. The educational system, and with it the education of the child, is usually one of the first victims of war. Whether in times of peace or during war, the absence of schools, or proper education, is a good prelude to children joining armed groups. This disruption or devalorization of education can create a vicious cycle of delinquency among children. 'I didn't get far at school', Birahima tells us. 'I gave up in my third year in primary school. I chucked it because everyone says education's not worth an old grandmother's fart any more . . . because nowadays even if you get a degree you've got no hope of becoming a nurse or a teacher in some fucked-up French-speaking banana republic.'[92] Almost all the children for whom Birahima provides an oration are school drop-outs. Sekou the Terrible quit school for want of money to pay his school fees; Johnny Thunderbolt quit school because of violence he received and committed at school; and Siponni the Viper quit school after only three years of attendance, then decided to become a fighter because he feared abuse at home if he returned there.[93]

Not even the children are oblivious to the value of education for their actual development or as a sign thereof. Birahima is cognizant of the dangers of inadequate education:

> [G]oing to primary school for three years doesn't make you all autonomous and incredible. You know a bit, but not enough; you end up being what Black Nigger African Natives called grilled on both sides. You're not an indigenous savage any more like the rest of the Black Nigger African natives 'cos you can understand the civilized blacks and the toubabs (. . . a white person) and work out what they are saying.[94]

At the end of his narrative, Birahima's most prized possessions are four dictionaries he inherits from a Malinké who served as interpreter at the UNHCR (High Commissioner for Refugees).

Unlike Birahima, Johnny believes he is an intellectual: 'I myself was already a bit of an intellectual . . . I had completed fourth grade, after all . . .'[95] In the course of the war, he collects books for his future library, one of which, a bible, is used by Laokolé to kill him. A tragic irony of sorts. We are not sure if Johnny intends the collection merely for display, or for his actual edification once the war is over. As for Ishmael, the chance to return to school after the long hiatus brings him great joy: 'I had forgotten what it felt

---

[91] Ibid.: 172.
[92] Kourouma 2006: 1–2.
[93] Ibid.: 110, 178–9 and 196–7.
[94] Ibid.: 2.
[95] Dongala 2005: 88.

like to be a student, to sit in class, to take notes, do homework, make friends, and provoke other students.'[96]

4.4 The Power to Be and to Have

In addition to the loss of family and the inability to stay in school, the lure of power, control, access to basic resources, as well as a sense of one's personal worth can also serve as powerful motivations to join armed conflict. When Yacouba tells Birahima that in Liberia street kids like him can become 'small-soldiers' and, with guns, can get everything they want, including 'American dollars . . . shoes and stripes and radios and helmets and even cars that they call four-by-fours', Birahima shouts 'Walahé! Walahé! I want to go to Liberia.'[97] Johnny reveals, in his characteristic crude fashion, the reasons he and his friends are fighting: 'To line our pockets. To become adults. To have all the women we wanted. To wield the power of a gun. To be the rulers of the world.'[98] In addition to helping him avenge his family, the gun allows Ishmael to be somebody:

> I stood there holding my gun and felt special because I was part of something that took me seriously and I was not running from anyone anymore. I had my gun now . . . your source of power in these times. It will protect you and provide you all you need, if you know how to use it well.[99]

In the absence of any viable alternatives, it is hard to fault the boys for gravitating towards these immediate and tangible 'benefits' of war.

5. OF VICTIMS AND FREE AGENTS

'When the ocean tide recedes from a beach, fish are often left stranded. Torn from their natural environment, exposed to the sun and the wind, they thrash desperately on the sand as they die.'[100] Laokolé is speaking here of the horde of humanity trying to escape attacks by militia forces (they are in front of the closed gates of foreign embassies), yet it is a useful metaphor for understanding the status of children in times of conflict. As juvenile fish to the tides are children to grown-ups; they use them as pawns in their politics. As Ishmael puts it, 'We had not only lost our childhood in the war but our lives had been tainted by the same experiences that still caused us great pain and sadness.'[101] All children in war, be they willing perpetrators of atrocities or casualties of them, are victims. Yet, as we hinted earlier in this chapter, the question as to why children become combatants assumes a certain degree of agency on the part of some of them. Indeed, we know for sure that, unlike Ishmael who has to be forced to carry arms (though he ends up enamoured of them), both Birahima and Johnny willingly join their respective ragtag armies.

---

[96] Beah 2007: 202.
[97] Kourouma 2006: 37.
[98] Dongala 2005: 64.
[99] Beah 2007: 124.
[100] Dongala 2005: 104.
[101] Beah 2007: 202.

Birahima refuses to deliver funeral orations for three child soldiers in his group. He tells us why: 'they were more like the devil's children than the Good Lord's. All three of them were bastards, druggies, criminals, liars. They were cursed. I don't want to say a funeral oration for the damned.'[102] And talking about what he calls his 'fucked-up life',[103] he cautions the reader:

> Don't go thinking I'm some cute kid, 'cos I'm not. I'm cursed because I did bad things to my maman ... I'm not some cute kid on account of how I'm hunted by the *gnamas* of lots of people ... And I killed lots of innocent victims over in Liberia and Sierra Leone where I was a child doing tribal warfare, and where I got fucked-up on lots of drugs. The *gnamas* of the innocent people I killed are stalking me, so my whole life and everything round me is fucked. *Gnamokodé*.[104]

What are we to make of this harsh judgement by Birahima of his fellow child soldiers and of himself? Why are the other children deserving of funeral orations, but not these three, though it is easy to see that all child soldiers are more or less 'bastards, druggies, criminals, liars?' How much weight should we give to the self-judgment of a pre-teen who, clearly, has not had the benefit of a strong moral education? Or maybe, the question to ask is: how did these particular children become bastards, druggies, criminals and liars? Was it a conscious choice on their part? How much free will do Birahima and other children have, and how much latitude do they have to exercise it? Moreover, should they be held accountable for actions committed under adult supervision and instigation? Is one's victimization an excuse to victimize others?

The victim-perpetrator question has become a particularly thorny one, especially given the current ICC trial of Dominic Ongwen for crimes of war and against humanity.[105] Abducted at around nine, Ongwen grew up to be a ruthlessly efficient fighter who became one of the loyal strategists and brigade commanders in Joseph Kony's now nearly defunct Lord's Resistance Army (LRA). The debate concerns the extent to which, if any, Ongwen should be held accountable for the atrocities he committed while a member of the LRA. In a more general sense, where do we set the threshold for culpability and innocence? Does the argument for moral exoneration become weaker the further up the adulthood ladder one moves? In other words, Ongwen would argue that because, to his mind, there is no temporal rupture between his capture and conscription and his arrest and arraignment, he should not be held responsible for the things he did in the interim. In an interview given just before leaving for The Hague, he reasoned thus: 'I was captured at a tender age, and went there as someone who was blind and deaf. It is the same way in which I returned.'[106] If we can, how do we assign moral responsibility? Did Dominic Ongwen know at the time of his abduction that something wrong was being done to him? If so (which is more than likely), did he completely forget this as he grew up into adulthood and his new role? Did Ongwen take any decision between the age of 18 and the time he was

---

[102] Kourouma 2006: 144.
[103] Ibid.: 3.
[104] Ibid.: 4.
[105] Ongwen is the 'first known person to be charged with the same war crimes of which he is also victim'. Baines 2008: 1. For a detailed review of the Ongwen case, see Ramos in this volume.
[106] Akena 2015.

arrested that demonstrated moral complexity? Erin Baines, in her field notes on Dominic Ongwen, observes that 'Ongwen grew up in one of the most brutal environments known to humanity, with little room for moral development that would enable him to later take decisions independent of the LRA.'[107] By saying that Ongwen had 'little room for moral development', as opposed to zero room, Baines allows us to see Ongwen as a 'complex political victim'.[108] Not being entirely bereft of conscience and agency, Ongwen could not have been a mere marionette in the hands of his LRA superiors. Indeed, Ongwen, it has been said, could be kind and merciful to his subordinates and victims. 'Reflecting on messages about amnesty'[109] and his eventual defection from the LRA reveal a capacity on his part to understand the irrationality, unreliability and wickedness of Joseph Kony.[110] While his capture by LRA forces 'may indeed have been a matter of bad luck' for little Dominic,[111] it could not have been a matter of simple luck that he rose faster than most of his colleagues within the LRA ranks to become brigade commander in his late 20s.[112] Ongwen certainly knew that by being hardworking, efficient and loyal, he would do more than just survive. Acknowledging that the 'environmental factors to which Ongwen was exposed' may have played a part in what he became, Matthew Talbert and Jessica Wolfendale caution against heading down a slippery slope: '[I]f we start down the road of excusing perpetrators because their moral vision is impaired and because they have been shaped by factors beyond their control, we may not find an obvious place to stop.'[113] Is it possible then to punish Ongwen appropriately for his cruel deeds while taking into account the cruelty he himself suffered? How could this be accomplished within the framework of the criminal justice system?

Mark Drumbl makes the case that criminal law, which sees things in binary absolutes –'guilty or not-guilty, persecuted or persecutor, abused or abuser, right or wrong, powerful or powerless' – can benefit significantly from 'literary accounts' which tend to 'unpack the subtleties of and contiguities among victims and perpetrators, including betrayals, loyalties, connivances and acts of resistance'.[114] Cautioning against dichotomous thinking, Nikki Bado-Fralick notes:

> In dichotomous thinking, light and dark function as absolutes, very much like the on/off light switch we're familiar with in our homes. In absolute darkness, we are blind. In absolute light, we are also blind. If sight is the point, neither absolute darkness nor absolute light gives us what we want. It is only through the dynamic play of light and dark – the shifting of lights and shadows –that sight exists.[115]

To be sure, if justice is the goal in cases such as Ongwen's, Drumbl's idea that 'the performance of international courts and tribunals could be tweaked to transcend reductionism

---

[107] Baines 2008: 2.
[108] Ibid.: 4.
[109] Akena 2015.
[110] A fact that is at least partly revealed in 'Dominic Ongwen Reveals Why He Left Joseph Kony'. NTV Uganda 2015.
[111] Drumbl 2016: 236–7.
[112] Chothia 2015.
[113] Talbert and Wolfendale 2018.
[114] Drumbl 2016: 218.
[115] Bado-Fralick 2005: 6.

and deliver a richer narrative'[116] makes a lot of sense. Fortunately, the potential for this is already present in the performance of courts. In presenting the prosecution's case against Dominic Ongwen, the ICC chief prosecutor argues that because 'each human being must be considered to be endowed with moral responsibility for their actions', Dominic Ongwen bears responsibility for 'crimes committed as an adult . . . the choice to embrace the murderous violence used by the LRA and to make it the hallmark of operations carried out by his soldiers'. Nonetheless, prosecutor Fatou Bensouda concedes the grey zones in Ongwen's biography:

> One aspect of this case is the fact that not only is Ongwen alleged to be the perpetrator of these crimes, he was also a victim. He . . . was abducted from his home by an earlier generation of LRA fighters . . . He . . . must have gone through the trauma of separation from his family, brutalisation by his captors and initiation into the violence of the LRA way of life.[117]

So while it is true that 'law fails to authenticate' multidimensional stories, law does not always have the capacity to exclude or silence them entirely. After all, those robed individuals and jurors who dispense sentences and punishment are humans, and as such, are prone to flexing their moral and empathic muscles in spite of what Drumbl calls criminal law's 'angularity'.[118] In Ongwen's case, prosecutor Bensouda concedes that the fact that Ongwen himself was victimized 'may perhaps amount to some mitigation of sentence in the event that he is convicted of these crimes'.[119]

The situation of the decommissioned child soldier is less complicated. Still, the case of a child soldier like Ishmael Beah could throw light on Ongwen's situation, especially given the difference between Ongwen (a grown man who refuses to assume responsibility for his crimes)[120] and Ishmael Beah (a teenager who acknowledges his blemished past). After his removal from the front,[121] Ishmael is mad at any adult who tells him 'it is not your fault'.[122] He hates the phrase because he knows what he has done is unforgettable and inexcusable. Talking about the war prisoners they tied to trees and executed, Ishmael underscores the impossibility of erasing evidence of one's past: 'Their blood stained the trees and never washed off, even during the rainy season.'[123] It is not until he meets Nurse Esther that his point of view shifts:

> It was the genuine tone in Esther's voice that made the phrase finally begin to sink into my mind and heart. That didn't make me immune from the guilt that I felt for what I had done. Nonetheless, it lightened my burdensome memories and gave me strength to think about things.[124]

---

[116] Drumbl 2016: 243.
[117] ICC 2016.
[118] Drumbl 2016: 243.
[119] ICC 2016.
[120] Ongwen has pleaded not guilty to all charges against him.
[121] Chosen by Lieutenant Jabati as a candidate for rehabilitation and released to the UNHCR, Ishmael left the front in January 1996. He completed eight months of rehabilitation in Freetown, mostly at The Benin Home Rehabilitation Center, before he was handed over to his uncle.
[122] Beah 2007: 160.
[123] Ibid.: 190.
[124] Ibid.: 165.

Ishmael knows that he cannot be held criminally culpable for his actions. However, by showing remorse for them, he acknowledges he is not 100 per cent innocent. The same is true of the fictional Birahima who never stops blaming himself for his mother's death and for the terrible things he did to his war victims.

6. ADAPTABILITY, MEMORY AND RESILIENCE

To survive in a new environment, children (like adults) are required to adapt, in one fashion or another, to their new reality. The Kapo trials, for example, expose the extent to which people can go to stay alive.[125]

Birahima tells us that '[t]he first time I smoked hash, I puked like a sick dog, but after a while I got used to it and soon it made me strong as a grown-up'.[126] The ability to normalize new realities, or become desensitized to their effects, constitutes a form of adaptability. Laokolé makes this salient observation on more than one occasion:

> The brain is an extraordinary organ. After an hour of fear and dread under the bombardment, mine adapted to the situation. It transformed the whistlings, shock waves, and explosions into routine sounds that were nothing more than familiar background noise. My terror faded and my body relaxed.[127]

The need for survival not only allows one to be chameleon-like, to be one with one's surroundings, as in the examples with Birahima and Laokolé above; it can also enable one to display abilities that one didn't know one had, or that one will never see again after the need has been satisfied. This is the case of Ishmael. Ishmael did not know how to climb coconut trees, until one day, hungry and thirsty, the only food available is coconuts. He finds himself at the summit of a coconut tree before he realizes what he is doing: 'It is difficult to explain how it happened, but I mounted the coconut tree quite fast and unexpectedly. By the time I realized what I was doing and thought about my experience in this particular art, I was already at the top of the branches and plucking coconuts.'[128] Ishmael tried climbing other coconut trees after that; he could not.

If children are able to adapt to a new environment, they are equally able to resist its stranglehold on them. This is resilience, the capacity to remain essentially oneself in adversity, or to spring back from it. More specifically, the ability to recover partially, if not fully, one's childhood.

In the *Souls of Black Folk*, W.E.B. Du Bois develops the notion of double consciousness in relation to blacks in America: 'One ever feels his two-ness,— an American, a Negro; two souls, two thoughts, two unreconciled strivings; two warring ideals in one dark body, whose dogged strength alone keeps it from being torn asunder.'[129] Resilience, indeed, is why blacks survived slavery in America, even though the struggle to be accepted as fully American continues. The 'two-ness' of the Black man is similar to the oxymoron of the

---

[125] See Drumbl 2016.
[126] Kourouma 2006: 71.
[127] Dongala 2005: 218.
[128] Beah 2007: 47.
[129] Du Bois 2007: 3.

child soldier. However, whereas Du Bois' subject 'simply wishes to make it possible for a man to be both a Negro and an American, without being cursed and spit upon by his fellows',[130] the children of war forced to be adults do not necessarily actively seek to be both child and adult at the same time. In fact, they routinely lament the loss of their childhood even as they acknowledge (sometimes embrace) the impossibility of fully returning to that prelapsarian state.

The reader encounters two powerful images of resilience in *Johnny Mad Dog*. The first is offered by Johnny. During a conversation he had with his grandfather and the latter's wife, Johnny learnt about a special tree: 'A mougheté was a fire resistant tree. It was the proud, solitary form you saw on the savannah after all the vegetation had been destroyed by a brush fire.'[131] During one of the darkest moments in her life, shortly after losing her mother and her mother's best friend in a series of bombardments, Laokolé finds pride and solace in a structure that she had helped her mason father build. 'My gaze fell upon the wall surrounding Mr. Ibara's house. A rocket had blown an enormous hole in the middle of it, but despite this damage it was still standing . . . this wall that had defied the bombs.'[132] Here they are, two structures, one made by nature, the other by humans, preserving their integrity in the midst of adversity. Yet, we are reminded by the rocket hole in the standing wall that while recovery is possible, total recovery is not. The child, like a palimpsest of Mr Ibara's wall, will show felt and/or visible traces of past trauma.

Ishmael also uses nature to talk indirectly about his potential for recovery and redemption:

> One night . . . I looked into the sky and saw how the thick clouds kept trying to cover the moon, yet it would reappear again and again to shine all night long. In some way, my journey was like the moon – although I had even more thick clouds coming my way to make my spirit dull.[133]

Throughout Ishmael's journey, the moon appears quite frequently (as it does also in Laokolé's) as a reminder of what he should not forget, his relatively happy childhood. Save for a significant portion of the time when the constant fighting and consumption of drugs left him no time to think about his previous life, happy memories of his childhood (with family and friends, at home and at school) have resurfaced to help him deal with the trauma of war.

Whereas adaptability could be an end in itself, that is, a point of no return (which seems to be so in Johnny's case), resilience is a necessary condition of rehabilitation (as is clearly the case with Ishmael, and somewhat with Birahima, both rescued from war). Resilience, like the sankofa,[134] is at once backward-looking and forward-projecting; it drags along from the rubble of the past the very soul of the future. The foundation of resilience is memory. Without memory, one can never be resilient enough to make it

---

[130] Ibid.
[131] Dongala 2005: 236.
[132] Ibid.: 244.
[133] Beah 2007: 69–70.
[134] Sankofa is an Akan (Ghanaian) expression meaning it is not forbidden to go back and fetch what you forgot. The concept, often symbolized in a mythic bird whose feet face resolutely forward while the head faces backwards, represents the necessity and willingness to go back to the past for the sake of the future. See University of Illinois Springfield 2018.

successfully into the future. For those with childhood memories that are better forgotten, the task of rehabilitation becomes that much harder. Of the three child soldiers, Ishmael is the one who stands the greatest chance of succeeding in the future. Birahima refuses to think about his pre-war past for, honestly, given 'the scar, on my arm, in my head, in my belly ... and in my heart' and 'maman's nauseating smell',[135] there are no good memories from it. Instead, he wishes he could remember how life was before his mother started suffering and before he was born ('it is a pity we don't know how the world was before we get born'), a time when his mother 'was a young virgin before her excision ... pretty as a gazelle, pretty as a *gouro* mask'.[136] Like Birahima, Johnny hardly talks about his past; which makes the reader suspect there is nothing in the boy's life to fall back on. On the contrary, Ishmael has more pleasant memories than unpleasant ones from his time before the war. Even though his parents were separated, and his father's subsequent wives showed him and his brothers hostility,[137] he received genuine love from both parents and from his grandmother. 'Whenever I get a chance to observe the moon now, I will see those same images ... I saw when I was six, and it pleases me to know that part of my childhood is still embedded in me.'[138]

7. CONCLUSION

The child soldier sits at the crossroads of childhood (theoretical or lived) and adulthood, often without wishing to be there. It is a dangerous place to be. Depending on the force of the wind and the way it is blowing, the child will live fully again or be damaged forever. As Ishmael reminds us, 'children have the resilience to outlive their sufferings, if given the chance'.[139] One of the best concrete examples of this, beyond Ishmael's true and exemplary story of rehabilitation, is what Laokolé does with the children at the UN compound where thousands of refugees are held until abandoned by the international community: thanks to her efforts,

> [t]he kids had forgotten the dreary camp in which they were stagnating. They had become children once more, doing what nobody in the world does better: playing. With their hands and boundless imaginations, they built houses and trucks out of bits of bamboo; from empty sardine tins mounted on beer corks, they made cars that they raced in the sand; out of scraps of iron, they fashioned airplanes; using empty tin cans and pieces of plastic, they erected structures I couldn't even name. No sooner had their brains thought of an object than their nimble fingers would set about making it, their creativity finding abundant raw materials in the piles of trash that lay all over the camp ...[140]

Phoenix-like, children are the ones most able to make a heaven of hell, after grown-ups have done the opposite. This image is not very different from the one that ends *Johnny Mad*

---

[135] Kourouma 2006: 7.
[136] Ibid.: 11.
[137] Beah 2007: 10.
[138] Ibid.: 17.
[139] Ibid.: 169.
[140] Dongala 2005: 298.

Dog. The reader may have hoped that Laokolé would get out of the Congo mess and head to America.[141] That would have been a very happy conclusion indeed. Nonetheless, the actual ending of the story, that sees the 16-year-old Laokolé adopting a little orphan girl and moving resolutely into the future, without any thoughts of fleeing her country, is quite satisfying. In the end, we see two traumatized children – one now fully grown and already a mother at 16, the other on Laokolé's back, freshly named 'Joy' – step into the night, guided by their faith in themselves, the future and the 'brilliant diamonds' in the sky.[142]

REFERENCED WORKS

Abani, C. 2007. *Song for Night* (Brooklyn, NY: Akashic Books)
Adichie, C. 2006. *Half of a Yellow Sun* (New York: Anchor Books)
Akena, M. 2015. 'Ongwen Speaks Out on Why He Quit LRA', *The Daily Monitor* (19 January) [available at: http://www.monitor.co.ug/News/National/Ongwen-speaks-out-on-why-he-quit-LRA/-/688334/2593818/-/5ox5ac/-/index.html (accessed 19 July 2018)]
Arendt, H. 1961. 'The Crisis in Education', in *Between Past and Future: Six Exercises in Political Thought* (New York: The Viking Press)
Bado-Fralick, N. 2005. *Coming to the Edge of the Circle: A Wiccan Initiation Ritual* (Oxford: Oxford University Press)
Baines, E. 2008. 'Complicating Victims and Perpetrators in Uganda: On Dominic Ongwen' (JRP Field Note 7) (July 2008) [available at: http://justiceandreconciliation.com/wp-content/uploads/2008/07/JRP_FN7_Dominic-Ongwen.pdf (accessed 19 July 2018)]
Beah, I. 2007. *A Long Way Gone: Memoirs of a Boy Soldier* (New York: Farrar, Straus and Giroux)
Berrey, S.A. 2009. 'Resistance Begins at Home: The Black Family and Lessons in Survival and Subversion in Jim Crow Mississippi' 3 *Black Women, Gender + Families* 65
Bloom, H. 2008. 'Introduction', in H. Bloom (ed.), *William Golding's Lord of the Flies* (New York: Bloom's Literary Criticism) 1
Child Soldiers International 2018a. 'Why 18 Matters: Executive Summary' [available at: https://www.child-soldiers.org/Handlers/Download.ashx?IDMF=f437c5d7-d897-46b7-8b01-5449f8ba9010 (accessed 25 July 2018)]
Child Soldiers International 2018b. 'Who are Child Soldiers?' [available at: https://www.child-soldiers.org/who-are-child-soldiers (accessed 30 May 2018)]
Chothia, F. 2015. 'Profile: Dominic Ongwen of Uganda's LRA', *BBC News* (26 January) [available at: https://www.bbc.com/news/world-africa-30709581 (accessed 10 July 2018)]
Couo-Zotti, F. 1998 *Charly en guerre* (Paris: Dapper) (originally published in 1996 as *Un enfant dans la guerre*, by Éditions Haho-ACCT-BRAO, Lomé, Togo)
Dongala, E. 2005. *Johnny Mad Dog* (New York: Farrar, Straus and Giroux)
Drumbl, M.A. 2012. *Reimagining Child Soldiers in International Law and Policy* (Oxford: Oxford University Press)
Drumbl, M.A. 2016. 'Victims Who Victimise' 4 *London Review of International Law* 217
Du Bois, W.E.B. 2007. *The Souls of Black Folk* (Oxford: Oxford University Press)
Feldman, R.L. and Arrous, M.B. 2013. 'Confronting Africa's Sobels' 43 *Parameters* 66
Golding, W. 1954. *Lord of the Flies* (New York: Perigree)
ICC [International Criminal Court] 2016. 'Statement of the Prosecutor of the International Criminal Court, Fatou Bensouda, at the opening of Trial in the Case against Dominic Ongwen' (6 December) [available at: https://www.icc-cpi.int/Pages/item.aspx?name=2016-12-06-otp-stat-ongwen (accessed 25 July 2018)]
Iweala, U. 2005. *Beasts of No Nation* (New York: Harper)
Kandeh, J. 1999. 'Ransoming the State: Elite Origins of Subaltern Terror in Sierra Leone' 26 *Review of African Political Economy* 349
Kourouma, A. 2006. *Allah Is Not Obliged* (New York: Anchor Books)
Mazrui, A. 1973. 'The Lumpen Proletariat and the Lumpen Militariat: African Soldiers as a New Political Class' 21 *Political Studies* 1

---

[141] An American aid worker offers to help Lao get to America to continue her education.
[142] Dongala 2005: 321.

Nguyen, K. (dir.) 2012. *War Witch* [film]
NTV Uganda 2015. 'Dominic Ongwen Reveals Why He Left Kony' [available at: https://www.youtube.com/watch?v=CDiCGf3xDWI (accessed 23 July 2018)]
Olopade, D. 2014. *The Bright Continent: Breaking Rules and Making Change in Modern Africa* (New York: Houghton Mifflin Harcourt)
Presley, M. 2017. 'Lord of the Flies and the Coral Island' [available at: http://www.william-golding.co.uk/lord-flies-coral-island (accessed 25 July 2018)]
Saro-Wiwa, K. 1994. *Sozaboy: A Novel in Rotten English* (New York: Longman) (originally published in 1985 by Port Harcourt, Nigeria: Saros International Publishers)
Sony PlayStation 2017. 'God of War – Be a Warrior' [available at: http://www.yousubtitles.com/God-of-War-Be-A-Warrior-PS4-Gameplay-Trailer-E3-2017-id-701700 (accessed 19 July 2018)]
Talbert, M. and Wolfendale, J. 2018. 'The Moral Responsibility of Child Soldiers and the Case of Dominic Ongwen', Stockholm Centre for the Ethics of War and Peace [available at: http://stockholmcentre.org/the-moral-responsibility-of-child soldiers-and-the-case-of-dominic-ongwen/ (accessed 25 July 2018)]
University of Illinois Springfield 2018. 'Sankofa' [available at: https://www.uis.edu/africanamericanstudies/students/sankofa/ (accessed 24 July 2018)]

2. Challenges for the protection of child victims of recruitment and use in an era of complex armed conflicts: the Colombian case
Ana María Jiménez

In the last two decades, the dynamics of international and non-international armed conflicts have changed radically.[1] An increase in terrorist incidents, modified tactics of armed groups, the deployment of smaller weapons and links between armed groups and criminal bands are just some examples of developments within the nature of armed conflict.[2] These developments challenge the application of international humanitarian law (IHL) in armed conflict situations. Colombia constitutes a stark example.

The goal of this chapter is to study developments in the Colombian armed conflict following the demobilization of paramilitary groups and the formation of so-called criminal bands (BACRIM – from the Spanish, 'bandas criminales'), as well as the implications of these developments for militarized children. In particular, this chapter examines issues that arise in the application of the international legal framework to child recruitment[3] and to the situation of child BACRIM combatants, as well as the ramifications for the legal status of children affected by forced recruitment. This chapter also analyses how shifts in paramilitary dynamics and BACRIM's emergence might affect the implementation of the peace agreement between the Colombian government and the Revolutionary Armed Forces of Colombia (FARC-EP) guerrilla group, specifically in terms of ending the crime of child recruitment and providing guarantees of non-repetition.

This chapter begins by discussing the generally shifting nature of armed conflict and identifying gaps between these operational developments and the content of the international legal framework. The chapter then analyses the case study of Colombia as a specific example of these changing realities. The text focuses on aspects in Colombia pertaining to the recruitment and reintegration of children associated with armed groups, as well as on how the characterization of a conflict as armed or criminal affects developments in transitional justice, reparations and other remedial goals.

---

[1] Quénivet and Shah-Davis 2010.
[2] UNICEF and SRSG 2009.
[3] The term child recruitment is used in this chapter as shorthand for all the ways in which children become associated with armed forces and armed groups, which could be enlistment, abduction, conscription, use in hostilities and being born into the armed groups in protracted conflicts. I deploy the term 'recruitment' in this regard without any normative or phraseological intention – this is purely for the purposes of expedience.

1. THE CHANGING NATURE OF ARMED CONFLICTS AND THEIR IMPACT ON CHILDREN

Several decades ago, it was easier to classify armed conflicts as international or non-international, and it was just as easy to categorize those armed groups which were parties to a conflict. Most conflicts were of an international nature, with the opposing group being the national army of the enemy country. However, the nature of many conflicts has changed. Not only does the world face an increase in the number of internal armed conflicts and terrorist attacks, but new types of war have emerged.[4] Winton explains that 'these new wars are characterized by multifarious networks of (increasingly indistinguishable) violent actors, who severely affect the community in which they function'.[5] Such groups have economic, social and political control over vast territories, especially those where state institutions are weak.[6] These groups have the ability to mutate, split into several groups and modify their military strategies. Consequently, monitoring, combating and punishing these groups becomes more complex.

In 1996, appointed expert, Graça Machel, presented the first report on the impact of armed conflict on children to the United Nations (UN) General Assembly.[7] At that time, she concluded that the characteristics of contemporary armed conflicts increase risks for children. The repeated collapse of governments in many countries as well as the vestiges of colonialism fomented inequality and conflict.[8] According to Machel, the percentage of civilian war victims has increased and children have become the targets of armed groups and of perpetrators of war crimes.[9] In her report, Machel adds that the real impact on children's lives remains invisible, especially in terms of child recruitment.

Ten years after the publication of Machel's report, the UN conducted a strategic review to identify advances and challenges regarding the protection of children affected by armed conflicts.[10] The review shows that, although the number of interstate armed conflicts has been declining, prolonged conflicts within states have proliferated. This review explains how the cross-border dynamics of these conflicts implicate a variety of non-state actors, and further observes an increased participation of paramilitary and proxy forces whose motivations 'may switch back and forth from armed conflict to criminal violence to other forms of armed political violence'.[11] The review also notes that non-state actors have several labels, including insurgents, resistance movements, opposition forces, militias, rebels and paramilitaries. Finally, the review analyses how the participation of paramilitary and proxy forces in armed conflicts increases the vulnerability of children due to weak accountability mechanisms.

According to Coomaraswamy, independent of their nature (international or non-international, intrastate or cross-border), armed conflicts represent a significant and

---

[4] Mundy 2011; Kaldor 2013.
[5] Winton 2004: 9.
[6] Quénivet and Shah-Davis 2010.
[7] UN General Assembly 1996.
[8] Ibid.: [22].
[9] Ibid.: [24].
[10] UNICEF and SRSG 2009.
[11] Ibid.: 10.

harmful threat to children. This is largely because children are used by armed groups in many ways. They participate in combat, in addition to carrying out support functions such as cooks, porters, bodyguards, messengers and spies. Most of these children are inexperienced in conducting hostilities and lack training, which increases their vulnerability.[12] Due to the availability of small weapons, children are seen as a useful tool as combatants.[13] Marginalized and especially vulnerable children, such as children that have been separated from their families and communities, are most likely to participate in armed groups.[14] Some children perceive armed groups as a way to escape from domestic violence or ensure their protection from attacks by other groups.[15] In countless cases, children are forcibly recruited and abducted by armed groups. The situation for girls is particularly critical: beyond being trained and put on the front line for combat, they are also used as domestic servants and sex slaves, where they are denied control over their reproductive rights as they are subjected to forced impregnation,[16] compelled to use contraception and endure abortion.[17]

2. APPLICATION OF INTERNATIONAL STANDARDS ON CHILD RECRUITMENT TO COMPLEX ARMED CONFLICTS

Child recruitment is a concern that has advanced in international standards over the past 20 years in the areas of international human rights law (IHRL), international humanitarian law (IHL) and international criminal law (ICL). It is a very complex issue not only because it violates children's rights, but also because legal, economic, political and psychosocial approaches are necessary to understand and address the problem. The participation of children in armed groups is characterized as a war crime according to the Rome Statute to the International Criminal Court, and is considered to be among the worst forms of child labour,[18] representing a multiple violation of children's rights.[19] It is acknowledged as a 'global phenomenon' that presently involves not only developing countries such as Colombia, Libya and Myanmar, but also rich nations such as the United Kingdom and the USA.[20] According to Wessells, the militarization of children is currently among the most contentious issues in the United Nations Security Council (UNSC).[21]

The changes brought about by international legal standards have specific implications for the analysis of child recruitment. The Optional Protocol to the Convention on the Rights of the Child on the Involvement of Children in Armed Conflict (OPAC) still allows for the voluntary recruitment of persons between 16 and 18 years old by state armed

---

[12] Coomaraswamy 2010: 536.
[13] Wessells 2002: 238.
[14] UN General Assembly 1996: [35].
[15] Brett and Specht 2004.
[16] ICC 2012: [14] and [18].
[17] Coomaraswamy 2010.
[18] ILO Convention 182 1999, art. 3(a).
[19] Convention on the Rights of the Child, art. 38.
[20] Wessells 2002: 237.
[21] Ibid.

forces (Article 3), but sets 18 as the minimum age for conscription into those armed forces, as well as for any kind of recruitment by armed groups.[22] As extensively detailed elsewhere in the book, international law regarding children and militarization is chronologically uneven. For example, concerning ICL, the Rome Statute of the International Criminal Court (ICC) classifies conscripting, enlisting or using children under the age of 15 to actively participate in hostilities as a war crime. Because this proscription applies in the context of war crimes (as opposed to crimes against humanity), the impugned conduct must be found to occur within 'the context of and associated with an armed conflict', whether of an international or non-international nature.

In the ICC's first conviction, the Lubanga Trial Chamber judgment analysed the elements of the crime of enlisting and recruiting children.[23] First, the Court began by establishing whether the situation taking place in the Democratic Republic of Congo (DRC) was an armed conflict. In this regard, the Chamber referred to paragraph 2 of the introduction to the section of Elements of Crime relating to war crimes under Article 8(2) of the Rome Statute, which states that elements for war crimes 'shall be interpreted within the established framework of the international law of armed conflict'. Taking into account the lack of a conventional definition of armed conflict, the Chamber employed the jurisprudence of the International Criminal Tribunal for the Former Yugoslavia (ICTY). According to the *Tadić Interlocutory Appeal* decision, 'an armed conflict exists whenever there is a resort to armed force between States or protracted violence between governmental authorities and organized armed groups or between such groups within a State'.[24]

Although it is clear that the principles of humanitarian law apply to any armed conflict (international or non-international), according to Kurth, 'the mixed nature of many contemporary armed conflicts in times of Failed States[,] or at least States[] which lose control over parts of their territory, poses a serious challenge for the proper application of principles of international humanitarian law'.[25] This mixed nature also challenges the establishment of a connection between child recruitment cases and armed conflict. Hence, one of the principal blind spots in the applicability of IHL and ICL is that an armed conflict (whether international or non-international) may not be technically found to exist in a context of systemic violence by criminal syndicates, whose activities, structures and conduct may not exactly map onto the template of 'armed groups'. This is all the more paradoxical in that many of the recruitment practices of groups such as criminal syndicates may share much in common with those of armed groups, such as the RUF, LRA and MILF, that are extensively discussed in this book.

The Colombia case offers an example of these knotty ambiguities and discomfiting gaps. But Colombia is not alone. At present, there are several examples of war and terrorism situations in which the application of international legal standards relating to child recruitment remains unclear. This is vexing since terrorist groups may use children in a way that resembles the methods deployed by illegal armed groups.[26] Some

---

[22] See Kaushik and Freeland in this volume; Odongo in this volume.
[23] ICC 2012.
[24] ICTY *Prosecutor v. Tadić*, cited by ICC 2012: [533].
[25] Kurth 2013: 2.
[26] Singer 2006; Moodrick-Even 2010.

such children are in conditions of extreme poverty while others are victims of violence; both situations can lead to recruitment. Children who participate in Al-Qaeda terrorist actions, who are known as the 'Birds of Paradise' or 'Youth of Heaven', present as an example.[27] These children are under the age of 14 and are used to 'spy, transport military supplies and equipment, videotape attacks and plant explosive devices', in addition to carrying out attacks against security forces and civilians and participating in suicide attacks.[28] However, some of these children are often not considered child combatants because of the nature of the attacks that they perpetrate and the armed groups which use them.

The use of children by terrorist groups is a new and serious threat to children.[29] Two fundamental principles of IHL are challenged by this new form of war, with serious consequences for children: the distinction between combatants and civilians and the doctrine of proportionality.[30] The lack of a clear definition of terrorism makes the distinction between acts of terrorism and liberation attacks in which children participate even more difficult. Chadwick considers it crucial to distinguish between acts of terrorism perpetrated during liberation struggles and those carried out separately from such struggles, since this distinction has legal and political implications in terms of the characterization of terrorist acts as serious breaches or war crimes.[31] In the context of such liberation struggles, Chadwick argues:

> States are afraid to recognize the existence of an armed conflict under these circumstances. States are unwilling to recognize some armed groups or liberation movements' forms of operation because this recognition implies the application of IHL. Instead they prefer to combat these groups as criminals and prosecute them under penal law.[32]

The result of this approach is that children who are used by terrorist groups in the context of an armed conflict often fail to be designated as combatants; rather, they are dealt with pursuant to the relevant terrorism standards. Treatment of these children as terrorists is particularly problematic in terms of their protection, legal proceedings and conditions of imprisonment.[33]

The situation of child recruitment in Haiti is another largely under-discussed example of a fluid context in which children have been subjected to recruitment. Despite the fact that the UN's Stabilization Mission in Haiti (MINUSTAH) was established in the country with the mandate to disarm, demobilize and reintegrate all armed groups, urban armed groups continue to be used by politico-criminal entrepreneurs of all types, including government members. These groups serve various purposes – including political functions – in the areas they control, mainly in popular neighbourhoods such as Bel Air and Cité Soleil. A notable characteristic of these groups is the fluidity between the different

---

[27] See Bloom in this volume; Casey-Maslen in this volume.
[28] UN Secretary-General 2011: [54].
[29] O'Neil and Van Broeckhoven 2018.
[30] SRSG 2008.
[31] Chadwick 1996.
[32] Ibid.: 10.
[33] SRSG 2008; Drumbl and Rona 2018.

functions they fulfil.[34] This fluidity has made the demobilization of children associated with these groups difficult, as children have continued to join their ranks. In 2007, the Special Representative of the Secretary-General for Children and Armed Conflict (SRSG) stated in this regard that 'children themselves have found their status changing – once considered victims unlawfully recruited, now they are seen as "gang members"'.[35]

On 14 October 2011, the UN Security Council unanimously adopted resolution 2012, which extended MINUSTAH's mandate for a year and recognized that the overall security situation in Haiti had improved since 2010.[36] As a result, the 2012 Annual Report of the UN Secretary-General on Children and Armed Conflict announced that Haiti had been removed from the list of parties which is committing serious violations against children in the context of an armed conflict.[37] At present, the situation is monitored by the Special Representative on Violence Against Children.

As this section has demonstrated, several characteristics of modern warfare complicate the application of traditional notions of armed conflict and the participation of armed groups in hostilities. A lack of clarity regarding the nature of some violent situations, such as armed conflicts or terrorist attacks, consequently constrains the application of international legal frameworks. If a group is not considered to form part of the armed conflict, children recruited by these groups may not then be considered as child combatants. They may be considered victims of exploitation by organized armed violence, gang members or terrorists. In these cases, IHL may not apply and the situation may be regulated by norms applicable to organized crime or terrorism. Victims can be prosecuted, and their status as victims of a war crime may be neglected.

These exact same questions and concerns arise in Colombia today. Although there was a paramilitary demobilization process and a peace agreement with the FARC-EP, several groups have emerged (BACRIM) which use child recruitment as an operational strategy. The victims of recruitment and use by such groups in Colombia face the same struggles as victims of recruitment and use by terrorist or urban armed groups.

3. THE TRANSFORMATION OF COLOMBIA'S ARMED CONFLICT

The Colombian human rights situation has been aggravated by 65 years of internal armed conflict. Some of the root causes of the conflict are inherited from Spanish colonization and derive from the high concentration of land ownership in rural areas. Further, Colombia has among the largest populations of internally displaced persons (IDPs) in the world.[38] According to Colombia's National Victims Unit, the 'armed conflict has displaced approximately 7 million people'[39] from 1985 to 2017. Child recruitment, sexual

---

[34] Schuberth 2017.
[35] SRSG 2007: 8.
[36] UN Security Council Resolution 2070 (12 October 2012).
[37] UN Secretary-General 2012.
[38] Norwegian Refugee Council & Internal Displacement Monitoring Centre 2017.
[39] Colombia Reports 2017.

violence, forced disappearances, killings and summary executions continue to be the country's most serious human rights violations.

The conflict has involved several parties: guerrillas, paramilitaries and the army. The FARC-EP, which has existed since the 1960s, was the largest Marxist–Leninist guerrilla force. The FARC's statutes establish anti-imperialism, Latin American unity and popular well-being as the bases of their cause.[40] The FARC-EP claims it fights to defend the rights of Colombia's rural poor against the rich. However, over time political interests have changed and become mangled to the point of justifying kidnapping, child recruitment and the killing of civilians. After more than 60 years of armed conflict, the Colombian government and the FARC-EP signed a peace agreement, preceded by a long process of peace talks.

According to an Amnesty International report on Colombia, in June 2016 the government and the FARC-EP agreed to a bilateral ceasefire and cessation of hostilities, although a de facto ceasefire had previously been set up in 2015. On 24 August 2016, the parties reached a peace agreement that was signed on 26 September 2016 in Cartagena. However, on 2 October 2016, the peace agreement was rejected in a nationwide referendum, in part because of concerns regarding the agreement's justice provisions.[41] This report continues:

> On 12 November, the two sides announced a revised peace deal, which was signed on 24 November. The agreement was ratified by Congress on 30 November, after which the FARC was due to begin a six-month process of demobilization and disarmament, to be monitored and verified in part by a mission of unarmed UN observers. By the end of the year, FARC combatants had yet to congregate in the concentration zones from where they were due to start the demobilization process, because of delays in making these areas habitable.
>
> On 28 December, Congress approved a law to provide amnesties or pardons to FARC combatants and the waiving of criminal prosecutions for security force personnel not under investigation for or convicted of crimes under international law. Those who had served at least five years in prison for crimes under international law will, under certain circumstances, be conditionally released. Ambiguities in the law could result in many human rights abusers evading justice.[42]

Since then, the government has undertaken several legal reforms to implement the agreement. The government has created the Integral System of Truth, Justice, Reparation, and Non-Repetition (ISTJRNR), which established three mechanisms: (1) a Special Jurisdiction for Peace to investigate and punish perpetrators of crimes under international law; (2) a truth commission; and (3) a commission to find and identify missing people in the framework of the armed conflict.[43] As a consequence, '[a]rmed violence between the Colombian military and FARC-EP reached its lowest level in 50 years'.[44] Additionally, the FARC-EP agreed not to recruit children according to the age standard established for armed groups in the OPAC, that is, 18 years.[45] As noted in the Report of the Secretary-General: 'Since the FARC-EP committed itself to ending child recruitment

---

[40] Statutes of FARC-EP 1993, art. 2.
[41] Amnesty International 2017a.
[42] Ibid.
[43] Ibid.
[44] UN Secretary-General 2017: 50.
[45] Avila 2016.

in the context of the peace talks, the overall number of recruitment cases has dropped.'[46] Afterwards, this issue was included in the final peace agreement in the Peace Special Jurisdiction chapter as one of the crimes that does not permit the granting of amnesties or pardons.[47]

The second largest guerrilla group is the National Liberation Army (ELN), with whom the government has attempted different negotiation processes with no success. 'The ELN began as a movement of students and Catholics, predominately radical priests, inspired by the Cuban Revolution. These individuals believed they represented the majority of Colombians.'[48] In other words, the group presented itself as the face of the poor in society who had been excluded from the state. The ELN has had relationships with different groups. It has been both a rival and ally to the M-19 (19th of April Movement) and the FARC-EP – both of which are currently demobilized groups – as well as the EPL (Popular Liberation Army), which also demobilized but maintains some dissidents still operating in the country.

All guerrilla groups have been responsible for extortions, kidnappings, homicides, sexual violence and child recruitment. Children from vulnerable groups, including indigenous peoples and IDPs, are the most affected. These groups have carried out child recruitment campaigns in schools and forced children to take part in the conflict.[49]

Colombian paramilitaries also recruited children into their ranks, and their recruitment dynamics were similar to those of guerrilla groups. However, there remain some differences between the two in terms of recruitment. First, paramilitary forces paid children wages, varying from US $300 to $400, in some cases per month, and in other cases every three months. They also paid bonuses for special assignments.[50] Second, although both guerrilla and paramilitary groups use girls as sex slaves, the number of cases of sexual violence committed by paramilitary forces against civilians is significantly higher.

Paramilitary self-defence groups used terror against what they perceived as the guerrilla's civilian support networks – for instance human rights' defenders – in the areas where guerrillas were active.[51] The Inter-American Court on Human Rights in several judgments delineated the links between paramilitary groups and units of the Colombian armed forces, politicians and business leaders.[52] Even though paramilitary groups had been declared illegal as early as 1989, the government continued supporting and tolerating them until the demobilization process that was carried out between 2005 and 2007.[53]

Following the demobilization, government agencies, NGOs and even international bodies such as the UN High Commissioner for Human Rights (OHCHR) and the Mission to Support the Peace Process in Colombia of the Organization of American States (MAPP/OAS), began to document changes in the armed conflict's dynamics and the emergence of considerable numbers of 'new' illegal armed groups.

---

[46] UN Secretary-General 2017.
[47] Republic of Colombia 2016 [numeral 5.1.2].
[48] Stanford University 2017: 2.
[49] UN Secretary-General 2009: [21].
[50] Ibid.: [41].
[51] Human Rights Watch 2003.
[52] IACHR 2002.
[53] Human Rights Watch 2003.

In 2009, two years after the demobilization of paramilitaries, the MAPP/OAS reported one of the main threats to peace as the existence of areas that are under the influence of armed factions and closely related to the development of illegal economies. Criminal organizations have established alliances with guerrilla and drug trafficking groups and continue to use violence to prevent the exercise of the law. Communities consider these groups to be a continuation of paramilitary forces.[54] The International Crisis Group has reported alliances between the ELN, Los Rastrojos (categorized as a BACRIM by the government) in Cauca, and dissidents from paramilitary groups created by Vicente Castaño and from the FARC-EP. These alliances result from the division of labour in the drug trafficking chain.[55] Most recently, in 2018, Amnesty International reported:

> Paramilitary structures continued to operate in various parts of the country, despite their supposed demobilization under the terms of Law 975, passed in 2005. There were reports of paramilitary attacks and threats against leaders of the Peace Community of San José de Apartadó in the department of Antioquia.[56]

It is important to note that BACRIM are comprised not only of former paramilitary members and dissidents from the United Self-Defense Forces of Colombia (AUC), but also of former guerrilla members (including the ELN and FARC-EP as mentioned above). The UN OHCHR describes BACRIM as groups 'linked to organized crime – including transnational crime – and local crime, as well as FARC-EP dissidents'.[57]

After the peace dialogues between the government and FARC-EP, the process of establishing temporary pre-grouping points for FARC-EP members to undergo disarmament and reintegration was very slow. This situation led to mistrust and FARC-EP vulnerability, and it also provided an incentive for desertion or joining BACRIM.[58]

Torrijos defines BACRIM as heirs of the private counterinsurgency forces. He distinguishes two types of BACRIM: one has emerged from paramilitary gangs, and the other is a FARC-EP/BACRIM hybrid which is called FARCRIM. Now FARCRIM are FARC-EP members who are not demobilized or who, if demobilized, continue operating and building alliances with illegal groups. From Torrijos' perspective, the FARCRIM are a continuation of the FARC-EP with permanent and formal alliances. Torrijos has demonstrated that the FARCRIM has a command structure and operates according to strategic plans.[59] BACRIM use child recruitment as a strategy. The 2016 Report of the UNSG on children affected by the armed conflict in Colombia stated:

> An increasing number of cases of recruitment and use by the five main post-demobilization groups and other local armed groups, such as La Empresa and Los Machos, were reported. According to the Early Warning System of the Office of the Ombudsman, these groups were present in approximately half of the departments and were responsible for grave violations against children in cities such as Buenaventura, Cúcuta, Medellín and Tumaco in 2015.[60]

---

[54] MAPP/OEA 2009.
[55] Prieto 2014.
[56] Amnesty International 2018.
[57] UN High Commissioner for Human Rights 2017: [44].
[58] Ibid.: [37].
[59] Torrijos, referenced in Ambos and Zuluaga 2015.
[60] UN Secretary-General 2016: [21].

In 2018, the Colombian government approved Law 1908. The purpose of Law 1908 is to facilitate the collective criminal investigation of BACRIM members who decided to surrender and collaborate with the General Attorney. This law requires that all children who were used by these groups be put under the protection of the Colombian Family Welfare Institute (ICBF).

4. BACRIM'S STATUS IN COLOMBIA

The nature of the illegal armed groups that appeared after the paramilitary demobilization is not clear, and there are different positions on the matter. The Colombian government considers these groups to be criminal gangs with no relation to the paramilitary structure and the armed conflict. According to Article 2 of Law 1908, these groups can be classified as:

> Organized Armed Groups (GAO) are those who, under the direction of a responsible command, exercise control over a part of the territory that allows the carrying out of sustained and concerted military operations. Organized Crime Groups (GDO) are structured groups of three or more people who exist for a certain period of time and who act in concert with the purpose of committing one or more felonies or offences established in accordance with the Palermo Convention, with a view to obtaining, directly or indirectly, an economic benefit or other material benefit. [Our translation]

Since their emergence, the government has combated these groups with the police and not with the army. However, after the FARC-EP's demobilization, the government announced the creation of a new military unit – named the Hercules Task Force – 'aimed at combating illegal armed groups that have begun to seize areas once controlled by Marxist FARC rebels in strategic drug-trafficking territory in the south of the Andean nation'.[61] It is important to note that despite the establishment of this military unit, these groups continue to be classified as criminal bands, and thus ordinary criminal jurisdiction is applied to them instead of the peace and justice jurisdiction, which applies to former paramilitaries and some members of the guerrillas included on the lists submitted by the government to the General Attorney according to Law 975 of 2005 (the Justice and Peace Law).[62] The United Nations Secretary-General (UNSG) in his 2010 Annual Report described these groups as:

> Not homogeneous in terms of their motivation, structure or modus operandi . . . Some of the groups have a military structure and chain of command, and are capable of exercising territorial control and sustaining military-type operations. Moreover, they have a political and ideological orientation similar to that of the former AUC.[63]

In its annual reports on Colombia, the Colombian Office of OHCHR refers to these groups as 'illegal armed groups that emerged after the demobilization of paramilitary

---

[61] Reuters Staff 2018.
[62] In Colombia, transitional justice mechanisms form part of two frames: (1) the transitional justice jurisdiction, formerly Justice and Peace Jurisdiction, mainly applicable to paramilitary and some FARC-EP members; and (2) the ISTJRNR, applicable to FARC-EP members and Armed Forces officials.
[63] UN Secretary-General 2010: [128].

organizations'.[64] It also states that post-demobilization groups have a coercive presence in communities and are identified by all sectors as one of the greatest threats to public order and human rights.[65] In contrast, several Colombian civil society organizations consider these groups to be a continuation of paramilitary structures. The Colombian Commission of Jurists labels them as 'neoparamilitary groups'[66] and Amnesty International still calls them paramilitaries. In their words: 'Despite their supposed demobilization a decade ago, paramilitaries continue to operate in various parts of the country.'[67]

Granada, Restrepo and Tobón have found that the nature of these groups is very complex and diverse.[68] In 2009 it was possible to identify within these groups new paramilitary armies, dispersed paramilitaries, newly annexed paramilitaries and criminal forces. All of these groups not only operate in territories formerly controlled by the Autodefensas Unidas de Colombia (AUC)[69] but also exercise control in areas that have not been subjected to such violence in the past. This has led to greater complexity in territorial control disputes.[70] These entities emerged between the paramilitary demobilization and the FARC peace process. The aforementioned illegal armed groups are mainly present in the areas controlled by paramilitaries. Avila classifies these armed groups in three different categories:

1. *Dissidents:* structures that never demobilized.
2. *The rearmed:* structures that participated in the paramilitary demobilization process and then subsequently rearmed.
3. *Emerging groups:* groups that are indirectly linked to paramilitary groups but have a new genesis.[71]

It was between 2006 and 2011 that the first generation of these groups appeared. In total there were up to 36 structures or networks across the country. After 2011, due to a process of cooptation between criminal structures, these organizations began a process of adaptation and several of them consolidated.[72]

The classification of BACRIM as armed groups that participate in the conflict or as criminal bands has legal and political implications. First, the applicable legal framework varies: if they are recognized as illegal armed groups that form part of the conflict, they may be subject to the transitional justice jurisdiction;[73] conversely, if they are simply considered to be members of organized crime, the applicable legal framework is the ordinary criminal jurisdiction. Second, how these groups (and their members) are classified bears upon the political treatment that they receive. If they are considered to be

---

[64] UN High Commissioner for Human Rights 2013: [83].
[65] Ibid.
[66] Colombian Commission of Jurists 2008.
[67] Amnesty International 2017b.
[68] Granada et al. 2009.
[69] The AUC was a paramilitary group demobilized between 2003 and 2006.
[70] Granada et al. 2009: 472–3.
[71] Avila 2016.
[72] Ibid.
[73] Created by Law 975 of 2005, arts 32 to 35.

combatants, they have political status that, in an eventual context of peace negotiations, would authorize their participation. If they are solely considered to be criminal bands, they have no political recognition, and thus they are treated solely as criminals according to Law 1908 of 2018.

5. CRIMINAL BANDS OR PARTIES TO AN ARMED CONFLICT?

The human rights situation in Colombia offers important insights into the complexity of modern conflicts. The situation is particularly interesting considering that Colombia is not a fragile state when compared to other countries characterized by a lack of democratic institutions that also confront long-term armed conflicts. Furthermore, the government has adopted a strong legal framework based on international human rights standards. It has also set up peace initiatives to facilitate the demobilization of paramilitaries, FARC-EP and the ELN, in addition to the release of children. Moreover, despite the problems revealed during the implementation of the Justice and Peace Law, Colombia's legal demobilization framework has been referred to as a transitional justice model by academics and also in countries such as Iraq.[74]

The convergence of several groups, including insurgent groups, paramilitaries, drug cartels, criminal gangs and official armed forces shows how IHL's boundaries regarding terrorism and organized armed violence are no longer easy to demarcate. In particular, the transformation of paramilitaries and the formation of BACRIM illustrate the difficulty of identifying these groups as parties to the conflict and of applying IHL rules to their crimes.

The long-term debate in Colombia about characterizing the groups formed post-demobilization shows that the arguments are not only legal but also political. The UNSC process to examine the situation of children affected by Colombia's armed conflict has revealed several political issues concerning the monitoring of crimes committed by BACRIM.[75] Some states aligned with Colombia's position, like India, China and Pakistan, consider that the reporting of these cases opens the door for the inclusion of similar situations into the UNSC's agenda. In this regard, after the debate on the adoption of UNSC Resolution 2068 (2012), India's permanent mission expressed the view that 'the Secretary-General's reports include situations that do not meet the threshold for being

---

[74] Cast 2011.

[75] Since 1999, the matter of children in armed conflicts has been an important topic on the agenda of the Security Council. Between 1999 and 2005 the Council adopted six resolutions which contain concrete measures to protect children. Resolution 1612 of July 2005 was one of the most important among the Council's achievements. This resolution created a monitoring and reporting mechanism (MRM) 'focused on six grave violations against children: recruiting and use of child soldiers; killing and maiming of children; rape and other grave sexual violence against children; attacks on schools and hospitals; abduction of children; and denial of humanitarian access to children'. This Resolution also created the Security Council Working Group on Children and Armed Conflict. The SRSG monitors the situation of children and the developments of the MRM. Every year the Secretary-General submits a report to the Security Council on the situation of children affected by the armed conflict in countries in which these violations take place.

an armed conflict or a threat to the maintenance of international peace and security. The facts . . . should have led to the removal of such situations, not their continued inclusion with a blasé disclaimer.'[76]

The UNSC argument to continue reporting cases of groups that are delisted – for example, paramilitaries in Colombia – is that it is important to follow up on the demobilization and disarmament of armed groups to ensure the protection of children. Consequently, if the UNSC determines 'that de-listed parties recruit and use children at a later point in time, or fail to allow continuous and unhindered access to the UN for verification, they will be re-listed onto the annexes, and the Security Council will be alerted to the non-compliance'.[77]

It is important to clarify that mentioning BACRIM in UNSG reports as a new group formed after the demobilization of paramilitaries cannot be interpreted as classifying these groups as parties to the conflict. As it is stated in all of the UNSG reports on children affected by armed conflict since 2004, 'the reference to a situation is not a legal determination, and reference to a non-State party does not affect its legal status'.[78] This statement's inclusion in UNSG reports as well as in UNSC Resolutions is a result of previous debates on the legal determination of the parties to conflict in Northern Ireland and Russia (regarding the situation of Chechnya).[79]

However, recognizing BACRIM's political character or their criminal status is not easy and comes with some risks. Human Rights Watch has expressed concerns about attributing a political status to BACRIM.[80] They argue that there is a high risk of impunity due to well-noted problems within the existing legal framework that facilitates paramilitary demobilization. BACRIM could be allowed to participate in potential peace negotiations, a situation that could complicate ongoing peace dialogues with the ELN.[81] The International Crisis Group (ICG) has a different opinion. Using the example of ERPAC's partial demobilization in 2011,[82] ICG argues that characterizing BACRIM as common criminals can affect the punishment of its members. ERPAC's demobilized members 'received less serious sentences for crimes such as "aggravated conspiracy" and were not charged with serious human rights violations'.[83]

Each alternative (considering BACRIM as political actors or as criminal bands) thus has different implications that must be carefully addressed, and thus each situation requires a case-by-case analysis, with permanent monitoring of the groups to document changes in their modus operandi, structures and territorial control. This is fundamental for identifying challenges in addressing the situation and guaranteeing the effective protection of children who have been forcibly recruited.

---

[76] Johnson 2012.
[77] UN Secretary-General 2003.
[78] See for example, UN Secretary-General 2012: [6].
[79] See UN Secretary-General 2003.
[80] Human Rights Watch 2012.
[81] Perez-Santiago 2012.
[82] The Ejecito Popular Anti-terrorista de Colombia – ERPAC – is a group that emerged after the demobilization of paramilitaries in Colombia.
[83] Perez-Santiago 2012.

6. PRACTICAL CONSEQUENCES OF THE CHARACTERIZATION OF BACRIM FOR CHILDREN

The debate on characterizing BACRIM as criminal bands or as parties to the armed conflict has serious implications for protection, reintegration and reparations for children recruited and used by these groups. First, the lack of recognition of children's active participation when they are recruited by BACRIM in the context of armed conflict relegates them to the sphere of organized armed violence. When categorized in this way, IHL does not apply to them. As long as these groups are considered criminal bands, children cannot be treated as combatants, and they will be treated in most cases as young criminal offenders. As a result, it may be very difficult to demonstrate that demobilized children are victims of BACRIM, according to Article 3 of the Victims and Land Restitution Law.[84] Finally, BACRIM will not be able to participate in peace negotiations or action plans drawn up pursuant to UNSC Resolutions on children and armed conflict that allow humanitarian agreements for children's liberation, a situation that hinders the reintegration of these children.

According to Article 162 of the Colombian Criminal Code, any person who 'recruits persons below the age of 18 years or forces them to participate directly or indirectly in hostilities or armed action' can be prosecuted for illicit recruitment of children. This article is defined in such a way that the perpetrator may either be a member of an illegal armed group or any other person that takes part in hostilities. This prohibition is also quite extensive. It applies not only to the act of recruitment, but also to the act of forcing minors to participate in hostilities.

Based on this article, BACRIM members could be prosecuted for recruitment of children if there is evidence that the events took place during the armed conflict or in connection thereto.[85] However, prosecutors may face the difficult task of proving the perpetrator's connection with the conflict and of linking this to the child recruitment case, given that there is a tendency to deny BACRIM participation status in the conflict.

Prosecutors have found another way to hold BACRIM members accountable for using children in their ranks. They use Article 188D of the Criminal Code, which establishes that using children to commit crimes is itself a crime. This article is not part of international humanitarian law, and it is intended to prosecute cases that are unrelated to armed conflict. Cases must be built upon the argument that the impugned conduct took place in the context of organized crime, committed by an actor who is not party to a conflict. Therefore, children will not appear in the judgment as child combatants but rather as child victims of exploitation or child labour.

Although both articles – one article using the perspective of illicit recruitment and the other using the perspective of criminality – aim to protect children from exploitation and consider them to be victims, the legal consequences differ in each case:

- *Route one:* If the case goes through Article 162, the trial might require proof of the child's active participation in the armed conflict and their status as a victim. In this

---

[84] Law 1448 of 2011.
[85] Constitutional Court of Colombia 2017.

case, there is precedent for closing or ceasing investigations of crimes committed by these children, taking into account their status as victims of one of the gravest war crimes.[86] The majority of these cases proceed to the Colombian Family Welfare Institute's (ICBF) special programme for demobilized children. These children are not put in prison. Article 175 of the Children and Adolescence Code provides that children who have participated directly and indirectly in hostilities, armed actions or crimes committed by illegal armed groups are subject to the principle of prosecutorial discretion. This means that the prosecutor has the power to withdraw charges after they have been presented and cease the process.

- *Route two:* If the case goes through Article 188D, the child will be considered as a victim of child exploitation and the perpetrator convicted. However, it is very probable that this child will be sent to the Juvenile Criminal Responsibility System (JCRS) to account for the crimes he or she committed. There is a large body of evidence on how the deprivation of liberty of people between 16 and 18 years old, especially those recruited by BACRIM in Colombia, has become JCRS' main sanction.[87]

7. REINTEGRATION

The ICBF special programme for demobilized children was instituted for the reintegration of children demobilized from recognized illegal armed groups: guerrilla groups and paramilitaries. In recent years, after the paramilitary structure's demobilization, the programme adopted a broader vision of recruitment and started receiving children who declare themselves to be part of the BACRIM, with the aim of re-establishing their rights. According to official ICBF information between 1999 and 2015, 208 children recruited by BACRIM have been demobilized.[88] The majority of these children have come from Antioquia, Meta, Nariño, Chocó and Casanare.[89] However, there are cases of children demobilized from BACRIM who have not been allowed to join the ICBF programme. For example, in 2012, The Coalition to Stop the Use of Girls, Boys, and Youths in the Armed Conflict in Colombia (Coalico) reported the recruitment of three boys by BACRIM in the central region of Colombia. They were part of the armed group for one to two years, and during that time, they were subjected to intensive military training. The children's families asked the government to reintegrate the children as former child soldiers. However, the government did not recognize the children as combatants given the nature of the armed group and they were not accepted onto ICBF's special programme for demobilized children.[90]

Additionally, a considerable number of cases regarding children who are part of BACRIM have been sent to JCRS, and criminal proceedings have been opened to investigate crimes committed by these children, despite evidence that they were exploited

---

[86] Ladisch et al. 2014.
[87] ICBF 2012a.
[88] ICBF 2018.
[89] ICBF 2012b.
[90] Watchlist on Children and Armed Conflict 2012.

and used by BACRIM structures. In several departments of Colombia, once prosecutors receive information concerning a child who has participated in an illegal activity that could be related to the modus operandi of a BACRIM, these prosecutors proceed within the juvenile criminal process but fail to investigate the command structure of BACRIM or the recruitment or illegal utilization of the child.[91] In this regard, the Committee on the Rights of the Child has expressed concern about the heavy recruitment of children by BACRIM and reports that some of these children are prosecuted by the state party as criminals and not treated as victims, and are therefore not included in the programme of the ICBF for demobilized children.[92]

The situation described previously demonstrates the legal uncertainties for BACRIM children after their demobilization from armed groups. There is no clarity on whether they will be treated as child combatants, and thus remitted to the ICBF special programme for demobilized children, or if they will be prosecuted as juvenile offenders.

Some children do not approach state institutions for fear of being interrogated, imprisoned or sent back to their home towns where the threat of armed groups persists. Instead, some children decide to return directly to their communities, confronting alone the serious effects of the armed conflict and their wounds. These children receive neither psychosocial assistance nor compensation for damage. Several national and international organizations, as well as the media, have reported cases of children who were not demobilized from paramilitary groups during the demobilization process. Such children continue to participate in BACRIM, while others have returned to their communities in a clandestine fashion.[93]

A similar situation might happen if the Colombian government fails to reintegrate and provide reparations for the 124 children released by the FARC-EP,[94] a process that began in 2016. At present, there is fear that these children who are in FARC-EP concentration areas might escape or reach adult age without their legal situation being resolved.[95] The delays and failures of the special child demobilization programme created by the government represent additional factors that might encourage children to leave the rural areas, feeling that the promises made to them have been broken, or in the most serious cases, even join BACRIM or FARCRIM.[96] In this regard, the UN verification mission in Colombia reported:

> As verified by the Mission, a sizeable number of former FARC-EP members have moved out of the territorial areas. The reasons are manifold, including family reunions, political activities and the search for more appropriate locations for reintegration. However, growing frustration with the lack of opportunities is also a major factor. In some locations, a significant number of former FARC-EP members have joined illegal or dissident groups.[97]

---

[91] Jimenez 2012.
[92] CRC Committee 2015: [67d].
[93] *El Tiempo* 2012.
[94] *El País* 2018.
[95] W Radio 2017.
[96] *Panam Post* 2017.
[97] UN Secretary-General 2017: [30].

8. REPARATIONS AND OTHER BENEFITS

Another consequence of refusing to recognize child victims of BACRIM as child combatants is that this makes it difficult for them to benefit from reparations. Until Constitutional Court Judgment C-069 of 2016,[98] children recruited by BACRIM did not receive reparations pursuant to the Victims and Land Restitution Law (Law 1448 of 2011), with some exceptions,[99] and could not be certified as former combatants. According to Decree 128 of 2003 (Article 2) and Law 418 of 1997 (Article 1), children recruited by BACRIM could not be certified as demobilized by the Comité Operativo para la Dejación de Armas (CODA).[100] This certification is dependent on the official classification of the groups as parties to the conflict. It is important to note that this certification is the basis for applying the special legal framework for the demobilization of illegal groups in Colombia, which carries legal and judicial implications.

It is also essential to entitle the affected children to legal and socioeconomic benefits. According to Decree 128 of 2003 (Article 13), legal benefits include the right to pardon, conditional suspension of the sentence's execution, cessation of proceedings and preclusion of the investigation or a restraining order, according to the state of the legal process. Socioeconomic benefits include educational programmes, monthly wages and a productive project, as well as special benefits for disabled persons. In this regard, the Committee on the Rights of the Child has expressed concern about the 'potentially discriminatory treatment of children depending on which illegal armed group they are demobilized from and that children who have been informally released from illegal armed groups do not receive assistance and recovery measures'.[101] However, with Constitutional Court Judgment C-069, the Court made an important statement on the recognition of the status of victims of children recruited by BACRIM, in the following terms:

> From the perspective of minors who are victims of recruitment, and based on the principle of equality, the difference that may exist between these groups is irrelevant in terms of defining the route of access to restitution mechanisms, because for that minor, what is relevant is having been forcibly recruited by an armed group or criminal organization that has certain characteristics and that takes action in the context of the armed conflict . . .
>
> [T]he facts attributed to the post-demobilization groups have been considered to have occurred in the context of the armed conflict, when it is possible to establish their relationship or connection with the real and historical complexity that has characterized the Colombian internal conflict, which is why the victims of such groups cannot be disqualified for the purposes of exercising their rights and the benefits recognized by Law 1448 of 2011. [Our translation][102]

Consequently, the Court ordered that the CODA certificate must be given to all victims of child recruitment in the context of the armed conflict who reach the age of majority,

---

[98] Constitutional Court of Colombia 2016.
[99] For instance, in order to access the Law 1448 of 2011 reparations, some victims of BACRIM declared they did not know the nature or name of the armed group that violated their rights (although they actually knew that information). In some cases they were advised to do so by the Victims Unit officials who would be granting those reparations. Giraldo and Jimenez 2015.
[100] Jimenez 2012.
[101] CRC Committee 2010.
[102] Constitutional Court of Colombia 2016: [9.22–9.31].

regardless of the illegal armed group from which they have been demobilized. Despite the Constitutional Court judgment that importantly recognizes children recruited by BACRIM as victims of the conflict, uncertainty persists about which groups CODA will consider to be illegal armed groups related to the conflict. Taking into account that the corresponding CODA certification determines all of the benefits of reintegration, and that not all of the groups that currently recruit children have the essential characteristics to be considered armed groups with a close relationship to the armed conflict, children recruited by BACRIM will continue to face the uncertainty of whether or not they will be recognized as demobilized persons, and whether their legal treatment will be as juvenile offenders or victims of the armed conflict.

Finally, although children recruited by BACRIM will be included in the Victims Unit Registry – which means they will be recognized by the state as victims of the armed conflict – no compensation will be given to them because the Victims and Land Restitution Law curtails the period of time in which victims can claim reparations.[103] Articles 155 and 208 thereof establish that all the cases that occurred between 1 January 1985 and 10 June 2011 should be declared before the Public Ministry before 10 June 2011. If the facts occurred after that date, the deadline to declare is two years after they took place.[104] Considering that the Court Judgment was issued in 2016 and it is not clear if the Court decision is retroactive, many of these children will not receive compensation.

9. CONCLUSION

The application of international legal standards has been challenged by the complex nature of today's armed conflicts. Some contemporary intrastate conflicts present a complex dimension that blurs the distinctions between criminality, terrorism and armed conflict. The mixed nature of armed groups and their connections to drug cartels, terrorist groups and other criminal structures is a major problem. This results in difficulties for children recruited and used by these groups. Principally, the condition of being considered a victim of child recruitment depends on the classification of the context in which the child is used during an armed conflict, in addition to the characterization of the recruiting group as a party to the conflict. If the nature of the group is unclear, it becomes difficult to discern whether children are victims of child recruitment or not. This situation creates great challenges for the international community in terms of effective protection of children affected by these complex contexts and in accordance with their reality and needs. The Colombian case offers important insights into understanding the changing nature of armed conflicts and the implications of these changes for victims of child recruitment.

The Colombian government has the authority to grant political and legal recognition to armed groups. However, there are several issues that restrict the recognition of these groups as parties to a conflict, which consequently affects the characterization of recruited children as victims. Recognizing these groups as combatants may award these children legal and economic benefits. On the other hand, classifying BACRIM as criminal gangs

---

[103] Law 1448 of 2011, art. 155.
[104] Victims Unit 2015.

may impede the recognition of children recruited by BACRIM as victims of the armed conflict. Although the Constitutional Court recognizes children recruited by BACRIM as victims and has ordered their certification as former child combatants, in practice, the recognition of these groups' operations as connected to the armed conflict is very difficult. This can lead to very few children being recognized as combatants, which seriously affects their reintegration and any reparations. Therefore, the situation of children victimized by BACRIM requires additional legal and political measures to protect these children from the impact of war and ensure that they receive the same treatment as other victims of child recruitment in terms of demobilization, prosecution, reintegration and reparations.

A greater understanding of the problem of child recruitment in the context of Colombia is needed in order to adopt measures that respond to the complexities of armed conflict, the changes in the tactics and structures of armed groups and the impact on children. To this end, the Colombian state must strengthen the child recruitment prevention policy in accordance with the needs of children at risk, taking into account the forms of urban and rural operations of armed groups and distinguishing the type of actors involved.

It is also necessary that Colombia advances in submitting BACRIM to the law, in addition to the state opening routes to achieve the disengagement of children in BACRIM's ranks through legal reform. To this end, the Office of the Prosecutor must focus its efforts on the analysis of organized power structures and the recruitment dynamics of BACRIM in order to prosecute the most responsible and shift the focus away from prosecuting the children. Likewise, greater clarity is required regarding the effects of the judgment of the Constitutional Court in terms of retroactivity, administrative reparation and practical procedures for accessing the benefits of demobilization. Victims and their families must know the scope of the law and jurisprudence to be able to demand their rights. Finally, the reintegration of and reparations for child victims of use and recruitment in Colombia should not be based on political considerations. The Colombian government has the obligation to restore the rights of these children and accord them the highest standards of protection. Effective care for these children should not be subject to the classification of perpetrators as part of the armed conflict. In the words of Radhika Coomaraswamy:

> Although it is important to garner a better understanding of the character and motivations of armed actors, it is critical to ensure that the child protection discourse does not become paralysed at the level of definitional semantics. For the child victims of violations the labels that apply to perpetrators make little difference. From a child protection perspective the primary analysis must be whether armed actors in situations of concern, regardless of their character and motivation, commit grave violations such as recruiting and using children or killing, maiming or raping them.[105]

REFERENCED WORKS

Ambos, K. and Zuluaga, J. 2015. 'Understanding Colombia's War' *Entwicklung und Zusammenarbeit* 2015/07, 34–35

Amnesty International 2017a. *Amnesty International Report 2016/17 – Colombia*, 22 February 2017, available at: https://www.refworld.org/docid/58b0340d13.html [accessed 4 April 2019]

---

[105] SRSG 2008: [35].

Amnesty International 2017b. 'Further Information: Paramilitary Build-Up in Peace Community' (AI Index: AMR 23/5614/2017) (3 February)
Amnesty International 2018. 'Report 2017/18: The State of the World's Human Rights' (AI Index: POL 10/6700/2018) (22 February)
Avila, A. 2016. 'Bacrim, Neoparamilitares y Grupos Post-Desmovilización Paramilitary', *Revista Semana* (30 March)
Brett, R. and Specht, I. 2004. *Young Soldiers: Why They Choose to Fight* (Boulder: Lynne Rienner Publishers)
Brodzinsky, S. 2017. 'Colombia's Armed Groups Sow Seeds of New Conflict as War with Farc Ends', *The Guardian* (18 April)
Cast, S. 2011. 'Iraq Seeks to Use Colombia's Demobilization, Reintegration Process as Model', *Colombia Reports* (6 October)
Chadwick, E. 1996. *Self-Determination, Terrorism, and the International Humanitarian Law of Armed Conflict* (The Hague: Martinus Nijhoff Publishers)
Colombia Reports 2017. 'Colombia Displacement Statistics' (17 February)
Colombian Commission of Jurists 2008. *Colombia: el Espejismo de la Justicia y la Paz* (Bogota: Colombian Commission of Jurists)
Constitutional Court of Colombia 2016. Judgment C-069. Magistrate: Luis Guillermo Guerrero (18 February)
Constitutional Court of Colombia 2017. Judgment T-163. Magistrate: Gloria Stella Ortiz (13 March)
Coomaraswamy, R. 2010. 'The Optional Protocol to the Convention on the Rights of the Child on the Involvement of Children in Armed Conflict – Towards Universal Ratification' 18 *International Journal of Children's Rights* 535
CRC Committee [Committee on the Rights of the Child] 2010. 'Concluding Observations: Colombia' (UN Doc. CRC/C/OPAC/COL/CO/) (21 June)
CRC Committee 2015. 'Concluding Observations on the Combined Fourth and Fifth Periodic Reports of Colombia' (UN Doc. CRC/C/COL/CO/4-5) (6 March)
Drumbl, M. and Rona, G. 2018. 'Navigating Challenges in Child Protection and the Reintegration of Children Associated with Armed Groups', in S. O'Neil and K. Van Broeckhoven (eds), *Cradled by Conflict: Child Involvement with Armed Groups in Contemporary Conflict* (New York: UN University)
El País 2018. 'En el Posconflicto, 124 Niños que Pertenecían a Farc Se Han Entregado' (28 February)
El Tiempo 2012. 'Empiezan a Aparecer los Niños que Escondieron los "Paras": Hay 236 Casos Identificados en 5 Bloques' (15 October)
Giraldo, J. and Jimenez, A.M. 2015. 'Garantías y Oportunidades para la Defensa de la Vida. Experiencias de Niñas, Niños y Adolescentes en la Ruta de Reparación Administrativa en Colombia' (Bogota: Benposta Nación de Muchachos)
Granada, S., Restrepo, J. and Tobón, A. 2009. 'Neoparamilitarismo en Colombia: Una Herramienta Conceptual para la Interpretación de Dinámicas Recientes del Conflicto Armado Colombiano', in J. Restrepo and D. Aponte (eds), *Guerra y Violencias en Colombia Herramientas e Interpretaciones* (Bogota, Editorial Pontificia Universidad Javeriana)
Happold, M. 2012. 'Protecting Children in Armed Conflict: Harnessing the Security Council's "Soft Power"' 43 *Israel Law Review* 360
Human Rights Watch 2003. *You'll Learn Not to Cry: Child Combatants in Colombia* (New York)
Human Rights Watch 2012. 'Colombia: Fix Flaws in Transitional Justice Bill' (June 12)
IACHR [Inter-American Court of Human Rights] 2002. *Case of the 19 Merchants v. Colombia*, Judgment of 12 June
ICBF [Instituto Colombiano de Bienestar Familiar] 2012a. 'Adolescentes en Conflicto con la Ley Sistema de Responsabilidad Penal para Adolescentes' *Boletín* 1
ICBF 2012b. Letter of Answer (Derecho de Petición) to the Questionnaire Submitted by Ana María Jiménez (3 August)
ICBF 2018. *Tablero desvinculados*
ICC [International Criminal Court] 2012. 'Situation in the Democratic Republic of the Congo in the Case of The Prosecutor v. Thomas Lubanga Dyilo, Dissenting Opinion of Judge Odio Benito' (ICC Doc. 01/04-01/06) (10 July)
ICTY [International Criminal Tribunal for the Former Yugoslavia] *Prosecutor v. Tadić*, Case No. IT-94-1-AR72, Appeals Chamber, Decision on the Defence Motion for Interlocutory Appeal on Jurisdiction, 2 October 1995 ('Tadić Interlocutory Appeal Decision')
Jimenez, A.M. 2012. 'Easier Said than Done: The Debate on the "Characterization" of Paramilitary Groups in Colombia in View of the Situation of Children Victims of Illicit Recruitment' (Bogota: Coalition to Stop the Use of Children and Youth in Colombia)
Johnson, T. 2012. 'Report on the Security Council Open Debate on Children in Armed Conflict' (Center for UN Reform Education) (28 September)
Kaldor, M. 2013. 'In Defence of New Wars' 2 *Stability: International Journal of Security and Development*

Kurth, M. 2013. 'The Lubanga Case of the International Criminal Court: A Critical Analysis of the Trial Chamber's Findings on Issues of Active Use, Age, and Gravity' 5 *Goettingen Journal of International Law* 431

Ladisch, V., Correa, C., Jiménez, A. and Salazar, G. 2014. *Reparación Integradora para Niños, Niñas y Jóvenes Víctimas de Reclutamiento Ilícito en Colombia* (Bogota: International Center for Transitional Justice)

MAPP/OEA [Organization of American States – Mission to Support the Peace Process in Colombia] 2009. 'Decimosegundo Informe Trimestral del Secretario General al Consejo Permanente Sobre la Misión de Apoyo al Proceso de Paz en Colombia' (OEA doc. Ser.G CP/doc. 4365/09) (9 February)

Moodrick-Even, H. 2010. 'Child Terrorists: Why and How Should They Be Protected', in N. Quenivet and S. Shah-Davis (eds), *International Law and Armed Conflict: Challenges in the 21st Century* (The Hague: T.M.C. Asser Press)

Mundy, J. 2011. 'Deconstructing Civil Wars: Beyond the New Wars Debate' 42 *Security Dialogue* 279

Norwegian Refugee Council & Internal Displacement Monitoring Centre 2017. 'Global Report on International Displacement' (May)

O'Neil, S. and Van Broeckhoven, K. 2018. *Cradled by Conflict: Child Involvement with Armed Groups in Contemporary Conflict* (New York: UN University)

Panam Post 2017. 'Según las FARC, Hay Menores de Edad que no Quieren Dejar sus Filas' (12 August)

Perez-Santiago, M. 2012. 'Colombia's BACRIM: Common Criminals or Actors in Armed Conflict?' *InSight Crime* (23 July)

Prieto, C. 2014. 'La Relación FARC-Bacrim y sus Lugares Communes', *Fundación Ideas para la Paz* (16 October)

Quénivet, N. and Shah-Davis, S. 2010. 'Confronting the Challenges on the International Law and Armed Conflict in the 21st Century', in N. Quenivet and S. Shah-Davis (eds), *International Law and Armed Conflict: Challenges in the 21st Century* (The Hague: T.M.C. Asser Press)

Republic of Colombia, Final Peace Agreement Between the Government of Colombia and the FARC-EP, 24 November 2016

Restrepo, J. and Aponte, D. 2009. *Guerra y violencias en Colombia, Herramientas e Interpretaciones* (Bogota: Editorial Pontificia Universidad Javeriana)

Reuters Staff 2018. 'Colombia Launches Military Task Force to Combat Crime Gangs', *Reuters* (12 January)

Revista Semana 2016. '¿Qué Significa el Nuevo Anuncio de las FARC Acerca del Reclutamiento de Menores?' *Semana* (2 October)

Schuberth, M. 2017. 'To Engage or Not to Engage Haiti's Urban Armed Groups? Safe Access in Disaster-Stricken and Conflict-Affected Cities' 29 *Environment and Urbanization* 425

Singer, P.W. 2006. *Children at War* (Berkeley: University of California Press)

SRSG [UN Office of the Special Representative of the Secretary-General for Children and Armed Conflict] 2007. 'Report to the General Assembly' (UN Doc. A/62/228) (13 August)

SRSG 2008. 'Report to the General Assembly' (UN Doc. A/63/227) (6 August)

Stanford University 2017. 'National Liberation Army (Colombia)' [available at http://web.stanford.edu/group/mappingmilitants/cgi-bin/groups/view/87 (accessed 9 November 2018)]

UN General Assembly 1996. 'Promotion and Protection of the Rights of the Children: The Impact of Armed Conflict on Children' (UN Doc. A/51/306) (26 August)

UN High Commissioner for Human Rights 2013. 'Annual Report on Colombia' (UN Doc. A/HRC/22/17/Add.3) (7 January)

UN High Commissioner for Human Rights 2017. 'Annual Report on Colombia' (UN Doc. A/HRC/34/3/Add.3) (23 March)

UN Human Rights Council 2009. 'Annual Report of the Special Representative of the Secretary-General for Children and Armed Conflict, Radhika Coomaraswamy', 30 July 2009, A/HRC/12/49 [available at: https://www.refworld.org/docid/4a9d1bf10.html]

UN Secretary-General 2003. 'The Amendment of the 2003 UNSG Annual Report' (UN Doc. A/58/546/Corr.1–S/2003/1053/Corr.1) (20 February)

UN Secretary-General 2009. 'Report on Children and Armed Conflict in Colombia' (UN Doc. S/2009/434) (28 August)

UN Secretary-General 2010. 'Annual Report on Children and Armed Conflict' (UN Doc. A/64/742–S/2010/181) (13 April)

UN Secretary-General 2011. 'Annual Report on Children and Armed Conflict' (UN Doc. A/65/820–S/2011/250) (23 April)

UN Secretary-General 2012. 'Annual Report on Children and Armed Conflict' (UN Doc. A/66/782–S/2012/261) (26 April)

UN Secretary-General 2016. 'Report on Children and Armed Conflict in Colombia' (UN Doc. S/2016/837) (4 October)

UN Secretary-General 2017. 'Annual Report on Children and Armed Conflict' (UN Doc. A/72/361–S/2017/821) (24 August)

UN Security Council 2008. 'Cross-Cutting Report No. 1: Children and Armed Conflict' (2 June)
UN Security Council Resolution 2070. 'The Situation in Haiti'. Adopted by the Security Council at its 6845th meeting on 12 October 2012
UNICEF and SRSG 2009. (April) (UNICEF)
Victims Unit 2015. '¿Cuáles son los Plazos para Declarar como Víctima del Conflicto Armado?' (23 October)
W Radio 2017. 'Gobierno Responde por Supuesta Fuga de Menor de Una Zona Veredal de las Farc' (10 October)
Watchlist on Children and Armed Conflict 2012. 'No One to Trust: Children and Armed Conflict in Colombia' (3 April)
Wessells, M. 2002. 'Recruitment of Children as Soldiers in Sub-Saharan Africa', in L. Mjøset and S. Van Holde (eds), *The Comparative Study of Conscription in the Armed Forces* (Oxford: Elsevier Science Ltd) 20
Winton, A. 2004. 'Urban Violence: A Guide to the Literature' 16 *Environment and Urbanization* 165

3. The construction of gender in child soldiering in the Special Court for Sierra Leone

*Valerie Oosterveld**

The West African country of Sierra Leone was embroiled in armed conflict from 1991 to 2002. During the war, tens of thousands of children were used as fighters by armed groups. Children were abducted, coerced and recruited in large numbers to fight with the Revolutionary United Front (RUF) and the Armed Forces Revolutionary Council (AFRC). In addition, children formed part of the pro-government Civil Defence Forces (CDF) militia. Following the conflict, the Special Court for Sierra Leone (SCSL) was created as a result of an agreement between the United Nations and the government of Sierra Leone, following consultation within the United Nations Security Council.[1] That court was tasked with prosecuting those 'bearing the greatest responsibility' for war crimes and crimes against humanity committed during the 1996–2002 portion of the Sierra Leone conflict.[2] Given the widespread nature of the recruitment and use of child soldiers, and the brutality these child soldiers both suffered and inflicted,[3] it is no surprise that the SCSL Statute included the war crime of 'conscripting or enlisting children under the age of 15 years into armed forces or groups or using them to participate actively in hostilities'.[4]

The SCSL became the first international criminal tribunal to prosecute individuals for the war crime of recruitment and use of child soldiers.[5] In the first case, three leaders of the rebel AFRC group were charged with this crime, and all were convicted.[6] In the second case, members of the pro-government Civil Defence Forces were charged, and one was convicted (with that conviction overturned on appeal).[7] In the third case, three leaders from the RUF were charged and two of the three accused were convicted.[8] The final case

---

* I wish to thank Milica Bijelic for her research assistance and Kirsten Stefanik for her feedback. I also wish to thank the University of Western Ontario, Faculty of Law and the Social Sciences and Humanities Research Council of Canada's Canadian Partnership for International Justice for their funding support for this research.

[1] SCSL Statute 2002.

[2] Ibid., art. 1. The SCSL's temporal jurisdiction controversially did not cover the entire armed conflict as a result of negotiations within the United Nations Security Council. See Smith 2004: 130–32.

[3] See, e.g., Sierra Leone TRC Chapter 4 2004: [126–40].

[4] SCSL Statute 2002, art. 4(c). The Prosecutor had jurisdiction to prosecute children over the age of 15 under art. 7 of the Statute, but decided not to do so: Special Court for Sierra Leone 2002.

[5] Special Court for Sierra Leone 2007.

[6] AFRC Trial Judgment 2007: [15, 2113, 2117, 2121]. This was upheld on appeal: AFRC Appeals Judgment 2008: 105 (Disposition).

[7] CDF Trial Judgment 2007: 290–91 (Disposition); CDF Appeals Judgment 2008: 190–91 (Disposition).

[8] RUF Trial Judgment 2009: 679, 683, 686 (Disposition); RUF Appeals Judgment 2009: [1169–80].

involved the former President of neighbouring Liberia, Charles Taylor, who was charged with, and convicted of, aiding and abetting the AFRC and RUF in the recruitment and use of child soldiers.[9] In all of the cases, the court heard testimony from former child soldiers about their experiences and the resulting impact. This chapter examines the narratives that emerged from the SCSL with respect to boy and girl soldiers. The SCSL's transcripts and judgments reveal that the soldiering experience was highly gendered for both boys and girls.

This chapter begins by examining the evidence provided to the court by boy soldiers affiliated with the AFRC and RUF. That evidence showed that both groups targeted boys for forced recruitment based on gendered assumptions about their obedience, aggression and agility. It also revealed that boys were sent to the frontlines more often than girls, and that boys were favoured over girls as bodyguards for rebel commanders and as guards at diamond mines. There are important silences, however: sexual violence committed against these boys was not examined by the SCSL.

The chapter then turns to consider the testimony provided by girls affiliated with the AFRC and RUF. That evidence demonstrated that girls were targeted for abduction to serve as fighters, but also to serve within a gendered socio-economic caregiving structure to cook, clean, launder and act as sexual slaves for the fighters. Additionally, girls were commonly subjected to other forms of sexual violence. Far fewer girls than boys testified at the SCSL about their training and combat experiences. However, girls testified about their sexual slavery and service as 'bush wives', bringing international legal attention to the issue. That said, due to the bifurcated consideration of the girls' evidence, the girl soldiers' specific experiences in this respect were somewhat obscured.

Finally, this chapter explores the exclusively male narratives by child soldiers affiliated with the CDF. It highlights the invisibility of girls within the CDF trial, and the lack of evidence from boy soldiers who were directly recruited into the CDF from within their own communities.

This chapter concludes that the SCSL is rightfully lauded for 'surfacing'[10] the gendered experiences of children affiliated with armed groups in Sierra Leone. At the same time, future tribunals need to be alert to gender 'blind spots', so as to render visible all child soldiers.

1. THE GENDERED CONSTRUCTION OF BOYS AFFILIATED WITH THE AFRC AND RUF

The evidence heard by, and findings of, the court on the use of boy soldiers by the AFRC and RUF illustrate that, while each male witness had a unique experience differing in terms of length of time with the rebels, temporal period of their service, exposure to combat and other variables, there were also similarities and parallels in their harsh histories. The Trial Chambers in the AFRC, RUF and *Taylor* cases carefully outlined these common

---

[9] *Taylor* Trial Judgment 2012: 2438 (Disposition); *Taylor* Appeals Judgment 2013: [272], 11070–71 (Disposition).
[10] This term is taken from Copelon 1994.

encounters with the rebels. The evidence ultimately shows that these experiences were significantly gendered in nature, but that some gendered experiences were left relatively unexplored by the court.

The RUF and AFRC both engaged in widespread and organized recruitment of child soldiers to serve as combatants.[11] Mazurana and Carlson estimate that the RUF used around 15,000 boy soldiers, while the AFRC used in the region of 3,300 boy soldiers.[12] The experience of boy soldiers often began with abduction. In the AFRC case, the Trial Chamber characterized the abductions as 'acts of coercion', 'forced recruitment' and 'particularly egregious form[s] of "conscription"'.[13] Abduction was then usually followed by training in AFRC or RUF camps, where boys were often assigned to Small Boys Units.[14] After training, many boys were assigned to fight in active conflict or serve as guards.[15] The training and deployment experience was largely one of physical and psychological violence.

The AFRC trial was the first to conclude and issue a judgment, and thus started the judicial narrative on child soldiers in the Sierra Leone conflict. In that trial, the story of two boys became particularly central to the description of the experiences of boy soldiers. Witness TF1-157 testified that he was abducted at approximately 13 years of age when AFRC rebels attacked his home village in Bombali District.[16] He watched the rebels commit atrocities against his family members, and then he was abducted by a man named Mohamed. The rebels abducted at least five other people that day, including three children younger than TF1-157. Mohamed forced him to carry rice and luggage along the route to the rebel camp, Camp Rosos, and other combatants forced him to fetch water, pound rice and carry other goods.[17] He was subsequently 'systematically exploited and abused' and 'witnessed the commission of numerous crimes by his abductors'.[18] In particular, he was required to undergo military training, during which he was compelled to take cocaine. Witness TF1-157 described being forced to kill people, burn vehicles and burn houses.[19] Resisting his situation, he eventually escaped during the retreat from the Freetown invasion and ended up in the care of UNICEF.

Witness TF1-157's younger brother served as Witness TF1-158, who was abducted in the same raid at 10 years of age.[20] He watched a rebel named Adama hack his father to death, and was forced by his captors to carry food for the troops as they journeyed to the rebel camp. The experience of abduction was followed by obligatory military training with other children as young as seven or eight years old. He escaped shortly after this military training – like his brother, demonstrating agency within his constrained situation – but

---

[11] AFRC Trial Judgment 2007: [1250]; RUF Trial Judgment 2009: [1614].
[12] Mazurana and Carlson 2004: 12.
[13] AFRC Trial Judgment 2007: [734, 1245, 1276].
[14] AFRC Trial Judgment 2007: [1275]; the RUF Trial Chamber noted that the term 'Small Boys Units' 'entered into common parlance in Sierra Leone', demonstrating 'the entrenched and institutionalized nature of the practice'. RUF Trial Judgment 2009: [1621, 1632].
[15] AFRC Trial Judgment 2007: [1244].
[16] Ibid.: [1253].
[17] Ibid.: [1254].
[18] Ibid.
[19] Ibid.: [1254–5].
[20] Ibid.: [1256].

was recaptured by the AFRC, made to carry loads for his captors and to undergo further military training.

The Trial Chamber judges noted additional evidence of boy soldiers capturing and abducting civilians, serving as guards at diamond mines and rebel bases, functioning as bodyguards for AFRC leaders, forcing civilians to undress, committing amputations and flogging civilians.[21] Additionally, the Trial Chamber noted that child soldiers described directly suffering or witnessing an array of violent acts, including being forced into hard labour and military training; being made to fight in active hostilities on the frontlines; being beaten; being pressed to watch the commission of crimes against family members; being injected with narcotics to reduce fear; being compelled to commit crimes including rape, murder, amputation and abduction; being used as human shields; and being threatened with death if they tried to escape or did not obey orders.[22] The AFRC Trial Chamber concluded that the AFRC targeted children for forced recruitment and use in hostilities because 'they were easy to manipulate and program, and resilient in battle'.[23]

The RUF and *Taylor* judgments provided additional detail about the recruitment, training and use of boys by the RUF and AFRC. They illustrate that an underlying theme of boys' experiences within the AFRC and RUF was the normalization of violence from the beginning of the boys' interaction with the rebels.

The evidence showed that children, many as young as 10 years of age, and some younger, were targeted for abduction by the RUF.[24] While most were abducted, some were instead coerced into joining the rebels through the RUF issuing a demand to the inhabitants of the city of Makeni that they must contribute 'young men' for training by the RUF.[25] The captured or coerced boys were screened into different roles, depending on their age, health and suitability for combat, and either underwent military training[26] in weapons use, ambushes and tactics, or were assigned to logistics such as cooking, laundry, food foraging and carrying loads.[27] The boys felt unable to refuse to participate in the training, as otherwise they would be killed.[28] The evidence pointed to a gender difference in the age of abducted boys versus abducted girls and their subsequent screening: boys as young as seven were assigned to the Small Boys Unit, while girls aged 9–15 years old were assigned to the Small Girls Unit.[29]

The military training usually lasted anywhere from two weeks to six months.[30] It included learning how to dismantle and reassemble a gun, firing weapons such as AK-47s and rocket-propelled grenades using live ammunition, dodging bullets in 'Halaka'

---

[21] Ibid.: [1262–5, 1268–70].
[22] Ibid.: [1275].
[23] Ibid.
[24] RUF Trial Judgment 2009: [1617, 1629–32].
[25] Ibid.: [1684].
[26] The RUF had training camps at different locations at different times during the conflict, including Bayama, Camp Lion (Bunumbu) and then Yengema. RUF Trial Judgment 2009: [1634, 1646, 1699, 1700].
[27] Ibid.: [1618–20]. The domestic chores were often done in the homes of their commanders: Ibid.: [1632]; *Taylor* Trial Judgment 2012: [1369, 1372].
[28] *Taylor* Trial Judgment 2012: [1387].
[29] Ibid.: [1369, 1372].
[30] Ibid.: [1369].

training,[31] mounting attacks on urban communities and setting fire to houses.[32] The court also heard evidence that some children were trained in reconnaissance, which included instructions to wear civilian clothing and carry wares on their head to sell in towns so as to go unnoticed.[33] Boys were injured and killed during the training, sometimes by falling onto barbed wire or being hit with live ammunition.[34] Those who did not succeed in the training were beaten or killed.[35] The RUF Trial Chamber cited evidence that the accused, Issa Sesay, told some boys during training that if they did not obey orders during battle he would personally execute them.[36] The *Taylor* Trial Chamber noted that abducted boys sent to the RUF training bases often had 'RUF' forcibly carved onto their foreheads or backs to prevent escape.[37] For example, witness TF1-143 described being captured by a mix of AFRC and RUF rebels when he was 12 years old and having 'RUF' carved into his chest with a razor blade.[38] All of the other children at his training base were also carved with 'RUF' or 'AFRC'. At some bases, branding did not occur immediately after abduction, but boys 'who tried to escape were either killed or branded on their faces or chests with the letters "RUF"'.[39] In some cases, just the individual who was trying to escape was branded; in others, all trainees at the base were branded after an escape attempt.

The boys who completed the military training were given a weapon (depending on their height: sticks, knives, cutlasses, guns or rocket-propelled grenades).[40] Some were assigned to act as spies to gather information from civilians and opposition camps, and act as bodyguards for commanders.[41] They were deployed throughout the country, and members of the Small Boys Units were mixed with other fighters to fight on the frontlines or to spy on enemy positions.[42] The youngest boys were tasked with carrying weapons for the RUF.[43]

The boy fighters were routinely given alcohol or drugs, with the drugs mixed into their food, given as pills, or ingested through cuts on their skin, sniffing or smoke inhalation.[44] The *Taylor* Trial Chamber stated that drugs, including cocaine, were used by the AFRC and RUF as a 'method of coercion used to make the children fearless and carry out orders without hesitation'.[45] Some of the children became addicted as a result.[46]

---

[31] Ibid.: [1370]. Halaka training 'was intended to train recruits to dodge bullets. It took place in a round area surrounded by bricks; the instructors stood around the circle holding canes. The recruits would enter the circle and would then have to dodge being beaten by the canes. Halaka training would sometimes last 1-1/2 to 2 hours, and recruits went through these exercises 2–3 times a week. Many incurred injuries or died, especially the [children] and the elderly.' Ibid.: [1241].
[32] RUF Trial Judgment 2009: [1637, 1640]; *Taylor* Trial Judgment 2012: [1599].
[33] RUF Trial Judgment 2009: [1648].
[34] Ibid.: [1640–42]; *Taylor* Trial Judgment 2012: [1370].
[35] RUF Trial Judgment 2009: [1640–42].
[36] Ibid.: [1643].
[37] *Taylor* Trial Judgment 2012: [1366].
[38] Ibid.: [1425–6].
[39] Ibid.: [1369, 1544].
[40] RUF Trial Judgment 2009: [1649].
[41] Ibid.: [1620, 1632, 1655, 1658, 1669–71, 1731, 1732, 1735, 1736].
[42] Ibid.: [1644, 1729].
[43] Ibid.: [1638].
[44] Ibid.: [1623]; *Taylor* Trial Judgment 2012: [1543, 1555, 1560].
[45] *Taylor* Trial Judgment 2012: [1600].
[46] Ibid.: [1601].

Once deployed to fight, the boys killed children, elderly men and women and teenagers.[47] They would also beat people, rape women and girls, capture girls for commanders to rape, commit amputations, flog civilians, behead corpses, help to abduct children, burn buildings and loot homes, vehicles, hospitals and businesses.[48] The court recorded acts of resistance: for example, witness TF1-143 refused orders to rape an old woman encountered on a food-finding mission.[49] He was slammed against a wall, forced to eat faeces and made to lie in the sun all day with his eyes open as punishment for disobeying orders.[50] In another example, witness Komba Sumana explained that he avoided participating in an attack by giving away his gun and hiding in a house.[51]

Sometimes boys were assigned to guard the RUF bases, captured civilians or forced labourers.[52] For example, two boys aged 9–12 years were assigned by the RUF defendant, Sesay, to guard civilians working at a farm he controlled in Kailahun in 1996–1997.[53] Their role was to supervise the forced farming done by civilians, 'and to ensure that civilians who refused to work were punished with severe beatings'.[54] Boys were also 'instructed to beat village elders during raids carried out to abduct civilians to bolster the labour forces for the government [i.e. RUF-controlled] mines'.[55] Other times, boys were assigned to guard diamond mining sites controlled by the RUF, intimidate the miners and force them to work.[56] They were selected for this assignment 'because they would obey orders or shoot miners who breached the mining rules, whereas the older soldiers tended to speak to adult miners first'.[57] Boy soldiers committed most of the documented killings in the Tongo mining area.[58] Some boys were also assigned to do armed patrols in RUF-held areas.[59]

Some of the younger boys had to drag their guns, as they did not have the strength to carry them.[60] Very young boys who could not carry arms, and boys who were not in combat, were often expected to carry out domestic work such as pounding rice, preparing food and laundering clothes for (male) RUF commanders.[61] Girls, on the other hand, were required to help the wives of senior RUF commanders, doing their cleaning, washing and cooking.[62]

Why were boys targeted for these experiences? Like the AFRC judges, the RUF Trial Chamber concluded that the RUF targeted young boys for abduction or coercion

---

[47] RUF Trial Judgment 2009: [1649, 1681].
[48] E.g., Ibid.: [1649, 1653, 1672, 1673, 1675, 1681, 1682, 1711, 1712, 1719]; *Taylor* Trial Judgment 2012: [1462, 1489–90, 1561, 1570, 1581, 1591].
[49] *Taylor* Trial Judgment 2012: [1517].
[50] Ibid.: [1517–18].
[51] Ibid.: [1532].
[52] RUF Trial Judgment 2009: [1683, 1726].
[53] Ibid.: [1656].
[54] Ibid.
[55] Ibid.: [1666].
[56] Ibid.: [1664, 1674, 1719]; *Taylor* Trial Judgment 2012: [1458–9, 1465, 1468].
[57] RUF Trial Judgment 2009: [1664].
[58] Ibid.: [1665].
[59] Ibid.: [1717–18].
[60] Ibid.: [1664] (original footnotes omitted).
[61] Ibid.: [1667].
[62] Ibid.

'due to their loyalty to the movement and their ability to effectively conduct espionage activities, as their small size and agility made them particularly suitable for hazardous assignments'.[63] Further, the younger boys 'were particularly aggressive when armed and were known to kill human beings as if they were nothing more than "chickens"'.[64] In other words, the RUF leadership concluded that young boys were the most pliable recruits. They tried to increase that pliability through the use of narcotics and by forcing the boys to commit acts that would destroy their homes or family bonds.[65] The *Taylor* Trial Chamber echoed these conclusions: 'children were of importance to the AFRC and RUF as they carried out orders "quickly" and "they followed their bosses' way"'.[66]

While the experiences of boys within the AFRC and RUF were discussed in depth by the court, there were certain aspects of those experiences that were largely invisible. In particular, sexual violence, when suffered by girl soldiers, was considered in detail through the sexual slavery and forced 'marriage' charges discussed below, and sexual violence committed by boy soldiers against civilian girls and women was noted.[67] For example, the court heard evidence that some boys in a Small Boys Unit captured girls, kept the girls captive as sex slaves and raped them.[68] However, sexual violence committed *against* boys affiliated with the AFRC and RUF was not examined, despite indications that such violations likely occurred.[69] For example, Betancourt et al. indicated that 5 per cent of boy soldiers and 44 per cent of girl soldiers surveyed reported being raped, and the statistical analysis of Guberek et al. demonstrated sexual violence directed against boys aged 10–19 years, though in much lower numbers than sexual violence directed against girls.[70] Human Rights Watch also recorded a case involving a female rebel inflicting sexual violence on male conscripts.[71] Low reporting rates of sexual violence committed against men and boys likely did not reflect actual occurrences: '[d]ue to the stigma attached to homosexuality in Sierra Leone, male victims of rape feared they would be perceived as homosexuals and therefore few boys were willing to report it'.[72]

In addition to silence on sexual violence directed against boy soldiers, the potential victim status of boys forced to commit rape or sexual violence was not discussed in the judgments. Sanin and Stirnemann indicate that one former child combatant who provided evidence to the SCSL suffered from repeated traumatic nightmares and feelings of guilt because he was forced to rape two young girls during the conflict.[73] Older boys who were given 'wives' could potentially simultaneously be a perpetrator and a victim of forced 'marriage' if they did not want this 'marriage' but felt that they had to comply. Forced

---

[63] Ibid.: [1616] (original footnotes omitted).
[64] Ibid.
[65] Richards 2002: 258.
[66] *Taylor* Trial Judgment 2012: [1602] (original footnotes omitted).
[67] E.g., RUF Trial Judgment 2009: [1675]; RUF Transcript 11 April 2005: 93–5. Marks (2013: 374) explains that young RUF fighters were inculcated into accepting or committing ongoing sexual violence, 'through their own perpetration of and complicity in violence'.
[68] *Taylor* Trial Judgment 2012: [1498, 1502].
[69] This was noted by Grey 2014: 605. See also Aijazi et al. in this volume.
[70] Betancourt et al. 2011: 23; Guberek et al. 2006: 20–23.
[71] Human Rights Watch 2003: 42.
[72] Ibid.
[73] Sanin and Stirnemann 2006: note 28.

'marriage' cannot be understood without an adequate understanding of relationality – in Uganda, some men were given, or forced to care for, 'wives' they did not choose or want.[74] This issue was made clear in the Extraordinary Chambers in the Courts of Cambodia, which recognized that both men and women were victims of forced marriage (in this case, a marriage under Khmer Rouge law).[75] That said, as noted above, the resistance of witness TF1-143 to orders to commit sexual violence was considered in the *Taylor* trial.[76]

The stories told by boys formerly affiliated with the AFRC and RUF to the SCSL, and the summaries of these experiences in the SCSL's AFRC, RUF and *Taylor* judgments, point to experiences that were gendered in a number of ways. The evidence outlined above showed that boys were deliberately sought by the rebels with the goal of expanding their fighting forces. They were usually trained for armed conflict. While girls were also trained as combatants, they were often targeted for other gendered reasons: for example, to serve as domestic or sexual slaves, as discussed in the next section. The roles played by boys differed in certain ways from those of girls, particularly in serving as bodyguards for rebel commanders or as guards in diamond mines. This differentiation was influenced by the social construction of maleness and femaleness in Sierra Leone prior to the conflict but was appropriated by the AFRC and RUF to create an internal system to meet their own ends.[77]

The commonalities in the stories told by boy soldiers outlined above also became, it is argued, the standard against which all other stories of child soldiering told to the SCSL were measured. The abducted boy brutally mistreated by the RUF or AFRC was the emblematic child soldier to the SCSL.[78] The next two sections compare this representation of the child soldier experience with the manner in which the court describes the experiences of girls affiliated with the AFRC and RUF and child soldiers in the CDF.

2. THE GENDERED CONSTRUCTION OF GIRLS AFFILIATED WITH THE AFRC AND RUF

Some have estimated that 5–10 per cent of the RUF fighters were female.[79] Others have assessed that 33 per cent of the children associated with RUF fighting forces were girls: 7,500 girl soldiers and 15,000 boy soldiers.[80] The same study estimated that a similar percentage of girls served with the AFRC: 1,667 girl soldiers and 3,333 boy soldiers, out of a total of 10,000 fighters overall.[81]

---

[74] Aijazi and Baines 2017: 476–7, 481.
[75] ECCC Closing Order 2010: [842].
[76] *Taylor* Trial Judgment 2012: [1517–18].
[77] On discrimination against girls and women in Sierra Leone prior to the conflict, see: Sierra Leone TRC, Chapter 3: [34–104]. This discrimination was replicated in the conflict, ibid.: [103, 326].
[78] Indeed, the emblematic child soldier overall. See Drumbl's description of traditional discourse typifying child soldiers: Drumbl 2012: 6–8.
[79] Richards 2002: 262.
[80] McKay and Mazurana 2004: 92. In total, the same study estimates that the RUF had 45,000 fighters overall. Half of these fighters were child soldiers: ibid. See also Mazurana and Carlson 2004: 12.
[81] McKay and Mazurana 2004: 92; Mazurana and Carlson 2004: 12.

The rebels abducted girls for two reasons. First, they wanted to add children to their overall ranks of fighters, as children were more pliable than adults – more easily transformed from regular civilians into rebel fighters. Girls were used to fight, spy, porter, run messages between rebel camps and assist with war-related communications.[82] They also received weapons training.[83] As a result, they carried out, were subjected to and witnessed the same or similar types of psychological and physical violence as their male counterparts, such as killing, torture and amputation.[84]

Second, the rebels wished to create a highly gendered socio-economic caregiving structure, in which the girls were forced to cook, clean, grow and harvest food, nurse the sick and wounded and serve as sexual slaves for the fighters.[85] Many of these girls were categorized by the rebels as 'bush wives', which meant inter alia that they were expected to submit to rape on demand by their 'husbands'.[86] A large number of them became pregnant as a result of rape by the AFRC or RUF fighters, and therefore bore and reared those children.[87] The roles of these girls were multifaceted: nearly all reported that, in addition to performing a primary role, for example as a fighter, they would also perform the secondary roles referenced above. Therefore, the categories of 'fighter' and 'bush wife' should not be considered as mutually exclusive.

The evidence provided by witness Akiatu Tholley demonstrates the multiple and interlinked roles played by girls within the AFRC and RUF. Tholley was abducted from Wellington by the AFRC in January 1999 when she was approximately 13 or 14 years old.[88] She was captured by a rebel named James, who made Tholley (as well as some boys captured with her) carry his ammunition to Allen Town.[89] She refused to have sex with James, so he raped her in a church in which many young girls were being raped, beaten and killed.[90] James damaged her vagina as a result.[91] She had not yet had her menses.[92] James took Tholley to Waterloo with his 'wives' and the captured boys. He continued to rape her and made her his 'wife'.[93] He then held her in Masiaka for more than two months.[94] James taught Tholley to use an AK-47 and a pistol, and she was also given military training in Port Loko District on how to load bullets, shoot and hide.[95] At one point, Tholley tried to flee, but was caught. James beat her and gave her drugs which 'changed her mind', making her 'brave enough to do wicked things' and made her forget about wanting to go home.[96]

---

[82] McKay and Mazurana 2004: 92.
[83] Ibid.
[84] E.g. see the evidence of Finda Gbamanja, explaining that she witnessed killing and mutilation: *Taylor* Transcript 29 January 2009: 23874–5.
[85] McKay and Mazurana 2004: 92; Sierra Leone TRC, Chapter 3: [335, 338].
[86] RUF Trial Judgment 2009: [460, 1154–5, 1211–13, 1293, 1295, 1413, 1460, 1472].
[87] Richards 2002: 273. See also Denov in this volume.
[88] *Taylor* Trial Judgment 2012: [1454].
[89] Ibid.: [1002].
[90] Ibid.: [1174].
[91] Ibid.: [1003].
[92] Ibid.
[93] Ibid.: [1004].
[94] Ibid.: [1175].
[95] Ibid.: [1451, 1508].
[96] Ibid.: [1451, 1507].

She subsequently used drugs on a looting raid and killed a female civilian when that civilian refused to join her group.[97] Tholley was later taken to Koinadugu District to fight, during which she participated in the killing of civilians.[98] She then ran away and surrendered to ECOMOG forces and eventually was reunited with her family.[99] During her time in captivity, Tholley became pregnant three times.[100]

The Prosecutor of the SCSL elected to divide the story of AFRC and RUF girl soldiers into two types of existence: first, the girl soldier subjected to the 'standard' boy soldier experiences outlined in section 1 above, and, second, the girl (who may or may not have been a soldier) who was subjected to sexual violence or forced to become a 'bush wife'. Therefore, the Prosecutor brought 'one set of charges for the conscription, enlistment and use of child soldiers, and another set of charges for the sexual violence and forced marriage of girls in armed groups' in the AFRC, RUF and *Taylor* cases.[101] Thus, the child soldier recruitment charges were not based on evidence of sexual violence, while the rape, sexual slavery, forced 'marriage' and outrages upon personal dignity charges were based, in part, on evidence from girls affiliated with the AFRC or RUF.[102] As a result of this bifurcation of charges, boys were most often called to testify about their experience as a child combatant, and girls about sexual violence.[103]

This division of charges was done deliberately by the Prosecutor, so as to 'surface' sexual and gender-based violence committed within the Sierra Leone conflict as crimes.[104] The SCSL Statute listed rape and sexual slavery as crimes against humanity and war crimes, and rape as a war crime,[105] so there was no need to consider these forms of violence specifically under the child recruitment and use charge.[106] As observed by Grey, 'this approach represents a successful application of the existing legal framework to prosecute sexual violence against girl soldiers by members of the same armed groups'.[107] However, it also tended to somewhat obscure the fact that sexual and gender-based violence was committed against girl soldiers.[108] This was because the prosecution identified the victims of sexual violence and forced 'marriage' as 'civilians' or 'women and girls', rather than specifically as members of an armed group.[109] Additionally, the Trial Chambers discussed the evidence presented by the girl soldiers in separate sections of the judgments on child soldiering, domestic slavery, rape, sexual slavery and forced 'marriage'. Thus, those reading the judgments need to read through various parts to gain a full picture of the experience of each girl soldier witness.

Stories told by the female child soldier witnesses about their abduction and integration

---

[97] Ibid.: [1507].
[98] Ibid.: [1456, 1513].
[99] Ibid.: [1514].
[100] Ibid.: [1178].
[101] Grey 2014: 608, citing Jørgenson 2012: 659, 686.
[102] Grey 2014: 608.
[103] Michels 2006: 135.
[104] Grey 2014: 608, citing Jørgenson 2012: 659.
[105] SCSL Statute, arts 2(g) and 3(e).
[106] Grey 2014: 608, citing Jørgenson 2012: 686.
[107] Grey 2014: 608.
[108] Ibid.
[109] Ibid.

within the AFRC and RUF show that the experiences of girl soldiers often included brutal sexual violence[110] as well as a somewhat gendered division of labour. For example, Edna Bangura testified that she was abducted by the RUF from her school when she was 10 years old.[111] She was taken to an RUF camp and forced to undergo two weeks of military training on how to use a gun, set an ambush and retreat.[112] She was then assigned to a Small Girls Unit with other young girls.[113] While in the Unit, she was made to undertake looting raids on villages and capture civilians, who were then forced to carry the looted goods.[114] Also while in the Unit, she was assigned to live with an RUF commander and his wife, for whom she did domestic chores.[115] She was raped during this time by another commander, became pregnant and gave birth twice (with one child surviving).[116] She then became the forced 'wife' of another commander.[117]

In the *Taylor* trial, another girl soldier, Witness TF1-026, provided a detailed account of her experiences. Nine RUF fighters came to her house in 1999 during the invasion of Freetown.[118] She was 14 years old at the time.[119] They shot her sister dead for crying and told TF1-206 that, if she cried, they would also kill her, and then they abducted her.[120] They told her mother, who was pleading for her daughter, that, if she said anything more, they would kill her.[121] The rebels also burned houses and committed amputations on civilians in the area, forcing TF1-026 to witness this, telling her that she would suffer the same fate if she tried to escape.[122] She was then taken to Calaba Town, where she was gang-raped by four armed RUF fighters and left bleeding in a room with eight other young women and girls who were also being raped.[123] She was also subsequently raped by another RUF fighter in a separate incident.[124] TF1-026 underwent six months of military training in Buedu with 19 other girls, learning how to use a gun, crawl, roll and escape.[125] Despite being told that she would be killed if she tried to escape, she did try to escape along with some other girls: two of the other escapees were shot dead in front of the trainees as examples, while all of the other girls, including the witness, had 'RUF' carved into their chests.[126]

---

[110] The RUF Trial Judgment noted that '[a]bducted female children, including girls less than 15 years of age[,] were forced into sexual partnerships with fighters. Those who resisted were liable to physical or sexual abuse or execution': RUF Trial Judgment 2009: [1622].
[111] *Taylor* Trial Judgment 2012: [945].
[112] Ibid.: [1396].
[113] Ibid.: [1394–5].
[114] Ibid.: [1395].
[115] Ibid.: [946].
[116] Ibid.: [947, note 2440].
[117] Ibid.: [949]. Note that Bangura's testimony was found by the court to refer to events outside of the indictment period and also that it contained inconsistencies, which Bangura pointed out were due to her very young age at the time of the events: ibid.: [949, 954, 1401–2, 1487].
[118] *Taylor* Transcript 14 February 2008: 3843.
[119] *Taylor* Trial Judgment 2012: [1403].
[120] *Taylor* Transcript 14 February 2008: 3843–4.
[121] Ibid.: 3847.
[122] Ibid.: 3844 and 3846.
[123] Ibid.: 3852–5, 3860.
[124] Ibid.: 3862.
[125] *Taylor* Trial Judgment 2012: [1405–6].
[126] Ibid.: [1407].

After training, Witness TF1-026 and the other captured girls did domestic chores, cooking and laundering for Issa Sesay and his wife.[127] She explained that she had to do this domestic work: 'He had captured us. We had no power. That was why whatever he told us we would do.'[128] Sesay told her and the other girls that 'a woman should not be among them without a husband' so she was forcibly 'married' to an 'RUF boy'.[129] She was regularly raped by her 'husband' and forced to do domestic chores for him.[130] She escaped to her home village after she became pregnant.[131] While this is where her story ends in the judgment, the transcripts reveal that, once in her home village, people ostracized her as a rebel, which made her afraid for her own safety.[132] This ostracism continued to the day of her testimony – more than nine years later.[133] Her mother and father, however, helped her.[134] TF1-026 had her baby and raised it, and her child is treated poorly: 'If the children will be playing and if mine did anything they will say, "Leave this place. You are a rebel". They treat my child with scorn.'[135] A non-governmental organization removed the letters 'RUF' from the witness' chest through surgery, though she still has scars.[136]

As can be seen from these examples, girls abducted into the AFRC and RUF were provided with military training like their male counterparts. While some were sent to fight, it was more common for girls to provide forced domestic labour:[137] '[o]n completion of their training, these young girls typically remained with the Commanders or their wives, undertaking cleaning, laundry and kitchen duties'.[138] They were also sent on food-finding missions.[139] They were often subjected to sexual violence such as rape and sexual slavery. They also exercised acts of resistance, escaping when possible.

In sum, the account told by the SCSL of the experiences of girls affiliated with the AFRC and RUF is simultaneously accurate and obfuscatory. It is accurate because it portrayed the gendered reality that girl soldiers underwent military training and were also pressed into domestic caregiving labour such as cooking, cleaning and laundry. They tried to escape when they could, often in groups. Additionally, they were extremely vulnerable to sexual violence and forced 'marriage'. The charges reflected this, with the positive outcome that sexual violence and forced 'marriage' directed against girls was highlighted during the AFRC, RUF and *Taylor* trials in ground-breaking, precedent-setting ways.[140]

---

[127] Ibid.: [1408]; *Taylor* Transcript 14 February 2008: 3874.
[128] *Taylor* Transcript 14 February 2008: 3874.
[129] *Taylor* Trial Judgment 2012: [1408], *Taylor* Transcript 14 February 2008: 3875.
[130] *Taylor* Transcript 14 February 2008: 3876.
[131] *Taylor* Trial Judgment 2012: [1408].
[132] *Taylor* Transcript 14 February 2008: 3878.
[133] Ibid.: 3879.
[134] Ibid.: 3878–80.
[135] Ibid.: 3879. See also Denov in this volume.
[136] Ibid.: 3880.
[137] The Small Boys Units were sent to the frontline, while the members of the Small Girls Unit were tasked with serving the commanders at base camp: RUF Trial Judgment 2009: [1647].
[138] Ibid.: [1622, 1667].
[139] For example, Witness TF1-314 was sent with 25 other girls in the Small Girls Unit – ten of whom were armed with pistol grips, AK-48s and AK-58s – to loot villages for food: ibid.: [1660].
[140] See Oosterveld 2011 and Oosterveld 2012. Note, however, criticism that more types of charges could have been brought: Aptel 2013: 341, 348, 358–9.

Yet the SCSL's account of the reality of girl soldiers is also obfuscatory. Far fewer girls than boys testified to the experience of serving as a child soldier, which meant that fewer details about their training and combat experiences were recorded in the trials.[141] On the other hand, in separate sections of the judgments, their subjection to sexual violence or forced 'marriage' was combined with the experiences of civilian girls. Thus, the girl soldiers' specific experiences in this respect were somewhat hidden, and not necessarily easily pieced together with their soldiering experiences. On the whole, though, the SCSL provided snapshots of the lives of girl soldiers which – prior to these trials – were virtually ignored in international criminal law.

3. THE GENDER CONSTRUCTION OF CHILDREN AFFILIATED WITH THE CIVIL DEFENCE FORCES

The Civil Defence Forces were militia fighting against the RUF and AFRC to restore the democratically elected government of Sierra Leone.[142] The CDF was composed of, inter alia, Kamajors, male traditional hunters 'normally serving in the employ of local chiefs to defend villages in rural parts of the country'.[143] During the war, Kamajors and other similar groups acted as allies to the elected government. After the 1997 AFRC military coup, the exiled President of Sierra Leone wished to coordinate and unify the efforts of these defence militia and thus created the CDF.[144]

For a time prior to the 1997 AFRC military coup, '[y]oung male fighters of good character were recommended and selected by the local chiefdom authorities for initiation' into the Kamajor society.[145] They were required to follow certain rules, including prohibitions on the killing of women and civilians not participating in the conflict; the killing of a surrendered enemy; and looting.[146] After the coup, there was a need to substantially increase the number of fighters within the CDF. Children were recruited in a number of ways, including abduction, coercion, demands to communities to provide a quota of fighters and decisions made by children in order to survive or to protect their communities from the AFRC and RUF.[147] The need to rapidly grow the CDF led to a hasty increase in initiations without recommendations by the chiefs and a breakdown in the transmission

---

[141] Aptel states: 'By calling as witnesses mostly male victims with regard to the crime of recruitment and use in hostilities, and girls as victims of sexual crimes and slavery, the prosecutors of the SCSL may have inadvertently contributed to a skewed understanding of the respective experience of boys and girls during conflicts.' Aptel 2013: 357.
[142] CDF Trial Judgment 2007: [2].
[143] Ibid. Kamajors were originally males of the Mende ethnic group who possessed specialized knowledge of the forest and were responsible for 'protecting communities from both natural and supernatural threats said to reside beyond the village boundaries': ibid.: [60]. The SCSL discussed the CDF as an organization of men – see the reference to 'men' in ibid. [355 and 358] – though (as discussed below) there were female CDF members.
[144] Ibid.: [80–81].
[145] Ibid.: [314].
[146] Ibid.
[147] Mazurana and Carlson 2004: 13; Sierra Leone TRC Chapter 4 2004: [270] (noting also that, in most cases of volunteerism, 'great pressure from their elders was brought to bear on them').

of the war-fighting prohibitions to the new recruits.[148] One study estimated that the CDF totalled 68,865 fighters, which included 17,216 children.[149]

In considering the war crime of recruitment of child soldiers, the Trial Chamber did not make a distinction between voluntary and forced enlistment into the CDF, finding that 'the distinction between the two categories is somewhat contrived'.[150] The Trial Chamber continued: '[a]ttributing voluntary enlistment in the armed forces to children under the age of 15 years, particularly in a conflict setting where human rights abuses are rife, is, in the Chamber's view, of questionable merit'.[151] The method of recruitment of the children was thus not at issue in the CDF trial. However, while many of the youth within the CDF fighting forces underwent an initiation ritual prior to fighting, the Trial Chamber concluded that initiation into the Kamajor Society did not necessarily amount to enlistment in an armed group, as 'some parents put their children through initiation for other reasons' such as gaining spiritual protection from bullets.[152]

The court heard evidence from three former child soldiers with broadly similar experiences. Witness TF2-140 was abducted by the RUF when he was 13 years old in an attack that also killed his father.[153] He was forced to fight with the RUF from 1996 to 1997, until he was captured by the CDF in an ambush in Koidu at age 14.[154] After being held in a cage made of palm tree thorns and tortured with biting ants, water and ashes, a Kamajor named Sandi offered him freedom if he agreed to help the CDF: he felt that he had no other choice but to do so.[155] He spent a month assisting the Kamajors, leading them to hidden RUF weapons caches and helping them to capture strategic points. As a result, he was initiated into the Kamajor society along with children as young as 10.[156] He then accompanied Sandi to Mano Junction and, along the way, fought in a battle.[157] He was re-initiated along with 28 other boys once he reached Mano Junction in order to provide additional immunity to bullets, because 'it was widely believed that little boys were more effectively immunized because they had not had any time with women'.[158] Witness TF2-140 eventually became a security guard for one of the CDF accused, Fofana, and also participated in more attacks.[159] It is at this point that he indicates some agency: he decided that he would link himself to the accused, Sam Hinga Norman, who was a significant person in the CDF hierarchy.[160] He gained the confidence of Norman, who took him

---

[148] CDF Trial Judgment 2007: [315].
[149] Mazurana and Carlson 2004: 12. The gender breakdown of boy and girl soldiers is discussed below.
[150] CDF Trial Judgment 2007: [192].
[151] Ibid.
[152] Ibid.: [969].
[153] Ibid.: [667].
[154] Ibid.; CDF Transcript 14 September 2004: 70.
[155] CDF Trial Judgment 2007: [667]; CDF Transcript 14 September 2004: 71–2.
[156] CDF Trial Judgment 2007: [668, 970]; CDF Transcript 14 September 2004: 74–5.
[157] CDF Trial Judgment 2007: [670].
[158] Ibid.: [670].
[159] Ibid.: [673]. Note, however, that Fofana was acquitted of the charge of recruitment or use of child soldiers: ibid.: [959, 962, 966, Disposition].
[160] Norman was the National Coordinator of the CDF appointed on 15 June 1997 by President Kabbah. Ibid.: [294].

on as a 'personal son of his'.[161] He was eventually handed over by the CDF to a child protection agency and transported to Moyami to undergo schooling, but that programme failed and he returned to Norman in Freetown.[162] After that, Norman paid his school fees (including during trial).[163] Kelsall noted that the evidence of Witness TF2-140 reflected a 'curious mix of helplessness, self-importance, pride, agency, regret and loyalty', which was likely reflective of the confusion of his life as a child soldier and SCSL witness testifying against his former guardian.[164]

The CDF Trial Chamber also heard evidence from witness TF2-021. He was abducted by rebels from his home village at 9 years old.[165] Two years later, he was captured by Kamajors, along with seven other young boys.[166] The Kamajors forced the boys to carry looted goods, and then brought them to Base Zero for initiation as fighters.[167] At Base Zero, TF2-021 was taught to shoot and made to go on missions to engage in battle with the rebels.[168] In one battle, he shot an unarmed woman, looted and helped to capture women and bring them back to Base Zero.[169] He gave evidence that girls or women were initiated into the CDF's Bondo society (characterized by one judge as 'a very big claim').[170] He was given drugs to get him ready to fight in armed conflict.[171] He also set a man on fire and participated in cannibalism following an attack on Kenema.[172] At age 13, he was again initiated, this time into the Kamajors' Avondo Society.[173] He entered a disarmament, demobilization and reintegration programme at age 14.[174]

The third former child soldier, witness TF2-002, was abducted by the rebels from his village when he was a small boy.[175] He was taught by the rebels how to use a gun and was involved in both food-finding missions and looting.[176] In a battle between the rebels and Kamajors, he was captured by the Kamajors, along with five other boys.[177] Armed with a machete, he subsequently participated in fighting against the rebels.[178] He was then initiated into the Kamajors for the purpose of fighting in the war, along with children as

---

[161] CDF Transcript 14 September 2004: 89–90.
[162] Ibid.: 100–101.
[163] CDF Transcript 14 September 2004: 104–5.
[164] Kelsall 2009: 168.
[165] CDF Trial Judgment 2007: [674].
[166] Ibid.
[167] Ibid.: [675].
[168] Ibid.: [676–80].
[169] Ibid.: [676].
[170] CDF Transcript 2 November 2004: 59–60. The Bondo society is a secret society within Sierra Leone providing rites of passage for girls to become women and teaching members about cultural traditions, histories, skills and trade: MacKenzie 2009: 254.
[171] CDF Trial Judgment 2007: [681].
[172] CDF Transcript 2 November 2004: 69, 77.
[173] CDF Trial Judgment 2007: [682]. The Avondo society had gendered norms: the male initiates 'did not want to be touched by or stand near female teachers ... They began to show violent behaviour.' Ibid.: [372].
[174] CDF Transcript 2 November 2004: 103–5.
[175] This witness did not know his age at the time. CDF Trial Judgment 2007: [683]; CDF Transcript 9 November 2004: 66, 68, 86.
[176] CDF Transcript 2 November 2004: 73.
[177] CDF Trial Judgment 2007: [683].
[178] Ibid.: [684].

young as 10.[179] He was given a gun, trained how to use it and was immediately required to fight the rebels in Zimmi.[180] He was also involved in other battles, and was with the Kamajors for a long time.[181] In his testimony, he did not discuss how his involvement with the CDF ended.

The Trial Chamber referred to evidence from other sources regarding the CDF's use of child soldiers, who were referred to as 'Small Hunters'.[182] Most of this evidence is referred to in a gender-neutral manner in the trial judgment, but it appears from the transcripts that the evidence related to boys (rather than both to girls and boys). For example, that evidence indicated that some children were used as bodyguards (including for the accused, Kondewa) or to monitor checkpoints.[183] They were also used to lead the CDF militia into combat, and children as young as seven years old danced in front of the Kamajors as they left for a battle.[184] As indicated elsewhere, these roles were perceived to be the domain of boys.

Why did the CDF use child soldiers? The evidence before the SCSL indicated that the child soldiers performed more reliably in combat: in a meeting at Base Zero in 1998 attended by both child and adult fighters, the accused Norman complained that the child soldiers were outperforming the adult soldiers.[185] As well, according to one witness, the CDF liked to use child soldiers in combat because they were obedient.[186]

Given the evidence considered by the Trial Chamber, the CDF Trial Judgment contained two types of invisibilities based on gender: first, a complete absence of the stories of girls affiliated with the CDF (despite hints in the evidence of such girls),[187] and second, the absence of stories of boys who joined the CDF from within their own communities. These lacunae need to be acknowledged because their absence skews the record of history created by the SCSL.[188]

The first invisibility relates to the absence of the stories of CDF girls. During and after the war, it was widely – and incorrectly – assumed 'that the CDFs were male-only secret societies that prohibited the presence of females or sexual contact with females'.[189] This was the message conveyed by the government of Sierra Leone.[190] However, in-depth study of the CDFs revealed that hundreds of girls served as fully initiated members and frontline fighters within the two largest groups, the Kamajors and the Gbethis.[191] Mazurana and Carlson estimate that the CDF contained 15,494 boy soldiers and 1,722 girl soldiers.[192]

---

[179] Ibid.: [685]. When initiated, he was told to obey certain laws to keep himself safe from bullets, including not to eat nut oil, electric fish or pumpkin, and not to jump over or sit on a mortar pestle. CDF Transcript 9 November 2004: 115.
[180] CDF Trial Judgment 2007: [686]; CDF Transcript of 9 November 2004: 77.
[181] CDF Trial Judgment 2007: [687]; CDF Transcript of 9 November 2004: 83.
[182] CDF Trial Judgment 2007: [688].
[183] Ibid.
[184] Ibid.
[185] Ibid. [689].
[186] Ibid. [688].
[187] E.g. CDF Transcript 2 November 2004: 59–60.
[188] There is a debate on whether international criminal trials serve the purpose of truth telling and recording history, given the focus of a trial on particular individuals: Cryer at al. 2014: 38–40.
[189] McKay and Mazurana 2004: 91, note 15.
[190] Ibid.
[191] Ibid.
[192] Mazurana and Carlson 2004: 12.

While the Kamajors were originally a male-only society, the pressures of combat with the RUF led to the enlistment of women and girls from the beginning of the war in the early 1990s.[193] The Gbethis were created in the mid-1990s in response to increased rebel attacks, and they enlisted and initiated women and girls 'as integrated members of the CDF'.[194] Women and girls within the CDF served as 'commanders, frontline fighters, initiators, spiritual leaders, medics, herbalists, spies and cooks'.[195] Some of these girls were abducted and conscripted into the CDF, 'some "joined" or became "wives" to male CDF fighters as a matter of survival', some joined at the request of their husbands or parents, and others joined because they wanted to protect their villages and towns from attack by opposing forces.[196]

There are interlinked reasons for the absence of the story of girl CDF soldiers from the SCSL. As mentioned above, the SCSL's Prosecutor bifurcated the girl soldier evidence into that which related to traditional fighting and that which related to sexual and gender-based violence. It was difficult for girls subjected to either type of experience within the CDF to come forward to the SCSL's Office of the Prosecutor, and thus there were few potential witnesses.[197] These girls were often ostracized within their communities due to their involvement in, or having witnessed, violent acts such as killing and human sacrifice.[198] They were also ostracized if they were subjected to rape due to the focus on female virginity at marriage within rural Sierra Leonean culture.[199] These experiences of violence 'went against traditionally acceptable roles for females' and thus all girls affiliated with the CDF involved in Mazurana and Carlson's study reported 'stigmatization, threats and abuse upon returning to the communities they had fought to protect'.[200] Additionally, there was popular support within Sierra Leone for the CDF, creating another social pressure on girls not to provide evidence to the SCSL against their own community members.[201]

Another crucial reason for the invisibility of girl soldiers in the CDF trial judgment is that a majority of the Trial Chamber judges excluded all evidence of sexual and gender-based violence from the CDF trials through a series of questionable decisions.[202] This meant that CDF 'wives' or girls within the CDF who were subjected to sexual violence were not permitted to testify about their experiences, even to support charges related to

---

[193] Ibid.: 13. See also Coulter 2009: 126.
[194] Mazurana and Carlson 2004: 13.
[195] Ibid.
[196] Ibid.; CDF Transcript 2 November 2004: 47; Sierra Leone TRC Chapter 4 2004: [270].
[197] Oosterveld 2015–2016: 139–40. Note that the Sierra Leone Truth and Reconciliation Commission (TRC) recorded sexual violence committed by the CDF against women and girls: Sierra Leone TRC Chapter 3 2004: [352–5]. The TRC noted the precarious position of female former combatants in Sierra Leonean society: 'Women thus suffer a "double victimisation"[,] having been compelled by circumstances to join the armed forces, they are further victimised by the same society for having done so. Non-disclosure facilitates their assimilation into their society and is yet another survival mechanism.' Sierra Leone TRC Chapter 3 2004: [410–11].
[198] Mazurana and Carlson 2004: 13.
[199] Coulter 2009: 224.
[200] Mazurana and Carlson 2004: 13.
[201] Oosterveld 2015–2016: 139–40.
[202] For an explanation and critique of these procedural moves, see Oosterveld 2007: 159–68, and Oosterveld 2009: 420–29.

The construction of gender in child soldiering in the SCSL 91

cruel treatment or inhumane acts.[203] The Appeals Chamber, while finding that the Trial Chamber erred in certain respects, did not order a new trial on charges of sexual and gender-based violence.[204]

The second invisibility relates to boy soldiers who were directly recruited into the CDF from within their own communities, although many children joined the CDF in this manner.[205] All three witnesses who had been boy soldiers within the CDF were originally boy soldiers within the AFRC or RUF and were captured by the CDF. They were not necessarily linked to the communities which they 'served'. Evidence from, for example, boys put forward by their parents at the request of the Paramount Chief for their area[206] would potentially present a more nuanced story than the three SCSL witnesses, given their link to the fighting forces and the civilians they were meant to protect.[207] The evidence of Witness TF2-140 comes the closest to reflecting the complicated mix of patriotism, the belief that one is fighting on the 'just' side of a conflict, the urge towards survival, and the ability to perpetrate violence that potentially might emerge in testimony from boy soldiers with close community ties to the CDF.

In sum, the narrative presented by the SCSL on child soldiers affiliated with the CDF is incomplete. It lacks the perspectives and experiences of girl soldiers, which is a large and worrisome absence. It also only hints at – but does not confront – the complexities of the experiences of boy soldiers who were recruited from within their own communities, as opposed to being captured from an opposing armed group. The SCSL thus only presented a partial glimpse into the gendered experiences of child soldiers affiliated with the CDF.

4. CONCLUSION

This chapter has considered the ways in which the testimony of child soldiers (and others) before the SCSL explicitly and implicitly brought their gendered experiences to light. The SCSL demonstrated that boys were specifically targeted by the AFRC and RUF based on gendered views about their obedience, agility and ferocity, and thus were trained and sent to the frontlines or to serve as guards. Girls were targeted based on gendered views about their utility for domestic work and sexual slavery, while also trained to serve as fighters. Importantly, given the historical silences in this regard, the SCSL highlighted the fact that girls were extremely vulnerable to sexual violence once within the power of the AFRC or RUF: most girls testifying at the SCSL had experienced many episodes of sexual violence during the war. However, experiences of boy soldiers as victims of sexual violence were not proffered for consideration. Finally, the SCSL only received a partial

---

[203] This caused these witnesses lasting negative psychological effects: Staggs Kelsall and Stepakoff 2007: 373. The Appeals Chamber summarized the evidence that the Prosecutor intended to elicit, but which was not permitted to be presented: CDF Appeals Judgment 2008: note 862.
[204] CDF Appeals Judgment 2008: [440–51].
[205] Sierra Leone TRC Chapter 4 2004: [270–72].
[206] Ibid.: [270].
[207] It is understandable that the prosecution focused on boys abducted from the RUF/AFRC. From a socio-cultural perspective, these boys were not testifying about crimes committed by people directly from within their own communities.

story of child soldiers within the CDF, as the court did not consider the recruitment or use of girls. Additionally, the full range of experiences of boy soldiers within the CDF was not necessarily examined.

It is important for international criminal tribunals to conduct contextualized gender analysis in any conflict under consideration. Such analysis provides crucial and more nuanced insight into many underlying questions – of motivation, targeting and impact – that are key to understanding the case at hand.[208] As well, a gender analysis assists with uncovering previously invisible experiences. The SCSL is rightly lauded for 'surfacing' the gendered experiences of child soldiers affiliated with armed groups in Sierra Leone. The SCSL not only developed international law in relation to the recruitment and use of child soldiers, as well as sexual and gender-based violence, it also brought attention to the actual experiences of Sierra Leonean boys and girls in a way that complemented and extended the work of Sierra Leone's Truth and Reconciliation Commission in this regard. At the same time, future tribunals need to be alert to the gender 'blind spots' evident within the SCSL's judgments, so as to render visible all child soldiers within international criminal law.

REFERENCED WORKS

Books, Articles and Reports

Aijazi, O. and Baines, E. 2017. 'Relationality, Culpability and Consent in Wartime: Men's Experiences of Forced Marriage' 11 *International Journal of Transitional Justice* 463

Aptel, C. 2013. 'Unpunished Crimes: The Special Court for Sierra Leone and Children', in C. Chernor Jalloh (ed.), *The Sierra Leone Special Court and its Legacy: The Impact for Africa and International Criminal Law* (New York: Cambridge University Press) 340

Betancourt, T.S., Borisova, I., de la Soudière, M. and Williamson, J. 2011. 'Sierra Leone's Child Soldiers: War Exposures and Mental Health Problems by Gender' 49 *Journal of Adolescent Health* 21

Copelon, R. 1994. 'Surfacing Gender: Re-Engraving Crimes Against Women in Humanitarian Law' 5 *Hastings Women's Law Journal* 243

Coulter, C. 2009. *Bush Wives and Girl Soldiers: Women's Lives Through War and Peace in Sierra Leone* (Ithaca, NY: Cornell University Press)

Cryer, R., Friman, H., Robinson, D. and Wilmshurst, E. (eds). 2014. *An Introduction to International Criminal Law and Procedure*, 3rd ed. (Cambridge: Cambridge University Press)

Drumbl, M. 2012, *Reimagining Child Soldiers in International Law and Policy* (New York: Oxford University Press)

Grey, R. 2014. 'Sexual Violence Against Child Soldiers: The Limits and Potential of International Criminal Law' 16 *International Feminist Journal of Politics* 601

Guberek, T., Guzman, D., Silva, R., Cibelli, K., Asher, A., Weikart, S., Ball, P. and Grossman, W. 2006. 'Truth and Myth in Sierra Leone: An Empirical Analysis of the Conflict, 1991–2000' (Palo Alto, CA: Benetech Human Rights Data Analysis Group and the American Bar Association)

Human Rights Watch 2003. '"We'll Kill You if You Cry": Sexual Violence in the Sierra Leone Conflict' (16 January)

Jørgenson, N. 2012, 'Child Soldiers and the Parameters of International Criminal Law' 11 *Chinese Journal of International Law* 657

Kelsall, T. 2009. *Culture Under Cross-Examination: International Justice and the Special Court for Sierra Leone* (New York: Cambridge University Press)

MacKenzie, M. 2009. 'Securitization and Desecuritization: Female Soldiers and the Reconstruction of Women in Post-Conflict Sierra Leone' 18 *Security Studies* 241

---

[208] This approach underlies the International Criminal Court's 2014 Policy Paper on Sexual and Gender-Based Crimes.

Marks, Z. 2013. 'Sexual Violence Inside Rebellion: Policies and Perspectives on the Revolutionary United Front of Sierra Leone' 15 *Civil Wars* 359

Mazurana, D. and Carlson K. 2004. 'From Combat to Community: Women and Girls of Sierra Leone' (Washington DC: Hunt Alternatives Fund)

McKay, S. and Mazurana, D. 2004. *Where Are the Girls? Girls in Fighting Forces in Northern Uganda, Sierra Leone and Mozambique: Their Lives During and After War* (Montreal: International Centre for Human Rights and Democratic Development)

Michels, A. 2006. 'As If It Was Happening Again: Supporting Especially Vulnerable Witnesses, in Particular Women and Children, at the Special Court for Sierra Leone', in K. Arts and V. Popovski (eds), *International Criminal Accountability and the Rights of Children* (The Hague: Hague Academic Press) 133

Office of the Prosecutor of the International Criminal Court 2014. 'Policy Paper on Sexual and Gender-Based Crimes' (June)

Oosterveld, V. 2007. 'The Special Court for Sierra Leone, Child Soldiers, and Forced Marriage: Providing Clarity or Confusion?' 45 *The Canadian Yearbook of International Law* 131

Oosterveld, V. 2009. 'Lessons from the Special Court for Sierra Leone on the Prosecution of Gender-Based Crimes' 17(2) *American University Journal of Gender, Social Policy & the Law* 407

Oosterveld, V. 2011. 'The Gender Jurisprudence of the Special Court for Sierra Leone: Progress in the Revolutionary United Front Judgments' 44 *Cornell International Law Journal* 49

Oosterveld, V. 2012. 'Gender and the *Charles Taylor* Case at the Special Court for Sierra Leone' 19 *William & Mary Journal of Women and the Law* 7

Oosterveld, V. 2015–2016. 'The Special Court for Sierra Leone: Initial Structural and Procedural Decisions on Sexual and Gender-Based Violence' 46 *Cambrian Law Review* 131

Richards, P. 2002. 'Militia Conscription in Sierra Leone: Recruitment of Young Fighters in an African War', in L. Mjøset and S. Van Holde (eds), *The Comparative Study of Conscription in Armed Forces* (New York: JAI Elsevier Science) 255

Sanin, K. and Stirnemann, A. 2006. 'Child Witnesses at the Special Court for Sierra Leone' (Berkeley, CA: University of California War Crimes Studies Center)

Sierra Leone TRC [Truth and Reconciliation Commission] 2004. *Witness to Truth: Report of the Sierra Leone Truth & Reconciliation Commission* (Accra, Ghana: GPL Press)
Volume Three B, Chapter 3, 'Women and the Armed Conflict in Sierra Leone'
Volume Three B, Chapter 4, 'Children and Armed Conflict in Sierra Leone'

Smith, A. 2004. 'Sierra Leone: The Intersection of Law, Policy, and Practice', in C. Romano, A. Nollkaemper and J. Kleffner (eds), *Internationalized Criminal Courts: Sierra Leone, East Timor, Kosovo, and Cambodia* (New York: Oxford University Press) 125

Special Court for Sierra Leone 2002. 'Press Release: Special Court Prosecutor Says He Will Not Prosecute Children' (2 November)

Special Court for Sierra Leone 2007. 'Press Release: Guilty Verdicts in the Trial of the AFRC Accused' (20 June)

Staggs Kelsall, M. and Stepakoff, S. 2007. '"When We Wanted to Talk About Rape": Silencing Sexual Violence at the Special Court for Sierra Leone' 1 *International Journal of Transitional Justice* 355

Judicial Proceedings

Extraordinary Chambers in the Courts of Cambodia (ECCC), *Prosecutor v. Nuon Chea, Ieng Sary, Khieu Samphan and Ieng Thirith* (Case No. 002/19-09-2007-ECCC)
- Closing Order (15 September 2010)

SCSL, AFRC, *Prosecutor v. Alex Tamba Brima, Brima Bazzy Kamara and Santigie Borbor Kanu* (Case No. SCSL-04-16)
- Trial Judgment (20 June 2007)
- Appeals Judgment (22 February 2008)

SCSL, CDF, *Prosecutor v. Sam Hinga Norman, Moinina Fofana and Allieu Kondewa* (Case No. SCSL-04-14)
- Trial Judgment (2 August 2007)
- Appeals Judgment (28 May 2008)
- Transcripts:
  14 September 2004
  2 November 2004
  9 November 2004

SCSL, RUF, *Prosecutor v. Issa Hassan Sesay, Morris Kallon and Augustine Gbao* (Case No. SCSL-04-15)
- Trial Judgment (2 March 2009)
- Appeals Judgment (26 October 2009)

- Transcripts:
  11 April 2005
SCSL, Taylor, *Prosecutor v. Charles Ghankay Taylor* (Case No. SCSL-03-01-T)
- Trial Judgment (18 May 2012)
- Appeals Judgment (26 September 2013)
- Transcripts:
  14 February 2008
  29 January 2009

4. 'We were controlled, we were not allowed to express our sexuality, our intimacy was suppressed': sexual violence experienced by boys

*Omer Aijazi, Evelyn Amony and Erin Baines**

Why are academic and policy discourses on child soldiers relatively silent on boys' experience of sexual violence in armed groups? In August of 2006, Erin Baines – one of the authors – accompanied journalists from the Canadian Broadcasting Corporation (CBC) to an internally displaced person's camp in Anaka, northern Uganda, to document the consequences of the ongoing war upon children. One of the interviewees was Fred, a young boy who had been abducted by the Lord's Resistance Army (LRA) at the age of 13 and coerced into their ranks. At the time of the interview, Fred had just escaped the LRA to reunite with his family in Anaka. Fred shared his unease: he was continuously disturbed by nightmares and often took to sleepwalking. Even though he was only in the LRA for a few months, Fred was forced to kill and rape civilians. He recalled one incident in which he was forced to rape an elderly woman. How should we approach Fred's experience? Can this event be considered a dual form of sexual violence inflicted on Fred and the elderly woman? This was the first time Erin had knowingly spoken to a male survivor of wartime rape. Fred challenged her conceptions of not only who should be considered a victim of sexual violence in wartime, but also the forms sexual violence may take.

Fred reminds us of the insufficient attention to the sexual harms men and boys endure in wartime. Literature and policy on sexual violence and 'child soldiers' pays less attention to the ways boys are victims.[1] Instead, scholarly and policy research has more often centred on girl's and women's experiences of sexual violence within an armed group, such as, for example, concubinage, forced marriage, pregnancy and sterilization or abortion, as well as rape and sexual mutilation.[2] A reason often cited for this exclusion is the social taboos regarding sexual violence against boys and men, where norms regarding gender and sexuality intersect to 'doubly silence' and render the experiences of these victims invisible. Another is the inadvertent (at times purposeful) exclusion of boys and men from the work of feminist legal scholars who are sometimes singularly focused on the inclusion of women and girls in the global agenda on sexual violence and in the development of international legal cases.[3]

---

* This research was supported by a Standard Research Grant from the Social Sciences and Research Council (SSHRC) of Canada, and the Conjugal Slavery in War (CSiW) SSHRC Partnership.

[1] We use the term 'child soldier' but are aware of the racialized infantilization such a label may suggest. See, Macmillan 2009.

[2] Coulter 2015; Baines 2017.

[3] See the following debate between Chris Dolan and Jeanne Ward: Dolan 2014a; Ward 2016; Dolan 2016.

Fred also reminds us of the insufficient language that exists on sexual violence. While an increasing number of studies of sexual violence in wartime urge closer attention to the ways state armed forces and non-state armed groups target men and boys, gender and age-based normative assumptions persist.[4] We use the terms 'boys' and 'men' to refer to an age-based spectrum in relation to experiences of wartime sexual violence. However, we are cognizant that these categorizations are vague and often rooted within Western conceptions of adulthood.[5] Some authors consider the causes of sexual violence against women and men, often drawing on the lens of masculinity to explain both its occurrence and underreporting.[6] Other studies document forms of sexual violence experienced – from rape, to genital mutilation, enforced sterilization, enforced nudity and enforced masturbation – and explore why such cases are underreported to service providers and judicial institutions.[7] Others consider how sexual violence against men and boys has failed to be prosecuted in international law,[8] or trace its recent evolution.[9] Still others consider the immediate and long-term social and health impacts of such violations for the victim and within communities where the violence took place.[10] Context-specific case studies have been increasingly documented to allow the consideration of actual lived experience within the otherwise sterile and generalized remits of academia and policy.[11] Across studies, focus and location, gendered and age-based assumptions of victimhood and guilt persist, even if the experiences of boys and men are now the focus. In legal narratives of sexual harm, men are most often assumed to be perpetrators, children are considered innocent and power is understood to exist as an absolute. Again, we ask, how should we approach Fred's violation(s)?

Drawing from the experiences of boys forcibly conscripted into the LRA, we seek to move beyond the gendered, limiting language of sexual slavery, concubines, forced pregnancy and rape in relation to child soldiers. We start with the premise that in settings of coercion – such as that of the LRA where forced conscription was endemic – most intimate and sexual relations were in themselves violent impositions. This allows us to reconsider our understanding of culpability and opens up an entry point for examining experiences of sexual violence without falling into the conceptual trap of girls and women as victims and boys and men as perpetrators found in second wave feminist legal studies.[12] In our opinion, this conceptual trap has been an obstacle for substantively understanding the experiences of sexual violence amongst boys and men in armed groups. We note the problematics of localizing the harms of sexual violence using the labels of 'child' and

---

[4] See, e.g. Solangon and Patel 2012.

[5] To this effect, we remain dissatisfied with the language of 'boys' and 'men' which lends to dualistic and binary thinking despite our intentions otherwise. This is a challenge: how to work against categories and categorical thinking in the absence of adequate language?

[6] Vojdik 2014; Grey and Shepherd 2013.

[7] Sivakumaran 2007.

[8] Lewis 2009; Touquet and Gorris 2016. See also Oosterveld in this volume who observes that sexual violence committed against boys was not examined by the Special Court for Sierra Leone, despite indications that such violations likely occurred.

[9] Oosterveld 2014.

[10] Christian et al. 2011; Chynoweth et al. 2017.

[11] Touquet 2018; Clark 2017; Chynoweth 2017.

[12] Buss 2009; Mibenge 2013.

'adult', knowing that there are no universal or fixed distinctions between children and adults – a transition less marked by age but by contextualized understandings of responsibility and kinship. We are also mindful of the inconsistent approaches to 'child soldiers' within the liberal imagination, which is heavily marked by a skewed racial representation of vulnerability and ethics.[13] We suggest a relational approach to sexual violence in settings of coercion and where one's sexuality is controlled, and intimacy is supressed. A relational approach enables us to move beyond an understanding of patriarchal power as totalizing by attending to the context-specific constructions of age, race, ability and sexuality as they intersect. This is crucial, we suggest, to develop analytical assemblages beyond ageist and gendered understandings of sexual violence.

1. METHODS

After her encounter with Fred, Erin continued to work in northern Uganda on a multi-year research project with female survivors of forced abduction and marriage in the LRA. Despite Fred's disruption of common feminist assumptions about sexual violence and victimhood, Erin did not think of including in her study the lived and felt experiences of men who were abducted as children. It was only when the participants in her study began to reference how *both* girls and boys were sometimes raped inside the LRA that Erin further considered how her own research design may be contributing to the erasure of boy's experiences in the armed group.[14] In 2014, Erin and community researcher and activist Evelyn Amony conducted a series of preliminary interviews and focus group discussions with men who had been forced to soldier at a young age in the LRA. The goal for these interviews was to generate discussion on the occurrence of sexual violence inside the group.

Exploratory in design, the study comprises unstructured focus group discussions (FGDs) and open-ended individual interviews conducted in 2014 and 2015. This research took place in Gulu town, Acholi-bur, Pader Town Council and Ngoto in northern Uganda. Most participants were men who were abducted by the LRA and who had fought for between one and 17 years following brutal processes of socialization and training. Most participants were abducted between the ages of 13 and 20 and hence came of age in the armed group. Participants fought and lived in South Sudan, northern Uganda, the Democratic Republic of Congo and Central African Republic. All but one – a Brigade commander – held junior to mid-level ranks in the LRA, ranging from private, second or first lieutenant and captain. The Women's Advocacy Network, a grassroots organization with 900 members of war-affected men and women throughout northern Uganda, assisted in the identification of participants for this study.

The fieldwork was completed in collaboration with a team of Ugandan research assistants. In the focus group discussions, participants were asked to speak of their experiences of sexual violence within the LRA. These discussions were then supplemented with individual interviews. Thirty-three demobilized male soldiers were interviewed or

---

[13] Moynagh 2014.
[14] On the multiple and intersecting institutions that silence male survivors – including academic institutions – see Schulz 2018.

participated in focus group discussions. All interviews and discussions were conducted in Luo-Acholi, the local vernacular. We left all discussions open ended, thereby allowing participants to lead the discussions and ended them promptly when they stated or indicted that they were done speaking. In the following sections, we present some lived experiences of this subset of purposefully identified participants and what they chose to narrate in response to our research interests.

2. WAR IN NORTHERN UGANDA

The war began in northern Uganda in 1986, shortly after the present-day President of Uganda, Yoweri Museveni and the National Resistance Army (NRA) assumed control of the state in a *coup-d'état*.[15] Resistance to NRA acts of terror against the predominantly Acholi inhabitants of the north came in the form of demobilized soldiers retreating and regrouping in the north, first coalescing around the leadership of Alice Lakwena, a spirit medium who hailed from the north and formed the Holy Spirit Mobile Forces (HSMF) which fought against the NRA.

In the late 1980s, Joseph Kony emerged as a spiritual leader in the north. Kony attracted different groups of rebels, including remnants of the HSMF, and followers to amass a significant army devoted to following the spiritual laws communicated through Kony and eventually forming the LRA. Following a series of military operations by the NRA – later renamed the Ugandan People's Defence Forces – against the LRA, the government entered peace talks with the rebels in 1993. When the talks failed, the LRA relocated to Sudan. The LRA received military support and aid from the Sudanese government and, in return, assisted the Sudanese Armed Forces in fighting the civil war in that country. The LRA built extensive bases in Sudan until 2003, when a Ugandan military-led offensive, Operation Iron Fist, led them to return to Uganda to fight the war there once more. The war ended in Uganda with a ceasefire in 2006 but remains ongoing in the Central African Republic, Democratic Republic of Congo and Sudan, where Kony relocated with the LRA following a failed attempt at peace talks in 2008.

3. SEXUAL GOVERNANCE IN THE LRA

Studies of the LRA in Sudan suggest that the group was organized around a military-familial unit, in which each commander acted as 'father' to new recruits, and the most senior wife acted as 'mother'.[16] Abducted children were socialized through physical labour, beatings and public displays of violence, such as the beating, murder or mutilation of other recruits or of civilians.[17] Such tactics were to harden the abducted child and replace their longing for home with loyalty to the movement. As one participant argued, 'We abducted young children, so they can grow into the system and adjust to the system.

---

[15] See also Akello; Barrett; and Denov, all in this volume.
[16] Baines 2014.
[17] Oloya 2013.

Just as a child starts in the nursery, they grow into primary and secondary school and university. That is why we abducted children.'[18]

Within the LRA, sexual relations were strictly regulated according to the spiritual dictates of Alice Lakwena as communicated through Kony. Participants emphasized both the normality of rules dictating behaviour but also the gross ramifications of failing to obey the rules that governed sexual and gender relations, which included a variety of ways men and women were to interact on a daily basis to minimize the possibility of sexual transgressions. Sex was only permitted between men and women within a 'marriage' sanctioned by senior commanders, at a time of their determination, and between two persons they selected for it. Rape was forbidden, as were extramarital affairs.[19] Nevertheless, participants acknowledged that soldiers raped newly abducted girls and women without the knowledge of commanders. Often male commanders themselves covertly raped newly abducted girls and women before their 'assignment as a wife' and would release them immediately being fully aware of the implications if they were caught. It is within this context of rules of marriage and sexual relations, and the ways these rules were broken, that participants discussed the ways they themselves or others experienced different forms of sexual violence against men and boys. We draw attention to the fact that all persons were subject to violent governance within the LRA. Therefore, most intimate and sexual relations were forged in a setting of coercion – albeit assuredly negotiated in a variety of ways which were in themselves deeply gendered. One participant explained, 'In the LRA, you can't just wake up and leave . . . every decision you make, you factor in how it will affect you and your life, every decision affects your life as it is confined within the LRA.'[20]

Mindfulness of the coercive settings within the LRA allows observers to approach the experiences of men and boys within the group with the same urgency as those of women and girls. We also encourage readers to take note of the deep involvement of Kony himself within the elaborate regulation of sexual relationships within the LRA. Kony's involvement indicates the centrality of sexual regulation to the political and spiritual imperatives of the LRA and the extraordinary conditions for unsanctioned forms of sexual relations and violations. This helps us to further appreciate the silences and erasures around sexual violence against boys and men in the armed group.

The next several sections of this chapter consider various coercive relationships – specifically, forced marriage, relationships in which senior women exploited boys and relationships in which senior men exploited boys.

3.1 Forced Marriage

One of the more commonly documented and analysed forms of sexual violence in armed groups, including the LRA, is the practice of forced marriage. Research on forced marriage is usually conducted from the perspective of women who were often abducted as girls. Cognizant of the setting of coercion described above in which all relationships

---

[18] Interview with 'Tony', former mid-level ranking LRA soldier who spent 17 years in the rebel group, Pader Town Council, 25 June 2015.
[19] Baines 2014: 410.
[20] FGD with nine former LRA soldiers, all abducted between the ages of 10 and 15 for three to eleven years, mid-level rank, Gulu District, 10 July 2014.

were forged, we draw attention to men's experiences of forced marriage to offer a more gender-inclusive understanding of sexual violence amongst boys within the LRA. We build on our previous argument that a relational approach reveals the entanglements of power, and 'the wider web of social entanglements through which power circulates and is contested, disrupting the problematic framework of men-as-perpetrators (and thus all-powerful and in need of restraint) and women-as-victims (and thus without agency and in need of rescue).'[21] In settings of coercion, a relational approach reveals the various ways relationships impinge or place demands upon each other. As such it 'lets go of the gender binary', to understand how vulnerability is shaped in a dynamic set of relationships that are never static, or merely defined by domination and subordination.[22]

Men spoke of the many ways they were assigned a wife in the LRA. One participant recalled how he fell in love with a young woman instructed by his superior to nurse him back to health after an injury. He was eventually granted the right to marry her. This was identified as a common enough occurrence. Others talked of approaching their commanders when they felt they were ready for marriage and appealed to them for a wife. Only those who were considered loyal, hardworking and obedient were given the right to take a wife – once again at their commander's discretion. These rules were unevenly applied. Some 'would apply pressure' on their commander until their request was fulfilled. As Richard, a former Brigade commander explained, others 'were jolly and liked by the big men, and that is why they were given a wife, because they favoured their behaviour.'[23] Richard also commented, 'At times it was like home, depending on status and who you were you were free to speak your mind, and it was respected.' Another participant reported:

> If you don't want that woman, and there is another you want, if you explain it well to the commander, they will release you [from that woman]. If you want the other one and she is fit for a specific commander, then they will remind you that she is for someone for a big commander. They will tell you that next time we will abduct another group and give you another, or next time in the field you can recruit a girl you like to keep as your wife.[24]

The distribution of young girls to their new homes was achieved under the oversight of the high command, often Kony himself. If a girl was premenstrual, she was taken into a commander's home to act as a *ting ting* – a caregiver for his children and assistant to his wives. *Ting tings* called the commander 'father'. When she menstruated, a *ting ting* was either forced to become the commander's wife or given to one of his escorts or to a new commander. Richard explained that, originally, wives were released by the LRA after they gave birth. But on relocation to South Sudan in 1994, the LRA began to enforce new marriage laws to prevent extra-marital sexual relations and the desertion of their male soldiers:

> Eventually, with the urge of nature, people hooked up, and there was rivalry. Say there was one woman, and then four or five people were trying to encroach on her, she would pick one and the

---

[21] Aijazi and Baines 2017: 468.
[22] Dolan 2014b: 498.
[23] Interview with 'Richard', a former LRA Brigade Commander, Gulu District, 9 July 2014.
[24] Interview with 'Tony', former mid-level ranking LRA soldier who spent 17 years in the rebel group, Pader Town Council, 25 June 2015.

rest would feel jealous – and would lose morale to fight. Some would even want to just go back home, because they had left their women and children at home . . . *Those at young age [boys abducted for fighting and domestic labour] grew up, we didn't want them to go back. That is why we did marriage.*[25]

Another important rationale for the regulation of marriage within the LRA was to promote distinctive forms of moral purity for the creation of a 'new' and superior Acholi nation. Sex outside marriage was strictly forbidden and enforced via public forms of punishment and humiliation, such as being beaten in front of an assembly, imprisonment or execution:

> In Congo, an escort to Kony slept with one of Kony's wives. The sex resulted in a pregnancy. Kony asked [his wife] how she became pregnant because they had not had sex for more than six months, so where did she get? The woman admitted that she went together with the escort. The wife and escort were both shot.[26]

Men regulated their interactions with women, for even the slightest of suspicions could be enough to solicit accusation, interrogation and punishment. Others stated they feared the spiritual ramifications of breaking the proclaimed rules, for it was believed – and many testified that they witnessed it to be true – that the spirits guided bullets to those who broke these rules. Such was the state of coercion in which sexual or familial relations were governed.

Only a small group of commanders close to Kony, or Kony himself, determined who could marry and when they could marry.[27] Even senior commanders often did not have a choice of whom they could take as a wife, or who the girl or young woman under their care was given to. Richard, the Brigade commander in this study, argues he himself was once subject to forced marriage. Richard describes an instance where he was instructed to accept a new wife he did not want. Richard illuminates the degree to which Kony regulated the sexual relations of all those under his control, even his senior commanders, as well as how Kony imposed marriages on both men and women:

> There was a time a lady was allocated to me by top leadership, I didn't want it [the marriage], I refused and explained a lot that I was not in the position to handle that lady and all that . . . but what came out for me from him [Kony], was that well, if I refused, it would mean I was looking for a lady amongst those he already he had, that I wanted his own wives . . . so I became afraid. There was no way I could refuse.[28]

While Kony insisted the LRA should live as one unified Acholi and publicly discouraged favouritism amongst kin relations, nepotism reportedly took place under various political machinations. This extended to who was afforded a wife, but had to be handled carefully since, as one participant observed, there were many powerful escorts who did not have wives and who might revolt against their commander if one was favoured over another.

---

[25] Interview with 'Richard', a former LRA Brigade commander, Gulu town, 9 July 2014.
[26] Interview with 'Tony', former mid-level ranking LRA soldier who spent 17 years in the rebel group, Pader Town Council, 25 June 2015.
[27] Carlson and Mazurana 2008.
[28] Interview with 'Richard', a former LRA Brigade Commander, Gulu town, 9 July 2014.

Still, lower-ranking men could wait 10 years or more to be assigned a wife if they failed to live up to the standard expected of them to receive one. Some men reported being as young as 14 when given a wife, although most were in their mid-20s and stated they were ready. A few understood themselves as victims of forced marriage:

> We used to abduct girls from an area and move with them to the position [a temporary base in the bush]. I was given a woman without being asked. I was just ordered to do it without any choice of who. I see that as being forced to marry. Our commander just distributed women to his men and told you to stay with her whether you wanted to or not. I was given to a very young girl to stay with as my wife.[29]

Participants recalled various times they escaped death following accusations by a commander that they coveted his wife or his prospective wife and were forced to marry someone they did not wish to wed to placate the jealousies of their commanders. It is important to be mindful of the coercive settings under which forced marriage was instituted and regulated. A participant explained: 'When you are confined, you can't just do as you please. So, if you were given a woman, you had to accept, there was no choice. It was only when we returned home, we learn this was against the law set by the Government of Uganda.'[30] A community social worker we spoke with recalled a dialogue he facilitated on reconciliation in which members accused one man who had been abducted by the LRA of forced marriage and rape. The accused responded by reminding community members of the settings of coercion and regulation which governed life in the LRA: 'I was abducted at a young age, I went to the bush knowing nothing about women. You accuse me of all these crimes [forced marriage, rape, killing, abduction, looting], but I learned all this in the bush – how was I to know right from wrong?'[31]

3.2 Senior Wives and Sexual Violence Against Boys and Young Men

Men described coercive sexual relations between senior ranking women and newly abducted boys. They gave an example of a female commander who took a boy of 13 to the bush and raped him while pretending to teach him how to ride a bike. They also gave an example of a boy who gave in to the sexual advances of a senior woman fearing that she would generate a rumour about him if he did not. Another participant discussed that some abducted boys agreed to have sex with senior women to gain better access to food and supplies that these women controlled. Others spoke of senior women singling out a favoured escort under their care: 'Some women had young boys as an escort – they would pick one to move to the gardens to have sex with.'[32]

Participants emphasized how senior women held a significant degree of decision-making power over the fate of boys under their command. This power sometimes led to

---

[29] FGD with four former LRA soldiers, all abducted at unknown ages, for an unknown timeframe and whose rank was undisclosed, Pader District, 26 June 2015.

[30] Individual interview with 'Kalen', LRA soldier for 9 years, abducted at age 14, Pader District, 26 June 2015.

[31] Interview with 'Mark', community worker, Gulu District, 19 July 2015.

[32] FGD with nine former LRA soldiers, all abducted between the ages of 10 and 15 for three to eleven years, mid-level rank, Gulu District, 10 July 2014.

coercive sexual relations. A participant explained, 'She is like your mother, so you accept because she is the one who provides for you.'[33] Another added,

> In the bush, sleeping with a woman that was not given to you is one of the biggest risks you can take. The more you do it the riskier it becomes to you. So, you must understand this context to consider the risk to the young boys entering a relationship with a sugar mummy.[34]

And for others, the line between coercion and choice was blurred, although relations of power remained:

> That is something that really used to happen. So many young boys were given to senior women and used. Even I was given to a senior woman and used. Once you are given, you didn't have to deny – there was even love. The time I was given, I was old enough and accepted. The head of the coy [a small military unit], would arrange for me to be with that lady.[35]

Patricia was one of the few female soldiers who rose to the rank of captain in the LRA. She was rumoured to regularly force boys into sexual intercourse but, since no one had any proof, these rumours were just considered hearsay. At one point, Patricia was caught and seriously beaten as punishment for violating the rules. In her defence, Patricia insisted, 'If old men are receiving young girls as wives, then why are senior women not given the liberty to also receive young boys?'[36]

Some participants believed that senior women preyed on young boys because they were sexually unsatisfied:

> Some commanders had numerous wives, six or more women. He could not satisfy them all sexually. Some of these commanders were not even active sexually, they were impotent, so they could not have sex – this made women want to have sex with younger boys.[37]

Another participant added, 'Sometimes the old, tired commanders were unable to satisfy their wives, so the wives sought young, vigorous boys.'[38]

Despite the backdrop of coercion and control, what approximated consensual affairs also happened. Men and boys risked meeting young girls in the garden or by the well, or would 'willingly' sleep with 'big women' or 'sugar mommies.' David aptly sums up this ambiguity: 'Human beings are very funny, even if there are rules and regulations and guidelines they would go ahead and break it, but if caught they were punished or even killed!'[39] He elaborates the dilemma faced by many young men coming of age in the LRA, and the regulation of their sexuality: 'As human beings, the way God created us, we want

---

[33] Ibid.
[34] Interview with 'Peter', a former LRA soldier, Atiak, 19 June 2015.
[35] FGD with two former LRA soldiers, abducted at unknown ages, with no or unknown rank or length of service, Omoro District, 18 June 2015.
[36] Evelyn, who spent 11 years inside the LRA, recalled this story when reviewing the draft to this chapter, 11 March 2017.
[37] FGD with nine former LRA soldiers, all abducted between the ages of 10 and 15 for three to eleven years, mid-level rank, Gulu District, 10 July 2014.
[38] Ibid.
[39] Ibid.

intimacy – but in the bush, *we were controlled, we were not allowed to express our sexuality, our intimacy was suppressed.*'[40]

As we discussed at the outset of the chapter, starting from the premise that all relationships in settings of coercion are violent provides one entry point to consider boys and men's sexual victimization. The inverse is also true: consensual affairs in such settings can be understood as a refusal of such violent impositions and call for attention to 'the ways in which relationships matter, how one acts *in relation* to others and how this conditions experience.'[41]

3.3 Male Commanders and Sexual Violence Against Boys

We also heard reports of sexual assault of boys by senior male commanders, both from within the LRA and other forces. Participants described instances when newly recruited boys were raped:

> In 1995, when Kony entered Sudan we were in a tight situation and we did not have food. It was at the border of Ethiopia, the LRA were confined in a barracks with 'the Arabs' [the Sudanese Armed Forces, or SAF] – some new recruits accepted to sleep with Arabs and given food to eat; those who refused to have sex were denied food.[42]

A participant narrated that an LRA soldier raped him shortly after his abduction. He also observed rape happening to other boys before they were given to the high command for 'distribution'. Some participants suggested that the rape of newly abducted boys happened frequently, but because of heterosexist ideals of manhood these incidents went underreported. One participant named Samuel also shared his experiences of sexual assault.[43] As a young boy newly abducted into the LRA, Samuel's role was to look after his commander. Samuel recalled that most nights he served dinner to his commander who would then rape him. Samuel did not report the incidents out of fear. He explained:

> One thing you should know it is hard for a man to open up because we are taken to be strong and courageous and we should be able to find a solution for ourselves and that is why at first, we do not want to open about such experiences.[44]

Other participants stated rape of boys occurred when 'there were no girls/women' to have sex with. One participant shared:

> On one occasion, several girls and boys were abducted. Before handing over the new recruits to their commander, they distributed the girls amongst the rebels who did not already have a wife. The girls were raped. But some men were still left without a girl. They turned to the boys. A boy was taken and asked: 'why didn't you bring your sisters with you? Now you will turn into a woman.' He was then raped.[45]

---

[40] Ibid.
[41] Aijazi and Baines 2017.
[42] FGD with nine former LRA soldiers, all abducted between the ages of 10 and 15 for three to eleven years, mid-level rank, Gulu District, 10 July 2014.
[43] Interview with 'Samuel', formerly abducted, LRA ex-combatant, Acholi-bur, 11 July 2014.
[44] Ibid.
[45] Interview with 'Bob', formerly abducted, LRA ex-combatant and long-term escort to Kony, Pader Town Council, 25 June 2015.

It was moreover recalled that young boys were raped when they went to collect water at isolated boreholes some distance from LRA bases. A participant told us,

> There used to be a lieutenant who raped an escort. He had two wives but still slept with this boy. He was caught and killed. Kony said 'God, doesn't want this kind of sex, it was very bad.' The lieutenant was shot in public, but the escort was spared and instructed never to repeat this experience.[46]

4. DISCUSSION

In this chapter, we have attempted to tackle the following question: why are academic and policy discourses on 'child soldiers' relatively silent on boys' experience of sexual violence in armed groups? Speaking from the experiences of men who were abducted by the LRA as boys and came of age under their commanders, we have sought to delineate the multiple intersecting reasons for these silences and erasures.

Feminist legal frameworks have yet to sufficiently make room for boys or men in their advocacy and policy efforts to prosecute sexual and gender-based harms as war crimes. We believe these omissions arise from a singular focus on girls and women based on a very particular reading of patriarchy which fails to consider the relational nature of sexual violence. This oversight is conceptual as well as intuitive, given the long history of the erasure of the situated and gendered experiences of women in wartime. We have attempted to show this by outlining how Erin's work with women led to this current project.

We also draw attention to our earlier work, where we have argued that sexual violence such as forced marriage within armed groups cannot be understood without examining the multiple relationalities on which it is contingent.[47] A relational lens draws attention to the problematic framework of men only as perpetrators in settings of coercion. Therefore, we must broaden the remit of men's relationships to women within armed groups to consider how men's relations to each other and to their children also shapes their experiences of forced marriage during wartime. A relational approach, further, enables us to move beyond an understanding of power as merely produced through patriarchy, but also to see it as infused with context-specific constructions of age, race, ability and sexuality as they intersect and shift in webs of relations that constitute power and its circulation. For instance, a soldier's relationship with a senior commander can, and does, shape his or her relationship with the person they were forced into a union with; as does the birth, life or death of a child. Understanding such interweaving and shifting relations is crucial, we suggest, to develop an adequate understanding of forced marriage as sexual violence from the perspective of boys and men.

Legalistic understandings of consent and culpability also impede our ability to imagine boys and men as victims of sexual violence. Our gaze fixates on boys and men as perpetrators. Again, this obstacle is both conceptual and intuitive, given the unequal relations of power that exist between men and women. However, our data indicate that men too, particularly boys, were also embedded within uneven relations of power, as

---

[46] Interview with 'Richard', a former LRA Brigade Commander, Gulu District, 9 July 2014.
[47] Aijazi and Baines 2017.

demonstrated by the sexual violence that senior women and commanders inflicted upon them. We believe that the reductionist language of victim/perpetrator does not offer any room to substantively engage with the violations inflicted on boys and men, or even girls and women. Such dyads are not only conceptually inaccurate[48] but exert a stranglehold on what is known or unknown, and seen or unseen, as consent in the sociality of violent settings,[49] and the possible antagonistic contestations of the subjugated[50] (such as consensual affairs as the refusal of a violently governed sexuality and intimacy).

The silences and erasures on sexual violence as experienced by boys and men can also be linked to heteronormative ideals of manhood and masculinity which discourage any conversation and inhibit reporting.[51] There seems to be a limited cultural vocabulary and resources to articulate these experiences. As noted by other scholars, this lack is indicative of historical and ongoing colonial suppression of alternate masculinities and sexualities in the region and elsewhere.[52] Our data indicate that within settings of sexual regulation in the LRA, sexual violence occurred within the interstitial gaps between forced marriage and allowable sexual relations. This made it even more difficult to bring these violations to light as these constituted multiple levels of rule breaking, further compounding secrecy and silence. The stakes within the LRA were far too high and the consequences of reporting sexual transgressions against boys and men far too extreme for both the victim and the perpetrator. Some of our participants also described how they felt compelled to sleep with senior men or women to gain access to material advantages. These 'choiceless decisions'[53] and pragmatism further contribute to the silences of sexual violence against boys and men.

Another major obstacle to bringing the experiences of boys into our analytical purview is the impulse to impose an age-based understanding of childhood. Age is at best a 'normative truth' rooted in Western and Euro-American traditions, which does not take into consideration wider circumstances that compel a child into adulthood, such as considerations of kinship and responsibility.[54] The insistence on an age-based approach to childhood also poses significant conceptual challenges because of the pressure to then categorically separate sexual violence experienced by boys from that experienced by adults. Most of our interview participants are adult men who were forcibly conscripted into the LRA at a young age (as 'children'). Many of them came of age within the LRA, enmeshed within settings of extreme sexual regulation. Should their experiences of sexual violence both as children and adults be separated and categorized or allowed to exist as a continuum of violations within our analytical purview? This complexity was frequently demonstrated during our fieldwork when adult men would refer to themselves as 'child soldiers'.[55] After all, they were abducted as children by the LRA and became adults within that group. Age and time therefore assume a rather

---

[48] Drumbl 2016.
[49] Hartman 1997.
[50] Simpson 2016.
[51] Dolan 2016.
[52] Epprecht 2008; Stoler 1989; Nyanzi 2013; Tamale 2011.
[53] Aretxaga 1997.
[54] See also Hanson and Molima in this volume; Kamara in this volume.
[55] See also Ramos in this volume.

spectral quality, one in which child soldiers can be 'made and unmade' in the liberal humanitarian imagination.[56]

Our data demonstrate that sexual violence in the LRA was contextual, dependant on a range of factors and occurred over a continuum from abduction as a child to release as an adult. Therefore, in this chapter we have purposefully and methodically included a wide range of experiences of sexual violence against boys and men in the LRA including that of rape, forced marriage and instances of being forced to inflict sexual harm on others. This enriches our conceptual understanding of sexual violence. Our reading of the data suggests that there is not much value in insisting on the category of the child within the LRA, a state that was dispelled as soon as one was abducted into that armed group.

At the beginning of this chapter, we mentioned Erin's encounter with Fred. Fred compels us to seriously consider that in the LRA many/most sexual relations, whether as child or adult, were forced to begin with. This provides us with an important entry point to open up the very remit of sexual violence and to engage more purposefully with instances when recruits were forced to inflict sexual violence on others. In being forced to rape an elderly grandmother, was Fred not only a perpetrator but also a victim? Erin had difficulties seeing Fred as anyone but a victim given his young age, whereas Omer was open to the possibility that Fred may be considered a victim and a perpetrator. Omer was not approaching Fred as a child simply because of his age while Erin was. We realized that, intuitively, we each had very different understandings of what constitutes childhood and how that intersects with culpability. We trace this difference to our own divergent life experiences and ontologies in relation to how each one of us is placed within and/or outside Western impulses to categorize and draw straight lines, such as ones that separate children from adults.

Nadje Al-Ali and Latif Tas write that 'war is like a blanket': some aspects remain hidden while others are revealed.[57] Silence on the sexual abuse of boys and men was pervasive within the LRA. One participant denied that boys were ever sexually assaulted within the group: 'I have never heard of a boy being raped.'[58] Another added, 'I have never heard of a senior wife having a sexual relationship with a boy.'[59] To us, these negations suggest silence rather than absence. A participant explained,

> Men who raped other men or boys kept it a secret. Why should they allow the conversation to occur? Most people see sex as something that happens between a man and a woman, not between two men. To avoid stigma, they [those who were raped] also kept it to themselves.[60]

Another participant added, 'When it comes to gender-based violence, most people think of women first, but boys were also raped.'[61] Another stated, 'I am so happy that at last men are being invited to speak. I am irritated by the NGOs who only focus on women, because some men have suffered even more than women.'[62]

---

[56] Moynagh 2011; Shaw 2014.
[57] Al-Ali and Tas 2017.
[58] Interview with 'Tom', formerly abducted LRA soldier, Palaro Sub County, 27 June 2015.
[59] Interview with 'Patrick', formerly abducted LRA soldier, Palaro Sub County, 27 June 2015.
[60] Interview with 'Tony', former mid-level ranking LRA soldier who spent 17 years in the rebel group, Pader Town Council, 25 June 2015.
[61] FGD with two former LRA soldiers, Palaro Sub County, 27 June 2015.
[62] FGD with four former LRA soldiers, Ngoto, 26 June 2015.

5. CONCLUSION

In this chapter, we have sought to understand sexual violence in armed groups from the perspective of men who were abducted as boys and came of age within the LRA. We have argued for the advancement of appropriate analytical assemblages that extend beyond ageist and gendered perspectives. We are cognizant that much additional careful work is needed to substantially reframe sexual violence from the perspectives of boys and men. This requires careful listening as well as a rethinking of the very conceptual scaffolding and normative assumptions on which current understandings of sexual violence rely. We take our participant's invitation to heart: 'Listen to our stories and document them well.'[63]

REFERENCED WORKS

Aijazi, O. and Baines, E. 2017. 'Relationality, Culpability and Consent in Wartime: Men's Experiences of Forced Marriage' 11 *International Journal of Transitional Justice* 463

Al-Ali, N. and Tas, L. 2017. '"War Is Like a Blanket": Feminist Convergences in Kurdish and Turkish Women's Rights Activism for Peace' 13 *Journal of Middle East Women's Studies* 354

Aretxaga, B. 1997. *Shattering Silence: Women, Nationalism, and Political Subjectivity in Northern Ireland* (Princeton, NJ: Princeton University Press)

Baines, E. 2014. 'Forced Marriage as a Political Project: Sexual Rules and Relations in the Lord's Resistance Army' 51 *Journal of Peace Research* 405

Baines, E. 2017. *Buried in the Heart: Women, Complex Victimhood and the War in Northern Uganda* (Cambridge: Cambridge University Press)

Buss, D.E. 2009. 'Rethinking "Rape as a Weapon of War"' 17 *Feminist Legal Studies* 145

Carlson, K. and Mazurana, D. 2008. 'Forced Marriage Within the LRA' (Feinstein International Centre, Tufts University) (May)

Christian, M., Safari, O., Ramazani, P., Burnham, G. and Glass, N. 2011. 'Sexual and Gender-Based Violence against Men in the Democratic Republic of Congo: Effects on Survivors, their Families and the Community' 27 *Medicine, Conflict and Survival* 227

Chynoweth, S. 2017. 'We Keep It in Our Hearts: Sexual Violence Against Men and Boys in the Syria Crisis' (UNHCR Report) (27 November)

Chynoweth, S.K., Freccero, J. and Touquet, H. 2017. 'Sexual Violence against Men and Boys in Conflict and Forced Displacement: Implications for the Health Sector' 2017 *Reproductive Health Matters* 1

Clark, J.N. 2017. 'Masculinity and Male Survivors of Wartime Sexual Violence: A Bosnian Case Study' 17 *Conflict, Security and Development* 287

Coulter, C. 2015. *Bush Wives and Girl Soldiers: Women's Lives through War and Peace in Sierra Leone* (New York: Cornell University Press)

Dolan, C. 2014a. 'Into the Mainstream: Addressing Sexual Violence against Men and Boys in Conflict' (Overseas Development Institute Briefing Paper)

Dolan, C. 2014b. 'Letting Go of the Gender Binary: Charting New Pathways for Humanitarian Interventions on Gender-Based Violence' 96 *International Review of the Red Cross* 485

Dolan, C. 2016. 'Inclusive Gender: Why Tackling Gender Hierarchies Cannot be at the Expense of Human Rights and the Humanitarian Imperative' 98 *International Review of the Red Cross* 625

Drumbl, M. 2016. 'Victims who Victimise' 4 *London Review of International Law* 217

Epprecht, M. 2008. *Heterosexual Africa? The History of an Idea from the Age of Exploration to the Age of AIDS* (Athens, OH: Ohio University Press)

Grey, R. and Shepherd, L.J. 2013. '"Stop Rape Now?" Masculinity, Responsibility, and Conflict-Related Sexual Violence' 16 *Men and Masculinities* 115

Hartman, S.V. 1997. *Scenes of Subjection: Terror, Slavery, and Self-Making in Nineteenth-Century America.* (Oxford: Oxford University Press)

---

[63] Interview with M, a survivor of sexual violence perpetrated by the Ugandan People's Defence Force, Koch Goma.

Lewis, D.A. 2009. 'Unrecognized Victims: Sexual Violence against Men in Conflict Settings under International Law' 27 *Wisconsin International Law Journal* 1

Macmillan, L. 2009. 'The Child Soldier in North-South Relations' 3 *International Political Sociology* 36

Mibenge, C.S. 2013. *Sex and International Tribunals: The Erasure of Gender from the War Narrative* (Philadelphia: University of Pennsylvania Press)

Moynagh, M. 2011. 'Human Rights, Child-Soldier Narratives, and the Problem of Form' 42 *Research in African Literatures* 39

Moynagh, M. 2014. 'Political Futurity and the Child-Soldier Figure: A Romance of Globalization' 16 *Interventions: International Journal of Postcolonial Studies* 655

Nyanzi, S. 2013. 'Dismantling Reified African Culture through Localised Homosexualities in Uganda' 15 *Culture, Health & Sexuality* 952

Oloya, O. 2013. *Child to Soldier: Stories from Joseph Kony's Lord's Resistance Army* (Toronto: University of Toronto Press)

Oosterveld, V. 2014. 'Sexual Violence Directed against Men and Boys in Armed Conflict or Mass Atrocity: Addressing a Gendered Harm in International Criminal Tribunals' 10 *Journal of International Law and International Relations* 107

Schulz, P. 2018. 'The "Ethical Loneliness" of Male Sexual Violence Survivors in Northern Uganda: Gendered Reflections on Silencing' *International Feminist Journal of Politics* (published online)

Shaw, R. 2014. 'The TRC, the NGO and the Child: Young People and Post-Conflict Futures in Sierra Leone' 22 *Social Anthropology* 306

Simpson, A. 2016. 'The State is a Man: Theresa Spence, Loretta Saunders and the Gender of Settler Sovereignty' 19 *Theory & Event*

Sivakumaran, S. 2007. 'Sexual Violence Against Men in Armed Conflict' 18 *European Journal of International Law* 253

Solangon, S. and Patel, P. 2012. 'Sexual Violence against Men in Countries Affected by Armed Conflict' 12 *Conflict, Security & Development* 417

Stoler, A.L. 1989. 'Making Empire Respectable: The Politics of Race and Sexual Morality in 20th-Century Colonial Cultures' 16 *American Ethnologist* 634

Tamale, S. (ed.) 2011. *African Sexualities: A Reader* (Cape Town: Pambazuka Press)

Touquet, H. 2018. 'Male Directed Conflict Related Sexual Violence in Sri Lanka' (International Truth and Justice Project Report)

Touquet, H. and Gorris, E. 2016. 'Out of the Shadows? The Inclusion of Men and Boys in Conceptualizations of Wartime Sexual Violence' 24 *Reproductive Health Matters* 36

Vojdik, V.K. 2014. 'Sexual Violence Against Men and Women in War: A Masculinities Approach' 14 *Nevada Law Journal* 923

Ward, J. 2016. 'It's Not about the Gender Binary, It's about the Gender Hierarchy: A Reply to "Letting Go of the Gender Binary"' 98 *International Review of the Red Cross* 275

5. Getting Tambo out of limbo: exploring alternative legal frameworks that are more sensitive to the agency of children and young people in armed conflict

Karl Hanson and Christelle Molima

In the summer of 2017, Christelle Molima undertook fieldwork for her doctoral dissertation on the criminal responsibility of children who left the armed forces and armed groups in eastern Democratic Republic of the Congo (DRC). She interviewed a former judge who recounted the intriguing story of Tambo, an ex-child soldier. Tambo had been prosecuted and convicted for desertion. During the 1998 war against Ugandan and Rwandan troops, the 14-year-old Tambo had integrated into the Congolese armed forces (Forces Armées de la République Démocratique du Congo – FARDC).[1] Tambo had been deployed in the territory of Uvira near the border with Burundi and Rwanda in the DRC's South Kivu province. After three years of service, he had had enough of the military life that no longer corresponded to his conception of the army and decided to run off, but without respecting the conditions for resigning from the armed forces. During his escape, Tambo found himself in the middle of a battle between the Congolese armed forces and a Mai Mai rebel group. He fell into the hands of the FARDC. Tambo was recognized by Congolese soldiers and was sent to the Military Tribunal of the Uvira legion which convicted him for desertion because, as the former judge explained, he had left the army in an illicit manner and, moreover, while in the presence of the enemy, which constituted an aggravating circumstance.

Tambo's case evokes the absurdity of military bureaucracy described in Joseph Heller's renowned satirical novel *Catch-22* from 1961 that narrates the story of Captain John Yossarian, a bombardier enrolled in the American Army during World War II and who is deployed in Italy. In the novel, the original Catch-22 rule states that to escape from flying dangerous military missions, one must ask for a mental evaluation that can determine if one is crazy, which is required for being dismissed from flying crazily dangerous missions. However, by demanding a mental evaluation to escape flying crazy missions, a pilot demonstrates his mental capacities, hence making it impossible to be declared crazy. Considering the current international legal framework concerning child soldiers, the prosecution and conviction of a child soldier for desertion indeed seems a Catch-22. At the time of his enrolment, Tambo was below the minimum age for recruitment into the armed forces and deployment in conflict both under national and international law. Under DRC legislation operative at the time, the minimum age for recruitment in the armed forces was established at 16 years.[2] The DRC ratified the

---

[1] For further discussion of the FARDC, see Parmar and Lebrat in this volume.
[2] Law No. 81-003 of 17 July 1981 on the staff regulations for state public service personnel and

United Nations Convention on the Rights of the Child (CRC) in 1990 (which sets 15 as the minimum age) and ratified the Optional Protocol to the Convention on the Rights of the Child on the Involvement of Children in Armed Conflict (OPAC) in 2001 (which increases that minimum age). How can a boy, who was not allowed to be a member of the military in the first place, be convicted for having deserted from the military? If Tambo's enrolment as a soldier was against the law, it is illogical that a law enforcement authority, here a military tribunal, convicts him for having escaped such an unlawful situation.

Tambo's fate raises questions as to how to cover the distance between the international normative framework that prohibits child soldiering under a certain age, and the social world where children and young people, regardless of their age, at times deliberately decide to join or to leave the military. International law and policy regarding children and armed conflict, which has largely been informed by humanitarian advocacy perspectives, is built on the presumption of children's victimhood and hence considers children incapable of voluntarily participating in the military.[3] According to Claudia Seymour, who conducted empirical research in eastern DRC, the nearly exclusive focus on children's vulnerability and victimhood renders the international protectionist approach to children in the context of war and armed conflict 'simplistic and decontextualized from the lived realities of children and young people'.[4] Such a protectionist view, indeed, forecloses the fact that children and young people, like many other human beings, often do make well-informed and conscious decisions to actively engage in armed conflict, as has been amply demonstrated in anthropological and ethnographic research on conflicts around the globe.[5] The denial of children's agency at times of social, economic and political instability also presents problems for dealing with the social implications and consequences of children's actions once the conflict ends.[6] One of the difficulties is how societies can honour those young persons who have contributed to ending violent oppression by their deliberate engagement and actions, but whose courage cannot be officially recognized because of the dominant image of child soldiers' victimhood. Another point is how victims and communities to which former child soldiers seek to return after the conflict can come to terms with individual children who have committed atrocities without being able to hold them accountable.[7] A manual edited by the International Committee of the Red Cross (ICRC) on the domestic implementation of international humanitarian law (IHL) provokes another Catch-22 in dealing with the criminal responsibility of child soldiers. This manual states:

> Children who are alleged to have committed war crimes should be primarily considered as victims and should be treated as such. On the other hand, to ignore their criminal responsibility could imply impunity and have the reverse and perverse effect of rendering them attractive to

---

Ordinance No. 72/060 of 25 September 1972 instituting the military code of justice, cited in: CRC Committee 2011: [43].

[3] Rosen 2007.
[4] Seymour 2012: 373.
[5] Hart 2006; Lee 2009; Rosen 2005. See also the references in: Hanson 2011: 58; Seymour 2012: 374; Drumbl 2012.
[6] Shepler 2014.
[7] Drumbl 2012.

armed forces and armed groups since crimes committed by them would go unpunished. A solution to this problem has yet to be found by the international community.[8]

The present chapter aims to explore alternative legal frameworks that could be more sensitive and responsive to young people's active agency throughout the peace–war–recovery continuum, without abandoning their rights to protection. What are, in other words, the challenges for international children's rights law of the 'conceptual shift' that is needed 'to embrace the possibility that the young may engage voluntarily in military action'?[9] In exploring such frameworks, we wish to contribute to 'reimagining child soldiers in international law and policy', as was the title of Mark Drumbl's book.[10] The first section herein presents the theoretical framework that informs our thinking. This framework actuates Hanson and Nieuwenhuys' proposal to include children's conceptions and enactments of their rights when studying particular children's rights claims and is composed of the notions of living rights, social justice and translations.[11] Next, we examine how international humanitarian and human rights law considers young people who are legally allowed to be recruited into the armed forces, such as children over 16 years of age who have, in compliance with international rules, voluntarily joined government forces. Building further on the findings from this legal analysis, we examine literature on youth activism and on citizenship to explore young people's rights to participate in violent political struggles or in the military. In conclusion, we contend that the right of children to participate in contexts of violence and armed conflict is not necessarily a violation of children's rights. In the local contexts in which they come to have meaning, rights that recognize children's subjectivities can even be understood as empowering if they do justice to children and young people's efforts and sufferings in the dramatic and adverse contexts of armed conflict.

1. LIVING RIGHTS, SOCIAL JUSTICE AND TRANSLATIONS

The claim that children's opinions need to be taken more seriously, which is frequently made by children's rights advocacy groups with reference to Article 12 of the CRC, generally aims at promoting children's participation in uncontroversial settings, such as schools, sport clubs or local politics. 'We need to recognize and enhance children's constructive roles in society, consider them as social actors and acknowledge their citizenship more fully, the main argument goes, in particular when children "do the right thing."'[12] However, in situations with an undesirable undertone, such as child labour or child soldiering, the same advocacy groups tend to defend the opposite viewpoint, and argue that when children 'don't do the right thing', high minimum ages should be established in order to protect them from participating in such hazardous activities. International legal and policy documents on child labour that set a minimum age for admission to work

---

[8] International Committee of the Red Cross 2015: 17.
[9] Hart 2006: 224.
[10] Drumbl 2012.
[11] Hanson and Nieuwenhuys 2013.
[12] Hanson 2016: 471.

are a case in point where protective concerns are preferred over participatory ones. The approaches adopted in relation to child labour do not leave much space for recognizing working children's agency: children under a certain age are deemed to be unable to decide for themselves if they want to work or not, or what kind of work they would like to do. For more than two decades, working children's organizations that disagree with the prevailing aim to prohibit all child labour and instead claim a right to work in dignity have relied on norms and discourses about the importance of children's participation to try to influence the discussions. However, they have met with only very limited success.[13]

The discussions among representatives of working children's organizations who argue in favour of a right to work in dignity and the UN agencies charged with developing international legal and policy responses in the field of child labour illustrate that there is not necessarily a consensus about the content, meaning and consequences of children's rights. Relying on perceptions of their own agency, child soldiers also might advance claims about their rights that do not necessarily correspond with how other people think of children's rights when related to political violence or armed conflict, such as the right to fight for their ideas or to defend their community from oppression. In order to investigate alternative pathways to understanding children's agency and their rights in armed conflict we take as a starting point the notions of living rights, social justice and translations that can open our thinking about alternative, child-centred approaches to children's rights.[14]

Instead of approaching children as the helpless objects of well-meaning interventions, this framework seeks to include children and young people's own conceptions of their rights in determining how legal and policy frameworks for children's themes are crafted. Starting from the lived experiences in which rights take shape, the notion of living rights suggests that children implicitly or explicitly understand what children's rights mean to them. This notion encompasses the idea that if children have rights, including agency and participation rights, they also have the right to participate in the production of knowledge about their rights. In addition, this notion encourages looking beyond abstract formulations of rights and focusing on the specific situations and circumstances where rights claims come alive. Children as well as other actors are active producers of knowledge about children's rights. The notion of living rights hence expresses the idea that 'all social practices that are conventionally identified as rights may be understood as "living rights". They are alive through active and creative interpretations, association, and framing of what constitutes in a given context a child's right in people's hearts and minds.'[15]

The notion of social justice refers to the underlying normative beliefs when human rights claims are invoked. Especially since the almost universal ratification of the CRC, there is a broad consensus that children have fundamental human rights. However, notwithstanding the CRC's detailed provisions and its authoritative interpretation by the UN Committee on the Rights of the Child, conflicting viewpoints over the precise meaning and consequences of children's rights persist. Academic literature on the CRC, for instance, still reveals divergence between those who abundantly praise the CRC and how the text is interpreted and implemented, and those who are very critical as to how the

---

[13] Hanson and van Daalen 2016; van Daalen and Hanson 2019.
[14] Hanson and Nieuwenhuys 2013; Hanson and Nieuwenhuys 2019.
[15] Hanson and Nieuwenhuys 2013: 11.

CRC and its monitoring is apprehended.[16] Social justice deals with discussions about the normative beliefs that make rights appear legitimate and beyond question for some but not for others. Diverging ideas about what children are, what they are capable of, what they deserve and the relative importance of the differences between adults and children all have a strong bearing on the way children's rights get interpreted.[17]

Struggles over interpretations of children's rights amount to translations that designate fluctuations between different beliefs and perspectives.[18] Challenging the idea that children's rights norms and their fixed meaning merely need to be implemented, the notion of translation expresses the idea that when rights are transposed from one context to another, for instance from international norms to national legislation, their sense can be altered. Translation of norms is what happens not only between international and national legislation, but also between children's conceptualizations of their rights and the rights as defended by spokespersons of social movements who speak on children's behalf; between national legislation and local administrators charged with putting the legislation into practice; between representations of children's rights upheld by donors and the actual work undertaken by development NGOs; and between decisions made at the headquarters of international organizations and the fieldworkers in country offices. Different series of translation processes take place, in varying directions, whereby rights are not only translated 'down' from international to national levels but are also translated 'up' from the local to the international level.[19] The translation of children's rights is not confined to the transfer of one idea into another context, but it is a dynamic process whereby meanings are actively reproduced and changed. By using the notion of translation over implementation or norm diffusion, the active reproduction of meaning of children's rights can be made more explicit and open for debate.[20]

Taken together, the notions of living rights, social justice and translations remind us that discussions on children's rights do not exist in a social vacuum but are inescapably related to specific themes and take place in distinct situations where different normative ideas around children's rights coexist. We mobilize this conceptual framework to take the opposite route compared to the one most travelled in international law and policy-making concerning child soldiering. Instead of looking at how to prevent children from becoming soldiers by declaring their enrolment in the military and participation in combat unlawful, at least under certain age limits, we want to look at the rights related to joining the military or engaging in violent conflicts, whereby 'the idea of living rights re-frames the way we think about rights, young people and citizenship'.[21] By looking at children's active roles in armed conflict, the aim is not to pass over children's suffering or to be blind to the potentially detrimental consequences of children's participation in warfare; on the contrary, as argued by Pamela Reynolds, recognizing children's agency and acknowledging their participation in society, including children and young people's participation in

---

[16] Arts 2014; Reynaert et al. 2009.
[17] Hanson 2012.
[18] Hanson and Nieuwenhuys 2013.
[19] Merry 2006.
[20] Freeman 2009; Hanson and Nieuwenhuys 2019; I'Anson et al. 2017; Zwingel 2012.
[21] Sanghera et al. 2018: 553.

wars and revolutions, might be the best way to protect them.[22] As with other vulnerable groups who are often considered to be 'non-citizens', the language of living rights might in fact enhance protection for child soldiers rather than increase their suffering.

2. CHILDREN LEGALLY ALLOWED TO BE INVOLVED IN ARMED FORCES OR ARMED GROUPS

Even though minimum ages for child soldiering have increased over the past few decades – especially with the adoption in 2000 of the OPAC – situations arise where it is not unlawful for young people to be involved in the military. Taking a similar approach to the analysis of children's rights in relation to education or the media,[23] we consider different aspects of children's rights related to the military and comment on children's rights to, in and through engagement in military activities.

At the time of the CRC's adoption in 1989, several states, UN agencies and humanitarian organizations were deeply disappointed by CRC Article 38 that sets 15 years as the minimum age for the recruitment of children into the armed forces and their direct participation in hostilities.[24] The dissatisfaction with this provision gave rise to revived efforts by a large coalition of humanitarian advocacy groups to raise the minimum age for recruitment and participation in hostilities to 18 years. This push coaxed the adoption, in 2000, of OPAC. The Committee on the Rights of the Child, the body established to monitor progress made by state parties in fulfilling their duties regarding CRC provisions and which played an instrumental role in the elaboration of OPAC,[25] had found that 'persons under the age of 18 should never be involved in hostilities, either directly or indirectly, and should not be recruited into armed forces, even on a voluntary basis'.[26] Most of the provisions contained in OPAC correspond with this 'Straight-18' position. OPAC Articles 1 and 2, which deal with state armed forces, require state parties to ensure that persons who have not attained the age of 18 years do not take direct part in hostilities and are not compulsorily recruited into their armed forces. OPAC Article 4 concerns armed groups which are distinct from the armed forces of a state, such as non-state rebel groups or private armed militias: these entities are forbidden to compulsorily and voluntarily recruit and to use in hostilities persons under the age of 18 years. However, OPAC is not totally aligned to the minimum age of 18 years, as it does not specify a minimum age for indirect participation in hostilities. Furthermore, OPAC Article 3 leaves states with the option to adopt a lower age than 18 as the minimum age for voluntary recruitment into armed forces and also exempts military schools from complying with the minimum age requirement.[27]

Regarding the minimum age for the voluntary recruitment of persons into their national armed forces, states must 'raise the minimum age' above that age set out in Article 38(3) of the CRC. Therefore, under OPAC states should set at least 16 years as

---

[22] Reynolds 1998: 55.
[23] Verhellen 2000.
[24] Hammarberg 1990; Kuper 2000.
[25] Hanson 2011.
[26] Commission on Human Rights 1996: [39].
[27] Sheppard 2000. See also Rosen; Crilley; Kamara; and Odongo, all in this volume.

the minimum age for voluntary recruitment.[28] According to OPAC Article 3(2), states must deposit a binding declaration that clarifies the minimum age at which voluntary recruitment into national armed forces is permitted and must also adopt safeguards that ensure that such a recruitment is neither forced nor coerced. These safeguards are detailed in OPAC Article 3(3). States must ensure that such recruitment is genuinely voluntary and is carried out with the informed consent of the recruit's parents or legal guardians. In addition, these young persons who are voluntarily recruited must be fully informed of the duties involved in military service and provide reliable proof of their age prior to their acceptance. OPAC Article 3(4) allows state parties to strengthen their initial declaration by raising the minimum age for voluntary recruitment, for instance from 16 to 18 years, but they cannot lower the minimum age that was announced in the initial declaration.[29]

As of 23 September 2018, out of the 167 state parties to OPAC, 37 states had declared that persons under 18 could voluntarily join their armed forces, while 23 countries have set the minimum age for voluntary recruitment at 17 years, 13 countries at 16 years, and one country at 15 years old.[30] The Committee on the Rights of the Child, which already before the adoption of OPAC had been trying to convince state parties to raise the minimum age of all forms of recruitment (including voluntary recruitment) to 18 years,[31] continued after the adoption of OPAC Article 3 to invite states to raise the minimum age to 18 years. For instance, in its Revised Guidelines regarding initial reports submitted by state parties under OPAC Article 8(1), the Committee on the Rights of the Child asks states that have submitted a declaration that allows voluntary recruitment under the age of 18 'to indicate whether there are plans to raise this age to minimum eighteen and a tentative timetable for doing so'.[32] Four countries, namely Japan, Luxembourg, Paraguay and Poland, have followed up on the Committee's recommendation by amending their initial declaration that had been made upon ratification of the Protocol and have raised the minimum age for voluntary recruitment to 18 years.[33] In the case of Paraguay, the withdrawal of its initial declaration allowing voluntary recruitment at 16 years and the subsequent increase to 18 years is attributed to the advocacy activities of the Coalition to Stop the Use of Child Soldiers in Paraguay, which have been undertaken with the support of UNICEF,[34] a decision that is positively welcomed by the Committee on the Rights of the Child.[35]

However, as shown above by the number of countries that have adopted a lower minimum age for voluntary recruitment, the Straight-18 position adopted by the Committee has not been followed by about 20 per cent of OPAC state parties. The proportion is, remarkably, higher amongst the permanent members of the UN Security Council, where only one country has set the minimum age at 18 (Russian Federation), whereas three

---

[28] Hanson 2011: 54.
[29] Vandewiele 2006: 37.
[30] See Status of Treaties. See also Crilley in this volume.
[31] Hanson 2011: 54.
[32] CRC Committee 2007a: [5].
[33] Note that Chile amended its declaration in 2008 to raise the minimum age from 16 to 17 years, and Guyana amended its declaration in 2010 to raise the minimum age from 14 to 16. See Status of Treaties.
[34] CRC Committee 2012a: [9–11].
[35] CRC Committee 2013a: [4].

countries (China, France and the United States of America) have established 17 years and one country has set 16 years (the United Kingdom of Great Britain and Northern Ireland) as the minimum age. The discussions between the Committee on the Rights of the Child and China, France, the US and the UK illustrate two competing approaches to the voluntary engagement of children under 18 years of age in the military. In its concluding observations concerning these countries' reports under OPAC, the Committee, holding on to a long-held view, systematically repeats its recommendation to review and raise the current voluntary recruitment age in the armed forces to 18 years 'in order to promote and strengthen the protection of children through an overall higher legal standard'.[36] To make this argument, the Committee does not refer to the precise wording of OPAC, which does not sustain its view as it allows state parties to adopt a minimum age below 18 years, but instead draws on 'the spirit and principles of the Optional Protocol and the Convention', with which it finds minimum ages under 18 years inconsistent.[37]

In its initial report under OPAC, France underscores its active international involvement to address the situation of children in armed conflict, including its financial contribution to the 'Coalition to Stop the Use of Child Soldiers' (now called 'Child Soldiers International'),[38] an NGO that defends a strict Straight-18 position and which has for instance been instrumental in raising the minimum age in Paraguay, as noted above. The Committee welcomes France's efforts on the international scene, but remains concerned that young people under 18 can be voluntarily recruited into the armed forces, including non-nationals who can be recruited at 17 into the Foreign Legion.[39] France does not give effect to this demand, and neither do China, the UK and the USA, which explicitly state that they have no plans to modify the extant age limitations for young people's voluntary recruitment.[40] During its latest dialogue with the Committee, the US representative found it 'worth recalling that the Optional Protocol provided for the recruitment of volunteers under the age of 18 to national armed forces, subject to parental consent'.[41] As these countries follow the ordinary meaning of the terms of OPAC Article 3(2) and hence respect Article 31 of the 1969 Vienna Convention on the Law of Treaties, they did not need to provide an elaborate legal argumentation to sustain their position. Arguments invoked to maintain lower minimum ages for voluntary recruitment refer to the benefits for the young people as well as to the needs of the armed forces. China for instance finds that voluntarily enlisting in the army at the age of 17 years old is not only an individual desire and honour for young people, but also that the army offers them a means 'to acquire greater knowledge, which made them more competitive in the labour market'.[42] In addition, the social realities in China also need to be considered.[43] During its dialogue with the Committee, the Chinese representative explained that, because of the deferment of the entry into armed service of students in higher education, the

---

[36] See, for instance, CRC Committee 2013b: [21].
[37] CRC Committee 2008: [54]; CRC Committee 2007b: 2.
[38] CRC Committee 2006: [29].
[39] CRC Committee 2007b: 2.
[40] CRC Committee 2012b: [17] CRC Committee 2016: [66]; CRC Committee 2017: [76].
[41] CRC Committee 2017: [63].
[42] CRC Committee 2013c: [41].
[43] CRC Committee 2012b: [17].

number of recruits had fallen, 'which was why it was not possible to raise the age of conscription to 18'.[44] The UK State Party report of 2007 provides similar arguments as to why young people aged 16 and above are attracted to pursuing careers in the armed forces and why the government welcomes their participation: 'the armed forces provide valuable and constructive training and employment to many young people, giving them a sense of great achievement and worth, as well as benefiting society as a whole'.[45] These discussions do not however mention a 'right' of young people to join the military but rather revolve around the right to leave the armed forces for military staff under 18 years of age.[46]

Regarding armed groups that are distinct from the armed forces of a state, OPAC Article 4 prohibits voluntary recruitment of persons under the age of 18 years and requests state parties to take measures to prevent, prohibit and even criminalize such recruitment. What contracting state parties found lawful for their national armed forces is criminalized if undertaken by competing non-state armed groups who cannot, as for instance the Chinese and UK governments did to justify the recruitment of 16- and 17-year-olds, refer to potential benefits for the young recruits in terms of educational training and skills. As in OPAC Article 3(2), the terms used are straightforward and do not leave much room for interpretation.

However, the Straight-18 position for voluntary recruitment by non-state armed groups gets complicated in cases where a rebel group succeeds in overthrowing the government in place and supplants the national army, as has been the case for example in Rwanda, Timor-Leste and the DRC.

In Rwanda, many children were incorporated into the ranks of the Rwandan Patriotic Front (RPF) that seized power in the aftermath of the 1994 genocide. Upon its victory, the RPF became a regular army, the Rwandan Patriotic Army. Many of the under-18s who were in the ranks of the RPF while it was still an armed group were retained in the national Rwandan armed forces, especially those in strategic positions.[47]

In Timor-Leste, many young people participated in the country's liberation process from an Indonesian occupation that was marked by many acts of violence. After the country's independence that came about after a popular referendum in 1999, the rebellion Armed Forces for the National Liberation of East Timor, with whom many young people had been associated, became Timor-Leste's national armed force. However, the young people who had participated in the fight for the liberation of the country were excluded from the peace process.[48]

Already at the time of its independence in 1960, the DRC was experiencing rebellions led by schoolchildren. These events prompted the enactment of legislation in 1981 that set 16 years as a minimum age for entry into the armed forces.[49] During the First Congo War of 1996–1997 that saw the Mobutu regime brought down by the Alliance of Democratic

---

[44] CRC Committee 2013c: [41].
[45] CRC Committee 2007c: [18]. For a different perspective, see Crilley in this volume.
[46] CRC Committee 2016: [66].
[47] Internationale des Résistant(e)s à la Guerre.
[48] Kurtenbach and Pawelz 2015.
[49] Art. 8 of the Law No. 81-003 of 17 July 1981 on the staff regulations for state public service personnel.

Forces for the Liberation of Congo, a significant number of people under 18 years of age joined the rebellion. Following the overthrow of the regime, the rebellion army morphed into the new national armed forces retaining all combatants between 16 and 18, in conformity with the 1981 law. Following pressure from the international community, the new Congolese government decided to order the demobilization of all children under 18 years of age from the armed forces.[50]

Would it be possible, under OPAC Articles 3(2) and 3(4), to 'legalize' the unlawful recruitment of 16- and 17-years-olds by non-state armed groups in cases where these rebellion groups become the national army? In the three countries described above, this question no longer applies as all three have declared upon their ratification or accession to OPAC that the minimum age for voluntary recruitment into their national armed forces is 18 years.[51] But the possibility of legalizing previously unlawful recruitment is not completely inconceivable and might be relevant in other situations where young people lawfully form part of the military.

The divergent outcome of the Committee's recommendation to follow the spirit rather than the letter of OPAC shows the persistence of asymmetries in international politics about young people's recruitment in armed forces and armed groups. Well-established democracies and permanent members of the Security Council who are generally confident about their place in the concert of nations do not feel compelled to change their national practices and yield to pressure from advocacy groups to raise the minimum age for voluntary recruitment to 18 years. Akin to social evolutions in the USA and the UK that – because of a backdrop of its enlistments in a concomitant context of persistent demands for military staffing – have increased efforts to attract young people into a future career in the military,[52] China, for instance, argues that the needs of the armed forces make it impossible to raise the age of conscription to 18. Conversely, less powerful regimes as well as more recent democracies are more disposed to showing the international community their willingness to depart from their past and look to the future where human rights must prevail, including the adoption of an outright Straight-18 position concerning children's involvement in the military.[53] The Coalition to Stop the Use of Child Soldiers provides an example of these contrasts: without impacting its own legislation, France has financially supported this NGO whose activities have been instrumental in raising the age of voluntary recruitment in Paraguay. An apparently unintended, but not impossible, consequence is that a 17-year-old Paraguayan national who can no longer voluntarily join his own country's armed forces can still be legally recruited to voluntarily serve in the French Foreign Legion.

International law and international humanitarian law prohibit the participation of child soldiers in hostilities. CRC Article 38(2) as well as Article 77(2) of Additional Protocol I and Article 4(3)(c) of Additional Protocol II to the Geneva Conventions establish the minimum age for participation in hostilities at 15 years; the active use of children under

---

[50] Decree-Law No. 066 of 9 June 2000 providing for the demobilization and reintegration of vulnerable groups present within fighting forces.
[51] See Status of Treaties.
[52] Hart 2006: 221. For a critique of recruitment campaigns in the UK, see Crilley in this volume.
[53] See Hathaway 2002; Hathaway 2007; Moravcsik 2000.

the age of 15 years to participate in hostilities constitutes a war crime under the Rome Statute of the International Criminal Court.[54] As discussed above, these age limitations have been raised to 18 years in OPAC Articles 1 and 4(1) which oblige both national armed forces and non-state armed groups to refrain from deploying in hostilities persons who have not yet attained the age of 18 years.[55] In countries that allow their national armies to recruit persons under 18 years of age, special provisions must be adopted to ensure that members of their armed forces who are younger than 18 are not deployed to any theatre of hostilities. This is the case in Canada, for example, that allows voluntary recruitment of persons under the age of 18 years but precludes them from being deployed into any area where hostilities are taking place.[56] However, the legal prohibition of the deployment of child soldiers does not preclude the fact that in many armed conflicts around the globe children do actively take part in hostilities. Even armed forces that themselves strictly abide by all international rules pertaining to minimum ages for the recruitment and deployment of their soldiers cannot avoid having to fight an enemy who engages child soldiers in their battles. In 2017, Canada for instance developed rules of engagement for its armed forces when they encounter under-18-year-old soldiers on the battlefield.[57] This Doctrine aims to offer the Canadian Armed Forces guidance on how to balance, in armed conflicts involving child soldiers, the rights of the child soldier to special protection with the attainment of military objectives as well as the soldiers' right to self-defence.[58] Where the CRC and OPAC are silent on how to deal with child soldiers from rival armies, international humanitarian law (IHL) does contain some relevant provisions but these do not settle this complex area of law.[59]

International law regarding the recruitment and deployment of children in armed conflict aims at ending the recruitment and deployment of young people and children under the age of 18 years and is built on the premise that persons under a certain age are unable to exercise agency.[60] Law and policy are characterized by a negative view of the military. This view presumes that children should not be associated with militaries, either as part of a wider undertaking that wishes to end all wars and bring peace to the world, starting with children, or out of a consideration to protect the vulnerable from conflicts for which they are too young. However, a detailed analysis of international human rights law, especially of the provisions contained in OPAC, reveals that some exceptions persist to this general view. We suggest that the study of the margins of the dominant protectionist doctrine can reveal interesting new insights and approaches to analyse, understand and evaluate the complex situation of children's involvement in armed conflict. Here we will analyse these exceptions as deriving from children's rights to, in and through engagement in military activities.

States that allow voluntary recruitment under the age of 18 years must provide

---

[54] Rome Statute, Article 8(2)(b)(xxvi) and (e)(vii).
[55] Note that the minimum age for participation in hostilities has also been established at 18 years under Art. 22 of the African Charter on the Rights and Welfare of the Child.
[56] CRC Committee 2005: [4].
[57] Canadian Armed Forces 2017. See also Rosen in this volume.
[58] See also Kuper 2008: 15.
[59] Henckaerts and Doswald-Beck 2005: 17.
[60] Hanson 2011.

safeguards that ensure that such recruitment is in every instance 'genuinely voluntary',[61] but no mention is made of any rights related to joining national armed forces. In the case of China, France, the USA and the UK, which we have inspected above and where young people can voluntarily join the military once they reach 16 or 17 years of age, no mention is made of a subjective right of the child to join the military. Reasons given to justify this arrangement refer to the primacy of the nation's own interests or *raison d'état* to maintain its capacity to defend the country's engagements, and to the military need to recruit young talents, who are much sought after in a competitive employment market. The only reference to a subjective right is to the negative corollary, namely, the right for young people *to leave or exit* the armed forces. But can there be a right to *leave* an institution without a pre-existing right to *join* it?

Rights *in* the military for young people are regularly mentioned in international law, for instance with regard to the special protection of young combatants who cannot under OPAC be deployed in any theatre of hostilities. Another example of special protection rights for young combatants concerns children who are accused, or recognized, as having infringed the penal law, or are alleged to have done so, whilst associated with armed forces or armed groups.[62] They must be 'treated in a manner consistent with the promotion of the child's sense of dignity and worth', which considers 'the child's age and the desirability of promoting the child's reintegration and the child's assuming a constructive role in society'.[63] In line with the 'cross-cutting standards' of the CRC,[64] there are indeed a whole set of rights available to juveniles in the military that relate to the right to be free from discrimination while serving, to be free from bullying, to respect for one's family life, the right to be heard, etc.

Finally, reference is also made to rights that can be realized *through* engaging in the military, especially related to children's education and vocational training. In contrast to the Straight-18 philosophy, OPAC Article 3(5) exempts state parties from the obligation to raise the minimum age for voluntary enrolment in military schools, where children must receive an education that is directed, in accordance with CRC Article 29, to the child's personal development, to the cultivation of respect for human rights and fundamental freedoms, as well as respect for the child's parents and for cultural and national values. In sum, the education offered in military schools must aim at 'the preparation of the child for responsible life in a free society, in the spirit of understanding, peace, tolerance, equality of sexes, and friendship among all peoples, ethnic, national and religious groups and persons of indigenous origin'.[65] The military thereby functions as 'a school for the nation'.[66] Armed forces may also provide work-based training and education for all young people, without any distinction, who can acquire qualifications and skills that are equally recognized outside the armed forces.[67] Working within the army can enable young people to acquire administrative and organizational skills and help develop a personal discipline,

---

[61] Art. 3(3) OPAC; see also International Committee of the Red Cross 2015: 14; Crilley in this volume.
[62] International Committee of the Red Cross 2015: 16.
[63] Art. 40(1) CRC.
[64] Hanson and Lundy 2017.
[65] Art. 29(1)(d) OPAC.
[66] Krebs 2004.
[67] CRC Committee 2007c: [19].

self-confidence and leadership skills, as in any civil trade. Empirical studies conducted in the USA show that amongst the reasons why young people enlist in the army, in addition to their commitment to serve their country, is precisely the goal to develop such skills.[68]

3. ON THE THIN LINE BETWEEN CHILDREN AND THE MILITARY: YOUTH ACTIVISM AND CITIZENSHIP

Studies in the field of youth activism and young people's engagement in political struggles indicate that consideration of children's voices is relatively uncomplicated in relation to issues that already benefit from broader community support, for instance the conservation of a community forest with which most civil society actors agree. But taking into account the perspective of children is less straightforward when children challenge extant community voices or broadly shared assumptions, such as when they want to work rather than go to school.[69] Because of the dominant view on children and young people as persons who lack the capacity for autonomous decision making, very few studies have examined the significant and autonomous nature of children's participation and their respective experiences in political violence. On the contrary, the direction has been to rather carelessly consider political violence as unvaryingly bad for them.[70] According to Barber, 'the dominant focus in the approach to the study of children's and youths' experience with political violence remains the chronicling of violence exposure and the documentation of its correlation with stress or other forms of psychological impact',[71] even if this narrowly focused linkage has often been found to be weak and inconsistent. Political action therefore habitually remains a privilege of adults whereby the entry of children into this universe is considered as being transgressive.[72]

From our review of literature on youth activism and political violence, we discern three possible ways of looking at children's involvement in political violence: these are characterized, respectively, by manipulation, compliance and difference.

The first approach maintains that children bluntly follow the instructions received from adults who manipulate them. Children do not have the required capacity to make political choices and to defend them. This is the position generally taken in international law, as discussed above, as well as in research on children and violence, whereby it is the manipulating adult who must pay for having transgressed the prohibition of engaging children in violent political struggles.[73]

Pursuant to the second approach, compliance, children who live in a violent environment share the same vision and understanding as their adult counterparts and comply with the latter's viewpoints. Here children's capacity for action is recognized because their views correspond with the aspirations of the entire community. As their autonomy is preserved, children are not considered as manipulated by adults, but owing to the dominance

---

[68] Eighmey 2006.
[69] Duncan 2016: 55.
[70] Barber 2008: 303; Hammack 2010: 180–81.
[71] Barber 2008: 298.
[72] Hermant 1995.
[73] Hermant 1995: 5.

adults exert over them, in effect they (the children) have no choice but to comply with the directives of the adults. The recognition of children's capacity is also limited as it is very often inclined to be ignored upon returning to peace. This latter aspect is highlighted by Kurtenbach and Pawelz who noted that, following the conflict in Timor-Leste, young people who had fought alongside adults for the liberation of their country were not permitted to participate in negotiating the peace process.[74] Adults wanted to maintain the political community's hierarchy by being the only persons allowed to dominate the public arena. Similar findings were revealed by Pamela Reynolds in her study of children who participated in the struggle against apartheid in South Africa. Analysing the functioning of the South African Truth and Reconciliation Commission, she found that 'the testimonies have added little to our understanding of the complexity of children's engagement, ... or the development of their political ideas and the range of their reflections on broad issues to do with morality, duty and the nature of society'.[75]

The third approach finds that children have a different understanding compared to adults with respect to political violence. This approach posits that children have an independent response to experienced political violence, a phenomenon Duclos terms as 'children's autonomous political violence'.[76] Studies on children and violence consider that youth violence is related to social obstructions such as the breakdown of the long-established organization of the traditional community,[77] or to the poverty of a population composed largely of young males between the ages of 15 and 35 who are unemployed, illiterate and live in poor socio-economic conditions.[78] Although under this optic young people have an ability to make choices, the scope thereof is tainted with a negative connotation that can reduce the efforts of these young people to merely reproducing violence rather than seeing such acts as a way of appropriating and subverting violence.[79] Moreover, this optic does not allow for consideration of the fact that young people 'have political knowledge through their lived experience' and that 'this knowledge may translate into actions in multiple ways', especially into small everyday actions.[80] Even if the second and third approach open up some space for considering children's collaborative and independent agency, we find that none of these three approaches deals in a sufficiently elaborate manner with children's involvement in political violence.

Besides providing nuanced empirical accounts of the active role played by young people in the mobilization, demobilization and reconciliation process,[81] the recognition of children's agency in terms of their being political actors also resonates with citizenship studies. Recent literature on childhood studies and children's rights has explored the intersection of children's agency and participation rights with the notion of citizenship. This literature

---

[74] Kurtenbach and Pawelz 2015: 148–9. For a discussion of very similar dynamics of exclusion that operated in the Truth and Reconciliation Commissions in South Africa, Sierra Leone and Liberia, see Drumbl 2012.
[75] Reynolds 1998: 50.
[76] Duclos 1995: 5 (writing in French, the author uses the words 'la violence politique autonome des enfants' or also 'la violence politique juvénile autonome').
[77] Hermant 1995.
[78] Özerdem and Podder 2015: 21–2.
[79] Argenti 2002: 133.
[80] Duncan 2016: 58.
[81] Özerdem and Podder 2015.

argues for a more inclusive form of citizenship.[82] But what are the consequences of an enlarged view of citizenship that encompasses children's political rights, and even their right to vote, for children's rights related to the military? If children are granted full citizenship rights, does that imply that they also have a right to join the military, which is one of the attributes of citizenship status? We will explore the links between children's citizenship and the military by following two countervailing directions. First, we consider soldiering as a pathway to citizenship and, second, we will reflect on how being a citizen might be linked to the right to join the military.

Historically, as Burk explains, 'members of groups not recognized as full citizens could improve their social standing by performing military service'.[83] There is generally a strong thread in public discourse that links the willingness and ability to undertake military service to citizenship, whereby the right to vote is seen as a marker of political inclusion and full citizenship.[84] Through their participation in armed conflicts, minority groups have been able to acquire citizenship status. This was, for instance, the case in granting women the right to vote in Britain which was explicitly linked to their contribution to the war effort during World War I.[85] In France, legislation enacted in 1999 facilitated the naturalization of foreigners who already could apply for French citizenship after having served in the Foreign Legion for at least three years. This development further illustrates the strong link between citizenship and the military. According to Law No 99-1141 of 29 December 1999, Article 21-14-1 of the French Civil Code stipulates that French nationality can be conferred by decree to any requesting non-national who is enlisted in the Foreign Legion and who has been wounded on mission during an operational engagement of the French Army. Not only have members of specific groups gained access to a country's citizenship by contributing to its war efforts, certain groups have also instrumentalized their participation in the military as a means to gain access to citizenship status. In the USA, citizenship aspirations have been fuelled by the military service of various groups including African Americans and other racial minorities, as well as undocumented migrants, women and lesbians and gays who 'have pressed for access to the risks and sacrifices of military service as a means to gain the privileges and benefits of full citizenship'.[86] The extensive participation in the Vietnam war of young Americans under 21 years old, which was the minimum voting age at that time, had a direct influence on extending the franchise in 1971 to 18-year-olds in the USA.[87] Student protests that led to lowering the voting age maintained that if young persons could fight and die for their country at 18 and 19 years old, they should not be denied the right to vote.[88] According to Sarabyn, debates went beyond the mere question of giving full citizenship to 18-year-old soldiers who had been fighting in Vietnam, but also:

---

[82] See e.g. Baraldi and Cockburn 2018; Cockburn 2012; Invernizzi and Williams 2008; Oswell 2012.
[83] Burk 1995: 504.
[84] Sarabyn 2008: 54.
[85] Carter 1998: 80.
[86] Hillman 2009: 1282; see also Sarabyn 2008; Burk 1995: 505.
[87] Amar 1991: 1164.
[88] Amendment XXVI – Right to Vote at Age 18, 1971.

[F]ocused on the role young people should take in civil and political society. Supporters considered young people mature and responsible, capable of bringing unique assets to the political order. Opponents, in contrast, saw young people as immature, needing a sheltered environment free from 'bad' influences.[89]

A similar movement took place in South Africa where young people's past efforts in the country's struggle against Apartheid were officially recognized, not via lowering the voting age but through the declaration of a public holiday to commemorate the 1976 Soweto uprising where black schoolchildren had taken the lead to demonstrate against the Apartheid regime. For President Nelson Mandela, this official public holiday, called South Africa Youth Day, was aimed at giving 'a fitting tribute to our young heroes'.[90]

Besides considering soldiering as a path to citizenship, citizenship confers rights related to the military. For a long time, serving in the military has been considered as the fulfilment of the social status of a citizen, amounting to a kind of rite of passage through which everyone learns and earns his or her citizenship.[91] Military service was seen as the means by which an individual could be recognized as a citizen by the members of his or her political community.[92] A number of minority groups have argued that not allowing them to join the military is not only discriminatory but also deprives them of full citizenship status.[93] Reserved for citizens, military service is one of the attributes of being a full member of a nation, together with active and passive voting rights, holding public office, pursuing a career in the administration and serving as jury members.[94] But is there also a right to join the military? The question of whether the American Constitution protects such a right to military service was discussed amongst American legal scholars in the wake of the United States Supreme Court decision in *District of Columbia v. Heller*,[95] which concerned the right to keep and bear arms. According to Justice Scalia, the right to be a soldier or to wage war would be 'an absurdity that no commentator has ever endorsed'.[96] In contrast, based on his analysis of the Second Amendment to the US Constitution, Riehl finds that there is a 'close relationship between the right of military service and full political participation in our democracy', and considers that 'the right to serve in the military is a fundamental political right'.[97] Noting that the issue of the right to military service has been left largely unexamined, Hillman agrees with this view, and asserts that access to the military is a fundamental but as of yet unacknowledged aspect of citizenship.[98] For Hillman, the protection of an individual's right to participate in the defence of the nation is 'a right rooted in the nature of citizenship itself'.[99]

---

[89] Sarabyn 2008: 30.
[90] Mandela 1995.
[91] Hays 1967: 19.
[92] Burk 1995: 505–8.
[93] Burk 1995; Hillman 2009; Riehl 1995.
[94] Amar 1991.
[95] 128 S. Ct. 2783 (2008). See Hillman 2009.
[96] Hillman 2009: 1278.
[97] Riehl 1995: 394.
[98] Hillman 2009: 1279.
[99] Ibid.: 1283.

In order to better frame the connection between citizenship and military service, two concepts need to be untangled: namely, the citizen-soldier from the free citizen. The citizen-soldier tradition is inherited from the Ancient Greeks[100] and was exalted by Rousseau for whom the idea of *pro patria mori* (to die for one's country) constitutes a fundamental component of his theory of the social contract.[101] This tradition rests on two core implications. The first is that military duties inherently assume the devaluation of biological life which makes it possible to enjoin citizens to sacrifice themselves for the nation.[102] The second is that a first-class citizen is the person who serves or has served in the nation's army, whereby military service produces better citizens[103] or even new forms of citizenship.[104] The citizen-soldier tradition comes into existence through conscription, which leaves an individual little room for manoeuvre as serving in the nation's army is constructed as an obligation backed up by sanctions.

Despite states' persistent militarization, a more liberal vision of the military has emerged, giving rise to the concept of the 'free citizen'. This vision, which originated during the Enlightenment and took shape through the adoption of the Universal Declaration of Human Rights in 1948, proposes new links between military service and citizenship based on individual freedom. Indeed, even if the idea that states must be defended against external or internal aggressors continues to be acknowledged, it is no longer accepted that the interests of the state can prevail over those of an individual.[105] The citizen must be able to judge freely the dangers to which she or he would be exposed if joining the military and can for instance perform civil service as an alternative to military service by accessing the status of conscientious objector or even avoid all military service on account of religious beliefs. In this case a balance is possible between the rights of the individual and those of the state: serving in the national army is an individual choice whereby enrolment should be voluntary. As both conceptions about the relationship between citizenship and the military co-exist, serving in the army can be seen as an attribute of citizenship for the citizen-soldier as well as an individual freedom stemming from the status of citizen.

Unanswered in this literature is the question of whether children's citizenship includes a right to join the military. This question has been almost entirely overlooked, and merits further exploration, especially considering the intense debates about the need to develop forms of citizenship that also include children and young people. Furthermore, the link between the military and citizenship posits a circular, reinforcing movement. Through their past efforts in armed conflicts, minority groups can gain access to citizenship, and through this newly acquired status they have a political base to further enlarge participation in the military which further facilitates enhancing their citizenship status.[106] In cases where full citizenship includes an individual's right to participate in the nation's defence, is obtaining full citizenship beyond the reach of persons under 18 years old because they are, according to international children's rights standards, principally excluded from

---

[100] Snyder 2003.
[101] Prélot 2003.
[102] Desmons 2001.
[103] Leal 1999.
[104] Catros 2007.
[105] Carter 1998.
[106] Cf. Burk 1995.

participating in the military? Or is there a different form of citizenship for children that would include some political rights but not the right to join the military?

4. CONCLUSION

In discussions about lowering the voting age in the USA following the Vietnam war, opponents of the 'old enough to fight, old enough to vote' argument reverted to Heller's *Catch-22* to make their point. For them, 'the thing called for in a soldier is uncritical obedience, and that is not what you want in a voter'.[107] Considering that young people's absence of maturity makes them unfit to vote but perfect soldiers, the main argument gets twisted and becomes 'young enough to fight, but too young to vote'. Today, arguments about children's capacity and incapacity for autonomous decision making continue to fuel debates over their relationship with the military. International law has been a catalyst for the present-day idea that children should never, under any circumstance, be associated with the military or warfare – children are 'too young to fight, but (not) old enough to vote'.

The perspective presented by Tambo, the child soldier who is the protagonist of the story with which this chapter began, is largely absent from these debates. Showing little concern for legal age categorizations but echoing instead a free citizen conception of his living rights related to the military, Tambo first exercised his right to join an armed group before turning to its corollary right to leave the military. Instead of being respected for his choices, he was convicted for desertion, in accordance with the citizen-soldier conception of the military. The translation of international law at work in the case of DRC is that of a fragile state that has learned to interpret international norms differently depending on whether the purpose at hand is external or internal in nature. Powerful states can resist pressure from advocacy groups, as we have seen in the case of the permanent members of the UN Security Council. The double standards they impose upon themselves and other nations illustrate how children's vulnerability and inherent weakness, which informs the language of humanitarian concern with child soldiering, can be put to use as an effective cover 'to allow activity around "child soldiers" to be placed in the service of powerful interests rather than children themselves'.[108] Because of the DRC's precarious position among states, its government presents itself to the international community as an obedient nation. On the international scene, the DRC conforms to the internationally hailed Straight-18 approach towards child soldiering that is based on the child's vulnerability, leading to a rejection of Tambo's potential status as a free citizen. However, the DRC takes a different response to young Tambo at the internal level, where he is convicted for desertion by a military tribunal, hence expressing a citizen-soldier conception that includes sanctions for citizens who breach their military obligations. Whereas the internal level takes the interests of the nation as a starting point, it is the child's perceived vulnerability that takes centre stage at the international level. Neither perspective seems to be truly concerned with doing justice to the living rights of Tambo, who is left in limbo.

---

[107] Sarabyn 2008: 57
[108] Hart 2006: 225.

In this chapter, we have explored avenues that can recognize children and young people's potentially voluntary engagement in military action, an activity for which conceptual work is needed that allows us 'to engage more fully with the realities of children's lives, which are inevitably shaped by ideas, practices, and power relations that are both local and global'.[109] Such conceptual work needs to attribute some legitimacy to Tambo's conceptions of his rights related to the military and that are at present lacking.

We have seen that international law does not contain a total ban on the participation of children in military life. Such participation remains possible through their voluntary recruitment as of 16 years onwards (provided certain safeguards are respected) or via their enlistment in military schools where no minimum age exists. For many observers, these possibilities are merely residual (and unattractive) exceptions which are contrary to 'the spirit' of the CRC and OPAC and that will be 'fixed' in the long and putatively progressive journey towards the universal ban of child soldiering.[110] For us, however, the study of these margins has permitted us the space to grow our reflections on the real, albeit tempestuous relationship between children and the military.

Taking the conceptualization of a right to join the military as a starting point, even if this right can be limited for persons under a certain age in view of protecting them, an aperture opens to an alternative entry portal into current child soldier discussions. This opening permits a stepping back from the almost exclusive 'protectionist' approach through which international law pertaining to children and armed conflict is generically understood. Even if such an approach expresses a consensus on the negative consequences of violent conflicts for children, it emerges at times in tension with the complex realities of children's experiences of political struggles and violent conflicts that are characterized not only by protectionist but also by emancipatory concerns. Relying on the notions of living rights, social justice and translations, we contend that the right of children to participate in contexts of armed conflict is not necessarily a violation of children's rights. In the local frameworks where lives are lived most intensely, rights that recognize children's subjectivities can even be understood as doing justice to children and young people's efforts and sufferings in the dramatic and adverse contexts of armed conflict.

REFERENCED WORKS

Amar, A.R. 1991. 'The Bill of Rights as a Constitution' 100 *Yale Law Journal* 1131

Amendment XXVI – Right to Vote at Age 18. 1971 [available at: https://system.uslegal.com/u-s-constitution/amendment-xxvi-right-to-vote-at-age-18-1971/ (accessed 1 September 2018)]

Argenti, N. 2002. 'People of the Chisel: Apprenticeship, Youth, and Elites in Oku (Cameroon)' 29 *American Ethnologist* 497

Arts, K. 2014. 'Twenty-Five Years of the United Nations Convention on the Rights of the Child: Achievements and Challenges' 61 *Netherlands International Law Review* 267

Baraldi, C. and Cockburn, T. (eds) 2018. *Theorising Childhood: Citizenship, Rights and Participation* (London: Palgrave Macmillan)

Barber, B.K. 2008. 'Contrasting Portraits of War: Youths' Varied Experiences with Political Violence in Bosnia and Palestine' 32 *International Journal of Behavioral Development* 298

---

[109] Ibid: 223.
[110] Sheppard 2000.

Burk, J. 1995. 'Citizenship Status and Military Service: The Quest for Inclusion by Minorities and Conscientious Objectors' 21 *Armed Forces & Society* 503
Canadian Armed Forces 2017. 'Canadian Armed Forces Sets Precedent with Child Soldier Doctrine', News Release (2 March) [available at: https://www.canada.ca/en/department-national-defence/news/2017/03/canadian_armed_forcessetsprecedentwithchildsoldierdoctrine.html (accessed 22 October 2018)]
Carter, A. 1998. 'Liberalism and the Obligation to Military Service' 46 *Political Studies* 68
Catros, P. 2007. 'Tout Français est soldat et se doit à la défense de la patrie [Retour sur la naissance de la conscription militaire]' 348 *Annales historiques de la Révolution française* (Armand Colin, Société des études robespierristes)
Cockburn, T. 2012. *Rethinking Children's Citizenship* (Basingstoke: Palgrave)
Commission on Human Rights 1996. 'Report of the Working Group on a Draft Optional Protocol to the Convention on the Rights of the Child on Involvement of Children in Armed Conflicts on its Second Session' (UN Doc. E/CN.4/1996/102) (21 March)
CRC Committee [Committee on the Rights of the Child] 2005. 'Consideration of Reports Submitted by States Parties under Article 8(1) of the Optional Protocol to the Convention on the Rights of the Child on the Involvement of Children in Armed Conflict. Initial Reports of States Parties Due in 2004. Canada' (UN Doc. CRC/C/OPAC/CAN/1) (29 July)
CRC Committee 2006. 'Consideration of Reports Submitted by States Parties under Article 8(1) of the Optional Protocol to the Convention on the Rights of the Child on the Involvement of Children in Armed Conflict. Initial Reports of States Parties Due in 2005. France' (UN Doc. CRC/C/OPAC/FRA/1) (6 November)
CRC Committee 2007a. 'Revised Guidelines Regarding Initial Reports to be Submitted by States Parties under Article 8, Paragraph 1, of the Optional Protocol to the Convention on the Rights of the Child on Involvement of Children in Armed Conflict' (UN Doc. CRC/C/OPAC/2) (19 October)
CRC Committee 2007b. 'Concluding Observations OPAC: France' (UN Doc. CRC/C/OPAC/FRA/CO/1) (15 October)
CRC Committee 2007c. 'Consideration of Reports Submitted by States Parties under Article 8(1) of the Optional Protocol to the Convention on the Rights of the Child on the Involvement of Children in Armed Conflict. Initial Reports of States Parties Due in 2007. United Kingdom of Great Britain and Northern Ireland' (UN Doc. CRC/C/OPAC/GBR/1) (3 September)
CRC Committee 2008. 'Summary Record of the 1357th Meeting. Consideration of Reports of States Parties: United Kingdom of Great Britain and Northern Ireland' (UN Doc. CRC/C/SR.1357) (9 October)
CRC Committee 2011. 'Consideration of Reports Submitted by States Parties under Article 8(1) of the Optional Protocol to the Convention on the Rights of the Child on the Involvement of Children in Armed Conflict. Initial Reports of States Parties Due in 2004. Democratic Republic of the Congo' (UN Doc. CRC/C/OPAC/DOC/1) (18 April 2011)
CRC Committee 2012a. 'Consideration of Reports Submitted by States Parties under Article 8(1) of the Optional Protocol to the Convention on the Rights of the Child on the Involvement of Children in Armed Conflict. Initial Reports of States Parties Due in 2004. Paraguay' (UN Doc. CRC/C/OPAC/PRY/1) (22 May)
CRC Committee 2012b. 'Consideration of Reports Submitted by States Parties under Article 8(1) of the Optional Protocol to the Convention on the Rights of the Child on the Involvement of Children in Armed Conflict. Initial Reports of States Parties Due in 2010. China' (UN Doc. CRC/C/OPAC/CHN/1) (6 June)
CRC Committee 2013a. 'Concluding Observations OPAC: Paraguay' (UN Doc. CRC/C/OPAC/PRY/CO/1) (25 October)
CRC Committee 2013b. 'Concluding Observations OPAC: USA' (UN Doc. CRC/C/OPAC/USA/CO/2) (26 June)
CRC Committee 2013c. 'Summary Record of the 1835th Meeting. Consideration of Reports of States Parties: China' (UN Doc. CRC/C/SR.1835) (19 November)
CRC Committee 2016. 'Summary Record of the 2115th Meeting. Consideration of Reports of States Parties: United Kingdom of Great Britain and Northern Ireland' (UN Doc. CRC/C/SR.2125) (1 June)
CRC Committee 2017. 'Summary Record of the 2196th Meeting. Consideration of Reports of States Parties: USA' (UN Doc. CRC/C/SR.2196) (24 May)
Desmons, E. 2001. *Mourir pour la patrie?* (Paris: PUF)
Drumbl, M.A. 2012. *Reimagining Child Soldiers in International Law and Policy* (Oxford: Oxford University Press)
Duclos, L.-J. 1995. 'Les enfants et la violence politique' 18 *Cultures & conflits* 3
Duncan, M. 2016. 'Children and Civil Society in South Asia. Subjects, Participants and Political Agents' in B. D'Costa (ed.), *Children and Violence: Politics of Conflict in South Asia* (New York: Cambridge University Press)
Eighmey, J. 2006. 'Why Do Youth Enlist? Identification of Underlying Themes' 32 *Armed Forces & Society* 307
Freeman, R. 2009. 'What is "Translation"?' 5 *Evidence & Policy* 429

Hammack, P.L. 2010. 'Identity as Burden or Benefit? Youth, Historical Narrative, and the Legacy of Political Conflict' 53 *Human Development* 173
Hammarberg, T. 1990. 'The UN Convention on the Rights of the Child – and How to Make It Work' 12 *Human Rights Quarterly* 97
Hanson, K. 2011. 'International Children's Rights and Armed Conflict' 5 *Human Rights & International Legal Discourse* 40
Hanson, K. 2012. 'Schools of Thought in Children's Rights', in M. Liebel, K. Hanson, I. Saadi and W. Vandenhole (eds), *Children's Rights from Below: Cross-Cultural Perspectives* (Basingstoke: Palgrave Macmillan) 63.
Hanson, K. 2016. 'Children's Participation and Agency When They Don't "Do the Right Thing"' 23 *Childhood* 471
Hanson, K. and Lundy, L. 2017. 'Does Exactly What It Says on the Tin? A Critical Analysis and Alternative Conceptualisation of the So-called "General Principles" of the Convention on the Rights of the Child' 25 *The International Journal of Children's Rights* 285
Hanson, K. and Nieuwenhuys, O. 2013. 'Living Rights, Social Justice, Translations', in K. Hanson and O. Nieuwenhuys (eds), *Reconceptualizing Children's Rights in International Development: Living Rights, Social Justice, Translations* (Cambridge: Cambridge University Press) 3
Hanson, K. and Nieuwenhuys, O. 2019. 'A Child-Centered Approach to Children's Rights Law: Living Rights and Translations', in J. Todres and L. King (eds), *The Oxford Handbook of Children's Rights Law* (New York: Oxford University Press) (forthcoming)
Hanson, K. and van Daalen, E. 2016. 'Can Campaigns to Stop Child Labour be Stopped?' (Open Democracy) (26 February) [available at: https://www.opendemocracy.net/beyondslavery/karl-hanson-edward-van-daalen/can-campaigns-to-stop-child-labour-be-stopped (accessed 1 August 2018)]
Hart, J. 2006. 'The Politics of "Child Soldiers"' 13 *The Brown Journal of World Affairs* 217
Hathaway, O. 2002. 'Do Treaties Make a Difference? Human Rights Treaties and the Problem of Compliance' 111 *Yale Law Journal* 1932
Hathaway, O. 2007. 'Why Do Countries Commit to Human Rights Treaties?' 51 *Journal of Conflict Resolution* 588
Hays, S.H. 1967. 'A Military View on Selective Service', in S. Tax (ed.), *The Draft: A Handbook of Facts and Alternatives* (Chicago: University of Chicago Press) 7
Henckaerts, J.M. and Doswald-Beck, L. 2005. *Customary International Humanitarian Law* (Vol. 1) (Cambridge: Cambridge University Press).
Hermant, D. 1995. 'L'espace problématique de la violence politique des enfants' 18 *Cultures & Conflits* 181
Hillman, E.L. 2009. 'Heller, Citizenship, and the Right to Serve in the Military' 60 *Hastings L.J.* 1269
I'Anson, J., Quennerstedt, A. and Robinson, C. 2017. 'The International Economy of Children's Rights: Issues in Translation' 25 *The International Journal of Children's Rights* 50
International Committee of the Red Cross. 2015. 'Annex XVI. Guiding Principles for the Domestic Implementation of a Comprehensive System of Protection for Children Associated with Armed Forces or Armed Groups' in *The Domestic Implementation of International Humanitarian Law: A Manual* (Geneva: International Committee of the Red Cross) [available at: https://www.icrc.org/eng/assets/files/publications/icrc-002-4028.pdf (accessed 10 September 2018)]
Internationale des Résistant(e)s à la Guerre. 'Rwanda: recrutement, desertion et repression des soldats' [available at: https://www.wri-irg.org/fr/story/2017/rwanda-recrutement-desertion-et-repression-des-soldats (accessed 19 August 2018)]
Invernizzi, A. and Williams, J. (eds) 2008. *Children and Citizenship* (London: Sage)
Krebs, R.R. 2004. 'A School for the Nation? How Military Service Does Not Build Nations, and How It Might' 28 *International Security* 85
Kuper, J. 2000. 'Children and Armed Conflict: Some Issues of Law and Policy' in D. Fottrell (ed.), *Revisiting Children's Rights: 10 Years of the UN Convention on the Rights of the Child* (The Hague: Kluwer Law International) 101
Kuper, J. 2008. 'Child Soldiers and Civilians – Some Controversial Issues' 29 *University of La Verne Law Review* 12
Kurtenbach, S. and Pawelz, J. 2015. 'Voting is Not Enough: Youth and Political Citizenship in Post-War Societies' 3 *Peacebuilding* 141
Leal, D. 1999. 'It's Not Just a Job: Military Service and Latino Political Participation' 21 *Political Behavior* 153
Lee, A.-J. 2009. 'Understanding and Addressing the Phenomenon of "Child Soldiers": The Gap Between the Global Humanitarian Discourse and the Local Understandings and Experiences of Young People's Military Recruitment' (Refugee Studies Centre, Working Paper Series No. 52, University of Oxford)
Mandela, N. 1995. 'Speech by President Nelson Mandela on South Africa Youth Day Ladysmith' (16 June) [available at: http://www.sahistory.org.za/archive/speech-president-nelson-mandela-south-africa-youth-day-ladysmith-16-june-1995 (accessed 16 June 2018)]
Merry, S.E. 2006. 'Transnational Human Rights and Local Activism: Mapping the Middle' 108 *American Anthropologist* 38

Moravcsik, A. 2000. 'The Origins of Human Rights Regimes: Democratic Delegation in Postwar Europe' 54 *International Organization* 217

Oswell, D. 2012. *The Agency of Children: From Family to Global Human Rights* (Cambridge: Cambridge University Press)

Özerdem, A. and Podder, S. 2015. *Youth in Conflict and Peacebuilding: Mobilization, Reintegration and Reconciliation* (London: Palgrave Macmillan)

Prélot, P.-H. 2003. '"Lectures critiques" (Éric Desmons, *Mourir pour la patrie?*, PUF, 2001, 116 p.)' 17 *Revue Française d'Histoire des Idées Politiques* 173

Reynaert, D., Bouverne-de-Bie, M. and Vandevelde, S. 2009. 'A Review of Children's Rights Literature since the Adoption of the United Nations Convention on the Rights of the Child' 16 *Childhood* 518

Reynolds, P. 1998. 'Activism, Politics and the Punishment of Children', in G. Van Bueren (ed.), *Childhood Abused: Protecting Children against Torture, Cruel, Inhuman and Degrading Treatment and Punishment* (Aldershot: Ashgate) 43

Riehl, C. 1995. 'Uncle Sam Has to Want You: The Right of Gay Men and Lesbians (and All Other Americans) to Bear Arms in the Military' 26 *Rutgers L.J.* 343

Rosen, D.M. 2005. *Armies of the Young: Child Soldiers in War and Terrorism* (New Brunswick: Rutgers University Press)

Rosen, D.M. 2007. 'Child Soldiers: International Humanitarian Law and the Globalization of Childhood' 109 *American Anthropologist* 296

Sanghera, G., Botterill, K., Hopkins, P. and Arshad, R. 2018. '"Living Rights", Rights Claims, Performative Citizenship and Young People – the Right to Vote in the Scottish Independence Referendum' 22 *Citizenship Studies* 540

Sarabyn, K. 2008. 'The Twenty-Sixth Amendment: Resolving the Federal Circuit Split Over College Students' First Amendment Rights' 14 *Tex. J. on C.L. & C.R.* 27

Seymour, C. 2012. 'Ambiguous Agency: Coping and Survival in Eastern Democratic Republic of Congo' 10 *Children's Geographies* 373

Shepler, S. 2014. *Childhood Deployed: Remaking Child Soldiers in Sierra Leone* (New York: NYU Press)

Sheppard, A. 2000. 'Child Soldiers: Is the Optional Protocol Evidence of an Emerging "Straight-18" Consensus?' 8 *The International Journal of Children's Rights* 37

Status of Treaties [available at: https://treaties.un.org/Pages/ViewDetails.aspx?src=IND&mtdsg_no=IV-11-b&chapter=4&clang=_en#EndDec (accessed 24 September 2018)]

Snyder, R.C. 2003. 'The Citizen-Soldier Tradition and Gender Integration of the US Military' 29 *Armed Forces & Society* 185

van Daalen, E. and Hanson, K. 2019. 'The ILO's Shifts in Child Labour Policy: Regulation and Abolition' 11 *International Development Policy* (forthcoming)

Vandewiele, T. 2006. 'Optional Protocol: The Involvement of Children in Armed Conflicts' in A. Alen, J. Vande Lanotte, E. Verhellen, F. Ang, E. Berghmans and M. Verheyde (eds), *A Commentary on the United Nations Convention on the Rights of the Child* (Leiden: Martinus Nijhoff)

Verhellen, E. 2000. *Convention on the Rights of the Child: Background, Motivation, Strategies, Main Themes.* 3rd revised edition (Leuven: Garant)

Zwingel, S. 2012. 'How Do Norms Travel? Theorizing International Women's Rights in Transnational Perspective' 56 *International Studies Quarterly* 115

6. This Is Belonging: children and British military recruitment

Rhys Crilley

The British Army's latest recruitment campaign has been the cause of much controversy within the United Kingdom. The 'This Is Belonging' campaign features videos that address questions like 'Do I have to be a superhero to join the Army?', 'Can I be gay in the Army?' and 'What if I get emotional in the Army?' This attention to people's reservations about joining the military appears to mark a shift in the Army's recruitment strategy, which has previously focused on depicting Army life as exciting, or on the educational, career and personal benefits of learning new skills and gaining qualifications as part of military service. As such, the 'This Is Belonging' campaign has been criticized by the likes of Colonel Richard Kemp – former commander of the British military in Afghanistan – as a sign that the Army has 'gone soft' and is now 'pandering to political correctness'.[1] These claims perhaps reveal more about the conservative beliefs of people like Kemp, someone who has opposed the inclusion of women in combat roles,[2] than they do about the evolution of the British Army. However, Kemp's suggestion that the current Army recruitment campaign obscures the fact that combat and the use of force remain the Army's priority is an important one, and it is one that resonates with critiques of contemporary 'Western' warfare being represented in a clean, bloodless and humanitarian way.[3] This gap between the representation and the reality of conflict and military service is important, especially given that it is through these representations in the media and in broader popular culture that young people find out about war and conflict. This chapter argues that British military recruitment practices should be included in debates about child soldiers. This is especially pertinent given that the United Kingdom is the only military force in NATO and Europe that recruits 16-year-olds.

This chapter explores the British military's practice of recruiting 16-year-olds and argues that such practices should be included in debates around child soldiers. Since 2011, over 12,000 under-18s have joined the British military. In the USA, approximately 7,000 17-year-olds join the military each year, and in Germany over 2,000 17-year-olds were recruited by the Bundeswehr in 2017. The study of child soldiers often focuses on the global South, at the expense of allowing the recruitment practices of militaries in the global North to escape proper scrutiny. I address this gap by focusing on the British military recruitment of under-18s and I demonstrate why this should be considered in debates about child soldiers. This chapter outlines the legal context, inquires into why the British military continues to recruit children, and documents how this has been challenged

---

[1] BBC 2018.
[2] Kemp 2014.
[3] Baudrillard 1995; Der Derian 2009; Butler 2010; Stahl 2010; Bourke 2014.

by various human rights groups. Specifically, I highlight how support for the recruitment of under-18s into the British military is reliant upon three myths. These are the notions that children do not fight in the British military; military service is not dangerous for soldiers that join the military as children; and children who enlist in the military gain skills for life. I then suggest that British military recruitment practices are reliant on broader cultural forms of outreach that specifically target children – at times as young as five – through the production of official HM Armed Forces toys, cadet programmes, school visits and social media campaigns. Here I pay particular attention to the Army's most recent recruitment campaign, and I discuss how the 'This Is Belonging' campaign, with its focus on camaraderie and community, is specifically aimed at recruiting young people. The chapter concludes by discussing two recent forms of counter-recruitment activity by the artist Darren Cullen and by the SNP Youth in order to demonstrate how Britain's child soldier culture can effectively be challenged and changed.

1. THE BRITISH MILITARY AND CHILD SOLDIERS

In the United Kingdom the minimum age of military recruitment is 16. Whilst this is permissible under international law, it is the youngest age of military recruitment of any NATO member or European state. The UK is in fact one of only 19 countries worldwide to recruit 16-year-olds, and other countries that do so include North Korea, Syria and Iran. Article 1 of the United Nations Convention on the Rights of a Child defines anyone under the age of 18 as a child. Though people under the age of 18 cannot serve in combat roles in the British military, the internationally accepted definition of children associated with armed forces extends well beyond combat roles. The 2007 Paris Principles, a non-binding yet influential instrument, offers the following definition:

> any person below 18 years of age who is or who has been recruited or used by an armed force or armed group in any capacity, including but not limited to children, boys and girls, used as fighters, cooks, porters, messengers, spies or for sexual purposes. It does not only refer to a child who is taking or has taken a direct part in hostilities.[4]

Anyone under the age of 18 who serves in the British military is thus 'a child associated with an armed force', or what we might, for the sake of succinctness, call a child soldier. Article 38 of the United Nations Convention on the Rights of a Child bans the use of children under the age of 15 in armed conflict. Whilst this means the UK's position of recruiting 16-year-olds is legal under international law, there has been a shift towards international law adopting the aspiration that the minimum age of military recruitment should be 18.[5] This 'Straight-18' approach draws upon UNICEF's recommendation that states 'adopt national legislation that sets a minimum age of 18 years for voluntary and compulsory recruitment'.[6] This makes the UK's decision to recruit 16-year-olds all the more remarkable. Before exploring how and why the UK continues to recruit child

---

[4] Paris Principle 2.1 (definitions).
[5] Drumbl 2012: 4–5.
[6] Cape Town Principles: 1.

soldiers, it is worth outlining several issues concerning the use of this label and why it ultimately should be used in the context of the British military.

The phrase child soldier often invokes several myths that simplify the experiences of children who serve in militaries or armed groups. Most notable of these are two popular representations. The first consists of child soldiers being seen as threatening and uncivilized, where 'the horror of childhood [has been] perverted from its "natural" course of innocence, fragility and purity'.[7] The second representation involves child soldiers being seen as passive victims that lack agency and are forced to fight by the adults that recruit them.[8] These representations cast children 'as wholly dependent, helpless and victimized – ultimately deserving of our sympathy'.[9] Further to this, there has been a tendency within scholarly study and in policy-making to focus on child soldiers in zones of conflict in the global South rather than on the ways in which the lives of children in the global North are militarized.[10] Together, these representations and focus have the effect of 'pathologizing poorer countries as the locus of all child soldier activity'[11] whilst also sheltering the military recruitment practices of states such as the UK from critique and scrutiny.

These representations of child soldiers therefore need to be contested. It is worth emphasizing that when the label of child soldiers is used to refer to those under 18 who serve in the militaries of the UK, the USA and Australia (where 17-year-olds can join), there is no implication that they are threatening, uncivilized, or that they are helpless victims who lack agency. This is not to imply that the experiences of children whose lives are militarized in the global North are equivalent to those experiences of children who have fought in conflicts in the global South. Rather, it is to recognize that viewing child soldiers as something confined to the global South sidesteps questions about how military actors in the global North are reliant on young people under the age of 18 who are legally defined as children.[12] As Katrina Lee-Koo has recently noted: 'once the stereotype of the child soldier is challenged, it becomes clear that the militarisation of children is not isolated to the global South'.[13] This chapter therefore contributes to a growing body of literature that takes the military recruitment of under-18s in the global North seriously.[14] Specifically, it explores how the British military's current recruitment practices are aimed at children and are reliant on a broader cultural form of militarization that functions 'as a normalising process to do with preparation for war – the social and cultural preparation for the idea of war, which relies on a gendered logic and takes place in the mediatised everyday'.[15] I now outline the legal context surrounding the British military's recruitment of under-18s.

In October 2017, figures revealed that the number of people joining the regular forces of the UK had declined by 10 per cent since October 2016.[16] According to a report on

---

[7] Denov 2010: 7.
[8] Drumbl 2012: 7. See also Shepler 2005; Dallaire 2011; Singer 2006.
[9] Denov 2010: 8.
[10] Beier 2011: 1.
[11] Harding and Kershner 2017: 11.
[12] Ibid.: 10.
[13] Lee-Koo 2011: 733.
[14] Harding and Kershner 2015 and 2017; Rech 2014 and 2017; Beier 2011; Strand and Berndtsson 2015; Crilley 2016a and 2016b; Basham 2016b.
[15] Åhäll 2016: 162.
[16] Ministry of Defence 2017b.

British military recruitment conducted by Mark Francois MP, this decline stems from several factors that include: near record employment; an aging population; the end of British land warfare operations in Afghanistan; government cuts to the armed forces; an increase in obesity in the UK; and an increase in 16-year-olds staying on in education.[17] The combination of these factors is described by Francois as 'a "perfect storm" against which military recruiters have had to battle'.[18] It is in this context that the British military continues to recruit under-18s despite calls for the minimum age of military recruitment to be raised to 18. The UK's child recruitment policy has been challenged by major child rights organizations, Amnesty International, medical professionals, the National Union of Teachers, the UN Committee on the Rights of the Child, military veterans themselves, the Equality and Human Rights Commission and the British Parliament's very own Joint Committee on Human Rights and its Defence Committee. In response, the British government has recognized that 'the prospect of the Armed Forces, especially the Army, being legally barred from taking U18 recruits would have a most significant effect upon manning'.[19] Here, statistics reveal that between September 2013 and September 2017 an average of 19 per cent of the Armed Forces' annual recruitment intake were between the ages of 16 and 18.[20] The majority of these recruits joined the Army,[21] which since 2011 has seen a total of 12,560 under-18s join. These figures show that since 2011 over a quarter (26.1%) of the Army's intake of new recruits were under the age of 18.[22] The Ministry of Defence views the recruitment of children as 'an opportunity to mitigate Standard Entry shortfalls, particularly for the Infantry'.[23]

The legal situation of these recruits warrants further inspection. Children can begin the application process to join the Army at the age of 15 years and 7 months, and all under-18s require parental consent when enlisting. Despite this, there are no requirements for recruiters to meet with parents or guardians at any point of the enlistment process, and child rights groups have expressed concern that many child recruits do not fully comprehend the enlistment process. A freedom of information request recently revealed that three-quarters of under-18 enlistees have a reading age of 11 or less and the briefing materials provided to parents and guardians contain no information pertaining to 'the risks and legal obligations that follow their child's enlistment'.[24] Consequently, Child Soldiers International has suggested that this practice may be unlawful as it does not meet the legal requirements of the Optional Protocol to the Convention on the Rights of the Child concerning full information and informed consent for military recruits under the age of 18.[25] Moreover, whilst those that join the British military under the age of 18 are

---

[17] Francois 2017: 2.
[18] Ibid.: 2.
[19] Ibid.: 12.
[20] Ministry of Defence 2017b.
[21] The Army functions as the land forces of the British military, whilst the Royal Navy and Royal Air Force service the sea and skies respectively. According to Child Soldiers International, the Navy and the RAF have 'effectively moved on' from being committed to recruiting 16- and 17-year-olds (Taylor and Gee 2016).
[22] Ministry of Defence 2017a.
[23] MoD quoted in Saville Roberts and Taylor 2018.
[24] Child Soldiers International 2016b.
[25] Child Soldiers International 2016a. See also Hanson and Molima in this volume.

able to leave the forces before their 18th birthday, they are legally required to serve a minimum of four years of service from the date of their 18th birthday. Therefore, 16-year-olds who join the Army are often required to serve a minimum of six years, whereas those who join over the age of 18 are only required to serve for four years. In June 2015, the British Royal Courts of Justice heard a case challenging this difference between the minimum service period for children and adults. Justice Kenneth Parker ruled that the Army was legally entitled to continue this practice, however, he noted that the rules discriminated against minors as they did 'treat those recruited under 18 less favourably'.[26]

Alongside these issues, those who join the British Armed Forces under the age of 18 face a higher level of risk than their older peers. The military often makes the case that the recruitment of children is legal and justifiable as under-18s cannot be deployed in combat. As will be recalled, however, under the internationally accepted definition, anyone who is enlisted in a military under the age of 18 is a child soldier. It is also worth remembering that the British military's recruitment of children is aimed to make up shortfalls in the number of infantry soldiers. The MoD has stated that it wants 16- and 17-year-olds 'particularly for the infantry',[27] which is by far the most dangerous role in the military. Whilst under-18s cannot be deployed in combat roles, research shows that those who join under the age of 18 are more likely to eventually be deployed to frontline combat. In the British Army's most recent conflict in Afghanistan, those who enlisted at 16 were more likely to end up in frontline combat and were twice as likely to be killed or injured as their counterparts who enlisted when they were over 18.[28] On top of this, young soldiers are more likely to suffer from mental health problems such as post-traumatic stress disorder than older enlistees or civilians of the same age.[29]

Alongside the higher risks faced by child recruits to the British Armed Forces, there are also issues concerning the outcomes of the training and education they receive. Child recruits to the military are exempt from the Education and Skills Act that sets out a minimum standard for participation in education to the age of 18, and the target set by the Army for recruits' educational attainment after 12 months of training is a reading age of 9–11 years. Furthermore, one-third of 16- and 17-year-old enlistees are discharged before the end of their training. Rather than giving young people skills for life, the evidence suggests that those who leave the education system early to join the military at 16 are at a very real risk of leaving the military early as well, thereby risking 'permanent disengagement from the education system and long-term unemployment as a direct consequence of enlisting prematurely'.[30]

Taken together it becomes apparent that the arguments for continuing to recruit children to the British military are based on weak foundations. Whilst it is not illegal under international law, the recruitment of under-18s contravenes an emergent international norm for the complete removal of all children under 18 from any military force or armed group. Furthermore, claims that it is legitimate for the British military to recruit children because they will not be deployed in combat fail to account for the risks that those

---

[26] Child Soldiers International 2015.
[27] Child Soldiers International 2016b.
[28] Hill 2016.
[29] Child Soldiers International 2016b.
[30] Ibid.: 2.

individuals face. Young recruits are more likely to be deployed in dangerous roles at the age of 18; more at risk of mental health problems; and end up with limited development and skills opportunities. A comprehensive understanding of British military recruitment in the context of debates around child soldiers requires going beyond the legal issues and also needs to take into account how military careers and the normalization of military force are engrained through popular culture.

2. BRITAIN'S CHILD SOLDIER CULTURE

In the UK the military recruitment of children takes place through various means. There are recruitment offices in many cities and towns, military personnel are present at school careers events, and recruitment campaigns are targeted directly at children. These direct methods of recruitment take place within a broader context of what is – I argue – ultimately a child soldier culture where the military recruitment of under-18s is normalized in everyday life. As one former head of recruitment for the Army has stated, military recruitment 'starts with a seven-year-old seeing a parachutist at an air show and thinking, "that looks great" . . . [f]rom then the army is trying to build interest by drip, drip, drip'.[31] The British military attempts to promote this interest by engaging with children in military activities in schools. The armed forces visit approximately 8,800 schools per year and engage with 900,000 students through presentations, lessons, away days, mentoring and careers events. These visits to schools enable the British military 'to reach a large proportion of children, and bypass parents and other gatekeepers'.[32] It is often claimed that these visits are not recruitment activities, as no children are signed up directly. However, rather paradoxically, the MoD has stated that these activities 'enable recruiters to access the school environments' and that these events are 'a powerful way to facilitate recruitment'.[33]

This direct form of recruitment activity is not the only way that schools are being utilized for recruitment purposes. Since 2010, Britain's government has encouraged and funded various initiatives aimed at children with a military ethos. These initiatives suggest that 'certain values and qualities are inherent to military personnel and veterans, as a direct result of their military socialization or "raising" and service',[34] and that such values can be shared with children for their benefit. These schemes include: a Military to Mentors programme for veterans to work with children who struggle in mainstream education; a Troops to Teachers initiative which fast-tracks veterans into teacher training; and the development of academies and schools run by ex-military personnel. To date, almost £20 million has been spent by the government on these schemes.[35]

Since 2012, the British government has allocated a further £11 million to increase the number of military cadet programmes in state schools. These cadet programmes involve children partaking in military drills, parades and activities similar to those that they

---

[31] Colonel David Allfrey quoted in Armstrong 2007.
[32] Sangster 2013: 89.
[33] Ministry of Defence quoted in House of Commons Defence Committee 2008: 27.
[34] Basham 2016b: 259.
[35] Ibid.: 259.

would undertake during military service. At present there are almost as many military cadets (130,000) as there are soldiers in the regular Armed Forces (138,000), and these cadet forces are seen by the government to not only 'provide an important opportunity for young people to experience the military ethos' but they also stand as 'the only remaining military footprint in towns across the UK'.[36] Such programmes are growing, and 350 new cadet units have been created in schools, mainly in deprived areas. According to the military, the targeting of children in poor parts of the UK is to provide opportunities to those that do not have many. Rachel Taylor has however highlighted how this strategic targeting is 'not about presenting the military as one of many options. It's about exploiting people who don't have a lot else going for them and taking advantage of that lack of opportunity to fill the ranks usually for the most dangerous and badly paid roles.'[37] Indeed, one of the largest teaching unions in the UK, the NASUWT, referred to the government's plans for military-run free schools and academies in deprived areas as 'national service for the poor'.[38]

Britain's child soldier culture permeates deeper into society than in schools and cadet forces. It is also present in other spaces such as events like Armed Forces Day and other military events in public, in toys aimed at children as young as five, and on social media sites used by young people. In 2000, the government introduced the Armed Forces Covenant which aimed to enable communities and companies to regularly pledge support for and pay respect to the armed forces. Sarah Ingham has detailed the impact of the Armed Forces Covenant on civil–military relations in Britain, and notes that it served to solidify British public support for military personnel, where, despite popular opposition to the government's mission in Iraq and Afghanistan, there was 'unprecedented levels of moral and material support'[39] for the troops. This has been most notably apparent in two places. The first is in the growing number of military charities within the UK, a phenomenon referred to by Joanna Tidy as 'conscience capitalism'[40] – where the proliferation of military charities and public support for them has served to render the British armed forces as 'a notionally apolitical social "cause"'.[41] The second is in the increase in the military's presence in public spaces, most prominent with the military's involvement in the security of the London 2012 Olympics, but also apparent in air shows and Armed Forces Day events.[42]

The increasing permeation of the military into everyday spaces does not serve a direct recruitment purpose in the sense that obviously the act of buying a poppy or visiting an air show is not the same as signing up for the military. Rather, such everyday practices function in an indirect way, whereby they 'obscure the military's core violent function, [and] facilitate its application by fostering less-questioning popular support for the armed

---

[36] Francois 2017: 10.
[37] Rachel Taylor quoted in Morris 2017.
[38] politics.co.uk 2012.
[39] Ingham 2014: 4.
[40] Tidy 2015: 221.
[41] Ibid.: 221.
[42] Rech 2017.

forces'.[43] As such, they represent the military as 'good, natural and necessary'[44] and it is in this context that acts such as the wearing of poppies in November – poppies which were originally sold to signify the remembering of war dead – have been appropriated to celebrate serving soldiers.[45] People in the public eye who do not wear poppies are seen as unpatriotic, and the pressure to wear poppies has at times bordered on the weird and absurd. For example, in his appearance on BBC One's *The One Show* in November 2016, *Sesame Street*'s Cookie Monster had a poppy pinned to his bright blue chest. These everyday forms of militarization serve to normalize the use of military force as a solution to social problems and make it harder to speak out against the use of armed force in the service of the national interest.[46] This everyday militarization should be a cause for concern for British society, especially when it is targeted at children. Two forms of everyday militarization that are emblematic of Britain's child soldier culture include the involvement of the Armed Forces in the creation of military toys for children as young as five, and the Armed Forces' targeting of children on social media platforms.

As a child I grew up playing with Action Man figures. In the 1990s, these figures lacked an explicit military theme and depicted Action Man as less of a soldier and more of an adventurer, where Action Man's antagonist was a mutant supervillain called Dr X, and Action Man himself came with a variety of outfits and equipment that ventured into the territory of science fiction rather than realism. Between 1993 and 2006, Action Man figures were produced by Hasbro. In 2006, Action Man was discontinued as a brand and toy. To fill the void left by the demise of Action Man, the British military commissioned the company Character Group plc to produce a series of figures that were explicitly based on serving soldiers and were designed to be as realistic as possible. Gone was any assertion of fantasy; instead, these were hyper-realistic action figures with hyper-realistic military equipment. These figures were created in order to 'fill the void caused by the current lack of authentic military-inspired toys in the action toy figure market'.[47] In 2011, the British military once again commissioned Character Group plc to release a range of Lego-like building block toy sets based on military personnel and equipment. The name of these products was 'HM Armed Forces: Character building', and they were aimed at children as young as five.[48] Sets available included a Royal Navy Type 45 Destroyer, an Army artillery set, and a Royal Air Force Reaper Unmanned Aerial Vehicle. These products are illustrative of three tropes that serve to normalize the use of military force.[49] First, they constitute a vision of 'clean war' where violence and fighting are erased from representations of what the military does. None of the sets feature any sense of what battleships, artillery and drones are used for, beyond euphemisms for killing such as 'engaging targets'. These toys are also representative of 'technofetishism', where high-tech military equipment is fetishized and made out to be something impressive, enjoyable and fun. Here, the focus is placed on the technologies themselves, with no thought given to

---

[43] Basham 2016a: 268.
[44] Jackson 2016.
[45] Basham 2016a: 885.
[46] Åhäll 2016: 892. See also Basham 2016a.
[47] HM Armed Forces 2018b.
[48] HM Armed Forces 2018a.
[49] Stahl 2010.

what those weapons actually do. For example, the box for the RAF Reaper Drone building block set features information about its wingspan, length, take-off weight, maximum altitude and maximum air speed. Finally, these toys are constructive of a 'support the troops' rhetoric where children are encouraged to actively play with military careers in a figurative and literal sense. This functions to promote the military in a way that indeed is 'character building', and imbues military values into the very character of young children long before they are anywhere near the minimum age of recruitment.

In addition, the British military attempts to engage with young children through social media. The various branches of the Armed Forces have been relatively quick to adapt to the growth of social media platforms and have utilized them for various purposes since 2009.[50] Nowadays, the British military utilizes a wide range of social media platforms on a daily basis. Several of these platforms, such as Snapchat, are almost exclusively popular with young people. According to the British media regulator OFCOM, a quarter of 8–11-year-olds and three-quarters of 12–15-year-olds have social media profiles.[51] In OFCOM's 2017 survey of young people and media, Snapchat was the most popular social media platform with children in the UK,[52] and whilst there are no figures available for the percentage of British Snapchat users under the age of 18, it is worth noting that 23 per cent of Snapchat users in the US are under 18.[53] Social media sites such as Snapchat are used by militaries to communicate directly with children. This is problematic because militaries can now 'disseminate their messages directly to their intended recipients without any filtering by the traditional media'.[54] As a result, any external editorial oversight that one would expect to be present in press or television coverage of the military is now lost. There is also evidence that children struggle to differentiate between advertisements and other forms of content (such as news) online,[55] and the Army's Digital Strategy outlines that the Army's use of social media is aimed at people over the age of 14 with the intention of making them 'join the Army'.[56] The Army's latest recruitment campaign is called 'This Is Belonging'. It places social media at the heart of its recruitment strategy and is directly targeted at children.

3. THIS IS BELONGING

The most recent Army recruitment campaign involves several television advertisements, YouTube videos and social media content that marks a shift in the Army's recruitment strategy. Throughout the 1990s, Army recruitment advertisements involved a character called Frank who was pictured participating in outdoor activities such as windsurfing, skiing or rock-climbing in videos that were accompanied by soft rock music. Such advertisements portrayed military service as glamourous and exciting. These videos have,

---

[50] Crilley 2016b.
[51] OFCOM 2017: 4.
[52] Ibid.: 12.
[53] Statista 2017.
[54] Banham 2013: 615.
[55] OFCOM 2017: 4–5.
[56] British Army 2016: A-2.

however, been criticized by veterans who recently watched the videos and suggested that 'that was nothing like my Army career'.[57] During the 2000s, Army recruitment adverts continued to portray Army life as exciting – at times asking people whether they were 'bored of the same routine?' – however they also shifted to focus on the skills and educational benefits of Army service. Such adverts built upon the 1994 slogan 'Be the Best' and presented the Army in a particular way to appeal to children who wanted to gain an education and skills through military service. Rather than appealing to the excitement of army life, or the skills and educational benefits of military service, the latest British Army adverts appeal to inclusivity and notions of belonging.

The Army's 'This Is Belonging' campaign involves five video advertisements that are shown on television and available to view on YouTube. Each video is set around a phrase such as 'having my voice heard', 'still playing the joker' and 'facing my kryptonite'. In each of the 40-second videos a scenario plays out that is based on the experiences of real soldiers. In the 'still playing the joker' video, soldiers are sat in the back of an armoured vehicle. As one soldier falls asleep his colleagues place ration packs on his head and shoulders. As the vehicle moves off he wakes up and jokingly throws the ration packs at his colleague whilst everyone in the armoured vehicle laughs and smiles as the text 'still playing the joker' and then 'this is belonging' are overlaid on the screen. In this particular instance the video echoes the widespread popularity of prank videos on YouTube[58] and appeals to a psychological desire to have fun with friends. Together the series of 'This Is Belonging' videos all depict army life as enjoyable and fun, where friends listen to each other ('having my voice heard') and cheer each other on as they do physical exercises ('facing my kryptonite'). In the context of these videos, a Twitter user recently tweeted 'war recruitment adverts are just lads on tour having top bants'.[59] This 'lads on tour' representation of military life focuses on boys, banter and belonging and serves to suggest that military service is 'the ultimate form of disciplined masculinity'.[60] Other videos, such as the 'expressing my emotions' advertisement where a soldier receives a letter and a tea bag, before rubbing his eyes and looking sad (he never actually cries) are also bound up with gendered logics. This video suggests that whilst traditional soldiering has been seen as the preserve of hyper-masculine men who keep calm and carry on, modern soldiers are allowed to express emotions and be human; even if this expression of emotion only goes as far as a sad face and a sigh.

These adverts have been critiqued by veterans and prominent Army figures as 'political correctness gone mad',[61] due to how they portray the Army as a safe space for everyone regardless of race, religion, gender or sexuality. These critiques are beside the point: indeed, the Army should be an inclusive and diverse place. This campaign is, in my estimate, troubling for three other reasons. First, the campaign is designed to play upon the psychological weaknesses of children and young people. Karmarama, the PR company behind the Army's campaign have explicitly stated that the 'This Is Belonging' campaign

---

[57] Interviewed on BBC One 2018.
[58] Tait 2017.
[59] 'Top bants' is a colloquial reference to banter: language and activities based on jokes, light-hearted teasing and playfulness.
[60] Higate and Hopton 2005: 435.
[61] Army veteran quoted on BBC One 2018.

is designed to exploit people's 'desire to belong', something they identify as 'one of psychology's most powerful drivers'.[62] This campaign is explicitly aimed at children from working-class backgrounds and deprived parts of the UK,[63] and it has been described as 'very cynical' in its attempts to take advantage of young, economically poor people's desire to belong.[64] This relates to a second issue with the 'This Is Belonging' campaign which concerns the ways in which the advertisements gloss over various inequalities in the Army. Younger recruits from disadvantaged backgrounds are over-represented in infantry positions and job roles that involve the highest amount of risk. In addition, there are stark class divisions in the Army's recruitment practices. Private schools and universities are targeted to recruit potential officers (who must be over the age of 18), and poorer neighbourhoods in Scotland, northern England and Wales are targeted for combat roles and low-skilled positions for under-18s.[65] The Army and the advertising company behind the 'This Is Belonging' campaign have outlined that the key target audience for the campaign are 16–24-year-olds in the poorest parts of British society.[66] Third, the campaign presents a sanitized representation of military service and war fighting that is out of step with reality.

The collective of 'This Is Belonging' videos function by playing on the psychological need to belong. In doing so they depict remarkably banal scenes with which most people can empathize. This banality is often at the heart of militarization processes, because as we relate with the soldiers in these videos, as we feel for them and become emotionally attached, 'questioning becomes difficult, and in the process we risk forgetting the politics of what we are watching'.[67] By suggesting that military service is *the* route to belonging to a community – one that is depicted as being diverse, equal, fun and adventurous – the series of 'This Is Belonging' videos exploits the insecurities of young people and projects a sanitized vision of military service. Through this sanitized representation, children come to 'imagine military needs and militaristic presumptions to be not only valuable but also normal'.[68] Consequently, such representations need to be studied and challenged by students and scholars interested in child soldiers.

4. CHANGING BRITAIN'S CHILD SOLDIER CULTURE: ACTION MAN BATTLEFIELD CASUALTIES AND #MAKEIT18

In the global North there are various counter-recruitment activities that are aimed at challenging and disrupting the recruitment practices of military actors that target children. Matthew Rech has recently highlighted how these generally fall into three categories of tactics. According to Rech, the first involves the production and dissemination of

---

[62] Karmarama 2017.
[63] Morris 2017.
[64] Rachel Taylor quoted in Morris 2017.
[65] Veterans for Peace 2017: 6.
[66] Morris 2017.
[67] Åhäll 2016: 164.
[68] Enloe 2000: 3.

information and materials that directly challenge military recruitment practices and are handed out in and outside schools. The second consists of legal challenges whereby activist groups take militaries to court. The third tactic is direct lobbying aimed at governments.[69] In the UK these activities are undertaken by a variety of activist groups such as ForcesWatch, the Quakers, Veterans for Peace, War Resisters International and Child Soldiers International. All of these groups have been involved in these forms of activism, and undoubtedly these tactics are important in challenging the military recruitment of child soldiers in states such as the UK. In their advocacy efforts these groups often frame the issue of British child soldiers as being exploited by the armed forces. Whilst they recognize that young people who enlist in the British military have agency and are not simply passive victims, the advocacy efforts of these groups are keen to point out that: (1) the military targets young people from disadvantaged backgrounds who have few opportunities; (2) the military does not provide these young people with adequate information about military service prior to enlistment; (3) the military unfairly forces under-18s to serve for a longer minimum period than adults; (4) the military recruits under-18s for high-risk roles; and (5) the military does not provide young people in these roles with adequate training and career development opportunities for civilian life after military service. The tactics of these groups often remain focused on the policy and legal domains, and whilst this form of activism is important in ensuring institutional and legal change it often overlooks and does not address the broader cultural forms of militarization which normalize the recruitment of children into the British military. In response to this, I now draw attention to two forms of counter-recruitment activism that do so.

4.1 Action Man Battlefield Casualties

The work of British artist Darren Cullen has recently centred around drawing attention to the British military's recruitment of children. By satirizing military recruitment advertisements, Cullen's work highlights how humour, aesthetics and popular culture can be used in order to counter the military recruitment of child soldiers. Working alongside the activist group Veterans for Peace, Cullen released a short video in 2015 titled *Action Man: Battlefield Casualties*. The video uses Action Man dolls and repurposes them in new scenarios that aim to draw attention to the side of war that is often hidden in military recruitment advertisements and in militarized toys for children. The video is an ironic advertisement for *PTSD Action Man* who comes 'with thousand-yard stare action', *Paralysed Action Man* whose 'legs really don't work' and *Dead Action Man* who has been 'blown to bits by bombs'. The videos provide a darkly comic critique of military recruitment and the ways in which militaries target young people by producing toys and presenting warfare in a clean and sanitized manner. According to Cullen, the videos were produced because 'It's not sick to show what actually happens in a war. It's sick to convince people to join that war without telling them what's possibly going to happen. Recruiting 16-year-olds into the army is sick.'[70] The *Action Man: Battlefield Casualties* video is available to view on the website battlefieldcasualties.co.uk, which also features more information about British

---

[69] Rech 2014: 253–6.
[70] Cullen quoted in Gilmour 2015.

military recruitment and encourages visitors to write to their MP and 'and ask them to put a stop to child recruitment in the British armed forces'.[71]

The video produced by Veterans for Peace and Darren Cullen therefore contributes to two traditional forms of counter-recruitment activism by providing information and by facilitating the lobbying of policy-makers. However, it also goes beyond these traditional forms in that it presents information and arguments in novel ways. This is done in a satirical fashion through the medium of popular culture. In this instance that form of popular culture is a social media video. Cullen's other work – such as his *Army: Be the Meat* comic book – also challenges military recruitment by drawing upon other forms of popular culture such as comic books and artistic prints. This suggests that in order to challenge the military recruitment of children, activists can and should deploy forms of popular culture in order to communicate with audiences in ways that are not based purely on formal information providing and rational argumentation. The national and international press coverage that the *Action Man: Battlefield Casualties* has received, alongside the 17,000 shares of the video on social media, demonstrate that such forms of counter-recruitment activity can be an effective way of engaging audiences and can perhaps contribute to changing attitudes about the military recruitment of children.

4.2 #MakeIt18

In early 2017 the youth organization of the Scottish National Party adopted a motion to commit their party to raising the age of British military recruitment to 18. This involved a campaign that utilized the traditional tactics of information sharing and political lobbying as the SNP Youth presented and defended a motion to their party's annual conference. The campaign also invoked a much wider form of cultural outreach that was designed to engage with young people through the media and through social networks. Throughout 2017 members of the SNP Youth submitted press releases to local and national press outlets in order to challenge the British military recruitment of under-18s. Further to this, SNP Youth activists utilized blogs, podcasts and social media to directly engage with young people. This social media campaign was built around the hashtag #MakeIt18 and involved activists highlighting how they themselves were targeted by military recruiters and drew attention to how 16-year-olds were unable to buy military video games such as *Call of Duty* but were able to join the military. Eye-catching infographics were also used to show popular support for raising the minimum age of military recruitment, and young activists shared selfies where they held signs featuring #MakeIt18. On the day that the SNP Youth motion was presented to the SNP conference, the motion was presented by the SNP Youth Convenor Rhiannon Spear, and supported by a cohort of other young activists such as Cailyn McMahon and Keir Low, who spoke about how they themselves had been targeted by military recruiters whilst under the age of 18. Their motion was opposed by the SNP's defence spokesperson Stewart McDonald MP, Carol Monaghan MP and other members of the SNP (only one of whom was below the age of 30). Despite this opposition from eminent and experienced politicians, the SNP Youth's motion to

---

[71] Veterans for Peace 2015.

commit the party to raising the age of military recruitment to 18 was supported by a sizable majority of members and is now SNP party policy.

The SNP Youth's campaign underscores two important issues for counter-recruitment activists and those who wish to challenge the military recruitment of child soldiers. First, beyond information sharing, legal campaigns and political lobbying, there is a need for cultural forms of activism that utilize the press and social media in order to directly address and challenge Britain's child soldier culture. Second, there is also a need for young people to formulate and lead their own campaigns in order to highlight how and why military recruitment practices need to change. In this case, this involved an explicitly grassroots approach, where the SNP youth activists themselves visited and talked about their motion at most SNP constituency branches prior to the SNP conference. By drawing upon social media and by ensuring that it was clear that their #MakeIt18 campaign was a grassroots campaign by and for young people, the SNP Youth were able to complement their more traditional forms of political lobbying and have ensured that the largest political party in Scotland is committed to raising the age of military recruitment to 18.

5. CONCLUSION

As the British military continues to recruit 16- and 17-year-olds, whilst also using toys, social media and traditional forms of media to attract children as young as five to military careers, it is imperative that the British military be included in debates around child soldiers. This chapter has demonstrated this by noting that transnational actors recognize anyone under 18 as a child, and anyone serving in the military under the age of 18 as a child soldier, regardless of whether they fight on the frontline or not. Arguments in defence of British military recruitment aimed at 16- and 17-year-olds are – in my view – flawed and based on problematic assumptions that do not reflect the realities of military service for these young people. The MoD themselves state that under-18s are recruited in order to make up a shortfall in the number of infantry soldiers. This is the most dangerous role in the military, and research proves that those who join the military under 18 are more likely to be deployed in dangerous combat roles when they are 18. Further to this, under-18 recruits are more at risk of mental health problems and have limited development and skill opportunities.

In light of this, the minimum age of military recruitment should be raised to 18 in the UK.[72] The same could also be said for other states that continue to recruit 16- and 17-year-olds, such as the USA and Australia. In order to change this there is a need to overcome the child soldier culture that persists in these places. This child soldier culture serves to normalize military careers for young people and suggests that the use of military force is 'good, natural and necessary'.[73] Military actors use forms of popular culture in order to recruit young people, and to counter this it is vital to include such forms of militarization in debates about child soldiers.[74] Child soldiers should not simply be seen as

---

[72] For a different perspective, see Rosen in this volume.
[73] Jackson 2016.
[74] Lee-Koo 2011; Harding and Kershner 2017.

a problem for the global South, and scholars and policy-makers should critique, challenge and work towards changing the military recruitment of under-18s in the global North. Addressing the issue of child soldiers in states such as the UK requires going beyond traditional forms of counter-recruitment activism that only focus on information sharing, legal challenges and political lobbying. These are limited in overcoming the permeation of militarization in popular culture. As the British military's production of toys and recruitment activities such as the 'This Is Belonging' campaign demonstrate, militaries have few qualms about using popular culture to exploit the psychological vulnerabilities and desires of young people. In highlighting how perverse this is, and by using forms of popular culture to do so, the likes of Darren Cullen and the SNP Youth have shown that new and novel forms of counter-recruitment activism can be effective in challenging and changing Britain's child soldier culture. Furthermore, public opinion in Britain is in favour of raising the minimum age of military recruitment. One recent poll showed that 77 per cent of respondents supported changing the minimum military recruitment age to 18.[75] By including the British military in debates about child soldiers, and by continuing diverse forms of counter-recruitment activism, a change in the age of military recruitment and in the broader child soldier culture is not only desirable, but increasingly possible.

REFERENCED WORKS

Åhäll, L. 2016. 'The Dance of Militarisation: A Feminist Security Studies Take on "The Political"' 4 *Critical Studies on Security* 154

Armstrong, S. 2007. 'Britain's Child Army', *New Statesman* [available at: https://www.newstatesman.com/politics/2007/02/british-army-recruitment-iraq (accessed 5 January 2018)]

Banham, C. 2013. 'Legitimising War in a Changing Media Landscape' 67 *Australian Journal of International Affairs* 605

Basham, V.M. 2016a. 'Gender, Race, Militarism and Remembrance: The Everyday Geopolitics of the Poppy' 23 *Gender, Place & Culture* 883

Basham, V.M. 2016b. 'Raising an Army: The Geopolitics of Militarizing the Lives of Working-Class Boys in an Age of Austerity' 10 *International Political Sociology* 258

Baudrillard, J. 1995. *The Gulf War Did Not Take Place* (Bloomington: Indiana University Press)

BBC 2018. 'Army Ads "Won't Appeal to New Soldiers"', *BBC News* (10 January) [available at: http://www.bbc.co.uk/news/uk-42629529 (accessed 3 February 2018)]

BBC One 2018. 'The One Show' [available at: https://www.bbc.co.uk/iplayer/episode/b09p1j9p/the-one-show-24012018 (accessed 3 February 2018)]

Beier, J.M. 2011. 'Introduction', in J.M. Beier (ed.), *The Militarization of Childhood: Thinking Beyond the Global South* (New York: Palgrave Macmillan) 1

Bourke, P.J. 2014. *Wounding the World: How Military Violence and War-Play Invade our Lives* (London: Virago)

British Army 2016. 'Army Digital Strategy' [available at: https://www.whatdotheyknow.com/request/318806/response/789192/attach/4/20160330%20FOI02603%2076845%20Raffal%20Digital%20Annex%20A%20O.pdf (accessed 3 February 2018)]

Butler, J. 2010. *Frames of War: When is Life Grievable?* (London: Verso)

Child Soldiers International 2015. Child Soldiers International vs. Secretary of State for Defence [available at: https://www.child-soldiers.org/news/judgment-child-soldiers-international-vs-secretary-of-state-for-defence (accessed 6 February 2018)]

Child Soldiers International 2016a. 'The British Armed Forces: Why Parental Consent Safeguards are Inadequate' [available at: https://www.child-soldiers.org/Shop/briefing-why-parental-consent-safeguards-are-inadequate-1 (accessed 6 February 2018)]

Child Soldiers International 2016b. 'The British Armed Forces: Why Raising the Recruitment Age Would

---

[75] Hill 2016.

Benefit Everyone' [available at: https://www.child-soldiers.org/shop/the-british-armed-forces-why-raising-the-recruitment-age-would-benefit-everyone (accessed 6 February 2018)]

Crilley, R. 2016a. 'Counter-Recruitment and Anti-Military Organizing: Lessons from the Field' 2 *Critical Military Studies* 267

Crilley, R. 2016b. 'Like and Share Forces: Making Sense of Military Social Media Sites', in C. Hamilton and L.J. Shepherd, *Understanding Popular Culture and World Politics in the Digital Age* (London: Routledge) 51

Dallaire, R. 2011. *They Fight Like Soldiers, They Die Like Children* (London: Random House)

Denov, M.S. 2010. *Child Soldiers: Sierra Leone's Revolutionary United Front* (Cambridge: Cambridge University Press)

Der Derian, J. 2009. *Virtuous War: Mapping the Military-Industrial-Media-Entertainment Network* (London: Routledge)

Drumbl, M.A. 2012. *Reimagining Child Soldiers in International Law and Policy* (Oxford: Oxford University Press)

Enloe, C. 2000. *Maneuvers: The International Politics of Militarizing Women's Lives* (Berkeley: University of California Press)

Francois, M. 2017. *'Filling the Ranks': A Report for the Prime Minister on the State of Recruiting into the United Kingdom Armed Forces* [available at: https://www.markfrancois.com/filling-ranks (accessed 6 February 2018)]

Gilmour, C. 2015. 'War Veterans Made Some Dark Films to Protest the British Army's Recruitment of Child Soldiers' [available at: https://www.vice.com/en_uk/article/xd7dba/action-man-battlefield-casualties-ptsed-soldiers-348 (accessed 7 February 2018)]

Harding, S. and Kershner, S. 2015. *Counter-Recruitment and the Campaign to Demilitarize Public Schools* (London: Palgrave)

Harding, S. and Kershner, S. 2017. '"A Borderline Issue": Are There Child Soldiers in the United States?' *Journal of Human Rights* (Online First) 1

Higate, P. and Hopton, J. 2005. 'War, Militarism, and Masculinities', in M.S. Kimmel, J. Hearn and R. Connell (eds), *Handbook of Studies on Men and Masculinities* (London: Sage) 432

Hill, A. 2016. 'Under-18s in Army "Face Greater Injury, Death and Mental Health Risks"' [available at: http://www.theguardian.com/uk-news/2016/oct/18/under-18s-in-army-face-greater-injury-death-and-mental-health-risks (accessed 7 February 2018)]

HM Armed Forces 2018a. 'HM Armed Forces Toys & Action Figures: Character Building' [available at: http://www.hmarmedforces.com/characterbuilding.htm (accessed 5 January 2018)]

HM Armed Forces 2018b. 'HM Armed Forces Toys & HM Armed Forces Action Figures' [available at: http://www.hmarmedforces.com/index.html (accessed 5 January 2018)]

House of Commons Defence Committee 2008. *Recruiting and Retaining Armed Forces Personnel: Fourteenth Report of Session 2007–08; Report, Together with Formal Minutes, Oral and Written Evidence* (London: The House of Commons)

Ingham, S. 2014. *The Military Covenant: Its Impact on Civil–Military Relations in Britain* (London: Routledge)

Jackson, S.T. 2016. 'Marketing Militarism in the Digital Age', in L.J. Shepherd and C. Hamilton (eds), *Understanding Popular Culture and World Politics in the Digital Age* (London: Routledge) 68

Karmarama 2017. 'Army: This Is Belonging', in: *Karmarama* [available at: https://www.karmarama.com/work/this-is-belonging/ (accessed 9 February 2018)]

Kemp, R. 2014. 'Female Soldiers Just Lack the Killer Instinct' [available at: http://richard-kemp.com/female-soldiers-just-lack-the-killer-instinct/ (accessed 3 February 2018)]

Lee-Koo, K. 2011. 'Horror and Hope: (Re)presenting Militarised Children in Global North–South Relations' 32 *Third World Quarterly* 725

Ministry of Defence 2017a. 'Freedom of Information Request: Personnel Recruited Under the Age of 18' [available at: https://www.gov.uk/government/uploads/system/uploads/attachment_data/file/659984/2017-10006.pdf. (accessed 5 January 2018)]

Ministry of Defence 2017b. 'UK Armed Forces Monthly Service Personnel Statistics 1 October 2017' [available at: https://www.gov.uk/government/statistics/uk-armed-forces-monthly-service-personnel-statistics-2017 (accessed 5 January 2018)]

Morris, S. 2017. 'British Army is Targeting Working-Class Young People, Report Shows', *The Guardian* (9 July) [available at: http://www.theguardian.com/uk-news/2017/jul/09/british-army-is-targeting-working-class-young-people-report-shows (accessed 7 February 2018)]

OFCOM 2017. 'Children and Parents: Media Use and Attitudes Report 2017' [available at: https://www.ofcom.org.uk/research-and-data/media-literacy-research/childrens/children-parents-2017 (accessed 9 February 2018)]

politics.co.uk 2012. 'Report Promotes National Service for the Poor, says NASUWT' [available at: http://www.politics.co.uk/opinion-formers/nasuwt-the-teachers-union/article/report-promotes-national-service-for-the-poor-says-nasuwt (accessed 5 January 2018)]

Rech, M.F. 2014. 'Recruitment, Counter-Recruitment and Critical Military Studies' 4 *Global Discourse* 244

Rech, M.F. 2017. 'Children, Young People, and the Everyday Geopolitics of British Military Recruitment', in M.C. Benwell and P. Hopkins (eds), *Children, Young People and Critical Geopolitics* (Abingdon: Routledge) 45

Sangster, E. 2013. 'The Military's Influence in UK Education', in O. Everett (ed.), *Sowing Seeds: The Militarisation of Youth and How to Counter It* (London: War Resisters' International) 86
Saville Roberts, L. and Taylor, R. 2018. 'The British Army is Targeting Teenagers in Wales – It Must Stop', in *Nation.Cymru* (18 January) [available at: https://nation.cymru/2018/the-british-army-is-targeting-teenagers-in-wales-it-must-stop/ (accessed 6 February 2018)]
Shepler, S.A. 2005. *Conflicted Childhoods: Fighting Over Child Soldiers in Sierra Leone* (Berkeley: University of California Press)
Singer, P.W. 2006. *Children at War* (Berkeley: University of California Press)
Stahl, R. 2010. *Militainment, Inc.: War, Media, and Popular Culture* (London: Routledge)
Statista 2017. 'U.S. Snapchat Users Demographics 2016' [available at: https://www.statista.com/statistics/326452/snapchat-age-group-usa/ (accessed 9 February 2018)]
Strand, S. and Berndtsson, J. 2015. 'Recruiting the "Enterprising Soldier": Military Recruitment Discourses in Sweden and the United Kingdom' 1 *Critical Military Studies* 233
Tait, A. 2017. '"It's Just a Prank, Bro": Inside YouTube's Most Twisted Genre', *New Statesman* (21 April) [available at: https://www.newstatesman.com/science-tech/internet/2017/04/its-just-prank-bro-inside-youtubes-most-twisted-genre (accessed 5 January 2018)]
Taylor, R. and Gee, D. 2016. 'The British Army Should Stop Recruiting 16-Year-Olds' (Child Soldiers International) [available at: https://www.child-soldiers.org/News/blog-the-british-army-should-stop-recruiting-16-year-olds (accessed 1 March 2018)]
Tidy, J. 2015. 'Forces Sauces and Eggs for Soldiers: Food, Nostalgia, and the Rehabilitation of the British Military' 1 *Critical Military Studies* 220
Veterans for Peace 2015. 'Action Man: Battlefield Casualties – A Veterans for Peace UK Film', in *Action Man: Battlefield Casualties* [available at: http://battlefieldcasualties.co.uk (accessed 7 January 2018)]
Veterans for Peace 2017. 'The First Ambush? Effects of Army Training and Employment' [available at: http://vfpuk.org/2017/report-the-first-ambush/ (accessed 9 February 2018)]

PART II

CONDUCT: AGENCY, CAPACITY AND RESILIENCE

7. Child soldiers in historical and comparative perspective: creating a space for data-driven analysis
David M. Rosen

In this chapter, I argue that the heart of the modern child soldier crisis is a problem of place, context and imagination. Despite the deeply felt concerns of humanitarian, human rights and children's rights organizations, and the embodiment of these concerns in contemporary international criminal law, there are far fewer child soldiers in the world today than there were in the past. Indeed, the evidence makes plain that the contemporary number of children under arms is a fraction of the vast numbers of children who had fought as soldiers in centuries past. Clear analysis of the actual circumstances and experiences of child soldiers has been made difficult by the dominance of narratives that confound evidence-based analysis.

Children's rights advocates consider the persistence of the use of child soldiers in conflicts across the globe to constitute a central problem. Frequently they understand the presence of children in the military to be a modern-day aberration.[1] But current understanding of child soldiers has been distorted by a kind of historical amnesia, which has erased the long history of recruitment of youngsters into the armies of the West and the factors which significantly curtailed child recruitment. Throughout much of the eighteenth and nineteenth centuries, children and young people were an unremarkable feature of military life. By the middle of the nineteenth century, powerful new ideas about children and childhood began to put pressure on the military recruitment of youngsters. The idea that childhood is a highly distinct stage of life characterized by innocence, vulnerability and the need for protection remains central to the Western understanding of the child. This concept has increasingly rendered childhood and military life incompatible in the public imagination. But these ideas alone did not bring about changes in child recruitment. Child recruitment was radically curtailed only when rich and powerful nation states such as the United States and Great Britain organized highly rationalized bureaucratized forms of national registration and conscription as part of the machinery of mass warfare.

To be sure, some voluntary child enlistment – but not conscription – still takes place in Western armies, including Germany, the United Kingdom and the United States: both Germany and the United States allow 17-year-olds to enlist, and the United Kingdom allows 16-year-olds to enlist.[2] Enlistment requires parental consent and precludes enlistees from direct participation in hostilities. This form of recruitment remains lawful under current international criminal law as well as the key children's rights treaties regulating child recruitment, the Optional Protocol to the Convention on the Rights of the Child on the Involvement of Children in Armed Conflict (OPAC) for those states that have

---

[1] Machel 1996.
[2] See Crilley in this volume.

filed declarations thereto.[3] Nevertheless, many observers and children's rights advocates still object to the lawful recruitment of youngsters in the West, even if they are excluded from combat. These objections are based less on concerns about the potential harm to these child soldiers than on the belief that the West should serve as a role model for the suppression of child recruitment elsewhere in the world.[4]

A comprehensive analysis of child recruitment requires an appreciation of several key elements. First, the armed forces of the West were once major recruiters of child soldiers, but over the last century, child soldiers have substantially disappeared from the ranks of Western and European armed forces and groups, and almost entirely from their actual combat forces. Child soldiers now fight almost exclusively in the poorest nations on earth. This shift was a long, complicated and uneven process, but the result is that child soldiers now participate in conflict on only one side of the great North–South socio-economic and political divide; they are almost exclusively in the part of the world that has half of the world's population and only one-fifth of the world's income.

Second, with some notable exceptions, such as Myanmar, today's child soldiers are predominantly recruited not by the armed forces of nation states, but by a variety of armed groups – rebels, freedom fighters, militias, terrorists and other groups that stand outside the system of formal state recruitment. This phenomenon is not new. In the Continental Army that fought the British during the American Revolution, the basic rank and file rebel foot soldiers were drawn from the young and the poor. Understanding the meaning and mechanisms of recruitment for both recruiters and recruited is central to understanding the involvement of children in armed conflicts from Africa to the Middle East.

Third, there have been major geographical shifts in patterns of recruitment. When the issue of child soldiers first gained public attention, the focus was largely on sub-Saharan Africa. The criminal prosecutions of recruiters of child soldiers that began both with the creation of the Special Court for Sierra Leone and the establishment of the International Criminal Court resulted in indictments and convictions against child recruiters from Liberia, Sierra Leone, northern Uganda and the Democratic Republic of the Congo. Even today, non-state actors in the DRC and the Central African Republic continue to recruit children. But the vast majority of armed groups recruiting children are now spread across North Africa, the Sahel, the Horn of Africa, the Middle East and South and South East Asia.[5] The recruitment of children has tracked the patterns of rebellion and revolt across the globe.

1. HISTORICAL PATTERNS OF RECRUITMENT

One useful way to think about child recruitment is to look at past practices. While there is no comprehensive database available for scholars, those instances in which data are available are particularly instructive. During the American Revolution, the armies, militias

---

[3] In the fiscal years 2013–2015 the United States recruited 49,035 (35,581 males and 13,454 females) 17-year-olds or about 6 per cent of its total voluntary enlistments. United States Department of State 2016.
[4] The Local 2018.
[5] See also Bloom in this volume; Casey-Maslen in this volume.

and partisan groups of both sides were filled with youngsters of all ages. Colonial militias played a vital role in the emerging youth culture in America. Organized in opposition to dominant Puritan values, youth culture began to take shape around militia training days, which afforded young people the opportunity to congregate, and (to the alarm of many adults), allowed youngsters to meet, smoke, carouse and swagger.[6] Between 30 and 40 per cent of adolescent males participated in armed conflict between 1740 and 1781.[7] Indeed, American Revolutionary leaders were much younger than loyalist leaders, and local militias were often organized at the nine colleges of the colonies including the then College of New Jersey (Princeton), New College (Harvard) and the Collegiate School (Yale), which were themselves cauldrons of revolutionary thinking.[8] Teenagers played a major role in American resistance to British rule. Between 1765 and 1769 at least 150 anti-British riots occurred in the American colonies – rioting mobs were filled with teenage apprentices and youthful labourers.[9] The focus of recruitment was on boys 16 years of age or older, but the Continental Army had no fixed policy as to who could serve as soldiers.[10]

Teenagers filled the ranks of the revolutionary forces, which were composed largely of men and boys drawn from the poor, the young, the marginal and the unfree.[11] With half the American population under age 16, it was not surprising that the Continental Army was filled with boys of every age.[12] Because of the fragmentary nature of record keeping during the American Revolution, it is not possible to fully know the precise age profile of all patriot troops during the American Revolution. Nevertheless, historians have been able to reconstruct the age distribution of groups of soldiers at particular times and places during the Revolution. For example, Caroline Cox's recent analysis of pension applications and memoirs of former revolutionary soldiers reveals the pervasive presence of boy soldiers under age 16 in the American Revolution.[13] Her data show that many of these soldiers were between 13 and 15 years of age and some were as young as nine or ten.[14]

Other data indicates a similar pattern. For example, of the 299 soldiers in General Smallwood's Maryland line, 76 (25.4%) were between the ages of 14 and 19.[15] The records of the many regiments camped at Valley Forge with Washington during the winter of 1777–1778, moreover, show that many youngsters from all over the country enrolled in regiments. In the 1st to 8th Connecticut regiments, 179 out of 655 soldiers (27.3%) were between the ages of 12 and 17. In the nine companies of the NY 2nd Regiment, 52 of 188 soldiers (27.6%) were between the ages of 12 and 17. In Rhode Island's 1st and 2nd Regiments, 35 of 109 (32%) were between the ages of 13 and 17. Of the 922 soldiers of the Pennsylvania Line of the Continental Army between 1775 and 1783, 113 (12%) were between the ages of 10 and 17. The age range of soldiers serving in the Revolutionary

---

[6] Mintz 2004: 29.
[7] Ibid.: 51. See also Selesky 1987.
[8] Mintz 2004: 69; Cremin 1970.
[9] Mintz 2004: 62.
[10] Royster 1996: 34.
[11] Mintz 2004: 63.
[12] Ibid.: 62.
[13] Cox 2009: 18.
[14] Cox 2016: 7–8.
[15] Papenfuse and Stiverson 1973: 117–32.

War was far wider than those of modern armies. In the Pennsylvania Line, there were four youngsters aged 10 and one man who was 73. The vast majority of young soldiers across the militias and regiments of the revolutionary forces were 15, 16 or 17 years old. Many of the youngest were fifers and drummers, but many also served as ordinary private soldiers. The age ranges differ to some degree by regional and other circumstances, but it is clear that the armies of the revolution were filled with youngsters under 18.[16]

Many of the regular foot soldiers in the Continental Army were significantly younger than those serving in the British armed forces, a pattern common in rebel armed groups even today. Baron Ludwig von Closen, an aide-de-camp of General Rochembeau (who commanded 7,000 French troops in the Continental Army), stated: 'I admire the American troops tremendously! It is incredible that men of every age, even children of fifteen, of whites and blacks, almost naked, unpaid, and rather poorly fed, can march so well and withstand fire so steadfastly.'[17] This all makes clear that children and teenagers were a regular and unremarkable part of the armed forces of the American Revolution.

Beyond this aggregate data, many individual youngsters stand out. Perhaps the best description of life in the Continental Army was written by Joseph Plumb Martin, who was only 15 years old when he enlisted along with many of his age-mates. In his autobiography *Private Yankee Doodle* Martin describes his urge to enlist and how he frequented the 'rendezvous' where many of his 'young associates' would join up. Of his decision to enlist, he said, 'I had obtained my heart's desire.'[18] Daniel Granger, a 13-year-old Revolutionary War soldier, wrote a lengthy memoir of his service.[19] Granger was involved in several battles, witnessed the execution of deserters and others and otherwise experienced all the pleasures and privations of an ordinary soldier. What is remarkable about Granger's memoir is how his age was seen as unremarkable.

Another boy soldier, Peter Francisco, joined the 10th Virginia Regiment at age 16 and became a widely known hero of the American Revolution. Because of his great strength and size, he was called the 'Virginia Giant' or the 'Hercules of Virginia' and fought in many battles.[20] He died in 1831 as a widely celebrated hero and folk legend, although today – along with most of the common soldiers of the American Revolution – he is largely forgotten. These are but a few examples of a widespread phenomenon. Given the pull of adventure and the clamour for patriotism, it is little wonder that so many youngsters fought in the revolution.

Available data on the ages of soldiers during the US Civil War (1861–1865) also point to startling mixtures of children, youth and adults on the front lines. About 2.1 million soldiers and sailors served in the Union forces during the Civil War, and about 882,000 soldiers and sailors served in the Confederate forces.[21] During the war, Benjamin Gould of the US Sanitary Commission undertook a statistical analysis of the ages of soldiers in the Union army as of 1864. He examined the recorded ages in military rosters of 1,049,457

---

[16] Selesky 1987.
[17] Acomb 2012: 102.
[18] Martin 2002.
[19] Quaifem 1930.
[20] Evans 1905.
[21] McPherson 2003: 306, note 4.

soldiers and concluded that 1.2 per cent of the soldiers were under 18 years of age.[22] But Gould's figures were likely unreliable because of the large numbers of volunteers who misrepresented their age. In 1905, George Kilmer reviewed Gould's data and pointed out a number of statistical anomalies that led him to assert that at least 100,000 boys who were listed as age 18 were often not even 16 or 17. This did not include the thousands who were officially listed as 16 or 17 or younger.[23]

In 1911, Charles King asserted that the Civil War was fought by a 'grand army of boys'. He claimed that 800,000 soldiers were below age 17; 200,000 were under 16; and another 100,000 were no more than 15 years old.[24] King did not explain how he obtained these figures. Moreover, it is difficult to fully accept his estimates, since it would mean that more than half the Union army of 2.1 million would have been below age 18, a figure which clearly seems exaggerated. King however had a long and distinguished career in the US military. He was a West Point graduate who participated in the Civil War and retired from active service in 1879. So even if the figures King presented do not seem entirely correct, it is fair to assume that he had a good understanding of the general age, makeup and composition of military units and that the widespread presence of children and youth in the ranks left a lasting, if only somewhat inaccurate, impression upon him.

More recent evidence nonetheless demonstrates a very large number of children implicated in the US Civil War – even if not quite the numbers suggested by King. In 2006, Pizzaro, Silver and Prause examined the full medical records of recruits from 303 randomly selected companies of the Union Army. These data were drawn from the descriptive roll books in the US National Archives, which yielded a sample of 35,730 individuals. From this sample, a smaller sample of 15,027 recruits who lived until at least 1890 were selected for the analysis of their medical histories.[25] Age at first enlistment was obtained from military records. These ages ranged from 9 to 71 years. This variable was categorized into five age cohorts of approximately equal size to highlight the effect of younger ages: 9 to 17 years (n = 3,013), 18 to 20 years (n = 3,694), 21 to 25 years (n = 3,435), 26 to 30 years (n = 2,225), and 31 years and older (n = 2,660). Of these 15,027, roughly 20 per cent (3013) were recruited into the Union ranks between ages 9 and 17.

Assuming the random sample is representative of all recruits across the armed forces, then approximately 420,000 of the 2.1 million soldiers in the Union forces were between ages 9 and 17. While this number is less than half of what King suggested, it indeed remains as very significant. The number of youngsters in the Union forces alone would have been greater than the numbers of child soldiers often said to exist in the entire world today. While we do not have comparable data for the armies of the Confederacy, it is not unreasonable to assume that the figures would be proportionately similar. The role of young cadets, aged 15–18, from the Virginia Military Institute in the Battle of New Market in 1864 has been widely noted and, as Mark Drumbl has pointed out, their valour is lionized to this day in a mural by Benjamin Clinedinst on the campus of the Virginia

---

[22] Gould 1969: 35.
[23] Kilmer 1905: 269–75.
[24] King 1911: 190.
[25] Pizzaro et al. 2006: 193–200.

Military Institute that shows the heroic cadets (all minors) fighting for the Confederacy in that battle.[26] Accordingly, even if it is impossible to pin down exact numbers, the presence of children and youth throughout the army was a well-known and accepted fact of life throughout the US Civil War. Moreover, these data make plain the significant degree of continuity between past and present in the matter of recruitment.

2. RETHINKING CHILDHOOD

Despite the large numbers of youngsters under arms, profound changes in ideas about children and childhood eventuated in Western life in the period between the American Revolution and the Civil War, and the recruitment of boys into Civil War armies was not without controversy. By the beginnings of the nineteenth century, new ideas about childhood were gradually taking root. These ideas articulated the growing belief that children were purer and more innocent than adults and hence were required to be treated with special care.[27] In both Great Britain and the United States, this new view of childhood prompted courts, legislators and parts of society to express greater concern for the interests of children and to articulate their own ideas about children's interests and needs. Cultural and social distinctions between childhood and adulthood began to harden. Childhood increasingly came to be regarded as a separate and distinct stage of life, characterized by innocence, vulnerability and the need for protection.

None of this happened quickly or evenly. Changing views about childhood spread far more rapidly among the middle class than among the working class and poor. These new sensibilities were overall incorporated into law, which was increasingly fashioned around middle-class sensibilities in both America and Britain.[28] Part of this change included the growing assumption in the West that children should be protected dependents and that military service was incompatible with childhood. Much of American society nonetheless remained indifferent to these legal developments. American society in the nineteenth century was also what Jon Grinspan has called 'the wild years of American youth'.[29] Children, especially boys, were expected to embody democratic virtues, which meant independence, autonomy and the rejection of authority. America was a society that prized assertiveness and risk-taking and there was little or no room for ideas about childhood vulnerability.[30] But these were also times of rapid and chaotic change for children and young people whose lives were often 'rootless, disparate and confusing'.[31] As important as the new ideas about childhood were to become in the twentieth and twenty-first centuries, these ideas were not deeply rooted in American society at the time of the Civil War, and they were set aside as a peacetime luxury. As a result, the Civil War offered up a strange paradox: the increasingly idealized and innocent child was also the object of increasingly aggressive military recruitment.

---

[26] Drumbl 2012: 28.
[27] Dolgin 1997: 1114.
[28] Friedman 2005: 70.
[29] Grinspan 2016: 7.
[30] Grinspan 2014.
[31] Grinspan 2016: 10.

Aggressive military recruitment was at the heart of the volunteer army that formed the core of the fighting forces during the Civil War. At the beginning of the Civil War, the peacetime US Army consisted of about 16,000 volunteers. Voluntary enlistment excluded minors, and recruitment was limited to those over age 21. Nevertheless, minors between 18 and 21 could enlist if they had parental consent. In fact, by 1850 Congress had also addressed a related problem of minors who had managed to evade the consent requirements. That legislation required the Secretary of War to order the discharge of any minor under the age of 21 upon evidence that the enlistment lacked the consent of a parent or guardian. While the statute did not impose a duty upon the army to seek out minors within its ranks, it imposed a duty upon the army to discharge a minor upon presentation of adequate evidence.[32]

The outbreak of the war completely altered this picture. The first major changes to army enlistment came in 1862, after President Lincoln issued General War Order No 1. This Order required US army forces to move against the southern insurgency. Shortly afterwards Congress repealed the provision of the 1850 law requiring the discharge of minors enlisted without the consent of their parents or guardians. Ostensibly, the new legislation set a minimum age of enlistment by declaring that no person under the age of 18 shall be recruited into the United States service. As a practical matter, however, the new legislation actually opened the door to underage enlistment by providing that the age sworn to by an enlistee at the time of the oath of enlistment would be taken as conclusive as to his age.[33] This meant that whatever age the recruit swore to at the time of enlistment (the so-called 'declared age') would be the final determinant of age, regardless of actual age, and none of these recruits would be subject to mandatory discharge even if their actual age were ultimately revealed. This situation was exacerbated by the fact that, as in previous generations, states and local communities raised volunteer units for the war, and enlisted men and boys and commissioned officers to lead them in accordance with local customs and standards. So, once a youngster got into the army he would remain in service regardless of the circumstances surrounding the recruitment. The need to raise an army of volunteers trumped other considerations. Once a child successfully enlisted, there was no obligation on the part of the military to release that child from military service.

As the war went on, even these relaxed recruitment standards could not fill the army's need for soldiers. A limited form of conscription was introduced, but this had little impact upon the recruitment of youngsters. The Enrollment Act of 1863 introduced conscription for men between ages 20 and 45, but this Act did not create a system of universal conscription. Unlike the national systems of conscription, which would later be established both in Great Britain and the United States during World War I, the real purpose of the Enrollment Act was to coerce or stimulate voluntary enlistment, but not to replace it.[34] Under the Enrollment Act, military conscription was based upon quotas assigned by congressional district. Conscription served to supplement the number of enrolees not otherwise filled by volunteers and members of the state militias.[35]

---

[32] An Act Making Appropriations for the Support of the Army.
[33] An Act Making an Appropriation for Completing the Defenses of Washington.
[34] McPherson 1982: 356.
[35] Enrollment Act 1863.

3. NATIONAL CONSCRIPTION: THE GREAT TRANSFORMATION

During World War I (1914–1918), both Great Britain and the United States introduced national conscription. By then, both countries were economic powerhouses with national institutions capable of registering and mobilizing millions of people for the war effort. Britain did not mandate conscription at the beginning of World War I. At the outbreak of the war in the summer of 1914, the British Army was roughly the same army of volunteers that had fought in the many colonial wars it had initiated in the nineteenth century. Army regulations provided that volunteers had to be at least 18 years old and that only those over 19 could be sent overseas to fight. At the beginning of the war, Britain implemented a nationwide campaign to recruit soldiers. A wave of patriotic and anti-German sentiment engulfed the country, so recruits flooded the army.

But the patriotic outburst for what many believed would be a short war was not long-lived. It was soon evident that mass warfare could not be sustained on a voluntary basis. Two key problems loomed large. First, there was a pressing need to mobilize populations for mass warfare without disrupting and damaging the national economy. It was plain that the sudden flood of men and boys moving from the factory floor to the front lines had seriously affected war production. Second, as the war dragged on and casualties reached grotesque proportions, voluntary enlistment rates began to plummet. Britain was desperate for recruits. It became clear that the chaotic boom and bust character of voluntary recruitment was not sufficient for this type of mass warfare, which demanded a more efficient bureaucratic system of organizing men and allocating labour between the shop floor and the trenches. Long before the war, supporters of mandatory national service had advocated national conscription, but Great Britain was finally moved to embrace the concept by the inability of the volunteer army to meet the combined needs of both full-scale national mobilization and efficient wartime production.

By 1915, conscription was in the air and Britain instituted a national registration system under the National Registration Act that required all persons between 15 and 65 to register.[36] This was organized in much the same manner as a national census with data collected and verified not by the military, but by the general population registration offices located throughout England, Ireland, Scotland and Wales; these bureaucracies were well-versed in managing vital statistics.[37] By 1916, Britain's volunteer army was abandoned. Parliament introduced national conscription for all single men aged between 18 and 40.

Conscription had a profound impact upon the recruitment of child soldiers in that it brought a virtual halt to the systematic enlistment of underage soldiers that prevailed in the volunteer armies of the past. Enterprising youngsters with the will to enrol could always figure out a means of disguising their true ages and evading enlistment regulations, but national conscription ended institutional incentives to enrol the young. In this context, the new ideas about childhood that emerged in the nineteenth century could be effectively implemented. The entire logic of recruitment changed with conscription. When

---

[36] National Registration Act 1915.
[37] Elliot 2010: 145.

the volunteer army ended in Great Britain, there simply was no longer any pressing need to systematically recruit youngsters.

Underage enlistment was at its highest at the beginning of the war, with between 10 and 15 per cent of recruits being underage.[38] Young people could enlist without providing any documentation relating to age, so boys between the ages of 14 and 18 joined the steady stream into the ranks and formed a substantial portion of the overseas fighting forces.[39] During the first two years of the war, when volunteerism was the norm, the army was filled with boy soldiers. Boys from all over the country sought to enlist in violation of army regulations. In the great rush to recruit, scant attention was paid any serious method of determining age. The army, hungry for soldiers, was a reluctant enforcer of its own regulations. During the course of the war some 8.9 million individuals served and, by conservative estimates, some 250,000 soldiers were underage. About 55 per cent of these children were killed or wounded during the war.[40] Thus in World War I, Great Britain alone recruited as many child soldiers as are estimated to exist in the world today.

4. MASS WARFARE, CONSCRIPTION AND THE END OF CHILD RECRUITMENT

One of the many arguments made in support of national conscription was that it would eliminate the problem of having large numbers of boy soldiers in the British military. This argument, however, was hardly the decisive factor in adopting conscription. Advocates of conscription asserted that the presence of underage boys had a pernicious effect upon the army. In particular, they argued that the sight of wounded boys evoked both compassion and mothering impulses among the adult troops, which interfered with their duties. They also argued that the killing and wounding of boys gave ammunition to views of pacifists and other so-called 'peace at any price' advocates and thereby undermined the war effort. In addition, conscription advocates claimed that the open lying and deceit involved in the recruitment of underage boys undermined the faith of the British people in the army and other institutions.

On the other side of the argument, however, many of those who opposed conscription also saw the recruitment of youngsters as an evil. Some argued that compulsory military service constituted a new form of tyranny against a free-born people and reflected a growing militarism in the state. In this light, the recruitment of underage boys was another sign that democracy had succumbed to militarism.

Before conscription was instituted, the War Office had rejected all attempts to modify recruitment policies. The War Office spurned the idea that enlistees be required to provide birth certificates to prove their eligibility for voluntary enlistment. It did so on the grounds of administrative efficiency and the overwork and confusion in governmental offices required to produce such records. The War Office rebuffed the

---

[38] Van Emden 2005: 319.
[39] Ibid.: 321.
[40] Ibid.

view that young recruits be accepted provisionally until actual birth certificates were obtained.[41] National registration and conscription brought a close to all these issues and thereby rang the death knell for the recruitment of boy soldiers. Those boys recruited before conscription was instituted were rarely released from service, but with conscription the flow of youngsters into the military came to a sudden and decisive end.

The American experience with recruitment in World War I was quite different from that of the British. The United States entered the war on 6 April 1917, almost three years after the war began. The US remained in the war until it ended on 11 November 1918 and therefore participated for a period of about 17 months in total. In the United States, unlike in Britain, there was no rush to volunteer at the beginning of the country's involvement in the conflict. President Wilson's original hopes to create a volunteer army were quickly dashed when only 73,000 out of the expected 1,000,000 volunteers actually enlisted. As a result, Congress passed the Selective Service Act of 1917. Between 1917 and the end of the war, the United States drafted nearly 2.8 million men. The total number raised was about 4.1 million, including voluntary enlistments and those who were part of the pre-war military.[42] The vast majority of American troops were conscripts and the new selective service system created a national system of registration in which all United States male citizens or persons who had declared their intention to become citizens between the ages of 21 and 35 were required to register for the draft. The US set the age of conscription at 21 and voluntary enlistment at 18. By 1918 Congress amended the Selective Service Act to require the registration of 18-year-olds. Selective service did not completely eliminate underage soldiers. Some youngsters continued to misrepresent their way into military service, but conscription allowed for the mass mobilization of society and left little need to dip into younger age cohorts for recruits. Turning a blind eye to child enlistment was no longer necessary.

The British Empire mobilized 8,904,467 persons during World War I: of these 908,371 died from battle death, disease and accidents; 2,090,212 were wounded; and 191,652 went missing or were taken prisoner. Total casualties were 3,190,235 persons. In the United States 4,355,000 individuals were mobilized: 116,516 died from battle deaths and other causes; 204,002 were wounded; and 4,500 went missing or were taken prisoner. Total casualties were 323,018 persons. Ironically, in the West, whatever the changing sentiments about children and war may have been, and however heartfelt the idea that childhood was incompatible with war, the recruitment of child soldiers for combat became radically curtailed only with the advent of mass warfare and the implementation of the bureaucratic and highly organized mobilization of the populace for war. Indeed, the horrific irony is that the effectiveness of the system of forced militarization of the entire society is what moved children off the battlefield but sent hundreds of thousands of adults to their deaths.

---

[41] Markham Papers 1915.
[42] Rinaldi 2005: 5.

5. THE MODERN CHILD SOLDIER

Today, millions of people around the world are involved in wars, rebellions, insurgencies and civil conflicts. Although it is widely asserted that between 250,000 and 300,000 child soldiers below the age of 18 are involved in contemporary armed conflicts, there are no reliable statistics to substantiate these numbers. In fact, the same figures have been bandied over and over for several decades, thereby making plain the paucity of real data about this issue. The figure of 300,000 was put forth by advocacy groups promoting a ban on child recruitment. It is very likely that the actual numbers are significantly lower.[43] Nonetheless, whatever the precise number, over the last several decades, the fact remains that many thousands of children have experienced and continue to experience war as soldiers.

The numbers are also very much a product of the definition of who is a child soldier. International criminal law proscribes conscripting, enlisting or using children under age 15 through the imposition of individual penal responsibility on the adult recruiter. This near-universal standard is embodied in the Rome Statute that established the International Criminal Court. Article 8(2)(b)(xxvi), relating to international conflicts, prohibits 'conscripting or enlisting children under the age of fifteen years into the national armed forces or using them to participate actively in hostilities'. Article 8(2)(e)(vii), relating to conflicts not of an international character, prohibits 'conscripting or enlisting children under the age of fifteen years into armed forces or groups or using them to participate actively in hostilities'. Virtually identical standards are found in the Statute of the Special Court for Sierra Leone where Article 4(c) prohibits '[c]onscripting or enlisting children under the age of 15 years into armed forces or groups or using them to participate actively in hostilities'. This standard is also regarded as a rule of customary international law.

The age that triggers individual penal responsibility for illicit recruitment differs from the age of unlawful recruitment for which the state may be held responsible, which is currently 18 in the case of armed groups, and for which there is an advocacy push to raise uniformly to 18 for national armed forces as well.[44] The United Nations and most humanitarian and children's rights groups routinely define a child soldier as anyone under age 18. Because of this discursive shift in the age at which soldiers are considered children, many persons who today are defined as child soldiers would not have been classified as children in years past. Lurking beneath these definitional controversies is a far blurrier and highly contested empirical reality. To give a simple example, as noted earlier, the United States allows youngsters aged 17 to enlist in the military with parental permission. This is fully compliant with US law and the US' treaty obligations. The US does not allow soldiers under 18 to be stationed in war zones. Compliance has not always been perfect, and during the war in Iraq some under-18-year-olds served in a war zone. No doubt some humanitarian organizations would accuse the US of recruiting child soldiers, but when they do so they are asserting their advocacy for the so-called Straight-18 position – a universal ban on the recruitment of persons under age 18 – rather than citing any breach by the United States of any rule of law or treaty obligation.

---

[43] Scott and Reich 2009.
[44] To be clear, the Straight-18 advocacy position also calls for individual penal responsibility to attach to those adults who conscript, enlist or actively use in hostilities children below the age of 18.

I argue that the real issue of modern child soldiers is primarily one of recruitment of children by non-state actors. This is abundantly clear in reports on children in armed conflict issued by the UN Secretary General. As of the 2017 report, only six nation states were designated by the United Nations as recruiters of child soldiers: the Tatmadaw Army of Myanmar (Burma) and its integrated border guard forces; the Afghan National Police; the Somalia National Army; Sudan's Government Security Forces and various allied defence forces and police; South Sudan's Sudan People's Liberation Army; and the Yemeni Armed Forces. Of these, the Afghan Police,[45] the Somalia Army and the Sudan Government Security Forces have already entered into agreements to curb or end child recruitment. In contrast to state recruitment, at least 52 distinct armed groups are now recruiters of child soldiers. Much like rebel groups in the past, they rely heavily upon the young. The vast majority of these armed groups – 39 in fact – are spread across North Africa, the Middle East, the Sahel, the Horn of Africa and South and South East Asia. With the exception of Myanmar and South Sudan, the emergence of these non-state armed groups is directly linked to the turmoil and upheavals in the Islamic world over the last decades. The countries affected by insurgencies are Afghanistan, Iraq, Mali, Nigeria, the Philippines, Somalia, Sudan, Syria and Yemen. South of the Sahel, 13 non-state armed groups are operating in the Central African Republic and the Democratic Republic of the Congo. In the rest of the world, there are only two armed groups, both remnants of the insurgency in Colombia,[46] which are listed as recruiters of child soldiers.[47]

It is, of course, extremely difficult to obtain direct data about the age composition of these armed groups. Such data as do exist suggest more continuity than rupture with historical patterns of recruitment. For example, Dodwell, Milton and Rassler's analysis of 4,600 Islamic State personnel records produced by ISIS (primarily between early 2013 and late 2014) showed that 400 (about 9%) of the foreign fighters flowing into Iraq and Syria were below the age of 18, and among these 41 (less than 1%) were below the age of 15.[48] These records constitute the largest primary source documents of their kind ever uncovered.[49] As a rebel movement aspiring to become a Caliphate, ISIS was a remarkably well-organized entity. The data were primarily composed of one-page processing forms of personal information put into Microsoft PowerPoint templates.[50]

Another recent study by Bloom, Horgan and Winter focuses on the range of ages within this younger category of fighters, although it does not address the issue of the overall percentage of young fighters. This study classified the ages of children and youth depicted in Islamic State's martyrdom propaganda between 2015 and 2016, and specifically included 89 recorded instances of children and young people depicted as martyrs in official Islamic State reports from 1 January 2015 to 31 January 2016.[51] Since the actual ages of those killed were not reported in the propaganda materials, age was inferred by examining photographs of the youngsters, which were classified into the categories of

---

[45] See also Van Engeland in this volume.
[46] See also Jiménez in this volume.
[47] UN Secretary-General 2017.
[48] Dodwell et al. 2016: 5.
[49] Ibid.: 6.
[50] Ibid.: 4.
[51] Bloom et al. 2016: 29–32.

'pre-adolescent' (ages 8 to 12), 'adolescent' (ages 12 to 16), or 'older adolescent' (ages 16 to 21). Based upon these inferences, this research concluded that 6 per cent of the youngsters were pre-adolescent, 34 per cent were adolescent, and 60 per cent were older adolescents.[52] To be sure, inferring age from digital images is a notoriously challenging task. If the accuracy of these inferences is assumed, however, then the evidence would show that the numbers of the very young involved remains relatively low as a percentage of overall recruits and is not remarkably different from volunteer armies of the past.

6. CHILD SOLDIERS: THE SHIFTING TERRAIN OF RHETORIC

The transnationalized understanding of child soldiers is largely grounded in the advocacy-based discourse of humanitarian imperatives, human rights and children's rights, and related law and policy.[53] The mobilization of public sentiment around the issue of child soldiers is partly based on the ability of advocates to manage the public discourse around which issues are discussed and engaged.[54] The very term 'child soldier' is itself an example of a form of a discourse created to frame public discussions. This discourse imagines and posits the existence of a universal child whose development, needs and well-being are all indifferent to context. The most striking features of this image of the child is its mobility, transferability and disconnection from history. Using this model, children's rights advocates have little difficulty in codifying simple and universally applicable bright-line distinctions between childhood and adulthood. In contrast, many fields involved in the study of children, such as anthropology and history, take as their central orientation the idea that there are a multiplicity of concepts of childhood and adulthood, each contextualized by age, ethnicity, gender, history, location and numerous other factors.

Whereas the idea of the 'rights of the child', a concept based upon a putative universal child, seems self-evident and obvious to modern-day children's rights advocates,[55] it may strike anthropologists and historians as facile, tendentious and ethnocentric. Concerns about childhood cast in the language of human rights and humanitarian imperatives tend to overlook the enormity of the social and cultural changes embedded in the transnational restructuring of age categories, thereby concomitantly tending to ignore or demonize historical experiences and cultural contexts.[56]

For rights advocates, aversion to the idea of the child soldier is a simple and logical extension of the concept of a universal child. Indeed, the very concept is intentionally constructed to conflate two contradictory and incompatible terms. The first, 'child', typically refers to a young person between infancy and youth and connotes immaturity, simplicity and an absence of full physical, mental or emotional development. The second,

---

[52] Ibid.: 30 (giving the full details of the methodology).
[53] See Drumbl 2012 for a critical and comprehensive analysis of the legal and policy issues surrounding the recruitment of child soldiers. Other useful sources include McBride 2014; Happold 2005; Waschefort 2014.
[54] Becker 2017.
[55] See also Hanson and Molima in this volume.
[56] Merry 1999: 55–77.

'soldier,' in the context of contemporary professional armies in the West, generally refers to men and women who are skilled warriors. As a result, the term 'child soldier' melds together two very contradictory and powerful ideas, namely the 'innocence' of childhood and the 'evil' of warfare. From the outset, the framing of the discourse renders the very idea of the child soldier both aberrant and abhorrent. The central problem with this view, and the one that has made it extremely difficult to operationalize in practice, is that most child soldiers are adolescents who have been legally redefined as children.

Both humanitarian discourse and international law categorize child soldiers primarily as victims of criminal adult abuse and perceive the child soldier's essential character as one of victimhood and vulnerability. Any variance in the real experience of child soldiers tends to collapse under this essentialist rubric. Clearly, there are some terrible and aberrant cases of child recruitment including the Islamic State in West Africa (Boko Haram), the Lord's Resistance Army in northern Uganda and, in the recent past, the Revolutionary United Front of Sierra Leone. Yet even within these invidious groups, considerable evidence exists of the diversity of experience among the children who end up fighting, making clear that child recruitment is not solely about abduction and abuse.[57] Nevertheless, these horrific cases often serve as proxies for the entire problem of recruitment. The child soldier who volunteers is conflated with the child soldier who is kidnapped; the teenager is conflated with the vulnerable toddler.

The gap between empirical description and humanitarian advocacy is vast. Humanitarian advocates insist that the issue primarily be framed as a matter of childhood innocence distorted and childhood vulnerability subverted by adult culpability. This approach does occasionally yield convictions in international tribunals, and for the worst abusers of children such convictions are appropriate and just, but virtually no ethnographers or other on-the-ground observers of war zones would agree that the issue of child soldiers can be reduced solely to adults abusing and terrifying innocent children into committing violent acts.[58]

Nevertheless, advocates for banning child recruitment equate childhood with vulnerability, and recognizing this equation is central to understanding humanitarian views of the child soldier. Although it is self-evident that young children are both vulnerable and in need of nurturing, it is only by international definition that these attributes of infancy, toddlerhood and early childhood have been extended to apply to all persons under age 18. From the perspective of the essential vulnerability of the child, recruiting child soldiers at any age is seen as the action of abusive and corrupt adults who thereby bring harm to innocent children. It is a model designed primarily to affix blame and assign culpability, and it frames virtually all discussions of child soldiers. In recent years, as Western armed forces have come to engage child soldiers in the Middle East and elsewhere, there has been a splintering of the rhetoric. While advocacy groups still largely focus on images of vulnerable and manipulated children, Western military forces that are faced with combat-ready lethal youngsters have added a new realism to the discussion. There is also an increasing emphasis on children recruited by armed groups labelled as 'terrorist' and

---

[57] See, e.g. Oloya 2013; Allen and Vlassenroot 2010.
[58] See, e.g. Coulter 2008; Denov 2012; Hoffman 2012; Honwana 2006; Jourdan 2011; Rosen 2005; Rosen 2015; Utas 2005; Vigh 2000.

subjecting such 'child terrorists' to severe sanctions.[59] A particularly egregious example of this was the treatment of child detainees in the US wars in Afghanistan and Iraq, where captured child soldiers were sometimes subject to extremely harsh treatment. I will discuss this in greater detail after first unpacking the delicate issue of how to engage with child soldiers on a battlefield.

7. RULES OF ENGAGEMENT WITH CHILDREN IN COMBAT SITUATIONS

Singer has pointed to an incident during the Civil War in Sierra Leone (1991–2001) in which the West Side Boys, a rebel 'rogue militia' that had many child soldiers, captured a 12-man patrol of the British Royal Irish Regiment brought to Sierra Leone in support of the Sierra Leone government. Singer affirms that this group was captured because they hesitated to fire on the child soldiers.[60] While other reasons have also been given for this capture, what is clear is that in the follow-up rescue of the patrol, many members of the rebel force – including child soldiers – were killed.[61]

The potential of engagements with large numbers of child soldiers has led to doctrinal and training changes in Canada. These take the form of a policy called the Canadian Armed Forces Joint Doctrine Note 2017-01 Child Soldiers. The development of this policy was influenced by former Canadian General Roméo Dallaire.[62] Dallaire was the head of UNAMIR (United Nations Assistance Mission for Rwanda) – the tragic entity tasked as the peacekeeping force for Rwanda between 1993 and 1994. UNAMIR did not stop the violence that metastasized into genocide. Dallaire had direct experience of the danger posed by child soldiers in the field and is deeply involved in organizations such as Child Soldiers International that seek to protect children in conflict zones.[63] The Canadian approach tries to balance the safety of its own soldiers with Canada's treaty commitment to the OPAC, which provides that combatants under 18 are entitled to special protection. Similar principles are incorporated into the Vancouver Principles on Peacekeeping and the Prevention of the Recruitment and Use of Child Soldiers, which are designed to operationalize these principles in UN Peacekeeping missions.[64]

But the Joint Doctrine Note makes plain that in any engagement, child soldiers must first and foremost be treated as combatants and not as children. It provides that Canadian forces be given 'clear direction' authorizing the use of force where armed child soldiers pose a valid threat.[65] The Joint Doctrine expresses concern that lightly armed Canadian units may be particularly vulnerable to groups of child soldiers using human wave tactics.[66] It authorizes the use of heavy weapons under these circumstances to counter these

---

[59] O'Neil and van Broeckhoven 2018.
[60] Singer 2001: 40.
[61] NATO 2011: section 5.3.9.
[62] Government of Canada 2017a.
[63] Dallaire 2010.
[64] Government of Canada 2017c.
[65] Government of Canada 2017b: §§ 2011 (b), 2013.
[66] Ibid.: § 2010 (b).

tactics.[67] The doctrine makes clear that Canadian soldiers are now trained to use deadly force when confronted with child soldiers, although it advises that child soldiers may be more easily defeated if adult leadership is sought and engaged. If soldiers ever expressed hesitation to use deadly force against child soldiers, that hesitation is now being mitigated by policy and training.

The second major prong of Canadian policy relates to the detention of child combatants. Canadian doctrine now requires that captured child combatants be held separately from and treated differently than adult combatants. This aligns with the precept of the UN Convention on the Rights of the Child as well as the 'best interests of the child' maxim. Basically, the Canadian doctrine bifurcates the child soldier issue by addressing child combatants together with adults during combat and separating them from adults upon detention. Training in the Canada armed forces focuses on preparing the military to do battle with child combatants, making it clear that armed forces can readily adapt to the presence of child combatants and can prevent the presence of child combatants from reducing soldiers' effectiveness.

8. THE ABUSE OF CHILD DETAINEES

The labelling of rebels and resistance groups as terrorists has often resulted in the widespread criminalization of combatants. One consequence of this is that captured child soldiers are sometimes treated primarily as terrorists and criminals and only reluctantly, if at all, as children in need of protection.[68] The ill-treatment of child detainees by US forces during the wars in Afghanistan and Iraq is instructive on this problem. It is a history that should make us extremely wary of embracing sweeping declarations about Western sensitivities about harming children. Clearly, Canada's detention policies as outlined in the Joint Doctrine highlight the pressing need to protect child soldiers from their captors, but the brutal treatment accorded to some child detainees by US forces illustrates the difficulties of embodying child protection principles in situations where combatant children are a lethal threat to Western forces.

In Afghanistan, virtually all detainees held by the United States, including juveniles, were labelled 'enemy combatants' by the Bush administration.[69] What the Bush administration meant by 'enemy combatant' was an unlawful combatant – essentially a criminal combatant – who would not be entitled to the protections legally afforded to prisoners of war under the Geneva Conventions. Indeed, the Bush administration announced that such combatants would not have even the minimal protections of Common Article 3, the only provision of the Geneva Conventions that was specifically created to provide humane standards for captured unlawful combatants. This was a complete subversion of the application of the laws of war that require captive prisoners to be treated as lawful combatants, and not as criminals, unless they are shown not to be entitled to

---

[67] Ibid.: § 2010 (d)(1).
[68] O'Neil and van Broeckhoven 2018. For discussion on the perception of children in the immigration and asylum context, see Rikhof in this volume.
[69] Executive Office of the President 2001.

prisoner-of-war status. Following Bush's decision, virtually all armed opposition to the US invasion of Afghanistan was criminalized. Moreover, President Bush ordered that when these detainees were put on trial, it would not be practical to 'apply the principles of law and the rules of evidence generally recognized in the trial of criminal cases in the United States district courts'.[70] On 2 February 2002, President Bush issued another order declaring that Common Article 3 of the Geneva Convention did not apply to al-Qaeda or Taliban detainees. These detainees, the President asserted, were not legally entitled to humane treatment.[71] This Presidential order led directly to the abuse of numerous detainees, including children. One of them, Yasser Talal al-Zahrani, hanged himself shortly after arriving at the prison camp.[72] But the most well-known instances are those of two child soldiers who came before US military commissions: Mohamad Jawed and Omar Khadr.

Mohammed Jawad was detained in Afghanistan as a child soldier and charged with attempted murder in relation to US service members. The United States alleged that he threw a hand grenade at a passing American convoy on 17 December 2002. There was a great deal of uncertainty about Jawad's age. No written records existed of his birth. His family claimed that he was 12 years old when he was detained. A bone scan done almost a year after his detention indicated that he was 18 at the time of the scan, which would have made him approximately 17 at the time of detention. Bone scan evidence is often unreliable, so the best that can be said is that he was somewhere between 12 and 17 when he was detained. Jawad was first arrested by the Afghan police and taken to an Afghan police station to be interrogated, where armed Afghan police officers and officials threatened him and his family with death if he did not confess to throwing the hand grenade. He allegedly confessed and was turned over to US authorities. Shortly thereafter, he was interrogated at a US military base, where he allegedly confirmed his confession. Jawad was transferred to the Bagram Theater Internment Facility in Afghanistan and later transported to Guantanamo Bay, where it is undisputed that he was systematically abused.

The abuse of Jawad took place in the context of the widespread ongoing abuse of detainees by the US military in Iraq and Afghanistan and at Guantanamo Bay. The abuses began early in the 'war against terror' and are directly linked to Presidential orders rejecting the legal right of detainees to humane treatment. Among the most extreme examples of abuse were the killings of two Afghan detainees, Mullah Habibullah and Dilawar from the town of Yakubi, who were chained and suspended from the ceiling and beaten to death over a five-day period in December 2002.[73] Both the US Army and the US Senate Armed Services Committee confirmed that these two detainee deaths were homicides.[74]

Because of widespread public reports of abuse of detainees, the Department of Defense initiated an investigation into the allegations. In 2005, Vice Admiral Albert Church, the Navy inspector general, issued a report that investigated cases of substantiated abuse of detainees by military personnel.[75] According to the Church Report, the abuses were

---

[70] Ibid.
[71] Bush 2002.
[72] Ibid.
[73] Jehl 2005.
[74] United States Senate Committee on Armed Services 2008.
[75] United States Department of Defense 2005.

perpetuated by members of all armed services, including active-duty, reserve and National Guard personnel. Most abuses took place in Afghanistan and Iraq, with a smaller number occurring at Guantanamo Bay. The report focused on serious abuse, meaning abuse that had the potential to lead to death or grievous bodily harm. These included actions that fractured or dislocated bones, created deep cuts, or seriously damaged internal organs, as well as sexual assaults and threats of death or grievous bodily harm. The report did not cover lesser injuries to detainees, such as black eyes and bloody noses.[76]

In 2008, the US Department of Justice issued a report of its investigation of FBI involvement in and observations of the interrogations of detainees in Afghanistan and Iraq and at Guantanamo Bay. At Guantanamo Bay, FBI agents saw or became aware of a variety of abusive techniques used against detainees, including depriving detainees of food, water and clothing; exposing them to cold and heat; death threats; short shackling to the floor to induce pain and stress; choking; and strangling. One FBI agent observed a female interrogator bending back the thumb of a detainee and grabbing his genitals while the detainee grimaced in pain.[77] The FBI also reported on a so-called pep rally where FBI agents observed Guantanamo Bay interrogators being told to get as close to the legal limits of torture as possible.[78]

This pattern of abuse was applied to juveniles like Jawad. When Jawad was first transferred to American custody, he was subjected to inhumane and degrading treatment. This pattern of abuse continued when he was transferred to Bagram. In fact, he arrived at Bagram only a few days after Mullah Habibullah and Dilawar from the town of Yakubi were beaten to death by US forces. At Bagram, he was forced into so-called stress positions. His interrogators forcibly hooded him, placed him in physical and linguistic isolation, pushed him down stairs, chained him to a wall for prolonged periods and subjected him to death threats. He also endured sleep deprivation and was so disoriented that he could not tell night from day and was psychologically pressured by the sounds of screams from other prisoners and rumours of other prisoners being beaten to death.

When Jawad was finally transferred to Guantanamo Bay, he was treated as an adult and housed with adults. Moreover, he never received rehabilitation treatment or special education. Instead, military records show that Jawad repeatedly cried and asked for his mother during interrogation, and that he fainted and complained of dizziness and stomach pain but was given an IV and forced to go through interrogation. A psychological assessment by the Behavioral Science Consultation Team at Guantanamo Bay was undertaken. This assessment was not intended for the purpose of treatment, but rather to learn about and exploit his vulnerabilities for further interrogation.

Among the abuses of detainees cited by both the Church Report and the FBI was the sleep deprivation programme dubbed by interrogators and guards as the 'Frequent Flyer Program'. At Guantanamo Bay, the FBI was briefed on the use of this technique, which was designed to disorient detainees so as to make them cooperative. The Detainee Incident Management System records at Guantanamo Bay revealed that Mohamad Jawad was subject to this programme. According to the records, Jawad was shackled

---

[76] Ibid: 88–9.
[77] United States Department of Justice 2008: 175.
[78] Ibid.: 174.

and moved 112 times from cell to cell over a period of two weeks – an average of eight moves a day. His abuse had no purpose, and his former military prosecutor described it as 'gratuitous mistreatment'. Major David Frakt (Jawad's defence counsel) stated that there was no special effort to collect intelligence from Jawad, nor any belief that he actually had any special intelligence. What is more, no interrogations were undertaken around the times he was being tortured. 'The most likely scenario', according to Major Frakt, 'is that they simply decided to torture Mr. Jawad for sport.'[79] The records also revealed that Jawad tried to kill himself by banging his head repeatedly against his cell wall.

The government's case against Jawad received a major setback on 28 October 2008, when Colonel Stephen Henley, the judge of the military commission set to try Jawad, ruled that the admission of guilt that Jawad allegedly had made to the Afghan police at the time of his detention was obtained by torture. According to the Military Commissions Rules of Evidence, statements obtained by torture cannot be admitted into evidence. As a result, any oral or written statements made by Jawad were suppressed.[80] In addition, on 19 November 2008, Henley ruled that statements subsequently made by Jawad to US authorities also were inadmissible as evidence, as they were also the result of the preceding death threats.[81]

Major Frakt petitioned US courts for a writ of habeas corpus, asking for an order that Jawed be released from custody. At the initial hearing, an exasperated Judge Ellen Segal Huvelle described the government case as 'unbelievable'.[82] Referring to Jawad's continued detention without any evidence, she stated, 'This guy has been there seven years, seven years. He might have been taken there at the age of maybe 12, 13, 14, 15 years old. I don't know what he is doing there . . . I don't understand your case.'[83] She demanded that the government produce any witness to testify that Jawad had thrown a grenade at anyone.[84] No witnesses were ever produced. No one was able to show that Jawad was ever a combatant for any military or terrorist group. On 30 July 2009, Judge Huvelle ordered that Jawad be released from detention, that he be treated humanely, and that he be returned to Afghanistan.[85] Jawad's return and resettlement to Afghanistan was at best a difficult experience, and he may well have fled into the tribal areas of Pakistan.[86]

The second case is that of Omar Khadr, the first child soldier tried in the West since World War II.[87] Omar Khadr, a Canadian citizen, was captured in Afghanistan at age 15 and charged with 'intentional murder by an unlawful combatant' of US Army Sergeant Christopher Speer. It was alleged that Khadr threw a hand grenade at US forces. As there was no eyewitness who could identify Khadr as having thrown the grenade that killed

---

[79] Frakt 2009: 417.
[80] *United States v. Mohammad Jawad* 2008.
[81] Ibid.
[82] *Bacha v. Obama* 2009a: 9.
[83] Ibid.: 4.
[84] Ibid.: 13.
[85] *Bacha v. Obama* 2009b.
[86] Paterniti 2011.
[87] Some child soldiers have been put on trial in other domestic jurisdictions. The Democratic Republic of the Congo has charged some child soldiers for various offences such as desertion and failure to obey orders as well as for the crimes of murder and rape. Child Soldiers International 2004; see also Coalition to Stop the Use of Child Soldiers 2002: 33.

Sergeant Speer, much of the case depended on his alleged confession. As in the Jawad case, a key element in Khadr's defence was that his confession was involuntary. Because Khadr was handled harshly as a detainee, the key question was whether his confession could be used as evidence against him despite this treatment. Khadr made numerous allegations that he was tortured and subjected to cruel, inhumane and degrading treatment throughout the course of his capture and ultimate detention at Guantanamo Bay. Among the most disturbing of his claims was that he was threatened with rape and sexual violence and that he was told that uncooperative detainees were sent to Afghanistan to be raped and that 'they like small boys in Afghanistan'. In a different interrogation, Khadr also alleged that he was told that someone identified as 'Soldier Number 9' would be sent to interrogate and rape him or that he would be sent to Egypt, Syria, Jordan or Israel to be raped.[88]

During his detention at Bagram, Khadr allegedly confessed to throwing the hand grenade that killed Sergeant Speer as well as to helping build and plant improvised explosive devices (IEDs). The principal issue prior to trial was whether Khadr's admissions were obtained through torture or other forms of abuse. Some of Khadr's claims of having been tortured or abused were corroborated at his pre-trial hearing in May 2010. Particularly important was the testimony of Interrogator No. 1, who was later identified as John Claus, the same interrogator who was involved in the beating to death of Dilawar. Claus' interrogation of Khadr took place in the summer of 2002 after Khadr had been released from a military hospital. Claus admitted that he had interrogated the badly wounded Khadr, who was 15 years old at the time, and that he had told Khadr a fictitious tale of an Afghan kid who was sent to an American prison where he was gang-raped and died. Claus testified, 'We'd tell him about this Afghan who gets sent to an American prison and there's a bunch of big black guys and big Nazis.' He said that he described the Afghan child as 'a poor little kid . . . away from home, kind of isolated'.[89] Claus went on to tell Khadr that he had sent the kid to an American prison because he was disappointed in his truthfulness and that when the American prisoners discovered that the Afghan boy was a Muslim, they raped him in their rage over the 9/11 attacks.[90]

Another of Khadr's allegations was corroborated by a former army combat medic identified as M, who treated Khadr. M testified that he found Khadr – hooded and weeping – chained by the arms to the door of a five-square-foot cage at a US lockup in Afghanistan. He also testified that Khadr's wrists were chained just above eye level although with enough slack to allow his feet to touch the floor. He did not remember whether Khadr's feet were shackled. When he pulled the hood from Khadr's head, the teenager was in tears.[91] Despite evidence of abuse, the military judge ruled that statements made by Khadr during his detention admitting his involvement were not the product of torture and/or abuse and were therefore voluntary.[92] The judge's ruling did not specifically reject the truthfulness of the witnesses' testimony of torture but rather ruled that whatever abuse Khadr may have suffered was unrelated to his admissions of involvement

---

[88] *United States v. Omar Ahmed Khadr* 2010a.
[89] Rosenberg 2010a.
[90] Ibid.
[91] Rosenberg 2010b.
[92] *United States v. Omar Ahmed Khadr* 2010b.

in Sergeant Speer's death. Ironically, on 23 April 2009, the Canadian Supreme Court ruled that Khadr had been illegally detained at Guantanamo Bay, that he had been tortured and deprived of legal counsel and that the government of Canada should seek his repatriation but the court did not order his repatriation.[93]

Following the military judge's ruling, both the government and the defence began to speak about a plea bargain. Khadr agreed to a prison sentence of eight years with no credit given for his detention since 2002. The agreement provided that the first of these years would be spent in US custody, but if so requested by the Canadian government, the remaining seven years could be spent in Canada. Under the procedural rules of the Military Commission, even after Khadr's guilty plea was entered, the military jury deliberated his sentence without knowledge of the plea bargain. The jury had no knowledge that Khadr would be entitled to the lesser of two sentences: the eight years agreed to or the one handed down by the jury. On 31 October 2010, the military jury sentenced him to 40 years in prison. In the humanitarian and human rights community, the sentence has been derided as 'stunningly punitive'.[94] Khadr began serving the first year of his eight-year sentence at Guantanamo Bay in January 2010. In 2012, he was transferred to Canadian custody, and in 2015 he was released on bail. He recently agreed to a settlement of 10.5 million Canadian dollars with the Canadian government, which now admits that it failed to protect his rights.

These two cases illustrate the tension between the rhetoric of child protectionism and the lived realities of actual encounters with child soldiers. In the case of Afghanistan, the Bush policies were not specifically directed at children. Children were swept up in the 'war on terror' which turned a blind eye to their protected status. But these cases also touch on the fact that the understanding of child soldiers is invariably framed by over-inclusive and exaggerated rhetoric. In humanitarian rhetoric the lethality of children is sometimes explained away by assertions that aggressiveness on the battlefield flows from their victimization. Children are said to fight because they have been kidnapped, brainwashed, physically and sexually abused or forced to ingest alcohol or drugs. This remains a common theme and serves to absolve children of their culpability. This rhetoric sometimes merges with and sometimes stands apart from concerns that children have become such deadly terrorists that it becomes impossible to sustain the innocence model.[95] Elsewhere, we are confronted with children who apply their own intelligence, strategize about situations and otherwise act in ways that make it hard to differentiate them from ordinary soldiers. The issue remains continuously unsettled because we insist on defining as children people who do not behave as children. Navigating this terrain, which in essence means safeguarding the human rights of young people without patronizing them or demonizing them has proven to be an extraordinarily difficult project. We need more historical perspective and less essentialized rhetoric from the perspectives of both human rights activists and from the counterterrorism and national security communities. At its heart, this is the central operational outcome that I hope to achieve in this chapter. A more nuanced perspective rooted in a data-driven analysis would yield better policy.

---

[93] *Khadr v. Canada* 2009.
[94] Rosenberg 2010c.
[95] Osborn 2017.

9. CONCLUSION

By the late twentieth century, humanitarian and human rights groups politicized the concept of the 'child soldier', a term that, in its contemporary sense, denotes a person too young to serve legitimately in the military. It is easy to lose sight of the fact that the term 'child soldier' was not created by historians or social scientists as a guide to empirical research and analysis. Rather, it is a legal and moral concept created by humanitarian and human rights organizations, law enforcement, criminal law codes and political leaders to help secure a set of normative goals. This language is now so deeply embedded in a Western discourse of deviancy that it is virtually impossible to treat it as a socially constructed codification. It is this perspective that leads to the exaggerated claims about the special crisis of child soldiering in the twentieth century. As I have tried to show, the problem of child soldiers is primarily not one of numbers but of changing ideas about children.

The overall concept of the child soldier is based upon a view of children as innocent and vulnerable. This is a powerful and pervasive idea that has served as a general platform for social reform in many areas of children's lives. It was the basis of the nineteenth-century Child Saver movement, which sought to rescue working-class children in Great Britain and America from the evils of their environment. Not long afterward, it was exported to the colonial world, where it became the template for saving innocent children from the 'evils' of their own societies and cultures. This view of children has become the foundation of virtually all contemporary international legal, humanitarian and human rights efforts to improve the lives of children, including severing any links between childhood and military service. But for historians, social scientists and others trying to engage in research and understanding of the issues surrounding the recruitment of the young, the adoption of the language of advocacy as the language of inquiry is, in my view, a major error. It risks divorcing researchers from the experiences of real children and youth. It may clash with local understandings about the involvement of young people in war as well as with historical patterns of recruitment.

One problem with this essentialized image of the child soldier as faultless passive victim is that it permits the emergence of a counter-narrative, when politically expedient, because of the lack of data-driven historical and ethnographic accuracy that undergirds the image in the first place. This counter-narrative is one of the purposeful and dangerous child terrorist, which becomes deployed when the interests of powerful Western states may be seen as threatened. The deployment of this image, in turn, permits gaps to open in the law and for the children that fall into these gaps to become subject to horrible and degrading treatment. While this chapter focuses on the US and the war on terror, similar patterns are now emerging in terms of the responses of other states to children suspected of affiliation with ISIS or Boko Haram.[96] Once again this is (from a different political perspective) the result when the language of advocacy (in this case, for 'our' security) becomes the language of inquiry.

In the West, our understanding of war has been affected by more than half a century of peace in the Western democracies. Accordingly, and luckily, we have lost a visceral

---

[96] See also Bloom in this volume; Casey-Maslen in this volume; O'Neil and van Broeckhoven 2018.

understanding of war. Instead, our experience of war has become mediated by cultural and geographical distance, professional volunteer armies, human rights organizations, and civil society more generally. All of these, in numerous ways, have served to ascribe war to an essentialized 'other'. As distant observers of far-away wars, we have scant comprehension of the kind of warfare at home that often thrusts children into combat. From the safety of the West, we have generated a humanitarian discourse about children that can barely comprehend the ability and resourcefulness of the children Anna Freud encountered during the years of the German air blitz of London in World War II.[97] Instead, passive imagery of victimization, innocence and vulnerability has distorted our ability to grapple with real children and to create realistic rules of engagement and properly protective policies and requirements for detention. There is also a pressing need for the international community to deal effectively with children who commit war crimes. Data-driven and more nuanced perspectives are clearly now emerging. The recruitment of children and young people today has many similarities with patterns of recruitment in the past by rebel and populist armed forces and groups. This should be the starting point of analysis. Imagery of faultless, passive victimhood and competing imagery of baleful menacing youth are each lacking in historical perspective. The extent to which these images continue to suffuse the imagined spaces, epistemologically, of who becomes a child soldier and why stifles the development of realistic rules of engagement as well as properly protective requirements for detention.

REFERENCED WORKS

Books, Articles, Reports and Legislation

Acomb, E.M. 2012. *The Revolutionary Journal of Baron von Closen, 1780–1783* (Chapel Hill: University of North Carolina Press)
Allen, T. and Vlassenroot, K. (eds) 2010. *The Lord's Resistance Army: Myth and Reality* (London: Zed Books)
An Act Making an Appropriation for Completing the Defences of Washington 1862, 25 Stat. 339
An Act Making Appropriations for the Support of the Army 1850, 9 Stat. 504
Becker, J. 2017. *Campaigning for Children: Strategies for Advancing Children's Rights* (Stanford: Stanford University Press)
Bloom, M., Horgan, J. and Winter, C. 2016. 'Depictions of Children and Youth in the Islamic State's Martyrdom Propaganda, 2015–2016' 9 *CTC Sentinel* 29
Bush, G. 2002. 'White House Memorandum: Humane Treatment of al Qaeda and Taliban Detainees' (7 February) [available at: http://www.pegc.us/archive/White_House/bush_memo_20020207_ed.pdf (accessed 31 July 2018)]
Child Soldiers International 2004. *Child Soldiers Global Report 2004 – Congo, Democratic Republic of the* [available at: http://www.refworld.org/docid/49880668c.html (accessed 24 May 2018)]
Coalition to Stop the Use of Child Soldiers 2002. 'Action Appeal: Child Soldiers on trial in the DRC' 3 *Child Soldiers* 33
Coulter, C. 2008. *Bush Wives and Girl Soldiers* (Ithaca, NY: Cornell University Press)
Cox, C. 2009. 'Boy Soldiers of the American Revolution: The Effects of War on Society', in J. Marten (ed.), *Children and Youth in a New Nation* (New York: New York University Press)
Cox, C. 2016. *Boy Soldiers of the American Revolution* (Chapel Hill: The University of North Carolina Press)
Cremin, L. 1970. *American Education: The Colonial Experience* (New York: Harper and Row)

---

[97] Freud and Burlingame 1943.

Dallaire, R. 2010. *They Fight Like Soldiers, They Die Like Children: The Global Quest to Eradicate the Use of Child Soldiers* (New York: Random House)
Denov, 2012. *Child Soldiers: Sierra Leone's Revolutionary United Front* (Cambridge: Cambridge University Press)
Dodwell, B., Milton, D. and Rassler, D. 2016. *The Caliphate's Global Workforce: An Inside Look at the Islamic State's Foreign Fighter Paper Trail* (West Point, NY: Combatting Terrorism Centre)
Dolgin, J. 1997. 'Transforming Childhood: Apprenticeship in American Law' 31 *New England Law Review* 1113
Drumbl, M. 2012. *Reimagining Child Soldiers in International Law and Policy* (Oxford: Oxford University Press)
Elliot, R. 2010. 'An Early Experiment in National Identity Cards: The Battle over Registration in World War I' 17 *Twentieth Century British History* 145
Enrollment Act 1863, 12 Stat 731
Evans, W. 1905. 'Peter Francisco: The American Soldier' 13 *William and Mary Quarterly* 213
Executive Office of the President 2001. 'Military Order of November 13, 2001: Detention, Treatment, and Trial of Certain Non-Citizens in the War against Terrorism' 66 *Federal Register* 57831–36 [available at: http://federalregister.gov/a/01-28904 (accessed 31 July 2018)]
Frakt, D. 2009. 'Closing Argument at Guantanamo: The Torture of Mohammed Jawad' 22 *Harvard Human Rights Journal* 401
Freud, A. and Burlingame, D. 1943. *War and Children* (London: Medical War Books)
Friedman, L. 2005. *The History of American Law*, 3rd Edition (New York: Touchstone)
Gould, B. 1969. *Investigations in the Military and Anthropological Statistics of American Soldiers* (New York: Hurd and Houghton)
Government of Canada 2017a. 'Canadian Armed Forces Sets Precedent with Child Soldier Doctrine' (2 March) [available at: https://www.canada.ca/en/department-national-defence/news/2017/03/canadian_armed_forces setsprecedentwithchildsoldierdoctrine.html (accessed 28 June 2018)]
Government of Canada 2017b. *Canadian Forces Joint Doctrine Note 2017-01 Child Soldiers* (Ottawa: Ministry of Defence)
Government of Canada 2017c. 'Vancouver Principles on Peacekeeping and the Prevention of the Recruitment and Use of Child Soldiers' (15 November) [available at: http://international.gc.ca/world-monde/issues_devel opment-enjeux_developpe-ment/human_rights-droits_homme/principles-vancouver-principes.aspx?lang=eng (accessed 31 July 2018)]
Grinspan, J. 2014. 'The Wild Children of Yesteryear', *New York Times* (14 May)
Grinspan, J. 2016. *The Virgin Vote* (Chapel Hill: University of North Carolina Press)
Happold, M. 2005. *Child Soldiers in International Law* (Manchester: Manchester University Press)
Hoffman, D. 2012. *The War Machines: Young Men and Violence in Sierra Leone and Liberia* (Durham: Duke University Press)
Honwana, A. 2006. *Child Soldiers in Africa* (Philadelphia: University of Pennsylvania Press)
Jehl, D. 2005. 'Army Details Scale of Abuse of Prisoners in an Afghan Jail', *New York Times* (12 March)
Jourdan, L. 2011. 'Mayi-Mayi: Young Rebels in Kivu, DRC' 36 *Africa Development* 89
Kilmer, G. 1905. 'Boys in the Union Army' 70 *The Century* 269
King, C. 1911. 'Boys of the War Days', in F.T. Miller (ed.), *A Photographic History of the Civil War, Volume 8* (Springfield, MA: Patriot Press)
The Local 2018. 'German Army Recruits More Minors than Ever Before' (9 January) [available at: https://www.thelocal.de/20180109/german-army-recruits-more-minors-than-ever-before-report (accessed 31 July 2018)]
Machel, G. 1996. *Impact of Armed Conflict on Children* (New York: United Nations)
Markham Papers 1915. 'Papers, Correspondence, and Press Cuttings Relating to the Life and Careers of Arthur Basil Markham' (London: British Library of Political and Economic Science, London School of Economics)
Martin, J.P. 2002. *Private Yankee Doodle* (Fort Washington, PA: Eastern National)
McBride, J. 2014. *The War Crime of Child Soldier Recruitment* (The Hague: Asser Press)
McPherson, J. 1982. *Ordeal by Fire: The Civil War and Reconstruction* (New York: Alfred A. Knopf)
McPherson, J. 2003. *Battle Cry of Freedom: The Civil War Era* (Oxford: Oxford University Press)
Merry, S. 1999. 'Human Rights Law and the Demonization of Culture (And Anthropology Along the Way)' 26 *Polar: Political and Legal Anthropology Review* 55
Mintz, S. 2004. *Huck's Raft: A History of American Childhood* (Cambridge, MA: Harvard University Press)
National Registration Act 1915, 5 & 6 Geo 5, Ch. 60 (Eng.)
NATO 2011. 'Child Soldiers as the Opposing Force (NATO RTO Technical Memorandum TM-HFM-159)' (January)
Oloya, O. 2013. *Child to Soldier: Stories from Joseph Kony's Lord's Resistance Army* (Toronto: University of Toronto Press)
O'Neil, S. and van Broeckhoven, K. 2018. *Cradled by Conflict: Child Involvement with Armed Groups in Contemporary Conflict* (New York: United Nations University)
Osborn, S. 2017. 'Boko Haram Increasingly Using Drugged Children as Suicide Bombers, Warns Unicef', *Independent* (12 April)

Papenfuse, E.C. and Stiverson, G.A. 1973. 'General Smallwood's Recruits: The Peacetime Career of the Revolutionary War Private' 30 *William & Mary Quarterly* 117

Paterniti, M. 2011. 'The Boy from Gitmo', *GQ* (10 March)

Pizzaro, J., Silver, R.C. and Prause, J. 2006. 'Physical and Mental Health Costs of Traumatic War Experiences Among Civil War Veterans' 63 *Archives of General Psychiatry* 193

Quaifem, M.M. 1930. 'A Boy Soldier under Washington: The Memoir of Daniel Granger' 16 *The Mississippi Valley Historical Review* 538

Rinaldi, R. 2005. *The United States Army in World War I – Order of Battle* (Takoma Park, MD: Tiger Lily Publications)

Rosen, D. 2005. *Armies of the Young: Child Soldiers in War and Terrorism* (New Brunswick: Rutgers University Press)

Rosen, D. 2015. *Child Soldiers in the Western Imagination: From Patriots to Victims* (New Brunswick: Rutgers University Press)

Rosenberg, C. 2010a. 'Interrogator Says Khadr Was Told He'd Likely Be Raped in U.S.', *Miami Herald* (6 May)

Rosenberg, C. 2010b. 'Medic: I Saw Omar Khadr Shackled as Punishment', *Miami Herald* (3 May)

Rosenberg, C. 2010c. 'Despite 40-Year Sentence, Khadr Likely to Go Home in a Year', *Miami Herald* (31 October)

Royster, C. 1996. *A Revolutionary People at War: The Continental Army and American Character, 1775–1783* (Chapel Hill: University of North Carolina Press)

Scott, G. and Reich, S. 2009. 'Think Again: Child Soldiers', *Foreign Policy* (22 May)

Selesky, H. 1987. *A Demographic Survey of the Continental Army that Wintered at Valley Forge, Pennsylvania, 1777–1778* (Washington, DC: National Park Service)

Selesky, H. 1990. *War and Society in Colonial America* (New Haven, CT: Yale University Press)

Singer, P. 2001. 'Caution: Children at War' 31 *Parameters* 40

UN Secretary-General 2017. 'Report of the Secretary-General on Children and Armed Conflict' (UN Doc. A/72/361–S/2017/821) (24 August)

United States Department of Defence 2005. 'Review of Department of Defence Detention Operations and Detainee Interrogation Techniques' (7 March)

United States Department of Justice 2008. 'Review of the FBI's Involvement in and Observations of Detainee Interrogations in Guantanamo Bay, Afghanistan, and Iraq' (May) [available at: https://oig.justice.gov/special/s0805/final.pdf (accessed 31 July 2018)]

United States Department of State 2016. 'U.S. Third and Fourth Periodic Report on the Children's Protocols' (8 February) [available at: https://www.state.gov/j/drl/rls/c70331.htm (accessed 31 July 2018)]

United States Senate Committee on Armed Services 2008. 'Inquiry into the Treatment of Detainees in US Custody' (22 April)

Utas, M. 2005. 'Victimcy, Girlfriending, Soldiering: Tactic Agency in a Young Woman's Social Navigation of the Liberian War Zone' 78 *Anthropological Quarterly* 403

Van Emden, R. 2005. *Boy Soldiers of the Great War* (London: Headline)

Vigh, H. 2000. *Navigating Terrains of War: Youth and Soldiering in Guinea-Bissau* (New York: Berghahn)

Waschefort, G. 2014. *International Law and Child Soldiers* (Oxford: Hart Publishing)

Judicial Proceedings

United States

Bacha v. Obama 2009a. Transcript of Hearing before the Honourable Ellen Segal Huvelle, United States District Court Judge, Civil Case No. 05-2385 (16 July)

Bacha v. Obama 2009b. Order Granting Petition of Habeas Corpus, Civil Case No. 05-2385 (30 July)

United States v. Mohammad Jawad 2008. Ruling on Defence Motion to Suppress Out of Court Statements Made by the Accused while in U.S. Custody (D-021) (19 November)

United States v. Omar Ahmed Khadr 2010a. Supplemental Defence Motion (D-094) (8 March)

United States v. Omar Ahmed Khadr 2010b. Ruling on Defence Suppression Motion (D-094) (17 August)

Canada

Khadr v. Canada (Prime Minister) 2009. 1 FCR 34, 2009 FC 405

8. The voiceless child soldiers of Afghanistan
Anicée Van Engeland

Despite the fact that Afghanistan has been a party to the UN Convention on the Rights of the Child since 1994, children and teenagers have been recruited and used by both the armed forces and armed non-state actors for decades, with a surge after 2002.[1] Recent conflicts provide prime examples: the first killing of a US soldier deployed in Afghanistan, Sergeant Nathan Ross Chapman, was the deed of a 14-year-old;[2] and in the summer of 2017, the authorities released a group of teenagers that had been abducted for the purposes of forced recruitment by the Taleban in south-eastern Ghazni province.[3]

To be fully understood, the issue of child soldiers in Afghanistan needs to be approached within the cultural and traditional context: most children do not themselves enrol to fight with armed non-state actors (including the Taleban and ISIS) or the armed forces. The choice is usually made for them by their family or the community. I therefore argue that they are deprived of agency and are subjected to the will of the group. In a context that has witnessed a surge in recruitment in the last few years,[4] male Afghan children and teenagers are often kidnapped, sold, exchanged for protection or coerced to join insurgent groups or the armed forces for a salary.[5] Once recruited, these children will be exposed to violence, drugs and sexual abuses: death or migration is the only way out.[6]

This chapter illustrates how these children are pawns in a game that is controlled by a variety of actors involved in the conflict. I aim to show that Afghan child soldiers are victims of the security context and thus have little agency when it comes to joining armed forces or groups. The originality of this chapter lies in its approach to children's unwilling contributions to conflict: I explore the concept of agency as influenced by traditions, culture, religion and customs. I locate agency by focusing mainly on recruitment. In Afghanistan this is the key moment at which the agency of children and teenagers is called into question. Through a focus on the cultural and religious factors that influence recruitment, I aim to provide a better understanding of the phenomenon of child soldiers in Afghanistan.

By taking account of traditions, culture, religion and custom, my contextualization of child soldiering in Afghanistan borrows from feminist literature, in particular the theoretical framework of intersectionality.[7] This piece also contributes to the discussion on liberal perspectives on the protection of child soldiers initiated by Quénivet.[8] My aim

---

[1] Quénivet 2017: 445.
[2] Singer 2010: 94.
[3] Behzan and Furogh 2017.
[4] HRW 2016.
[5] Hartjen and Priyadarsini 2012: 106; Obaid-Chinoy 2009; Boon et al. 2011: 287.
[6] Badie 2018.
[7] See also Drumbl 2012: 58.
[8] Quénivet 2013.

is to propose an innovative approach to child soldiering, building on the work done by Drumbl and Rosen.[9] My argument is that the recruitment of child soldiers in Afghanistan is the outcome of a security context that has shaped traditional, religious, cultural and customary behaviours, making it acceptable, if not normal, to recruit children as combatants. I thus explore how the macro context has an impact on the micro context in the field of recruitment of child soldiers, expanding Singer's assessment of factors contributing to the existence of child soldiers.[10] This need for understanding the context has already been stressed by Drumbl in his 2004 research on women in Afghanistan.[11] Whilst the contextual factors that influence recruitment of child soldiers in Afghanistan may be unique to this country, I would suggest that there are similarities between Afghan child soldiers and other children around the world who are implicated in long-running conflicts. Shedding light on the Afghan case will thus allow us to better understand how a context, namely that of a war, shapes traditions and culture to encourage and support the recruitment of children as combatants.[12]

1. OVERVIEW OF THE AFGHAN CONTEXT: THE IMPACT OF AN ENDLESS CONFLICT

1.1 Afghanistan, a Decades-Long Conflict

Afghanistan has been at war through most of its existence as an attempted nation state, with a series of modern conflicts starting at the end of the 1970s. The focus in this chapter will be on events that have occurred since 2002. There is a multiplicity of actors who all have different stakes. The most well-known armed non-state actor remains the Taleban. Through their intervention in 2002, the Allies intended to put an end to the Taleban regime established in 1996. However, this was unsuccessful, and the group continues to operate in the country. The Taleban began a counter-offensive against the Allies in 2005, looking at Iraq for insurgency models. They have fought NATO forces and Afghan authorities ever since, using suicide bombings and improvised explosive devices (IEDs), and have caused many deaths among NATO soldiers, governmental forces but also and mainly civilians. In 2009, Obama launched a strategy that sought to protect civilians by targeted killings of Taleban insurgents. However, this again was unsuccessful, leading instead to an increase in US combat deaths. This period was coined the 'Afghan War Diary' by WikiLeaks and involved the killing of civilians and the involvement of Special Forces. The situation began to spiral out of control in 2012, and in 2014 US and NATO troops formally ended their mission in Afghanistan (although residual forces remained in the country until mid-2017). The country has sunk into endemic violence including attacks against foreigners, international organizations and governmental institutions.[13]

---

[9] Drumbl 2012; Rosen 2015.
[10] Singer 2006.
[11] Drumbl 2004.
[12] See Almarez et al. in this volume.
[13] UNHCR 2016: 13–14; UNAMA 2017.

The 2016 UN Secretary General's report and other reports[14] have stressed that civilians are more than ever targeted by armed non-state actors.[15]

In terms of key parties, the Taleban established the Islamic Emirate of Afghanistan in 1996. They held power over 75 per cent of the territory from 1996 to 2001, until the United States and its Allies intervened. Their governance system relied on hard-line interpretations of Islam. They combine Deobandi fundamentalist beliefs with radical Salafi views, mixed with traditional norms found in Pashtunwali. Most of the Taleban are Pashtun, but they have recently recruited fighters from minorities in order to strengthen security deals to protect communities. The Taleban are divided into several branches, and leaders are in competition with each other, as illustrated by the Spring 2013 tensions[16] over the successor to Mullah Omar.[17] Further, they operate differently in different regions of the country. For example, they collaborate with the Al Haqqani network in some areas.[18] ISIS is also now well established in Afghanistan and seeks to defeat the Taleban in its territorial conquest, with the aim of creating a caliphate that would stretch from Afghanistan to Iraq. The rise of ISIS in Afghanistan has taken a dramatic turn since 2016. The group has spread quickly in the country and has conducted a series of deadly attacks, targeting mainly civilians.[19] A Royal United Services Institute report asserts that there is a competition among Taleban and ISIS commanders to cause the maximum number of civilian casualties.[20] Some civilian deaths are, however, caused by US and Afghan airstrikes.[21] Drug lords thrive as the country has blossomed into a narco state.[22] There are also warlords who are either affiliated with an armed non-state actor or who act alone. Finally, there are militias in charge of the security and protection of individuals and groups. State actors struggle to keep control of all these groups.

As a result of this multiplicity of actors all vying for the control of the country, the security situation and who holds the balance of power are in constant flux. As an example, in Parwan province, and in particular the Ghorband valley, security has declined significantly: militants of different groups such as ISIS, the Taleban, Hezb-e Islami, the Islamic Movement of Uzbekistan, Al Qaeda and Al Haqqani are all fighting for territorial control,[23] and militias working for local warlords terrorize the population. Meanwhile state security forces fight to gain control. Parwan held a special place in the security project of the Allies before 2014 as it is close to the capital city, Kabul, and Bagram Airbase. The region, once a symbol of success, is now under heavy political scrutiny, as

---

[14] UN Secretary-General 2016: 1; ICRC 2015.
[15] UNHCR 2016: 14-15.
[16] Rubin 2015.
[17] Mullah Omar was the spiritual leader of the Taleban as well as their commander. He was in control of Afghanistan between 1996 and 2001, when the Taleban were ousted by the Allies. He died in 2013 and his succession created schisms amongst the Taleban.
[18] In Pashto and Dari, which are the primary languages in Afghanistan and neighbouring Pakistan, 'al' means 'the'. The editors have elected to retain the phrase 'the Al Haqqani network' for ease of reading in English despite the repetition.
[19] EASO 2017.
[20] Farrell and Semple 2017: 10.
[21] UN Secretary-General 2017: [15]; UNAMA 2017: 44; Bendix 2017.
[22] Carr 2010: 51; McNally and Bucala 2015.
[23] Landinfo 2014: 20.

it constitutes a prime example of the failure to tackle security issues in the country. This decline in the security situation is what led the US to bomb the valley in 2014, the aim being to eliminate the Taleban stronghold.[24] However, at the time of writing, the Taleban has strengthened its grip on Ghorband valley at the door of the capital city. For example, Sah Darah-e Wazghar, a village located in the Ghorband valley, is reportedly used as an ammunitions cache for the Taleban. As a result, the Taleban come in and out of villages in the area, ransacking or occupying homes, forcing locals to flee. One of the outcomes of this change in the security situation has been internal displacement: the UNHCR has observed that families have started moving towards Kabul.[25] This example highlights the complexity of the situations on the ground and showcases the variety of actors playing a role in fuelling the conflict.

1.2 Impact on the Afghan Population

The impact of the conflict has been deadly for civilians. Returning to the example of Parwan province, there has been constant fighting between the Afghan security forces and the Taleban, but also among different armed non-state actors in the Ghorband valley.[26] The Taleban have established a shadow provincial government in the valley, absorbing pre-existing Hezb-e Islami (an Islamic organization that fought communism) structures. The role of this shadow government is to win the hearts and minds of the local population, collect taxes through bribes and arbitrate local feuds.[27] The shadow government has been in place since 2009 and operating properly since 2012, which means that the Taleban are well anchored in Parwan and know the locals well.[28] The same has been noted for a large part of Afghanistan in 2018: the Taleban have succeeded in establishing shadow governments in many of the provinces.[29] This would not have been possible without two of the elements examined in this chapter: manpower via recruitment, including of child soldiers, and the support – willing or not – of the community.

Recruitment has been, and is still, crucial for the Taleban as they aim to establish a government in Afghanistan: they are in constant need of new recruits to control hard-won territories and expand. The Taleban's main competitor in terms of recruitment of

---

[24] Unfortunately, the strike led to apparent civilian deaths and it emerged that the airstrike had not been authorized by Afghan authorities. The Afghan authorities' report on the incident contained fake evidence and it soon became clear that no fact-finding mission had ever been sent to Wazghar to collect evidence and testimonies. Photos of the casualties included in the report proved unreliable, with some even depicting other events. Villagers were brought in to testify, but it soon became clear they were lying as they identified photos that were linked to a 2009 attack. The government also took unverified material from a Taleban website. The report on the airstrike was disavowed by a Parwan senior Afghan official. The International Security Assistance Force later released a statement stating the same views and explaining that one or two civilians who were in the same building as the Taleban were killed. Yet, the event happened at a time when President Karzai was asking foreign troops to leave, and the Wazghar event gave him an opportunity to make a point. See Rosenberg 2014.
[25] UNHCR 2014.
[26] Ibid.
[27] Dorronsoro 2012: 9.
[28] International Crisis Group 2011: 23; Giustozzi 2012: 71–80.
[29] Jackson 2018.

manpower is ISIS and other armed non-state actors. The Taleban strategy to control the country and the rivalry with other groups such as ISIS has had a direct impact on recruitment: for example, the conflict between ISIS and the Taleban (supported by the Al Haqqani network) has ripped the Paktia province apart, with some Taleban switching sides and joining ISIS. As a result, Paktia has become a zone for recruitment, where even young male adults working for the Afghan Local Police are regularly approached by the Taleban to join them.[30] The Taleban recruit children and teenagers at schools and at the mosques. There has also been a surge in the recruitment of locals, males and females, to work in illegal mines that finance the conflict. In the northern province of Kunduz, the Taleban have been going from door to door in villages, towns and cities to recruit all the boys and men of fighting age. They have also begun attacking schools and madrasas where young men are studying, enrolling all boys and men.[31] Herat province is often seen as one of the most secure areas to live in, yet the United States Institute of Peace reports signs of growing extremism.[32] The report points to the madrasas, mosques, universities and prisons of Herat as having become places for recruitment. Part of the success in recruiting children, teenagers and young adults in Herat comes from the fact that local structures have either collapsed or do not function properly, leaving a vacuum for the Taleban to fill. The situation worsened in January 2015 when President Ghani came to Herat and fired many officials, including district police chiefs, in a bid to fight corruption: their positions were not filled, leaving a police gap in the province. This power vacuum has allowed the Taleban to prosper. Kandahar province is at the heart of the Taleban's ideology as the group was created there. As the population is more sympathetic to the Taleban, there is less use of coercion in recruitment. The Taleban are seeking a comeback in Kandahar, currently controlled by the authorities, by destroying local infrastructures so that locals must turn to them for assistance.

Throughout Afghanistan, and for all parties to the conflict, there is a dire need for fresh fighters as most young males living in non-urban areas have departed for larger cities or abroad when faced with the danger of being recruited. Groups, including the Taleban, are now therefore taking the risk of recruiting inside cities. As will be illustrated in the next section, recruitment takes all forms and is endemic in Afghanistan. Given the intensity of the conflict, and the need of the many warring parties for manpower, the recruitment of children has, and remains, unavoidable. Whilst some elements of the security context are unique to Afghanistan, the inevitability of child recruitment is, I suggest, common to other countries.

Other than an impact on recruitment, the context – that of decades-long conflict – has also shaped the relationships between the local population and security actors. War has changed traditions, religion, culture and customs, just as it has where other children are recruited into armed forces or groups, such as in Iraq, the Philippines, South Sudan, Yemen and Colombia.[33] As I will illustrate in the next section, this shift has had consequences for children, who are now considered as fighters from a younger age.

---

[30] Roggio and Weiss 2015.
[31] HRW 2016.
[32] Fazli et al. 2015: 4.
[33] See also Almarez et al.; Bloom; and Jiménez, all in this volume.

The relationship existing between security actors and communities is one of mutual benefit. This is especially true in places the authorities have vacated. The Taleban are skilled at filling governmental gaps and ensuring recruitment in the process. Again, the Ghorband valley, where the Taleban has established a shadow government, provides an excellent example. As a result of the presence of multiple warring actors, tensions among locals run high. Some families have sent their children to join local militias; others have sent their children to the Taleban, and yet others have sent them to join governmental forces. Each family unit, each community, each village and each town located in the Ghorband valley has sought out the best security deal with the actor of their choice, which makes life as a societal unit unbearable. Firearms have been widely distributed to locals since 2014 by insurgent groups or militias (political or attached to warlords) in an effort to buy loyalty. This has caused a surge in criminality.[34] As a result, disputes amongst villagers over land, marriage or an insult are amplified, and traditional local feuds mutate into conflicts that the Taleban claim they will adjudicate. The Taleban remain the leading force in the Ghorband valley and they use locals' feuds to establish their authority. In addition, as already noted, they have been effective in creating a shadow government. Consequently, the Taleban have found a fertile ground in the remote villages of Parwan.[35] This local support is hardly surprising: in places like Parwan province, locals tend to turn to the Taleban as they are seen as the only local actors who can bring peace and security.[36]

The Taleban have also been skilled at exploiting resentment against foreign troops and Afghan authorities: NATO airstrikes, followed by Afghan governmental airstrikes, have been a cause for rebellion against the authorities. The Taleban explicitly condemned the US airstrike on Wazghar in 2014 and tried to exploit the resentment it caused to their advantage, publishing mostly on their website. In a YouTube video, the Taleban encouraged the local population to take revenge and tried to exploit their anger at the overall fighting by suggesting they side with them. Additionally, locals have complained about the presence of militias attached to warlords. Such militias, which protect the warlords, have been attacking civilians to extort money and have been vandalizing homes and shops. The Taleban are very much aware of this local opposition to conflict and have tried to influence villagers and townsmen.[37] This assists with recruitment into the Taleban. There is a trade-off: children versus security. Also, by ensuring local loyalty instead of occupation, this enables the Taleban to maintain control despite a lack of manpower. The Taleban, which remains the main opponent to the government, has expanded its area of control and continues to seek a return to power.

The Taleban, and those working in tow such as the Al Haqqani network, however, have a complex approach to their interactions with the Afghan population: they use violence, entering villages at night and killing everyone; but they also engage in dialogue with the local population. This twofold approach is the result of disagreements among the Taleban: there is no uniformity of approaches to war among the various branches. Further, the Taleban encounter different challenges in different areas of Afghanistan and

---

[34] APPRO 2015: 5.
[35] EASO 2016a: 54.
[36] Cesaretti 2017.
[37] Dorronsoro 2009: 16–17.

thus must adapt to local circumstances. One key issue of contention between different Taleban branches is recruitment.

2. RECRUITMENT OF CHILD SOLDIERS IN AFGHANISTAN

All children have been severely affected by the decades-long war in Afghanistan. As I will show in this section, children often find themselves forced into joining armed groups by their family, by their community, or by values and circumstances over which they, as individuals, have little control. This is reminiscent of the key moment in Faye's award-winning book on Burundi, when Gaby, a wealthy mixed-race child engulfed in the 1993 Burundi genocide, realizes he has no other choice but to embrace violence and leave his childhood behind:

> In normal times, I'd have turned back. But the war was in our homes now, it was threatening us directly, together with our families. Armand's father had been murdered, and I no longer had a choice . . . Death had just stolen our street. There was no sanctuary left on earth. I lived here, in this city, in this country. There was nothing else for it.[38]

Torn between their childhood and their duties towards their family, their community, their warlords or the nation, Afghan children suffer from what Zyck has called the imposition of childhood on children who adhere to the 'But I am a man' narrative.[39] Zyck, who interviewed child soldiers in Afghanistan, concluded that child soldiers who already perceived themselves as adults were being required to submit to this imposed concept of childhood.

2.1 Targeted Recruitment to Fuel an Endless Conflict

Generations of children have been recruited to fight by armed non-state actors or the authorities.[40] According to a survey cited by Singer, 'roughly 30 percent of all Afghan children have participated in military activities at some point in their childhood'.[41] Others report that half of Afghan combatants might have started their career as child soldiers.[42] The recruitment of child soldiers has gone from cyclical (according to the fighting seasons) to permanent over the last few years, the result of increased fighting among the various warring factions. The outcome has been a surge in the recruitment of children.[43] This is due to the harsh territorial competition between insurgents – mainly ISIS and the Taleban – that has fuelled a need for manpower. There has also been a change in the techniques used by armed non-state actors in Afghanistan: as the armed non-state actors seek to conquer territories, children are considered as a fighting asset. This perception of the child is not confined to non-state actors. The poster child for the phenomenon was 11-year-old Wasil Ahmad, whose commitment to fighting the Taleban, standing by the

---

[38] Faye 2018: 168.
[39] Zyck 2011: 163.
[40] Boutin 2014: 143–4.
[41] Singer 2006: 26
[42] Zyck 2011: 161.
[43] HRW 2016.

side of the Afghan Local Police, was made public. Photos of the child dressed and armed like a soldier circulated to celebrate his engagement. Wasil Ahmad was then executed on his way to school by the insurgents he fought. His case is not unique in a country where children are deeply impacted by the conflict, as perpetrators or as victims, or indeed as both.[44]

In Afghanistan, it is not so much the use of these children as the recruitment that is striking. Any male child and any male teenager of any social and ethnic background is a potential target for state forces or insurgents. Children living in villages but also towns and cities have been targeted, to the point that it is rare to meet a young male child or teenager who has not been approached by the Taleban, ISIS, the Al Haqqani network or the state forces. In the case of insurgency, children and teenagers are often forcibly recruited through violent means, and such techniques leave no room for will or agency: some children are kidnapped, and others are blackmailed or bribed into joining.[45] When abducted, the children are taken to a hidden place to be trained and cannot escape. The insurgents threaten to kill the families of those who try to run away and execute anyone trying to escape. There have been cases where children have successfully returned home, only to find the insurgent group at their doorstep a few hours later.

In some cases, the Taleban storm into a village at night and kill everyone except those of fighting age.[46] At other times, insurgent groups trawl through the streets of cities looking for homeless children and teenagers. These are often either war orphans or youngsters who have been returned from the West and do not dare to return home for fear of bringing shame for their failed expatriation attempts.[47] Others are children who were sent by their parents to work in towns but failed to secure employment. As many street children are addicted to drugs, it is not difficult for armed non-state actors to bribe them into joining their group. Insurgents also often target other vulnerable children, who have no family or no community support, such as those in orphanages or, who have been internally displaced. Insurgent groups also enter madrasas (religious schools) to kidnap children who have been either sent there by their parents to study or who have been sold by their families.[48] This has particularly been the case for Pakistani madrasas located on the border with Iraq, a region where state authority is weak, and where groups like the Taleban and Al Haqqani operate more or less freely. It has also occurred in Kabuli madrasas, whether urban or non-urban:

> Some madrassas serve as propaganda and recruiting grounds for the Taleban. Reports of this can be found in Qarabagh district in Kabul province; a madrassa named Kokcha in the Shinwari area in the district of Dasht-e Archi in Kunduz, run by Pakistanis under the supervision of the Haqqani network; in Warduj district (Badakhshan), Deobandi madrasas have been present since long [sic]; and many Taleban individuals studied in the Nur-ul-Mudaris in the district of Andar (Ghazni). . . . Most young rural boys, as well as some urban boys, go to madrassas, at some point in their education. Taleban, almost always[,] have had some sort of a madrassa education.[49]

---

[44] UNAMA 2017.
[45] Hartjen and Priyadarsini 2012: 106.
[46] Ibid.
[47] Van Engeland and Schockaert 2015; Asylos 2017: 45.
[48] Boutin 2014: 155. See also Almarez et al. in this volume.
[49] EASO 2016b: 17.

Throughout Pashtun areas, madrasas are used to recruit into the Taleban movement.

Finally, parents may send their children to work on a farm or in town without knowing that their offspring will actually be trained by the Taleban. In such situations, the absence of a parent figure means that these children are easy prey. In other circumstances, Afghan children and teenagers appear to join the insurgents or the state forces willingly: a Taleban recruiting officer has explained that he would show weapons to young men to entice them to join, with often a positive outcome.[50] The Taleban use videos that encourage these children and teenagers to join, seeking to impress them with weapons.[51] The fact that some children join the Taleban 'willingly' demonstrates that these children exercise some agency; nonetheless, any such agency is sharply constrained due to the circumstances in the country, an endless conflict and a need to find protection or income.

ISIS works along similar lines: it attracts children by promising a salary and accommodation, although it also abducts them. This strategy of encouraging recruitment has proved successful to some degree, as the children approached lack life options such as education or employment. Some of these youngsters are brain-washed;[52] others are told they will pay off their families' debts by joining. For some children, being recruited is an opportunity to leave 'dead-end' localities where there is no future for them. While some have pointed at the cult for martyrdom, it is important to understand that the concept of honour and pride through martyrdom usually develops later in the process, once the child is indoctrinated.[53] Yet, there are children and teenagers willing to join the insurgency to become martyrs, often in exchange for large sums of money. The Taleban also offer large sums of money in exchange for a child who will become a suicide bomber. Also, the Taleban often visit parents to convince them that having a child who becomes a martyr by fighting for their insurgency will be a social benefit, as they will climb up the social ladder. In a society based on honour, such a discourse has power in villages.

Children who work for the state forces do so for the same reasons they join (ostensibly voluntarily) insurgent groups: for a salary or a life prospect. However, these boys (very few girls are recruited)[54] are not compelled to join by state authorities. Rather the family or the community volunteer or encourage the child to join to honour the family or community or earn a salary. In such cases, even though the child chooses to join, it can be questioned whether he does so with real intent. Families sometimes falsify identity cards so that some children as young as 12 years old join state forces. It has been noted that those who falsify the cards do so for economic reasons: they are in need of the salary that comes with the employment. Economic and social incentives thereby play a role in recruitment, raising yet again the question of agency: as asked by Singer in his 2006 report, is a child who is hungry empowered to refuse to join a group?[55] This question is not only relevant to Afghanistan but to all child soldiers around the world.

Children are considered a fighting asset. They are nimble and can therefore access areas that are now restricted to adults, such as the heart of Kabul. Their size and innocence

---

[50] Obaid-Chinoy 2009.
[51] See also Bloom in this volume.
[52] Boon et al. 2011: 287.
[53] Brett and McCallin 1996: 64.
[54] Dominguez 2016; UN Secretary-General 2015.
[55] Singer 2006: 4.

are key for suicide attacks but also crucial for collecting intelligence, smuggling weapons and planting mines and IEDs. Children may also perform roles related to security such as spies, guards, decoys, scouts and messengers, and also serve as tea boys, drug dealers or cooks. The Taleban have also used them as part of the morality police. As a result, some have called the children 'force enablers'.[56]

In 2015, President Ashraf Ghani signed a presidential decree criminalizing the recruitment of child soldiers to end the recruitment of Afghans under 18 years old into the security forces. Despite this decree, and despite denials to the contrary, there is evidence that both the military and the police force still recruit children.[57] Further, the decree does not prohibit the recruitment and use of children by armed non-state actors, which, as illustrated, are the main recruiters of children.

2.2 The Role of the Community

Forced recruitment takes another turn when it is imposed by the family or the community. In some cases, children from a Pashtun background will be exchanged or sold to the Taleban. This happens when the Taleban seeks to gain control of some territories while gaining new manpower: they request that those of fighting age join them and, in exchange, the Taleban will protect the family, the community and/or the village. One of the Taleban's strategies is to force an agreement out of a village's elders:[58] they threaten to destroy an entire village, burn the crops or kill some or all inhabitants if the men (and boys) do not join them. As a result, an agreement is made whereby food, protection, weapons and/or men/children are provided to the Taleban, in exchange for peace. Such tribal agreements constitute an interesting case study when it comes to forced recruitment and intent: a recruitment based on an agreement with tribal leaders does not mean that all recruits are willing to join. Some obey the agreement with the Taleban willingly, for pride and honour.[59] Some obey because of tribal pressure.[60] Others obey because they know that if they do not join, the entire village might be destroyed, the crops might be burned or the women might be raped. In such dealings, the child has no agency: prompted by the collective, the child cannot refuse to join the insurgents. Children are aware that a refusal will not be tolerated and the price paid for rebellion is high. The Taleban usually leave a male behind in each household, as in Afghanistan a home cannot function without a man. They will return to the same family if the father, uncle or brother who was recruited is killed, arrested, wounded or disappeared. As a result, the Taleban sometimes find themselves recruiting male children as young as seven. For the collective peace bargain to hold, the family must surrender the last male child.

In some cases, there is resistance: the mother, usually with the support of the maternal uncle, will sell the family's land or possessions to have sufficient means to send the child abroad.[61] There may also be negotiations between the families and the Taleban. As outlined

---

[56] Dominguez 2016.
[57] Child Soldiers International 2015 and 2016.
[58] Borchgrevink 2010.
[59] EASO 2012: 30.
[60] UNHCR 2012.
[61] This is an interesting phenomenon. Hanafi law relies mostly on the paternal side of the family,

earlier, there is a complex relationship between the Taleban and the Afghan population, with the approach taken depending on the branch of Taleban in ascendancy and the particular context. Currently, the faction that has been controlling the Taleban are those who seek to establish legitimacy in Afghanistan to re-conquer the country; they believe that the support of the population is key to this strategy. This position leads to complex stances, such as the attempt to have a dialogue with the locals while requiring them to give up a child to the Taleban. This explains why some children find themselves recruited after negotiations.

The outcome of having a child fighting for an armed non-state actor is that a family or a community has no other choice but to support the insurgent group, the warlord or the militia. This explains how entire villages, towns or areas support a group like the Taleban or ISIS without adhering to their ideology or goals. I would argue that it is consequently not only the child who is deprived of their agency: the whole family and/or community are taken hostage by the conflict and the different actors at play. Tribal structures have been deeply impacted by such agreements and by the competition for recruitment between state security forces, insurgent groups and militias, but also by the presence of foreign troops and organizations.[62] This has led tribal elders to sell their youngsters to buy some relative and temporary peace in an environment where conflict lines evolve rapidly. When the recruitment results from a tribal agreement with the Taleban, the child is voiceless, treated as an object that will buy peace for the community, a community that finds itself with its hands tied. This has to be read within a cultural context where the communal interests override those of the individual.

It is of interest to note that while children are considered as assets during the conflict, they become a hindrance when demobilized and are unable to return home. Communities and families reject them, and they are left destitute.[63] When they are demobilized after being wounded, these children face rejection on the grounds of *bad tarbia* (translated as 'bad manners')[64] which means that they have been socially corrupted and do not belong anymore. A recent collection of testimonies from former ISIS child soldiers brings this to light:[65] the outcome is that '[t]here is no turning back a soldier into a child from an Afghan perspective'.[66]

In summary, many children and teenagers join insurgent movements because of family pressure, a community decision, honour, the lack of employment, the lack of educational opportunities and poverty: very few join of their own volition.

3. THE DEBATE ABOUT AGENCY AND INTENT

Children are often depicted in the expert literature as deprived of agency, resulting in the de facto and *de jure* endorsement of the status of victim. In the case of Afghan children,

---

leaving the maternal family with no influence. Yet here, a maternal uncle becomes the protector of the male child on the run, the financial enabler for the migration or the organizer of the migration.
[62] Kilcullen 2009: 243.
[63] Asylos 2017: 108.
[64] See also Landgren 2007: 202.
[65] Video from Channel 4 available on YouTube: https://www.youtube.com/watch?v=EVxZfP1fC_I.
[66] Singer 2006: 183.

this perspective is put to the test at the time of recruitment: as I have illustrated, most children and teenagers who are recruited either by the authorities or by the insurgents have little choice in the matter, yet in many cases, it appears that they join voluntarily.

As evinced above, children's protectors – parents, families and/or the community – play an important role in the recruitment of children in Afghanistan, either coercing the child into joining an insurgent group or the state forces, or exchanging the child for collective security. This is the outcome of cultural and social factors, with values being shaped by decades of conflict. Children's agency is lost in a trade-off between actors in the quest for manpower (state forces and the insurgents) and community leaders in the quest for security. Afghan children are in that regard 'immediately conceptualised as victims of the new modes of warfare, and their agency gets lost in the macro-context of political and social crisis'.[67]

Some commentators argue that some children who join the non-state actors are motivated by honour,[68] pride or cultural values. However, I would again argue that agency is missing because of the context: the child operates within traditional parameters that have been defined for him since early childhood, and little is left to an actual will or intent to join.[69] Is it really volunteering when there is no alternative?[70] The question was put forward by Afghan asylum seekers interviewed in 2013–15 by the UNHCR: many interviewees were puzzled by the European asylum system that did not seem to comprehend that decades of conflict had deeply impacted societal values and legitimized child recruitment for war, depriving them of a voice.[71] These children and teenagers were outraged at the thought that they could have any agency, rejecting outright the idea that they had any control over their life, often blaming parents and leaders for becoming fighters or migrants to avoid recruitment.[72]

Further, the conflict has pushed children into roles that are characterized by suffering, such as child soldiers, *bacha bazi*[73] or migrants. Afghan children and teenagers therefore fall prey to a context shaped by war that dictates their destinies. Culture, customs, traditions and religion have adapted to war and have transformed male children and teenagers into societal objects used by others for survival, which questions children's status as rights-bearing subjects.[74] Such children provide an excellent illustration of children affected by armed conflict, as highlighted in the much-discussed Machel report:

> More and more of the world is being sucked into a desolate moral vacuum. This is a space devoid of the most basic human values; a space in which children are slaughtered, raped, and maimed; a space in which children are exploited as soldiers; a space in which children are starved and exposed to extreme brutality. Such unregulated terror and violence speak of deliberate victimization. There are few further depths to which humanity can sink.[75]

---

[67] Lee 2009: 12.
[68] Dupree 2002: 978.
[69] Boutin 2014: 159.
[70] Ibid.
[71] Van Engeland and Schockaert 2015.
[72] Ibid.
[73] *Bacha bazi* is a traditional form of prostitution of male children. The literal interpretation is 'child games' but it has become the slang word for paedophilia.
[74] Derluyn et al. 2015: 29.
[75] Machel 1996: 7.

As stressed by Lee,[76] the recruitment and use of child soldiers in the Afghan conflict is also an illustration of Kaplan's views of conflicts that pervade culture.[77] Here, the pervasion of culture is anchored in a broader traditional environment where the collective supersedes the individual. In Afghanistan, children belong firstly to the community and the family, and are expected to contribute to social life from a young age.[78] Because of the decades-long conflict, this contribution has taken the shape of a contribution to the fighting. I therefore argue that children are culturally stripped of agency due to societal expectations.

Yet, the depiction of children as being solely victims of the context and societal values could be an error akin to Western imperialism or paternalism.[79] As Bodineau states:

> Reinforcing victimhood and leaving little room for children and youth's agency, and the process that invalidates any ideological justification of voluntary enlistment enforces the idea that children can only be manipulated, making them voiceless.[80]

Wars have always been barbaric, and children have always played a role in them. Whilst children can be seen as victims deprived of agency, they could also be perceived as children who have become fighters to survive within the given context. It could thus be argued that Afghan children's resilience should be interpreted as agency. This tension between Afghan children as victims or as actors is seen in British courts, when matters of asylum are brought to the attention of the judges. British judges tend, as do their international counterparts, to consider children as deprived of agency either because of their age or their lack of control over events. This is what Lee calls the 'Beah syndrome'.[81] When judges do this, the risk is of superimposing a colonial narrative when seeking to rescue a child who was destined to serve the community in any event. We might therefore be imposing a discourse of victimhood on children and teenagers who would have lacked agency because of the culture, whether there was a conflict or not.

While those words ring true, they ignore the fact that culture, customs, traditions and religion have morphed during the conflict. The concept of *bacha bazi* is a good illustration of how tradition transforms during wartimes. This centuries-long practice involves young boys being sold into sexual slavery to men. The practice is well explained in the bestselling book by Hosseini:[82] Hosseini's fictional work tells the story of a young boy, Amir, who, as an adult, seeks to rescue his friend's son from the clutches of a Taleban leader who sexually abuses him. Over the last few centuries, boys have been asked to cross-dress as little girls and dance in front of male adults. They are then given for sex to the highest bidder. It is rife in Afghanistan and some powerful men sometimes have a small harem of boys to show their power. While this practice was limited to warlords, it has become an endemic practice in post-Taleban society. *Bacha bazi* is an example of a limited traditional practice that expanded because of the context, becoming an instrument of war. The Taleban and

---

[76] Lee 2009: 12.
[77] Kaplan 1994, as cited by Lee 2009: 13.
[78] Ventevogel et al. 2013: 53.
[79] Breen 2006: 3.
[80] Bodineau 2014: 115.
[81] Lee 2009: 10.
[82] Hosseini 2003.

state authorities have tried to contain the phenomenon by forbidding the presence of children in military headquarters. While child prostitution is not to be equated with child soldiering, part of breaking the will of a child can include being a *bacha bazi* or being subjected to rape. This demonstrates how a traditional practice that goes back centuries, but was always limited, has become almost a norm in a fighting context.

Another example of how traditions have evolved in war is the abusive use of authority by community elders to compel children to enrol with security actors or an armed non-state actor. It is customary to have the community elders decide the fate of the small society they lead. Yet, in a context of crisis, leaders have accepted compromises, relying on their own understanding of customary law and traditional values: in Afghan society, children are socialized from an early age and are expected to shoulder social duties from the age of 12 years. Controlling the population has been key for the elders and they have relied on such traditional values to ensure compliance with forced recruitment. This explains why children and teenagers who have left the country to avoid forced recruitment cannot return to their original home: not only have they betrayed Afghan cultural values, they have also challenged authority. This power play is important to understand as it too explains why children are often disempowered and voiceless in the recruitment process: authority is at stake.[83] Groups like the Taleban are very much aware of this authority element and rely on it to recruit the children. This is how and why room for negotiation is created between the elders and the local armed non-states actors (ISIS, as a foreign entity does not have this local anchor): children become a vehicle to reassert authority on both sides without losing face.

I would thus suggest that these cultural and societal changes are crucial to an understanding of agency in the Afghan child soldier context. Children and teenagers who enrol or are compelled to join armed groups or forces have known no other situation than war: how can they make an informed decision when the context dictates their every move and when the community decision-makers rob them of their view to protect the group? This raises the question of how we evaluate intent: do we evaluate a child's intention to become a child soldier based on the opportunities offered in the local context or do we use international standards applicable to all child soldiers, not considering the local context? This question has been raised by Hanson, who calls for a better consideration of the 'lived realities' of young people participating in conflicts.[84] I argue that, in the best interests of the child, the local environment should be taken into account when considering the issue of choice at the time of recruitment. Contextualization allows for this. An example is to be found in the recruitment of Hazara children by the Iranian authorities to fight in Syria: these children obey a religious pattern whereby Iran exchanges its protection of the Afghan Shia communities for these services. It is the same motivation that pushes Pashtun teenagers to join the state forces or the Taleban: the social and cultural context trumps the individual interests, forcing youngsters to comply and enrol to fight. The predicament of Tajik children is even more acute: as a minority ethnic group in Afghanistan, the recruitment of these children into armed groups is often seen as necessary to protect the minority.

---

[83] Vautravers 2008: 102.
[84] Hanson 2011: 43.

As I call for a contextualized understanding of the phenomenon of child soldiers, just as Drumbl called for contextualization to understand the plight of women in Afghanistan,[85] I believe that consideration of how the context shapes agency and intent is key. One of the ways to fully comprehend the status of child soldiers in Afghanistan is to use intersectionality: we should consequently include culture, customs, traditions, religion, conflict, politics, drugs, economics and many other areas to develop a local understanding of the recruitment of young men and children in Afghanistan, and before talking about agency.

The key question is to know whether there is intent and agency when all the elements above come into play: can a child be empowered to choose to join a fighting group when he is hungry or scared, or where society requires this of him? As highlighted by Save the Children:

> Although children may come forward to join an armed group without conscription or press-ganging, this type of recruitment is rarely truly voluntary. Children may have no other option for survival in a conflict where they have lost family members or access to other forms of protection. Finally, children do not yet have the cognitive developmental skills to fully assess risk and choices that they may make under these conditions.[86]

We consequently need to examine what Bodineau calls 'binding contingencies'[87] when discussing agency and intent. In my view, such contingencies negate any agency of the child: the child becomes a vehicle for the provision of protection (for the family and/or the community when exchanged) or money (when a salary is included). I therefore suggest that the issue of child soldiers in Afghanistan should rather be discussed in terms of objectivization versus empowerment or agency in a conflict zone; this can be observed elsewhere in the world and is not unique to Afghanistan.

Part of the answer to the discussion on agency and objectivization is to be found in the way Afghan children are perceived in the local culture. One of the issues in the debate on child soldiers is indeed the definition of who is a child.[88] For the international community, a child is an individual under the age of 18 years old and '[a]ge is taken as a universal indicator of a child's moral agency'.[89] However, while international standards have adopted a politics of age when shaping the concept of childhood, reality is different in the field, in different parts of the world.[90] The Taleban judge the age of a child by his facial hair: the moment a male child grows facial hair, he can be recruited as a fighter. The Taleban produced their guidelines for combat in 2009:[91] the Code of Conduct is entitled *Afghanistan Islamic Emirate Rules and Regulations*.[92] These guidelines reflect the Taleban's approach to striking a balance between their aim to conquer the country through force and winning the hearts and minds of the people. The code has been understood as prohibiting the use

---

[85] Drumbl 2004.
[86] Save the Children 2010.
[87] Bodineau 2014: 117.
[88] Zyck 2011: 163.
[89] Lee 2009: 9.
[90] Rosen 2007: 296.
[91] Giustozzi 2009: 60.
[92] The Taleban 2009.

of child soldiers by some,[93] as it states that only children who have reached the age of puberty can be recruited and fight. Mullah Omar was more thorough in his edict, stating that only children with stubble can be allowed to join, as a beard is considered as a sign of maturity in line with customary law.[94] In reality, both instructions seem rather to aim at preventing the presence of child soldiers so as to control practices such as *bacha bazi*.[95] And, as children over the age of puberty, pursuant to this definition, yet under 18, can be recruited, there is no prohibition on the use of children in conflict. In that regard, the Taleban and other insurgent groups align themselves with the hard-line interpretations of Muslim classicist and neo-classicist scholars that allow the contribution of children to conflict.

Moving away from the battlefield to childhood more generally, in Afghanistan a child is usually defined as such by looking at Islamic law and customary law: in Hanafi law, the main school of Islamic law in Afghanistan, the age of puberty is established at 18 for boys and 17 for girls. The narrative of adulthood at 18 years old is also established in state law. A fringe of Hanafi law interpreters believe that the age of puberty is 12 years old and that this constitutes the threshold into adulthood.[96] This minority interpretation also reflects customary law: an individual of 12 years of age is considered old enough to marry and fight.[97] Both the minority interpretations of Islamic law and customary law therefore contribute to reinforcing the authority of the tribal elders over communities when it comes to child soldier recruitment, as they legitimize the recruitment of children under 18. Additionally, the early socialization of Afghan children that emphasizes the collective over the individual also leads to lack of empowerment. Children are expected to contribute to the family and communal life from a young age. As discussed earlier, parties to the conflict exploit this cultural pattern that focuses on the collective to render children vulnerable to forced recruitment and a career as a child soldier.

As a result, there is no golden age depiction of childhood that Rosen describes as a rather modern perception[98] and that Drumbl challenges as being artificial:[99] Afghan children are not expected to be innocent, educated and entrusted to adult care.[100] Their childhood is one that is owned by the community. There is therefore an issue with the very concept of child soldiers: they are not perceived as children anymore, consequently challenging our 'fundamental assumption of a universal notion of childhood and children's lack of social and political agency'.[101] The reality in Afghanistan, but also elsewhere, is that children become adults sooner and are expected to actively contribute to society early on. Studies have demonstrated that Afghan children and teenagers do picture themselves as adults

---

[93] Giustozzi cited in EASO 2016b: 40
[94] The use of physical attributes to determine age is not so different from the Western technique of measuring a wrist when deciding whether or not an asylum-seeker is an adult. See Van Engeland and Schockaert 2015.
[95] Johnson and DuPee 2012: 82
[96] As already demonstrated, the armed non-state actors operating in Afghanistan have a tendency to embrace minor views in Islam.
[97] Zyck 20011: 163; Dupree 2002 cited in Chrobok 2005: 21.
[98] Rosen 2015.
[99] Drumbl 2012: 47.
[100] Lee 2009: 12.
[101] Ibid.: 13.

and are very much aware of the expectations weighing on them.[102] Nonetheless, from the arguments I have made above, becoming an adult does not equate with empowerment: the collective nature of Afghan life reduces any agency or empowerment that might usually accompany adulthood. Age is thus not defined in legal terms but in social terms.[103] Some would say that this is the outcome of conflict; yet, historical reports show that children have been instrumentalized and socialized from early on. For example, the *bacha bazi* practice has existed for at least four centuries.[104]

Looking in more detail at agency, it has been argued that children are able to make strategic choices during conflicts to survive, but also at the time of recruitment: children may join armed groups because it is popular to be a fighter (as stressed by Kourouma in his fiction),[105] because of duty, or because they are forced into it. Lee speaks of opportunities that have led children to join.[106] Honwana talks of children exercising 'tactical agency',[107] which is 'the agency of the weak within structural confinements',[108] to deal with the immediate circumstances of their situation. Her view is that children sometimes opt to join as the alternative is worse, an observation also made by Rosen.[109] Drumbl speaks of 'circumscribed action' where the individual has 'the ability to act, the ability not to act, and the ability to do other than what he or she actually has done' but the range of these abilities is 'delimited, bounded and confined'.[110] Accordingly to Drumbl, child soldiers can be placed along a spectrum: at one end children exercise considerable volition in joining armed groups; at the other, they are subject to overwhelming coercion. I would argue that Afghan children are at the extreme of the coercion end of that spectrum. Drumbl believes that when child soldiers actively negotiate their context and show resilience, they display agency and a choice to participate in the conflict.[111] I suggest that Drumbl's idea functions in an environment where children have room to manoeuvre: as stated here, I believe that Afghan children do not benefit from that opportunity.

4. CONCLUSION

As illustrated in this chapter, children are perceived as duty-bearers born into a world of expectations, rather than rights-bearing subjects. This is particularly the case in non-urban areas, and this is why insurgents and militias tend to mostly recruit outside cities. This approach to child soldiers who are not considered to be children once they have hit puberty is shared by the community, the militias, the insurgents and, indirectly, by the security forces. Yet, at the same time, state authorities must comply with international law

---

[102] Zyck 2011: 163; Van Engeland and Schockaert 2015.
[103] Francis 2007 cited in Lee 2009: 6.
[104] Solter 2014: 187; Kapur 2014.
[105] Kourouma 2000: 83.
[106] Lee 2009: 25.
[107] Honwana 2006: 51.
[108] Lee 2009: 25.
[109] Rosen 2005: 85
[110] Drumbl 2012: 17 and 98.
[111] Ibid.: 17.

and thus domestic law provides for the transition to adulthood at the age of 18 years. As such, the Afghan case study questions the idea that agency is a universally shared value and it questions the concept of the 'child' in the term 'child soldier'.

REFERENCED WORKS

APPRO [Afghanistan Public Policy Research Organization] 2015. 'Afghanistan: Monitoring Women's Security in Transition' (Cycle 5) (January)
Asylos 2017. 'Afghanistan: Situation of Young Male "Westernised" Returnees to Kabul' (August)
Badie, B. 2018. 'Interview sur l'ère des nouveaux conflits' (International Committee of the Red Cross)
Behzan, F. and Furogh, S. 2017. 'Afghan Police: Children Kidnapped to be Suicide Bombers for Taliban' *Radio Free Europe* (10 July)
Bendix, A. 2017. 'Civilian Deaths in Afghanistan Reached Record High', *The Atlantic* (17 July)
Bodineau, S. 2014. 'Vulnerability and Agency: Figures of Child Soldiers within the Narratives of Child Protection Practitioners in the Democratic Republic of Congo' 4 *Autrepart* 111
Boon, K., Huq, A.Z. and Lovelace, D.C. 2011. *Terrorism: Commentary on Security Documents – Al Qaeda, the Taleban, and Conflict in Afghanistan* (New York: Oxford University Press)
Borchgrevink, K. 2010. 'Beyond Borders: Diversity and Transnational Links in Afghan Religious Education', Peace Research Institute Oslo (PRIO) Paper.
Boutin, D. 2014. 'Child Soldiering in Afghanistan', in J. Heath and A. Ashraf Zahedi (eds), *Children of Afghanistan: The Path to Peace* (Austin, TX: University of Texas Press) 153.
Breen, C. 2006. *Age Discrimination and Children's Rights: Ensuring Equality and Acknowledging Difference* (Leiden/Boston: Martinus Nijhoff)
Brett, R. and McCallin, M. 1996. *Children: The Invisible Soldiers* (Stockholm: Save the Children)
Carr, S.C. 2010. *The Psychology of Global Mobility* (New York: Springer)
Cesaretti, L. 2017. 'Afghanistan's Militias: The Enemy Within?' *The Diplomat* (4 January)
Child Soldiers International 2015. 'Briefing to the All Party Parliamentary Group on Afghanistan' (September)
Child Soldiers International 2016. 'Ongoing Recruitment and Use of Children by Parties to the Armed Conflict in Afghanistan' (March)
Chrobok, V. 2005. 'Demobilizing and Reintegrating Afghanistan's Young Soldiers: A Review and Assessment of Program Planning and Implementation' (Bonn International Center for Conversion)
Derluyn, I., Vandenhole, W., Parmentier S. and Mels, C. 2015. 'Victims and/or Perpetrators? Towards an Interdisciplinary Dialogue on Child Soldiers' 15 *BMC International Health and Human Rights* 3
Dominguez, G. 2016. 'Child Soldiers – What's their Role in the Afghan Conflict?' *DW* (13 February)
Dorronsoro, G. 2009. *The Taleban's Winning Strategy in Afghanistan* (Washington DC: Carnegie Endowment)
Dorronsoro, G. 2012. 'Waiting for the Taleban in Afghanistan' (Carnegie Endowment) (September)
Drumbl, M. 2004. 'Rights, Culture, and Crime: The Role of Rule of Law for the Women of Afghanistan' 42 *Columbia Journal of Transnational Law* 349
Drumbl, M. 2012. *Reimagining Child Soldiers in International Law and Policy* (Oxford: Oxford University Press)
Dupree, N.H. 2002. 'Cultural Heritage and National Identity in Afghanistan' 23 *Third World Quarterly* 977
EASO [European Asylum Support Office] 2012. 'EASO Country of Origin: Afghanistan' (July)
EASO 2016a. 'EASO Country of Origin Information Report: Afghanistan Security Situation' (January)
EASO 2016b. 'Afghanistan Recruitment by Armed Groups' (September) [available at: https://www.ecoi.net/en/file/local/1131093/90_1474353951_2019-09-easo-afghanistan-recruitment.pdf]
EASO 2017. 'Afghanistan: Individuals Targeted by Armed Actors in Conflict' (December)
Echavez, C.R., Mosawi, S.M. and Pilongo L.W. 2016. 'The Other Side of Gender Inequality: Men and Masculinities in Afghanistan' (Afghanistan Research and Evaluation Unit and Swedish Committee for Afghanistan Issues Paper) (January)
Farrell, T. and Semple, M. 2017. 'Ready for Peace? The Afghan Taleban after a Decade of War' (RUSI Briefing Papers) (31 January)
Faye, G. 2018. *Small Country* (London: Penguin)
Fazli, R., Johnson C. and Cooke P. 2015. 'Understanding and Countering Violent Extremism in Afghanistan' (United States Institute for Peace) (September)
Francis, D. 2007. 'Paper Protection Mechanisms: Child Soldiers and the International Protection of Children in Africa's Conflict Zones' 45 *Journal of Modern African Studies* 207
Gal, S. 2012. *War Against the Taleban: Why It All Went Wrong in Afghanistan* (London: Bloomsbury)
Giustozzi, A. 2009. *Decoding the New Taleban: Insights from the Afghan Field* (London: Hurst)

Giustozzi, A. 2012. 'Hearts, Minds, and the Barrel of a Gun: The Taliban's Shadow Government' 3 *PRISM* 71
Hanson, K. 2011. 'International Children's Rights and Armed Conflict' 5 *Human Rights and International Legal Discourse* 40
Hartjen, C.A. and Priyadarsini, S. 2012. *The Global Victimization of Children: Problems and Solutions* (Boston: Springer).
Honwana, A. 2006. *Child Soldiers in Africa* (Philadelphia: University of Pennsylvania Press)
Hosseini, K. 2003. *The Kite Runner* (New York: Riverhead Books)
HRW [Human Rights Watch] 2016. 'Afghanistan: Taleban Child Soldier Recruitment Surges' (17 February)
ICRC [International Committee of the Red Cross] 2015. 'Afghanistan: Concern over Growing Number of Civilian Casualties' (30 April)
International Crisis Group 2011. 'The Insurgency in Afghanistan's Heartland' (Asia Report No. 207) (27 June)
Jackson, A. 2018. 'Life under the Taliban Shadow Government' (Overseas Development Institute (ODI)) (June)
Johnson, T.H. and DuPee, M.C. 2012. 'Analysing the New Taliban Code of Conduct (*Layeha*): An Assessment of Changing Perspectives and Strategies of the Afghan Taliban' 3 *Central Asia Survey* 77
Kaplan, R. 1994. 'The Coming Anarchy: How Scarcity, Crime, Overpopulation, and Disease are Rapidly Destroying the Social Fabric of Our Planet', *The Atlantic* (February)
Kapur, R. 2014. 'Bacha Bazi: The Tragedy of Afghanistan's Dancing Boys', *The Diplomat* (August)
Kilcullen, D. 2009. 'Taleban and Counter-Insurgency in Kunar', in A. Giustozzi (ed), *Decoding the New Taleban: Insights from the Afghan Field* (New York: Columbia University Press) 231
Kourouma, A. 2000. *Allah is Not Obliged* (London: Vintage)
Landgren, K. 2007. 'Protection: The United Nations Children's Fund Experience', in M. O'Flaherty (ed), *The Human Rights Field Operation: Law, Theory and Practice* (London: Ashgate) 183
Landinfo 2014. 'Temanotat Afghanistan Sikkerhetsoppdatering' (9 January)
Lee, A-J. 2009. 'Understanding and Addressing the Phenomenon of 'Child Soldiers': The Gap between the Global Humanitarian Discourse and the Local Understandings and Experiences of Young People's Military Recruitment' (Refugee Studies Centre, Working Paper Series No. 52, University of Oxford)
Machel, G. 1996. *Promotion and Protection of the Rights of Children: Impact of Armed Conflict on Children* (New York: United Nations)
McNally, L. and Bucala, P. 2015. *The Taleban Resurgent: Threats to Afghanistan's Security* (Washington DC: Institute for the Study of War)
Obaid-Chinoy, S. 2009. 'Pakistan's Taliban Generation' [available at: http://www.pbs.org/frontlineworld/blog/2009/04/pakistanas_tali.html (accessed 16 October 2018)]
Quénivet, N. 2013. 'The Liberal Discourse and the "New Wars" of/on Children' 38 *Brooklyn Journal of International Law* 1053
Quénivet, N. 2017. 'Does and Should International Law Prohibit the Prosecution of Children for War Crimes?' 28 *European Journal of International Law* 433
Roggio, B. 2014. 'Afghan, US Forces Target Haqqani-Linked Taleban Leader in Parwan', *FDD's Long War Journal* (17 January)
Roggio, B. and Weiss, C. 2015. 'Taleban Touts Camp in Paktia Province', *FDD's Long War Journal* (5 August)
Rosen, D.M. 2005. *Armies of the Young: Child Soldiers in War and Terrorism* (Camden: Rutgers University Press)
Rosen, D.M. 2007. 'Child Soldiers, International Humanitarian Law, and the Globalisation of Childhood' 109 *American Anthropologist* 296
Rosen, D.M. 2015. *Child Soldiers in the Western Imagination: From Patriots to Victims* (New York: Rutgers University Press)
Rosenberg, M. 2014. 'False Claims in Afghan Accusations on U.S. Raid Add Doubts on Karzai', *New York Times* (24 January)
Rubin, B. 2015. 'Turmoil in the Taliban', *New Yorker* (31 July)
Ruttig, T. 2011. 'Ghorband, a Valley Once Friendly' *Afghanistan Analysts Network* (19 July)
Save the Children 2010. 'Child Soldiers: Care and Protection of Children in Emergencies – A Field Guide Online' [available at: https://resourcecentre.savethechildren.se/sites/default/files/documents/2386.pdf]
Singer, P.W. 2006. *The Enablers of War: Causal Factors behind the Child Soldier Phenomenon* (Washington DC)
Singer, P.W. 2010. 'The Enablers of War: Causal Factors behind the Child Soldier Phenomenon', in S. Gates and S. Reich (eds), *Soldiers in the Age of Fractured States* (Pittsburgh: Pittsburgh University Press) 93
Solter S. 2014. 'Children's Health: The Challenge of Survival', in J. Heath and A. Zahedi (eds), *Children of Afghanistan: The Path to Peace* (Austin, TX: University of Texas Press) 187
The Taleban 2009. *Taleban Handbook. Afghanistan Islamic Emirate Rules and Regulations*
UN Secretary-General 2015. 'The Situation in Afghanistan and Its Implications for International Peace and Security' (A/70/359–S/2015/684) (September)
UN Secretary-General 2016. 'The Situation in Afghanistan and Its Implications for International Peace and Security' (A/70/775–S/2016/218) (7 March)

UN Secretary-General 2017. 'The Situation in Afghanistan and its Implications for International Peace and Security' (UN Doc. A/72/392– S/2017/783) (15 September)
UNAMA [United Nations Assistance Mission in Afghanistan] 2016. 'Afghanistan: Protection of Civilians in Armed Conflicts: Annual Report' (February)
UNAMA 2017. 'Protection of Civilians in Armed Conflict: Midyear Report' (July)
UNHCR [United Nations High Commissioner for Refugees] 2012. 'Forced Recruitment by the Taleban in Afghanistan: UNHCR's Perspective' (July)
UNHCR 2014. 'Conflict-Induced Internal Displacement' (February)
UNHCR 2016. 'Eligibility Guidelines for Assessing the International Protection Needs of Asylum Seekers from Afghanistan'
Utas, M. 2003. *Sweet Battlefields: Youth and the Liberian Civil War* (PhD Uppsala University)
Van Engeland, A. and Schockaert, L. 2015. 'All Born on 01/01' (Brussels/Geneva: UNHCR)
Vautravers, A.J. 2008. 'Why Child Soldiers are Such a Complex Issue' 27 *Refugee Survey Quarterly* 96
Ventevogel, P., Jordans, M.J.D., Eggerman, M., van Mierlo, B. and Panter-Brick, C. 2013. 'Child Mental Health, Psychological Well-Being and Resilience in Afghanistan: A Review and Future Directions', in C. Fernando and M. Ferrari (eds), *Handbook of Resilience in Children of War* (New York: Springer) 51
Zyck, S.A. 2011. '"But I Am a Man": The Imposition of Childhood on and Denial of Identity and Economic Opportunity to Afghanistan Child Soldiers', in A. Özerdem and S. Podder (eds), *Child Soldiers: From Recruitment to Reintegration* (Basingstoke; New York: Palgrave Macmillan) 159

9. Weaponizing the weak: the role of children in terrorist groups
*Mia Bloom**

Violent extremist organizations have increasingly mobilized children into their ranks. The Islamic State of Iraq and Syria (ISIS), for example, has trained hundreds, if not thousands, of young children for front-line military engagement.[1] As ISIS has lost control of significant territory, it has come to refocus its efforts on affiliates in the AfPak (Afghan–Pakistan) region and the Sinai. In doing so, the group continues its exploitation of children in their Khorasan Wilayah (the ISIS Province (Wilaya) for Afghanistan). In the past three years, ISIS has sent over 400 children to their deaths in a variety of roles, from suicide car bombers (including children as young as 10 driving the vehicle) to propagandists, to commandoes in joint operations with adults.[2] In October 2013, the Taliban kidnapped 100 Afghan and Pakistani children to train them as suicide bombers.[3] In January 2014, the group posted a photo on Facebook showing their youngest Mujahid balancing an automatic weapon on barricades in Aleppo. That same month, the younger sister of an Afghan Taliban commander admitted to being forced to wear a suicide belt at a border police checkpoint in Kandahar.

By exploiting children, terrorist groups gain what they see as comparative advantages, notably the element of surprise and increased media attention for breaching societal norms and psychological barriers. The exploitation of children represents an alarming new development, both tactically and strategically. These groups are grooming the next generation of terrorist operatives.[4] Throughout the Middle East, children's soccer teams, streets, parks and summer camps are routinely named after suicide bombers.[5] Recruitment efforts have been uncovered in diaspora communities in the United States and United Kingdom. Perhaps the most well-known case was the disappearance of 17-year-old Burhan Hassan and six of his friends (Somali-American adolescents from Minneapolis) between 2007 and 2009, who were eventually found to have travelled to

---

* This work was supported by research grant ONR N00014-16-1-2693 'Preventing the Next Generation: Mapping the Pathways of Children's Mobilization into Violent Extremist Organizations' under the auspices of the Office of Naval Research. The views and conclusions contained in this document are those of the author and should not be interpreted as representing the official policies, either expressed or implied, of the Department of Defense, the Office of Naval Research, or the US government. The author thanks Tanya Zayed, Madhavi Devasher and Danielle Douez for their assistance on previous drafts. All images in this chapter were captured by the author from ISIS networks on their encrypted platform, Telegram. The images are disseminated publicly on the platform.

[1] Alalam News 2013.
[2] See Grooming the Next Generation.
[3] Zia 2014.
[4] Bloom and Horgan (forthcoming).
[5] Mekhennet and Warwick 2016.

Somalia to serve as suicide bombers.[6] In an October 2013 ISIS recruitment video that targeted young boys, some youthful al-Shabaab members from East London (UK) were featured with their infamous tagline: '*This* is the *real* Disneyland.'[7]

Attacks in Afghanistan and Pakistan involving child suicide bombers have shocked the world. The median age of suicide bombers continues to decrease.[8] A noticeable trend in the past three years has been the involvement of not only adolescents but also pre-pubescent children. Terrorist groups employ 12-year-olds and occasionally children as young as seven as suicide bombers. Schools specifically dedicated to training bombers have been established in Iraq, Pakistan, Syria and the Sudan. The growth of child soldiers in Africa has also been well documented (including by many of the contributors to this volume), and the broader exploitation of children by organizations such as the Liberation Tigers of Tamil Eelam (LTTE) has garnered international condemnation. Yet, our knowledge of how, why and when children become involved in terrorist movements has been limited. This chapter aims to help redress this gap.

This chapter contrasts child soldiers and children recruited by militant terrorist organizations. While some literature draws parallels between child soldiers in armed groups and child soldiers in terrorist groups, I prefer to maintain these distinctions. Also, with regard to terminology, I prefer not to search for totalizing vocabulary or phraseology to define 'terrorist groups'. This means I recognize that there is no clear or consistent language to describe such groups, nor am I convinced that efforts should be undertaken to develop such language. I therefore deploy a variety of terms such as terrorist groups, militant organizations, violent extremists and militias throughout this chapter. Mostly, however, I simply identify the group in question by its name. While I focus on ISIS, I make comparative references to a number of other groups, with a particular focus on Sri Lanka, Nepal and Sierra Leone. This chapter thereby contributes to the discussion of children's involvement in militant activities in these other jurisdictions as well.

In addition, this chapter suggests an innovative approach to understanding how ISIS, in particular, exploits children (see Figure 9.1). Child Soldiers International, the primary

Figure 9.1   Cubs of Khilafah (Caliphate) banner on Telegram

---

[6] Temple-Raston 2018.
[7] Ross.
[8] Yogev and Schweitzer 2016.

NGO focused on this subject, published a report in 2012 stating that there were no child soldiers in Syria, there were merely reports of children used as human shields.[9] To this day, media and NGOs have vastly underreported the number of children involved in the conflicts in Syria and Iraq[10] and have failed to demonstrate that virtually every militant group in the conflict, including those who enjoy the support of the United States and other Western countries, have exploited children on the front line.[11]

Issues of data collection are complicated when studying this phenomenon. Barry Ames notes that much of the literature on children and conflict has taken an advocacy position. Accordingly, most statistics, including the oft-cited number of 300,000 children under arms, cannot be independently verified.[12] While one cannot authenticate the actual number or percentages of children involved in ISIS as cited by NGOs and the UN,[13] the reality of their involvement holds true.

There is a further debate as to whether ISIS will be able to sustain its recruitment activities indefinitely with its loss of territorial control in Iraq and Syria. For several years ISIS ran a slick, modern social media campaign from its centres in Mosul and Raqqa – distributing messages across a variety of open Application Programming Interface (API) and encrypted social media platforms (for example: Twitter, Kik, Pinterest, Whatsapp, Viber, Surespot, Wickr, Ask.fm.) in as many as 25 languages, including American Sign Language.[14] On the surface, ISIS recruitment emulates a funnel characterized by 'milestones, such as hazing rituals and group identity-building exercises or validation of commitment to its principles through the recruits' demonstrated knowledge of radical Islam and the use of violence to achieve its goals'.[15] Yet, according to Richard Le Baron, the former director of the Center for Strategic Counterterrorism Communications, from ISIS' viewpoint:

> [S]ocial and other media are useful but not critical elements in radicalization and recruitment. Social media provides access to a large audience but it rarely is an independent force that mobilizes an individual to take off. . . . The motivation of a former Iraqi army major is quite different from that of a teenager from Wales. And only in the rarest cases does the religious/political ideology of ISIS appear to be a determining factor.[16]

Significantly, some of the conventional wisdom about child soldiers does not hold true for the children involved with ISIS, while other experiences complement each other. Gates and Reich's research has identified common themes across a variety of cases, to wit, that 'children become especially vulnerable with the breakdown of the traditional extended family', that 'schooling can mitigate the risk of child soldiering' and that 'females constitute a significant proportion of child soldiers'.[17] Ames has found that 'children

---

[9] Child Soldiers International 2012: 11.
[10] Motaparthy 2014; see also Reuters 2015a.
[11] Bloom 2017.
[12] Ames 2010; Rosen 2005. See also Rosen in this volume.
[13] Motaparthy 2014; see also Ashawi 2014.
[14] Stalinsky and Sosnow 2015.
[15] Gerwehr and Daly 2006: 77.
[16] LeBaron and McCants 2015.
[17] Gates and Reich 2010: 8, 10 and Ames 2010: 15.

are more likely to become child soldiers if one or both parents are dead'.[18] This chapter underscores the commonalities and differences between ISIS recruitment and how child soldiers have traditionally been recruited. By developing a model of violent extremist recruitment, the chapter seeks to examine the micro-processes at work for transforming children from casual bystanders into fully committed front-line fighters. This mobilization process constitutes an institutionalized form of child abuse, comprising six discrete phases: socialization, schooling, selection, subjugation, specialization and stationing.[19] This chapter addresses these phases. First, though, it provides some background to ISIS.

1. BACKGROUND

ISIS features children in virtually all of its propaganda. Between May and July 2015, the group released three videos involving children ranging from 10 to 15 years old. One video depicted young boys in a live-fire exercise inside an ISIS 'kill house' – an indoor firing range to train recruits to infiltrate residential structures and take control. The children were taught how to approach and enter the property before moving from room to room. They learned how to subdue and remove an occupant who is likely to be a potential hostage. In the videos, children are trained as snipers and taught how to ambush moving targets. Another video from February 2015 depicted 80 children, some as young as five, wearing camouflage, standing in formation and engaging in military exercises with guns. These children were allegedly taught how to behead people and how to use AK-47s.[20]

ISIS has even showcased children executing prisoners (see Figure 9.2). In January 2015, 12-year-old Ryan Essid from Toulouse, France executed two Russian prisoners accused of being spies from the FSB (Federal Security Service of the Russian Federation Федеральная служба безопасности Российской). A follow-up video featured a 13-year old boy shooting Muhammad Mossalam (an Arab Israeli from Jerusalem accused of being a Mossad spy) multiple times, including once in the head.[21] Smiling children led prisoners

Figure 9.2   Banner for video featuring child executioners

---

[18] Ames 2010: 16.
[19] See Horgan et al. 2016: 645–64.
[20] Engel 2015.
[21] Labott 2015.

to a beheading and handed out knives to adults in Hama, Syria, in March 2015. Months later, on 4 July 2015, 25 boys shot 25 regime soldiers before a packed crowd at the ancient Roman Amphitheatre in Palmyra, Syria. In yet another 22-minute video released from the Speicher massacre[22] (in Tikrit), children were the executioners.[23] The film showed a 'handcuffed soldier who confessed to being a Syrian army captain' and a child, '[c]lad in camouflage and clutching a small knife', who 'jerked the man's head back by his hair and put the blade to his throat'. After the execution the child posed holding the severed head.[24]

While the actual number of children recruited and fighting in Syria and Iraq remains unknown, for reasons explained above, a Syrian monitoring group (Violations Documenting Center) recorded 194 deaths of non-civilian male children between September 2011 and June 2014.[25] In June 2015, the United Nations reported that '271 boys and seven girls were recruited by militant groups affiliated with the Free Syrian Army, Kurdish People's Protection Units, ISIS, and al-Nusra Front'.[26] In 77 per cent of these cases, children were armed or used in combat. Almost one-fifth of these children were under the age of 15. In July 2015, the Syrian Observatory for Human Rights documented the deaths of 52 'Cubs of the Caliphate' (ISIS' term for child militants) and alleged that over 1,100 more children had been recruited in 2015 alone.[27]

Exploiting children is not merely advantageous for shock value and propaganda; children additionally are considered fully-fledged militants. After careful analysis of propaganda, social media use and interviews with child escapees, a clearer picture emerges of the ISIS recruitment and training model and how it differs from other organizations such as African militias.

2. RECRUITMENT

ISIS child recruits come from five sources: (1) children born to foreign fighters ('*emigrants*' according to ISIS); (2) those born to local Syrian or Iraqi fighters; (3) children who have been orphaned or abandoned; (4) those abducted from parents; and (5) those who 'voluntarily' join the Islamic State. The children in ISIS training camps tend to be those who have been taken from their families or found (abandoned or lost) in orphanages.[28] By contrast, the children in ISIS-controlled schools tend to be those whose families have volunteered them. An increasing percentage of children join ISIS as the result of a

---

[22] The Speicher massacre occurred on 12 June 2014 during which ISIS murdered 1,700 army recruits in a former palace compound of Saddam Hussein on the banks of the Tigris River near Tikrit.
[23] Jenkins 2015.
[24] Kavanaugh 2015.
[25] Violations Documentation Center in Syria.
[26] Opponents of ISIS have used child recruits. Human Rights Watch compiled a list of 59 children, 10 of them under 15, who were recruited by or volunteered for YPG or YPJ forces since July 2014. Human Rights Watch confirmed seven of these cases by speaking directly with the children's relatives. In some cases, the groups enlisted children without their parents' consent; see Human Rights Watch 2015.
[27] Al Jazeera 2015.
[28] Horgan et al. 2016.

200 *Research handbook on child soldiers*

Figure 9.3   Toddler featured in propaganda wearing camouflage fatigues and ISIS hat

grooming process in which the organization instils a sense of commitment to its cause and camaraderie among its young recruits. Foreign fighters encourage their own children to join the Cubs of the Caliphate but few of the children of foreign fighters are used as suicide bombers (see Figure 9.3). The vast majority of children are local or from the Middle East and North Africa (MENA) region. ISIS effects a distinction between children who are expendable and those who are featured repeatedly in their propaganda.

I conclude that the pattern of child recruitment into ISIS differs from recruitment patterns elsewhere, particularly in sub-Saharan Africa, where children were disproportionately orphaned or isolated from family prior to recruitment. Often the children's parents are dead (perhaps because children might have been forced to kill a parent as part of the recruitment process to ensure that the children can never return to their extended families and thereby exit the group) or the children were abducted or separated from their caregivers. As a general rule, parents or guardians in sub-Saharan Africa were not willing participants in the recruitment process. Militias subsequently re-socialized the children to form close ties to the group, replacing family with members of the militia to create a new 'family unit'.

Alfredson notes that when children are separated from their families, they become particularly vulnerable to recruitment and re-recruitment by militias, illustrating the connection between absence of parents and child soldiering. According to Betancourt, the death of a caregiver has particularly pernicious effects such as depression and anxiety in former child soldiers.[29] The death of parents or caregivers is the most frequently stated motivation for children to 'voluntarily join' militant movements. For example, in Sri Lanka, Kanagaratnam interviewed youth who voluntarily joined Tamil rebel groups and found that the death of family members was a key driving force in their mobilization. One

---

[29] Betancourt et al. 2011: 21–8.

former member of the LTTE rationalized: 'I needed security and I wanted to take revenge for what they did to my father. Only boys with personal losses are able to withstand military life for a long time. They have this determination to take revenge.'[30]

Kanagaratnam et al.'s interviews highlight how personal loss feeds individual motivations to become a suicide bomber or join dedicated *thatkodai* (martyrdom) brigades.[31] Gates and Reich note that the absence of parental authority is a precursor or root cause for youths' desire to avenge the death of loved ones.[32]

Parents who are part of ISIS appear not just willing to permit children's participation in all levels of violence but to encourage it. Muhajiroun (*emigrant*) parents have taken to Western social media to post images of their children posing with mutilated corpses or severed heads,[33] and encourage their children to become martyrs in ISIS video propaganda. ISIS has released several videos of fathers bidding their sons goodbye as they depart for a suicide mission. In this regard, ISIS recruitment parallels that of the Philippines' Moro Islamic Liberation Front (MILF),[34] more so than the LTTE or child soldiers in Africa. Many members of MILF encourage their children to engage in militant activities along with the family unit.

With other militant groups, the parents might sell their children to the terrorists voluntarily or because they were coerced to do so. According to a media report:

> In 2009, Pakistan's then Taliban leader, Baitullah Mehsud, was buying children aged 7 to 16 to serve as suicide bombers against American, Pakistani and Afghan targets. In a nation where the per capita income is $2,600 per year, the children could be sold for $7,000 to $14,000, Pakistani officials confirmed at the time.[35]

Based on field research in Malakand and the Swat Valley, Pakistan, Taliban commanders did not give parents an option. Against a background of widespread poverty, the Tehrik Taliban Pakistan (TTP) would demand financial payments equivalent to one year's salary from the local civilian population in return for protection. If families could not pay this extortionate amount, the group demanded a child for the movement instead.[36]

In addition to the presence or absence of parental authority, a significant difference between ISIS children and child soldiers elsewhere revolves around narcotics and alcohol. Myriam Denov and Richard Maclure describe the role played by drugs and alcohol in the preliminary stages of initiation to sow confusion and fear, and to prepare children for violent attacks.[37] Drug use was prevalent in the Revolutionary United Front (RUF) in Sierra Leone, where some children reported being injected with cocaine,[38] or taking

---

[30] Kanagaratnam et al. 2005: 515.
[31] Bloom 2005: 63.
[32] Gates and Reich 2010.
[33] Saul 2015.
[34] For a detailed review of child soldier recruitment in the Philippines, see Almarez et al. in this volume.
[35] *Washington Times* 2009.
[36] Horgan 2013.
[37] Denov and Maclure 2007: 243–61.
[38] Betancourt et al. 2008: 565–87.

hallucinatory drugs, alcohol, or gunpowder[39] as a means of gearing up for fighting. According to Tanya Zayed, formerly of the Romeo Dallaire Child Soldier's Initiative, among the first instructions for new child recruits in the Democratic Republic of the Congo (DRC) was how to roll a joint, smoke drugs and rape a woman.[40] By contrast, there are virtually no reports of ISIS children using drugs, and herein lies an important difference between child soldiers and ISIS Cubs. In ISIS, as an aside, such is not the case in terms of reports about the use of narcotics as well as sexual-performance-enhancing drugs by adults.

Zayed and Conradi explain the complex processes of recruitment in the Great Lakes region of Africa, which involve exploiting at-risk children or compelling them to engage in activities that will ensure future isolation:

> Some of these children tote automatic rifles and are forced to commit massacres. Others who are desperately poor or orphaned may choose to assist an armed group in a support capacity, as cooks or porters or messengers. In all of these cases, a whole host of international laws are being grievously broken.[41]

In some instances, perpetrating acts of violence is a crucial element of the recruitment process, including, for example, forcing children to kill their own parents or perpetrate acts of extreme brutality against family members. Dara Cohen writes that these acts of extreme violence by a group – for example mass rape or gang-rape – helps cohere the recruits to one another, foster kinship, build bonds and create a macabre 'band of brothers', especially when recruitment was coerced.[42] Forcing children to kill members of their own family can cause a psychological break and result in attachment to a new entity – the militia. This intimate form of violence also cuts the child off from a possible exit strategy from the militia, thereby leaving him or her with nowhere to go in the event of any escape.

In contrast, ISIS facilitates recruitment by branding itself as a utopian society and ideal way of life, luring in parents who bring their children or children who might run away from home. Many European *emigrants* to the Islamic state insist that the Caliphate provides a better environment for their children than the licentious, drug-infested West. One woman, Asiya Ummi Abdullah, left her husband, Sahin Akhtan and took their three-year-old to Raqqa, claiming that she did not want her son growing up in Turkey surrounded by rampant homosexuality, drunkenness and a permissive environment. According to Asiya's Facebook post: 'The children of that country [Turkey] see all of it and become either murderers or delinquents or homosexuals or thieves. . . . [L]iving under Shari'a, means that my 3-year-old boy's spiritual life is secure. [My son] will know God and live under his rules . . .'[43]

British ex-punk rock singer Sally Jones, who was killed by an American drone in 2017, left Kent for Raqqa in 2013 (with her 10-year-old son Jojo) to marry Junaid Hussein, a

---

[39] Maclure and Denov 2006: 119–35.
[40] Interview with the Author, New York City, May 2015. See also Parmar and Lebrat in this volume for a discussion of child soldiering and related violations committed against children in armed conflict in the DRC.
[41] *National Post* 2013.
[42] Cohen (forthcoming).
[43] Associated Press 2014.

computer hacker from Birmingham and ISIS' master of social media.[44] There are numerous other examples of parents willingly bringing their children to a war zone, such as the Dawood sisters, who left their respective husbands in the UK to join ISIS, abducting their nine children to Syria. The women joined their brother Ahmed who was already a member of ISIS and in the Caliphate.[45]

ISIS appeals directly to young people to defy and disregard parents who are not supporters.[46] They encourage the children to flout usual parental authority if parents refuse to adhere to ISIS' principles or ideology (a number of parents support their children in joining ISIS, to be clear). ISIS even encourages girls to travel without a chaperon to the so-called Caliphate (which would theoretically violate strict codes of conduct for single women and girls). In February 2015, for example, three girls from London's Bethnal Green Academy disappeared, following a classmate who had vanished a few months prior. For these teenage Muslim girls, Raqqa is 'a world in which teenage rebellion is expressed through a radical religiosity that questions everything around them. In this world, the counterculture is conservative. Islam is punk rock. The headscarf is liberating. Beards are sexy.'[47]

Hundreds of foreign children arrived in Syria from Europe, the Middle East and South Asia between 2014 and 2017.[48] To date, the estimated number of foreign fighters who have joined ISIS exceeds 30,000 from over 100 different countries.[49] When foreign fighters arrive in Syria, they enrol their (male) children in one of the many religious schools, two of which cater specifically to English speakers. The schools are the setting for the recruitment process and funnel youth into the 'Cubs of the Khilafah'. The transformation of children from bystanders to committed militants thereby begins.

On ISIS social media the Cubs are shown to play a critical role and are regularly featured to promote encrypted ISIS channels and other memes. In October 2017 as ISIS began to lose control of vast stretches of territory in Syria and Iraq, ISIS online propaganda began to emphasize affiliated groups in Afghanistan, Sinai and South East Asia as the new focus for their operations, especially those involving children.

In ISIS chat rooms, recruiters code-named Muhd-Ata abdulkarim, Sniper Wolf and Alnasseri posted the following message:

> Remember this, 'Marawi is just the beginning!' as of those who survives Walahi we will train those new cubs and soldiers migrated from different countries for the knowledge we gain inside for more than 4 month of intense fighting agaisnt [sic] your crusader forces. Walahi the next seige [sic] you will never see it coming bi'idnillah.[50]

---

[44] Hussein was killed by a US drone strike on 27 August 2015. See BBC News 2015.
[45] Whitehead and Sawer 2015.
[46] Bentley et al. 2014.
[47] Benhold 2015.
[48] Byman and Shapiro 2014.
[49] Mamoun 2015.
[50] Alnasseri 2017.

3. SOCIALIZATION

ISIS targets children in unique ways that differ from those deployed by other terrorist groups. Historically, a number of terrorist groups have formalized the inclusion of young people by creating youth wings or children's brigades. Examples come from Hamas, Ogra Sinn Fein and Hezbollah, where such structures have generally been created with the intention of providing ideological preparation to ensure consistent and unified revolutionary political views. In most of these groups, children are not 'activated' for front-line activities until after they turn 16. In fact, some left-wing European groups like the Red Brigades refused to engage youth altogether. By contrast, ISIS targets children from a young age and engages them on the front lines early on.

ISIS has recruited children in mosques, schools and public areas where execution by stoning, beheading, crucifixion and other violent acts are carried out. According to Rami Abdulrahman, the head of the Syrian Observatory for Human Rights, '[ISIS] uses children because it is easy to brainwash them. They can build these children into what they want, they stop them from going to school and send them to ISIS schools instead.'[51] While the view may be that children are brainwashed, ISIS inveigles children using non-coercive indoctrination, through a gradual socialization into ISIS' ideology and worldview (see Figure 9.4). The organization socializes children in a number of ways – most

Figure 9.4 Two young boys posing with their finger raised (Tawhid) with the ISIS flag, December 2017

visibly through public events aimed at raising awareness of ISIS' apocalyptic vision and the purported benefits of membership. Some of these events attract children by offering

---

[51] Reuters 2015b.

them free toys, candy or ice cream just for showing up.[52] Local children help out at these 'meet and greet' events by waving the ISIS flag or distributing leaflets to passers-by: 'Such enticements serve as a kind of macabre ice-cream truck, beckoning local kids to come out and learn more about what life is like with the Islamic State.'[53]

4. DESENSITIZATION

Another stage involves a process of desensitization to violence. Initially, children are encouraged to conduct mock executions using dolls.[54] Then they attend public viewings of filmed executions (see Figure 9.2). Eventually, ISIS requires the children to attend live events including corporal punishment and executions. The routine spectacle of such events internalizes and normalizes the violence. Although some children may get physically ill from attending the beheadings,[55] the vast majority become immune to violence. This follows from what psychologist Albert Bandura described as moral disengagement and the process of desensitization:

> In early phases of child development conduct is largely regulated by external dictates and social sanctions. In the course of socialization people adopt moral standards that serve as guides and major bases for self-sanctions regarding moral conduct. ... In the face of situational inducements to behave in inhumane ways, people can choose to behave otherwise by exerting self-influence.[56]

ISIS children who have gone through this socialization process lose their capacity for self-sanctioning.

ISIS also provides rewards. ISIS teaches the children of foreign fighters that even peripheral participation will be rewarded. Human Rights Watch has verified that children are compensated. 'Amr received US$100 and monthly salaries of up to $135, while others said they participated without pay.'[57] Other children reported compensation of up to $150 a month, in contrast to adults who receive up to $1,000.[58]

Many attend training camps where they learn military tactics and receive weapons training. In propaganda, the children are carefully posed and coached by those filming as to how to behave and what to say. In some cases, the children are praised for wielding a weapon or holding up a decapitated head.

---

[52] http://www.liveleak.com/view?i=b0b_1428844789 (this thread was deleted after the account was deleted by the user).
[53] Horgan and Bloom 2015.
[54] Karam and Janssen 2015.
[55] Damon 2014.
[56] Bandura 1999: 193–4.
[57] Motaparthy 2014.
[58] Damon 2014.

Figure 9.5   Children studying an ISIS curriculum in Afghanistan

5. SCHOOLING

ISIS recruitment often occurs at schools (see Figure 9.5).[59] As a result of the civil war, the Syrian state descended into chaos and ISIS assumed de facto authority over schools and mosques in the areas under its control. Although a significant portion of Syrian teachers remained in their positions, they were forced to teach an ISIS-controlled curriculum to gender-segregated pupils. The curriculum included weapons training and intense ideological conditioning. Although attendance at these schools was not mandatory, many parents sent their children. There were a few reported instances in which ISIS threatened parents who refused to comply.

At school, children are indoctrinated into the group's ideology, thereby bringing the children closer to each other and providing ISIS recruiters access and opportunity to scout for talent. Students earn Cub status in one of the dedicated training camps (for example, Camp Farouq).[60] Educational programmes organized in ISIS-controlled schools stand in contrast to the experience of child soldiers in Africa, who received little to no 'education'. During their respective military campaigns, neither Liberian nor Ugandan militias ran schools to groom the next generation. If anything, the militias were not interested in creating an ideological legacy. Gates and Reich acknowledge that in such cases 'former child soldiers suffer from a lack of educational and vocational skills'.[61] In

---

[59] See also Almarez et al. in this volume on the role of Islamic education in the recruitment of child soldiers.
[60] Associated Press 2015.
[61] Gates and Reich 2010: 6.

this respect ISIS shares some characteristics with the Tamil Tigers, who used propaganda in schools to attract young recruits.

Maoists in Nepal similarly turned to such methods during the decade-long civil war in 1996 when they fought the country's monarchy. According to Rajenda Shakya of the SNV Netherlands Development Organization, Maoists used mass schooling to foster a sense of identity in young children through a standardized curriculum. The rebels provided mandatory education for girls, eliminated discrimination based on caste, forced teachers to comply with their rules and regulations, and banned the study of Sanskrit.[62] The Maoists' fundamental view was that education was essential to create a new generation of enlightened revolutionaries. Shakya notes that: 'Recruitment campaigns of youth (both voluntary and forced) were expedited, many were taken directly from schools, reportedly 10–200 at a [single] time.'[63] In Nepal, schools were transformed from educational providers to recruitment centres, and the Maoists urged students to form unions to disseminate propaganda using cultural programmes and leftist rhetoric.[64] The 'empowerment' rhetoric encouraged children to join voluntarily, while older students were taken by force to participate in the campaigns. Recruiters on both sides of the conflict approached schools strategically to gain access to children. About 32,000 individuals registered as combatants after the end of the conflict in 2006; the United Nations Mission in Nepal verified 19,602 of these as combatants and disqualified over 4,000 persons for being under-age. The disqualified were discharged from the cantonments in 2010.

Like Tamil and Nepalese groups, ISIS engenders a sense of pride, prestige and competition among the students to achieve status as a Cub. Not every child is eligible for the honour of membership. Younger students may be groomed as spies and encouraged to inform on family members or neighbours who criticize the group or violate Shari'a law.

6. SELECTION AND TRAINING

If the child is selected for Cub training, he (no girls are trained) will undergo a systematic process that involves indoctrination and physical conditioning. Newly graduated Cubs are paraded in full regalia with ample weaponry to signal strength and discipline. In propaganda videos, children are instructed to stand still while suffering beatings from adult commanders. In the background, dozens of younger children look on admiringly. The cycle repeats itself with each wave of graduates attracting new child recruits. Accounts of former ISIS Cubs paint a bleak picture of daily life in ISIS training camps. The daily schedule included praying, religious instruction and military tactics instruction, as well as weapons training.[65] Children were pushed to their mental and physical limits during the training sessions, beaten to 'toughen them up' and forced to sleep on flea-infested mattresses. Yet despite the hardships, or maybe as a result of them, the experiences fostered an intense sense of camaraderie among the cohort.

---

[62] For girls, *voluntarily* joining the Maoist struggle became their only option to escape the gender discrimination and sexual violence of traditional Hindu culture in Nepal.
[63] Shakya 2011: 558.
[64] Hart 2001: 26.
[65] Motaparthy 2014.

The Tamil Tigers also trained young recruits with a wooden rifle to prepare them for using a real gun. Maslen, as well as Charlu Lata Hogg (Chatham House's Asia Fellow), state that children first served as messengers and spies.[66] By age 10, they were used as combatants, when they were strong enough to shoot a gun. Tamil Tiger boys received combat training earlier than girls.[67] Among the Palestinian terrorist groups, the Popular Front for the Liberation of Palestine (PFLP) recruits children for cultural and educational activities, during which they are evaluated for membership. However, official membership in the PFLP is permitted only at 18.[68]

In contrast, Maslen contends that child soldiers in Africa received little training and were frequently massacred. Those children who refused to follow orders or tried to escape were killed.[69] Children were often perceived as low-skilled members of the military who were valuable because of their youth and availability. Child soldiers in African conflicts generally were not gradually introduced into military life. In respect of the RUF in Sierra Leone, Maclure and Denov note that the speed of engagement with the group was not uniform: 'For some, learning how to engage in armed conflict was a relatively slow and methodical process. For others, weapons training was a ruthless sink-or-swim process, with only the most cursory demonstrations provided before they were led into combat.'[70] Nonetheless, there was often a progression. As Denov and Maclure note:

> The process of becoming full-fledged child soldiers involved a progression from the status of frightened and disoriented recruits who were often forcibly taken from their homes and communities to that of ruthless destroyers who became steeped in a sense of collective purpose and power. It was a progression that effectively perpetuated a violent social system.[71]

Child soldiers tended to be separated and isolated from their families at the outset – moved from their traditional villages or, as previously mentioned, even at times forced to kill family members in order to destroy their option of fleeing home.

7. SPECIALIZATION AND STATIONING

Although Cubs may have had multiple or overlapping roles within the organization, many underwent training for specialized tasks. Some children were assigned to checkpoints or bodyguard duties, which required them to wear a suicide vest even if they were not suicide bombers. One 15-year-old interviewed by CNN's Arwa Damon said that he was strapped with an explosive belt, given a pistol, an AK-47 and a radio and ordered to protect a base in the eastern Syrian city of Deir Ezzor.[72] Yasir (not his real name) worried his belt might accidentally detonate but the organization insisted he wear it to show his allegiance. ISIS began using 14-year-old suicide bombers starting in the summer of 2015. At that point,

---

[66] Bloom 2015.
[67] *The Telegraph* 2009.
[68] Defence for Children International 2012.
[69] Coalition to Stop the Use of Child Soldiers 2000.
[70] Maclure and Denov 2006: 125.
[71] Ibid.: 129.
[72] Damon 2014; Bloom 2015.

IED vests became more than decorative signs of commitment. ISIS training camps in Aleppo included children as young as 13 being deployed as suicide car bombers.[73]

Children who demonstrate an aptitude for communication and a grasp of ISIS ideology are occasionally deployed as recruiters, adopting public speaking roles to conscript other children. Child recruiters not only spur adults into action, they lure more children into the fold with the promise of status, purpose and admiration from adult militants and the public alike.

ISIS has pioneered a new form of resilience and longevity by combining intense physical and military training with unusually deep levels of ideological and psychological indoctrination. ISIS designed a systematic process of cultivating competent young militants who genuinely embrace ISIS ideology. ISIS' priority is to ensure the continuity and longevity of the group,[74] thereby rendering it more multifaceted than the terrorist organizations of the past.

8. THE ILLUSION OF VOLUNTARINESS

One of the thorniest issues regarding the recruitment of children by terrorist groups is whether children can ever freely choose to become involved? Questions about the 'voluntariness' of recruitment into ISIS, upon which this chapter has elaborated, can be discussed in relation to the 'voluntariness' demonstrated by youthful members of other groups.[75] In Kilanochi, Sri Lanka, for example, children often sought out involvement with the LTTE.[76] At a very early age, children emulated the behaviour and dress of the militants. Both boys and girls envisioned joining the organization as a way to demonstrate their allegiance to the movement, their family, their community and to the Tamil people, and may have considered it 'cool'.[77] This would be equivalent to what some analysts refer to as 'Jihadi cool' among European Muslim youth.

Alfredson argues that 'voluntary' group participation may be only an illusion in situations where political or economic forces may leave children with no other option.[78] Children may see joining violent organizations willingly as a safer option when compared to being preyed upon.[79] Myriam Denov stresses that girls join violent extremist groups to satisfy basic needs for food and protection or to exact revenge for lost loved ones.[80] In Sierra Leone, girls joined the Civil Defence Forces as fighters along with their boyfriends or husbands. Girls may join for real or perceived empowerment. In Africa, some women joined the very groups that abused them sexually, the logic being that only such groups were powerful enough to provide the protection they needed. The desire for

---

[73] Motaparthy 2014: 20.
[74] Jawahar and McLaughlin 2001: 397–414.
[75] See also Rosen in this volume, who, when discussing the concept of the child soldier, concludes that the language of advocacy has become the language of inquiry.
[76] Author's field research in Sri Lanka, November–December 2002.
[77] Ibid.
[78] Alfredson 2002: 17–27.
[79] Rosen 2005.
[80] Denov and Ricard-Guay 2013: 473–88.

protection may have also inspired girls to join the FARC in Colombia (Fuerzas Armadas Revolucionarias de Colombia), to escape domestic abuse at home, develop skills and meet basic human needs for food, shelter and protection.[81]

Even in Afghanistan, the need for food and shelter motivated children to enlist. As reported in an Afghan newspaper: 'Taliban insurgents are bribing starving children to plant roadside bombs, act as decoys and to be suicide bombers against Afghan and foreign forces in the country. They recruit the young boys from the ranks of homeless and orphaned children.'[82]

Shakya illustrated this point when describing the experiences of an orphaned child who joined the Maoist rebels in Nepal with his siblings after witnessing the murder of his parents by a state military helicopter.[83] Additionally, his sister was raped and killed by government forces. The local community abandoned the children – this is not a unique experience. In desperation, the children sought sanctuary with the Maoist rebels who took them in. Ordinarily however, children who joined the Maoists did so with the encouragement or example of their parents and especially of older siblings.

For young people who joined the Tamil armed rebels, Kanagaratnam found that interviewees claimed multiple motivations – in particular feelings of discrimination or inequality. Often the provision of state benefits, or lack thereof, especially education, instilled a sense of outrage. One interviewee explained:

> Youngsters [of] school age know about the standardization system in our country. As Tamils they are discriminated [against]. Even if you study you are going to be under suppression. Tamils need a higher cut off point than the Sinhalese to get to the University. So we see that we have no future.[84]

Jordans et al. report that, in Burundi, 69.4 per cent of the youth joined voluntarily, while 16.3 per cent were recruited by force and 8.4 per cent were abducted. For those that reported 'voluntary' armed group participation, the most frequently cited reason was for material benefits, followed by fear and the prestige of being part of the group. Fewer of Jordans' respondents were influenced by their peers, by ideology, desire for vengeance, or as a result of social exclusion.[85]

Pugel's research on Liberia found that children's induction was not uniform and varied by organization. In MODEL (Movement for Democracy in Liberia), most child soldiers reported that they 'went looking for the group', while most LURD (Liberians United for Reconciliation & Democracy) recruits joined when a 'friend/relative joined the group'.[86] However, more than a quarter of LURD respondents joined after the 'group attacked my village'. Reasons for joining were comparable across all groups, with the most frequently

---

[81] Rice 2013. For details of child soldier recruitment and use in the armed groups/criminal bands in Colombia, see Jiménez in this volume.
[82] Zia 2014.
[83] Shakya 2011.
[84] Kanagaratnam et al. 2005: 515.
[85] Jordans et al. 2012: 905.
[86] Pugel 2010. For details of the conflict in Liberia and an account of disarmament, demobilization and reintegration programmes and former girl child soldiers, see Vastapuu in this volume.

cited one being the desire to 'protect family'. Nevertheless, one-quarter of all children across each group admitted they had been abducted.

9. GENDER AND ROLE DIFFERENTIATION

ISIS' parent organization, Al-Qaida in Iraq (AQI), inspired the group's ideology.[87] One critical area of difference between the Islamic State and AQI arises, however: the exclusion of women on the front lines. Women in ISIS are almost exclusively used for recruitment, reward, retention and reproduction. This contrasts with how other terrorist organizations have used women and girls (for example, Red Brigades, IRA, LTTE, Al Aqsa Martyrs Brigade, PFLP, Imarat Kavkaz). Overall, girls constitute as much as 30 per cent of child soldiers. The roles for girls in armed groups vary by age and individual, but tend to involve 'domestic work, sexual slavery, and combat activities. Importantly, in all of the contexts, girls' roles were multiple and fluid most often carrying out a variety of roles and tasks simultaneously'.[88]

Denov and Maclure's life history of two RUF child soldiers in Sierra Leone outlines the process of role development and compares the experience of a male and a female RUF fighter.[89] Isata was abducted at the age of nine. She was gang-raped and sexually abused until she became the 'wife' of a commander. Isata's initial role was mostly domestic and included cooking, cleaning and portage. After a year, she received weapons training and became a combatant, which she found to be empowering. She eventually took part in killings and mutilations and used drugs and alcohol along with the rest of the group. She exited the group after being abandoned by the commander who had impregnated her and was rescued by UN troops.[90]

Mohamed was similarly abducted at the age of nine. His first experiences included being forced to use drugs and being beaten. During his recruitment, he formed close bonds with the other children and their commanders. Violence was a form of socialization into the group and its norms. Mohamed eventually became a commander of a 'small boys' unit, which was a source of great pride and contributed to his feelings of self-worth. In both cases, Isata and Mohamed experienced 'role shifts' that triggered obedience to the organization under threat of punishment for failing to perform or not fulfilling roles that were assigned to them.

Betancourt et al. explain that in Sierra Leone regular camp duties (for example, portage, cooking and laundry) were the 'main duties' for both male and female child soldiers, who spent much of their waking hours working.[91] Maclure and Denov note that even while having combat roles, boy soldiers' jobs included 'manning military checkpoints, carrying out "domestic" chores (for example, fetching firewood and water), serving as porters (carrying weapons, ammunition, looted goods and wounded comrades) and acting as

---

[87] Weiss and Hassan 2015.
[88] Denov 2008: 819.
[89] Denov and Maclure 2005.
[90] Maclure and Denov 2006: 119–35.
[91] Betancourt et al. 2011: 21–8.

bodyguards for their commanders'.[92] Interviews given by Black Diamond, a well-known female commander of LURD's women's auxiliary corps, demonstrate how fighting was the best way for women to protect themselves from being raped. Indeed, Black Diamond explains: 'Becoming a fighter was the best thing I could do under the circumstances.'[93] The fact that most girls and women were not treated differently from the boys was an assertion made by Mairead Farrell, a leading female commander of the Provisional IRA.[94]

ISIS is also unique in that it enforces hyper-segregation of boys from girls, and men from women, and refuses to engage women in any meaningful way (beyond a handful of morality enforcers, the now infamous *Al Khansaa* Brigade). It's worth noting that Jihadi Salafi ideology is not the key factor accounting for this difference. AQI, ISIS' parent organization, and many other Jihadi groups, including Boko Haram, its African affiliate in Nigeria, have used women (and little girls) to deadly effect and with great enthusiasm.[95] Whereas Jihadi groups have historically employed female bombers and women on the front lines, ISIS remains reticent to tap 50 per cent of its population, even after suffering terrible territorial losses.[96] As Warner and Matfess note: 'Between April 2011 and June 2017 Boko Haram deployed 434 bombers in 238 suicide-bombing attacks. At least 56 percent of the bombers were women (243) and at least 81 were children or teenagers.'[97] ISIS, in contrast, does not use girls. Despite Boko Haram's pledge of allegiance (*bay'ah*) to al-Baghdadi in March 2015, the two organizations remain worlds apart in terms of strategy. In 2014, prior to its *bay'ah*, UNICEF reported that Boko Haram used women and girls to carry out three-quarters of the attacks in Nigeria.[98] Boko Haram has used girls as young as seven to carry out attacks. One girl blew herself up along with a baby strapped to her back.[99] This is also true of ISIS' other affiliates, for example in the Philippines and Marawi where entire families participate in suicide attacks, including women and children.[100] In this respect, there is no consistency within ISIS and its affiliates with regard to using women and girls on the front lines.

---

[92] Maclure and Denov 2006: 128.
[93] Taylor 2012.
[94] *Belfast Telegraph* 2014.
[95] There were 63 female suicide bombers for Boko Haram over the first 14 months after women became suicide bombers in 2014, the vast majority of the women were assumed to be kidnapped (e.g. from Chibok). The number of female bombers doubled the following year; see Bloom and Matfess 2016: 104. See also Casey-Maslen in this volume.
[96] There has only been one video in which veiled women are video-taped shooting (badly) on the battlefield during the so-called 'Battle to Avenge Chaste Women'. Dearden 2018. Nevertheless, analysis of ISIS social media is clear that women serve an instrumental and symbolic purpose rather than a strategic one. Lahoud: 2018.
[97] Warner and Matfess 2017.
[98] UNICEF 2015.
[99] Warner and Matfess 2017.
[100] Moore 2017.

10. CONCLUSION

The literature on child soldiers in Africa shows that children are recruited not for the future but for the present. Many children are killed in battle and few progress up the ranks to become adult leaders of the group.[101] From its tactics, strategies and the posted propaganda (above), I argue that ISIS takes a longer-term view of their child recruits.

What seems to have worked for several Disarmament, Demobilization and Reintegration programmes in Africa[102] – transformative roles for children aided by family, community and educational and religious authorities – may not work in Syria, as these institutions have been co-opted, controlled and distorted by ISIS. Families are not especially helpful for demobilization and preventing recidivism if the children's relatives are the ones who gave the terrorists access to the children in the first place.

If the international community is to have any hope of reintegrating those children who survive and leave ISIS, one thing is certain: it will require a level of coordination and creativity not seen in any de-radicalization programme to date. Demobilization will require a multi-pronged approach that addresses the psychological trauma suffered by the children from watching executions, in addition to the effects of having participated in acts of violence.

The children will need to unlearn the distortions of the Islamic faith (for example, that Islam sanctions suicide or killing civilians) and learn vocational training. They will likely encounter challenges with socialization. They may lack empathy and suffer from attachment problems. Programmes to treat children in militant organizations exist. However, reintegration will be all the more challenging with ISIS. It is often the family that encouraged the children and exposed them to the violence in the first place, and I argue children will likely have to be separated from the family members. While this process/endeavour will certainly be complicated, there is no choice but to begin planning for it now.

REFERENCED WORKS

Al Jazeera 2015. 'Scores of ISIL Child Soldiers "Killed" in Syria in 2015' (15 July) [available at: http://www.aljazeera.com/news/2015/07/scores-isil-child-soldiers-killed-syria-2015-150715132745980.html (accessed 16 June 2018)]

Alalam News 2013. 'ISIL Terrorists Recruit Children for War in Syria' (25 December) [available at: http://en.alalam.ir/news/1548067 (accessed 16 June 2018)]

Alfredson, L. 2002. 'Child Soldiers, Displacement and Human Security' 3*Children and Security* 17

Alnasseri 2017. 'Sons of the Khilafah', *Telegram*, posted 17 October

Ames, B. 2010. 'Methodological Problems in the Study of Child Soldiers', in S. Gates and S. Reich (eds), *Child Soldiers in the Age of Fractured States* (Pittsburgh, PA: University of Pittsburgh Press) 14

Ashawi, K. 2014. 'Syria: Armed Groups Send Children into Battle' (Human Rights Watch) (22 June) [available at: https://www.hrw.org/news/2014/06/22/syria-armed-groups-send-children-battle (accessed 23 June 2018)]

Associated Press 2014. 'Woman Leaves Turkey for "Family-Friendly" ISIS' (24 September) [available at: http://english.alarabiya.net/en/perspective/features/2014/09/24/Woman-leaves-Turkey-for-family-friendly-ISIS.html (accessed 23 June 2018)]

Associated Press 2015. '"They Beat Us Everywhere": Inside ISIS Training Camps for Terror's Next

---

[101] See Wratto; Wheeler 2015.
[102] On DDR programmes in Africa, see Casey-Maslen in this volume; Wessells in this volume.

Generation' (20 July) [available at: http://www.foxnews.com/world/2015/07/20/beat-us-everywhere-inside-isis-training-camps-for-terror-next-generation/ (accessed 23 June 2018)]

Bandura, A. 1999. 'Moral Disengagement in the Perpetration of Inhumanities' 3 *Personality and Social Psychology Review* 193

BBC News 2015. 'UK Jihadist Junaid Hussain Killed in Syria Drone Strike, Says US' (27 August) [available at: http://www.bbc.com/news/uk-34078900 (accessed 16 June 2018)]

Belfast Telegraph 2014. 'Mairia Cahill: In Fairness, When It Came to Killing, the IRA Were Always Keen on Equal Opportunities' (27 October) [available at: http://www.belfasttelegraph.co.uk/opinion/debateni/mairia-cahill-in-fairness-when-it-came-to-killing-the-ira-were-always-keen-on-equal-opportunities-30695137.html (accessed 16 June 2018)]

Benhold, K. 2015. 'Jihad and Girl Power: How ISIS Lured 3 London Girls', *New York Times* (17 August) [available at: http://mobile.nytimes.com/2015/08/18/world/europe/jihad-and-girl-power-how-isis-lured-3-london-teenagers.html?smprod=nytcore-iphone&smid=nytcore-iphone-share&_r=1&referrer= (accessed 23 June 2018)]

Bentley, P., Williams, D. and Marsden, S. 2014. 'British Jihadists Bidding to Recruit Boys as Young as 15 on Social Media Sites', *Daily Mail* (12 August) [available at: http://www.dailymail.co.uk/news/article-2723346/Youre-not-young-die-British-jihadists-bid-recruit-boys-young-15-social-media-sites.html (accessed 16 June 2018)]

Betancourt, T., Borisova, I., de la Soudière, M. and Williamson, J. 2011. 'Sierra Leone's Child Soldiers: War Exposures and Mental Health Problems by Gender' 49 *Journal of Adolescent Health* 21

Betancourt, T., Simmons, S., Borisova, I., Brewer, S., Iseala, U. and de la Soudière, M. 2008. 'High Hopes, Grim Reality: Reintegration and the Education of Former Child Soldiers in Sierra Leone' 52 *Comparative Education Review* 565

Bloom, M. 2005. *Dying to Kill: The Allure of Suicide Terror* (New York: Columbia University Press)

Bloom, M. 2015. 'Cubs of the Caliphate: The Children of ISIS', *Foreign Affairs* (21 July) [available at: https://www.foreignaffairs.com/articles/2015-07-21/cubs-caliphate (accessed 23 June 2018)]

Bloom, M. 2017. 'ISIS Terrorism Targets Children in Unthinkable Ways', *Newsweek* (25 May) [available at: http://newsweek.com/islamic-states-terrorism-targets-children-unthinkable-ways-614573 (accessed 23 June 2018)]

Bloom, M. and Horgan, J. (forthcoming). *Small Arms: Children and Terrorism* (New York: Cornell University Press)

Bloom, M. and Matfess, H. 2016. 'Women as Symbols and Swords in Boko Haram's Terror' 6 *Prism: A Journal of the Center for Complex Operations* 104

Byman, D. and Shapiro, J. 2014. 'Be Afraid, Be a Little Afraid: The Threat of Terrorism from Western Foreign Fighters in Syria and Iraq' (Brookings Institute) (November) [available at: http://www.brookings.edu/~/media/research/files/papers/2014/11/western-foreign-fighters-in-syria-and-iraq-byman-shapiro/be-afraid--web.pdf (accessed 16 June 2018)]

Child Soldiers International 2012. *Louder than Words: An Agenda for Action to End State Use of Child Soldiers* (London: Child Soldiers International)

Coalition to Stop the Use of Child Soldiers 2000. 'The Use of Children as Soldiers in Africa: A Country Analysis of Child Recruitment and Participation in Armed Conflict' (1 August) [available at: https://reliefweb.int/sites/reliefweb.int/files/resources/C157333FCA91F573C1256C130033E448-chilsold.htm (accessed 23 June 2018)]

Cohen, D. (forthcoming). *Sexual Violence During War* (New York: Cornell University Press)

Damon, A. 2014. 'Child Fighter Tormented by ISIS', *CNN* (13 November) [available at: http://www.cnn.com/2014/11/12/world/meast/syria-isis-child-fighter/ (accessed 16 June 2018)]

Dearden, L. 2018. 'Isis Propaganda Video Shows Women Fighting for First Time Amid "Desperation" to Bolster Ranks', *The Independent* (8 February)

Defence for Children International 2012. 'Recruitment and Use of Palestinian Children in Armed Conflict' (February) [available at: http://arabic.dci-palestine.org/sites/default/files/recruitment_report_-_final.pdf (accessed 16 June 2018)]

Denov, M. 2008. 'Girl Soldiers and Human Rights: Lessons from Angola, Mozambique, Sierra Leone and Northern Uganda' 12 *The International Journal of Human Rights* 813

Denov, M. and Maclure, R. 2005. 'Child Soldiers in Sierra Leone: Experiences, Implications and Strategies for Community Reintegration' (Canadian International Development Agency) (August)

Denov, M. and Maclure, R. 2007. 'Turnings and Epiphanies: Militarization, Life Histories, and the Making and Unmaking of Two Child Soldiers in Sierra Leone' 10 *Journal of Youth Studies* 243

Denov, M. and Ricard-Guay, A. 2013. 'Girl Soldiers: Towards a Gendered Understanding of Wartime Recruitment, Participation, and Demobilisation' 21 *Gender & Development* 473

Engel, R. 2015. 'Child Soldiers, or "Cubs," Shown in Latest ISIS Video' (*NBC News*, 22 February) [available at: http://www.nbcnews.com/storyline/isis-terror/child-soldiers-or-cubs-shown-latest-isis-video-n310646 (accessed 23 June 2018)]

Gates, S. and Reich, S. 2010. 'Introduction', in S. Gates and S. Reich (eds), *Child Soldiers in the Age of Fractured States* (Pittsburgh, PA: University of Pittsburgh Press) 3

Gerwehr, S. and Daly, S. 2006. 'Al-Qaida: Terrorist Selection and Recruitment', in D. Kamien (ed), *McGraw-*

Hill Homeland Security Handbook: Strategic Guidance for a Coordinated Approach to Effective Security and Emergency Management (New York: McGraw-Hill Publishing)

Grooming the Next Generation. 'Preventing the Next Generation: Mapping Children's Mobilization into Violent Extremist Organizations' [available at: https://groomingthenextgeneration.-weebly.com (accessed 23 June 2018)]

Hart, J. 2001. 'Conflict in Nepal and its Impact on Children' (Refugee Studies Centre) [available at: http://www.rsc.ox.ac.uk/files/publications/other/dp-children-armed-conflict-nepal.pdf (accessed 16 June 2018)]

Horgan, J. 2013. 'Child Suicide Bombers Find Safe Haven', *CNN* (27 March) [available at: http://www.cnn.com/2013/03/27/world/asia/pakistan-anti-taliban/index.html (accessed 16 June 2018)]

Horgan, J. and Bloom, M. 2015. 'This is How the Islamic State Manufactures Child Militants', *Vice News* (8 July) [available at: https://news.vice.com/article/this-is-how-the-islamic-state-manufactures-child-militants (accessed 23 June 2018)]

Horgan, J., Taylor, M., Bloom, M. and Winter, C. 2016. 'From Cubs to Lions: A Six Stage Model of Child Socialization into the Islamic State' 40 *Studies in Conflict and Terrorism* 645

Human Rights Watch 2015. 'Syria: Kurdish Forces Violating Child Soldier Ban' (15 July) [available at: https://www.hrw.org/news/2015/07/10/syria-kurdish-forces-violating-child-soldier-ban-0 (accessed 23 June 2018)]

Jawahar, M. and McLaughlin, G. 2001. 'Toward a Descriptive Stakeholder Theory: An Organizational Life Cycle Approach' 26 *Academy of Management Review* 397

Jenkins, L. 2015. 'Isis Video Shows Killing of Syrian Troops at Palmyra Amphitheatre', *The Guardian* (4 July) [available at: https://www.theguardian.com/world/2015/jul/04/isis-video-killing-palmyra-amphitheatre (accessed 16 June 2018)]

Jordans, M., Komproe, I., Tol, W., Ndayisaba, A., Nisabwe, T. and Kohrt, B. 2012. 'Reintegration of Child Soldiers in Burundi: A Tracer Study' 12 *BMC Public Health* 905

Kanagaratnam, P., Raundalen, M. and Asbjørnsen, A. 2005. 'Ideological Commitment and Posttraumatic Stress in Former Tamil Child Soldiers' 46 *Scandinavian Journal of Psychology* 511

Karam, Z. and Janssen, B. 2015. 'In an ISIS Training Camp, Children Told: Behead the Doll', *Associated Press* (20 July) [available at: http://www.seattletimes.com/nation-world/in-an-isis-training-camp-children-told-behead-the-doll/ (accessed 23 June 2018)]

Kavanaugh, S. 2015. 'The Uphill Battle to Saving ISIS' Child Soldiers', *Vocativ* (22 July) [available at: http://www.vocativ.com/news/212945/the-uphill-battle-to-saving-isis-child-soldiers/ (accessed 16 July 2018)]

Labott, E. 2015. 'New ISIS Video Claims to Show Child Killing Palestinian Captive', *CNN* (11 March) [available at: http://www.cnn.com/2015/03/10/middleeast/isis-video-israeli-killed/ (accessed 23 June 2018)]

Lahoud, N. 2018. 'Empowerment or Subjugation? An Analysis of ISIL's Gendered Messaging' (UN Women) (June) [available at: http://www2.unwomen.org/-/media/field%20office%20arab%20states/attachments/publications/lahoud-fin-web-rev.pdf?la=en&vs=5602 (accessed 27 November 2018)]

LeBaron, R. and McCants, W. 2015. 'Experts Weigh In: Can the United States Counter ISS Propaganda?' (Brookings Institute) (17 June) [available at: http://www.brookings.edu/blogs/markaz/posts/2015/06/17-lebaron-us-counter-isis-propaganda (accessed 23 June 2018)]

Maclure, R. and Denov, M. 2006. '"I Didn't Want to Die So I Joined Them": Structuration and the Process of Becoming Boy Soldiers in Sierra Leone' 18 *Terrorism and Political Violence* 119

Mamoun, A. 2015. 'ISIS has 30,000 Foreign Fighters from More Than 100 Countries', *Iraqi News* (29 May) [available at: http://www.iraqinews.com/arab-world-news/isis-30000-foreign-fighters-100-countries/ (accessed 16 June 2018)]

Mekhennet, S. and Warrick, J. 2016. 'For the "Children of ISIS," Target Practice Starts at Age 6. By Their Teens, They're Ready to Be Suicide Bombers', *The Washington Post* (7 October) [available at: https://www.washingtonpost.com/world/national-security/for-the-children-of-isis-target-practice-starts-at-age-6-by-their-teens-theyre-ready-to-be-suicide-bombers/20-16/10/06/3b59f0fc-8664-11e6-92c2-14b64f3d453f_story.html?utm_term=.7-934edf4b6-61 (accessed 23 June 2018)]

Moore, J. 2017. 'Women and Children Taking Up Arms for ISIS in Marawi, Philippine Army Says', *Newsweek* (4 September) [available at: https://www.newsweek.com/women-and-children-taking-arms-isis-marawi-philippine-army-says-659068 (accessed 23 August 2018)]

Motaparthy, P. 2014. 'Maybe We Live and Maybe We Die: Recruitment and Use of Children by Armed Groups in Syria' (Human Rights Watch) (22 June) [available at: https://www.hrw-.org/report/2014/06/22/maybe-we-live-and-maybe-we-die/recruitment-and-use-children-armed-groups-syria (accessed 16 June 2018)]

National Post 2013. 'Carl Conradi & Tanya Zayed on Bosco Ntaganda: A Commander of Child Soldiers Now Headed to The Hague' (21 March) [available at: http://news.nationalpost.com/full-comment/carl-conradi-tanya-zayed-on-bosco-ntaganda-a-commander-of-child-soldiers-now-headed-to-the-hague (accessed 16 June 2018)]

Pugel, J. 2010. 'Disaggregating the Causal Factors Unique to Child Soldiering: The Case of Liberia', in S. Gates and S. Reich (eds), *Child Soldiers in the Age of Fractured States* (Pittsburgh, PA: University of Pittsburgh Press) 160

Reuters 2015a. '"Cubs of the Caliphate" – ISIS Recruits 400 Children since January', *The Jerusalem Post* (24 March) [available at: https://www.jpost.com/Middle-East/Cubs-of-the-Caliphate-ISIS-recruits-400-children-since-January-394908 (accessed 23 June 2018)]

Reuters 2015b. 'Islamic State Recruits 400 Children Since Jan – Syria Monitor' (24 March) [available at: http://in.reuters.com/article/2015/03/24/mideast-crisis-syria-children-idINKBN0MK0U620150324 (accessed 16 June 2018)]

Rice, J. 2013. 'Girls at War: Historical Perspectives and Representations', in H. Embacher, G. Prontera and A. Lichtblau (eds), *Children and War: Past and Present* (Warwick, UK: Helion & Company Limited)

Rosen, D. 2005. *Armies of the Young: Child Soldiers in War and Terrorism* (New Brunswick, NJ: Rutgers University Press)

Ross, B. 'Al-Shabaab's American Pipeline for Terrorism', ABC News [available at: http://abcnews.go.com/WNT/video/al-shabaabs-american-pipeline-terrorism20351030 (accessed 23 June 2018)]

Saul, H. 2015. 'Khaled Sharrouf: Mother of Boy Pictured Holding Severed Head "Wants to Return to Australia" – But PM Warns Family Will Face Full Force of Law', *The Independent* (28 May) [available at: http://www.independent.co.uk/news/world/australasia/khaled-sharrouf-mother-of-boy-pictured-holding-severed-head-wants-to-return-to-australia--but-pm-warns-family-will-face-full-force-of-law-10281994.html (accessed 16 June 2018)]

Shakya, A. 2011. 'Experiences of Children in Armed Conflict in Nepal' 33 *Children and Youth Services Review* 557

Stalinsky, S. and Sosnow, R. 2015. 'Encryption Technology Embraced by ISIS, Al-Qaeda, Other Jihadis Reaches New Level with Increased Dependence on Apps, Software—Kik, Surespot, Telegram, Wickr, Detekt, TOR: Part IV – February–June 2015', *MEMRI* (15 June) [available at: http://www.memri.org/report/en/print8610.htm (accessed 16 June 2018)]

Taylor, D. 2012. 'Black Diamond: A Female Victim of Charles Taylor's Crimes Speaks Out', *The Guardian* (28 May) [available at: http://www.theguardian.com/lifeandstyle/2012/may/28/female-victim-charles-taylor-speaks (accessed 23 June 2018)]

The Telegraph 2009. 'Life as a Female Tamil Tiger Guerrilla Relived by One of First Female Soldiers' (8 May) [available at: https://www.telegraph.co.uk/news/worldnews/asia/srilanka/5283438/Life-as-a-female-Tamil-Tiger-guerilla-relived-by-one-of-first-female-soldiers.html (accessed 23 June 2018)]

Temple-Raston, D. 2018. 'Missing Somali Teens May Be Terrorist Recruits', *NPR* (28 January) [available at: https://www.npr.org/templates/story/story.php?storyId=99919934 (accessed 16 June 2018)]

UNICEF 2015. 'Northeast Nigeria: Alarming Spike in Suicide Attacks Involving Women and Girls' (26 May) [available at: http://www.unicef.org/media/media_82047.html (accessed 16 June 2018)]

Violations Documentation Center in Syria. 'Martyrs' Database' [available at http://www.vdc-sy.info/index.php/en/martyrs (accessed 16 June 2018)]

Warner, J. and Matfess, H. 2017. 'Exploding Stereotypes: The Unexpected Operational and Demographic Characteristics of Boko Ḥaram's Suicide Bombers' (Combatting Terrorism Center) (9 August) [available at: https://ctc.usma.edu/posts/report-exploding-stereotypes-the-unexpected-operational-and-demographic-characteristics-of-boko-harams-suicide-bombers (accessed 23 June 2018)]

Washington Times 2009. 'Taliban Buying Children for Suicide Bombers' (2 July) [available at: https://www.washingtontimes.com/news/2009/jul/02/taliban-buying-children-to-serve-as-suicide-bomber/ (accessed 16 June 2018)]

Weiss, M. and Hassan, H. 2015. *ISIS: Inside the Army of Terror* (New York: Regan Arts)

Wheeler, S. 2015. '"We Can Die Too": Recruitment and Use of Child Soldiers in South Sudan' (Human Rights Watch) (14 December) [available at: https://www.hrw.org/report/2015/12/14/we-can-die-too/recruitment-and-use-child-soldiers-south-sudan (accessed 23 June 2018)]

Whitehead, T. and Sawer, P. 2015. 'Missing Dawood Sisters and 9 Children "Already in Syria" and May Never Return, Police Warn', *The Telegraph* (17 June) [available at: http://www.telegraph.co.uk/news/uknews/terrorism-in-the-uk/11681007/Missing-Dawood-sisters-and-9-children-already-in-Syria.html (accessed 23 June 2018)]

Wratto, C. 'If We Didn't Pick Up the Guns, We Would Have Been Killed' (Child Soldiers International) [available at: https://www.child-soldiers.org/news/if-we-didnt-pick-up-the-guns-we-would-have-been-killed (accessed 16 June 2018)]

Yogev, E. and Schweitzer, Y. 2016. 'Suicide Attacks in 2015' (Institute for National Security Studies) (26 January) [available at: http://www.inss.org.il/publication/suicide-attacks-in-2015/ (accessed 16 June 2018)]

Zia, H. 2014. 'The Psychological Effects of War on Children', *Daily Outlook Afghanistan* (17 March) [available at: http://www.outlookafghanistan.net/topics.php?post_id=9665 (accessed 23 June 2018)]

10. Retracing the journey of child soldiers and looking for the path to return them home: a report from southern Philippines

David N. Almarez, Ajree D. Malawani, Sittie Akima A. Ali, Princess Mae S. Chua and Primitivo C. Ragandang III

This descriptive-qualitative study on child soldiers in the Lanao provinces,[1] located on Mindanao island in southern Philippines, looks into the factors that influenced children to join the armed struggle against the government. The study considers the influence on the children of their *madrasah* education, their recruitment process, the training they underwent and the duties and responsibilities given to them by the militant group with which they were affiliated. Data were gathered through personal interviews and focus group discussions. Participants were selected through purposive and snowball sampling. The concept of 'Multi-stakeholder Processes' was used as a study framework. The study found the educational background of participants to correlate with their entry into the armed struggle. Moreover, family and peers have a strong influence. The participation of child soldiers in armed struggles in southern Philippines is influenced by family and community values which recently have been reinforced through many militant groups being united by the professed objective of establishing an Islamic state. To put an end to child soldier recruitment in the Philippines, it is recommended that the curricular offerings in the *madrasah* system be streamlined to align with the mission of Philippine education. Furthermore, other stakeholders, such as parents, teachers and religious leaders must be involved in the process of peace-building in the Philippines.

Mindanao is the second largest island of the Philippine archipelago. It has six regions that include the Autonomous Region in Muslim Mindanao (ARMM), which is inhabited by most of the Filipino Muslims, also known as Moro people. Moro people, who constitute 6 per cent of the total Filipino population, are divided into 11 ethnic groups, in which the major tribes are the Maranao, the Maguindanao and the Tausug.[2] The territory of the Moro people in southern Philippines, which includes parts of Mindanao,[3] part of Palawan and the Sulu Archipelago, is commonly referred to as the Moroland.

The involvement of children in armed conflict in southern Philippines has a long history that dates back to the Moro struggle against Spanish colonial rule. In 1637, Sultan Kudarat fought the forces of Governor-General Hurtado de Corcuera in Lamitan, where many children were seen fighting with their warrior-parents.[4] Like their elders, the Moro

---

[1] These are Lanao del Norte and Lanao del Sur.
[2] Bara 2015.
[3] These are the provinces of Maguindanao, Lanao del Sur, parts of Lanao del Norte, parts of North Cotabato and parts of Sultan Kudarat.
[4] Majul 1999: 150.

children faced significant challenges brought about by the protracted struggle against colonialism. During the three-month siege by the Spaniards of the Tausug *cotta*[5] at the foot of Mt Tumantangis in Sulu in 1638, children stood with their parents.[6] The exposure of Moro children to armed conflict during the colonial period is an inevitable part of a people's struggle for self-determination in an era where the conduct of armed conflict was not regulated by any legal norm. During this period, at least on the part of Moro people, the involvement of children in armed struggle was more of an obligation to fight for freedom and self-determination rather than exploitation or manipulation of people for any ideological agenda. What is more, at the time, the community was considered as a single entity without disaggregation of inhabitants according to gender and age. And, of course, this was a period before the distinction between combatants and non-combatants had been advocated and accepted.

The perspective on the involvement of children in armed conflict has changed completely since the promulgation of the Declaration of Human Rights in 1948. Since then, international humanitarian law (IHL) has evolved to identify and protect non-combatants, including children, from the effects of armed conflicts. Consequently, the recruitment and engagement of children in armed conflict is prohibited and therefore illegal. These developments coincided with the proliferation of insurgency movements in many new independent states after World War II, which were divided along ethnic, religious and ideological fault lines. In the context of the Bangsa Moro struggle for self-determination in the southern Philippines,[7] children were nevertheless continuously engaged in the armed struggle.[8] In this contemporary period, key factors that influence some children to become child soldiers are their *madrasah* education and the socio-cultural dynamics in their community and their family.[9]

Between 23 May and 23 October 2017, Marawi City in Lanao del Sur was under siege as a result of an attempt by pro-Islamic State groups (including the Maute and Abu Sayyaf) to make it the seat of their rule in South-East Asia. There are indications that young boys participated in the five-month siege: pictures and video clips showing the involvement of boys were released by the groups to the public through social media as a part of their propaganda.[10] The siege claimed the lives of 974 militants,[11] 168 members of the security forces and around 68 civilians. What is more, the siege caused the forced evacuation of an entire city of more than 200,000 residents and the declaration of martial law in Mindanao.[12] In the history of the Philippines, this is the first occurrence of the mass exodus of an entire city population in just a few days.

---

[5] *Cotta* is a term used in southern Philippines to refer to a defensive camp which was common among Moro people during the colonial period. The term is still used today to refer to a hideout of rebels and bandits.

[6] Majul 1999: 152.

[7] Bangsa is a local term that translates into 'nation', hence Bangsa Moro is Moro Nation, referring to Islamized Filipinos in southern Philippines.

[8] Almarez 2010: 143.

[9] Ibid.

[10] See also Bloom in this volume.

[11] Hincks 2017; *South China Morning Post* 2017.

[12] Morales 2017.

1. BACKGROUND

The engagement of children in armed conflict is a longstanding phenomenon in many parts of the world.[13] But in the contemporary period, advanced technology, blending with the strategies of terrorism, magnifies the impact of a child soldier in conflict. Children's participation in conflicts which are not their creation demonstrates a global trend in the changing landscape of the battlefield in present-day armed conflicts where the underlying philosophy, rules, technology and even nature of participants have changed. Part of the change in the nature of conflict is the intensified and systematic recruitment of children to feed the ranks of combatants.

Whenever armed conflicts occur, children are vulnerable to recruitment as soldiers. Modes of recruitment vary in different countries. In Sierra Leone, children were abducted and forcibly integrated.[14] This is also the case in the Democratic Republic of Congo, although there were also some cases of voluntary enlistment in return for promises of money, jobs and other benefits by recruiters.[15] In the long history of insurgency in Burma, children were deliberately recruited by the warring parties.[16] In Rwanda, thousands of children were recruited by the Hutu leadership in the effort to exterminate the Tutsi minority.[17] Children also participated in mass killing in Cambodia during the Pol Pot regime. In Sri Lanka, the recruitment of children aged between nine and 12 into the Liberation Tigers of Tamil Eelan (LTTE) is a result of the interplay of many factors. First is the discrimination experienced by the minority Tamils from the Sinhalese majority. Sinhala security forces targeted children 'in their checking, cordon and search operations, and they are often detained for interrogation, torture, execution, or even rape'.[18] Parents within LTTE-controlled territories also cooperated due to tangible benefits: for example, when they lose a child, they are granted the special status of a 'hero family', receive job preferences, are not required to pay taxes and are allocated special seats during public events.[19] These enticements are difficult to resist in poverty-stricken communities such as in Sri Lanka.

Aside from adding fuel to the flame of conflict, children also help prolong conflict. Having learned limited survival skills aside from the use of force, the children face impediments when it comes to reintegrating them into civilian society.[20] With limited survival skills other than soldiering, fighting a war or insurgency becomes a livelihood. In some instances, a well-indoctrinated child soldier is programmed to see enemies lurking in the immediate environment. Growing up in a context of armed struggle sustained by the culture of violence and hatred develops a self-perpetuating violent personality that is difficult to subsequently reintegrate.[21]

---

[13] Gray and Matchin 2008.
[14] Denov 2005: 3. See also Oosterveld in this volume.
[15] MONUSCO 2013: 5. See also Hanson and Molima in this volume; Parmar and Lebrat in this volume.
[16] Risser et al. 2003: 10.
[17] Klemensits and Czirjak 2016: 215–22.
[18] Gray and Matchin 2008: 110, quoting Somasundaram 2002.
[19] Singer 2006: 5.
[20] Klemensits and Czirjak 2016. See also Wessells in this volume.
[21] See also Akello in this volume.

In the Philippines, moreover, the child warrior is a cultural phenomenon deeply engrained in the way of life of people, particularly in the south. Reports from Marawi City during the May–October 2017 siege revealed the participation of some children. This is not surprising in light of the historical involvement of children in armed conflict in the Lanao provinces.[22] The involvement of children in armed conflict in southern Philippines is deeply rooted in the four centuries of armed struggle by the Moro people against the Spaniards where general mobilization of entire communities was inevitable and seen as necessary. In this period, no distinctions were drawn between combatants and non-combatants. Accordingly, women and children were targeted. To prepare them for the ruthlessness of a serial war, Moro women and children were trained to fight like regulars.

In 1637, the forces of the Maguindanao Sultan Kudarat and Governor-General Sebastian Hurtado de Corcuera fought in Lamitan.[23] The wives and children of the Moro warriors stood with the fighting men until they were forced to evacuate their *cotta*. One of the wives of Sultan Kudarat died in this encounter. The following year, a strong Spanish force attacked Sulu.[24] Together with women and children, the Tausug warriors endured a three-month siege in their *cotta* at the foot of Mt Tumantangis. In 1845, during a Spanish attack on the Island of Balangingi, the Samal defenders resorted to killing many of their women and children to save them from becoming prisoners of the Spaniards. The arrival of the Americans did not change the overriding preoccupation to subjugate the Moros, as manifested by the series of military excursions the Americans undertook into the Moroland.[25] In the battles against the Maranaos in Bayang, Butig, Masiu, Bacolod, Calawi and Taraca from 1902 to 1903 and in the 1906 Bud Dajo and 1913 Bud Bagsak battles in Sulu,[26] the victorious Americans counted many children and women among the casualties.

Moving to the present day, the extent of the involvement of child soldiers in Mindanao can be gleaned from the pronouncement of Sheik Abdulhadie Gumander, the team leader of the Moro Islamic Liberation Front (MILF) Focal Persons on para-social workers, that the MILF is disengaging 1,869 child warriors.[27] The MILF, which signed a peace agreement with the government in 2014, is however only one of the insurgent groups in Mindanao. The Moro National Liberation Front (MNLF), which signed a peace agreement with the Philippine government in 1996, still maintains its own camps in Sulu. The Bangsa Moro Islamic Freedom Fighters (BIFF) group is a faction that broke away from the MILF when the latter signed the peace agreement. Abu Sayyaf,[28] another insurgent group, is engaged in kidnap-for-ransom and extortion activities in southern Philippines.

---

[22] Almarez 2010: 154.
[23] Madale 1997: 142.
[24] Refers historically to the island of Jolo, which is the seat of a Tausug Sultanate; Tausug (literally, 'people of the waves') is the dominant tribe inhabiting the Sulu Archipelago which is now divided into two provinces: the Province of Sulu and the Province of Tawi-tawi.
[25] Moroland is a collective term referring to the geographic territories occupied by Muslims in southern Philippines during the colonial period. The Spaniards referred to the Islamized people of southern Philippines as Moors, a designation that evolved into the local term Moro.
[26] Gowing 1979: 35.
[27] Jannaral 2018.
[28] An Islamist group based in Jolo that is engaged in piracy and kidnap for ransom. Recently it allied itself with the Maute group during the Marawi siege.

Abu Sayyaf joined the jihadist Maute group[29] which pledged allegiance to ISIS in 2015. Both groups were active participants in the 154-day Marawi Siege. Considering that all of these groups could be harbouring minors in their ranks, the figure given by the MILF is just a fraction of the whole picture.

While the presence of minors on the battlefield had earlier been viewed as tolerable, if not inevitable in the absence of commonly accepted conventions that distinguish civilians from combatants, the modern concept of human rights views the military involvement of children with grave concern. Bringing children into the conflict zone '. . . is a violation of the rights of boys and girls to a healthy life, within the shelter of their families and communities; it is a violation of their rights to education, love, affection, adequate and appropriate care, freedom of movement and expression'.[30] However, even if the involvement of children in armed conflict is now viewed as unacceptable and illegal under IHL, the fact remains that their presence in military conflicts continues, reflecting the current global transformation of the objective of armed conflicts and the manner in which they are waged. The involvement of child soldiers in Marawi City and more generally in the Lanao provinces is a characteristic of that global transformation which is also manifested in the cases of the Democratic Republic of Congo, Sierra Leone, Sri Lanka and elsewhere in Africa, South-East Asia and Latin America. In some instances, the objectives of waging war have changed from victory to mere revenge or terrorism. The aspiration may no longer be self-determination, freedom or sovereignty to be enjoyed by the living but something attainable only in the afterlife, as shown by the prevalent use of child soldiers in suicide missions where they certainly end up dead. Many groups that are waging war against their governments like the Maute group and the Abu Sayyaf in the Philippines may not have the prospect of winning due to the apparent lack of resources. Nevertheless, they inflict a great deal of terror upon the populace by conducting unconventional war and resorting even to illegal means like the use of land mines, suicide bombers, kidnappings and assassinations. They use religion to recruit and develop fighters with the enticement of salvation.

2. STRUCTURE OF RESEARCH

2.1 Objective

This study scrutinizes the involvement of minors in militant groups in the Lanao provinces. It identifies the factors that influence the recruitment of children into these groups. One of the critical factors that this study investigates are the roles of *madrasah* education and the community in the propagation of militancy among the Moro youth. Likewise, this study also looks into the possible reasons why these militant youths separated from their groups.

---

[29] This is a group led by the Maute brothers (Omarkhayam Maute and Abdullah Maute) from the municipality of Butig, Lanao del Sur, who founded the Dawlah Islamiyah, an Islamist group that has pledged allegiance to ISIS and which was responsible for the Marawi siege in 2017.
[30] MONUSCO 2013: 2.

2.2 Significance

The findings and recommendations of this study could serve as inputs in decision-making and policy review by the Department of Education of the Philippines. The research outputs could also help improve the management and administration of *madaris* (the plural form of *madrasah*) and guide the local government units in Lanao provinces in improving the operation and quality of *madrasah* education. In addition, this research could help broaden the perspectives of Filipino legislators, academics, community organizers and other stakeholders in their peace-building initiatives in southern Philippines. Finally, the study sheds light on the phenomenon of child soldiers in the Philippines in order to contribute to enriching available literature on an issue that has received little academic attention internationally.

2.3 Research Methodology

This is a descriptive-qualitative study on child soldiers in the Lanao provinces, southern Philippines. Data were gathered through personal interviews and focus group discussions. Participants were identified through purposive and snowball sampling. The project interviewed child soldiers, former child soldiers and their relatives. Child soldiers in this study refers to individuals who have been affiliated to armed groups like the MNLF, the MILF and the Maute group and who were less than 18 years old when interviewed for this study. On the other hand, 'former child soldiers' refers to those participants of this study who were older than 18 when interviewed but had started their engagement with armed groups when they were younger than 18.

Data gathering such as interviews and focus group discussions were conducted from November 2017 up to June 2018. For confidentiality and for the convenience of respondents, interviews were conducted in neutral places where respondents felt safe to engage in spontaneous conversations and the researchers could extract relevant data. Anonymity among participants is maintained because of the sensitivity of the topic: actual names were not asked. Names voluntarily given were not recorded. All names of child soldiers, former child soldiers and their relatives mentioned here are not their real names. Thirty-two respondents were interviewed. Of these, ten were child soldiers, six were former child soldiers, 15 were relatives of child soldiers and one a prisoner (a captured combatant from the Maute group).

Twelve *madaris* were visited. Copies of their curricular offerings were requested for comparative analysis. Interviews with administrators or owners were conducted to obtain information on the administration of these schools. Focus group discussions were also conducted among teachers to know more about their school activities and the relationship between teachers and students and teachers and administrators. Secondary data were taken from contemporary studies about child soldiers in the Lanao provinces.

2.4 Conceptual Framework

In advancing their political agenda, some groups like the MNLF and MILF in the Philippines resorted to an armed struggle against the security forces of the government. Inability to match the firepower of the police and army usually compels armed groups to adopt the strategy of sowing terror amid the civilian population in order to extract support in terms of money, supplies and safe havens that would help sustain their struggle. Threats of violence to and violent attacks on non-combatants or civilians are acts of terrorism which make armed groups or the individuals affiliated to them terrorists. To understand how an individual becomes a terrorist, Huesmann proposed some characteristics that may predispose an individual to become a terrorist.[31] These are: (1) the need to defend one's sense of entitlement and to achieve recognition and admiration; (2) negative emotional states; (3) reduced emotional arousal in response to violence; and (4) negative beliefs about the world and beliefs that violent extremism is necessary and justified. Huesmann suggested that these characteristics may 'arise from innate predispositions' but often they are learned 'from early exposure to violence and oppression, which desensitizes individuals and teaches them violent scripts'.[32] Considering that child soldiers nowadays are used to undertake terror acts like suicide bombings, planting land mines and even participating in direct assaults on the civilian population, this study posits that the induction of Moro children into militant groups is influenced by similar factors that lead to the making of a terrorist. A child soldier in the Lanao provinces joins a militant group like the MILF or the Maute group because they are indoctrinated to believe that violent extremism is necessary and justified. Moreover, their perceptions and attitudes are products of their experiences and training. Finally, their emulation of their elders as role models is a strong influence on what they want and are willing to do. The armed struggle of the Moros in Mindanao against the Philippine government has already entered into its fifth decade. Many children have been orphaned along the way and some of them were adopted by their relatives who are fighting the government. Armed groups in southern Philippines occupy territories where they have established their camps and within these camps are families with children who are exposed to the daily activities in the camp. Growing up in a belligerent environment influences the development of a child soldier. Since the child soldier is a creation of his or her environment, changes in the same environment are needed to guide the child to a 'normal' life. Re-socialization is important but other external factors may include demobilization and cessation of hostilities among warring groups. A personal decision like the desire to settle down and study or work is also a factor that reintegrates a child soldier into society.

2.5 Scope and Limitations of the Study

This study was conducted in the two Lanao provinces, which are inhabited by the Maranaos. Data were gathered through interviews, focus group discussions and analyses of documents obtained from the Department of Education (DepEd) and from various *madaris* located in these two provinces. Other secondary data were taken from previous studies on child soldiers in the Lanao provinces.

This study has geographic limitations having included only the Maranao child soldiers; child soldiers from other Moro tribes like the Maguindanao and Tausug were not included. Although Moro tribes in the Philippines are all Muslims, they have significant

---

[31] Huesmann 2010, cited in Beardsley and Beech 2013.
[32] Ibid.

cultural differences. Further, given security considerations, we were able to interview only a limited number of child soldiers, former child soldiers and their relatives. It was also difficult to find respondents who were willing to participate in the study for fear of exposure while the armed conflict in southern Philippines is still unresolved. In many instances, the researchers were suspected as infiltrators or government agents so there was a need to look for common friends or 'gatekeepers' who could facilitate the establishment of a trusted connection with prospective participants. Given the limited number of research participants, it is difficult to make generalizations, but our findings are nonetheless valuable for an understanding of factors that influenced these Maranao children to join the armed struggle, their training and roles, and factors leading to their departure from armed groups.

3. RESEARCH RESULTS: FACTORS THAT INFLUENCE CHILDREN TO BECOME CHILD SOLDIERS

A child is a human being below 18 years of age.[33] A child soldier therefore is a person who is associated with an armed force or armed group who is below 18 years of age and who has been recruited or used by an armed force or armed group as a fighter, cook, porter, messenger, spy or for sexual purposes.[34] In 2004, it was estimated that approximately 300,000 children were serving as child soldiers, guerrilla fighters, or in support roles in more than 50 countries around the world.[35] It is noted that an increasing number of children are being recruited into armed forces[36] in many countries, especially in Africa, the Middle East, Latin America and South-East Asia. In the Philippines alone, particularly in Mindanao, it is estimated that 15 per cent of the 6,000 to 10,000 armed members of the MILF are under the age of 18.[37] This figure attests to the UNICEF statement that 'Mindanao is home to a number of armed groups who use and recruit combatants under the age of 18.'[38] In 2009, the MILF signed an action plan with UNICEF to stop the recruitment of children into their ranks. However, it took eight more years for the MILF to finally implement the plan in order to be delisted from the UN Secretary-General's report on children and armed conflict, presented annually to the UN Security Council.[39]

In South-East Asia, children are radicalized and recruited through schools, especially religious boarding schools or *pesantrens*, which in Lanao are locally called the *toril*.[40] In Lanao, some of these boarding schools are not supervised by the government. They do not adhere strictly to the standard curriculum prescribed by the Department of Education (DepEd). What they teach and how they teach are left to the creativity and innovation of their administrators, who, in most cases, are also the owners.

---

[33] Art. 1, UN Convention on the Rights of the Child.
[34] Paris Principle 2.1 (definitions).
[35] Derluyn et al. 2004: 861. See, however, Rosen in this volume.
[36] Cherwon 2014: 1.
[37] Barrete and Lischin 2017.
[38] Al Jazeera News 2017.
[39] Brago 2017.
[40] Homeland Security Institute 2009.

3.1 The Evolution of the Child Soldier in Mindanao

The long history of armed struggle by the Muslims in the Philippines against colonial rule led to a fractious Mindanao when national independence was granted in 1946. The uneasy relationship between the Muslims and Christian settlers from Visayas and Luzon triggered a situation known as the 'Mindanao Crisis'. The long-simmering Mindanao Crisis erupted with the establishment of the Muslim Independence Movement (MIM) in 1968, which envisioned a Muslim state independent of the Philippines comprising Mindanao, Sulu and Palawan. This movement was later renamed the 'Mindanao' Independence Movement to imbue it with an air of inclusivity in terms of the non-Muslim inhabitants of Mindanao, Sulu and Palawan. A year before (1967), a paramilitary extremist group of Christians called 'Ilaga' was organized with the avowed intention of eliminating Muslims in their areas. Then another paramilitary group called 'Blackshirts' emerged as the armed group of the MIM. With two armed groups operating in overlapping jurisdictions, 'pocket wars' were inevitable in the province of Cotabato, the province where both armed groups emerged. The expansion of Ilaga operations to other provinces with Muslim inhabitants, including Lanao del Norte, led to bloody confrontations with the Barracudas, an armed group that emerged in Lanao del Norte in the 1970s.

The MIM was dominated by older traditional Muslim elites. In 1972, the MNLF was born, consisting of young Muslim leaders, many of whom are students. This was headed by Nur Misuari and Hashim Salamat. A rift between Nur Misuari and Hashim Salamat later developed: this led to Hashim Salamat breaking away and the creation of the MILF in 1977. Nur Misuari is a Tausug by ethnic affiliation and Hashim Salamat is a Maguindanao. In 1996, the MNLF signed a peace agreement with the government while the MILF continued its armed struggle until 2014 when it signed the Comprehensive Agreement on the Bangsa Moro with the Philippine government.

The troubled decade of the 1970s showed that Mindanao was indeed in crisis. This perilous situation served as the backdrop for the eventual declaration of martial law on 21 September 1972. A phenomenon that is associated with this troubled period is the belief in *anting-anting* (amulet) propagated by both Ilagas and Blackshirts. The *anting-anting* culture made people believe that they can be invulnerable in battle provided they perform the required rituals and carry their *anting-anting* with them. Belief in invulnerability turned fighting among adventurous youngsters into somewhat of a fad. In some instances, in 1970 and 1971, some active fighters of the Ilagas fought suspected Blackshirts who likewise believed in their invulnerability, and in some cases were their classmates in high school. Professor Muhammad Kurais, an anthropologist who taught at the Central Mindanao Colleges of Kidapawan, North Cotabato, once commented that 'whoever invented the concept of "anting-anting" for the Ilagas is so successful in creating monster warriors among the young'.[41] The case of the Ilaga child soldier manifests a shift in motivation. Whereas earlier generations of child soldiers in Mindanao during the colonial period fought side-by-side with their parents for self-determination, the young fighters of the 1960s and 1970s were motivated more by adventurism propped up by a belief in their invulnerability. A similar shift can also be inferred in the recruitment of

---

[41] Interview with Muhammad Kurais by the first author on 7 May 1972.

child soldiers in the Lanao provinces. To some extent, some of the children are no longer fighting in defence and preservation of their communities but to destroy the existing structure, which is characterized by things forbidden (*haram*), and instead establish one that is acceptable in Islam.

The Maranao child soldiers are recruited by their parents, friends, MILF recruiters and relatives; one major factor that influences their recruitment is their *madrasah* education.[42] In Butig, Lanao del Sur, the place of MILF's Camp Busra and the hometown of the Maute brothers, who led the Islamic-State-inspired rebellion in Marawi in 2017, studies show that children have been taught in *madaris* that jihad is an Islamic obligation. A study of former girl soldiers in the municipalities of Munai and Tangcal in Lanao del Norte revealed similar educational processes.[43]

3.2 Former Child Soldiers

All of the former child soldiers in this study revealed that they were taught to believe that Mindanao belongs to Muslims. The fact that the population has retained its religion is presented as a result of the failure of the Spaniards to subjugate them despite over three centuries of efforts to colonize the entire Philippines. By virtue of the Treaty of Paris on 10 December 1898, the entire Philippine archipelago was ceded to the United States. The American effort to establish effective control over southern Philippines, which the US designated as the 'Moro Province', resulted in further hostilities when the defiant Moros resisted what they considered as intrusions by outsiders into their territories. In 1903, Datu Ali of Maguindanao, despite inferiority in arms, led his 15,000 men in battles against the Americans which ended in his eventual defeat and death.[44] These bloody events were kept fresh in the mind of young Moros through oral traditions which in turn can easily be exploited by recruiters of child soldiers. The mantra is simple: 'Mindanao is for the Moro people, non-Muslims are land grabbers.' The bloody history of Mindanao has created this great divide between 'we' and 'they' among inhabitants.

Although they remained sympathetic to the cause of the MILF, which is to establish an autonomous region for the Moros, all six former child soldiers interviewed have returned home and are no longer active in the armed struggle against the government, in pursuance with the comprehensive peace accord forged with the government in 2014. Two child soldiers, Mamalangcas and Abutalib, revealed that they had been recruited in 2007 and that they had participated in the MILF attack of Kolambugan, Lanao del Norte in 2008. They stated that they were offered PhP15,000 (US$283) a month in remuneration. Their parents, who consented to their recruitment, received the first month's pay, but no further payments followed.

Another former child soldier, Asnawi, grew up in an MILF camp since his father is one of the commanders. He grew up watching the activities of MILF combatants in their camp and, when he was old enough to handle weapons, he was allowed to carry one of his father's handguns. Like some children living in the MILF camp, he performed auxiliary

---

[42] Almarez 2010.
[43] Montud and Nadjmah 2012: 31.
[44] Becket 1977: 56.

functions of cleaning, fetching water and cooking. He was also trained to dismantle, clean and assemble firearms. He had not been involved in a firefight but he had engaged in several missions for providing supplies to men on front-line duty.

Abedin is an orphan who was adopted by his uncle, who himself had 12 children from three marriages. He has to live with the poverty that surrounds the family that adopted him. When he was six years old, he was sent together with his cousins to a nearby *madrasah* where the concept of jihad was discussed. He remembered that, one time, a foreigner, who came to discuss the topic, explained that *jihad* is obligatory. This same notion was further expounded by local *madrasah* teachers in the context of Mindanao, which according to them belongs to Muslims who were dispossessed by non-Muslim settlers from the North (Visayas and Luzon). These teachers urged their students to fight for the recovery of what rightfully belongs to them. Accordingly, taking the properties of the non-Muslims and even conducting violent actions against them are justified. Repeated coaching along these lines and the seemingly unending poverty prompted this former child soldier to begin considering other possible options for himself: at age 11, he joined older friends in a visit to a nearby MILF camp and, instead of returning home, he ended up staying there for ten years. He said that there was no compelling reason to return to his uncle's poor neighbourhood. This respondent started doing auxiliary functions in the camp. He said he was happy because food was always available in the camp.

Usop, the fifth former child soldier, was a volunteer who was allowed by his parents to join the MILF to contribute to the cause of the movement which everybody in their farming village believed to be fighting for the legitimate entitlements of the Muslims. At an early age he saw MILF combatants passing by the village and heard them talk of their exploits in battles. He looked at these men as heroes and he wanted to be like them. At 14 years old, he decided to join the group, which readily accommodated him. He had to undergo three months of training under an experienced trainer who personally supervised his daily activities, such as gun handling, intelligence gathering, physical conditioning and basic military operations. He recalled three enemy engagements, one when he was still a child soldier and two when he was already over 18 years of age. As proof of his fighting experience he proudly showed a big scar below his right ear, which, according to him, happened in a 25 minute-long firefight when his group encountered an army patrol.

Ayesha, the sixth former child soldier, is female. She does not remember exactly when she joined the MNLF. The sprawling MNLF camp (later turned MILF camp) in Lanao del Norte lies within their *barangay* (village). Like most of the inhabitants of their *barangay* who are relatives and supporters of MNLF combatants, Ayesha also counted many MNLF members among her relatives. She observed that it was difficult to make a distinction between members and non-members of the MNLF because whenever armed engagements occurred in the vicinity or a need for reinforcements arose in other places every able-bodied inhabitant seemed to be part of a supportive mobilization. This former child soldier thinks that she just responded to a call of duty. As to her training, she said that the life of a 'freedom fighter' is the way of life in her *barangay*.

3.3 Child Soldiers

In the case of the ten child soldiers (under 18 at the time of the interview) who participated in this study, seven have seen action in Piagapo, Butig or in Marawi City, while three served as auxiliaries. These three are all 12-year-old classmates in Marawi. According to Saidali, the most articulate of the three, they were invited by Ugalingan, a *mujahedeen* affiliated to the Maute group, to join them in fighting for the true Islamic community that would soon arise in Marawi. Since they had not undergone any combat training when the siege of Marawi started, they were instructed to provide support services, particularly transporting ammunitions and securing provisions from abandoned stores in the city. They were promised that they would be given remuneration for their services. They performed their role for around two months. When air strikes became more frequent, however, they were encouraged by relatives to disengage and escape from Marawi. They maintained communication with friends and relatives through their mobile phones until electric power in the city was completely shut off. They confided that they did not have the opportunity to receive the money promised them because of constant movement around the city and, what is more, they witnessed the death of Ugalingan in an air strike. They too narrowly escaped death several times from aerial strikes and ground bombardment. While looking for their parents, they had to survive with the money that they had collected from the safes of two houses that were hurriedly abandoned at the start of the siege.[45] They had a total of PhP27,000 (US$513) divided among themselves. With the help of friends, neighbours and relatives, they were able to locate the parents of Macaurog in an evacuation camp in Lanao del Norte after two weeks of searching. They learned that the parents of Macadatar are in Iligan while those of Saidali are in Cagayan de Oro.

Ombra revealed that he is from Lanao del Norte. He was invited by a neighbour to help reinforce embattled militants during the February 2016 battle in Butig. He also participated in the 2017 battle in Piagapo, Lanao del Sur. He was 16 years old during the battle in Butig and eager to go to the battlefront. He had undergone combat training in a nearby MILF camp in 2014. A cousin who is working as an engineer in Saudi Arabia bought him an assault rifle as a gift when this cousin went home for a vacation in 2015. When they arrived in Butig, the Maute fighters were already withdrawing. Their engagement was brief, and they slipped back to their home town as hostilities in Butig subsided.

Badron is the 15-year-old son of a Maute combatant. He saw his father die in an encounter with the military in Butig in November 2016. While other fighters moved the body of his father to safety, he took the rifle his father had left and joined the other fighters in delaying the advance of the military. After this experience and the bloody events that led to the death of his father, he began feeling a sense of emptiness without him. He moved out of Butig and tried to locate his Christian mother, whom he believed to be in Iligan. But relatives told him that his mother had left, with her three younger daughters, for Cebu to find employment. As of the date of interview (5 May 2018), he had not heard any news about his mother or his siblings. As an internally displaced person (IDP), he was living as a home-based evacuee with the sister of his mother in Iligan when interviewed. In the light of his harrowing encounter with the military in Butig, Badron swore not to fight again.

Two other child soldier respondents are siblings: Kadil is 11 years old and his brother Angni is 13. Their parents are farmers in Munai, Lanao del Norte. In 2015, they were invited by a religious leader to follow him so that he could enrol them in a *madrasah*.

---

[45] Most Maranaos do not save in the bank. They keep their money and other valuables like jewellery and heirlooms in their homes.

Since their parents could not afford to send them to a boarding school, they agreed to part with their children. For four months Kadil and Angni were regular students in a *madrasah*. Then one of their teachers began to lecture on *jihad* and other obligations of a Muslim; this was followed by two months of indoctrination on how to fight oppressions perpetrated by non-believers. These respondents were also given basic combat training so as to be able to defend themselves from aggressors identified as including the police and the military. When the Marawi event erupted they were joined by other young fighters. These respondents were in Marawi for 47 days when they were cut off from their main unit and they had to abandon their position to avoid capture. When their five remaining adult companions died one by one from sniper shots and they realized the preponderance of military power in the city, the brothers and three other minors decided to disengage. They travelled incognito and followed a group of people who had been trapped in the city for weeks in their evacuation. They were in an evacuation centre in Lanao del Norte when they were interviewed. They participated in psychosocial activities administered by the Catholic Relief Services (CRS) and the Institute of Peace and Development in Mindanao (IPDM) of the Mindanao State University-Iligan Institute of Technology (MSU-IIT). The older brother said that he experiences uncontrolled trembling whenever he remembers the thunder of cannons and airstrikes. He also revealed that his younger brother is suffering from nightmares and uncontrolled urges to urinate. Both confided that they have had enough of fighting and all they want is to be reunited with their parents.

Three child soldiers, Dimasangcay, aged 12, Abdul, 14, and Kareem, 15, are friends who said that *mujahidin* are their 'idols' and they always wanted to be like them. They like hearing lectures on *jihad* during weekends in a nearby *madrasah* and they believe that Mindanao is a land for Muslims. They were taught by their teachers that it is their obligation to fight the land-grabbers who took lands owned by Muslims. Accordingly, the use of force purportedly becomes justified to advance the cause of *jihad*. When the Battle of Marawi erupted in May 2017, these respondents discovered that some of their older friends in their school were participants in the hostilities. They asked to join their friends but because they did not have appropriate combat training, they were refused. However, their persistence was rewarded when the team leader of the group agreed that they could join as auxiliaries. They were told to produce their own guns and ammunition and be ready to move out at any time. The following day, they moved to the battlefront, where they stayed for 23 days. During the first week, their front-liners were nearly wiped out by an airstrike. In the second week, their group was ordered to block an advancing convoy of military transports, which they did, resulting in more deaths among their adult comrades. On the 22nd day, they saw only three adult men as they gathered for breakfast. Kareem, the oldest, called his friends for a discussion and they decided to disengage. The following day, they crawled away under cover of darkness. Abdul was familiar with the environs and in half an hour they reached the lakeshore. It was 3:30 a.m. and the lake with its elevation of 700 metres above sea level was icy cold. Yet, still, they started swimming. After couple of hours in the water, they reached safer ground and located relatives who gave them shelter.

3.4 Relatives of Child Soldiers

As a part of their training, some child soldiers are taught in their camp and in the madrasah that jihad is obligatory and needed in the establishment of a dar-ul-Islam or Islamic state.[46] This brings them into a violent environment which they are made to believe is inevitable. The majority of the relatives of child soldiers who were interviewed concurred that jihad is indeed perceived as obligatory. No distinctions were made among the three jihads: Jihad Akbar, Jihad Kabeel and Jihad Asghar. Jihad Akhbar, the 'Greatest Jihad', pertains to self-purification; Jihad Kabeel, the 'Great Jihad' pertains to the struggle against Satan and Satanic teachings; and Jihad Asghar, the 'Lesser Jihad' pertains to a holy war. In waging jihad, the use of arms is necessary only in the case of holy war. In the context of the Lanao provinces, however, emphasis seems to be placed on armed struggle.

No relative of the child soldier respondents expressed any opposition to the decision of their young relatives to join the MILF or the Maute Group. There was concurrence that these children should fight for their communities against intruders or foreign ideologies contrary to Islam. Five relatives reported that they were aware that the children had been offered money in exchange for their services; they were not aware however of any instance where the offer had been fulfilled, except in cases where an initial payment was made, as noted by three parents. One mother said that when a recruiter asked her to allow her son to join them, the initial offer was monthly remuneration and the opportunity for their son to study. She allowed her son to go with the recruiter to another municipality to study. After few months she was surprised to hear that her son was in Marawi with the Maute group. Since then, she has not heard any further news.

Abdulgani, an uncle of one child soldier who participated in the February 2016 Butig Battle, revealed that, as early as 2005, when he was a student of one of the universities in northern Mindanao, he was approached by two individuals who introduced themselves as azatids (Muslim teachers). Abdulgani learned later that the two were also enrolled in the university and that they were conducting regular group discussions among Muslim students on the concept of Ummat Al-Islamiyah.[47] The two also introduced themselves as MILF members. Discussions were conducted in the prayer room provided by the university, the cafeteria and in places where Muslim students congregate. These discussions occurred publicly and were known about even by the university administration. In 2006, Abdulgani was informed that around 20 Muslim students of at least 14 years of age[48] from his university had successfully undertaken 40 days of training somewhere in Lanao del Norte. Three of the trainees later went to the Middle East for further studies. By then the two teachers had declared separation from the MILF. Two years later, the three trainees returned and revealed that the teachings of their former recruiters were more political in nature. These recruiters were advocating for separation from the Philippine state and joining a global Islamic State. This goal prompted the three to disengage from the group formed by their erstwhile teacher-recruiters. During the Marawi Siege, while looking at Facebook, Abdulgani saw pictures of casualties posted in his account. He was

---

[46] Almarez 2010: 148.
[47] Islamic community.
[48] Before the implementation of the Republic Act 10533 of 2013 that established the two-year senior high school, basic education in the Philippines lasted only ten years. A person who starts Grade 1 at five years old becomes a freshman at college at 14 years old. Most parents enrol their children in Grade 1 at the age of seven but there are many cases of enrolment at the earlier ages of six and five. In the school year 2018–2019 that started in June 2018, the first batch of graduates of senior high school under the new system joined as college freshmen.

disturbed upon seeing that two pictures of dead members of the Maute group looked like two of his former schoolmates who were among the 20 trainees in 2006. He realized that the battles in Butig and Marawi in 2016 and 2017 had been preceded by at least a decade of preparation. He remembered that in one group discussion in 2006, he asked the azatids about the timeline when the global Islamic state may be realized and he was told 'in 10 years'. Abdulgani was able to evade recruitment into an extremist group and he is now an engineer, but his nephew, Saidali, was unable to refuse the invitation of the recruiter Ugalingan to join those who fought in Marawi in 2017.

While no respondent opposed the participation of their young relatives in battles against the government, the majority were against the establishment of a Caliphate (global Islamic state) and were disturbed by the methods of its supporters, in particular the summary executions of those perceived to be *kafir* or unbelievers by beheading and shooting in the head. However, they noted that such realizations came late and only when they had already witnessed the depredations caused by this group in Marawi. According to some respondents, the Maute group had initial support from many Maranaos but many withdrew their support when they began to feel the consequences of the effort to establish a Caliphate. Instead of uniting the Maranaos into an Islamic community, the death of many people as a consequence of the siege resulted in potential *ridu* awaiting eruption in the future.[49]

4. TRAINING AND ROLES OF CHILD SOLDIERS

Child soldiers have undergone rigid physical training that included daily jogging, crawling, swimming, martial arts, mountain climbing, river crossing, rappelling and firearms target practice. They were taught first aid and were trained to identify various firearms, from pistols to rocket-propelled grenades (RPGs), and they learned how to dismantle and assemble them. Few child soldiers were selected to go into bomb-making. This is a highly specialized training which, according to Acmad,[50] takes three years to master.[51] Because so much has been invested in their training, trainers are very selective when choosing trainees. Only the best and the brightest are selected. Only very few child soldiers were able to 'make it'. Acmad was accepted only when he was already 17 years old. He (along with others) was trained to improvise by using unexploded cannon shells and bombs retrieved from the battlefield. Acmad counted at least two foreign bomb experts among his trainers. Bomb-making is a dangerous trade and Acmad recalled cases of trainees losing body parts due to accidents.

Training usually starts early in the morning before recruits pray for *soboh* (dawn prayer). Trainees wake up at 3:00 a.m. and perform the *tahajjud* prayer (special prayer after *Isha*, the obligatory night prayer) before they undergo their physical training. They cook their

---

[49] *Ridu* is a family or clan vendetta triggered by any serious wrongdoing like murder, rape, robbery and arson. Conflict may last for generations or until settled in a traditional ceremony among Maranaos.

[50] Acmad (nickname: Bobby) was a former child soldier interviewed on 1 September 2010 (Almarez 2010: 158).

[51] Almarez 2010: 149.

food, but their survival training includes eating raw vegetables and the identification of fruits and root crops that can be eaten raw, because smoke in cooking can give away their location during aerial reconnaissance or during military patrols.

In some instances, Badron, while in a camp in Butig with his father, observed that the foreign instructors were the ones conducting the training. Some of them could not speak English which necessitated translators. Badron reported an instance when a Tagalog-speaking trainer was introduced as a member of the Special Action Force of the Philippine National Police. It is possible that this person was either a discharged policeman or one who had gone absent without filing leave of absence (AWOL) due to wrongdoing. The presence of these individuals in the Maute camp indicates the ability of the group to recruit through cash inducement. Samanodin, a boy of 14 when he joined the Maute group, said that they had only ten days of combat training and five days of indoctrination on Islamic creed when the February 2016 Butig Battle erupted. He was very scared, but he was forced to follow his team for fear of capture. Looking back, he considered his first battle experience as part of his training: for him, it was the most dangerous part, but it is where he learned the most.

Child soldiers are regularly indoctrinated. Male child soldiers are given rest before they perform their ablutions for the mandated daily prayers and there are also breaks to allow time for reading and memorizing the Qur'an. Trainees are conditioned not to fear death and are taught that dying while fighting will make them martyrs (*shahids*). A noontime siesta is allowed before another rigid physical training in the late afternoon. At night time trainees take shifts for perimeter patrols and night sentinel duties.

Ombra recalled that he was assigned to perform intelligence gathering for the *Dawlah*, the ISIS-inspired group established by Abdullah Maute. As such he had to visit places like Marawi City to validate the data that were filtering into their camp. In addition, this respondent related that he acted as a sniper during the battles in Butig in 2016 and Piagapo in 2017. Intelligence gathering is taught during the training and it accompanies training in night movements, escape, evasion, mountain climbing and river crossing, which are important skills in eluding pursuers once detected or in conducting offensive operations.

Abedin, the former child soldier who joined the MILF when he was 11 years old, revealed that, when he was 16 years old, he was assigned the task of stealing cars. According to him, stealing the property of non-Muslims is allowed by his group as long as it helps the cause of *Mujahideens*. He indicated that this is a part of *jihad*. However, this appears to be contradictory to the Qur'anic injunction (Qur'an 60:8–9) that peace and harmony between Muslims and non-Muslims shall be practised, and protection to non-Muslims shall be provided in the event that they seek protection from Muslims (Qur-an: Surah Al-Taubah 9:6). Article 60 paragraph 8 of the Holy Qur'an provides that 'Allah does not forbid you to deal justly and kindly with those who fought not against you on account of religion nor drove you out of your homes. Verily, Allah loves those who deal with equity.' The foregoing provision of the Holy Qur'an is clear that non-believers who are not engaged in religious war against Muslims should be treated fairly. Moreover, Article 9 paragraph 6 of the Holy Qur'an states that: 'And if anyone of the Mushrikun (polytheist, idolaters, pagans, disbelievers in the Oneness of Allah) seeks your protection then grant him protection so that he may hear the Word of Allah (the Qur'an) and then escort him to where he can be secure, that is because they are men who know not.' Instead of dealing with non-believers in a violent way, paragraph 6 of Article 9 enjoins Muslims to protect non-Muslims so that they be given the opportunity to learn about Islam.

Considering Abedin's ignorance of the foregoing provisions of the Holy Qur'an, it is clear that he has undergone extremist indoctrination. Note that this is not unique to the MILF: it is also true of the Maute group.[52] Abutalib, one of the two former child soldiers who participated in the attack of the municipality of Kolambugan in 2008 while still a child soldier, recalled that he was tasked by his group to take over and burn a church. This testimony attests to the extreme radicalization among child soldiers in the MILF.

Child soldiers who fought government troops bore scars on their bodies purportedly resulting from battle wounds. Tales of near-death experiences are apparent sources of pride, and the opportunity to be a martyr sustained their willingness to continue with their armed struggle. Some showed no emotions while discussing bloody encounters where people were shot in the head or beheaded.

The MILF has female child soldiers who are assigned tasks like housekeeping, food preparation and paramedic duties.[53] Although they perform auxiliary services, they are also given combat training to prepare them for action if needed. While Ayesha, a former child soldier who is now 33 years old, never saw action in battle, her training made her an expert in martial arts. This qualification made the Maute group recruit her as their trainer in hand-to-hand combat for their fighters, some of whom saw action in the Battle of Marawi.

Pendatun is a combatant from the Maute group who was captured while on patrol two weeks before the Marawi siege. In a prison interview, he shared that, during the early months of 2016, he noticed at least seven child soldiers in their camp situated at Butig, Lanao del Sur. The ages of these child soldiers ranged from 13 to 17 years old. Some looked frail and even appeared to be younger than their age. Pendatun further shared that during his stay in Butig there were children in the camp whom he identified as children of the combatants who had been brought along as they all moved to the front line. Older children performed auxiliary functions such as cleaning the camp, gathering firewood, making tents and foxholes and carrying ammunitions. Unlike military camps which are exclusive of civilians, camps of Moro armed groups in Mindanao are sprawling communities where civilian families reside. This fact also helps explain why children are present. The early exposure of children to armed conflict is a part of their experiential learning that makes them vulnerable to being recruited as child soldiers. In some instances, children who grew up in the insurgent camps were unconsciously integrated into an armed group by simply mimicking what their elders were doing. This pattern unfolds like a natural process in many areas in Muslim Mindanao where insurgency has simply become a part of community life.

5. FACTORS LEADING TO SEPARATION FROM SOLDIERING

Some child soldiers were later separated from the armed struggle they had previously espoused. Others, however, seemed to take a temporary leave while no active armed

---

[52] For accounts of indoctrination in other countries, see Bloom in this volume and Casey-Maslen in this volume.
[53] Ali et al. 2002.

encounter was underway. Usop and Badron were frustrated that none of the objectives set by their leaders had yet been achieved. They were told that only *jihad* can restore Mindanao to its rightful owners. However, years passed, and they had not seen victory: still, their elders exhorted them to be more patient. The total defeat of the Maute group in Marawi made them rethink their position. When granted leave by their commander, they decided not to return to their camp. Others were unhappy that, despite their achievements in battle, they received no appreciation. However, they said that they harboured no regrets for being part of an armed struggle.

Most of the child soldiers during the MILF struggle were recruited on the platform of *jihad* at the local level. They believed in the struggle for self-determination by the Moro people. But these fighters were later disillusioned by the influx of other fighters who propagated political ideology supportive of the Caliphate. This change in motivation made some of them decide not to participate in the Marawi siege. The 'cash for war' approach of the Maute group also eroded the foundations of the Moro armed struggle for self-determination. Some respondents testified that amounts ranging from PhP15,000 (US$283) to PhP30,000 (US$566) were given to some fighters, which made them appear as mere mercenaries. The involvement of large amounts of money brought into question the commitment of many people to the struggle. Currently, the line is drawn between the pro-ISIS group and other Muslims in the Lanao provinces. Having witnessed the cruelty of the Maute group in pursuing their aim of establishing an Islamic state, some Muslims distanced themselves from them. However, poverty and adventurism continue to play in the Maute group's favour while they have the funds to entice people, including children, to join their ranks. In the meantime, many child soldiers are demobilized as a consequence of the on-going peace negotiations between the government and the MILF and the move of the latter to be delisted by UNICEF from the roster of armed groups that are recruiting child soldiers. By 19 February 2017, the MILF had begun releasing its 1,858 child soldiers, with the initial release of 50 child soldiers in the municipality of Sultan Kudarat, Maguindanao. As a proof of demobilization, the MILF gave certificates of disengagement and turned the children over to their parents. Lotta Sylwander, the country representative of UNICEF, lauded the Bangsa Moro Armed Force (BIAF, the military arm of the MILF) for being the only armed group in the world that turned over its child soldiers to their parents.[54] By December 2017 the MILF was formally removed from the UN's list of armed groups recruiting child soldiers. But this is just the beginning. The children released still have to be reintegrated into mainstream society.

6. *MADRASAH* EDUCATION

The Muslim Mindanao Autonomy Act No. 279 defines madrasah as an Arabic term for school, which is operationally defined as a community-based and privately-run educational institution where the medium of instruction is the Arabic language and the core emphasis is on Islamic studies and Arabic literacy. In the same statute, three types of madaris are introduced, namely:

---

[54] Fonbuena 2017.

1. ***Madrasah*, developmental or formal** – a type of *madrasah* that offers hierarchically structured education and sequential learning generally attuned to the formal education system of the Philippines;
2. ***Madrasah*, integrated or pilot** – a type of *madrasah* that offers a complete basic unified instructional programme such as Arabic Language, Islamic Values Education, education in Islamic Studies and the core learning areas of the Restructured Basic Education Curriculum; and,
3. ***Madrasah*, traditional or weekend** – a type of *madrasah* wherein the instruction is basically religious. It is considered as non-formal education due to the following characteristics: (a) classes are held on Saturdays and Sundays or days agreed upon by the teacher and students/pupils; (b) it does not have a formal curriculum; (c) it is non-graded and may have multi-age grouping; and (d) it requires only a simple qualification for its teachers, such as being graduates of a *madrasah* or being an *imam* (Muslim religious leader).

Madrasah education in the Philippines has been operating from around the year 1380 CE when Muslim foreigners started arriving and converting people in the southern Philippine islands in the process known as the Islamization of the Philippines, which was accompanied by the establishment of Islamic political and educational institutions in southern Philippines. In most cases, *madaris* in the Philippines follow a foreign curriculum adopted from the country where their respective founder and/or teachers graduated. This curriculum may not be responsive to the educational needs of the school and of the community, but it continues to exist due to a lack of supervision from the government and despite the efforts of the Department of Education (DepEd) and other non-government organizations.

Madaris that are not supervised by the DepEd are suspected of being responsible for the radicalization of their students and for teaching them violent extremism. This suspicion is now being addressed by the government of the Philippines through DepEd by institutionalizing traditional or weekend *madaris* through prescribing a unified curriculum and textbooks and having them registered to DepEd. But the problem of human resources and lack of budget hamper successful implementation.

Respondents denied the influence of their *madrasah* education on their involvement in armed struggle against the government. All of our respondents had attended the second and third types of *madrasah* education mentioned above. Mamalangcas, for example, who was in the second year of high school when he became a child soldier, attended the *madrasah* at weekends together with some high school classmates, at the same time as also undertaking his formal education under the Department of Education. Whilst denying that the *madrasah* had influenced his decision to join the armed group (referring instead to the influence of activist relatives who advocate self-rule for Mindanao), he said that his teachers in the *madrasah* emphasized the concept of the 'Greatest Jihad'. Asnawi, for his part, stated that indeed *jihad* was regularly discussed by one teacher in the *madrasah* he attended. But his understanding of *jihad* was enriched more by discussions outside the classroom with some teachers and enthusiastic students. The narrative on the experience of Asnawi of meeting people who tried to convince him and his classmates to take up the armed struggle in fighting for their rights and in establishing an Islamic community is consistent with the narrative of Abdulgani who also underwent a similar experience in college. The effort to radicalize some students as a mode of recruitment by some armed groups appears to be widespread, at least in the Lanao provinces, over past decades. Cairoden attended the second type of *madrasah* and he remembers attending at least four sessions of lectures on the obligations of Muslims that were delivered by a foreign teacher. These lectures were conducted in the nearby house of a teacher who invited students after his class in the afternoon. The administrator of their *madrasah*, when interviewed, said that since his *madrasah* is strictly against radical ideas, topics like the use of force in pursuing one's entitlement or in advancing perceived interests have to be discussed outside. He stressed however that administrators do not interfere with the advocacies of their teachers when propagated outside school.

Teachers and administrators of three *madaris* concurred that they were against violent extremism. According to them, they conducted an active campaign against the Caliphate during the Battle of Marawi. Nevertheless, they admitted that some of their students participated in the battle. Similar denials are made by administrators and teachers of the other *madaris* included in the study. However, some administrators and teachers accepted that there were teachers who introduced the concept of the justified use of violence. Intentionally or unintentionally, it is possible that their efforts resulted in the radicalization of some students who later joined the MILF or the Maute group, but these efforts were undertaken outside the school, as asserted by *madaris'* administrators.

7. CONCLUSION AND RECOMMENDATIONS

The centuries-old unrest in Mindanao has engendered a culture of violence that provides systematic conduits for the induction of Moro children into the armed struggle. The *madrasah* has become one of the platforms for the propagation of an ideology that provided a rationale for the continuing rebellion in Mindanao. It is clear therefore that the problem of child soldiering in Mindanao has both political and educational dimensions.

The government should continue the on-going peace-building process with the Moro people. It must address the grievances of these people which pushed them into rebellion since 1968 with the establishment of the MIM and later the MNLF. Initially, the goal of the rebellion was independence, but this was later scaled down into regional autonomy for the Moro people with the signing of the Tripoli Agreement on 23 December 1976. This agreement led to the birth of the MILF in 1977 after the faction of Hashim Salamat (who continued to advocate for independence) separated from the MNLF. However, the implementation of the agreement did not satisfy even the MNLF. In 1989, the Republic Act (RA) No. 6734 was passed by Philippine Congress establishing the Autonomous Region of Muslim Mindanao (ARMM). Again, issues were raised on its implementation, but on 2 September 1996, the MNLF and the Philippine government signed the 1996 Final Agreement. The MILF, on the other hand, continued with armed rebellion, but after the death of Hashim Salamat in 2003 it also toned down its demands into those seeking autonomy. In 2012, the Framework Agreement on Bangsa Moro (which later formed part of the Comprehensive Agreement on Bangsa Moro (CAB)) was signed. The CAB became the basis of the Bangsa Moro Basic Law (BBL) Bill which failed to pass under the administration of President Benigno Aquino.

On 27 July 2018, a version known as the Bangsa Moro Organic Law (BOL) was signed by President Rodrigo Duterte as the Republic Act No. 11054. This law seeks to establish a political entity that is responsive to the aspirations of the Moro people. Hence it is seen by many as a positive development in peace-building in southern Philippines. This political entity gives the Moro people a political system in which they can manage their own political affairs in accordance with Islam. As early as 2014, after the signing of the CAB, the MILF reported that it had already started demobilizing its armed wing, the Bangsa Moro Armed Forces (BIAF), to which its 1,858 child soldiers were attached.

In our view, the passage of the BOL enhances the trust of the Moro people in this government, thus improving the atmosphere of peace-building. The many agreements between the government and the MNLF and MILF in the past did not end the Moro rebellion in southern Philippines; both armed groups accused the government of insincerity and fraud in their implementation. Hope is rising for the passage of the BOL; however, the law still has to go through a plebiscite, as provided by the constitution, before it is implemented. Thus, there is the need to put in place safeguards for the exercise of the right of suffrage in affected places where the plebiscite is to be conducted, all of which have a history of electoral fraud and violence. The sincere implementation of this law would eliminate the main reason for the armed rebellion of the Moro people and consequently enhance prospects for the demobilization of child soldiers.

On the educational dimension, it should be noted that the *madrasah* system is operating parallel to the Philippine education under the DepEd. With the exception of the first type of *madrasah*, the products of the other types are not accredited in the DepEd, thus they cannot be incorporated into the mainstream educational system in the Philippines. It is therefore recommended that the government, through DepEd, fast-track its policy of institutionalizing the third type of *madrasah* and intensify government supervision over all types of *madrasah*. Eventually, the DepEd should mainstream the curricular offerings and management of *madrasah* education. This entails a shift into the first type of *madrasah* where a standard curriculum aligned to the mainstream educational system is prescribed so that students can attend any school in the Philippines without any curricular deficiency. Resources should be made available to upgrade infrastructure and improve the competence of teachers and administrators. The end point, we posit, should be the integration of *madrasah* education into the national educational system, which means free tuition for students and the upgrading of the salary of teachers to the level of the DepEd. Upgrading teachers means sending them, through scholarship grants, to accredited higher educational institutions (HEIs) to earn their advanced degrees in line with their specialization as determined by the courses they teach. The competence of school administrators can be upgraded in a similar fashion by providing them with grants to study school administration. Likewise, infrastructures should be designed to be responsive to the needs and requirements of *madrasah* education. This will address the grievance of the Moro people with respect to having been consistently neglected under the Philippine Republic, thus reducing their list of reasons to rebel against the government.

With an autonomous state organized in accordance with Islamic governance, it is hoped that the political motivation for insurgency movements in southern Philippines will abate. Close supervision and full support for Islamic education will hopefully deny a platform to anybody who desires to propagate their own ideologies among unsuspecting young students.

Finally, a programme for the reintegration of former child soldiers should be crafted by the government to ensure that young people traumatized by the unrest in Mindanao will be welcomed and accepted as assets of society. First, a special educational programme should be designed for those demobilized child soldiers, including former child soldiers, who are still interested in studying. This programme should emphasize skills development in preparation for earning a livelihood. Second, training should be provided for those who desire to follow entrepreneurial pursuits and agricultural activities, considering that some child soldiers were recruited from agricultural communities. Some child soldiers grew up without learning any trade, hence livelihood training is important for their readjustment into mainstream society. Third, the government should provide technical and financial support to all certified demobilized members of the armed forces of Moro groups, including child soldiers, in terms of training, coaching, farming tools and non-collateralized and interest-free capital loans. Fourth, the government should involve the parents of child soldiers by providing them with coaching on child rearing and providing them with livelihood support so that they can be more productive and independent. The local government should be given technical support in the preparation of development plans that address economic issues in southern Philippines. Lastly, we recommend the organization of demobilized fighters into cooperatives that would include among their members demobilized child soldiers. Cooperatives are self-governing organizations supervised by the government. They differ from other kinds of popular organizations because they focus on livelihood and require cooperative education as a requisite for membership. Well-managed cooperatives are better conduits for government financial and technical support than local governments managed by corrupt local officials.

REFERENCED WORKS AND ADDITIONAL READINGS[55]

Al Jazeera News 2017. 'Hundreds of MILF Child Soldiers Released in Philippines' (11 March)
Ali, C., Bari, S.R. and Paraguya, G.M.F. 2002. *The Roles of Moro Islamic Liberation Front (MILF) Bangsa-Bai Women Rebels in Poona Piagapo, Lanao del Norte During the March 2000 Mindanao Conflict* (Undergraduate thesis in AB Political Science, College of Arts and Social Sciences, MSU-Iligan Institute of Technology)
Almarez, D.N. 2010 'Child Soldiers in Lanao Provinces: A Case of Human Rights Violation' 23 *Mindanao Forum* 133
Bara, H. 2015. 'The History of the Muslim of the Philippines' (National Commission for Culture and the Arts) (30 April)
Barrete, R.J. and Lischin, L. 2017. 'Coming of Age in Conflict: Child Soldiers in the Philippines', *UCA News* (31 October)
Beardsley, N.L. and Beech, A.R. 2013. 'Applying the Violent Extremist Risk Assessment (VERA) to a Sample of Terrorist Case Studies' 5 *Journal of Aggression, Conflict and Peace Research* 4
Becket, J. 1977. 'The Datus of the Rio Grande de Cotabato Under Colonial Rule' 5 *Asian Studies* 46.
Brago, P.L. 2017. 'MILF Stricken Off UN List vs Child Recruitment', *The Philippine Star* (7 October)
Cherwon, B. 2014. *Child Soldiers in Africa: A Case Study of Uganda and South Sudan* (University of Nairobi)
Denov, M. 2005. 'Child Soldiers in Sierra Leone: Experiences, Implications and Strategies for Rehabilitation and Community Reintegration' (Canadian International Development Agency) (August)
Derluyn, I., Broekaert, E., Schuyten, G. and De Temmerman, E. 2004. 'Post-Traumatic Stress in Former Ugandan Child Soldiers' 363 *The Lancet* 861

---

[55] The authors have included a broader list of additional readings of pedagogical value to the reader in the spirit of sharing informational sources about the Philippines with a global audience.

Fonbuena, C. 2017. 'Unicef Lauds MILF for Releasing Child Soldiers', *Rappler.com* (20 February) [available at: https://www.rappler.com/nation/162049-milf-release-child-combatants (accessed 27 November 2018)]

Gowing, P.G. 1979. *Muslim Filipinos – Heritage and Horizon* (Quezon City: New Day Publisher)

Gray, D.H. and Matchin, T.O. III. 2008. 'Children: The New Face of Terrorism' 3 *International NGO Journal* 108

Hincks, J. 2017. 'The Leaders of the ISIS Assault on Marawi in the Philippines Have Been Killed', *Time* (16 October)

Homeland Security Institute 2009. 'Recruitment and Radicalization of School-Aged Youth by International Terrorist Groups' (23 April)

Huesmann, L.R. 2010. 'How to Grow a Terrorist Without Really Trying: The Psychological Development of Terrorists from Childhood to Adulthood', in D. Antonius, A.D. Brown, T.K. Walters, J.M. Ramirez and S.J. Sinclair (eds), *Interdisciplinary Analyses of Terrorism and Political Aggression* (Cambridge, UK: Cambridge Scholars Publishing) 1.

Jannaral, J.I. 2018. 'MILF to Disengage 1,869 Child Warriors' *The Manila Times* (13 April)

Klemensits, P. and Czirjak, R. 2016. 'Child Soldiers in Genocidal Regimes: The Cases of the Khmer Rouge and the Hutu Power' 15 *Academic and Applied Research in Military Science (AARMS)* 215

Madale, A.T. 1997. *The Maranaws: Dwellers of the Lake* (Rex Bookstore, Inc.)

Majul, C.A. 1999. *Muslims in the Philippines* (Quezon City: University of the Philippines Press)

Montud, N.M. and Nadjmah S.L.M. 2012. *Former Girl Soldiers: The Effects of Soldiering to their Development and their Rights* (Undergraduate thesis in Political Science, MSU-Iligan Institute of Technology)

MONUSCO [UN Organization Stabilization Mission in the Democratic Republic of the Congo] 2013 'Child Recruitment by Armed Groups in DRC from January 2012 to August 2013' (24 October)

Morales, Y. 2017. 'Duterte Declares Martial Law in Mindanao', *CNN Philippines* (24 May)

Muslim Mindanao Autonomy Act No. 279, An Act Providing for a System of Basic Education for the Autonomous Region in Muslim Mindanao, Amending Muslim Mindanao Autonomy Act Numbered Fourteen Therefor, and for Other Purposes, Short title: ARMM Basic Education Act of 2010 (Republic of the Philippines), 4 August 2010

Republic Act No. 6734, An Act Providing for an Organic Act for the Autonomous Region in Muslim Mindanao (Republic of the Philippines), 1 August 1989

Republic Act No. 10533, An Act Enhancing the Philippine Basic Education System by Strengthening its Curriculum and Increasing the Number of Years for Basic Education, Appropriating Funds Therefor and For Other Purposes, Short Title: Enhanced Basic Education Act of 2013 (Republic of the Philippines), 15 May 2013

Risser, G., Ohm, K. and Htun, S. 2003. *Running the Gauntlet: The Impact of Internal Displacement in Southern Shan States* (Bangkok, Thailand: Humanitarian Affairs Research Project, Asian Center for Migration, Institute of Asian Studies, Chulalungkorn University)

Singer, P. 2006. *Children at War* (Los Angeles: University of California Press)

Somasundaram, D. (2002). 'Child Soldiers: Understanding the Context' *British Medical Journal* 3

South China Morning Post 2017. 'Battle Over: Philippines Declares End of Marawi Siege after Dozens of Militants Die in Final Showdown' (23 October)

11. Children born of conflict-related sexual violence within armed groups: a case study of northern Uganda

Myriam Denov

While children have been implicated in armed conflict for centuries – whether as participants, witnesses or victims – the definition and conceptualization of what and who constitutes a 'child soldier' have evolved and shifted over the decades. The 1977 Additional Protocols to the Geneva Conventions of 1949 prohibited the military recruitment and use of children under the age of 15. The Optional Protocol to the United Nations Convention on the Rights of the Child raised the minimum age of military recruitment, prohibiting the conscription and participation of children under 18 years in non-state armed groups.[1] Within a parallel time frame, in an attempt to recognize, acknowledge and address the critical, complex and multifaceted roles of children living within the context of armed groups, the Cape Town Principles broadened the definition of 'child soldier' to include those not only participating directly in hostilities, but also those associated with armed groups in a variety of roles and contexts, including cooks, porters, messengers and children recruited for sexual purposes and forced marriage. In 2007, the Paris Principles[2] dropped the use of the term 'child soldier' and instead employed 'a child associated with an armed force or armed group'.[3] The Paris Principles introduced the following designation, which represents the most current internationally recognized definition of the phenomenon of children's involvement in war:

> 'A child associated with an armed force or armed group' refers to any person below 18 years of age who is or who has been recruited or used by an armed force or armed group in any capacity, including but not limited to children, boys, and girls used as fighters, cooks, porters, messengers, spies or for sexual purposes. It does not only refer to a child who is taking or has taken a direct part in hostilities.[4]

As the complexity of armed conflict persists, endures and evolves, so do the situations of children's involvement within it. One such situation is the reality of children born within the context of armed groups, specifically, children born of conflict-related sexual violence. While these children may, in some ways, 'fit' within the above-noted definition

---

[1] Art. 4, OPAC.
[2] The Paris Principles were designed to guide interventions for the protection and well-being of children, to assist in making policy and programming decisions, to prevent unlawful recruitment or use of children, and to facilitate the release and reintegration of children associated with armed forces and armed groups. Paris Principle 1.11.
[3] Paris Principle 2.1 (definitions).
[4] Ibid.

of a child associated with an armed group, their situations and realities are relatively unique. These children are born of wartime rape, and in some cases, raised during their formative years within contexts of war and within armed groups. Moreover, these children may, as they age and grow, engage in many of the war-related activities referred to in the Paris Principles, such as acting as fighters, cooks, porters, spies, medics, messengers and, in addition, they may also be used for sexual purposes. However, in the aftermath of armed conflict, these children may not necessarily self-identify as 'former child soldiers' in the same way as those children who have been abducted into, or actively join, armed groups. In fact, given the complex circumstances of children born of war, and the fact that the setting of the armed group may be all they have ever known, many of these children may identify the armed group and the surrounding context as 'home'. Children born of conflict-related sexual violence and their presence within armed groups is not a 'new' phenomenon, as this reality has existed across time and armed conflicts.[5] However, given their overall invisibility and voicelessness in scholarly and policy discussions, their positionality as 'child soldiers' has rarely been considered.

A case in point are children who were born of conflict-related sexual violence in the context of the Lord's Resistance Army (LRA) in northern Uganda. Under the leadership of Joseph Kony, the LRA sought to overthrow the Ugandan government and became well known for its atrocities against civilians. Kony formed the LRA to counter the consistent and palpable abuse, exclusion and oppression that the Acholi people of northern Uganda experienced at the hands of the Ugandan government.[6] In their battle against the Ugandan government, the LRA abducted between 60,000 and 80,000 children into armed conflict.[7] However, variance and under-reporting in these estimates exist due to the many challenges in measuring and operationalizing child abduction during the war. An estimated 30 per cent of abducted children were girls who were used as combatants, porters and domestic workers, and were forced to 'marry' male commanders.[8] These girls became the exclusive property of commanders, and were required to obey any and every command and to never refuse their 'husbands' sexual services.[9] Roughly 10,000 abducted girls became pregnant from sexual violence, giving birth to two or more children.[10] While not all of these children born of conflict-related sexual violence survived the brutality and hardship of the war, thousands are currently living in post-conflict northern Uganda.[11]

For the most part, scholarly literature in the context of northern Uganda has focused and shed light on the abducted women and girls who were victims of repeated sexual violence, and gave birth to children in the context of the LRA.[12] However, an emerging literature on northern Uganda has begun to document the realities of their children who were born of conflict-related sexual violence, and in some cases, raised within the LRA.

---

[5] Mochmann and Lee 2010; Denov 2015: 61–8.
[6] Finnström 2008; Schomerus and Walmsley 2007.
[7] Shanahan and Veale 2016: 72.
[8] Carlson and Mazurana 2008; Veale et al. 2013: 839.
[9] Denov forthcoming.
[10] Akello 2013: 149.
[11] Watye Ki Gen 2014.
[12] Akello 2013; Carlson and Mazurana 2008; Shanahan and Veale 2016; Worthen et al. 2010.

Researchers have explored the wartime experiences of children born in LRA captivity,[13] the stigma, violence and marginalization that these children continue to face in the post-war period,[14] as well as the unique protection needs of these children.[15] These children represent a unique group of war-affected children who deserve greater research, policy and practice attention.

In response, the current study sought to further understand the realities of children born of conflict-related sexual violence, both during and following their captivity in the LRA. Data collection was carried out between June 2015 and December 2017 in the Gulu, Pader, Nwoya and Agago districts of northern Uganda. Interviews were conducted with 71 children born in captivity (CBC). All participants were recruited through a partner organization who had ongoing contact with children formerly in the LRA as a result of their continuing work and advocacy for women and children born in LRA captivity.[16] Child and youth participants (39 male and 32 female) were between the ages of 12 and 19 at the time of the data collection and were living in Gulu (27), Pader (23), Agago (20) and Nwoya (1).[17] Participants had often spent their formative years in captivity, ranging from a few months after being born, to seven years.

All interviews for the study were conducted in Acholi,[18] audio-recorded with permission and then translated and transcribed into English. Questions explored during interviews included: What are children's perceptions of life in the bush and within an armed group as compared to life in the post-war period? What challenges do children face in the post-war period and what opportunities are available to them? What are the implications of their experiences for the realities of child soldiers more generally? Drawing from these interviews, this chapter traces the experiences of children who were born within, and in many cases raised in the context of, the LRA. The chapter draws upon the direct voices of children born in LRA captivity to explore their perspectives on home, family, identity, belonging and post-war reintegration. The chapter concludes with a discussion of programmatic recommendations, as suggested by the children themselves, as well as the implications of the study findings for policy with regard to children born in captivity and our understanding of child soldier reintegration more generally.

---

[13] Green and Denov 2019.
[14] Denov and Lakor 2017; Denov 2015.
[15] Apio 2007; Denov and Lakor 2018.
[16] This research was funded by the Pierre Elliott Trudeau Foundation and was a partnership between researchers at McGill University and Watye Ki Gen. Watye Ki Gen is made up of a collective of women who were abducted by the LRA and held in captivity. In the post-conflict period, the organization is working to strengthen the rights, needs and collective voice of former abductee women and their children, particularly within mechanisms of transitional justice.
[17] The study received ethical approval from two research ethics boards: the first from the Uganda National Council for Science and Technology/Office of the President of Uganda, and the second from the Research Ethics Board of McGill University, Canada.
[18] Interviews conducted by non-Acholi speakers included Acholi–English translation.

1. 'PLACE' AND THE LRA: THE BUSH AS 'HOME'

The notions of 'place' and 'home' become important concepts when considering the lives of children born in LRA captivity. Casey suggests that the notion of 'place' cannot be conceptualized as having a fixed or single meaning, essence or structure.[19] Instead, place is dynamic and changing. Relph conceptualizes 'place' as theoretically organized around three basic elements: physical setting, activity and meaning.[20] As a physical setting, place can be a geographic centre, site or location for events.[21] The conceptualization of place as a physical setting is particularly relevant for children born in captivity. For participants, 'the bush' was a physical place imbued with meaning and memories (both good and bad), ultimately representing a place that held deep significance. However, it should be noted that for participants, given that the LRA was constantly on the move, 'the bush' did not represent a single place or setting, but instead meant multiple physical places and territories. As this participant explained:

> You know, in the bush we were never settled because any time you would be surprised by attacks from government soldiers. We would never settle in one place. I remember there was a certain period spanning three weeks when the government soldiers had intensified their attacks on our position. We would hardly stay in one place for more than an hour, then the UPDF would attack us. So we shifted from one location to another. Life was so difficult and hanging in balance. We were always on the move, walking long distance from one location to another as opposed to certain times when at least we would settle in one place for up to three months. Life was difficult around that time. We would trek day and night for long distances and sometimes on an empty stomach. (Female)

Importantly, place can be understood as more than a mere setting. Emphasizing a people–place dyad, place can also be defined by the activities and social interactions that occur in a given location.[22] Reflecting the connection between people, place, activities and interaction – for participants – the bush represented a place of danger, fear and violence:

> [Do you have memories of life in the bush?] I remember an incident whereby a helicopter gunship was dropping bombs in our direction. We were also being confronted by the government soldiers on foot. The assault on us by the government soldiers was so intense; both from the helicopter and the ground troops, with the bushes burning down. I remember we hid, but escaped narrowly. I think we would have been killed if we were to be found by the government soldiers. (Male)

> I have drawn here where the LRA are fighting with some soldiers . . . Secondly, this is my picture when I was shot in my leg and my leg was broken. Here is my mother tying my leg . . . Here after I had been shot in the leg, the LRA soldiers came and they are shooting those people and they are standing by my side and they are not running away. Then here is where my brother's bag he was carrying was shot by the plane [above] and the bag started burning his back. He dropped the bag with all his shirts inside. (Male)

> My mother had been shot while carrying me on her shoulder. . . . My mother was shot and fell down, while I also fell lying next to her, so one of the people who was running alongside her carried me away and continued running with me. (Male)

---

[19] Casey 1997: 37.
[20] Relph 1976.
[21] Ibid.
[22] Fullilove 1996: 1517.

Highlighting the ways in which children born in LRA captivity were, in some cases, trained to use weaponry and participate directly in hostilities, this participant explained the meaning of the bush and the potential danger and fear it incited:

> As a boy raised in the bush, they would hand me a gun and anything could have happened to me . . . When they [boys] reach sixteen years then they are given guns to carry on with the work of those who are killed in battles. (Male)

Conceptualizations of place as physical setting and activities ultimately lead to Relph's third element of place: *meaning*.[23] Relph asserts that place is 'a territory of meanings' and that people are an important vehicle for this meaning-making process, as well as a way we connect with others.[24] As Mumford notes, 'people are as attached to places as they are attached to families and friends. When these loyalties come together, one then has the most tenacious cement possible for human society.'[25] Highlighting the complexity of place and its deep connections to family, relationships and interactions, for participants, the bush also represented – somewhat paradoxically – a meaningful place of ease, togetherness and enjoyment:

> [Interviewer: You have drawn a beautiful picture. I am seeing picture of trees, flowers, and even pictures of children . . . Can you explain the picture before us?] [Participant:] I drew the picture of children playing, showing the time when we were still in the bush. Life was easy while we were in the bush. We would play all the time, I was also in company of both my parents . . . When I was young and in the bush, life was very enjoyable. (Male)

In addition to representing physical spaces, activities and meaning, for many participants the bush ultimately represented 'home'. Blunt and Dowling suggest that 'home' is both a space and a concept that can be reflected in the realms of the body, a physical structure, city or nation.[26] Blunt and Dowling argue that 'home' should be considered as a spatial imaginary, representing the relationship between feelings, attachment and dwelling, as well as a political space of negotiation and contestation.[27] Denov and Akesson assert that home can be considered a symbolic place that often embodies togetherness, individual and family growth, memories and personal and familial connections with land and territory.[28] The deep connection between conceptualizations of 'home' and 'the bush' was evident in the participants' narratives:

> The bush was not seen as the bush to me. It was home. (Male)

> [During the war] I did not think about anything. I thought that was home . . . I felt I loved staying in the bush because I felt that was home. (Female)

Importantly, place can also be linked to identity. Place identity is a bi-directional process whereby a place may help to confer identity upon one who inhabits, visits and uses it,

---

[23] Relph 1976.
[24] Relph 1993: 36.
[25] Mumford 1961: 287.
[26] Blunt and Dowling 2006: 1–2.
[27] Ibid.: 2.
[28] Denov and Akesson 2016: 339.

as well as the process by which one attributes their identity to a place.[29] Feld and Basso note that '[a]s people fashion places, so, too, do they fashion themselves'.[30] In relation to children, Ackroyd and Pilkington have noted that 'children do not have one essential identity, but switch identities in different contexts and, subject to diverse cultural influences, often produce new identities'.[31] Reflecting this idea, participants' identities were often recast over time, their experiences propelling them to rethink and re-evaluate the role of place and its meaning to their identity:

> I just learned on my own without someone telling me that I am a CBC [child born in captivity]. [When in] the bush I thought we were staying at home, but when we reached home, I realized that there is another home . . . I realized that the bush wasn't our home, but it was a place for fighting, where we were abducted and taken there. And where we were born from. Then that made me ask my mother. She told me that this is our home (post-war Gulu). [I asked her:] What about the bush where we lived? Then she explained it to me and I understood. (Female)

For children born in LRA captivity, 'the bush' was a place that held great significance, memories, meaning and contributed to identity formation. As such, leaving the bush often brought conflicted feelings for participants. Akesson, Basso and Denov note that loss of 'home' can negatively impact family structure and community ties, and can lead to increased vulnerability, family breakdown and ultimately displace a family from an environment that may provide cohesion, support, protection, cultural grounding and identity.[32] While life in the bush was characterized by participants as a place of violence, pain, sorrow and grief, paradoxically, the bush was simultaneously viewed with nostalgia, as a place of love, cohesion and as 'a way of life':

> When I was young and in the bush, life was very enjoyable. I had all my siblings around me, we would play in a group most of the time. Also our father was around us most of the time . . . My fatherly love was the best thing about life in the bush. Also food and play time . . . I would eat the food brought for my father and also I would eat from my father's plate. It would make me feel so happy. (Male)

> We were used to the situation and life in the bush. We looked at fighting as a way of life . . . We did not mind living in the bush. (Female)

The narratives of participants suggest a unique relationship to life and place in the bush. Given the circumstances of their birth, and in some cases, being raised in the context of captivity, participants' relationship to the bush and the LRA appears to be distinct to the perspectives of children and youth who have been abducted and/or join armed groups. This unique perspective is further underscored when examining participants' conceptualizations of 'family' within LRA captivity.

---

[29] Denov and Akesson 2013: 62.
[30] Feld and Basso 1996: 11.
[31] Ackroyd and Pilkington 1999: 445.
[32] Akesson et al. 2016: 377.

2. 'FAMILY' IN THE LRA: RELATIONSHIPS WITH FATHERS AND MOTHERS IN CAPTIVITY

For children affected by war, vital 'systems' – whether family, community or peers – are key determinants of developmental outcomes.[33] To understand the complexity of an individual's life, scholars must incorporate the views of family and community, given that they profoundly influence their long-term well-being.[34] As Boothby notes:

> An ecologic approach to understanding children and war thus begins with a thorough examination of the protective capacities (and deficits) of key people and systems that surround them. It should form the basis for thinking with appropriate breadth of potential influences on children's well-being.[35]

Understanding the lives of children within the LRA thus requires an exploration of family structures and family relationships. This is particularly important as, during interviews, child participants highlighted the importance of their 'bush family' within the LRA. While marriages within the LRA were forced, children born in captivity were often too young to fully understand the interactions and relationships between LRA commanders and their 'wives'. Moreover, participants may have only seen their fathers within the domestic context and did not know the details of their father's actions at the warfront. Significantly, in comparison to their lives post-conflict – where they reported a fragmented sense of family – for those participants who remembered their time in the bush, they reported a strong sense of family, togetherness, love and unity in LRA captivity. As these children explained:

> I used to consider us a big family while we were in the bush because I was with my father and other siblings, unlike the family [now] where I am just with my mother and a few of my siblings. To me, the family I am in now [post-war] is a weaker family than the one I had in the bush. (Male)

> Families in the bush were united with each other, unlike here at home where there is too much hatred. Not everyone will like you equally. In the bush it was different. People loved each other and they were united. (Male)

> [W]hen our father was there, we used to feel good because he cared for us a lot. At home [now], our mother cannot care for us as it used to happen in the bush when our father was there . . . The good thing I got from the bush was love from both of my mother and my father when he was still alive. (Male)

Participants outlined family structures in the bush, which were characterized by unique roles, and yet a sense of collective work and responsibility:

> Each family would collectively participate in performing different roles. For example, a family with all its members who were old enough to work would collectively go and tend to their gardens. But also, individuals would also carry out their roles as they may feel like. My mother had her own garden of sorghum which she cultivated herself. (Female)

---

[33] Boothby et al. 2006.
[34] Kostelny and Wessells 2013: 119–29; Denov et al. 2019.
[35] Boothby 2008: 502.

Regardless of the roles that families were undertaking, participants frequently commented on the 'harmony' and mutual support that families provided one another while in captivity:

> Families in the bush lived in peace and harmony with each other. For example, when one family was lacking food, another family that had something to spare would happily be able to share with the family without food. Also the loot is shared with those that did not have [anything]. Families considered themselves as one, because of the circumstances they were in. They all considered themselves to be at the same level and in the same situation. Even children were living together without quarrels or fights. Unlike here at home where I see families fighting with each other, or hating one another. This was not common in the bush. (Female)

The importance of family and family structure was underscored by participants:

> To me, the most special thing about my family in the bush was the fact that I was under the care of both my father and mother. (Male)

2.1 Fathers in the LRA: Protection and Love

Within the LRA, children produced through rape and forced marriage were understood to belong first and foremost to their fathers, and these fathers lavished great attention on them.[36] Moreover, children born within forced marriages were highly valued by the LRA, oftentimes much more so than their mothers, and the children were a source of pride for fathers. The value attributed to children was linked to their perceived roles as the potential next generation of LRA fighters.[37] While participants' biological fathers were physically absent from their post-conflict lives (most children's fathers had either been killed, were still in the bush, or were estranged), a key element in participants' narratives was the central role and figure their biological fathers represented, both during and following the war. Scholarly literature has addressed and focused mainly on the violence and atrocities committed by LRA commanders, which has been documented extensively.[38] This body of research is important and necessary to understand the culture of violence, *raison d'être* and command structure of the LRA. However, the empirical literature has generally overlooked the roles that these men played within the domestic context and their relationship to their children born of conflict-related sexual violence. Aijazi and Baines highlight the exclusion of men's experiences of wartime forced marriage, pointing towards the use of victim/perpetrator and consent/coercion dichotomies.[39] In stark contrast to the narrative of LRA commanders as violent, coercive and abusive, participants spoke of their fathers with nostalgia and longing, highlighting their fathers' central role in providing security and love during captivity. Many participants reported that, from their perspective, their father was a powerful figure who played a caring and protective role in the bush:

> My father used to move in our company and he would protect us because he held a high rank [in the LRA]. You never know – maybe if he had died before my mother, we would all not be living

---

[36] Denov and Lakor 2017.
[37] Denov and Lakor 2018.
[38] Kramer 2012.
[39] Aijazi and Baines 2017. See also Aijazi et al. in this volume.

[now]. He was very protective of us. So when my father was arrested because he was planning to escape, he handed us over to his close friend and he instructed him to take us to World Vision . . . [His friend] took us and the information reached our grandfather who came and got us from World Vision. (Female)

I remember one day my mother beat me and I cried . . . [She] picked up a stick and caned me. I threw myself down and began crying endlessly until my father returned home. My father asked me what the problem was, but I chose not to tell him. I then saw my father pick up a cane and caned my mother. I was actually happy seeing my father beating my mother . . . I felt so loved and special by my father . . . When I returned [after the war], I was sometimes beaten by mother when I misbehaved. I have no father to defend me now. (Male)

When questioned about their relationships with their biological fathers, participants viewed the love of their father as one of the most important aspects of their time in captivity. The importance of what was often referred to as 'fatherly love' was reported consistently by participants:

My fatherly love was the best thing about life in the bush . . . I would eat from my father's plate. It would make me feel so happy . . . I love him [father] so much and needed his attention . . . I think he knew that . . . He is the best father . . . Personally, I love my father so much . . . I miss my father . . . I miss his fatherly love . . . If I am to choose between my mother and my father, then I would choose my father. (Male)

My father loved me. He would always give me something to eat. He would also tell me stories that would make me laugh. I was always happy being around my father . . . I remember my father promising to take me home. He also promised to take me to school when we returned home. This showed that my father cared about me and my future. His desire was for me to start school and have a better future . . . I miss my father so much. I miss his fatherly love . . . I am certain that if my father were to be around, he would have solved most of the problems that we are facing at home now. He would pay my school fees, he would take care of my medical bills, and he would teach me the good ways that a child requires to develop well. (Male)

While participants emphasized their love for their fathers and deeply appreciated the protection they provided them during the war, a minority of participants had witnessed their fathers engaging in or ordering brutal forms of violence. In the war's aftermath, this often brought confusion and ambivalence regarding their understandings of their fathers. However, this did not ultimately alter participants' love for their fathers. The following participant articulates this ambivalence and confusion in the post-war period:

I remember my father had a wife who was linked to sorcery. So she was dragged over thorns by my father's escorts and she was later killed. She had a child who was also killed by my father's escorts . . . That was one thing that I witnessed that was so bad involving my father . . . he was the one who ordered that . . . My friends at school keep asking me about my father. They tell me of how they fear my father so much. They say that if there is anyone they fear in life, then it is my father and I wondered what they were talking about. It also makes me feel good that my father is unique . . . Sometimes when I imagine the crimes that my father has committed, I think it is a good thing if the world is given justice for the crimes committed by my father. But again, as his son, I would sympathize with him as much as he was involved in committing crimes against humanity. So basically I feel confused . . . My father will always be my father. I know he did many wrong things and I believe that if someone told me what he did, I would feel guilty. But that does not change the fact that I love him and nothing changes! (Male)

As noted earlier, children's perspectives and views of their fathers are likely to reflect that they saw their fathers mainly in the domestic context and were often not aware of their wartime activities. Moreover, children whose biological father was a high-ranking LRA commander were taught from a young age that they were 'superior' to other children and became used to a certain degree of status and power.[40] This unique context can help to explain children's understandings of their fathers and the deep respect and admiration they held for them.

2.2 Relationships with Mothers: Bonded Through Adversity

Participants' connection with their biological mother – though often fraught with complex relational dynamics – emerged consistently in the data as one of participants' most important and powerful relationships. Many participants described being bonded with their mothers through adversity, and felt their mother was, in the aftermath of the war, their sole source of love, protection and financial and emotional support:

> As Acholi folks state that 'your mother is your richness' so when you are near your mother, she would not wish to see you suffering so much compared to when you are living with your step mother. (Female)

> I feel it is my mother [who is the most significant figure] because she is the one who gave birth to me, and she persevered all the hardship in the bush with me and she knows how it was hard. I do feel that if I tell my problems to her, she could help me faster because she knows what happened to my father, she also knows that I am an orphan and there is no one that I can go to apart from her. (Male)

Participants had an acute awareness of the ways in which their mothers protected them and kept them alive during captivity. Participants frequently used language referring to the 'struggle', 'sacrifice' and 'suffering' their mothers endured on their behalf to maintain their survival and to care for them:

> I stayed hungry for one week and my mother said she thought I was not going live. So my mother decided to escape . . . She carried one AK 47 . . . She never shot dead anybody during the escape. When we reached some garden, my mother saw the LRA moving and she hid in the bush. She entered a cassava garden and we uprooted some for [us]. We continued with the journey. We were seen [by a vehicle]. It seems that it was a Red Cross vehicle . . . The vehicle was carrying dead bodies. They saw my mother and she ran back to the bush. They found her and captured her . . . She held my hands. She never left me. (Male)

Participants remembered or were told detailed stories of what their mothers went through with them in the bush, and child participants described incidents of their mothers defending them at great cost and risk to their mother's own well-being:

---

[40] Denov and Lakor 2017.

> I asked her when we were still in the bush: 'Mother, is this our home?' She replied, 'This is not our home.' [Interviewer: What made you ask her that question?] It is because I saw my mother being beaten several times. Whenever she was to receive any beatings, she would first remove me from her back. She would be beaten and later she would carry me back on her back. That's when I asked her, 'Mother, don't we have a home? Who are these people?' (Female)

Participants often expressed being bonded and indebted to their mothers because of what they went through, and they sought to provide for and protect their mothers in the future:

> With the suffering we have endured together, when I am grown and having a job, I will buy for her something nice to make her happy. (Female)

It was also important to recognize, however, that given the complexity of the mother–child relationship and the fact that children were born of conflict-related sexual violence, the mother–child relationship was often fraught with complexity and ambivalence.[41] During LRA captivity, for some mothers, the birth of their child was seen as a 'gift from God' or a reason to persevere and overcome their difficult circumstances. However, for others, a child was unwanted and hated, as the arrival of a child represented a profound burden in the bush. Girls abducted into the LRA were aware that having a child to care for would significantly reduce her chances of a successful escape from the LRA and would potentially threaten her survival. Having a child could be dangerous, an encumbrance slowing girls down during ambushes and fighting when they were required to run with children on their backs or at their sides. Mothers were also harshly punished, including being severely beaten if their babies cried, drawing attention to their position in the bush. Under such circumstances, mothers had varying responses to motherhood and towards their children.[42] In this sense, children born in captivity were met simultaneously with hatred and love, being perceived as sources of both resentment and joy. As such, while some child participants experienced great love and bonding with their mothers, many also experienced significant marginalization, rejection and stigma from their mothers, an issue that is addressed further below.

3. POST-WAR MARGINALIZATION AND STIGMA

Interviews revealed that in the war's aftermath, stigma and marginalization, based on participants' biological origins and identity as children born in LRA captivity, were pervasive factors that extended into every aspect of participants' post-war lives – whether at the individual, family, school and/or community level. At the individual level, in the home, participants reported being stigmatized and marginalized by their mothers, stepfathers, caregivers and siblings born after the war. Within their extended family networks, they reported facing stigma by grandparents, cousins, aunts and uncles. Outside the home, when their identity as a child born in captivity was known, they faced discrimination from neighbours, community members, community leaders, their peers, teachers and

---

[41] Denov et al. 2018; Woolner et al. 2019.
[42] Denov et al. 2018.

school administrators. Participants reported that they were commonly perceived to be violent, psychologically disturbed, dangerous 'rebel children', who had brought bad 'bush behaviours', chaos and bad spirits from the bush, which were believed to have a harmful influence on the family and other children.[43] These participants described the stigma that they faced in the post-conflict period within the home, school and in the larger community:

> [My mother] would make harsh statements like: 'You children have become a very big burden to me; I wish you had died in the bush.' My grandmother is also fond of discriminating me against other children who are at home. Normally on market days, she picks on other children to go with and buys for them clothes while we are left behind. She goes ahead to tell us that we should look for our own money because she is not the one who killed our mother. She buys for her daughter clothes; but for me, I have to raise money by myself to buy my clothes. (Female)

> It is the teachers who keep saying that we are the CBCs and they like insulting us. [They say] that we are wasting our money [for sending us to school]. If our mother is paying [for school fees] they say that we don't show interest in our studies. That is the thing that makes us so annoyed. (Female)

> At home where I am staying, I do not get enough food. We are normally told to leave to go to where our father is. They say that we do not belong at the home where we are staying. They also tell it to our face that we were born in the bush, and that we are useless. Sometimes we are sent away from home and we end up spending a night in a nearby bush. (Female)

While the rejection and mistreatment participants experienced was a constant source of hardship and frustration, participants developed their own insights into the reasons they, as a group, are so widely stigmatized within their communities post-conflict:

> They [community members] imagine what the LRA used to do to them and their families and friends. They want to retaliate against us. Yet it was not our wish to be abducted and to make them unhappy. Sometimes they think that what we did or have seen in the bush, we will do to them. Yet they don't know that it is the environment that makes people behave differently. (Male)

4. WHEN WAR IS BETTER THAN PEACE: IMPLICATIONS FOR POST-CONFLICT REINTEGRATION

Given participants' post-war experiences of marginalization and disempowerment, when comparing their post-war lives to their life during war, many participants declared that their lives were actually *better* during the war than in the post-conflict period. Despite the profound violence and deprivation that these children experienced during their time in LRA captivity, children individually and collectively articulated that 'war was better than peace':[44]

> The way we were loved and treated by our parents in the bush was better than now. [What was the difference?] While in the bush we were not insulted like here at home. When we were born, we had both our mother and father. We also had better clothes to wear unlike here where our

---

[43] See also Akello in this volume; Barrett in this volume.
[44] Denov and Lakor 2017.

> clothes are not nice . . . We also had nice food to eat while we were in the bush. Here, we cannot eat peacefully without our grandmother grumbling about how feeding us has become a burden to her. (Male)

> At home here life is easy in some ways . . . there is no war compared to life in the bush. But when our father was there, we used to feel good because he cared for us a lot. At home [now] our mother cannot care for us as it used to happen in the bush when our father was there . . . The hardest thing was war. We would not have any time to rest even at night or day time in case of an attack from the government soldiers. The good thing I got from the bush was love from both of my mother and my father when he was still alive. (Male)

> We did not have anything like stigmatization against us like here at home. Here at home, we are told: 'you are a rebel child', 'your mother returned from the bush', 'you do not own land' . . . So sometimes I think we would be freer with life in the bush . . . we were living free without having to worry about the challenges that we are now facing at home. (Female)

Participants' perceptions that 'war is better than peace' have important implications for post-conflict reintegration. Some participants asserted that as a result of post-conflict marginalization and stigma by family and community members, children born in captivity were at risk of re-recruitment into armed groups, or at risk of engaging in future violence:

> I think that CBC as a group stands a high chance of retaliation because they feel marginalized and rejected in their own communities. I believe they would want to express their anger through retaliation. (Male)

On the other hand, other participants declared that their horrific and terrifying experiences in the bush would inherently prevent them from wanting to return to a life of violence and deprivation:

> Some of them [CBC] have tasted the bitter experience of life in the bush and they would not want to go back to those same harsh conditions. Also, being home makes one have some peace of mind and one also receives good advice from different people; you get an opportunity to learn from those who are knowledgeable. So all this gives you hope for the future and may not give you chance to think of developing any wrong ideas that would put your life at risk. (Male)

5. PROGRAMMATIC RECOMMENDATIONS

In northern Uganda, to date, there have been minimal government programmes or policies to acknowledge and recognize victims of the conflict or provide them with adequate redress.[45] In the aftermath of the war, the Ugandan government instituted an amnesty for all formerly abducted persons,[46] which was accompanied by 263,000 Ugandan shillings (approximately US$ 75). However, beyond the amnesty, no law exists that protects the rights and freedoms of formerly abducted persons and their children. Programmes

---

[45] Ibid.
[46] This does not include children born in captivity.

of support have existed, including government development programmes for recovery. However, in practice, multiple barriers, including lack of information, stigma, restrictive criteria and gender norms have precluded women's and children's access.[47] According to Apio, programmes that focused on the reintegration of children affected by armed conflict were inadequate as they did not focus on the specific needs of children born of conflict-related sexual violence.[48] Moreover, there is very limited compliance and enforcement of the Children's Act, the Local Government Act and other government policies that protect the rights and welfare of children. The Probation and Social Welfare Officers and Community Development Officers, who are responsible for protecting the rights of children, are said to be limited in their ability to support these children due to a lack of financial support and corruption.[49]

As part of this research project, participants were asked what they believed to be critical to their protection and long-term security and well-being. They identified education and training, access to land and livelihood, sensitization and protective laws as the key pathways to protection, prevention and well-being.

5.1 Access to Education and Vocational Training

Education was the top priority of all CBC, whether formal education or vocational schooling. Education was viewed by CBC as the path to a bright future, as finding employment is extremely difficult without completing both primary school and senior school. Among young people who are unable to attend school, they expressed the need for vocational training programmes for hopes of future employment, including tailoring, mechanic and computer training programmes.

5.2 Access to Land and Livelihood

In Acholi culture, land inheritance and access is normally patrilineal in descent. For CBC, given the absence of their fathers, access to land is a significant barrier. CBC identified the need to access land to cultivate, as well as livelihood opportunities to help them and their families generate income for food, health care and school fees. CBC suggested support in the form of start-up capital, such as goats, chickens or oxen for each child born in captivity, in order to help them raise money for school and other requirements through livestock farming.

5.3 Sensitization: Family, School and Community

Participants emphasized that sensitization at all levels – home, school, community and government – would benefit them and fight stigma.[50] According to participants, sensitization should include programmes and workshops with school administration and with

---

[47] Ladisch 2015.
[48] Apio 2007.
[49] Ladisch 2015.
[50] For a different perspective, and a critique of sensitization practices, see Akello in this volume.

students, as well as targeted workshops for their mothers, caregivers, family members (including stepfathers) and for local leaders and community members. Sensitization should centre on (1) the history of CBC and formerly abducted persons and to inform them that it was not their mother's choice to be abducted and forced into marriage, nor their choice to be born in the bush, and (2) the challenges faced by CBC.

5.4 Protective Laws

CBC suggested that the government could institute bylaws to protect them from stigma and violence, as well as teach people in the community the effects of stigmatization. CBC desired to be treated like other children in the community, and to be treated with dignity and respect and live free from threats of and direct forms of violence and abuse. Participants called for the creation of official policies or bylaws against CBC discrimination, affording them some security and the possibility for recourse when their rights are being violated.

6. CONCLUSION

The realities of children born of conflict-related sexual violence and raised within the context of armed groups have garnered minimal attention. While these children may fall within the definition of a 'child soldier' and 'children associated with armed groups', their distinct circumstances, life histories and post-conflict realities call for responses that are unique to their needs and realities. And yet, this group of war-affected children has been largely neglected in global politics and post-conflict peacebuilding.[51] The silence surrounding the issue of children born of conflict-related sexual violence is not only reflected in research, but also policy-making. Scholars have emphasized that children born of conflict-related sexual violence have been largely invisible when it comes to the development of national and international policies to assure their protection and well-being.[52] Instead, policy and protection efforts have centred largely on women as the victims/survivors of sexual violence and not on the children born of sexual violence. This focus has often been regarded as an intentional advocacy strategy, or is implemented with the assumption that the benefits of programmes designed for women will inevitably trickle down to their children.[53] Some humanitarian actors have argued that the invisibility of children born of conflict-related sexual violence is important as it ensures the anonymity of these children who may face stigma – ultimately representing an important protection mechanism. However, other researchers and advocates have noted the potential harm of this silence and denial, arguing that neglecting to pay attention to the specific dimensions of these children's vulnerabilities may result in further marginalization and discriminatory treatment.

The fact that participants often identified the state of war and captivity – when

---

[51] Seto 2015; Carpenter 2010.
[52] Carpenter 2010.
[53] Ladisch 2015.

violence, upheaval, deprivation and ongoing terror were at its height – as *better* than life during peacetime is highly disconcerting and demonstrates the extent of their perceived marginalization. Not only does it point to a failure to integrate children born in LRA captivity in meaningful, cohesive ways in the post-war context, but also demonstrates the urgent need for long-term, targeted support and services for these children that reflect their own expressed needs.

In developing any such programming or policies it is essential that the unique context that children came from and experienced be taken into account. This means that children's views of the bush as 'home', and as a place of meaning and significance in terms of physical setting, activities, interactions and relationships need to be considered and integrated into concerted efforts to respond to their post-war situations. Moreover, the importance and influence of the LRA 'family' on children born in captivity cannot be understated. The unique family structure and set of relationships with their mothers and fathers have had a vital impact on children's sense of identity, community and belonging – all of which continue to have implications for the post-conflict period, and ultimately their sense of isolation and marginalization in the aftermath of the conflict. Ensuring the inclusion of culture and context in policy and programming are indeed consistent with international discussions on child protection, which demonstrate that service providers' approaches need to be more consistent with young people's context and realities.[54] Moreover, given young peoples' essential knowledge and expertise, they should not be considered merely as policy and service 'beneficiaries', but as key players in its development.

There is currently a strong policy and practice focus on the prevention of child recruitment into armed conflict – whether through force or non-force.[55] This focus is both important and understandable given the unacceptable numbers of children recruited into armed groups. However, the focus on child recruitment may unwittingly obscure the realities of children born into and raised within armed groups. And while children born into armed groups technically 'fit' within and correspond to the conceptualization of 'children associated with armed groups', their experiences and perspectives on place, home, family and post-war integration highlight their unique realities and life circumstances. These realities call for a more nuanced understanding of and responses to children born into armed groups and their unique origins, histories, post-war circumstances and needs.

REFERENCED WORKS

Ackroyd, J. and Pilkington, A. 1999. 'Childhood and the Construction of Ethnic Identities in a Global Age' 6 *Childhood* 443

Aijazi, O. and Baines, E. 2017. 'Relationality, Culpability and Consent in Wartime: Men's Experiences of Forced Marriage' 11 *International Journal of Transitional Justice* 463

Akello, G. 2013. 'Experiences of Forced Mothers in Northern Uganda: The Legacy of War' 11 *Intervention* 146

Akesson, B., Basso, A. and Denov, M. 2016. 'The Right to Home: Domicide as a Violation of Child and Family Rights in the Context of Political Violence' 30 *Children and Society* 369

---

[54] Boothby et al. 2006; Wessells 2009: 843.
[55] Barstad 2008: 146.

Apio, E. 2007. 'Uganda's Forgotten Children of War', in C. Carpenter (ed.), *Born of War: Protecting Children of Sexual Violence Survivors in Conflict Zones* (Bloomfield, CT: Kumarian Press)

Barstad, K. 2008. 'Preventing the Recruitment of Child Soldiers: The ICRC Approach' 27 *Refugee Survey Quarterly* 142

Blunt, A. and Dowling, R.M. 2006. *Home* (Routledge: New York)

Boothby, N. 2008. 'Political Violence and Development: An Ecologic Approach to Children in War Zones' 17 *Child and Adolescent Psychiatric Clinics* 497

Boothby, N., Strang, A. and Wessells, M. 2006. *A World Turned Upside Down: Social Ecological Approaches to Children in War Zones* (Bloomfield, CT: Kumarian Press)

Carlson, K. and Mazurana, D. 2008. Report: 'Forced Marriage within the Lord's Resistance Army' (Medford, MA: Feinstein International Center, Tufts University)

Carpenter, R.C. 2010. *Forgetting Children Born of War: Setting the Human Rights Agenda in Bosnia and Beyond* (New York: Columbia University Press)

Casey, E. 1997. *The Fate of Place: A Philosophical History* (Berkeley, CA: University of California Press)

Denov, M. 2015. 'Children Born of Wartime Rape: The Intergenerational Complexities of Sexual Violence and Abuse' 11 *Ethics, Medicine and Public Health* 61

Denov, M. forthcoming. '"Mother, Is this Our Home?" Mothering in the Context of Lord's Resistance Army Captivity: Understanding the Perspectives of Both Mothers and Children', in S. Lachance and T. Cassidy (eds), *Maternal Ambivalence* (Halifax: Demeter Press)

Denov, M. and Akesson, B. 2013. 'Neither Here nor There: Placemaking in the Lives of Separated Children' 9 *International Journal of Migration, Health and Social Care* 56

Denov, M. and Akesson, B. 2016. 'Children and Political Violence: At the Intersection of Rights and Realities' 30 *Children & Society* 337

Denov, M., Fennig, M., Rabiau, M. and Shevell, M. 2019. 'Intergenerational Resilience in Families Impacted by War, Displacement and Migration: "It Runs in the Family"' 22 *Journal of Family Social Work* 17

Denov, M., Green, A., Lakor, A.A. and Arach, J. 2018. 'Mothering in the Aftermath of Forced Marriage and Wartime Rape: The Complexities of Motherhood in Post-War Northern Uganda' 9 *Journal of the Motherhood Initiative* 156

Denov, M. and Lakor, A.A. 2017. 'When War is Better than Peace: The Post-Conflict Realities of Children Born of Wartime Rape in Northern Uganda' 65 *Child Abuse & Neglect* 255

Denov, M. and Lakor, A.A. 2018. 'Post-War Stigma, Violence, and "Kony Children": The Responsibility to Protect Children Born in Lord's Resistance Army Captivity in Northern Uganda' 10 *Global Responsibility to Protect* 217

Erjavec, K. and Volčič, Z. 2010. '"Target", "Cancer" and "Warrior": Exploring Painful Metaphors of Self-Presentation Used by Girls Born of War Rape' 21 *Discourse & Society* 524

Feld, S. and Basso, K.H. 1996. *Senses of Place*, 1st ed. (Santa Fe, NM; School of American Research Press)

Finnström, S. 2008. *Living with Bad Surroundings: War, History, and Everyday Moments in Northern Uganda* (Durham and London: Duke University Press)

Fullilove, M.T. 1996. 'Psychiatric Implications of Displacement: Contributions from the Psychology of Place' 153 *The American Journal of Psychiatry* 1516

Green, A. and Denov, M. 2019. 'Mask-Making and Drawing as Method: An Arts-Based Approach to Data Collection with War-affected Children' 18 *International Journal of Qualitative Research* 1.

Kahn, S. and Denov, M. forthcoming. '"We are Children Like Others": Pathways to Mental Health and Healing for Children Born of Genocidal Rape in Rwanda' *Transcultural Psychiatry*

Kostelny, K. and Wessells, M. 2013. 'Child Friendly Spaces: Promoting Children's Resiliency Amidst War', in C. Fernando and M. Ferrari (eds), *Handbook of Resilience in Children of War* (New York, NY: Springer) 119

Kramer, S. 2012. 'Forced Marriage and the Absence of Gang Rape: Explaining Sexual Violence by the Lord's Resistance Army in Northern Uganda' 23 *The Journal of Politics and Society* 11

Ladisch, V. 2015. 'From Rejection to Redress: Overcoming Legacies of Conflict-Related Sexual Violence in Northern Uganda', International Centre for Transnational Justice [available at: www.ictj.org/sites/default/files/ICTJ-Report-Uganda-Children-2015.pdf]

Mochmann, I.C. and Lee, S. 2010. 'The Human Rights of Children Born of War: Case Analyses of Past and Present Conflicts' 35 *Historische Sozialforschung* 268

Mumford, L. 1961. *The City in History: Its Origins, Its Transformations, and Its Prospects* (New York: Harcourt, Brace & World)

Relph, E. 1976. *Place and Placelessness* (London: Pion)

Relph, E. 1993. 'Modernity and the Reclamation of Place', in D. Seamon (ed.), *Dwelling, Seeing, and Designing: Toward a Phenomenological Ecology* (Albany, NY: SUNY Press) 25

Schomerus, M. and Walmsley, E. 2007. *The Lord's Resistance Army in Sudan: A History and Overview* (Geneva: Small Arms Survey)

Seto, D. 2015. 'Children Born of Wartime Sexual Violence and the Limits of Existence' 3 *Peacebuilding* 171

Shanahan, F. and Veale, A. 2016. 'How Mothers Mediate the Social Integration of their Children Conceived of Forced Marriage within the Lord's Resistance Army' 51 *Child Abuse & Neglect* 72

Veale, A., McKay, S., Worthen, M. and Wessells, M. 2013. 'Participation as Principle and Tool in Social Reintegration: Young Mothers Formerly Associated with Armed Groups in Sierra Leone, Liberia, and Northern Uganda' 22 *Journal of Aggression, Maltreatment & Trauma* 829

Watye Ki Gen. 2014. 'Documentation of Children Born in Captivity' (Gulu, Uganda: Unpublished Report)

Wessells, M. 2009. 'Do No Harm: Toward Contextually Appropriate Psychosocial Support in International Emergencies' 64 *American Psychologist* 842

Woolner, L., Denov, M. and Kahn, S. 2019. '"I Asked Myself If I Would Ever Love My Baby": Mothering Children Born of Genocidal Rape in Rwanda' 25 *Violence Against Women* 703

Worthen, M., Veale, A., McKay, S. and Wessells, M. 2010. '"I Stand Like a Woman": Empowerment and Human Rights in the Context of Community-Based Reintegration of Girl Mothers Formerly Associated with Fighting Forces and Armed Groups' 2 *Journal of Human Rights Practice* 49

12. Social reintegration following armed conflict in northern Uganda: how former child soldier young mothers use symbolic resources
Fiona Shanahan and Angela Veale

The capacity to integrate experience and have a sense of coherence is an important part of psychological well-being.[1] The research literature has documented many of the processes that make achieving a sense of coherence challenging for children formerly associated with armed forces and armed groups. Honwana argues that child soldiers exist in a liminal space between 'child' and 'soldier', wherein they negotiate multiple and conflictual identities.[2] Preston found that even though aspects of former child soldiers' pre-abduction experiences played a role in their life narratives, young people developed a split rebel/civilian identity which was characterized by a strong dissociation between these two identities.[3] When discussing former child soldiers in Sierra Leone, Shepler noted the multiple identities taken on by youth:

> Among their friends and fellow soldiers, they try to maintain the status that being part of the fighting gives them. They wear combat clothes and sunglasses and brag about firing rocket-propelled grenade launchers. With NGOs [non-governmental organizations] they adopt the persona of the traumatized innocent, usually requesting aid in furthering their education. With community members and in school they try to act like normal kids, never mentioning the past. Thus their 'reintegration' is achieved in social practice across a variety of contexts using a variety of strategically adopted identities.[4]

These accounts differ in the degree of intentionality ascribed to the break between civilian and rebel identities. However, the notion of *discontinuity* of experience is central to many accounts of child soldiers, including a distancing of the former child soldier from their narrative of child soldiering,[5] a making and unmaking of a militarized identity,[6] and a need to break entirely with a former military role, identity and related bad feelings and memories in order to maintain well-being.[7]

Yet other evidence suggests there is developmental *continuity* and coherence in identity construction among former child soldiers. Goins, Winter, Sundin, Patient and Aslan explored self-constructions of former child soldiers in Sierra Leone.[8] They used a repertory

---

[1] Antonovsky 1979; Siegel 2012: 14; Wagoner et al. 2015: 1.
[2] Honwana 2006.
[3] Preston 2015.
[4] Shepler 2014: 90.
[5] O'Callaghan et al. 2012: 87.
[6] Denov and Maclure 2007: 243.
[7] Vindevogel et al. 2013: 2421; Wessells 2016: 105.
[8] Goins et al. 2012.

grid method, which elicits and ranks personal constructs or meanings as part of asking participants to rate their sense of self before the war, their self now, their ideal self ('how I should be') and a future self. Former combatants viewed their sense of themselves in the present as closer to their ideal self than was the case with their pre-war self. Furthermore, they anticipated that in the next decade they would move even further towards how they perceived their ideal self. Drawing on Shepler,[9] the authors hypothesized that the developmental transition from childhood to adult roles in Sierra Leone traditionally involved an apprenticeship or fosterage model. Within armed groups, an apprenticeship role under a powerful adult was available to former child combatants yet this was simply not available to many of their displaced peers: therefore it may be that they managed this role transition to an adult self more seamlessly than other conflict-affected youth. The findings of the Mozambique Longitudinal Study which tracked 39 former child soldiers for 16 years also observed developmental continuity as former child soldiers successfully negotiated the developmental transition from childhood to productive adulthood roles.[10] Former child soldiers were found to be faring as well as, and often better than, national averages on indicators of home ownership, socio-economic status, marital relationships and the ability to send their children to school. The author noted 'In the same way an oyster transforms a raw irritant into a valued pearl over time, so too have most of these former child soldiers emerged from violent childhoods to become trusted and productive adult members of their communities and nation.'[11]

Qualitative research which explores the process of becoming a child soldier indicates that entering military life is experienced as an often-traumatic rupture in children's lives.[12] This rupture is followed by a period of adaptation to life within the armed group and, for those that return, a period of transition back to civilian life.[13] How has the research to date sought to explain processes of developmental continuity, discontinuity and change?

1. SYMBOLIC RESOURCES

Research to date has captured the importance of the relational and socioecological context in supporting former child soldiers to transition out of armed forces and groups back to civilian community settings. Family and community acceptance, social support and school access have been identified as key mediators of psychological well-being.[14] Further insight into developmental processes is evident in accounts which examine the experiences of former child soldiers in context. Vindevogel, Broekaert and Derluyn explored the meaning to former child soldiers of resources that they drew on to support their reintegration.[15] Resources were defined as encompassing intra-personal resources (e.g., self-esteem, health, inner peace, own behaviour), relational resources (e.g., close

---

[9] Shepler 2005, cited in Goins et al. 2012.
[10] Boothby 2006: 252.
[11] Ibid.: 256.
[12] Harnisch and Montgomery 2017: 103.
[13] Denov and Maclure 2007: 243.
[14] Betancourt et al. 2010: 606; Vindevogel et al. 2012: 2413; Wessells 2006: 204.
[15] Vindevogel et al. 2013.

attachments) and external resources which could be used as a means to an end (e.g., food, clothing, shelter), as well as political resources such as the amnesty act and community sensitization campaigns.[16] Vindevogel, Broekaert and Derluyn's analysis provided important insight into the processes by which former child soldiers strove to break with their child soldiering past and forge a future to which they aspired.

This chapter aims to complement and extend these important findings to examine how former child soldiers integrate their accumulated experiences as they move from home to a military environment and back to civilian life by focusing upon intra-psychological mediators of thought. We explore an under-researched but important element in reintegration, namely the use of *symbolic resources*.

According to Zittoun, symbolic resources are specific cultural elements used intentionally by people to facilitate developmental change.[17] In order to qualify as a symbolic resource, a person must be using a cultural element (such as an image, song, a prayer) with some intention, in ways that transcend the immediate cultural value or meaning of that cultural element. This requires an imaginary experience, that is, the creation of a sphere of experience beyond the here and now in ways that allow the person to act on their own mind or the minds of others.[18] In this way, a cultural element acts as a semiotic resource mediating experience. An individual may choose to use a specific cultural element as a symbolic resource to manage a particular challenge. The choice of resource relates to the physical or sociocultural context and what is available to that individual in that moment, but the way in which he or she makes use of the cultural element may be unique to them. In this way, some personal agency is exercised in the choice and use of symbolic resource. A symbolic resource can be deployed to regulate emotions, create meaning or manage identity. Memories can also act as symbolic resources as, in this instance, cultural elements can be internalized and memorized and then 'used' at a later time for a particular purpose in a specific situation. In this case, it is not the initial memory-making moment that is of interest but, rather, how memories are re-mobilized in thought and action at the point they are called on as a resource.[19]

Gillespie and Zittoun suggest that the use of symbolic resources can be most useful at times of rupture and transition, when facing an unfamiliar situation or at times of great need. In the rupture–transition process, familiar and habitual modes of action are disrupted, and cultural elements used as symbolic resources can be deployed for multiple purposes such as enabling dreaming, planning or self-talk, and in this way can enable developmental transition and adaptation.[20] This is of interest here as young women within and returning from armed groups find that the resources at their disposal are often highly constrained. An examination of the use of symbolic resources refocuses attention on the formerly abducted young woman as she turns the bits and pieces of material and symbolic means available to her into psychologically relevant symbolic resources which she uses to

---

[16] Hobfoll 2002, cited in Vindevogel et al. 2013.
[17] Zittoun 2007.
[18] Ibid.: 344.
[19] Zittoun 2004: 133.
[20] Gillespie and Zittoun 2010: 50.

mediate her own experience and her action in the world. Of interest also is how the use of symbolic resources may lead young women to develop new skills and understandings.[21]

The research question explored in this chapter is as follows: through an examination of formerly abducted young women's accounts, how did they use symbolic resources at times of developmental transition to integrate their experiences and maintain a sense of coherence as they moved across contexts?

2. METHOD

2.1 Design

This qualitative study was part of a mixed methods research strategy[22] linked to a three-year, multi-country community-based Participatory Action Research project 'Girl Mothers in Armed Groups and their Children in northern Uganda, Sierra Leone and Liberia: Programming and Action Research to Improve their Situations' (referred to as PAR).[23] The three-country PAR project included 658 young mothers, of whom 76 per cent of women were formerly associated with armed forces or groups and 24 per cent were war-affected young mothers in communities. Of the 658 young mothers, 240 participants were from northern Uganda. The 11 participants in the research reported in this chapter were a self-selected subset who had been formerly associated with armed forces or groups and who were participants in the PAR in northern Uganda. Additional ethical and informed consent procedures were developed for this study and approval was granted by the Social Research Ethics Committee of University College Cork. Autobiographical interviews were conducted with the 11 participants as part of a larger participatory study[24] in six Internally Displaced Person's Camps in northern Uganda. The qualitative analytic approach used was Interpretive Phenomenological Analysis which is an idiographic method that aims to provide detailed examinations of personal lived experience.[25]

2.2 Participants

This chapter focuses on data derived from 11 mothers of 15 children who were conceived in the Lord's Resistance Army (LRA). Table 12.1 summarizes participant characteristics (all names are pseudonyms). Some of the participants had additional children conceived in civilian relationships after their return from the LRA. The 11 formerly abducted mothers in this study were part of a larger self-selected sample of 53 young mothers (29 formerly abducted, 24 never abducted) and their data were selected for inclusion in this chapter because they had children who were conceived within the LRA. This is therefore a very specific sample of self-selected young women who had initially been identified as particularly vulnerable and isolated in their communities and had then participated

---

[21] Zittoun 2004.
[22] Shanahan 2012.
[23] McKay et al. 2011.
[24] Shanahan 2012.
[25] Smith and Osborn 2008.

Table 12.1   Participant information

Name	Age at last interview	Associated with LRA	Marital status	Children	Household
Sophie	21	Yes	Single	One son – Obiya, 4 years	Lives with mother and son
Alicia	18	Yes	Single	One son – Joseph, 3 years	Lives with mother and son
Aber	21	Yes	Married	Two sons – Robert, 5, Opit, 3 and 1 daughter Ayaa, 6 months	Lives with husband and children
Juliette	22	Yes	Married	Daughter – Love, died. Daughter Asha, 4 years	Lives with daughter and grandmother
Maya	22	Yes	Separated	Three sons – 6 years, 3 years and 6 months. Jackson, Ocan and Obonyo	Lives with two youngest sons
Sarah	24	Yes	Married	Three daughters – 9 years, 3 years, 6 months. Laruni, Lucy and Polly	Lives with husband and children
Lamara	22	Yes	Single	Two daughters – Aber Poppy, 7 years, Afua Rejoice, 6 years	Lives with her two daughters
Auma	20	Yes	Single	One daughter – Loved One, 3 years	Lives with parents and her child
Sunday	23	Yes	Single	One daughter – Thank You, 5 years	Lives with her mother
Serena	20	Yes	Married	One son – James, 4 years	Lives with husband. Her son lives with her mother
Phionah	23	Yes	Married	One son – Charlie, 3 years	Lives with son and husband

in a three-year Participatory Action Research programme (PAR) that had an explicit empowerment approach. Their accounts should therefore be viewed in light of their distinct experiences, both in relation to their initial vulnerability and to their engagement with a community-based psychosocial intervention that sought to link them to local resources and structures.[26]

---

[26]   McKay et al. 2011.

Social reintegration following armed conflict in northern Uganda 263

> **BOX 12.1 AUTOBIOGRAPHICAL INTERVIEW GUIDE**
>
> Autobiographical Interview – Timelines Outline
>
> I'm interested in your own personal experiences of moving from one place or role to another, for example becoming an adult, becoming a mother, coping with living during a time of war, and I would like you to tell me, in as much detail as you can about how you experienced changes in your life. I would very much like to learn about the dramas, songs and poems you've developed and to hear about your experiences from your point of view.
>
> To facilitate the participant in telling her story, if useful, introduce timelines – use markers to show turning points – times where things changed in my life.
>
> If we put this stick/leaf here to represent that time (if formerly abducted – leaving the LRA/if never abducted – becoming a mother) could you tell me in as much detail as you like what happened next.
>
> Different prompts were used in different interviews in response to the participants' story and a copy of the full schedule is available in Shanahan (2012). Prompts were not used as a list of questions, rather they were developed during fieldwork based on areas of interest that had arisen as interviews progressed – an emergent theme related to the use of cultural elements as semiotic or symbolic resources to mediate emotional well-being, identity and reintegration, and prompts related to this theme included the following: asking about things young mothers may have brought with them in the process of return from the bush; missing friends or other people; drawing on resources. For example: Did you ever think about people away from you? What made you strong? What use did you make of ceremonies or rituals? How did you understand certain events and what did [an event] mean to you? How did (use of a resource) change how you felt? Was [resource] significant? What marked a turning point? What was different after a turning point? What relationships were important? Each interview ended by asking if there was anything important that had not been asked.

2.3 Materials

An autobiographical interview guide was designed to evoke rich personal narrative accounts. A full schedule is available in Shanahan.[27] The questions that relate more specifically to the material reported in this chapter are detailed in Box 12.1.

2.4 Procedure

Sites in Internally Displaced Persons camps in northern Uganda acted as the setting for the research. Interviews were conducted by research assistants who lived locally and had been known to participants as research assistants within the PAR project for over three years. An initial information group discussion was organized in each of the sites for self-selected young women who were part of the PAR and who had expressed an interest in being involved in this study. These discussions were structured around a question and answer format covering the background and purpose of the study, modalities, voluntariness, confidentiality, data protection, disclosure of risks and procedures for managing risk. After volunteering to participate in the study, young women self-selected for the activities that interested them among methods that included storytelling, group

---

[27] Shanahan 2012.

discussions, drama, photo-ethnography and an autobiographical interview. This chapter presents data from autobiographical interviews. The Social Research Ethics Committee of University College Cork and the Uganda National Council for Science and Technology approved this study.

Demographic data collected for the PAR project at its inception identified children born or conceived in the LRA. However, the first author did not identify such children in conversation with their mothers until their mothers had told her of this fact. Young mothers guided the discussion and they were not asked any questions about the circumstances of their child's conception or birth. All interviews were concluded on a positive note, such as a discussion prompted by the request to 'tell me what you love most about your child'. Participants were debriefed and asked how they were feeling after the interview, and psychosocial referral was available for anyone who experienced distress after the interview or at follow-up. None of the participants reported distress or requested psychosocial support.

The transcript of one case was examined in detail before moving on to other cases. The process may be characterized as moving from the specific to the general, starting with particular examples of themes in a participant's transcript, gradually developing more generally applicable categories for the themes in that transcript, moving on to other participants' transcripts to do the same and then deriving overarching themes applicable to the participants as a group. A selection of some of the first level themes developed from Juliette's transcript is presented in Box 12.2.

The next stage of the analysis involves looking for connections and similarities among the first level themes to then produce from among these a list of super-ordinate themes to later develop a final list of master themes. The table of master themes derived from Juliette's case study is presented in Box 12.3.

A set of final themes emerged once all the transcripts were analysed. With respect to the analysis presented here which focuses on the role of symbolic resources in developmental transitions, these final themes were:

1. Formerly abducted young women use symbolic resources to mediate and integrate their sense of self before, during and after their abduction experiences.

BOX 12.2   LISTING OF THEMES (LEVEL 1)

Naming as a resource – meaning of Asha to mobilize inner responses and a public function – transform psychological and social space
Dismissing negative talk
Support from husband in bush and continues to now – continuity of relational resources
Drawing on people in authority as resources for protection
Family context with grandmother
Meaning of grandmother coming for me at reception centre – the relational aspects of this
Taking control of process of return
In control of activities of return process – finding friends, talking to them, singing together, sharing ideas, going for schooling
We-collectively using rituals and ceremony
Drawing on existing resources

> **BOX 12.3   MASTER THEMES FROM JULIETTE'S TRANSCRIPT**
>
> 1. **Transitional moments in the construction of self and identity**
>   Being a soldier
>   Finding meaning in role within LRA
>   Alienation from LRA
>   Continuity of LRA skills/roles in civilian life
>   Discontinuity of LRA skills/roles in civilian life
>   Ex 'rebel' identity as an unwelcome intrusion
> 2. **Suffering**
> 3. **Cultural/symbolic resources for change**
> 4. **Negotiating power in the process of return**

2. Formerly abducted young women use rituals as symbolic resources.
3. Formerly abducted young women use symbolic resources to cultivate resiliency in their children.

3. ANALYSIS

While military and civilian settings have frequently been understood as fundamentally disparate socio-cultural worlds, the analysis focuses on the ways in which formerly abducted young women used symbolic resources to maintain a continuity of identity as they managed transitions in and out of armed groups. These women drew on symbolic resources developed in civilian settings to adapt to conditions of extreme hardship within the LRA. Similarly, upon release from the LRA they continued to draw on these symbolic resources in reintegration and in their post-war lives. This continuity in the use of symbolic resources is central to understanding how former abductees adapted to adversity and cultivated resilience across the changing contexts of pre-abduction, living within armed groups and subsequent return.

3.1 Formerly Abducted Young Women Use Symbolic Resources to Mediate their Sense of Self Before, During and After their Abduction Experiences

Young women's autobiographical accounts delineated turning points when they, as abducted children, were able to utilize symbolic resources from their life before abduction to integrate their sense of self. Young women who were separated as children from their families and friends were able to keep the memories of these relationships and deploy them to transform the meaning of their circumstances within the LRA. Alicia, who was abducted at the age of 10, gave the following example of a turning point in her life during her autobiographical interview to the first author (FS):

> *Alicia:* I stayed there for six years. Because I was young it was my job to take care of the children, the children of a commander, I would look after them like babysitting.

FS: How did you feel towards those children?

Alicia: Sometimes if the commander was away fighting I would think of my own family and I would pretend that the commanders' children were my little brother and sister. I'd pretend that they were my family. Then I would love them and want to take care of them. It wasn't so bad at those times . . .

FS: That's very brave that you were able to do that, that you were able to take care of them and be good to them although things were difficult.

Alicia: Thank you.

FS: It's like even when you are suffering you can make something good out of it . . .

Alicia: I used to think like it's not their fault . . . and also just think all the time about my own family. It was hard to have freedom to think, but within myself I would think of my Mum and my brothers and coming home. If I could think about the time I will come home someday it helps you not to feel it so much . . . that suffering.

In an extraordinary leap of imaginative understanding Alicia used the memory of her family and particularly her love for her younger brother and sister as a symbolic resource to change the meaning of her relationship with the LRA commander's children. As a result, these children benefited from a caring relationship with another person. Alicia engaged in a process of perspective taking, whereby she identified and empathized with the children and felt that they were not at fault. She also engaged in a process of psychological 'distantiation',[28] whereby she disengaged from the immediate situation to think of her own family and a future 'coming home'. Alicia used the resources at her disposal (her memories and feelings towards her own family) as an imaginary or 'as if' experience to bridge a gap between her current and past life which allowed her to continue to relate to her absent family. These resources helped Alicia to manage her rupture from her family and her transition to life in the LRA and effected change not only in her own psychological experience but also changed her feelings towards the children of the commander, which, in turn was likely to have brought about a transformation in the experiences of the children in her care.

Alicia contrasted her ability to use memories of home as a form of present-absence, which served a purpose of keeping alive the possibility of developmental change and of having another life in the future, with the lack of such a resource for children born in captivity within the LRA.

Alicia: Those who they [the commanders] respect more who are the children who have been born into the bush, who have grown there and have been trained there. They [the commanders] like those who have been born into the bush more than those who have been abducted because they feel no need to get free, they don't think of escaping. They know nothing to go to.

Knowing 'nothing to go to' captures a reality that children born in the bush did not have another world to escape to in their imagination. They could not 'step outside' their current reality and have a different future to aspire towards. They lacked such a

---

[28] Gillespie 2012: 34.

symbolic resource that might direct or mobilize change. Children abducted from their communities of origin and those born in the bush, while living side by side, had two different imaginative universes. Unexpectedly, for those abducted from their communities, the imaginative possibility of escape fuelled a motivation to be a brave and strong fighter, as evidenced in the following account by Maya. Maya was already married and had a young baby when she was abducted at the age of 16 and later escaped from the LRA.

> *Maya:* Whenever Kony needs to call the army to come for battle, you will gather because he comes to select the troops. All those who need to escape when they reach Uganda, they are the ones who need to be selected. Because they find that, whenever they reach [Uganda], at least they will have a chance to escape. You will find that if they do not select you, you feel ah . . . you feel pain.
>
> *FS:* What kinds of things could you do to make sure they would select you?
>
> *Maya:* When you are brave, healthy and strong . . . A beautiful lady, a commander could come and say that we should have to go with you. They select only the brave fighters, but as a lady you may also be selected by a commander to help them; 'You are going to cook for me when I'm there'.

As Zittoun and Gillespie note, 'the loop of imagination entails a "stepping out" of the immediate situation which can have consequences for the immediate and future situation'.[29] Paradoxically, imaginings of home meant an abductee might have placed herself in danger in the quest to turn an imagined possibility into actuality.

The use of symbolic resources was a means by which participants maintained a sense of continuity of self to manage the rupture from home and removal to the LRA.[30] In the following extended extract from an interview with Sophie, a formerly abducted young woman, she describes her resistance to assimilation within the LRA during abduction through the use of prayer, which she used to change her own psychological orientation and transform the meaning of her experiences.

> *Sophie:* I never stayed quiet or looked like I was thinking. But inside myself I prayed.
>
> *FS:* What kinds of things did you pray about?
>
> *Sophie:* I prayed to God for my family that I would find them alive one day. I prayed to be forgiven also.
>
> *FS:* Were there ways you had to hide it from them?
>
> *Sophie:* I would show one face to them [LRA] eh? Be quick and let them think that I supported what they were doing. On the inside I would just think 'No.' They would tell you this is the way it is, this is what the people are doing, this is what we must do to them. I pushed that thing away. I knew it wasn't right. They have control over you, maybe your actions, you must do or they will kill you. But you have your own mind and in my own mind I was still my own person. I never

---

[29] Zittoun and Gillespie 2016: 122.
[30] See also Denov in this volume; Akello in this volume.

changed what I believe, my real life, my family, my home . . . it's like they could not have control over that part, eh? . . . They can't take it away, yeah.

FS: Like in what kinds of situations would you be able to pray or think of home?

Sophie: Like I would be doing something like on a march, working in the camp, and it's hard – you really suffer. At that same time I was having that feeling in my heart that I would just not agree with them. Inside I would still just really despise the kinds of things they were doing and just wait for my chance to escape . . . just fight back against that thing and keep your mind free of it. . . . In my own mind I knew what was right. I could just think of my Mum and sister and what life would be like in the future if I managed to make my escape.

FS: It is you know, that you were able to think about somewhere else, imagine the future that you could keep that for yourself.

Sophie: Yeah it's like if you can think about your own life inside, you are not totally belonging to those people, much as you are in captivity you are not truly one of those people – they cannot force you to think the way they need you to think like supporting them in all their things. But you could never let them see how you felt. You do your work, talk, laugh with them, but in your heart you are not one of them. I was never one of them.

In this extract, Sophie elucidated how she continued to maintain an independent intellectual and spiritual life despite severe constraints on her freedom. Through the use of prayer she sought to bring about a change in her psychological and spiritual experience and to resist the control of the LRA. Through prayer, she sought the forgiveness of her God. She utilized prayer as a symbolic resource for resistance, to reject or 'push away' an identification between herself and the LRA on moral grounds, and in this way she retained a sense of continuity of self. This could be regarded as a form of 'tactical agency' in which tactics are 'the art of the weak', a limited but agentive response to an extreme curtailed environment.[31] The concept of agency has been attached to the notion of successful or effective action.[32] This presents a problem particularly in relation to the conceptualization of actions of youth that are unsuccessful at bringing about change in their *external* circumstances – it is then an act of agency to change the symbolic, *internal* experience. Sophie used the sense of self developed in the bush when she returned to civilian life, as she explained in another part of her interview: 'I am the one who survived . . . If you never even suffer, it's like you are not really living in this world, this world is full of suffering.'

For Sophie, like many of the formerly abducted young women in our study, her capacity to withstand and survive extreme suffering was central to her sense of self. Rather than understanding suffering as having interfered with her development, suffering interacted with her development.[33] Sophie described a lived experience of developmental continuity and coherence of self.

Back in civilian life, symbolic resources such as songs and stories were useful to manage difficult times and mediate reintegration. Lamara and Serena explained that an important

---

[31] Honwana 2006: 70–71.
[32] Ibid.; Boyden 2003: 17.
[33] See also Aijazi et al. in this volume.

resource for them in their community was meeting up with other young people who like them also were formerly abducted to tell stories and to sing.

> *FS:* What kinds of things help you get through things that are difficult?
>
> *Lamara:* Me and my friends from the bush. I go to meet with them, boys and girls together, we take time together . . .
>
> *FS:* Yeah?
>
> *Lamara:* Yeah, it helps.
>
> *FS:* Because they were there too?
>
> *Lamara:* Because they know, if you were not there, you can never really know.
>
> *FS:* What kind of things do you do?
>
> *Lamara:* We begin just creating stories. Sometimes we sing. We make up stories about a new life.
>
> *FS:* (To Serena) Do you ever meet with friends from there [life in LRA]?
>
> *Serena:* Yeah. For us we just come together and say 'let us not talk about Olum Olum [Acholi language referring to the bush, the rebels] let us forget about it'.

The experience of shared past experiences served as an important basis for young women coming together to support each other when they found things difficult, and they found making up imaginative stories and songs to be an enjoyable activity. While they came together in this way because of a shared past, they choose to focus not on the past or present but rather on 'stories about a new life'. In Gergen's terms, they engaged in a form of world-making. Gergen asks 'what if we closed our eyes and began to imagine the worlds of our hopes? What if we replaced the persistent rush to establish "what is the case" and began to ask, "what kind of world could we build"?'[34] Gergen argues this shift is needed for a 'future forming orientation' that can result in the creation of new practices.[35]

While Lamara and Serena met with those with whom they shared a similar past to tell stories about the future, formerly abducted young women recognized that they had developed skills through adversity within the LRA that were adaptive back in the civilian environment to which they returned.

> *FS:* Like maybe a schoolgirl who had never went to the bush, what are the things that I can do that she can't do? What do you think about that?
>
> *Alicia:* Like coming to camps we have been able to get involved in generating money.
>
> *Aber:* You can get involved in digging people's gardens and you get paid.
>
> *Sunday:* Or you can go making local brew, anything and you can get money. Like those who have

---

[34] Gergen 2015: 294.
[35] Ibid.: 294.

been in the bush you can do things like using these bits of plastic around broken cups and things, plastics for fuel to cook with it. I can light a match on a plastic cup and I put the saucepan and the flame will go up and the water will boil and I can make tea eh? See that, it is a new technology that is developed.

FS: So when did you work this out?

Sunday: It was from the bush there.

Serena: But nowadays here, in the camp, when there is a broken plastic just lying on the ground there you pick it and make a great fire. So there is change in lives both for abducted and not abducted, much as you have suffered there are good experiences.

These young women participants noted their self-representation as having an ability to generate an income as a particularly adaptive response to life in the camps. Sunday raised an interesting example of the ability to use bits of rubbish to construct a makeshift stove and boil tea, as she had done in the LRA. Thus, using tools to act directly on the world had, for Sunday, also become a sign of her resourcefulness and ingenuity. Serena built on this example saying that they continued to use these skills in the camps. The ability to boil water and make tea in a context of scarce resources had great social significance and was symbolic of self-sufficiency and enterprise for these young women. As Serena went on to note, the knowledge that she can rely on herself to earn a living and provide for her family was particularly important to her:

If supposing my child is sent away from school because of lack of school fees, what am I to do? At least I know that I can use my own hands to earn a living. I will always be able to do that, if I have to go to people's garden to dig, I can go and dig. Because I have developed that kind of life in myself.

The phrase, 'I have developed that kind of life in myself' has a sense of an embedded past, present and future self; it conveys a subjective experience of a past and present self as competent, resourceful and resilient while containing a future orientation that she expects always to be able to use her own hands to earn a living. Suffering is closely related to resilience.

3.2 Formerly Abducted Young Women Use Rituals as Symbolic Resources

Rituals are cultural elements that can become symbolic resources in the process of being used by people to act upon the world, another person or themselves. Schultz and Weisaeth found that a local cleansing ritual in northern Uganda was effective as it facilitated a process of collective forgiveness (through the symbol of a goat).[36] Rituals are not effective as resources in themselves; they become effective through subjective meaning-making processes.[37] They do not have inherent power or meaning, but the person who uses a particular cultural practice as a symbolic resource gives it meaning through its use to change their experience. Sunday, a formerly abducted young woman who returned at the age of 17 when she was pregnant with her daughter, participated in a

---

[36] Schultz and Weisaeth 2015. See also Barrett in this volume.
[37] Shanahan and Veale 2015: 78.

ritual involving a *tumu* or sacrifice, whereby a goat was slaughtered. Participation in that ritual supported her in her reintegration. The imposition of practices that have not been designed or chosen by participants was sometimes experienced ambivalently, however, as explained by Sunday and another formerly abducted young woman, Sarah, both of whom experienced a ceremony of burning clothes and possessions in a reception centre run by a Christian NGO.

> *FS:* In [the reception centre run by an international NGO] when you arrived there had you brought anything with you, had you kept anything from before?
>
> *Sarah:* I never carried anything, I just came without. Even the clothes I came with they were all burnt. They just picked everything and burnt.
>
> *FS:* Yeah I've heard that from other girls, how did you feel about that?
>
> *Sarah:* I took it as not so bad, because they immediately gave me other ones.
>
> *FS:* Yeah, how did you feel about that?
>
> *Sunday:* The staff there at the rehabilitation centre thought we were carrying ghosts in our clothes. [Laughs]
>
> [All laugh]
>
> *Sunday:* They think that 'those people they are using lots of Satanic forces' so they want to burn our things.
>
> *FS:* Really? Do you think that's what they were thinking?
>
> [All laugh]
>
> *Sarah:* They are born again that's why they assume eh? That whatever you come with from the bush 'Ah ah no'
>
> *FS:* And did you have a choice or do they just take it?
>
> *Serena:* You don't have a choice, they just take it and destroy it. They just need everything you have.
>
> *Sunday:* They were afraid of everything that came from the bush, even us.
>
> *FS:* When you say ghosts in the clothes, was it something about memories, they were doing it to stop you from thinking about it [memories]?
>
> *Sarah:* You know in the centre there, they say if those clothes are burned it will help you not to think about what happened there.

The clothes were army uniforms. The act of burning them was not only a practical act but also a symbolic act. In this account, reception centre staff used the act of burning the clothes to engage in a symbolic action to bring about a rupture for the young women with their past experiences. Some of the participants interpreted the act of burning the clothes as expressing fear and rejection of themselves, however, noting: 'They [reception centre staff] were afraid of everything that came from the bush, even us.' Significantly, the clothes did not have a shared meaning for staff and young women. As such, the practice of burning the clothes was ineffective at best as a change strategy for these participants and may have done harm in signifying that they should disown their former selves. Juliette, for example argued that she felt no loss of coherence of self in her identity before and after being in the LRA. She observed: 'I can feel both these things [someone who is experienced in war activities and someone who is a civilian suffering during the war] because when I was there I still had that heart of suffering with civilians in war.' She herself felt no need to make a symbolic act of discontinuity with the past for an identity she had never taken on. Similarly, Aber, when asked to compare herself now with when she was in the bush, said:

> I have the same personality, I am still the same person that I was when I was in the bush. When I was in the LRA I could see guns and even now I still see guns. In the bush we could erect shelters and even now I can still do it. It has made me strong.

In the extract above, it is clear the young women recognized what was not permissible in the broader social imagination.

3.3 Formerly Abducted Young Women Use Symbolic Resources to Cultivate Resiliency in their Children

Becoming a mother to a child born or conceived within the LRA interacted with the developmental trajectories of young women in ways that were profoundly significant to many formerly abducted young mothers' sense of self, meaning and purpose. Auma, a formerly abducted young woman discussed how, even if it was possible, she would not go back in time and change things in her life: 'If I had never been to the bush, I would not even have my child. I couldn't live without my daughter . . . I wouldn't change it, no . . . this is the life I have.'

Young women used cultural elements such as stories, jokes and humour intentionally to provide children with tools to make them smart or keep them safe. One young woman, Lamara, said she liked to tell her children riddles, to pass things on to them to make them smart and to laugh with them. She gave an example of her favourite riddle to tell her children:

> *Lamara:* I am very thin, but people like me, what am I?
>
> *FS:* (giving traditional riddle response): I don't know.
>
> *Lamara:* A bicycle!

This riddle is funny but smart. The purpose of telling riddles is to be a good mother, and the riddles and stories link back to the women's own childhood and experiences with their mother. Lamara gave an example of another riddle that had a message in its meaning:

> *Lamara:* There is a story that one day a rooster said to his friend the millipede that they should go swimming in the river, so the two went to the water point. Then they bathed and the millipede's legs were very clean and shiny but the rooster's legs came dirty no matter how hard he tried. Millipede came out boasting 'My legs are so shiny.' But the rooster's were very dirty still. So the rooster now happened to swallow the millipede.

FS: To swallow him?

Lamara: To eat him [laughs]. So, on reaching home Mother Millipede was asking for the baby but the rooster couldn't answer – for him he said that he had left millipede behind because millipede was walking slowly but yet the thing was inside the stomach. Much pressure on the rooster to tell the whereabouts of the millipede from other birds and animals so at last the rooster had to vomit the millipede so the thing just comes out alive.

FS: And what kind of thing does that tell children, that story?

Lamara: Children can learn that you always should have a very good friend, not a jealous friend. So you shouldn't have a friend like a rooster who can't wash his leg clean and will be jealous. You need a nice friend who will be very good to you and who will not hurt you.

Telling riddles in the immediate post-war context creates an experience of psychological safety, a moment of light heartedness where vigilance is put aside, and a joke can be shared. Telling riddles also functions as a symbolic resource to transmit to the child a lesson about friendship; that not everyone who acts as a friend is really your friend and you must be careful who to trust or you could get hurt. Furthermore, it is not just the telling of a story but the telling of a story in a way that exceeds the cultural context in which it first evolved in the woman's own childhood. Unlike her mother, Lamara had experienced abduction with its own lessons of trust, distrust and hurt, while her mother may have told that riddle to her in a more innocent time. In the context in which Ali told the story to her child, it had the 'accent' of her own experience of the need to be careful who you trust, and therefore was a resource for her child on how to be safe (pick those you trust carefully). Simultaneously it knitted together the past of the mother and future of her child.

4. DISCUSSION

This chapter considers formerly abducted young women as they turned the bits and pieces of material and semiotic means available to them into psychologically relevant symbolic resources which mediated their action in the world and on the minds of themselves and others. This chapter presents examples of the intentional use of symbolic resources by former abductees to mediate their own reintegration, in particular adapting to suffering and adversity by maintaining a sense of continuity of self through the meaning they conferred on their experiences of the past and their imaginings of the future.

This research thereby sheds light on some aspects of the social reintegration of former child soldiers that are not yet sufficiently understood, such as a shift from a perspective on reintegration as located in formal interventions and in family and community relationships to an examination of informal private activity enacted by formerly abducted young women themselves as they sought to act on their own minds and the minds of others (such as their children). In the majority of accounts of reintegration, abduction experiences tend to be categorized as belonging to a separate, distinct world.[38] Nevertheless, in examining young women's accounts of their abduction and return experiences, we locate

---

[38] Ibid.

fluidity and porous boundaries between the LRA and civilian communities that capture development as an ongoing process. Young women drew on cultural resources developed in civilian settings to adapt to conditions of extreme hardship within the LRA. Similarly, upon release from the LRA, formerly abducted young women kept and continued to draw on symbolic resources they had earlier used to adapt to adversity in the LRA, in the process of reintegration and in their post-war lives. This continuity in the use of symbolic resources proves central to understanding how former abductees adapt to adversity and cultivate resilience without denying suffering. A key takeaway point is that formal reintegration programmes that encourage former abductees to break from and disavow the past may, in some cases, risk overlooking significant opportunities to build on how former abductees leverage their own resourcefulness and adaptive coping. Experiences of continuity, stability and integration promote positive mental health while a failure to integrate experiences is associated with disassociation and instability.[39]

The analysis also shows how an exploration of symbolic resources contributes to a greater understanding of agency in highly constrained contexts. If a young formerly abducted person engages in a particular form of action, but is unsuccessful at effecting external change, does her action constitute agency? The literature offers many examples of the agency of child soldiers: feigning illness, planning to escape and deliberately not fulfilling duties properly were all strategies cited in the literature that placed boy soldiers within what Honwana terms the 'dialectic of control'.[40] In Liberia, girls were found to use relationships with high-ranking commanders to secure access to food, aid and other resources, and to avoid sexual violence perpetrated by other men.[41] This is agency exercised on the external environment. Gillespie puts forward a narrow definition of agency as 'the degree to which an agent can act independently of the immediate situation' that is, a form of agency that concerns activity that is not constrained by the 'here and now'.[42] In the analysis presented here, young women used cultural elements as symbolic resources to enable distantiation from their immediate environment, which facilitated cognitive and emotional self-regulation and creative action as it allowed them to 'step out of' and act beyond the immediate context.[43] We saw this in the case of Alicia, who was abducted at the age of 10 and worked as a caregiver to an LRA commander's children in Sudan, and the way in which she used her memories of her own family as a symbolic resource to pretend that the children she cared for were her own brother and sister. This invited an imaginary or 'as if' experience that facilitated feelings of empathy for the commander's children. These feelings allowed Alicia to act to change her own experiences and those of the children in her care. This transformation of her own experience, which occurred in a context where Alicia lacked access to external material or social resources, still directly contributed to her resiliency. Formerly abducted young women's lives in the LRA were often characterized by experiences of adversity and they engaged in symbolic activity to adapt to that adversity. Sophie, for example, prayed and maintained a rich mental life, which allowed her to transcend her daily experiences of adversity and give meaning to

---

[39] Siegel 2012: 14.
[40] Honwana 2006: 70.
[41] Utas 2005: 413.
[42] Gillespie 2012: 32.
[43] Ibid.

her suffering. Through this mediated symbolic activity, she practised a kind of 'inner immigration' and found strength in her resistance to the dominant ideologies of the group.

Hobfoll et al. distilled five essential elements of psychosocial trauma interventions as those that promote: (1) a sense of safety; (2) calming; (3) a sense of self- and community-efficacy; (4) connectedness; and (5) hope. Our data provide insight into how young women mobilized these processes themselves. With respect to hope, one may critique the most common definitions of hope in the psychological literature, such as a 'positive, action orientated expectation that a positive future goal or outcome is possible'[44] as overly action orientated, individualistic and unreflective of the severe constraints with which people live. Yet the ways in which young women expressed hope as detailed in our analysis may be overlooked as the mundane everyday activities involved to support themselves and their children. In meeting with other former abductees to sing and tell stories and in recounting riddles to their children, these women cultivated a sense of coherence and optimism imbued with imaginings of the future. Hobfoll et al. propose Antonovsky's description of this hopeful state as 'a pervasive, enduring, though dynamic feeling of confidence that one's internal and external environments are predictable and that there is a high probability that things will work out as well as can reasonably be expected'.[45] This definition resonates with the Acholi concept of *'piny maber'*, which can be translated as 'good surroundings' or 'good environment' and has been defined by the anthropologist Sverker Finnström as a state of meeting and overcoming challenges.[46]

5. CONCLUSION

An examination of formerly abducted young women's use of symbolic resources illuminates the creativity and imagination with which they adapt to adversity and shows that they are not solely dependent on external interventions. This examination draws attention to developmental processes of continuity and integration that are important to a sense of coherence and well-being and the capacity to 'go on' in the world. The analysis has important implications for formal reintegration programmes. It offers insights into local coping strategies outside those formulated formally and often exogenously. Arguably, formal programmes failed to sufficiently understand the needs of former abductees to integrate their experience as they navigate different contexts. Participants created this developmental experience through their informal relationships such as meeting up with other former abductees to tell stories of the past and simultaneously make up stories of new lives. By seeking to understand local coping strategies and the role they play in important developmental transitions, formal interventions can build on and support local coping strategies rather than marginalizing or disavowing them.

This chapter raises a question about the boundaries of agency in very highly constrained environments. The child research literature has made a very significant contribution to understanding agency and the gendered nature of agency. This chapter has extended this

---

[44] Haase et al. 1992 cited in Hobfoll et al. 2007: 298
[45] Antonovsky 1979: 123, cited in Hobfoll et al. 2007: 298.
[46] Finnström 2008.

literature by exploring agency in the symbolic and imaginative realm, yet it must be kept in mind that the participants in this study managed to escape the confines of their captivity. For those that are unable to escape in the medium or long term, can the symbolic and imaginative world support development and be a motivator of change? Is it possible to hold in mind the 'here and now' and, over the long term, sustain the possibility of a different future? Also, what are the implications for those born into and raised within armed forces and groups? Further research is needed to understand the role of the symbolic resources and the imaginative world in the lives of children who may have never known a life outside armed forces and groups.

REFERENCED WORKS

Antonovsky, A. 1979. *Health, Stress, and Coping* (San Francisco: Jossey-Bass)
Betancourt, T., Brennan, R., Rubin-Smith, J., Fitzmaurice, G. and Gilman, S. 2010. 'Sierra Leone's Former Child Soldiers: A Longitudinal Study of Risk, Protective Factors, and Mental Health' 49 *Journal of the American Academy of Child and Adolescent Psychiatry* 606
Boothby, N. 2006. 'What Happens When Child Soldiers Grow Up? The Mozambique Case Study' 4 *Intervention* 244
Boyden, J. 2003. 'Children Under Fire: Challenging Assumptions About Children's Resilience' 13 *Youth & Environment* 1
Denov, M. and Maclure, R. 2007. 'Turnings and Epiphanies: Militarization, Life Histories, and the Making and Unmaking of Two Child Soldiers in Sierra Leone' 10 *Journal of Youth Studies* 243
Finnström, S. 2008. *Living with Bad Surroundings* (Durham, NC: Duke University Press)
Gergen, K. 2015. 'From Mirroring to World-Making: Research as Future Forming' 45 *Journal for the Theory of Social Behaviour* 287
Gillespie, A. 2012. 'Position Exchange: The Social Development of Agency' 30 *New Ideas in Psychology* 32
Gillespie, A. and Zittoun, Z. 2010. 'Using Resources: Conceptualizing the Mediation and Reflective Use of Tools and Signs' 16 *Culture & Psychology* 37
Goins, S., Winter, D., Sundin, J., Patient, S. and Aslan, E. 2012. 'Self-Construing in Former Child Soldiers' 25 *Journal of Constructivist Psychology* 275
Haase, J.E., Britt, T., Coward, D.D., Leidy, N.K. and Penn P.E. 1992. 'Simultaneous Concept Analysis of Spiritual Perspective, Hope, Acceptance and Self-Transcendence' 24 *Image – The Journal of Nursing Scholarship* 141
Harnisch, H. and Montgomery, E. 2017. 'What Kept Me Going: A Qualitative Study of Avoidant Responses to War-Related Adversity and Perpetration of Violence by Former Forcibly Recruited Children and Youth in the Acholi Region of Northern Uganda' 188 *Social Science & Medicine* 100
Hobfoll, S. 2002. 'Social and Psychological Resources and Adaptation' 6 *Review of General Psychology* 307
Hobfoll, S.E., Watson, P., Bell, C.C., Bryant, R.A., Brymer, M.J., Friedman, M.J., Friedman, M., Gersons, B.P.R., de Jong, J.T.V.M., Layne, C.M., Maguen, S., Neria, Y., Norwood, A.E., Pynoos, R.S, Reissman, D., Ruzek, J.I., Shalev, A.Y., Solomon, Z., Steinberg, A.M. and Ursano, R.J. 2007. 'Five Essential Elements of Immediate and Mid-term Mass Trauma Intervention: Empirical Evidence' 70 *Psychiatry* 283
Honwana, A. 2006. *Child Soldiers in Africa* (Philadelphia: University of Pennsylvania Press)
McKay, S., Veale, A., Worthen, M. and Wessells, M. 2011. 'Building Meaningful Participation in Reintegration Among War-Affected Young Mothers in Liberia, Sierra Leone and Northern Uganda' 9 *Intervention: International Journal of Mental Health and Psychosocial Support in Conflict Affected Areas* 108
O'Callaghan, P., Storey, L. and Rafferty, H. 2012. 'Narrative Analysis of Former Child Soldiers' Traumatic Experiences' 29 *Educational and Child Psychology* 87
Preston, J. 2015. 'If They Abduct You, You Don't Come Back: Understanding Ugandan Former Child Soldiers in the Context of their Life' 21 *Peace and Conflict: Journal of Peace Psychology* 432
Schultz, H.H and Weisaeth, L. 2015. 'The Power of Rituals in Dealing with Traumatic Stress Symptoms: Cleansing Rituals for Former Child Soldiers in Northern Uganda' 18 *Mental Health, Religion & Culture* 822
Shanahan, F. 2012. 'The Use of Cultural Resources in Cultivating Resilience in the Post-Conflict Reintegration Processes of Formerly Abducted Young Women and their Children Born or Conceived within the Lord's Resistance Army in Northern Uganda' (Unpublished doctoral thesis, University College Cork, Ireland)

Shanahan, F. and Veale, A. 2015. 'How Mothers Mediate the Social Integration of their Children Conceived of Forced Marriage within the Lord's Resistance Army' 51 *Child Abuse & Neglect* 72

Shepler, S. 2005. 'Conflicted Childhoods: Fighting Over Child Soldiers in Sierra Leone.' (Unpublished doctoral thesis, University of California at Berkeley)

Shepler, S. 2014. *Childhood Deployed: Remaking Child Soldiers in Sierra Leone* (New York: New York University Press)

Siegel, D. 2012. *The Developing Mind: How Relationships and the Brain Interact to Shape Who We are* (New York: Guilford Press).

Smith, J.A. and Osborn, M. 2008. 'Interpretative Phenomenological Analysis', in J. Smith (ed.) *Qualitative Psychology: A Practical Guide to Research Methods* (London: Sage) 53

Utas, M. 2005. 'Victimcy, Girlfriending, Soldiering: Tactic Agency in a Young Woman's Social Navigation of the Liberian War Zone' 78 *Anthropological Quarterly* 403

Vindevogel, S., Broekaert, E. and Derluyn, I. 2013. 'It Helps Me Transform My Life from the Past to the New: The Meaning of Resources of Former Child Soldiers' 28 *Journal of Interpersonal Violence* 2413

Vindevogel, S., Wessells, M., De Schryver, M., Broekaert, E. and Derluyn, I. 2012. 'Informal and Formal Supports for Former Child Soldiers in Northern Uganda' 2012 *The Scientific World Journal*

Wagoner, B., Chaudhary, N. and Hviid, P. 2015. *Integrating Experiences: Body and Mind Moving between Contexts* (Charlotte, NC: Information Age Publishing, Inc).

Wessells, M. 2006. *Child Soldiers: From Violence to Protection* (Harvard: Harvard University Press).

Wessells, M. 2016. 'Reintegration of Child Soldiers: The Role of Social Identity in the Recruitment and Reintegration of Child Soldiers', in S. McKeown, R. Haji, and N. Ferguson (eds), *Understanding Peace and Conflict through Social Identity Theory* (Peace Psychology Book Series, Switzerland: Springer).

Zittoun, T. 2004. 'Symbolic Competencies for Developmental Transitions: The Case of the Choice of First Names' 10 *Culture and Psychology* 131

Zittoun, T. 2007. 'The Role of Symbolic Resources in Human Lives', in J. Valsiner and A. Rosa (eds), *Cambridge Handbook of Socio-Cultural Psychology* (Cambridge: Cambridge University Press) 343

Zittoun, T. and Gillespie, A. 2016. *Imagination in Human and Cultural Development: Cultural Dynamics of Social Representation* (Hove, UK: Routledge)

PART III

ENCOUNTERS WITH THE LAW

13. The regional African legal framework on children: a template for more robust action on children and armed conflict?
Godfrey Odongo

Children often have borne the brunt of armed conflict. The phenomenon of child soldiers – which involves the recruitment, enlistment and use of children as fighters and in non-combatant roles – and its impact on children, including physical and psychological trauma and general stolen childhoods, is the most publicized effect. While the issue of child soldiers is not a recent phenomenon,[1] the magnitude and scale of the use of children as active combatants escalated in the late twentieth century with hundreds of thousands of children estimated to have been involved as soldiers or participants in hostilities in over 25 countries of the world. Although it is estimated that the total number of child soldiers has dipped in the first decades of the twenty-first century, even the most cautious estimates point towards there being currently '[a]t least 100,000 people under the age of 18 [who] serve in various capacities in armed groups around the world'.[2]

Millions of children are moreover affected by armed conflicts around the world and are often victims of internal or external displacement placing them out of school and with no access to other social amenities as well as separating them from their families, among other abuses.

In post-colonial Africa the use of children as soldiers on a noticeably larger scale appears traceable to a much more recent time in the 1980s during the early stages of an internal armed conflict between rebel fighters and government forces in Mozambique.[3] The use of child soldiers as a 'new technology'[4] of warfare subsequently became a prominent feature in most of an ever-increasing number of armed conflicts in Africa including in Somalia, Angola, Congo, Uganda, Sudan, Central African Republic and South Sudan.

Child soldiering is and has been a global and not just an African phenomenon. At present, the involvement of children as soldiers is a growing feature of conflict situations outside Africa in countries such as the Philippines and Colombia, and children under the age of 18 continue to be recruited into state armed forces in the UK and US.[5] That said, considerable innovative legal and policy work has occurred within Africa. The

---

[1] Vautravers 2008: 98 (stating that 'in Modern European societies, it was formerly commonplace for children to be enrolled in field regiments, although society was then substantially different. By the end of the eighteenth century in certain regions of France, up to a third of children were killed or abandoned, in particular in towns and in times of famine or hardship').
[2] Talbert and Wolfendale 2018.
[3] Gettleman 2007.
[4] Ibid.
[5] See Almarez et al.; Jiménez; and Crilley, all in this volume.

African Union (AU) (formerly known as the Organization of African Unity (OAU)) is the umbrella continental body that brings together 55 African states with the aim of greater integration and regional collaboration on norms and policies in social, political, economic and other matters. In the late 1980s, the OAU sought to develop a specific Pan-African legal instrument to combat child soldiering. The adoption in 1990 by the OAU of the African Charter on the Rights and Welfare of the Child (hereinafter referred to as the 'African Children's Charter' or 'the Charter') is a significant and positive example of a regional effort to use a legal framework to combat child soldiering. As of April 2018, only seven of the AU's 55 African states had not ratified the Charter.[6] Among other issues, the Charter deals with the involvement of children in armed conflict and war's impact on children as one of its priority issues.

Considering the panoply of various other global normative standards on the use of child soldiers and legal regimes on the protection of children's rights during conflict, this chapter analyses the contribution of the Charter. The chapter assesses the still nascent practice of the Charter's monitoring by the African Committee of Experts on the Rights and Welfare of the Child. I argue that the African Children's Charter provides a template for more robust action to ensure the protection of children's rights in the context of armed conflict in Africa and, ideationally, well beyond.

1. AN UNEQUIVOCAL STRAIGHT-18 PROHIBITION ON THE USE OF CHILDREN IN ARMED CONFLICT

One of the higher levels of the protection of children's rights found in the Charter as compared to its United Nations (UN) equivalent, the Convention on the Rights of the Child (the CRC), and other relevant international treaty provisions, is the absolute prohibition of the recruitment and other involvement of children in armed conflict,[7] with Article 2 of the Charter defining a child as 'every human being below the age of 18 years'.[8] Article 22(2) of the Charter provides thus: 'States Parties to the present Charter shall take all necessary measures to ensure that no child shall take a direct part in hostilities and refrain in particular, from recruiting any child.' The legal effect of this provision is that African state parties to the Charter are obliged to ensure that no person under 18 is recruited or allowed to take part in hostilities by any party of fighting groups within their jurisdiction. State parties should also refrain from recruiting anyone under the age of 18 into their armies.

At the broader international law level, measures to regulate the involvement of children

---

[6] See Ratifications of the Charter. The seven states yet to ratify are: the Democratic Republic of Congo, Morocco, the Sahrawi Arab Democratic Republic, Somalia, South Sudan, Sao Tome and Principe and Tunisia.

[7] Viljoen 2001: 22–3 (highlighting 'some of the most dramatic differences' between the Charter and the CRC and noting in this regard that 'each of these aspects resonates with the precarious position in which children find themselves in Africa. Although not restricted to Africa, child soldiers, child marriages and child refugees are recurring problems on the African continent').

[8] The CRC defines a child as every human being below the age of 18 years unless, under the laws applicable to the child, majority is attained earlier.

in armed conflict can be traced to the codification in 1977 of legal norms in the two Additional Protocols to the Geneva Conventions of 1949.[9] The Protocols prohibit the recruitment and use of children of tender years (defined as under 15 years of age) in both international and non-international armed conflict. Subsequent child-rights-specific international legal standards including the CRC and its subsequent Optional Protocol on the Involvement of Children in Armed Conflicts (OPAC) have lower thresholds than the African Children's Charter. The CRC obliges state parties to take measures to ensure that 'persons who have not attained the age of 15 years do not take a direct part in hostilities and to refrain from recruiting persons who have not attained the age of 15 years into their armed forces'.[10] OPAC obliges state parties to undertake to raise the minimum age of recruitment and participation into national armed forces from the CRC level of 15 to at least 16 years of age.[11] The Protocol however leaves a window for the 'voluntary recruitment' in contrast to 'compulsory recruitment' of children between the ages of 16 and 18.[12] Child rights advocates have criticized the lower-than-18 standard for children that may be recruited into national armed forces in the Optional Protocol (a lingering product of non-consensus between states regarding a 'Straight-18' ban) as the Protocol's 'ultimate failure'.[13]

The ban on the recruitment and involvement of persons under the age of 15 in national armed forces has evolved into customary international law. Thus, this ban on the recruitment and use of children under the age of 15 in hostilities is binding on all states as well as non-state actors (irrespective of agreement or acquiescence to treaties). The ban has subsequently been adopted in the Statute of the Special Court for Sierra Leone (SCSL) and the Rome Statute establishing a permanent International Criminal Court (ICC) which makes the conscription, enlistment or use of children under 15 in hostilities a war crime.[14] Indeed the very first conviction in March 2012 at the ICC relates to the use of children as soldiers by one of the militias headed by the accused Thomas Lubanga (convicted in the case) in the ongoing armed conflict between armed militia and government and allied forces in the eastern part of the Democratic Republic of Congo (DRC).[15]

The uniqueness of the African Children's Charter's Straight-18 prohibition is thus clear: it is a higher threshold than that found in the CRC or customary law. UNICEF, the leading UN agency on the protection of children's rights has consistently joined other organizations, child rights advocates and NGOs in advocating for a 'Straight-18 ban' on all recruitment, compulsory or voluntary, and participation of children under that age in hostilities. The comparatively lower age threshold in the CRC, and subsequently adopted in the ICC's Statute, represents a compromise between states. During the drafting process of the CRC, Article 38 provisions relating to the issue of children and armed

---

[9] Abitria (undated): 2–3.
[10] CRC, arts 38 (2)–(3).
[11] OPAC, arts 2–4.
[12] OPAC, art. 3.
[13] Jesseman 2001: 148.
[14] Rome Statute, arts 8(2)(b)(xxvi) and 8(2)(c)(vii) (considering as a war crime in international or non-international armed conflict 'conscripting or enlisting children under the age of fifteen years . . . or using them to participate actively in hostilities').
[15] Lubanga 2012: [1358].

conflict were identified as some of the most disputed.[16] The lack of unanimity originated from the practical reality that saw, and still sees, states legislating for lower ages for the recruitment and deployment of children into armed conflict. The reality of a lower age threshold under the CRC and international humanitarian law regimes remains an area of continuing global concern.

2. THE SIGNIFICANCE OF THE AFRICAN HIGHER AGE THRESHOLD OR PROHIBITION

It may be taken for granted that African states that negotiated and adopted the African Children's Charter were a less diverse and varied group sharing a common socio-economic and political context compared to a more diverse global structure inherent in the adoption process of a UN treaty, the Rome Statute or the Additional Protocols to the CRC. Hence there may have been fewer grounds for both legal and practical variances in contrast to a more global process underpinning the CRC. This is especially relevant bearing in mind the reality of the limited active participation of African states during the process of drafting the CRC, very few African countries being actively involved throughout the Convention's drafting process.

However, such a view would be far too simplistic not least because current state practice reveals that, at the domestic level, many African states have still not legislated for a Straight-18 ban on the recruitment of children into armies. Additionally, there have been arguments for the involvement of children in armed conflict drawing in part from the legitimacy of some African cultural beliefs that put children in the context of social institutions which would view them as having key societal roles including social cohesion.[17] Other contemporary factors also drove the use of children in armed conflict at the time of the Charter's adoption. There is anecdotal evidence that suggests the possibility that children have at times identified with a cause rooted in some African armed struggles. Yet against this background the message under the African Children's Charter is unequivocal that it is 'not in the best interests of the child to fight'[18] – a position enunciated by the African Committee of Experts on the Rights and Welfare of the Child, charged with monitoring state compliance with the Charter, in its adjudication of a case concerning Uganda, discussed later in this chapter. The African Committee has broadly interpreted the obligation of states with regard to the prohibition of children's 'direct' participation in hostilities as follows:

---

[16] Jesseman 2001: 141. ('The question of the nature of the special protection afforded to children in armed conflict has been described as the most controversial issue debated during the course of the CRC negotiations.')

[17] Bennett 1998: 10 (stating that this argument would be especially relevant in the context of acephalous societies; Bennett defines 'acephalous' polities as decentralized structured African societies, 'with no particular person or group wield[ing] absolute power, and without the organizing potential of a political superstructure' in contrast to centralized or 'state' or hierarchically structured ones and positing that such a society must 'depend for its cohesion on bonds of kinship . . . with families more or less autonomous').

[18] Lloyd 2002: 20.

Emerging international jurisprudence and practice points [to the conclusion] that 'direct part in hostilities' should cover both direct participation in combat and also active participation in military activities linked to combat such as scouting, spying, sabotage and the use of children as decoys, couriers or at military checkpoints. The implication of this is that a wider definition is being offered for the notion 'child soldier' than one who has a combatant status only.[19]

Speaking to potential cultural or contextual arguments about African children's possible commitment to an armed struggle or societal cause, the Committee, while adjudicating the aforementioned case against Uganda, is of the following view:

> 57. ... As a matter of principle, the African Committee supports children's participation in matters that affect them, and their views being given due consideration. The African Committee also recognizes children's evolving capacities. However, as far as consent to join the armed forces, or armed groups is concerned, the African Committee and the Charter take a more protectionist approach than one that promotes children's participation. The African Committee is of the view that children cannot give 'informed' consent to actively participate in activities related to armed conflict. This is due to the fact that they generally lack a nuanced and comprehensive understanding of the long-term and short-term impact of their involvement, as well as because their participation rights need not compromise their protection rights.
> 58. As a result, the African Committee supports the view that 'the line between voluntary and forced recruitment was both legally irrelevant and practically superficial in the context of children in armed conflict'. ...
> 59. Under Article 31 of the African Children's Charter captioned 'Responsibility of the Child', it is provided that every child shall have the duty, among others, 'to preserve and strengthen the independence and the integrity of his country'. However, the application of this Article is subject to the child's 'age and ability, and such limitations as may be contained in the present Charter'. As a result, in the presence of Article 22 of the Charter that absolutely prohibits the recruitment and use of children in armed conflicts, there is no legally and textually sound argument that can be made to support the involvement of children in armed conflict ... .[20]

Beyond the Charter's absolute prohibition of child soldiers as a phenomenon, the resilience of the practice of child soldiers provides ample evidence that the legal prohibition of recruitment cannot be looked at as a magic wand to the solution of an issue that is rooted in deeper social, political and economic contexts. For example, according to Human Rights Watch's monitoring of the practice subsequent to the International Criminal Court's 2012 conviction of Lubanga for child soldiering as a war crime, the recruitment and use of child soldiers by some rebel groups continued unabated, in spite of the goal of deterrence inherent in such prosecutions.[21] This highlights the need to address the broader socio-economic and political factors that motivate the use or involvement of children as soldiers.

Moreover, the enforcement of the legal prohibition requires the implementation of further measures by states – including the establishment of functional birth registration systems to ascertain children's ages; monitoring and oversight of military recruitment; and the domestic criminalization and enforcement of the act of recruitment of children into conflict. Indeed, even the lower age thresholds under the CRC and OPAC are yet to be fully enforced in domestic contexts, in part because of gaps in these regards. For

---

[19] Hunsungule Communication 2013.
[20] Ibid.: [57–9].
[21] Human Rights Watch 2012.

example, the UN Committee on the Rights of the Child in its monitoring of Uganda's compliance with the UN treaty framework noted that Uganda has made a declaration under OPAC accepting the Straight-18 prohibition rule. The Committee acknowledged Uganda's efforts to eliminate the recruitment of those under 18 years of age but was concerned about the continued presence of children in the armed forces. It noted that the country faces 'challenges presented by the very low rates of birth registration, less than 10 per cent', which made it difficult to determine children's age.[22]

3. THE BROAD GAMUT OF THE AFRICAN CHARTER'S LEGAL PROVISIONS ON CHILDREN AND ARMED CONFLICT

Research exists that asserts that the discourse regarding children's involvement in armed conflict is predicated on an over-emphasis on the prohibition of recruitment. Ah-Jung asserts that the global discourse on children affected by armed conflict is predicated on five theoretical philosophies: (1) the quest for a 'Straight-18' prohibition of child soldiers, with an underlying related pursuit of a universal definition of children as persons under the age of 18; (2) condemnation of all forms of children's involvement in military activities in any form or fashion, without a distinction between children's various or differing roles; (3) the underpinnings and assumptions of a homogeneous and unquestionable 'vulnerability' of all children involved in armed conflict (that children involved in armed conflict are homogeneous in lacking social and political agency); (4) a vision of a 'normal childhood' in which military recruitment is outside the domain of children; and (5) that the phenomenon of child soldiering is something new.[23] Hence, there is criticism that the lack of nuance in academic and related discourses ignores the potential for children's social and political agency in participating in conflicts (rooted in children's rights to participation and not merely predicated on the assumption that all such children are vulnerable and in need of protection).

It is true that a more complex and nuanced analysis is warranted. However, the criticism that the overall approach of the normative discourse is overly 'proscription-' or 'condemnation-based' (based on the condemnation of the child soldier phenomenon) may be an exaggeration when viewed in light of the full gamut of treaty provisions including those contained in the African Children's Charter. Beyond the Straight-18 prohibition of the involvement of children in armed conflict, the Charter further makes provisions that are relevant to all children affected by armed conflicts.

Article 22(1) of the African Children's Charter provides that: 'States Parties to this Charter shall undertake to respect and ensure respect for rules of international humanitarian law applicable in armed conflicts which affect the child.' Article 22(3) further provides:

> States Parties to the present Charter shall, in accordance with their obligations under international humanitarian law, protect the civilian population in armed conflicts and shall take all feasible measures to ensure the protection and care of children who are affected by armed

---

[22] UN Committee on the Rights of the Child 2008: [16].
[23] Lee 2009: 7–12.

conflicts. Such rules shall also apply to children in situations of internal armed conflicts, tension and strife.

By virtue of these provisions, the Charter reiterates existing norms under international humanitarian law. Under this legal regime, in the event of armed conflict, children benefit from the general protection provided for civilians not taking part in the hostilities.[24] Civilians are guaranteed humane treatment and covered by the legal provisions on the conduct of hostilities.[25] Further, because of children's vulnerability they benefit from special protection by virtue of the Fourth Geneva Convention of 1949 which states that children are entitled to 'special care', with such care further defined in the context of international armed conflict under the Additional Protocol I obliging state and non-state actors to the effect that: 'Children shall be the object of special respect and shall be protected against any form of indecent assault. The Parties to the conflict shall provide them with the care and aid they require, whether because of their age or for any other reason.'[26]

This principle also applies in non-international armed conflicts.[27] The nature of the special protection that children are entitled to is further detailed through the Fourth Geneva Convention and the two Additional Protocols. These include provisions on evacuation; assistance and care; identification, family reunification of unaccompanied children; education, and standards on the treatment of arrested, detained or interned children; exemption from the death penalty; and, as already discussed, protection against recruitment and participation in hostilities.[28]

The African Children's Charter has been criticized for its silence regarding measures for the disarmament, demobilization and reintegration of children involved in armed conflict which find expression under Article 39 of the CRC.[29] CRC Article 39 provides:

> States Parties shall take all appropriate measures to promote physical and psychological recovery and social reintegration of a child victim of: any form of neglect, exploitation, or abuse; torture or any other form of cruel, inhuman or degrading treatment or punishment; or armed conflicts. Such recovery and reintegration shall take place in an environment which fosters the health, self-respect and dignity of the child.

However, this critique is unfair. As discussed in the next section of this chapter, the implementation practice of the Charter's monitoring body – the African Committee of Experts – has read the Charter's provisions progressively, considering relevant international treaties, including the CRC, which state parties are equally bound by.

Articles 23 and 25 of the Charter are also integral to state parties' obligations with respect to the protection of the rights of children affected by armed conflict. Article 23 reiterates the right of refugee children to protection, including processes towards the tracing of the child's parents or other close relatives and their reunification with families.[30]

---

[24] ICRC 2011: 375.
[25] Ibid.
[26] Additional Protocol I, art. 77.
[27] ICRC 2011: 375 citing art. 4(3) of Additional Protocol II.
[28] Ibid.: 376.
[29] Jesseman 2001: 146–7; Olowu 2002: 127.
[30] For a discussion of children's rights and realities in the asylum and refugee context, see

It is significant that under Article 23(4) the Charter extends these provisions to internally displaced children who are displaced through 'natural disaster, internal armed conflicts, civil strife, breakdown of economic and social order or howsoever caused'.[31] Article 25 further amplifies that any child who is permanently or temporarily deprived of his/her family environment is entitled to 'special protection and assistance', including 'necessary steps to trace and re-unite children with parents or relatives . . .'.[32]

Beyond the provisions of Articles 22, 23 and 25, interpretations of the Charter effected by the Committee of Experts, such as in the case concerning Uganda, have considered that all the Charter's obligations (including with regard to children's rights to education, health and protection from abuse and violence) apply equally during situations of conflict or strife. Put another way, the state obligations to guarantee children's rights are neither suspended nor eliminated by the fact of conflict, even though the realization by children of or the capacity of governments to guarantee these rights would no doubt be affected or inhibited by the facts of insecurity, fatalities, destruction of homes, schools, hospitals and other effects of conflict.

As with the Charter's provisions prohibiting recruitment, the practice is such that children continue to be killed, maimed, sexually abused, or deprived of humanitarian assistance in the context of most (mainly internal) armed conflicts on the continent. This reality means that ongoing monitoring of the Charter's provisions remains vital. The next section of this chapter discusses the mandate and emerging practice of the Charter's monitoring body – the African Committee of Experts on the Rights and Welfare of the Child – 11 experts nominated and appointed by African Union member states, albeit that they serve in their independent professional capacity.

4. THE AFRICAN COMMITTEE'S MANDATE, PRACTICE AND JURISPRUDENCE ON CHILDREN AND ARMED CONFLICT

The Committee has a mandate to examine state reports akin to that of its UN counterpart (the UN Committee on the Rights of the Child). Article 43 obliges every state party to submit reports for examination to the Committee, initially within two years of the Charter's entry into force and thereafter 'every three years'. The Committee is also tasked with the adjudication of complaints of children's rights violations[33] and must conduct investigations and give views and make recommendations pursuant to these investigations.[34] The Charter's provisions empower the Committee to: collect and document information and commission 'inter-disciplinary assessment[s] of situations of African problems in the field of the rights and welfare of the child'; 'formulate and lay down principles'; 'interpret

---

Rikhof in this volume.

[31] African Children's Charter 1990, art. 23(4).
[32] Ibid., art. 25(2)(b).
[33] Ibid., art. 44, which empowers the Committee to receive communications from any person, group or non-governmental organization recognized by the African Union, by a member state or the United Nations.
[34] Ibid., art. 45, which gives the Committee powers to 'resort to any appropriate method of investigating any matter falling with the ambit of the Charter'.

the provisions of the Charter'; and 'perform such other tasks as may be entrusted to it' by the African Union or the United Nations.[35] Further the Committee has the power to cooperate with other African, international and regional institutions with a mandate to undertake further observance of children's rights.[36]

For Africa, the normative protection for children from the impact of armed conflict could be more robustly enforced at the regional level than through international mechanisms at the UN level. This argument draws mainly from the wide and broad institutional mandate that the African Children's Charter confers upon the Committee as its enforcement mechanism. A first indication is that the adjudicative or complaints determination jurisdiction is automatic upon ratification of the Charter. This differs from the CRC which requires additional ratification of an Optional Protocol on the complaints mechanism. Second, a broad range of persons or organizations can submit such complaints for determination including any person, group or NGO recognized by the AU and the UN. Third, the Committee's mandate to cooperate with organizations with similar mandates to protect children's rights is significant because it is through such cooperation that the Committee's work may be informed by and build on existing UN-level processes related to the protection of the rights of children involved in or affected by armed conflict.

5. PROVIDING DETAIL REGARDING STATE OBLIGATIONS THROUGH THE ADJUDICATION OF COMPLAINTS: THE UGANDA EXAMPLE

Thus far, the Committee has adjudicated and issued decisions on three complaints regarding cases of children's rights violations. These complaints concern Kenya, Uganda and Senegal. There are also several pending cases. In April 2013, the Committee issued its decision after adjudicating a complaint centred on the impact of a long-standing conflict between the government and armed rebels in northern Uganda (the Uganda case).[37]

The background to the complaint was the 20-year (1986–2006) conflict between Ugandan government forces and the rebel Lord's Resistance Army (LRA), led by Joseph Kony, and now largely depleted. This conflict was tragically characterized by extensive kidnapping and recruitment of children.[38]

The complainants alleged that a number of the rights of children in northern Uganda that are guaranteed in the African Children's Charter were violated as a result of the actions or omissions of the Ugandan government.[39] These rights include protection of children from being involved in armed conflict (Article 22); the right to education (Article

---

[35] Ibid., art. 42.
[36] Ibid., art. 42(a)(iii), which provides that one of the functions of the Committee shall be 'to cooperate with other African, international and regional institutions and organizations concerned with the promotion and protection of the rights and welfare of the child'.
[37] Hunsungule Communication 2013.
[38] For background on the Ugandan conflict and details of child abduction, see Aijazi et al.; Akello; Barrett; and Denov, all in this volume.
[39] Hunsungule Communication 2013: [11].

11); the right to life, survival and development (Article 5); the right to enjoy the best attainable state of physical, mental and spiritual health (Article 14); and the right to be protected from sexual abuse and violence (Articles 16 and 2).

In relation to violations of children's rights to education and health, the Committee took cognizance of the number of legislative, administrative and other appropriate measures taken by Uganda that it considered 'reasonable' in the fulfilment of the Charter's standards that required states to exercise 'due diligence' to meet their obligations.[40] It also held that neither had it found evidence nor had the complainants provided evidence to substantiate the allegations regarding government soldiers' alleged complicity in the commission of sexual abuse and violence and the abduction of children, or government failure to undertake its obligations to investigate, prosecute and punish perpetrators of these abuses.[41]

However, the Committee did find a violation of Article 22 (and, as a fundamental duty, Article 1(1)) of the Charter relating to the obligation to ensure that there is no recruitment and involvement of children in armed conflict. Article 1(1) of the Charter provides for the general obligation of state parties to undertake steps to adopt legislative and other measures. The Committee made substantive recommendations to the government to ensure: the criminalization of the recruitment or use of children in situations of conflict; the full implementation of procedures for the reception and handover of children separated from armed groups or forces, including DDR programmes, in collaboration with the AU, the UN and other partners in a 'child-centred manner'; and effective nationwide birth registration procedures. The Committee further recommended that Uganda puts in place administrative procedures and practices for all armed and auxiliary forces not to recruit any persons where there is no credible proof of age or there is conflicting or inconclusive evidence of age until there is determinative proof of age; and ensures that the accountability for children accused of violations or crimes in the context of conflict takes the best interests of children and the goal of reintegrating such children into consideration, including the appropriate role for restorative measures, truth-telling, traditional healing ceremonies and reintegration programmes.

The detailed and exhaustive nature of the Committee's consideration of this case demonstrates that the Committee's adjudicative mandate offers it the most discretion in providing, in sufficient detail, an authoritative interpretation of the Charter's obligations.

The decisions of the Committee are of a legally binding nature on state parties. However, as per general treaty law, the Committee's findings and recommendations, while legally binding, are to be implemented in good faith by governments of the state in question. The Uganda case is unique because, for varied reasons, it took eight years (2005–2013) from the filing of the complaint to the issuance of the final decision. During this time lag, Uganda had made progress with regard to legal amendments and policies such as military standard operating procedures to prohibit the recruitment of all children under the age of 18 into the armed forces. Since the Committee's decision, Uganda has made further progress in implementing other aspects of the Committee's decision that urged it to ensure that there is no recruitment of persons under 18 into armed or

---

[40] Ibid. [69–71] (about education) and [74–5] (health).
[41] Ibid. [78–80].

auxiliary forces (such as private security groups). Gradual progress has arisen in the level and extent of birth registration that would improve certainty regarding the age of children in Uganda. Official processes for the reintegration of former child soldiers, which have involved the assistance of international, UN and non-governmental agencies, have also continued. On the other hand, there appears to be limited progress on other fronts. This includes the overall question of how to hold children and other persons accountable for conduct that may have been criminal during their involvement in conflict. The Committee had recommended that Uganda should rely on forms of accountability other than detention and criminal prosecution and promote the reintegration of such children into their families, community and society, including the use of restorative measures, truth-telling, traditional healing ceremonies[42] and reintegration programmes. There is an ongoing process in Uganda to develop an overall transitional justice policy that would comprehensively include these issues.[43]

Besides, even though there is legal compliance with the prohibition of child recruitment, the extent to which Uganda is now fully compliant in practice with the Committee's decision remains unclear. This is partly because the Committee has not published its consideration (if any) of its follow-up on implementation of the decision. Also, experiences across Africa show that legal compliance does not translate into practical compliance. Globally, by dint of law, about fifty states (most of them in the Global North or outside Africa), allow under-18s to join the armed forces.[44] In practice, even though few African countries are on that list, some African states were still included in the UN Secretary General's annual list of countries where there was evidence that armed forces or groups still recruited children in 2017. These were: the Central African Republic, the Democratic Republic of Congo, Mali, Nigeria, Somalia, South Sudan and Sudan.[45] Yet the Central African Republic's 1994 Constitution, for example, stipulates the age of 18 as the minimum age to join the armed forces, and there is subsidiary legislation in abundance, across the continent, that sets a minimum age for military service at 18.[46]

In Uganda's case and equally in most of its recent decisions, the Committee recommends, in line with its rules of procedure, that the government of the state against which the Committee has issued a decision should report back to it within six months regarding progress that has been made in terms of implementation. Article 45(2) of the African Children's Charter empowers the Committee to provide reports to the collective AU Heads of State and Government organ on its activities, including adjudication, and thereafter publish its deliberations and decisions.[47] This organ is the highest-level political organ in the AU. Article 45(2) thereby opens the way for the Committee to develop a framework for the enforcement of its decision. Given the African Committee's relatively young record with adjudication of communications or cases, the Committee's practice in this regard is still developing.

---

[42] See Barrett in this volume on the use of traditional healing ceremonies in northern Uganda.
[43] For a critique of Uganda's transitional justice approach, see Akello in this volume.
[44] Child Soldiers International (undated).
[45] Ibid.
[46] Mezmur 2017: 139 (citing the examples of laws in Madagascar, Zimbabwe, Malawi, Algeria and Angola, among others).
[47] Hunsungule Communication 2013: [81]; Salem Communication 2017: [98].

6. AMPLIFYING THE NEED FOR ACTION THROUGH FACT-FINDING MISSIONS AND RESEARCH: SOUTH SUDAN, CENTRAL AFRICAN REPUBLIC AND BEYOND

The Committee has shown a willingness to carry out fact-finding missions to countries that are undergoing armed conflict, often in real time, with a view to highlighting the plight of children. This mandate is drawn from Article 45 of the Charter. It is also in keeping with the broad remit of the Committee's powers in other provisions of the Charter, such as Article 42 which, as will be recalled, provides for information-gathering and interdisciplinary assessments. The combined effect of these provisions is that the Committee can highlight for the attention of the government(s) of the states in which the armed conflict is ongoing (as well as the AU and the international community) the need for urgent or immediate remedial attention to ongoing violations of the human rights of children entangled in armed conflict.

It is noteworthy that while the Committee's investigative mandate is general to all matters related to children's rights, most of its fact-finding missions have involved situations of armed conflict. As far back as 2004 and 2005 the Committee undertook such missions to assess the situation of children's rights during armed conflicts in Darfur, Sudan and northern Uganda. These missions noted widespread violations of children's rights. However, owing to the very nascent stages of the Committee's work there was no follow-up of the results of these missions. This silence also arose in part because the Committee had not promulgated the relevant guidelines to guide its practice with these missions including report-back and follow-up action.[48]

In 2014, the Committee decided to use its investigative mandate to conduct missions in South Sudan and the Central African Republic, two countries roiled by ongoing fighting between government forces and rebel groups. The Committee explained the basis for the proposed missions in the following terms:

> The Committee is deeply concerned about the scale of the humanitarian challenges in the Central African Republic (CAR) and South Sudan, which have implications for the protection and well-being of children. While other departments of the African Union have conducted missions to the CAR and South Sudan, they have not focused specifically on the plight of children affected by armed conflict. Articles 22, 23, and 25 of the [Charter] explicitly recognises the need to respect international law as it applies to the effect of armed conflict on children, particularly those who are displaced and separated from their parents. Children in CAR and South Sudan are among the most vulnerable to a broad range of serious violations, including being involved with armed groups. It is therefore crucial that a detailed assessment of the situation of children occurs, both to bring the Committee in harmony with the positions of the [AU] Peace and Security Council, and to ensure that solutions to strengthen both States address the needs of children according to the Rights established under the Charter, OAU Convention Governing the Specific Aspects of Refugee Problems in Africa, the Convention for the Protection and Assistance of Internally Displaced Persons in Africa, and other relevant instruments of the African Union . . .[49]

It is significant that, based on a reading of the wide and open-ended nature of the Committee's mandate and the lived reality of children in the context of ongoing wars

---

[48] The Committee has since adopted such detailed guidelines to govern its conduct and follow-up action on investigative missions, see African Union (undated).

[49] African Committee of Experts on the Rights and Welfare of the Child 2014a.

in Africa, the Committee decided to undertake these fact-finding missions despite both South Sudan and CAR not being parties to the African Children's Charter in 2014 (CAR subsequently ratified the Charter in 2016). In justifying its mandate to conduct these missions, specifically in the case of states that have not ratified the Charter, the Committee cites its powers deriving from Article 42(a)(i) of the Charter to collect information and conduct 'inter-disciplinary assessment[s] of situations on African problems in the fields of the rights and welfare of the child . . .'.[50]

The Committee concluded its fact-finding trip to South Sudan in August 2014. The conflict pits the South Sudan government's armed forces against opposition rebel forces and has led to the killings of thousands of people and the displacement of over one and half a million people in the period since December 2013. The Committee found several violations of children's rights.[51] It published its report following the mission. The report documents the deliberate targeting of children for killing by both parties to the conflict;[52] killings of parents and care-givers that has left uncounted numbers of children parentless, orphaned and having to take to the streets;[53] the massive displacement of people, including children from their homes, leading to immense challenges including huge numbers of unaccompanied children who have no access to education;[54] abductions and sexual violence;[55] increased malnutrition leading to up to 50,000 infants and young children facing death;[56] lack of access to education, with over 1,000 schools closed down in areas affected by conflict;[57] worsening health and sanitation indicators;[58] and the blockade of emergency humanitarian aid, especially to areas under control of the rebel forces.[59]

The Committee focused on the involvement of children in hostilities, noting 'unverified reports of an upsurge in the recruitment of children by armed groups' and observed 'the existence of visible involvement of children in the conflict' including 'girls in military uniform'.[60] It reminded South Sudanese authorities of the commitment that they had made to the Committee and to the UN Special Representative of the Secretary-General (SRSG) for Children and Armed Conflict in June 2014 to desist from mobilizing child soldiers and to demobilize those children already affected.[61]

Noting that children constitute up to 60 per cent of the inhabitants of South Sudan, the Committee recommended that the South Sudanese authorities take measures to put in place child protection mechanisms envisaged under its domestic legislation (the Child

---

[50] Ibid.: 2–3.
[51] South Sudan Report 2014.
[52] Ibid.: [8] (noting that 'the exact number of children killed was not yet known but reports estimate that 490 killed children were identified in the many mass graves . . . These deaths are not accidental or unfortunate by-products as the Delegation was reliably informed that children are being targeted deliberately').
[53] Ibid.: [9].
[54] Ibid.: [10–12].
[55] Ibid.: [22–5].
[56] Ibid.: [26–7].
[57] Ibid.: [28].
[58] Ibid.: [29–32].
[59] Ibid.: [33].
[60] Ibid.: [13–21].
[61] Ibid.: [16].

Rights Act 2008) and further specific measures including: the reintegration of thousands of children separated from their families; the disarmament, demobilization and reintegration of child soldiers; and support for communities affected by violence to create resilience in families to be able to support their children. The Committee called on South Sudan to act on its already-stated intention, expressed to the Committee, to ratify the African Children's Charter. Based on these findings, the Committee subsequently provided its recommendations, including potential individual criminal accountability for recruitment of children and other abuses to a Commission of Inquiry established by the African Union to investigate conflict-related human rights abuses. In turn, this Commission recommended that South Sudanese authorities (with the assistance of the AU and the international community) establish a specialized tribunal – drawing from international and national expertise – to investigate and prosecute these conflict-related crimes. As of April 2018, the AU and the South Sudan government were in the early stages of setting up the mechanisms and appointment of staff for this specialized tribunal.

Following a similar mission to the Central African Republic (CAR), the Committee published a report in December 2014.[62] The latest ongoing CAR armed conflict has been marked by fighting since 2012 between the government and two separate armed rebel groups (the *Séléka* and 'anti-balaka' rebel groups) which control vast areas of CAR. The fighting has led to thousands of civilian casualties – including ethnic targeted killings and the internal displacement and forced migration of hundreds of thousands of people.[63] A peace deal followed by presidential elections in 2016 brought an initial lull in the fighting before renewed hostilities broke out in late 2016 and early 2017. A few parts of the country, such as the capital, have become more secure or free of hostilities, but peace remains elusive across the country. In its 2014 report, the African Committee expressed concern regarding, among other issues, how the conflict has denied access to education for thousands of children, decimated the justice system (and any chances for recourse or accountability for children's rights violations) and led to the displacement of thousands of children, separated from their families. Regarding the recruitment of children into armed conflict, the Committee received information that 'nearly 10,000 children, including girls, were recruited, exploited and used by the two rival armed groups'.[64] Among other recommendations, the Committee urged CAR to ratify the Charter (which CAR subsequently did in August 2016). It also urged CAR to implement a security sector reform process which includes the prevention of the recruitment and use of children by armed groups.[65] Amidst ongoing peace negotiations involving the government, rebel forces, the AU and the UN, there has been some progress in setting up processes to deal with the impact of the conflict, including justice needs. In June 2017, a specialized court/tribunal was formally created as part of the country's justice system to adjudicate conflict-related crimes. Like the proposed specialized court for South Sudan, the tribunal will involve international and national jurists and staff applying a mix of international and domestic law. As of April 2018, the tribunal's investigations into crimes, including abuses of children's rights, were ongoing.

---

[62] CAR Report 2014.
[63] For recent analysis of the CAR conflict, see International Crisis Group 2017.
[64] CAR Report 2014: [21].
[65] Ibid.: [36].

The regional African legal framework on children 293

Other than fact-finding missions, the Committee has prioritized general research about children and armed conflict in Africa. At its 28th Ordinary session in 2017, it released a comprehensive study on the impact of conflicts and crisis on children in Africa, which considered country situations of conflicts and crises over a 10-year period until 2016.[66] The Committee's research considered the plight of children in different armed conflict settings, including Burundi, Central African Republic, Libya, Nigeria, Somalia and South Sudan, which the Committee classified as countries in active conflict situations, while characterizing the Democratic Republic of the Congo, Guinea-Bissau, Liberia, Mali, Sierra Leone and Sudan as fragile post-conflict situations.[67] In this study, the Committee notes gaps between law and practice. It also affirms that the nature of conflicts in Africa is changing to involve more non-government armed groups (with little or no incentive to respect the legal norms, including on recruitment and the nature of weaponry),[68] and calls for improvements in the high-level commitment of member states to establish effective and functioning mechanisms to address the impact of conflict and crises on children and provide for the care and protection of children affected by armed conflict.[69]

Thus, the Committee's role in fact-finding research and the related publication and dissemination of findings, while departing from the adjudicative function, serves an important fact-establishing platform for specific policy recommendations to African governments, the African Union and international organizations and transnational agencies. This way, the Committee augments the role of other international mechanisms and procedures. The Committee has demonstrated that it is aware of its mandate to cooperate with other institutions, such as the UN Committee on the Rights of the Child and the broader UN framework that involves the UN Security Council and the UN Special Representative of the Secretary General on Children and Armed Conflict. For example, in its 2017 research study referred to above, the Committee offers specific recommendations not only to the African Union and African governments, but also to UN agencies and international organizations on a rights-based framework for the protection of children's rights in the context of armed conflict.

7. EXAMINING THE PROTECTION OF CHILDREN AFFECTED BY ARMED CONFLICT IN THE CONTEXT OF STATE REPORTS

Under Article 43 of the African Children's Charter, every member state is required to submit a progress report for the Committee's examination on the state's compliance with the Charter. In considering the state reports submitted to it, the Committee has consistently sought to examine how domestic legal and policy frameworks impact children's rights, including the prohibition of the recruitment of children into armed conflict. After examining the implementation report Uganda had submitted, the Committee

---

[66] African Committee of Experts on the Rights and Welfare of the Child 2017a.
[67] Ibid.
[68] See also Jiménez in this volume on the changing nature of armed conflicts.
[69] African Committee of Experts on the Rights and Welfare of the Child 2017a.

recommended that 'for a better protection of the child', Uganda should ensure the 'harmonization of [various laws] with the definition of the child as stated in the [Charter]'.[70] On occasions the Committee has reiterated the absolute Straight-18 prohibition of the recruitment of child soldiers. For example, it responded in the following manner to Tanzania's initial implementation report:

> The Committee observes that section 29 (6) of the National Defence Force Act provides that: 'No person under the apparent age of eighteen years shall be enrolled without the consent in writing of one of his parents or guardian or, where the parents are dead or unknown, by the District Commissioner of the District in which that person resides'. The Committee is of the firm view that this provision of the law is contrary to Article 22 (2) of the [Charter], which obliges State Parties thereto to 'take all necessary measures to ensure that no child shall take a direct part in hostilities and refrain, in particular, from recruiting any child'. The Committee urges the State Party to repeal the foregoing provisions of the National Defence Act so as to align it along the provisions of Article 22 of the Charter.[71]

Despite the endemic nature of the problem of children impacted by armed conflict in Africa, the Committee has noted that states have not been providing it with information on this subject even in contexts where this is pertinent. For example, it explicitly expressed concern at the paucity of information provided by Uganda and urged it to provide 'enough data on the status of child soldiers' in its subsequent reports.[72]

There is a paucity of research and data which makes it difficult to draw specific conclusions on the extent to which states are implementing the Committee's findings and recommendations resulting from its examination of state reports. In fact, most states have only submitted, or are in the process of submitting, their first or initial reports to the Committee. As of late 2017, only six countries had submitted two reports (an initial report followed by a second report), making it difficult to judge the extent to which African countries are implementing the Committee's recommendations derived from the reporting procedures. However, from its 2017 research study on recent conflict settings in Africa, the Committee is of the view that most African countries are far from compliant with the Charter's normative rights-based obligations. The Committee has called on member states to mainstream a rights-based approach, which includes legal and institutional frameworks that should contain strong and adequate norms to clarify rights, obligations and institutional roles and provide remedies for violations of rights through clear mechanisms and strengthened mandates of national human rights institutions.[73] In the Committee's view this would respond to the situation where most child protection response mechanisms face similar challenges to many African states, which would mean

> ... essentially abandon[ing] this terrain to NGOs, each of which has its own agenda and mandate. The result is a fragmented approach leading to spotty coverage, lack of coordination and inconsistency of services. The plight of victims is worsened by inadequate, inappropriate

---

[70] Recommendations and Observations sent to the Government of the Republic of Uganda 2010: 2.
[71] Concluding Recommendations Tanzania 2010: 5.
[72] Recommendations and Observations sent to the Government of the Republic of Uganda 2010: 8.
[73] African Committee of Experts on the Rights and Welfare of the Child 2014a: 8.

or nonexistent protection mechanisms; lack of awareness of services; and victims' reluctance to make use of services due to threats from perpetrators, fear, stigma and other obstacles.[74]

8. CONCLUSION

The Charter's normative framework sets out a vision in which all persons under the age of 18 should not be recruited into armed groups and involved in hostilities. This Straight-18 prohibition is singularly noteworthy as the Charter's unique contribution to international law. In addition, the Charter's incorporation of the relevant corpus of international law regarding the protection of children's rights in the context of armed conflict ensures that the Charter's legal regime is comprehensive.

This chapter has unpacked the role of the monitoring body – the African Committee of Experts – which has unparalleled powers to monitor the implementation of the African Children's Charter's provisions. The Charter has ensured in effect that the Committee is able to take unique steps to document, highlight and recommend requisite action regarding the violations of children's rights in conflict settings. Such steps entail rigorous processes for a treaty monitoring body (such as the powers to conduct fact-finding missions and unfettered authority to examine complaints) and build on the work of other institutions, including UN agencies and bodies whose work the Committee can draw from and provide further publicity and recommendations for action on. The Committee has demonstrated its willingness to bolster the domestic protection of children affected by armed conflict through its examination of this issue in state reports, conducting investigative missions (including in the context of countries that are not yet party to the Charter) and adjudicating complaints. Through these procedures, the Committee can provide African states with further detailed guidance on their legal obligations in relation to children impacted by armed conflict.

The Committee's nascent practice indicates that it is sensitive to the need for the exercise of its mandate as a complementary mechanism to the panoply of other mechanisms within the UN/global infrastructure of institutions and mechanisms that seek to enforce and implement treaty frameworks detailing legal norms that seek to ameliorate the impact of conflict on children.

REFERENCED WORKS

Abitria, R.A. (undated). 'The Contribution of the Case of Thomas Lubanga to the Development of International Law on the Protection of Child Soldiers' [available at: http://www.academia.edu/3808285/The_Contribution_of_the_Case_of_Thomas_Lubanga_to_the_Development_of_International_Law_on_the_Protection_of_Child_Soldiers (accessed 13 July 2018)]

African Committee of Experts on the Rights and Welfare of the Child 2010a. *Concluding Recommendations by the African Committee of Experts on the Rights and Welfare of the Child on the Republic of Tanzania Report on the Status of Implementation of the African Charter on the Rights and Welfare of the Child* (November 2010) [available at: http://www.refworld.org/docid/54608eb0c.html (accessed 16 November 2018)] [cited as Concluding Recommendations Tanzania 2010]

---

[74] Ibid.

African Committee of Experts on the Rights and Welfare of the Child 2010b. *Recommendations and Observations Sent to the Government of the Republic of Uganda by the African Committee of Experts on the Rights and Welfare of the Child on the Initial Implementation Report of the African Charter of the Rights and Welfare of the Child* (November 2010) [available at: http://www.refworld.org/docid/5460931eea.html (accessed 16 November 2018)] [cited as Recommendations and Observations sent to the Government of the Republic of Uganda 2010]

African Committee of Experts on the Rights and Welfare of the Child 2013. 'Michelo Hunsungule (Centre for Human Rights, University of Pretoria) and others (on behalf of Children in northern Uganda) versus The Government of Uganda', Communication No. 1/2005 (21st Ordinary Session, 15–19 April 2013) [cited as Hunsungule Communication 2013]

African Committee of Experts on the Rights and Welfare of the Child 2014a. 'Background, Terms of Reference: Missions to Assess the Situation of Children Affected by Armed Conflict in the Central Africa Republic and South Sudan' (April 2014) [on file with the author]

African Committee of Experts on the Rights and Welfare of the Child 2014b. 'Mission Report of the ACERWC to Assess the Situation of Children Affected by the Conflict in Central African Republic' (December 2014) [available at: http://www.refworld.org/docid/555c51244.html (accessed 16 November 2018)] [cited as CAR Report 2014]

African Committee of Experts on the Rights and Welfare of the Child 2014c. 'Report on the Advocacy Mission to Assess the Situation of Children in South Sudan' (August 2014) [available at: http://www.refworld.org/docid/545b4e384.html (accessed 16 November 2018)] [cited as South Sudan Report 2014]

African Committee of Experts on the Rights and Welfare of the Child 2017a. 'Continental Study on the Impact of Conflicts and Crisis on Children in Africa: Executive Summary' [available at: http://www.acerwc.org/download/executive-summary-acerwc-study-on-the-impact-of-conflicts-on-children/?wpdmdl=10161 (accessed 14 July 2018)]

African Committee of Experts on the Rights and Welfare of the Child 2017b. 'Decision on the Communication Submitted by Minority Rights Group International and SoS-Esclaves on Behalf of Said Ould Salem Against the Government of the Republic of Mauritania' (Communication No: 007/Com/003/2015 Decision No: 003/2017, 30th Ordinary Session, 15th December 2017) [cited as Salem Communication 2017]

African Union (undated). 'Guidelines on the Conduct of Investigations by the African Committee of Experts on the Rights and Welfare of the Child under Article 45 of the African Charter and Article 74 of the Rules of Procedure' (ACERWC/8/5) [available at: https://www.crin.org/en/docs/Guidelines_Investigation.pdf (accessed 16 November 2018)]

Amnesty International 2014. 'Nowhere Safe: Civilians under Attack in South Sudan' (AI Index: AFR 65/003/2014)

Bennett, T.W. 1998. 'Using Children in Armed Conflict: A Legitimate African Tradition?' Institute for Security Studies Monograph Series No 32 [available at: http://www.issafrica.org/uploads/Mono32.pdf (accessed 14 July 2018)]

Child Soldiers International (undated). *Where Are Child Soldiers?* [available at: https://www.child-soldiers.org/where-are-there-child-soldiers (accessed 14 July 2018)]

Gettleman, J. 2007. 'The Perfect Weapon for the Meanest Wars', *The New York Times* (29 April)

Human Rights Watch 2012. 'DR Congo: Bosco Ntaganda Recruits Children by Force' (16 May)

Human Rights Watch 2014. 'South Sudan's New War: Abuses by Government and Opposition Forces'

ICRC [International Committee of the Red Cross] 2011. 'Guiding Principles for the Domestic Implementation of a Comprehensive System of Protection for Children Associated with Armed Forces or Armed Groups' (Geneva)

International Criminal Court, *Prosecutor v. Thomas Lubanga Dyilo*, Situation in the Democratic Republic of the Congo, Judgment pursuant to Article 74 of the Statute (5 April 2012) [cited as Lubanga 2012]

International Crisis Group 2017. 'Avoiding the Worst in Central African Republic' (Report No. 253/Africa)

Jesseman, C. 2001. 'The Protection and Participation Rights of the Child Soldier: An African and Global Perspective' 1 *African Human Rights Law Journal* 140

Lee, A. 2009. 'Understanding and Addressing the Phenomenon of "Child Soldiers": The Gap between the Global Humanitarian Discourse and the Local Understandings of Young People's Military Recruitment' (Refugee Studies Centre, Working Paper Series No. 52, University of Oxford)

Lloyd, A. 2002. 'A Theoretical Analysis of the Reality of Children's Rights in Africa: An Introduction to the African Charter on the Rights and Welfare of the Child' 2 *African Human Rights Law Journal* 11

Mezmur, B. 2017. 'Happy 18th Birthday to the African Children's Rights Charter: Not Counting its Days but Making its Days Count' 1 *African Human Rights Yearbook* 125

Olowu, D. 2002. 'Protecting Children's Rights in Africa: A Critique of the African Charter on the Rights and Welfare of the Child' 10 *The International Journal of Children's Rights* 127

Ratifications of the Charter [available at: https://au.int/sites/default/files/treaties/7773-sl-african_charter_on_the_rights_and_welfare_of_the_child_1.pdf (accessed 12 April 2018)]

Talbert, M. and Wolfendale J. 2018. 'The Moral Responsibility of Child Soldiers and the Case of Dominic Ongwen' (Stockholm Centre for the Ethics of War and Peace) (March 5, 2018) [available at: http://stockholmcentre.org/the-moral-responsibility-of-child-soldiers-and-the-case-of-dominicongwen/ (accessed 12 July 2018)]

UN Committee on the Rights of the Child 2008. 'Concluding Observations: Consideration of Reports Submitted by State Parties under Article 8 of the Option Protocol to the Convention on the Rights of the Child on the Involvement of Children in Armed Conflict (Uganda)' (17 October 2008) (CRC/C/OPAC/UGA/CO/1)

Vautravers, A.J. 2008. 'Why Child Soldiers are Such a Complex Issue' 27 *Refugee Survey Quarterly* 96

Viljoen, F, 2001. 'Africa's Contribution to the Development of International Human Rights and Humanitarian Law' 1 *African Human Rights Law Journal* 18

14. Minors and miners: accountability beyond child soldiering in the Democratic Republic of Congo
Sharanjeet Parmar and Yann Lebrat

Syria, Burundi, Yemen, Myanmar and Venezuela: in every corner of the world, children suffer considerable anguish as a result of situations of armed conflict and political violence. This chapter argues that efforts to prevent human rights violations against children, in order to be truly effective, must directly target the underlying drivers of armed conflict, in particular, economic crimes. Armed conflict triggers developmental difficulties that haunt children throughout their lives, while also affecting their long-term ability to realize their economic, social and political rights due to the damage wrought on the basic functioning of state and society. Despite renewed international engagement with the children affected by armed conflict (CAC) agenda, current approaches to prevention, response and accountability do not appear to be successful in stemming the tide of CAC violations and their impact on children and young people.[1]

This chapter highlights the shortcomings of the CAC agenda through a case study of the use of child labour in gold mining in conflict-affected areas of the eastern Democratic Republic of Congo (DRC). We first demonstrate how the pernicious nature of CAC violations links to complex conflict drivers that include economic crimes such as illicit mining of conflict minerals. Through field research in conflict-affected gold mining areas in South Kivu, we show the active involvement of the Congolese army in economic crimes that are directly related and/or contribute to the continued commission of CAC violations. We further find that anti-impunity and institutional reform efforts have largely overlooked this important driver of serious violations against children. Instead, UN-sponsored accountability mechanisms have rewarded the DRC government for having lowered rates of child recruitment by the Congolese army (known as the Forces Armées de la République Démocratique du Congo, FARDC). In conclusion, we find that the CAC agenda remains funnelled through a child soldier lens, which is a necessary but insufficient starting point to prevent CAC violations. We conclude that the CAC agenda must be expanded and applied not only to the crime of child soldiering but also to related CAC violations that children suffer, such as child labour in conflict-affected mining areas.

Section 1 of this chapter presents an overview of the cycles of armed conflict in the DRC and the consequent impact on children. This part also examines the role of the economic crime of illicit mining operations in eastern DRC. In so doing, we demonstrate

---

[1] Throughout this chapter, 'CAC accountability mechanism' refers to any institution, programme, policy, legislation or other arrangement that is designed to address a specific aspect of accountability for serious violations against children in armed conflict (Conflict Dynamics International 2015a). They can operate in multiple forums simultaneously, including local, national, regional (including sub-regional), and/or international.

how long-standing violations against children in eastern DRC are linked to the commission of economic crimes.

Section 2 presents research findings on the prevalence of child labour in conflict-affected gold mining areas in eastern DRC. The research demonstrates the role of armed forces, in particular the Congolese army in perpetuating economic crimes and how these crimes extend to violations against children, primarily in the form of child labour.[2]

Section 3 analyses the effectiveness of accountability mechanisms in the CAC agenda in the light of findings from the DRC case study of child labour in illicit gold mining. Nonetheless, we note how the Congolese army has been delisted from the UN Secretary-General's annexes of actors responsible for grave violations against children for progress to date on its reduced rates of child recruitment and use. In so doing, we reveal how the CAC agenda operates with an unduly narrow focus on child soldiering. Our evidence of the extensive involvement of the FARDC in illicit mining control and taxation of mines where child labour is rampant points to the limits of these mechanisms. We encourage accountability mechanisms to go beyond the child soldier lens to include other forms of CAC violations. Without which, accountability efforts fall short of their ultimate objective of preventing CAC violations.

The chapter concludes with a survey of potential avenues through which anti-impunity efforts can more effectively target the economic impulses behind the recruitment and use of children and youth. Additionally, this chapter offers policy recommendations to improve the coordination of institutional reform efforts, which must be conducted in parallel to anti-impunity efforts at the national, regional and international level to effectively prevent CAC violations.

This chapter is based on two research methods. First, qualitative field research was undertaken in the DRC. This research consisted of first-hand observations, semi-structured key informant interviews and the use of a questionnaire in mining areas in the province of South Kivu. The objective of the field research was to examine the extent to which artisanal mining affects the lives of children and consider the potential links between armed conflicts in the region and mining operations. A total of 11 mining sites were visited out of a total of 19 sites identified in the Misisi region of South Kivu. A total of 55 individuals were interviewed through a combination of key informant interviews and focus group discussions. This included interviews with gold mining diggers, gold mining managers/overseers, children and their families working in mining areas, as well as with members of local militias/armed groups. Additional key informant interviews were also conducted, which included justice and child protection actors in Goma, Bukavu and Kinshasa to assess existing child rights violations as well as child protection needs. Finally, informal interviews were held with researchers and analysts working on conflict dynamics, including armed groups and economic crimes in eastern DRC. Throughout, data was triangulated to ensure the integrity of our findings.

Second, the research methodology comprised extensive analysis of open source data on two issues. Specifically, the research canvassed UN-sponsored and NGO reporting on the commission of serious violations, including CAC violations, in eastern DRC, particularly

---

[2] On the interplay between and among criminal groups and armed groups in Colombia, see Jiménez in this volume.

in known illicit mining areas. Moreover, extensive open source data on mining practices by armed groups was sourced and analysed against current conflict dynamics. As part of validating research findings from the field, the results from the review of open source data was then compared with the field research results. Together, we produced the picture presented herein of how economic crimes committed in the gold mining sector implicate CAC violations, in particular, child labour. Finally, desktop research was extended to a mapping and analysis of existing CAC accountability mechanisms.

1. AN OVERVIEW OF CONFLICT DYNAMICS IN THE DRC

Through this contextual overview, we show that long-standing human rights violations against children in the DRC demonstrate why CAC prevention efforts necessitate a multifaceted approach that must extend to targeting economic crimes.

1.1 History of Conflict and its Impact on Children

Successive wars and cycles of violence in the DRC since the 1990s have disproportionately afflicted children.[3] Today, children in conflict-affected areas of the DRC continue to suffer serious violations of international and national law, including killing, recruitment and use by armed forces and groups, abduction, sexual violence, maiming and other forms of physical violence, as well as attacks on schools and hospitals.[4]

All parties to the armed conflict largely act with impunity.[5] Many of these groups are involved in armed criminal activities, including exploitation of natural resources, whilst committing serious violations against children. As described in detail below, armed groups in eastern DRC and elements of the FARDC have historically relied heavily on natural resource exploitation to sustain themselves.[6] Unfortunately, many perpetrators of serious violations against children in armed conflict remain unidentified and are not held to account. Even where accountability programmes are implemented, they often fail to achieve tangible outcomes that benefit conflict-affected children and their communities. As a result of this 'accountability gap', violations against children continue to be committed with impunity.

1.2 Children and Economic Crimes Involving Conflict Minerals

Child labour and its role in the economic dimension of the DRC's wars is neglected in contemporary CAC reporting. Since 2014, the UN Group of Experts reports have not referred to child labour in mining despite extensively covering the issue of child soldiers. In 2014, the Group of Experts' mid-term report only made a passing mention of the

---

[3] Amnesty International 2003; OHCHR 2010; and HRW 2016.
[4] UNSC 2018 and UN Organization Stabilization Operations in the DR Congo 2017.
[5] Several of these groups have been designated as 'persistent perpetrators' of grave violations against children as they have been listed for more than five years in the annexes of the UN Secretary-General's annual report on children and armed conflict. See UNSC 2016.
[6] UNGoE 2016a.

issue, while the Secretary-General's CAC report in the DRC does not even refer to it. And yet child labour in mining remains a highly publicized concern, especially amongst international NGOs. Most of the coverage is focused on the former province of Katanga, which hosts the DRC's copper and cobalt reserves, both of which are key components in electronics. For example, Amnesty International's 'This Is What We Die For' report published in 2016 highlighted the widespread use of children in cobalt mines in southern DRC, a region mainly unaffected by the contemporary cycles of conflict that plague eastern DRC.[7]

No comprehensive study has been made on child labour in artisanal mining in DRC. Estimates on the proportion of children amongst artisanal miners vary from 10 per cent to upwards of 40 per cent of the total artisanal mining workforce.[8] A comprehensive study by the OECD of artisanal mining in eastern DRC in 2014 estimated that 216,000 artisanal miners worked over 1,088 sites.[9] This can be considered a low estimate as more than double this number of sites (2,403) have been identified by the International Peace Information Service (IPIS) in its latest mapping exercise of mine sites in eastern DRC (which does not include the copper belt sites on which Amnesty International was reporting).[10] According to interviews with UN officials, the difficulty in assessing the extent of the problem is the fluctuating nature of the industry: miners migrate and activity is affected by seasonal changes. Moreover, children can be involved at certain times of the year or even particular days of the week (especially if they also attend school). The poor availability of data on the subject also derives from limited attention on the part of international actors working on mining issues, whose interest has been focused on identifying sites and armed group interference, rather than conditions in the mines themselves and their impact on local populations.[11]

Thus, although child labour is generally neglected, mining has paradoxically been a key issue of interest for the international community. 'Conflict minerals' are widely considered to be drivers of the conflict; these minerals finance armed groups, underpin a large-scale untaxed black market, provide an incentive for conflict between various groups, and instigate overall instability in the region.[12] The UN Group of Experts systematically reports on natural resources, dedicating a whole section of its reports to the issue, in particular minerals such as the 3Ts (tin, tantalum and tungsten) and gold.[13] The attention around conflict minerals, although at times argued excessively to the exclusion of other conflict drivers, has been a key feature of the conflict and the international response in eastern DRC.[14]

Mining in DRC has historically been based on the industrial extraction of copper in southern DRC's Katanga province, where the state-owned Union Minière and its

---

[7] Amnesty International 2016.
[8] Ibid.: 6; Tsurukawa et al. 2011: 32.
[9] OECD 2015: 15. Note this does not include the southern Copperbelt or central diamond producing region where mining is also prevalently practised.
[10] IPIS 2018.
[11] OECD 2015: 34.
[12] CRS 2012: 3.
[13] UNGoE 2017b: 18.
[14] Autesserre 2012: 202.

post-independence successor the Gécamines contributed in large parts to funding the Congolese state.[15] The latest data from the Extractive Industries Transparency Initiative demonstrates the enduring economic weight of the extractive industry, which accounts for 24.7 per cent of government revenue, 20 per cent of GDP and 97.5 per cent of exports, primarily from industrial mining.[16] However, this formal revenue comes mainly from the south of the country. The east is fundamentally different in its make-up.

Eastern DRC primarily has reserves of gold as well as the 3Ts. These minerals were mined industrially during the colonial era, but by the 1990s a combination of investor disengagement following independence and a collapse in the price of tin led to the closure of the last remaining industrial mines.[17] Artisanal mining of these minerals gradually took over following the liberalization of the sector in 1982. It is estimated that up to 10 million people live directly or indirectly off the proceeds of artisanal and small-scale mining in DRC.[18] This is primarily due to the high value of these commodities, driven by a rise in commodity prices linked to the increased use of these resources in electronics, as well as their ease of extraction and ability to process locally. While the 3Ts present particular challenges in processing, gold is especially easy to process and smuggle.[19] For example, a block of 30 kilogrammes of 83 per cent pure gold is no larger than a 'tissue box' and would be worth around US$1 million at $1,200/ounce (prices in 2018 hovered around $1,300).[20]

Considering the predominance of artisanal mining in the east and the ease of smuggling, artisanal mining became a major source of funding and even a point of contention for armed forces and groups as the Second Congo War failed to reach an early resolution. Having fallen short of wresting control of Kinshasa or Katanga in the early days of the conflict, the Rwandan and Ugandan backed Rally for Congolese Democracy turned to artisanal mining to support its prolonged war effort.[21] At the official end of the country-wide conflict in 2003, the UN Panel of Experts reported '[i]llegal exploitation remains one of the main sources of funding for groups involved in perpetuating conflict . . . Over the last year, such exploitation has been characterized by intense competition among the various political and military actors as they have sought to maintain, and in some instances expand, their control over territory.'[22] The conflict also increased the involvement of the population in mining: in certain areas, such as Masisi in North Kivu, a third of the population worked in mines.[23] The chaotic environment of the war incentivized people to turn to mines to make a quick profit, while the slow work of farming was made all the more difficult by continued pillaging and displacement due to the activity of armed forces and groups.

Far from marking the end of interference in mining, the 2003 peace agreement simply

---

[15] Tsurukawa et al. 2011: 16
[16] EITI 2017.
[17] IPIS 2012: 8.
[18] Ibid.: 12.
[19] UNGoE 2017a: 18.
[20] The US dollar (US$) is used as the reference currency throughout this text, notably as the US$ is widely used in the DRC.
[21] IPIS 2012: 9.
[22] UNGoE 2003: 14.
[23] IPIS 2012: 10.

heralded a new chapter in which non-state actors now had to contend with competition from units of the Congolese armed forces (FARDC), which had re-established their presence in the east of the country and also became involved in the illicit exploitation of natural resources.[24] The FARDC remains in much need of reform due to an early political practice of reintegrating armed groups as part of the peace deals. The 2003 peace agreement prescribed the integration into state security bodies (such as the army) of members of several existing armed groups, including the Congolese Rally for Democracy (RCD, the Rwandan proxy rebel group that held most of the east) and the Congolese Liberation Movement (an armed group that held the north-east of the country under the command of Jean-Pierre Bemba).[25] Far from realizing a professional army, integration efforts failed to adequately integrate armed actors, some of whom continued to interfere in mining in eastern DRC.

Armed groups and members of the FARDC used a mixture of direct control of mine sites (involving the cooperation or coercion of miners), taxation, trade monopolies, road blocks, access fees and pillaging to extract revenue.[26] As the conflict evolved and international efforts were made to reduce interference in the mining sector (described below), direct interference in 3T mining was reduced by around 55 per cent between 2009 and 2013 (direct interference includes taxation of minerals, trade monopoly, forced labour and other efforts to exercise control on a site).[27] However, despite what may appear as an increase in public accountability for interference in mining, FARDC units were by far the most involved in mining. In 2013/14, 52 per cent of gold production in South Kivu and 54 per cent of 3Ts production in North Kivu came from sites with FARDC interference.[28]

Once a source of revenue for insurrectionary forces, artisanal mining is now mainly a source of personal profit for numerous FARDC units, officers and patrons. These state actors operate with limited accountability despite sustained efforts by the UN Group of Experts to highlight misdeeds, most recently identifying Major General Gabriel Amisi Kumba as illegally exploiting an alluvial gold site in Tshopo province (west of the Kivus).[29] In these reports the UN Group of Experts regularly cites the government's unwillingness to prosecute interference in mining notwithstanding the *de jure* illegality of such conduct under the DRC's military code and mining code.

Despite the grave concerns raised by international NGOs over children's involvement in mining, accountability efforts by the Group of Experts, or even military prosecutors, generally do not seem to refer to the issue of child labour. Their approach focuses on the economic dimension of these crimes, thereby leading to attempts to limit illicit financial

---

[24] CRS 2012: 25.
[25] ICG 2004 and ICG 2012. In the wake of this agreement, eastern DRC saw the continued activities of the Democratic Forces for Liberation of Rwanda (FDLR, composed of former Rwandan Armed Forces members involved in the perpetration of the Rwandan genocide), as well as the mushrooming of a plethora of local self-defence militias locally known as 'Mai Mai' (generally named after their commanders, such as the 'Mai Mai Yakutumba' operating in the region of our case study).
[26] IPIS 2012: 11.
[27] OECD 2015: 7.
[28] Ibid.: 28.
[29] UNGoE 2017a: 22.

flows, rather than addressing the human impact of these illicit activities on the miners themselves.

1.3 Measures Mitigating the Impact of Illicit Economic Activity

The most dramatic impact on reducing armed group interference has come from external demand-side efforts. These set the terms for the purchase of minerals originating from DRC. A variety of concurrent initiatives have strengthened due diligence efforts, the most prominent having been Section 1502 of the Dodd Frank Act 2010, which required until recently that all US-listed companies carry out due diligence to determine if they are sourcing 'conflict minerals' from DRC.[30] The law remains in place but has come under pressure from the current US administration under President Trump; specifically, the Securities and Exchange Commission has declared it would stop enforcing the law and an attempt was made to repeal the law in Congress.[31] Despite these efforts, it remains true that the original provision of Dodd Frank set an important norm globally. For example, the European Union has now adopted its own, more stringent, conflict minerals traceability regulation, against which local and multinational actors operating in the sector will find themselves subject to compliance.[32] Further, in 2010, the International Conference for the Great Lakes Region (ICGLR) endorsed the OECD Due Diligence Guidance on Conflict Minerals, launching a regional certification scheme requiring traders to undertake due diligence according to OECD standards.

The immediate effect of these policies was a boycott by the major buyers of the 3Ts and gold from DRC, and a temporary ban by the Congolese state on all artisanal mining from September 2010 to March 2011.[33] The policies however pushed trade further into illegality, away from nascent traceability initiatives. The reduced demand forced traders to sell to less reputable buyers at lower prices and harmed the livelihoods of tens of thousands of miners. By reducing overall demand, funding for armed groups was also reduced; as a result, the greater focus on due diligence had a limited but still significant deterrent effect on armed group interference.[34] Since then a more robust set of traceability initiatives has emerged, with sites being monitored by industry- or donor-funded organizations, such as the International Tin Supply Chain Initiative (iTSCi) which has been monitoring incidents of interference.[35]

Although child labour remains a key concern, the actors involved have primarily approached the issue from an economic crimes lens and have consequently directed accountability efforts towards international buyers. Of note, the OECD Due Diligence Guidance for Responsible Supply Chains of Minerals from Conflict-Affected and High-Risk Areas, on which all these initiatives are based, specifically indicates that companies should not source from parties with connections to the worst forms of child labour. The issue is of notable importance to the OECD, which has published a standalone guide to

---

[30] OECD 2015: 35.
[31] Graham 2017.
[32] European Commission 2017.
[33] CRS 2012: 11–13.
[34] Ibid.: 12.
[35] Global Witness 2017: 14.

identify and address the worst forms of child labour in mineral supply chains.[36] But in effect these initiatives seek to avoid sites with child labour rather than directly tackle the practice. By focusing on buyers and the economic dimension of these crimes, the current traceability efforts have an indirect impact on child labour in mining but fail to render perpetrators of conflict-related child labour accountable. In the next section we highlight the limited impact these initiatives have had on the gold trade and the persistent abuse of children's rights by armed groups in the mining sector.

2. DRC CASE STUDY: CHILDREN AND GOLD MINING IN MISISI

Our field research conducted in eastern DRC shows the extent to which violations against Congolese children continue to be linked to illicit mining by both state and non-state armed groups. In addition to elements of the FARDC, non-state armed groups include Mai Mai Yakutumba (a militia active in South Kivu and Tanganyika) and the Democratic Forces for the Liberation of Rwanda (FDLR) (former members of the Rwandan armed forces who became active in North Kivu after the Rwandan genocide).[37] Specifically, our research demonstrates how child labour remains endemic in the artisanal mining sector in DRC, particularly in the gold sector. Through the DRC case study, this section describes how the gold sector is exposed to sustained interference from armed forces (specifically, elements of the FARDC) and groups who exploit these mine sites directly or indirectly for their own benefit. These entities, most notably the FARDC, thereby become involved in the exploitation of children on a mass scale in very hazardous environments.

2.1 The Prevalence of Gold Mining in Eastern DRC's Armed Conflict

Gold mining is the gaping hole in international efforts to improve mineral traceability in DRC. Gold is found in abundance throughout eastern DRC and 64.8 per cent of artisanal mine sites in the region are focused on its extraction.[38] Only 61 of 1,556 gold sites have been certified as conflict-free for exports (16% of overall certified sites) and 47 per cent of gold sites report ongoing interference from armed forces and groups. More than half of these interferences are from FARDC soldiers, generally in the form of mine entry taxes or direct management of sites, that lead to monopolies on the trade of minerals and even forced labour.

Misisi is a region on the border between the South Kivu and Tanganyika provinces. It lies on the road between Uvira and Kalémie (see Figure 14.1). The region is one of the main artisanal gold mining sectors in South Kivu: a 2015 study identified 11 sites noted as having more than 500 diggers, locally referred to as '*creuseurs*'.[39] In our research, we identified 19 significant mine sites. In the late 2000s and early 2010s, gold revenue from the

---

[36] OECD 2017.
[37] See UNGoE 2017a. and UNGoE 2018:10. For more detail on Mai Mai Yakutumba see note 42.
[38] IPIS 2018.
[39] Ibid.

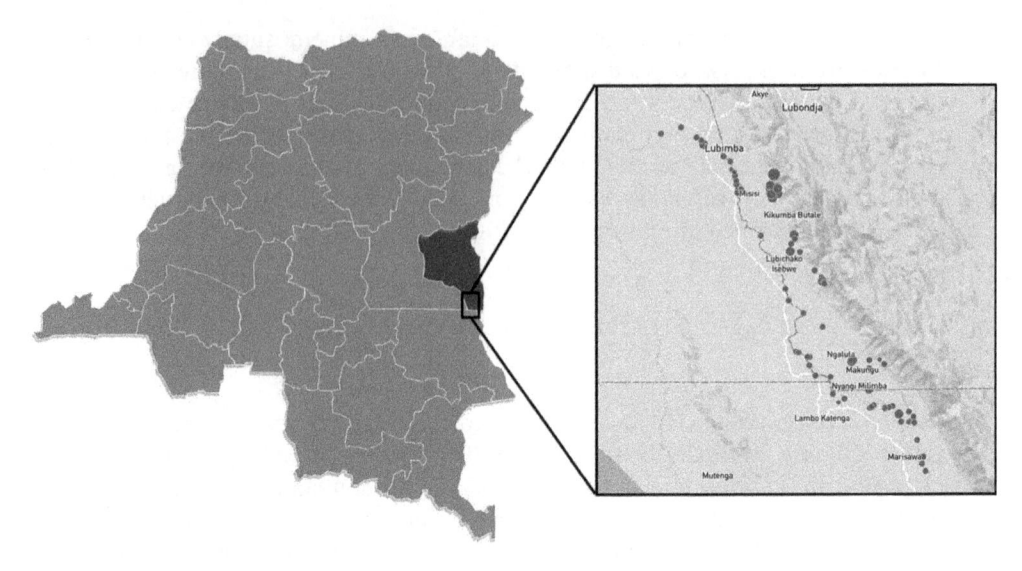

Source: IPIS 2018.

Figure 14.1 Misisi map highlighting gold mine sites

area was critical to the war effort of the region's main rebel group, Mai Mai Yakutumba.[40] Misisi's remoteness from the urban centres of Uvira and Kalémie, as well as its proximity to Lake Tanganyika and the porous borders with Burundi and Tanzania, make it ideal for illegal gold exploitation and smuggling by armed groups.[41] As of December 2017, the region has been under the control of the FARDC, with a limited influence from the erstwhile dominant Mai Mai Yakutumba.[42]

2.2 The Involvement of Children in Gold Mining

Our site visits highlighted the presence of children in the 11 mines visited, without exception and regardless of the presence of armed groups or forces. Although an estimate of the number of children is not possible without a systematic survey, we could ascertain that in each mining site groups of children were involved in arduous and hazardous tasks around extraction. Based on direct observation and site interviews, our field research found that young boys, often clearly below 15 years of age, are involved in digging pits, breaking stones, sifting, washing and carrying heavy loads of rocks. Beyond the strenuous nature of working long hours in a tropical climate, these children are exposed to a range

---

[40] Stearns et al. 2013: 37.
[41] Ibid.
[42] Mai Mai Yakutumba is a militia that emerged in southern South Kivu following failed demobilization efforts in 2007. Led by William Amuri Yakutumba, a former militia commander during the Second Congo War against Rwanda, the militia has based its politics on an anti-Tutsi, anti-Rwandan and anti-Banyamulenge platform (Stearns et al. 2013: 27).

of potentially deadly hazards including pit collapses, mercury used in processing the ores and inhalation of dust.

Girls are on the other hand mainly involved in commerce in and around the mine site. Women in general are often present on mining sites due to a lack of access to education and extreme poverty, as well as to accompany male relatives or partners.[43] Many women are also young abandoned single mothers and/or victims of sexual violence.[44] Girls are generally aged between 15 and 17 years; they sell water, food and other necessities in mining areas. While being insulated from the most immediate hazards of mining, interviews with *creuseurs* revealed that young girls are frequently the victims of rape and other forms of sexual violence, including forced marriage, by *creuseurs* and armed forces and groups alike. Regardless of the presence of the police, the exposure of young girls to these violations has become normalized by members of the community interviewed for this study.

Children working on the sites are subject to what can be identified as some of the 'Worst Forms of Child Labour' under ILO Convention 182, to which the DRC is signatory.[45] The tasks relating to mining qualify under Convention Article 3, in particular 'work which, by its nature or the circumstances in which it is carried out, is likely to harm the health, safety or morals of children'.[46] These practices have also been classified as such by the United States Department of Labour in its global report on the Worst Forms of Child Labour.[47] Considering the persistent exposure to gender-based violence, underage female small traders present on sites are likewise exposed to a hazardous environment which may also qualify as a Worst Form of Child Labour under ILO Convention 182. Outside domestic work, child labour under 15 is illegal under Congolese laws and as such can be considered illegal in the cases mentioned above (note that the ILO Convention extends to 15–18-year-olds).

Our research did not reveal evidence of armed groups or forces directly recruiting children into the mines. According to interviews with *creuseurs* and child protection actors, many children work in the mines of their own accord, having been forced to leave their families due to poverty and/or displacement due to armed conflict. Other children were observed to be mining alongside their family members. On the other hand, in a 2014 USAID study on human trafficking in artisanal mining generally in eastern DRC, only 12 per cent of respondents surveyed reported having witnessed 'child labour'. This finding stands in stark contrast to what our field research in conflict-affected gold mining revealed – we found a much higher prevalence of child labour.

In the 2014 USAID study, respondents described 'forced labour' as practices being perpetrated by the mine manager.[48] It would appear that local perceptions may influence what gets characterized as 'forced labour'. Moreover, local community members interviewed indicated that local fears of repercussion (from mine owners and armed forces and groups) persist even when it comes to discussing these topics. Together, these dynamics

---

[43] Côté 2014: 16.
[44] Ibid.: 17.
[45] The DRC signed the Convention on 20 June 2001.
[46] ILO Convention 182 1999.
[47] USDOL 2016: 2.
[48] USAID 2014: 34.

suggest that incidences of child labour and gender-based violence against children are underreported. Furthermore, our research confirmed that perpetrators of these violations often take measures to hide violations from potential inspections.

2.3 The Direct and Indirect Involvement of Armed Groups and the FARDC

This depiction of the situation facing children and their families in conflict-affected mining areas demonstrates how persistent violations of children's socio-economic rights are not necessarily always direct or linear results of acts committed by local armed groups, armed forces or otherwise. Rather, these violations remain part of a broader collective experience of children who live in areas of active armed conflict *and* other parts of the region that remain conflict-affected and/or conflict-prone.[49] Although child labour occurs on all sites investigated in Misisi, armed groups and forces are only directly interfering with a small fraction of the sites (at least openly). Nonetheless, armed actors benefit from these violations and may exacerbate them. In certain clear-cut cases, moreover, armed actors exercise direct control over mine sites and directly employ children in the extraction of gold. In other cases, armed groups and armed forces (specifically, units of the FARDC) illegally tax the work of *creuseurs* and thus benefit indirectly from these mines whilst also perpetuating predatory and exploitative conditions therein.

Our findings on the predatory role of the FARDC in the area indicate a systemic impact that compounds the issue of child labour.[50] By illegally engaging in the actual management of the mine sites, FARDC units directly exploit child labour and encourage it in its worst forms.[51] Secondly, when armed groups and forces restrict access to sites or control them, they create 'dark zones' or spaces in which state laws and oversight mechanisms cannot be implemented. Thirdly, by taxing access to mining sites, FARDC units benefit from this exploitation and reinforce the conditions of economic deprivation that lead to child labour.

Direct control of mine sites by armed actors (which can include members of armed groups or members of the FARDC) is not as common as it was in the 2000s; however, our research in Misisi revealed that the practice is nonetheless ongoing. Based on interviews on site, the 'Nyange' mine, 50km from Misisi centre, is one of the largest gold-mining sites in the area and is currently under the direct control of a FARDC unit. Direct control over a mine site involves either a monopoly over the trade of gold, direct management of *creuseurs* (including forced labour) or even the practice of soldiers digging themselves. The FARDC unit in Nyange holds a monopoly on the local gold trade, coercing local

---

[49] Indeed, child labour in the artisanal mining sector extends to other parts of the country that are not conflict-affected. For example, child labour in mining was reported by Amnesty International in Kolwezi in 2015, an urban centre situated in a relatively conflict-free area in the southern DRC province of Katanga.

[50] See also UNGoE 2016a: 29 and UNGoE 2016b (implicating the FARDC in illegal taxation in South Kivu) and UNGoE 2017a: 22 (detailing exploitation and trade of gold by FARDC and armed groups in eastern DRC).

[51] These findings have potential implications for the issue of state responsibility for any serious violations resulting from the conduct of members of the FARDC. Consider, e.g., judgments by Congolese courts finding the Congolese government responsible for the payment of reparations to victims of serious violations committed by the FARDC. ICTJ 2012.

creuseurs to sell to them. The soldiers also control access to the site through road blocks. With no alternative other than moving to another site, *creuseurs* are effectively managed by the security forces present on site who set the price and conditions for all those present. Groups also impose a monopoly on small trading of local goods, for example on water and cigarettes.[52] Following common practice in the region, the FARDC unit sets a price in an agreement, locally known as a 'convention', with the local miners. However, access to weapons via the security forces gives these managers more bargaining power than most, who reportedly resort to the intimidation of local diggers. However, contrary to findings by IPIS in the same area in 2015, we did not find any hard evidence of forced labour, either by FARDC or mining managers. Evidence of state failure and endemic poverty resulting from years of armed conflict in the region suggest nonetheless that diggers and children find themselves working in punishing conditions on their own 'volition' simply because they have no other livelihood and/or economic alternatives. The situation mirrors similar findings related to the independent exercise of agency by children in armed conflict by joining armed groups out of issues of necessity, survival and/or identity.[53]

This form of exclusive control by armed actors is not necessarily the norm. Nonetheless, it has been noted in sites throughout eastern DRC by the UN Group of Experts: for example, Colonel John Unega and Brigadier General Muhindo Akili Mundos are both illegally involved in gold mining in the northeast province of Ituri.[54] This form of direct involvement is banned under the Mining Code and military regulations, and as such constitutes an economic crime. The use of children greatly aggravates this issue by adding another dimension to the crime being committed. By directly managing these sites for personal gain these FARDC officers and their units are responsible for the exploitation of children and the harm which they suffer in these hazardous conditions. Due to the status of these units and officers and their ability to use force, the police or the SAESSCAM (Ministry of Mines body in charge of ASM) make no efforts locally to keep them accountable. And yet, as we will address later, the CAC dimension of these crimes is generally treated as a peripheral issue that is left for NGOs and, what is more, is generally left unaddressed by UN reports, in particular those of the UN Secretary-General's reports on children and armed conflict.

The indirect control of mines by armed actors is far more common, notably, illegal taxation either on- or off-site instead of exercising a monopoly on trade or forced labour. Our research revealed that all the 19 mine sites visited had some form of military road block on their access road. These road blocks create a bottleneck to levy some form of

---

[52] Of note, conditions are not reported to be necessarily any worse than at any other sites which may be managed by other groups.

[53] Consider Drumbl 2012b: 482 ('approximately two-thirds of child soldiers exercise some (at times considerable) initiative in coming forward to enroll'); Drumbl 2012a: 101 (proposing alternatives to the discourse of victimhood of child soldiers which can 'aid in restoring the dignity of children involved in armed conflict'); Wessells 2016 (highlighting how conflicts fought on ethnic or related lines of identity can stimulate views among children that violence is justified and necessary for survival of one's identity group); and Lasley and Thyne 2011: 156 (describing Wessells' argument on agency: 'Wessells goes beyond the "forced recruitment" scenario, discussing children's rational decisions to join armed forces in order to gain protection, a sense of family, education, training, power, money and prestige').

[54] UNGoE 2016b: 14–16.

tax, either in cash or in kind, to access the mine site. Our findings mesh with those of a 2017 study on road blocks in the Kivus which identified 122 road blocks dedicated to controlling access to mine sites and collecting a tax on *creuseurs*.[55] Although we were unable to ascertain the exact nature of this kind of taxation in Misisi, a case study from Walikale (western North Kivu) revealed a well-established system under the control of a local armed group.[56] It includes a yearly pass in cash and a weekly tax of 1 gram of gold per week, with a parallel taxation system imposed by the FARDC further down the road from the site.

This form of indirect control of mine sites exempts armed groups from direct responsibility for the exploitation of children. Nevertheless, road blocks are designed to enforce territorial control: through their operation, the road blocks enable the security forces to exercise access to and control of mine sites, and therefore participate in the governance of these areas. Strictly speaking, these road blocks are illegal, especially in the way they are used to impose taxes on minerals.[57] By restricting access to certain areas, these road blocks create areas of lawlessness where human rights violations can occur; and by precluding access to potential accountability actors these road blocks allow these violations to fester. Child labour would not end with the end of illegal road blocks, but their ongoing presence is a major obstacle to improvements in the situation.

Whether it be through direct or indirect control, the model of illegal taxation contributes to the impoverishment of *creuseur* communities. *Creuseurs* are generally migrants from nearby provinces, such as Maniema and Tanganyika. They become miners out of economic necessity. A previous USAID study established that the weekly income of male miners is $33 per week: 71.3 per cent of respondents claimed this amount was generally insufficient to cover basic living expenses; 86.3 per cent of female respondents, who are generally involved in less lucrative petty trading activities, affirmed their earnings as insufficient.[58] Our research in Misisi indicated children are generally present due to poverty and lack of economic options, with families unable to send children to school and requiring the additional income to meet basic needs. The extortion of funds and underpayment for the minerals actually extracted further reduce the income of *creuseurs*. In doing so armed groups reinforce the underlying drivers that bring children into the mines, and lock those already in the mines into a cycle of destitution.

The impact of FARDC on children in mining is stark. It is nonetheless worth noting that the FARDC contribute to a broader economic system: child labour in mining is the result of demand from external markets.[59] Gold produced in Misisi is smuggled to sub-regional trading hubs such as Kalémie, Uvira and Bukavu to be sold to international exporters.[60] The gold extracted around Misisi arrives on international markets to the benefit of international consumers. This creates a nexus between the responsibility exercised by the FARDC and the broader responsibility of international companies, who are notably expected to adhere to OECD Due Diligence Principles in sourcing minerals

---

[55] IPIS 2017: 34.
[56] Ibid.: 35.
[57] Ibid.: 7.
[58] USAID 2014: 15.
[59] See also Kamara in this volume; Hanson and Molima in this volume.
[60] IPIS 2018.

from DRC. Not only does the international community have the ability to act, it has a responsibility to do so.

3. ASSESSING THE EFFECTIVENESS OF CAC ACCOUNTABILITY MECHANISMS IN THE DRC

The DRC CAC case study on conflict-related child labour in gold mines demonstrates the complexity underpinning the nature and scope of CAC violations. CAC prevention efforts must in turn respond to this complexity in order to be truly effective. We therefore assess the effectiveness of 'accountability mechanisms' in responding to and preventing CAC violations by targeting the underlying drivers thereof. We rely on the definition proposed by Conflict Dynamics International, where 'accountability' can be understood as an action or series of actions taken to achieve outcomes in one or more of four categories: (i) imposing legitimate consequences for perpetrators; (ii) assigning responsibility for violations committed; (iii) preventing or deterring future violations; and (iv) reconciling and repairing traumatized societies and individuals.[61] We assess mechanisms that operate through both judicial and non-judicial means and that seek to realize objectives under the first three categories: imposing legitimate consequences, assigning responsibility and preventing or deterring CAC violations.

Current accountability efforts are insufficient in effectively neutralizing perpetrators and the underlying drivers of CAC violations. Specifically, this section identifies the shortcomings inherent in two types of approaches to CAC accountability: (i) the treatment of the CAC agenda by the UN Security Council (non-judicial mechanisms); and (ii) investigations and prosecutions in national and international criminal cases (judicial mechanisms).

3.1 The CAC Agenda at the UN

As a result of sustained engagement with the CAC agenda, a set of CAC-specific non-judicial accountability mechanisms have been in operation at the UN. These primarily fall under the auspices of the UN Security Council (UNSC).

The subject of children affected by armed conflict was cemented in the agenda of the international community following the landmark report by Graça Machel in 1996 on the impact of armed conflict on children,[62] and subsequently affirmed in the 10-Year Strategic Review of the Machel Study.[63] The adoption of a series of UNSC resolutions has since established a trio of initiatives that form the bedrock of UN-mandated CAC accountability mechanisms, designed to facilitate both national and international responses to grave violations against children.[64] These initiatives operate through the Office of the Special

---

[61] Conflict Dynamics International 2011: 4.
[62] Machel 1996.
[63] UNICEF and SRSG 2009.
[64] Key CAC-related UN Security Council Resolutions include 1261 (1999), 1379 (2001), 1612 (2005), 2225 (2015), as well as others cited in this section.

Representative to the UN Secretary-General on Children and Armed Conflict[65] and are facilitated by the high-level UN Working Group on Children and Armed Conflict.[66]

3.1.1 Monitoring Reporting Mechanism (MRM)[67]

The MRM provides for the systematic gathering of 'accurate, timely, objective and reliable information' regarding grave violations committed against children in identified situations of armed conflict. These violations are published in an annual report of the Office of the Special Representative and submitted by the Secretary-General (SG) to the UNSC. The 2016 report recorded 2,334 grave violations in the DRC, with the number of child casualties having increased by 75 per cent since 2015.[68] The Report notes the number of child casualties reported for the DRC over 2016 to have been 'the highest recorded since 2012'.[69] Indeed, the 'magnitude and nature of allegations received was alarming', whilst sexual violence against girls was also found to be highly prevalent.[70] These reports may in fact mask the actual scope of CAC violations. Child protection actors have 'consistently raised the issue of the UN's insufficient capacity to verify incidents using UN standards of verification'.[71]

3.1.2 Listing mechanism

Actors who are responsible for the commission of at least one of the six grave violations against children reported annually by the UN Secretary-General are named and listed in two annexes to the report. Annex I lists parties to armed conflict situations on the agenda of the UNSC; Annex II lists parties in relation to armed conflict situations not on the Council agenda but that persist as situations of concern regarding children. For the DRC, Annex I of the UN Secretary-General's (UNSG's) 2016 report to the UNSC lists 12 non-state armed groups responsible for committing all five grave violations against children.[72] Six of the 12 belong to local militias known as 'Mai Mai' (or 'Mayi Mayi') which are generally known as 'self-defence militias formed on an ad-hoc basis by local leaders who arm young men in villages, often along ethnic lines'.[73] An overwhelming majority (82 per cent) of cases of recruitment and use of children were documented in North Kivu. Listed perpetrators including the FDLR and Nyatura (both of whom operate in North Kivu), along with the listed Mai Mai groups, as well as the Force de résistance patriotique de l'Ituri (FRPI).[74] These practices follow findings in 2014 by the UN Group of Experts,

---

[65] Created under UN General Assembly Resolution A/RES/51/77.
[66] Created under UNSC Resolution 1612 (2005).
[67] UNSC Resolution 1539 (2009).
[68] UNSC 2017: 10.
[69] Ibid.: 2.
[70] Ibid.: 10. Children have been directly targeted in the escalating violence in the central Kasaï region since mid-2016.
[71] Child Soldiers International 2014a: 4.
[72] The report lists 65 parties in total for all situations under review, including nine government forces and 55 non-state armed groups. UNSC 2017: 37.
[73] IRIN 2010.
[74] It is important to note that the FRPI continues to recruit and use children despite the 2012 guilty verdict by the International Criminal Court (ICC) against Thomas Lubanga for the recruitment and use of children in the Ituri region, as well as the ICC's conviction of the group's former commander, Germain Katanga, for one count of a crime against humanity (murder) and four

which reported ongoing recruitment and use of child soldiers by several armed groups operating in eastern DRC.[75] Annex II of the 2016 report also lists the FARDC as an armed force responsible for committing rape and other forms of sexual violence against Congolese children (though the body of the report also cites the FARDC as responsible for abductions).[76]

The listing process entails significant reputational risk to states parties. Moreover, a direct consequence for listed state actors is that they become subject to UN conditionality policies that can preclude their armies from contributing to UN peacekeeping missions (which can be lucrative for national armies). The listing mechanism recently sparked controversy when the Israeli Defence Forces were removed from the list in 2015; controversy also ensued with the removal of the Saudi-led coalition in Yemen following threats from the Saudi government to withhold UN funding in 2016. Ultimately, the SG reoriented the annexure format in the 2017 report to include two subsections to each annex: Section A, which lists parties that have not put measures in place to improve the protection of children over the reporting period; and Section B, which lists those that have.[77]

3.1.3 National action plans

The CAC agenda includes measuring progress on action plans adopted by parties who find themselves listed in the annexes of the SG's annual report.[78] Established under UNSC Res. 1612 (2005), the CAC Working Group is comprised of state parties whose work includes the review of country situations and assessing progress by groups on the design and implementation of action plans.[79] The DRC signed a national Action Plan concerning child recruitment and other violations of international humanitarian law; this plan was concluded in 2012.[80] In 2014, the implementation of the DRC Action Plan was reported to be 'slow and piecemeal', 'hampered by insufficient funding and [suffering] from poor communication between Kinshasa and the affected provinces, as well as between government and other partners'.[81]

3.1.4 DRC sanctions committee and Group of Experts

The Group of Experts is mandated to conduct research and analysis to assist the DRC sanctions committee. Based on information produced by a nominated Group of Experts, the DRC sanctions committee advises the UNSC on monitoring and implementing the

---

counts of war crimes (murder, attacking a civilian population, destruction of property and pillage). See Parmar 2017; Bueno 2014.

[75] Specifically, the responsible armed actors and numbers of children identified with these groups included: Mai Mai groups (194, including 43 girls), Nyatura (112, including four girls), Mai Mai Kata Katanga (39), FDLR (30), Raia Mutomboki (25), M23 (24), APCLS (13), PARECO (12), FARDC deserters (seven girls), LRA (two girls) and ADF (one).

[76] UNSC 2017: 11.

[77] Of note, the Saudi-led coalition was placed in Section B of Annex 1, following two measures that were undertaken in 2016.

[78] See UNSC Resolution 1539 (22 April 2004) UN Doc S/RES/1539 and UNSC Resolution 1612 (26 July 2005) UN Doc S/RES/1612.

[79] For a detailed analysis of the Working Group operations, see Security Council Report 2017.

[80] UNSC 2014: 15 and HRW 2016.

[81] Child Soldiers International 2014a: 4.

sanctions. The UN Charter provides for the establishment of subsidiary bodies such as sanctions committees to facilitate its work (Article 29). Sanctions committees support the UNSC in particular situations to establish and monitor the implementation of sanctions. Sanctions can extend to economic and trade sanctions, as well as more targeted measures such as arms embargoes, travel bans and financial or diplomatic restrictions. In 2006, the UNSC extended the DRC sanctions regime to individuals recruiting or targeting children in situations of armed conflict.[82] The Group of Experts' 2016 annual report included information on the activities of Congolese and foreign armed groups operating in the DRC, as well as on their involvement in the illicit trade in natural resources, particularly gold.[83]

3.2 Assessing the Effectiveness of the UN CAC Agenda in the DRC

This overview highlights how predominantly the DRC figures on the CAC agenda at the UN, in particular in terms of the violation of recruitment and use of children. To date, only few initiatives have studied the efficacy of accountability efforts for CAC violations. One such study found a 'fundamental lack of a rigorous approach to accountability at all levels. Despite evidence of some genuine commitment and notable achievements, there is a poor record of concrete results for children'.[84] A more recent 2017 study of the efficacy of the UN Security Council's engagement with the CAC agenda found that 'when the political environment is right, the tools available for the protection of children in armed conflict can be effectively deployed'.[85] In 2015, Conflict Dynamics published a mapping of CAC accountability initiatives that were ongoing in the DRC. This publication noted 'insufficient linkages among judicial and human rights mechanisms working to enforce laws and standards, such as national courts, and those mechanisms working to empower children and assign responsibility for CAC violations, such as child protection working groups and/or the Monitoring and Reporting Mechanism (MRM) Country Task Force'.[86] Our DRC case study highlighting how the FARDC remains linked to practices of child labour in gold mining provides an opportunity to test whether the findings from these prior studies continue to apply.

3.2.1 Delisting of the Congolese army
Our findings on the active involvement of the FARDC in the exploitation of child labour as part of gold mining in South Kivu and the commission of conflict-related economic crimes is linked to deeper institutional reform issues. The DRC government has faced persistent difficulties in reforming its security sector into one that prioritizes protection of the civilian population over private interests, and refrains from committing grave violations against civilians, including sexual violence and the recruitment/use of children.[87] Since 2003, Congolese security forces have been comprised of a mix of professional soldiers

---

[82] UNSC Resolution 1698 (31 July 2006) UN Doc S/RES/1698.
[83] UNGoE 2016a.
[84] Conflict Dynamics International 2011: v.
[85] Security Council Report 2017: 2
[86] Conflict Dynamics International 2015b: 5.
[87] ICG 2012.

working alongside former rebels and militia members who had been integrated into the army and police as a condition of past peace agreements.[88] These actors are known perpetrators of crimes against civilians including children.[89] Despite these challenges, the FARDC has recently managed to succeed in dramatically lowering the number of children in its ranks.[90] Strong operational incentives have facilitated the realization of the norm prohibiting the recruitment and use of children.[91]

In 2017, the DRC was delisted after having been found to have implemented its national Action Plan for the recruitment and use of children.[92] The UNSG report on children and armed conflict in 2016 found no new cases of child recruitment by the FARDC for two consecutive years. This report further cites progress in the realization of the country's Action Plan. Of note, the 2017 study on the CAC agenda found that 'a number of parties have been willing to employ these tools in order to be delisted when the right factors are in place'.[93] In addition to the delisting mechanism, local sources cited the reputational interest of the DRC authorities in avoiding being listed by the US government, which also employs a conditionality policy with respect to bilateral military assistance under the US Prevention of Child Soldiers Act (PCSA).[94]

This progress by the Congolese army in terms of recruitment and use of children points to a positive impact of the CAC agenda in the DRC; although, the 2017 SG report nonetheless still lists the FARDC as responsible for rape and other forms of sexual violence against children (and the body of the text describes other violations such as abductions). More critically, however, our field research in conflict-affected gold mining areas in South Kivu points to the active involvement of the FARDC in economic crimes that are directly related and/or contribute to continued CAC violations *notwithstanding the army's progress on child recruitment*. Moreover, the use of forced labour of children in artisanal mining sites is well documented in public sources in addition to our own field research.[95]

---

[88] At the end of nationwide hostilities, the 2003 Sun City Accord established a transitional unity government that included Parliament and Senate appointments based on representatives from rebel groups, as well as the integration of members of the former warring factions into the security forces. This practice has since been repeated as part of subsequent peace deals with armed groups in eastern DRC. See Lemarchand 2009 and ICG 2012.

[89] OHCHR 2010.

[90] For example, in 2013, UNICEF's MRM Unit reported 113 cases of children that were recruited by FARDC, representing 12.4 per cent of the overall number of cases of recruitment and use. FARDC members explained that the occasional cases that may arise are due to the ignorance of lower-ranking army members and dealt with immediately. The latest UNSG's report notes no new cases of recruitment or use by the FARDC.

[91] Parmar 2017: 249.

[92] The website of the UN Special Representative on Children and Armed Conflict notes that the DRC was '[d]elisted in 2017 following compliance with Action Plan to end and prevent the recruitment and use of children. Action Plan on ending and preventing sexual violence against children under implementation' (https://childrenandarmedconflict.un.org/tools-for-action/action-plans/).

[93] Security Council Report 2017: 2.

[94] In September 2014, the US government under the Obama administration issued a partial waiver of the application of the PCSA to the DRC, under which the US government continued to provide inter alia military training to the FARDC as well as assistance to UN peacekeeping mission operations, which extend to supporting the FARDC. Obama 2014 and Child Soldiers International 2014b.

[95] See section 2.3.

Progress on the reduction of child recruitment and use merits recognition. However, the entrenched nature of broader CAC violations in the DRC persists and demands attention, particularly since these violations drive deeper dynamics that keep children vulnerable to further cycles of exploitation and abuse. In our field interviews, child protection actors strongly denounced the continued commission by FARDC elements of a range of children's rights violations, including sexual violence, forced labour, physical violence and in some cases killings.[96] They expressed overwhelming frustration with the manner in which perpetrators of CAC violations such as the FARDC are absolved from accountability while children continue to be victimized.

Applying a broader lens of CAC violations demonstrates how progress on the national action plan to reduce child recruitment and use by the FARDC is insufficient in the overall prevention of CAC violations. The additional attention on sexual violence violations (as noted under Annex II of the UNSG 2016 report) is welcome but by no means complete in terms of violations against children for which the FARDC is responsible. This is particularly the case in light of the extent to which the FARDC is implicated in a broader range of economic crimes that drive conflict dynamics and state fragility in eastern DRC.

3.2.2 Sanctions regime

Various UN sanctions regimes have played an important role in targeting key actors for sanctions as well as providing detailed identification of local and regional dynamics underpinning the commission of economic crimes in situations of armed conflicts. As outlined earlier, in addition to reporting on recruitment and use, the reports of the UN Group of Experts have focused on the role of armed forces and groups in conflict minerals with little attention paid to secondary violations such as child labour in illicit mining activities.

3.2.3 Conclusions on the CAC agenda's present effectiveness in the DRC

The DRC case study demonstrates the limits of narrowly applying accountability efforts to a circumscribed set of CAC violations. The six grave violations used in monitoring and reporting of the CAC agenda at the UN Security Council comprise: (i) recruiting and/or use of child soldiers (triggered for listing since 2002); (ii) killing and/or maiming of children (triggered for listing since 2009); (iii) sexual violence against children (triggered for listing since 2009); (iv) attacks against schools and/or hospitals (triggered for listing 2011); (v) abductions of children (triggered for listing since 2015); and (vi) denial of humanitarian access for children.

To be truly effective, accountability mechanisms should identify and target more nuanced constructions of CAC violations such as those described under the DRC case study. In this case, the dominance of the child soldier narrative for the CAC experience has had the effect of limiting the potential impact of the UN's CAC accountability agenda. In sum, the needs and interests of vulnerable groups are not adequately addressed when one violation tends to dominate an entire agenda.[97]

The same tendency can be said of the focus of the donor community and international

---

[96] See also UNSC 2014.
[97] See also Aijazi et al; Oosterveld; and Denov, all in this volume.

media on the commission of sexual and gender-based violence (SGBV) in eastern DRC. Indeed, as noted by Rift Valley Institute researchers Cuvelier and Bashwira, '[c]ontrary to what is often believed, women's roles in the Congo's violent conflicts are not invariably passive'.[98] The result of the focus on SGBV has been less attention on other equally critical aspects of the gender justice agenda. These issues include the exclusion of Congolese women from political participation and the formal exercise of public authority, as well as gender-sensitive approaches to their economic empowerment beyond the lens of SGBV programming.

3.3 Judicial Accountability Efforts for CAC Violations in the DRC

Beyond the CAC accountability mechanisms surveyed above, judicial efforts also deserve analysis. This section considers findings on prosecutions by the International Criminal Court (ICC) as well as judicial steps undertaken at the national level.

A number of CAC stakeholders have called for stronger efforts to fight impunity for CAC violations. In 2014, Child Soldiers International urged national and international actors to: '[p]rioritise criminal investigations and prosecutions of individuals suspected of recruiting or using children in hostilities', as well as to '[r]egularly publish information on the number of prosecutions and convictions for recruitment and use of children in armed conflict'.[99] More recently, Conflict Dynamics International in partnership with local child protection NGO, Rebuild Hope for Africa, distributed a pictorial leaflet to deter armed groups in the central and eastern regions of the DRC from recruitment and use. The leaflet depicts the criminal liability implications for the recruitment and use of children by referencing the ICC's conviction of Thomas Lubanga for the recruitment and use of children in hostilities.[100]

A recent 2017 study on the deterrence value of the ICC's *Lubanga* case found that the impact of ICC prosecutions on the crime of child soldiers was in fact mitigated by underlying conflict dynamics.[101] In terms of impact on targeted deterrence:

> [L]ocal actors shared the view that the Lubanga case raised awareness to a certain degree amongst some commanders of local armed groups that recruitment and use of child soldiers is a crime for which you can be punished. Interviewees explained that the ICC did play a role in this awareness through visits by the Prosecutor and the diffusion of ICC proceedings in the region. Child protection actors recounted dealing with some warlords who feared being caught for using child soldiers; in apparent reference to the Ituri cases, they noted 'some are horrified of experiencing the same fate as the others arrested'. Indeed, they attributed some of the shift in use of children to the ICC *Lubanga* case, which served as '*une connotation pédagogique*' – that is, a learning moment for armed actors. The impact of the Lubanga case that was most widely cited was the recent drop of children in the ranks of the Congolese army.[102]

---

[98] Cuvelier and Bashwira 2016: 2 and Parmar 2013.
[99] Child Soldiers International 2014a: 7.
[100] See also Kaushik and Freeland in this volume.
[101] Parmar 2017.
[102] Parmar 2017: 242–3 (footnotes omitted).

Notwithstanding this progress, the study further found that when faced with external security threats, local communities admitted that they would once again resort to child recruitment and use despite knowing the practice to be a crime. In particular, the study noted the continued commission of child recruitment and use by armed groups operating in the region, particularly the FRPI, a group routinely listed in the UNSG's reports on children and armed conflict.

These findings reflect broader discussions on the operation of deterrence in relation to international crimes,[103] in particular how situations of armed conflict present very different circumstances for the calculus by perpetrators: 'deterrence is based on the essentially unproven assumption of perpetrator rationality in the chaos of massive violence, incendiary propaganda, and upended social order . . . Nor is it evident that the risk of punishment will deter people from engaging in violent behavior that they, at the time, believe is morally justifiable and perhaps even necessary.'[104]

The 2017 study concluded, 'targeting warlords for prosecutions remains necessary but insufficient. Investigations must extend to economic crimes, including targeting actors who support proxy militias whilst sitting in business, political and regional circles of power. If not, any deterrent potential of the ICC will remain limited when the root causes behind violations persist.'[105] Once again, the situation in eastern DRC demonstrates how complex conflict dynamics can persist in driving the commission of serious violations over the long term.

International prosecutions for CAC violations remain further limited to the extent that they operate on the principle of complementarity, which places the initial responsibility for pursuing judicial accountability on the shoulders of national jurisdictions. The UNSG's 2017 CAC report to the UN Security Council noted that in the DRC:

> [T]he United Nations documented the arrest of at least 15 FARDC and 5 Congolese National Police officers, including for child recruitment and use of children offences before 2016, while 41 individuals (23 FARDC, 11 Congolese National Police, 1 Mouvement du 23 mars and 6 Nyatura) received sentences ranging from three years of imprisonment to the death penalty for sexual violence against children. The Government indicated that perpetrators of sexual violence against children were sentenced in 129 instances.[106]

A 2018 report by the UNSG on children in armed conflict in the DRC further reports that two actors have since been convicted of recruitment and use, with 11 remaining in custody.[107]

Field research seeking more detail about the 11 cases of individuals in pre-trial detention for child recruitment and use cited by the UNSG proved extremely difficult. We learned from military justice and child protection actors that *some* of the individuals in custody had already been in pre-trial detention for charges related to the commission of other serious violations, prior to the addition of the charge of child recruitment and use. Having been in detention for some time already, military justice prosecutors expressed

---

[103] Smeulers 2014.
[104] Drumbl 2005: 590–91.
[105] Parmar 2017: 255.
[106] UNSC 2017: 11.
[107] UNSC 2018: 13.

uncertainty as to what extent their cases will progress. Moreover, CAC stakeholders expressed concern that other more notorious individuals currently responsible for serious violations against children, including the crime of recruitment and use of children, continue to operate with impunity.

An interesting example of how local governance dynamics can thwart accountability efforts is that of Ntabo Ntaberi Sheka. Sheka is known as the political leader of the group 'Mayi Mayi Sheka', which operates from bases in the Walikale region of North Kivu, eastern DRC. In addition to attacking and controlling mining areas, the group has been found to commit serious violations targeting children, including forced labour, abductions, recruitment and use, and sexual violence. Wanted under a Congolese arrest warrant for crimes against humanity in January 2011, Sheka was later placed on the UNSC sanctions list in November 2011. In August 2017, he surrendered to the UN peacekeeping mission, MONUSCO.[108] The UN Secretary-General's 2018 report on children and armed conflict in the DRC cited Sheka as currently being in detention.[109] During interviews, local CAC stakeholders expressed deep scepticism that the DRC government possesses the political will to pursue meaningful accountability for the crimes for which Sheka is responsible. Specifically, in the past, the DRC government has in many instances brokered deals with warlords to secure political support from their militias in exchange for posts through integration into security sector organs as well as through the use of amnesties.[110] In other instances, armed actors have managed to 'escape' from detention and remain at large.[111]

4. CONCLUSION: NEXT STEPS FOR CAC ACCOUNTABILITY

Our analysis confirms that both CAC-specific and broader accountability mechanisms for serious violations have indeed made certain progress in promoting the protection of the rights of children affected by armed conflict. However, the DRC case study demonstrates that the impact of these mechanisms has been insufficient in preventing ancillary CAC violations, particularly in relation to deeper, sustained cycles of violence perpetuated against children as a result of economic conflict drivers.

What options are available to better target these crimes and slow persistent drivers of CAC violations?

---

[108] HRW 2017.
[109] UNSC 2018: 13.
[110] ICTJ 2009; RFI 2014.
[111] Consider, for example the case of Kyungu Mutanga, known as Gidéon, a notorious militia commander operating in the former province of Katanga. Convicted by a Congolese court for having committed inter alia war crimes and crimes against humanity, Gidéon mysteriously escaped from prison with many others in 2011, only to later turn himself in in 2016 along with a contingent of his men. Gidéon presently enjoys freedom of movement with no apparent intention by the Congolese authorities to return him to prison.

4.1 Pursuing Criminal Liability for Economic Crimes in Armed Conflict

In practice, there are very few examples of cases successfully pursuing judicial accountability for economic crimes in situations of armed conflict. However, some crucial developments deserve mention.

4.1.1 Pillage

International criminal jurists continue to pursue the theoretical development around pillage as an economic crime. Traditionally, 'the term pillage covers the individual and violent taking of property in wartime; generally an unauthorized taking of property, whether private or public'.[112] Under the Elements of Crimes of the Rome Statute of the International Criminal Court, the crime of pillage includes the element that the 'perpetrator intended to deprive the owner of the property and to appropriate it for private or personal use'. However, numerous scholars (and courts) have contested this requirement.[113]

A number of civil society initiatives are underway to support prosecutions of pillage as a means to hold actors accountable for economic crimes committed in relation to illicit exploitation of natural resources.[114] Notably, amongst these initiatives has been the case against Argor, a Swiss precious metals refiner over its alleged role in processing almost three tons of illicitly mined gold from the DRC. Ultimately, the Swiss federal prosecutor decided not to pursue charges;[115] however, civil society actors nonetheless continue to advocate further efforts of this nature to build on the strategic gains from the Argor case.[116] While not related to the pursuit of economic crimes, it should be noted that the International Criminal Court convicted Germain Katanga, then commander of the FPRI militia in Ituri, for the war crime of pillage committed in February 2003 during an attack on the village of Borgoro that targeted civilian members of the Hema ethnic group.[117]

4.1.2 Corporate criminal liability

Domestic efforts have also pursued novel cases alleging corporate criminal liability for international crimes: for instance, cases against Lafarge (for alleged crimes in Syria) and Riwal (for involvement in the construction of the Wall bordering Israel and Palestine). However, cases of this nature are notoriously difficult to build. Indeed, '[t]ough requirements of personal, territorial, temporal, and subject-matter jurisdiction requirements must still be met, particularly in the context of individual corporate officers who could be investigated and prosecuted'.[118]

---

[112] Carducci 2009: 2.
[113] Specifically, Stewart argues, '[b]y restricting pillage to appropriation "for personal or private purposes," the ICC Elements of Crimes depart from the vast majority of relevant World War Two cases that condemned acts of pillage perpetrated in furtherance of the Axis war effort.' Stewart 2010: 20.
[114] See, e.g., Open Society Foundation's Conflict Awareness Project, The Pillage of Eastern Congo Gold: A Case for the Prosecution of War Crimes, November 2013.
[115] For a detailed analysis of the case and the decision of the Swiss federal prosecutor, see Stewart 2015.
[116] de Moerloose 2016.
[117] ICC, *Prosecutor v. Katanga*: [926–32].
[118] Scheffer 2016: 36. For a deeper discussion of this subject, see de Vos 2017 and Keenan 2014.

4.2 Pursuing Economic Crimes Implicating Children at the National Level

Field interviews with Congolese military justice actors emphasized ongoing challenges to pursuing accountability for actors responsible for CAC violations. Political interference, which curtails prosecutorial independence and discretion, remains the most pressing concern. An acute political crisis persists in the DRC, with current leaders and elites beholden to a complex clientelist network that extends to members of the FARDC. For this reason, pursuing FARDC members for economic crimes may be politically implausible for military justice actors despite evidence of persistent violations of the Congolese military and mining codes. Nonetheless, an internationally sponsored initiative is looking to provide much needed capacity-building support to military justice actors in the pursuit of economic crimes.[119] Interviews with stakeholders, including military justice actors, on this initiative raised a strong interest in considering strategic litigation around child rights violations, which can be more politically palatable than pursuing economic violations directly.

4.3 Towards Cohesion and Creativity on the CAC Agenda

This chapter points to numerous challenges to pursuing judicial accountability for crimes of this nature, and underscores the need for comprehensive approaches of both a judicial and non-judicial character. Unfortunately, relevant CAC prevention efforts have been undertaken without coordination across multiple initiatives. This practice has been to the detriment of approaching CAC accountability in an integrated, holistic manner that transcends the lens of child soldiers.

First, following our analysis, it is clear that the delisting mechanism should not only be conditioned on child recruitment and sexual violence but on the overall role of listed armed forces in perpetuating cycles of violations against children. Beyond the six grave violations that underlie the MRM, CAC violations such as forced labour should also be given consideration.

Second, our analysis demonstrates the lack of a cohesive approach to the prevention of CAC violations in the mining of conflict minerals. On the one hand, actors involved in improving working conditions in the artisanal mining sector have drawn attention to the practice of child labour, advanced norm-setting and pursued reporting. However, UN-sponsored accountability actors and mechanisms working in the DRC are yet to include child labour in illicit gold mining in their scope of work. The situation calls out for a forum where these separate but related threads may be intertwined.

In light of the complexity of the DRC situation, it is important to recall the recommendation of the Security Council Report's 2017 study on the CAC agenda: 'the architecture for the protection of children needs to be used more creatively. It is time to see how the information already within the children and armed conflict monitoring and reporting mechanism can be used to deal more effectively with these new challenges.'[120] We propose that the UN Working Group on Children and Armed Conflict presents a unique platform

---

[119] USIP 2016.
[120] Security Council Report 2017: 2.

through which a more cohesive and creative approach can be promoted as part of the prevention of CAC violations in the DRC.

Specifically, the Working Group is in a strong position to reach out to multiple stakeholders, including members of the donor community, national governments, child protection actors, as well as actors working on the economic crimes angle. On the donor side, the Working Group can help orientate the multiple judicial assistance and rule of law efforts to more strategic forms of litigation on CAC violations. Likewise, the Working Group presents a unique platform to influence the exercise of prosecutorial discretion by the ICC and national level actors with evidence on how to better respond to drivers of CAC violations. This extends to ongoing judicial assistance support being providing by the Department for Peacekeeping (in the DRC through the operation of Prosecution Support Cells under the auspices of MONUSCO, the UN Stabilization Mission to the DRC). To guide this work, a recommendation from 'Bridging the Accountability Gap' is useful: identify and implement 'incremental and sequential steps in accountability processes for children and armed conflict according to pre-defined and agreed benchmarks'.[121]

Regardless of the extent to which judicial and non-judicial accountability mechanisms can slow the operation of underlying drivers of CAC violations, children living in conflict-affected parts of the DRC require sustained protection and support. Simply put, the 'task of restoring the lives of war-affected children must . . . involve redress for social and economic violations, as well as for violations of children's physical well-being'.[122] Having experienced decades of continued violence and instability, the men, women and children of eastern DRC deserve continued, constructive engagement from both the international community and their national government to realize meaningful responses to peacebuilding and the reconstruction of their communities.

REFERENCED WORKS

Amnesty International 2003. 'DRC: Children at War, Creating Hope for the Future' (AI Index: AFR 62/034/2003) (8 September)
Amnesty International 2016. 'This Is What We Die For: Human Rights Abuses in the Democratic Republic of the Congo Power the Global Trade in Cobalt' (AI Index: AFR 62/3183/2016) (January)
Autesserre, S. 2012. 'Dangerous Tales: Dominant Narratives on the Congo and their Unintended Consequences' 111 *African Affairs* 202
Bueno, O. 2014. 'In Ituri, Katanga Verdict Viewed as a Limited Success' *International Justice Monitor* (21 March)
Carducci, G. 2009. 'Pillage', *Max Planck Encyclopedia of Public International Law*
Child Soldiers International 2014a. 'Briefing on the Recruitment and Use of Children in the Democratic Republic of the Congo (DRC) to the UN Security Council Working Group on Children and Armed Conflict' (31 July)
Child Soldiers International 2014b. 'US Restricts Military Assistance to Some States that Recruit and Use Children' (1 October)
Conflict Dynamics International 2011. 'Bridging the Accountability Gap' (June)
Conflict Dynamics International 2015a. 'Children in Armed Conflict Accountability Framework' (June)
Conflict Dynamics International 2015b. 'Practical Application of the CAC Accountability Framework: Case Example, Democratic Republic of Congo'

---

[121] Conflict Dynamics International 2011.
[122] Parmar 2010: 366.

Côté, G. 2014. 'Women in the Artisanal Gold Mining Sector in the Democratic Republic of Congo' (Partnership Africa Canada) (November)
CRS [Congressional Research Service] 2012. 'Conflict Minerals in Central Africa: US and International Responses' (20 July)
Cuvelier, J. and Bashwira, M. 2016. 'Women, Conflict and Public Authority in the Congo' (Rift Valley Institute PSRP Briefing Paper) (13 June)
de Moerloose, B. 2016. 'Challenging the Pillage Process: Argor-Heraeus and Gold from Ituri' (Open Society Foundations) (November)
de Vos, D. 2017. 'Corporate Criminal Accountability for International Crimes' (Just Security) (30 November)
Drumbl, M. 2005. 'Collective Violence and Individual Punishment: The Criminality of Mass Atrocity' 99 *Northwestern University Law Review* 539
Drumbl, M. 2012a. *Reimagining Child Soldiers in International Law and Policy* (Oxford: Oxford University Press)
Drumbl, M. 2012b. 'Child Soldiers and Clicktivism: Justice, Myths, and Prevention' 4 *Journal of Human Rights Practice* 481
EITI [Extractive Industries Transparency Initiative] 2017. 'Rapport ITIE RDC 2015' (December)
European Commission 2017. 'The Conflict Minerals Regulation – The Regulation Explained' (13 December)
Global Witness 2017. 'Time to Dig Deeper' (August)
Graham, L. 2017. 'Congress Must Maintain Ban on Conflict Minerals and Oppose H.R. 4248' (Amnesty International USA) (14 November)
HRW [Human Rights Watch] 2016. 'Submission on the Democratic Republic of Congo to the Committee on the Rights of the Child' (17 March)
HRW 2017. 'Congolese Warlord Wanted for Mass Rape Surrenders' (26 July)
ICC. *Prosecutor v. Katanga* (Case No. ICC-01/04-01/07) Judgment pursuant to Article 74 of the Statute (7 March 2014)
ICG [International Crisis Group] 2004. 'Back to the Brink in the Congo' *Africa Briefing* No. 21 (17 December)
ICG 2012. 'Eastern Congo: Why Stabilization Failed' *Africa Briefing* No. 91 (4 October)
ICTJ [International Center for Transitional Justice] 2009. 'RDC: Loi d'Amnistie de 2009' [available at: http://ictj.org/sites/default/files/ICTJ-DRC-Amnesty-Facts-2009-French.pdf (accessed 5 November 2018)]
ICTJ 2012. 'Judgment Denied: The Failure of Congolese Courts to Fulfill Court-Ordered Reparations for Victims of Serious Crimes in the DRC' (18 June)
IPIS [International Peace Information Service] 2012. 'The Formalisation of Artisanal Mining in the Democratic Republic of the Congo and Rwanda' (December)
IPIS 2017. '"Everything that Moves Will Be Taxed": The Political Economy of Roadblocks in North and South Kivu Roadblocks' (November)
IPIS 2018. 'Carte de l'exploitation minière artisanale dans l'Est de la RD Congo' [available at: http://ipisresearch.be/publication/interactive-map-artisanal-mining-exploitation-eastern-drcongo-2018-update/ (accessed 5 November 2018)]
IRIN 2010. 'Who's Who Among Armed Groups in the East' (15 June)
Keenan, P. 2014. 'Conflict Minerals and the Law of Pillage' 14 *Chicago Journal of International Law* Article 6
Lasley, T. and Thyne, C. 2011. 'Developments in the Study of Child Soldiers' 13 *International Studies Review* 155
Lemarchand, R. 2009. *The Dynamics of Violence in Central Africa* (Philadelphia: University of Pennsylvania Press)
Machel 1996. 'Impact of Armed Conflict on Children' (New York: United Nations) [Machel Report]
Obama, B. 2014. 'Determination with Respect to the Child Soldier Prevention Act of 2008' [Memorandum]. (Washington, DC: The White House Office of the Press Secretary) (30 September) [available at: https://obamawhitehouse.archives.gov/the-press-office/2014/09/30/presidential-memorandum-determination-respect-child-soldiers-prevention- (accessed 5 November 2018)]
OECD [Organisation for Economic Co-operation and Development] 2015. 'Mineral Supply Chains and Conflict Links in Eastern Democratic Republic of Congo' (19 November)
OECD 2017. 'Practical Actions for Companies to Identify and Address the Worst Forms of Child Labour in Mineral Supply Chains' (May)
OHCHR [Office of the High Commissioner of Human Rights] 2010. 'Democratic Republic of the Congo, 1993–2003; Report of the Mapping Exercise Documenting the Most Serious Violations of Human Rights and International Humanitarian Law Committed Within the Territory of the Democratic Republic of the Congo between March 1993 and June 2003' (April)
Parmar, S. 2010. 'Realizing Economic Justice for Children: The Role of Transitional Justice in Post-Conflict Societies', in S. Parmar, M. Roseman, S. Siegrist and T. Sowa (eds), *Children and Transitional Justice* (Human Rights Program, Harvard Law School)
Parmar, S. 2013. 'Women's Agenda Key to Stabilizing Eastern Congo' (African Arguments) (19 August)
Parmar, S. 2017. 'Dissuasive or Disappointing? Measuring the Deterrent Effect of the International Criminal

Court in the Democratic Republic of the Congo', in J. Schense and L. Carter (eds), *Two Steps Forward, One Step Back: The Deterrent Effect of International Criminal Tribunals* (Brussels: Torkel Opsahl Academic EPublisher)

RFI [Radio France Internationale] 2014. 'RDC: loi d'amnestie pour faits de guerre et infractions politiques' (4 February)

Scheffer, D. 2016. 'Corporate Liability under the Rome Statute' 57 *Harvard International Law Journal* 35

Security Council Report 2017. 'Children and Armed Conflict: Sustaining the Agenda' (27 October)

Smeulers, A. 2014. 'Preventing International Crimes' in W. de Lint, M. Marmo and N. Chazal (eds), *Criminal Justice in International Society* (Abingdon; New York: Routledge) 267

Stearns, J. et al. 2013. 'Mai-Mai Yakutumba, Resistance and Racketeering in Fizi, South Kivu' (Rift Valley Institute Usalama Project)

Stewart, J.G. 2010. 'Corporate War Crimes: Prosecuting Pillage of Natural Resources' (Open Society Foundations) (October)

Stewart, J.G. 2015. 'The Argor Heraeus Decision on Corporate Pillage of Gold' (19 October)

Tsurukawa, N., Prakash, S. and Manhart, A. 2011. 'Social Impacts of Artisanal Cobalt Mining in Katanga, Democratic Republic of Congo' (Freiburg: Öko Institut) (November)

UN Organization Stabilization Operations in the DR Congo 2017. 'MONUSCO Strongly Condemns the Persistent Violence in the Kasai Provinces' (February)

UNGoE [United Nations Security Council (Group of Experts)] 2003. 'Letter Dated 15 October 2003 from the Chairman of the Panel of Experts on the Illegal Exploitation of Natural Resources and Other Forms of Wealth of the Democratic Republic of the Congo Addressed to the Secretary-General' (UN Doc. S/2003/1027) (23 October)

UNGoE 2016a. 'Final Report of the Group of Experts on the Democratic Republic of Congo' (UN Doc S/2016/466) (23 May)

UNGoE 2016b. 'Midterm Report of the Group of Experts on the Democratic Republic of the Congo' (UN Doc. S/2016/1102) (28 December)

UNGoE 2017a. 'Final Report of the Group of Experts on the Democratic Republic of the Congo' (UN Doc S/2017/672) (10 August)

UNGoE 2017b. 'Midterm Report of the Group of Experts on the Democratic Republic of the Congo' (UN Doc S/2017/1091) (22 December)

UNGoE 2018. 'Final Report of the Group of Experts on the Democratic Republic of the Congo' (UN Doc S/2018/513) (4 June)

UNICEF and SRSG [United Nations Office of the Special Representative of the Secretary-General for Children and Armed Conflict] 2009. 'Machel Study 10-Year Strategic Review, Children and Conflict in a Changing World' (New York)

UNSC [United Nations Security Council] 2014. 'Report of the Secretary-General on Children and Armed Conflict' (UN Doc. S/2014/339) (15 May)

UNSC 2016. 'Report of the Secretary-General on Children and Armed Conflict' (UN Doc. A/70/836–S/2016/360) (20 April)

UNSC 2017. 'Report of the Secretary-General on Children and Armed Conflict' (UN Doc. S/2017/821) (24 August)

UNSC 2018. 'Children and Armed Conflict in the Democratic Republic of Congo: Report of the Secretary-General' (UN Doc. S/2018/502) (25 May)

USAID [United States Agency for International Development] 2014. 'Assessment of Human Trafficking in Artisanal Mining Towns in Eastern Democratic Republic of the Congo'

USDOL [United States Department of Labor] 2016. 'DRC: 2016 Findings on the Worst Forms of Child Labor'

USIP [United States Institute for Peace] 2016. 'Prosecuting Economic and Environmental Crimes: USIP's Work in the DRC' (1 December)

Wessells, M. 2016. 'Reintegration of Child Soldiers: The Role of Social Identity in the Recruitment and Reintegration of Child Soldiers', in S. McKeown, R. Haji and N. Ferguson (eds), *Understanding Peace and Conflict Through Social Identity Theory: Contemporary Global Perspectives* (Switzerland: Springer) 105

15. Crimes committed by child soldiers: an argument for coherence
Nikila Kaushik and Steven Freeland

Criminal justice systems around the world rest on the principle that, in order for persons to be punished and held responsible for their actions, their behaviour must have contained both physical and fault elements. The prosecution must prove that at the time of committing a criminal offence, an accused person performed a particular physical act (*actus reus*) while holding a particular state of mind (*mens rea*).

Many jurisdictions presume a lack of *mens rea* for children below a certain age by defining a minimum age of criminal responsibility. Domestic jurisdictions identify an age – usually between 10 and 14 – above which a person has the capacity to be held criminally responsible. For the most part, children between the minimum age of criminal responsibility and the age of adulthood (usually 18, but 21 in some jurisdictions) proceed in a juvenile justice system that is differentiated from the regular judicial and correctional system for adults.[1]

In international criminal law the treatment of children, including child soldiers, is less certain. International jurisprudence does not identify an accepted age at which criminal responsibility begins, nor does it clearly answer the question of whether international law recognizes any minimum age of criminal responsibility at all. In the first section of this chapter, we outline the framework of instruments that have created this uncertainty about the minimum age for recognition of international criminal responsibility.

While this uncertainty may be surprising, it does not necessarily pose an urgent problem for international lawyers. This is because of emerging acceptance of the position, at least as a matter of practice, that children under 18 will not be prosecuted for international crimes before international courts or tribunals. In section 2, we track the development of that norm. In theory, it could represent a positive and legally defensible development, and eventually pave the way for domestic jurisdictions to increase the minimum age of criminal responsibility for international crimes recognized within their own legislation.

Although we agree that this would be a desirable outcome, in section 3 we reflect on the reasons for which the *way* that the standard is developing within international law is problematic and could have a damaging impact on the development of international criminal law in the longer term. As various legislative instruments and their drafting histories show, recognition of 18 as the minimum age of criminal responsibility in international law was not a deliberate assertion of principle by lawmakers. To the contrary, it has been borne, in many cases, of a determination to avoid answering the difficult question of when child soldiers should be held criminally responsible for their actions. There appears to have

---

[1] See Freeland 2008: 28–9.

been almost accidental movement towards that position, rather than the development and acceptance of a principled human rights stance.

This is unfortunate, because the development of international criminal law should be guided by principled decisions, the theoretical implications of which have been carefully scrutinized. Preserving integrity in law making is fundamental to ensuring the place of the rule of law at the centre of any legal system.[2] In our view, this is especially important for international criminal law, a relatively young body of law.

Ad hoc law making is not to be celebrated, even if the results might appear to be sound on their face. This is fundamental to the ongoing development of international criminal law. As with any system of law, the rules of international criminal law will be continually tested and challenged in the course of prosecutions. Permitting rules that lack coherent theoretical foundations to be enshrined into international criminal law will jeopardize its continuing influence.

1. THE AGE OF CRIMINAL RESPONSIBILITY IN INTERNATIONAL CRIMINAL LAW

Uncertainty about the age at which child soldiers can be held criminally responsible for their actions emerges as a result of there being no consistent approach enshrined across instruments of international law and the rules of international courts and tribunals. Although a number of instruments are specifically directed towards regulating child soldiers, they do not, individually or together, set an authoritative and internationally accepted standard for approaching the criminal liability of child soldiers. Nor does state practice in its approach to minors more generally reveal a standard that is accepted by the majority of nations, inhibiting the crystallization of general principles of law as a source of international law on this subject. This means that, in any given case, there may not be a clear answer to whether a child soldier can be prosecuted for his or her actions.

The rules governing the liability of minors before international courts and tribunals are contained primarily in the instruments or treaties that establish those institutions. These rules are informed, in turn, by other international legal instruments and the practices of domestic jurisdictions.

1.1 International Instruments

The majority of international legal instruments dealing with child soldiers aim to regulate states' recruitment practices as they apply to young people, or deal with the criminalization of certain actions, such as conscripting or enlisting child soldiers or using child soldiers in hostilities. Others set more general standards about who falls into the category of a child, without directly dealing with questions of criminal responsibility. While these disparate standards may bear upon the development of international criminal law, for the purposes of this chapter we have focused on instruments and authorities that deal directly

---

[2] Dworkin 1977.

with the age of criminal responsibility, rather than those that deal with child soldiers more generally.[3]

The Convention on the Rights of the Child 1989 (CRC) is the most prominent instrument regulating juvenile justice. Article 40 of the CRC requires, amongst other things, that any child suspected of having committed crimes is treated in a manner that 'takes into account the child's age and the desirability of promoting the child's reintegration and the child's assuming a constructive role in society'.[4] Article 40(3) provides that states must establish distinct juvenile justice systems that do not permit capital punishment or life imprisonment without parole, and specifically requires that states establish a minimum age of criminal responsibility:

> States Parties shall seek to promote the establishment of laws, procedures, authorities and institutions specifically applicable to children alleged as, accused of, or recognised as having infringed the penal law and, in particular: (a) The establishment of a minimum age below which children shall be presumed not to have the capacity to infringe the penal law.[5]

Notably, the Convention does not go so far as to identify a specific age of criminal responsibility. That matter is left to states to determine.

Further guidance as to the standards that the drafters of Article 40 intended to create can be taken from the non-binding UN Standard Minimum Rules on the Administration of Juvenile Justice (the 'Beijing Rules') and their commentary. Article 40 of the CRC was drafted to reflect the Beijing Rules,[6] with Rule 4 directly concerning the age of criminal responsibility:

> In those legal systems recognising the concept of the age of criminal responsibility for juveniles, the beginning of that age shall not be fixed at too low an age limit, bearing in mind the facts of emotional, mental and intellectual maturity.

The commentary to Rule 4 states:

> The modern approach would be to consider whether a child can live up to the moral and psychological components of criminal responsibility; that is, whether a child, by virtue of his or her individual discernment and understanding, can be held responsible for antisocial behaviour. If the age of criminal responsibility is fixed too low or if there is no lower age limit at all, the notion of responsibility would become meaningless.

The Committee on the Rights of the Child, established to monitor states' compliance with the provisions of the CRC, has provided further insight into the substantive standard enshrined in the CRC. In concluding observations to various state reports, the Committee has stated that the absolute minimum age for criminal responsibility should be 12, commended states that have adopted the ages of 14 or 16, and approved of a Nigerian proposal to set the minimum age of criminal responsibility at 18.[7]

---

[3] For a comprehensive review, see Freeland 2008.
[4] Art. 40(1), CRC.
[5] Art. 40(3), CRC.
[6] Happold 2008: 70.
[7] CRC Committee 1995; CRC Committee 1996; Happold 2008.

1.2 Domestic Jurisdictions

The rules governing proceedings before international courts and tribunals are inevitably shaped by approaches taken within domestic jurisdictions, most directly through consistent state practice contributing to the establishment of principles of international law.

Since the early 1990s there have been a number of attempts by domestic courts to prosecute children for international crimes committed during conflict.[8] In circumstances where child soldiers are brought before domestic courts for international crimes, the domestic laws of the jurisdiction in which they were charged guide any decision to prosecute. As noted above, Article 40(3)(a) of the Convention on the Rights of the Child provides that states must seek to establish a minimum age below which a child shall be presumed not to have the capacity to infringe the criminal law. States are given a broad discretion to determine what that age should be.

While most states have complied with the obligation to identify a minimum age of criminal responsibility, there is substantial divergence between states as to what the appropriate age should be. The UK, New Zealand and most states in Australia set the minimum age of responsibility at 10 years.[9] Canada sets the minimum age at 12, France at 13, Ireland at 7, Norway and Demark at 15 and Scotland at 8.[10] In addition to recognizing a minimum age of criminal responsibility, many jurisdictions also protect a *doli incapax* presumption, in which special protections and a higher prosecutorial burden of proof apply to accused juveniles (those between the minimum age of criminal responsibility and the age of adulthood).[11]

1.3 The European Court of Human Rights (ECHR)

The European Court of Human Rights has reviewed the state of domestic laws governing the age of criminal responsibility in considering an appeal from the United Kingdom,

---

[8] Examples of such proceedings have emerged against the backdrop of the UN Security Council repeatedly condemning the use of children in conflict, and urging states to deal with the problem directly. President of the Security Council 2005.

[9] Section 50 Children and Young Persons Act 1933 (UK – England and Wales); Sections 21(1) and 21(2) Crimes Act 1961 (New Zealand); Section 4M Crimes Act 1914 (Cth) (Australia – Federal); Section 5 Children (Criminal Proceedings) Act 1987 (Australia – New South Wales); Section 344 Children, Youth and Families Act 2005 (Australia – Victoria); Section 29 Criminal Code Act Compilation Act 1913 (Australia – Western Australia).

[10] Section 13 Criminal Code (Canada); Article 122-8 Criminal Code (France); Article 14 Penal Code (Ireland); Section 46 General Civil Penal Code (Norway); Section 15 Criminal Code (Denmark); Sections 41 and 41A(1)–(2) Criminal Procedure (Scotland) Act.

[11] In Australia, for example, the recognized minimum age of criminal responsibility means that a child under 10 cannot be charged with a crime. Full criminal responsibility, however, is recognized as beginning at the age of 14. While criminal proceedings can be brought against children aged between 10 and 14, the principle of *doli incapax* operates to create a rebuttable presumption that the child does not yet have the capacity to know right from wrong. The prosecution bears the onus of rebutting the presumption, by proving that the child was able to form the requisite intent to commit a criminal act. Section 4M, Crimes Act 1914 (Cth); Div 7.1 Criminal Code (Cth).

T v. the United Kingdom and *V v. the United Kingdom*.[12] Robert Thompson and Jon Venables were 10 years old when they abducted and brutally murdered a two-year-old boy, James Bulger, who had been with his mother in a shopping centre. When they were 11, Thompson and Venables were tried in a public, adult court before a jury in the United Kingdom.[13] Although some allowances were made for the boys' age, their names and faces were released along with closed circuit television footage of the abduction. Both boys were convicted of abduction and murder and sentenced to indefinite periods of detention.

In their application to the ECHR, Thompson and Venables asserted that the UK had violated Article 3 of the European Convention on Human Rights, which prohibits torture or other degrading treatment or punishment. The ECHR approached the appeal through the question of the degree to which the UK's practice diverged from any kind of 'norm' in dealing with children charged with serious criminal offences. The Court reviewed the standard amongst member states in the Council of Europe and concluded that:

> Even if England and Wales is among the few European jurisdictions to retain a low age of criminal responsibility, the age of ten cannot be said to be so young as to differ disproportionately from the age-limit followed by other European states.[14]

The Court found that the attribution to the applicants of criminal responsibility for their acts did not violate the European Convention on Human Rights. Happold observes that by 'basing its conclusion on the lack of consensus amongst contracting States, the Court granted States a wide margin of appreciation in respect of an issue within the scope of Article 3, which is an absolute, non-derogable right'.[15]

Five judges dissented in part:

> Only four Contracting States out of forty-one are prepared to find criminal responsibility at an age as low as, or lower than, that applicable in England and Wales. We have no doubt that there is a general standard among the member States of the Council of Europe under which there is a system of relative criminal responsibility beginning at the age of thirteen or fourteen – with special court procedures for juveniles and providing for full criminal responsibility at the age of eighteen or above. . . . Even if Rule 4 of the Beijing Rules does not specify a minimum age of criminal responsibility, the very warning that the age should not be fixed too low indicates that criminal responsibility and maturity are related concepts. It is clearly the view of the vast majority of Contracting States that this kind of maturity is not present in children below the age of thirteen or fourteen.[16]

The majority's conclusion was firmly based on the wide margin of appreciation granted to national legislatures in respect of the minimum age of criminal responsibility, which revealed both the way in which these standards are decided and the considerations that might form the basis of real and meaningful disagreement between states.

---

[12] *T v. United Kingdom*, No. 24724/94 and *V v. United Kingdom*, No. 24888/94, 30 EHRR 121 (2000).
[13] *The Queen on the Application of Ralph Bulger v. The Secretary of State for the Home Department* (2001) 3 ALL E.R. 449.
[14] *T v. United Kingdom* and *V v. United Kingdom* (2000): [74].
[15] Happold 2006: 5.
[16] *T v. United Kingdom* and *V v. United Kingdom* (2000).

1.4 International Courts and Tribunals

The enabling instruments of international criminal courts and tribunals are the primary source of the international regulation of children's criminal liability for international crimes. On the whole, they offer little clarity as to whether and how to prosecute minors. This is because during the negotiation of these statutes, the question of minors' criminal responsibility was often avoided or ignored by states.

1.4.1 Rome Statute of the International Criminal Court (Rome Statute)

The Rome Statute establishing the International Criminal Court deals with children's criminal responsibility in a somewhat superficial way. Article 26 of the Statute provides: 'The Court shall have no jurisdiction over any person who was under the age of 18 at the time of the alleged commission of the offence.'

The origins and interpretation of this provision are contested. According to one view, Article 26 is a purely procedural measure.[17] That is, it is only the jurisdiction of the ICC that is excluded, leaving the prosecution of juvenile offenders to domestic courts (where permitted by the laws governing the responsibility of minors within that state).[18] Indeed, at least for some international crimes, such as genocide or grave breaches of the Geneva Conventions, states are obliged to prosecute and punish offenders.[19] Happold observes that, in circumstances where the ICC's jurisdiction is excluded by Article 26 but a prosecution would be permitted by the domestic laws of a state, states would have some scope to determine the breadth of their own international obligations by deciding what the minimum age of criminal responsibility for those offences should be.[20]

An alternative reading of Article 26 provides that the Rome Statute articulates a substantive principle of international law, which is that criminal responsibility begins at the age of 18. Advocates for this interpretation argue that the drafters of the Rome Statute negotiated Article 26 to reflect the fact that 'no one under the age of 18 was charged with any crime by any of the Nuremberg Courts' and that, as a matter of customary international law, such prosecutions should not occur.[21] This reading of Article 26 was supported by advocacy groups present at the Rome Conference where the Statute was negotiated.[22]

On balance, however, the language of the article and the drafting history of the provision suggest that no substantive decision about the minimum age of criminal responsibility was made at the Rome Conference.[23] Although the Preparatory Committee for the Rome Statute considered a range of ages (between 12 and 21) at which criminal responsibility might begin, no agreement on the issue could be reached among the delegates. The jurisdictional bar to prosecuting children under 18 appears to be the result of political compromise and disinclination to engage with the issue, rather than a substantive

---

[17] Happold 2006: 10, citing Clark and Triffterer 1999: 494.
[18] Happold 2008: 79.
[19] Art. 8, Rome Statute; art. 1, Genocide Convention.
[20] Happold 2006: 4.
[21] Paoletti 2008: 11–12, citing Clark and Triffterer 1999: 494.
[22] Happold 2008: 79.
[23] Clark and Triffterer 1999; Happold 2006; Freeland and Walther 2017: 40.

assertion about the age at which children can be held responsible for international crimes. As in other areas of international concern, the effort to create principles or standards that can be applied on a global basis saw international law proceed down a path of compromise and generalization.[24] As one of the authors has observed elsewhere, it appears that the Rome Statute has simply avoided confronting the issue of the criminal responsibility of child soldiers in a meaningful way.[25]

1.4.2 The International Criminal Tribunal for the former Yugoslavia (ICTY) and the International Criminal Tribunal for Rwanda (ICTR)

The statutes of the ICTY and ICTR did not make any specific provision for the minimum age of criminal responsibility. A 1993 Report of the UN Secretary General concerning the text of the ICTY Statute states that the Tribunal 'itself will have to decide on various personal defences which may relieve a person of individual criminal responsibility, such as minimum age or mental incapacity, drawing upon general principles of law recognised by all nations'.[26]

It has been argued that the silence of both instruments on the minimum age for criminal responsibility was deliberate, indicating that if either body sought to exercise jurisdiction over a minor, she or he could raise age as an affirmative defence.[27] That reading is not supported by the text of either statute and, as neither body has ever sought to indict a person who was under 18 at the time of offending, has not been tested.

1.4.3 The Special Panels for Serious Crimes Established by the United Nations Transitional Authority in East Timor

The legislation that governed the Special Panels operating under the UN Transitional Authority in East Timor (UNTAET) provided special protections relating to the prosecution of minors. Section 45.1 of the Transitional Rules of Criminal Procedure provided: 'A minor between 12 and 16 years of age may be prosecuted for criminal offences only in accordance with such rules as may be established in subsequent UNTAET regulations on juvenile justice.'[28]

These rules clearly contemplated the prosecution of juvenile offenders, establishing the minimum age of criminal responsibility at 12. Minors between 12 and 16 were required to be prosecuted in accordance with specific regulations on juvenile justice,[29] unless they were charged with offences constituting murder, rape or a crime of violence resulting in serious injury to the victim. Proceedings were brought against one 14-year-old, but the charge was downgraded from crimes against humanity to a domestic murder offence upon a plea being entered on the first day of trial.[30]

The age for prosecution as an adult, with full punitive consequences, was 16. The regulations provided that any prosecution of a minor over the age of 16 (i.e., between 16

---

[24] Freeland and Walther 2017: 40.
[25] Ibid.: 40.
[26] UN Secretary-General 1993: [58]; see also Holá and Bouwknegt in this volume.
[27] Paoletti 2008: 15.
[28] Section 45.1 of the UNTAET Regulation 2000/30.
[29] Ibid.
[30] See Holá and Bouwknegt in this volume with regard to this case, *Prosecutor v. 'X'*.

and 18) must 'accord with the UN Convention on the Rights of the Child, and shall consider his or her juvenile condition in every decision made in the case'.[31] That Convention, as noted above, provides that the response to crimes committed by children must take into account the 'desirability of promoting the child's reintegration and the child's assuming a constructive role in society'.[32]

1.4.4 Extraordinary Chambers in the Courts of Cambodia (ECCC)

The legislation establishing the Extraordinary Chambers was drafted with cognizance of the fact that the Pol Pot regime oversaw numerous crimes committed by children.[33] It limits the jurisdiction of the ECCC to 'those who were most responsible' for crimes committed during the period of Democratic Kampuchea.[34] Article 33 provides:

> The Extraordinary Chambers of the trial court shall exercise their jurisdiction in accordance with international standards of justice, fairness and due process of law, as set out in Articles 14 and 15 of the 1966 International Covenant on Civil and Political Rights.

Article 14(4) of the International Covenant on Civil and Political Rights provides that criminal process over minors must 'take account of their age and the desirability of promoting their rehabilitation'. The sum of these provisions has led some commentators and advocates to the conclusion that any exercise of criminal jurisdiction over minors by the court should be intended to promote rehabilitation rather than retributive punishment.[35]

1.4.5 Special Court for Sierra Leone (SCSL)

The civil war in Sierra Leone saw prominent examples of child soldiers committing acts that amounted to atrocities, which led the drafters of the SCSL Statute to devote considerable attention to the appropriateness of prosecuting child soldiers and to grapple with the challenges involved. The SCSL Statute reflects the fact that, while child soldiers may perpetrate atrocities, they are also frequently the victims of abduction, forced recruitment and sustained abuse.

In his report establishing the SCSL, the UN Secretary General acknowledged the difficulties associated with prosecuting child soldiers. He noted the disagreement within the international community about how to deal with juvenile offenders:

> It was said that the people of Sierra Leone would not look kindly upon a court which failed to bring to justice children who committed crimes of that nature and spared them the judicial process of accountability. The international non-governmental organizations responsible for child-care and rehabilitation programmes, together with some of their national counterparts, however, were unanimous in their objections to any kind of judicial accountability for children below 18 years of age for fear that such a process would place at risk the entire rehabilitation programme so painstakingly achieved.[36]

---

[31] Section 45.4 of the UNTAET Regulation 2000/30.
[32] Art. 40(1), CRC.
[33] Drumbl 2012: 84; Paoletti 2008: 12, citing Ea and Sim 2001.
[34] Art. 1, ECC Law.
[35] See, for example, Paoletti 2008: 14.
[36] UN Secretary-General 2000a: [35].

Members of the Security Council who visited Sierra Leone in 2000 reported that: 'In the view of the Government of Sierra Leone, the Court should prosecute those child combatants who freely and willingly committed indictable crimes.'[37]

Ultimately, Article 7(1) of the SCSL Statute provided that the SCSL would have jurisdiction over persons aged 15 and over at the time of commission of a crime:

> The Special Court shall have no jurisdiction over any person who was under the age of 15 at the time of the alleged commission of the crime. Should any person who was at the time of the alleged commission of the crime between 15 and 18 years of age come before the Court, he or she shall be treated with dignity and a sense of worth, taking into account his or her young age and the desirability of promoting his or her rehabilitation, reintegration into and assumption of a constructive role in society, and in accordance with international human rights standards, in particular the rights of the child.

The reason for fixing 15 as the minimum age was not made clear, but could have drawn on the provisions of Additional Protocol I to the Geneva Conventions (see next section) and the CRC.[38] The SCSL Statute makes clear that if jurisdiction is exercised over children aged between 15 and 18, juvenile offenders must be treated differently from adults, with account taken of their young age and with a focus on rehabilitation and reintegration.[39] Despite jurisdiction over minors being conferred by the terms of the Statute, there remained a general consensus amongst members of the Security Council that juvenile offenders were better dealt with in other forums, such as the Sierra Leone Truth and Reconciliation Commission.[40]

1.5 Conclusions about the Standards Created

From the instruments above, it is clear *lex lata* that no definitive minimum age of criminal responsibility for international crimes is recognized at international law. However, some tentative principles about the criminal responsibility of child soldiers can be extracted from this framework.[41]

First, the minimum age of criminal responsibility should not be so low as to result in the punishment of children for offences which they could not understand the nature or consequences of at the time of their commission.[42] Second, there seems to be some consensus about a standard minimum age of 13 to 15 – an approach summarized by the Secretary General in drafting the SCSL Statute and considered by the minority of the ECHR in the *T v. UK* and *V v. UK* cases.[43] Third, children who are accused or convicted of crimes should be treated differently to adults.[44]

Beyond these general conclusions, it remains unclear what the minimum age of criminal

---

[37] UN Secretary-General 2000b: [50].
[38] Happold 2006: 7.
[39] Art. 7(2), SCSL Statute.
[40] UN Secretary-General 2001, cited by Freeland 2008: 83.
[41] Happold 2006: 9; Freeland 2008: 31–41.
[42] Commentary to the Beijing Rules 1985.
[43] *T v. United Kingdom* and *V v. United Kingdom* (2000).
[44] Art. 40, CRC; Happold 2006: 9.

responsibility for international crimes actually is, or indeed whether international law fixes a minimum age at all. There have been attempts to attain further clarity on these questions by inferring an international minimum age of criminal responsibility from standards regulating other aspects of child soldiering. For example, it has occasionally been argued that Article 77(2) of the first Additional Protocol to the Geneva Conventions (Additional Protocol I), which states that no child under 15 is to be recruited into, or to fight in, armed forces, fixes a minimum age of criminal responsibility for war crimes at 15.[45] The rationale underlying this argument is that if a child under 15 is too young to be recruited into armed forces, then he or she is also too young to be held responsible for actions done in the context of war.

This reading of Article 77(2) conflates two separate matters – the age of recruitment and the age of criminal responsibility – and is unsupported by both the text of the Article and the intentions of the drafters.[46] By attempting to infer international standards about the minimum age of criminal responsibility through instruments that are directed towards addressing other issues, we circumvent the theoretical debate that ordinarily accompanies law making.

2. CURRENT PRACTICE

Despite the uncertainty surrounding the prosecution of child soldiers, there is remarkable consistency in international legal practice: from Nuremberg onwards, no child under 18 has been prosecuted before an international court or tribunal.[47] Although the sources above reflect varied standards, it seems that 18 is gaining traction, both politically and operationally, as the appropriate minimum age of criminal responsibility for international crimes. In Manirakiza's words, the 'dominant view' in international law is that minors who have committed serious international crimes are not legally culpable.[48] Calls for 18 to be formally recognized as the minimum age of criminal responsibility for international crimes are increasingly shaping the international legal imagination.[49]

Such a result is, perhaps, predictable. The ambition of international criminal justice is to hold to account those most responsible for mass atrocities. As a matter of common sense, this should almost never lead to the indictment of a child soldier. Further, international criminal law is at a relatively early stage in its development, resources are

---

[45] Happold 2006: 3.
[46] Happold 2006: 3. During negotiations on Additional Protocol I, the Brazilian representative proposed that art. 77(5) be amended to add the sentence 'Penal proceedings shall not be taken against, and sentence not pronounced on, persons who were under sixteen years at the time the offence was committed.' The Italian representative sought to amend it further to include a paragraph prohibiting the criminal prosecution of and conviction of a child for any offence of which, at the time of commission, he or she was too young to understand the consequences. These amendments were rejected by the Committee, which decided to leave the issue to national regulation.
[47] Though note that proceedings were initially commenced in the East Timor Special Panels in *Prosecutor v. 'X'* – see Holá and Bouwknegt in this volume.
[48] Manirakiza 2009, cited by Drumbl 2012: 133.
[49] Drumbl 2012: 135.

limited and the scale of international conflicts is vast. Commencing proceedings against persons over whom there may be doubts about culpability would be strategically unwise for prosecutors, and divert resources away from the prosecution of adults accused of similar offences. The ongoing process of international criminal justice mechanisms gaining public acceptance and support may also lead prosecutors to err away from politically divisive matters.

These considerations might explain why the ICTY and ICTR did not indict any juveniles, though their statutes did not preclude such proceedings. As noted above, specific provision was made in the SCSL Statute to permit the prosecution of persons between the ages of 15 and 18 in certain circumstances.[50] Yet, early in his tenure as the first prosecutor of the Special Court, David Crane stated that he did not intend to charge anybody for crimes committed while under the age of 18.[51] He reaffirmed his mandate to prosecute those bearing the greatest responsibility for war crimes committed during Sierra Leone's Civil War, saying 'I want to prosecute the people who forced thousands of children to commit unspeakable crimes.'[52] It is an open question whether the prosecutor's approach should be taken as an expression of his personal views and intentions while in tenure, or as a matter of international legal principle that should be taken on notice by other jurisdictions.

The approach of international courts and tribunals can be contrasted with the practice of domestic jurisdictions, where there have been a number of efforts to prosecute child soldiers for international crimes.[53] Notably, following the 1994 genocide in Rwanda, the Rwandan government sought to deal with children suspected of taking part in the genocide by applying existing provisions within Rwanda's domestic law. These laws precluded criminal responsibility for any child under 14 and made provision for the sentences imposed on any child between 14 and 18 to be mitigated to account for age. In practice, the scale of the genocide made implementation of these provisions difficult. For example, both UNICEF and the Rwandan government formed the view that it would not be in the best interests of children under 14 who were suspected of having been involved in the genocide to be released straight back into the community, leading to those children being placed in 're-education centres'. Despite ostensibly being motivated by social welfare concerns, reports emerged suggesting that the centres were akin to prisons. Following the introduction of the more informal *gacaca* jurisdictions, there were reports of children under 14, and those between 14 and 18, going through the trial procedure in the same way as adults.[54] Their age was only taken into account at the end of the process, in deciding whether to send children under 14 to re-education centres or in determining the sentences of children over 14.[55]

While similar stories do emerge from other post-conflict societies, instances of children being prosecuted for international crimes appear to be in decline – a process that may have been catalysed by the efforts of international human rights organizations.

---

[50] Art. 7(1), SCSL Statute.
[51] Special Court for Sierra Leone 2002.
[52] Ibid.
[53] Happold 2006: 1.
[54] Barrett 2014: 20–21.
[55] Ibid.

A decline is also observable in cases involving the prosecution of children for domestic offences which, by their nature, could have also amounted to international crimes. In the Democratic Republic of Congo (DRC), children have been tried under national and military law for acts of child soldiering and, in some cases, harshly sentenced.[56] In 2001, Human Rights Watch urged the DRC not to carry out death sentences that had been pronounced against four child soldiers, who were between 14 and 16 at the time that they were arrested and tried before the Court of Military Order.[57] Legislation was subsequently enacted by the DRC to prohibit children under the age of 18 being brought before military courts.[58] In 2008, the government of Sudan brought treason charges against 99 children aged between 11 and 17 for their roles in an attack on Sudanese government forces. UNICEF offered legal advice to the Sudanese government, which was factored into a presidential decree issued three months later pardoning the children.[59]

These developments may herald a trend in post-conflict societies declining to prosecute children for extraordinary international crimes. This could indicate a wider recognition of a higher age of criminal responsibility at international law, and prevent the prosecution of child soldiers for acts committed before reaching the age of 18. It is important to recognize, however, that there remain serious questions about how 'international' these attitudes actually are. As demonstrated by the drafting process of the SCSL Statute, the view that children should be prosecuted for international crimes is firmly held within some communities. In perceiving a shift in the international legal imagination towards recognizing 18 as the minimum age of criminal responsibility, it might be that we are only hearing the views of a vocal community of transnational activists concerned with these issues. Speaking generally, these groups are often well-resourced and from the Global North, representing only a fraction of the actors shaping the development of international law.

Although caution needs to be exercised in concluding that the 'international community', however conceived, is moving towards recognition of 18 as the minimum age of criminal responsibility for international crimes, there is evidence that post-conflict societies are likely to trend away from the prosecution of children for serious international crimes, and that the practice of international forums avoiding prosecutions of minors will grow more entrenched.

2.1 Origins of the Standard

For many transnational advocates and human rights organizations, emerging recognition of 18 as the standard minimum age of criminal responsibility means that there is little incentive to continue making the argument for its formal recognition in international law. There is a discernible shift amongst international lawyers towards acceptance of that standard; reviving advocacy efforts now might only serve to draw attention to its somewhat shaky origins.

Instead, human rights groups have moved towards the position that, while international

---

[56] Drumbl 2012: 176.
[57] Human Rights Watch 2001a; Human Rights Watch 2001b, cited by Happold 2006: 1.
[58] Redress Trust 2006: 28, citing Law No. 023/2002 of the Military Justice Code (DRC).
[59] Drumbl 2012: 176; UNICEF Innocenti Research Centre 2010: 14.

instruments do not consistently or unequivocally preclude the exercise of criminal jurisdiction over child soldiers in an international setting, international law nevertheless is clear that without exceptional circumstances and a clear rehabilitative intent, such prosecutions should not occur.[60] In some instances, they go so far as to suggest that it is nearly accepted, as a matter of international law, that 18 is the appropriate age for recognition of criminal responsibility for international crimes.[61]

In doing so, advocates draw selectively on aspects of the legal framework set out above. Grossman states that 'The Rome Statute and the Optional Protocol to the CRC arguably demonstrate an emerging consensus that children aged fifteen to eighteen should also be shielded from criminal liability.'[62] Machel claims that '[b]ased on the Statute of the International Criminal Court, the Special Court for Sierra Leone and the practice of the *ad hoc* tribunals, there is an emerging standard that children under eighteen should not be prosecuted by international courts and tribunals'.[63] Radhika Coomaraswamy, the former UN Special Representative for Children and Armed Conflict, has said that '[t]he UN position is that children should not be prosecuted for war crimes'.[64] David Crane has been reported to have stated that '[n]o child has the *mens rea* – the criminal mind – to commit war crimes',[65] impliedly referring to children under the age of 18.[66] It is clear that international legal instruments, particularly the Rome Statute, are being called on to play an important role in cementing emerging standards around the minimum age of criminal responsibility.

However, the historical and legal origins of these provisions are simply not robust enough to support such arguments. The contexts in which they were negotiated reveal that they were borne largely of political manoeuvring and compromise, rather than as the result of debate about when international law should recognize criminal culpability. Article 26 of the Roman Statute, in particular, resulted from a decision to ignore questions about the minimum age of criminal responsibility rather than to make any positive statement about it. Each instrument, taken in its own context, does not reflect the principles which it is being increasingly cited as creating.

This process is catalysed by the fact that standards set at international law may be absorbed into domestic law: international criminal law may play a powerful 'trendsetting role' in modelling appropriate legal standards for domestic jurisdictions.[67] Although in theory, Article 26 appears to leave open the possibility for states to prosecute alleged child perpetrators of international crimes in domestic courts,[68] it is rational for states and other international bodies to emulate the approach of the ICC to legal questions, directly incorporating its rules into their own laws.[69] The ICC represents an attractive

---

[60] See Paoletti 2008: 11.
[61] Ibid.; Grossman 2007.
[62] Grossman 2007: 8.
[63] Machel 2010.
[64] Quoted in Finn 2010.
[65] Interview with NBC quoted in Isikoff 2010; see also Crane 2008: 15.
[66] Lee 2008.
[67] Drumbl 2012: 127, citing Goodman and Jinks 2005.
[68] Clark and Triffterer 1999: 774.
[69] Drumbl 2012: 127.

and respectable international standard, despite the fact that Article 26 emerged from a disinclination to formulate substantive rules. In this environment, any attempt by a state to prosecute a minor for international offences would undoubtedly lead to criticism from human rights groups.

As readers will appreciate, the way in which the norms of international law are developed and crystallized means that this process will lead, albeit slowly, to political compromises becoming substantive law.[70] That process is already visible. In 2009, Human Rights Watch decried attempts by Bangladesh to enact legislation that would allow juveniles to be tried for war crimes, referring to Article 26 of the Rome Statute and recommending that Bangladesh introduce a 'similar provision' into its domestic legislation.[71] The Paris Principles, which elaborate on the Commitments initially endorsed by 58 states at the 2007 'Free Children From War' conference,[72] include the provision that '[c]hildren should not be prosecuted by an international court or tribunal', and explicitly cite Article 26.[73] The Principles go on to provide, in respect of national prosecutions, that 'all relevant international laws and standards must be respected, with due consideration to the defendants' status as children' and that 'alternatives to judicial proceedings should be sought for children at the national level'.[74]

2.2 Reflections on the Emerging Standard

While the foundations of these standards might be questioned, the emerging consensus that children under 18 will not be prosecuted for international crimes before international courts and tribunals might nevertheless be a positive and defensible development. It is uncontroversial that children who are recruited, conscripted or enlisted into armed forces suffer as the victims of crimes, including international crimes. This is a matter that looms large in the international legal imagination, because it is well known that child soldiers endure horrific violence, indoctrination and abuse, due in part to their 'attractiveness' as recruits. Children can be intimidated and moulded relatively easily, and child soldiers can be more quickly trained than adults to perform dangerous and brutal tasks through sheer manipulation, and often under the influence of drugs or alcohol.[75]

In the context of questions about criminal responsibility, those factors would appear to support strong cases to mitigate the sentences of young offenders – circumstances of abuse and deprivation are routinely taken into account in sentencing children before domestic courts.[76] But the increasingly accepted stance of the international advocacy community goes beyond any suggestion that a child's background and experiences will reduce criminal culpability. Instead, the argument is that a child's background and

---

[70] Ibid.: 121.
[71] Human Rights Watch 2009.
[72] Conference held on 5 and 6 February 2008, co-hosted by the French government and UNICEF.
[73] Paris Principle 8.6.
[74] Paris Principle 8.9.
[75] Freeland 2008: 26.
[76] Drumbl 2016: 21, citing Delgado 1985.

experiences should operate as a complete defence, or a bar to the commencement of a prosecution.

Drumbl comments on this position, recognizing that international criminal law offers a 'clumsy fit with the etiology of collective violence and organizational massacre', incapable of responding to the complexity of modern-day and future armed conflicts.[77] At a more practical level, it has been observed that international criminal justice institutions simply lack the resources and scope to prosecute child soldiers.[78] The current state of international institutions, and as Drumbl argues, the state of the international legal imagination, means that the prosecution of child soldiers is seen by activists as 'unimportant, embarrassing and unhelpful'.[79]

But putting practical considerations to one side, it is difficult to see why, as a matter of principle, children who commit crimes at international law should be treated differently to their domestic counterparts. It has been argued that the *mens rea* for international crimes is more complex than for domestic offences, and that children are prima facie unable to form the requisite intent to commit international crimes.[80] That is not consistently true of all international crimes, and, as Happold argues, is a matter that goes to proof, rather than principle.[81] It might also be observed that the circumstances of abuse that child soldiers experience in the course of their recruitment and indoctrination into armed forces are difficult to separate from acts that they commit as part of those same armed forces. By comparison, it might appear easier to separate a domestic juvenile offender's background from his or her crimes. Again, this does not support a principled difference in approach. Drumbl has raised penetrating questions about the reliability of our suspicions that the circumstances of child soldiers, as faultless victims of distant broken societies, are relevantly different to the perceived 'aberrant delinquent' youth who emerges from a 'blameworthy, dysfunctional family' within an 'otherwise salutary' Western community.[82]

Indeed, although children are routinely prosecuted in domestic jurisdictions for serious offences, there is growing recognition amongst advocates and commentators in domestic settings that *all* children who commit serious crimes have been failed by society at some level.[83] Increasing acceptance of sociological and neurobiological evidence suggests that young offenders should be treated as victims by default. Such findings are slowly reversing the tendency of observers to assume that the criminal behaviour of Western 'delinquents' is the product of rational choice alone and cannot be traced back to their social environments.[84] That understanding has also been referred to by the Committee on the Rights of the Child, which frequently vets states' criminal law regimes against the requirement in

---

[77] Drumbl 2012: 127.
[78] Crane 2008.
[79] Drumbl 2012: 127.
[80] Happold 2006: 2.
[81] Ibid.: 4.
[82] Drumbl 2012: 128.
[83] For example in Australia, a recent Royal Commission into a notorious juvenile detention facility, Don Dale, drew attention to the fact that 80% of girls in prison had been victims of sexual or physical abuse. A 2009 survey of young people in custody in New South Wales found that 81% of girls had a reported history of child abuse, 92% were reported to have two or more psychological disorders and 23% had attempted suicide.
[84] Justice Health New South Wales 2009.

the Beijing Rules that children are prosecuted only where they 'can live up to the moral and psychological components of criminal responsibility'.[85] As noted earlier, while the Committee has not expressed a firm view, it has indicated that 14 is an appropriate age for recognizing criminal responsibility, and suggested that limiting the prosecution of offenders under 18 is consistent with human rights norms.[86]

2.3 Looking Forward

The push towards recognizing 18 as the minimum age of criminal responsibility at international law for international crimes has not been the result of a deliberate decision by the international community to protect human rights norms. To date, these conversations have regrettably been more jurisdictional than jurisprudential, and the arguments surrounding the appropriate age for recognition of criminal responsibility have barely been ventilated on the international stage at all. We urge the development of a rigorous jurisprudence. It is not enough to wait for these norms to quietly become part of international criminal law without the international community grappling with the values underlying them.

In the remainder of this chapter, we argue that the theoretical uncertainty underlying the emerging norm of criminal responsibility beginning at the age of 18 is in itself problematic. Permitting substantive rules of international criminal law to be developed from a jurisdictional limitation risks a degree of irregularity and malleability being folded into our approach to the difficult questions surrounding the culpability of child soldiers. In our view, it is important for both lawmakers and practitioners to engage squarely with the difficult questions surrounding the criminal responsibility of child soldiers, before asserting that 18 is the agreed standard. Failure to do so risks standards that are not deliberate being folded into our laws. As stated earlier, there is no value in an ad hoc approach to law making.

We agree that in almost all cases there will be a human rights imperative to protect child soldiers as victims of conflict, and little imperative to prosecute them for their actions before an international court or tribunal. Nevertheless, the gaps in the reasoning underpinning that view are dangerous and could ultimately lead to the *under*-protection of child soldiers' status as victims. In the following section, we explore two particular ways in which the development of this part of international criminal law is already falling short.

3. THE ARGUMENT FOR COHERENCE

The theoretical gaps that have been incorporated into the current legal regime have been revealed in some troubling features of the international response to child soldiering. At present, the only way in which international criminal courts consider acts perpetrated by child soldiers is through the clumsy (in our view) framework of offences committed by those who recruit, enlist or use child soldiers in hostilities. The result of this indirect approach is that an incomplete picture of child soldiers' experiences is created in two

---

[85] Commentary to the Beijing Rules 1985.
[86] CRC Committee 1995; CRC Committee 1996; Happold 2008.

Crimes committed by child soldiers: an argument for coherence 341

distinct ways: first, the narrative that emerges about child soldiers as victims is excessively simplistic and fails to acknowledge children's agency; and second, any inquiry into the acts perpetrated by child soldiers themselves is perfunctory and unsatisfying for the victims, who may themselves be children.

Inquiry into these failings calls for the fundamental aspirations of international criminal justice to be revisited to ensure that they are being developed in a principled way. In the discussion below, we adopt the word 'coherence' to capture this approach.

3.1 Child Soldiers as Victims

The current disinclination to prosecute child soldiers is built, at least in part, on the premise that child soldiers are exclusively the victims of international crimes. These narratives were cemented during the *Lubanga* trial, in which the former ICC prosecutor Luis Moreno-Ocampo argued that Lubanga 'stole the childhood of the victims by forcing them to kill and rape'.[87] In Moreno-Ocampo's words, Lubanga 'victimised children before they ever had the chance to grow up into full human beings, who could make their own decisions'.[88]

The two-dimensionality of this approach, and the failure to grapple with the full complexity of child soldiers' actions and experiences, have seen our understanding of child soldiers become dangerously simplified. Drumbl has compellingly argued that the perception of child soldiers as helpless, passive victims is incomplete and misleading.[89] That perception is reinforced by the fact that child soldiers' experiences and conduct are generally only considered in the somewhat removed context of prosecuting their recruiters. Drumbl's call for a renewed approach to child soldiers and recognition of their agency and resilience is gaining increasing traction amongst international lawyers. We welcome this development.

A second damaging consequence of simplified, one-sided depictions of child soldiers, however, is in their failure to capture the full extent of child soldiers' victimhood. This is particularly true of the approach taken by the ICC in *Lubanga*. The case has been characterized as a 'thematic prosecution', with a narrow focus on the recruitment and use of child soldiers in particular contexts.[90] Lubanga was found guilty of conscripting and enlisting children under the age of 15 into armed forces or groups and using them to participate actively in hostilities between early September 2002 and 13 August 2003. Jorgensen observes that this was only a thin slice of his offending, which did not include, in her words, the 'killings or violations of physical integrity, such as torture or rape, that have characterized the conflict in which he was an actor'.[91] Notably, the Court did not determine whether rape, sexual slavery and forced marriage could properly be included within the offence of using children under the age of 15 to participate actively in hostilities. As a result, the victimhood of the child soldiers who Lubanga conscripted

---

[87] Moreno-Ocampo 2009.
[88] Ibid.
[89] Drumbl 2012: 58.
[90] Jorgensen 2012: 659, citing Bergsmo and Cheah 2012: 2.
[91] Jorgensen 2012: 659.

and enlisted was explored narrowly, encompassing only a portion of their suffering and its impact on their lives.

This approach can be contrasted with that taken by the SCSL, which oversaw numerous prosecutions under Article 4(c) of the Statute, as well as separate charges mentioning both women and girls who had been victims of rape, sexual slavery and/or forced marriage, with the latter recognized as a crime against humanity.[92] The prosecutorial strategy of bringing multiple charges allowed for a more complete picture of the fate of child soldiers to emerge.[93] Additionally, more complete accounts of the actions that child soldiers were forced to perpetrate were brought before the Court.

The ICC's approach might be explained, as Jorgensen suggests, by the fact that the Court is not primarily concerned with creating a historical record of a conflict. Given the nature and workload of the ICC, focused indictments may be completely defensible. However, a serious consequence of the failure to capture the extent of child soldiers' participation in conflict, as both perpetrators and victims, is that little action results for the child soldiers themselves. Their exclusion from the frameworks of liability and limited recognition as victims allow the international community to sideline and ignore their experiences.[94] This is a damaging result. The *Lubanga* reparations judgment failed to adequately support transitional justice ventures to facilitate the reintegration of former child soldiers, despite allowing them procedural recognition as victims.

In our view, a path towards addressing these gaps lies in richer narratives of child soldiers being brought into the framework of international criminal justice. This need not, and should not, involve full criminal trials of child soldiers, but might take the form of a mechanism for hearing about the extent of their participation in a conflict and for recognizing the impact of those actions on both the children and their communities. This view aligns with the growing acceptance within domestic jurisdictions in some parts of the world that incarceration and punishment are inappropriate responses to juvenile offending generally, and that rehabilitation and reintegration programmes are fundamental to ensuring that child soldiers become productive and functional members of their communities.

The SCSL Statute (excerpted above) might most closely model this approach. The Statute provides limited jurisdiction in respect of persons who are aged 15 and under, and does not allow juvenile offenders to be incarcerated.[95] Instead, it provides that the SCSL may 'order any of the following: care guidance and supervision orders, community service orders, counselling, foster care, correctional, educational and vocational training programmes, approved schools and, as appropriate, any programmes of disarmament, demobilization and reintegration or programmes of child protection agencies'.[96]

Such procedures would have the function of ensuring formal recognition of crimes committed by child soldiers, and processes created and enforced to ensure that all child soldiers are consistently diverted into rehabilitation programmes. However, in practice, the SCSL's approach converged with the formal law of the ICC, with the Court deliber-

---

[92] See also Oosterveld in this volume.
[93] Jorgensen 2012: 659.
[94] See Holá and Bouwknegt in this volume.
[95] Art. 19 SCSL Statute.
[96] Art. 7, SCSL Statute.

ately avoiding the prosecution of any person under the age of 18.[97] This highlights the importance of creating laws built on comprehensive theoretical foundations, so that their consistency with human rights agendas is not re-litigated each time they are applied. In the longer term, stating these principles clearly will promote reliability in approaches to child soldiers who commit international crimes.

Considering the actions of child soldiers through the lens of prosecuting those responsible for their recruitment or enlistment will almost always lead to a one-dimensional, simplistic and incomplete picture of their experiences being formed. In Drumbl's words, justice for child soldiers will need to go beyond 'sporadic criminal convictions of stigmatised adult recruiters'.[98] Until structures are put in place to consistently divert children into a forum where their experiences are recognized and responded to, no complete understanding of their acts will be formed. This need not happen in a criminal setting and, in our view, is better placed in an environment that is focused solely on rehabilitation and reintegration, and not on retribution or punishment. But until that occurs, any suggestion that simply excluding criminal liability for persons aged under 18 protects and promotes human rights norms is false.

3.2 The Experiences of Victims of Crimes Committed by Child Soldiers

A second troubling consequence of a simplistic understanding of child soldiers lies in the plight of the victims of acts perpetrated by child soldiers.

The Rome Statute makes provision for the victims of crimes to access reparations, either through an order against a convicted person or through a separate Trust Fund for Victims.[99] The Statute also provides for the victims of offences to give evidence of the atrocities perpetrated against them.[100]

The determination of who falls into the category of a victim in proceedings involving child soldiers is contested.[101] During the *Lubanga* proceedings, applications to participate in the trial were submitted by victims of child soldiers' actions during conflict. The Office of the Prosecutor supported these applications, on the basis that the applicants could be considered 'indirect' victims, having suffered harm as a result of the harm suffered by 'direct victims' – the child soldiers.[102] Defence counsel opposed the application, arguing that 'the commission of war crimes, crimes against humanity or acts of genocide cannot be considered to be the normal or natural consequences of participation in hostilities, whether or not the combatants are children below the age of fifteen'.[103]

Trial Chamber I ruled that victims of child soldiers' actions could not be recognized as such for the purpose of participating in the criminal proceedings.[104] The child soldiers themselves, the Chamber declared, were the only recognized victims. The Court referred

---

[97] See Isikoff 2010.
[98] Drumbl 2012: 112.
[99] Arts 75 and 79, Rome Statute.
[100] Art. 68, Rome Statute.
[101] ICC, *Prosecutor v. Lubanga* 2009.
[102] Ibid.; Jorgensen 2012: 673.
[103] ICC, *Prosecutor v. Lubanga* 2009.
[104] Ibid.: [2].

to Additional Protocol I and the CRC in holding that the offences charged against Lubanga were clearly framed to protect the interests of the children he recruited.[105]

The Trial Chamber considered the class of indirect victims, and held that they 'must establish that as a result of their relationship with the direct victim, the loss, injury or damage suffered by the latter gives rise to harm to them', before stating:

> Excluded from the category of 'indirect victims' ... are those who suffered harm as a result of the (later) **conduct** of direct victims ... Indirect victims ... are restricted to those whose harm is linked to the *harm* of the affected children when the confirmed offences were committed, not those whose harm is linked to any subsequent conduct by the children, criminal or otherwise ... [T]he person attacked by a child soldier is not an indirect victim for these purposes because his or her loss is not linked to the *harm* inflicted on the child when the offence was committed.[106]

The category of 'indirect victims' has been interpreted to include those with close personal relationships to child soldiers, such as their parents. That approach renders the victims of violent crimes committed by child soldiers, in Jorgensen's word, 'invisible'.[107] Many of these victims face a tenuous future, especially in cases involving sexual offences. Without acknowledgment of their experiences and accountability for offences perpetrated against them, the path to social reintegration for women and girls who were raped and forced into marriages, as well as for any children that they had, is even more precarious.[108]

3.3 The Problems with Incoherence

The importance of a principled, theoretically sound approach to the development of international criminal law, particularly in these relatively early years, is demonstrated by commentary surrounding the prosecution of Dominic Ongwen. Ongwen is currently being tried by the ICC for 70 counts of war crimes and crimes against humanity that he is alleged to have committed as an adult (over the age of 18).[109] However, Ongwen was himself a child soldier, abducted at the age of nine and forcibly recruited into the LRA.

These issues were recently considered by the Trial Chamber in the context of questions raised about Ongwen's mental health. In response to a notice filed by Ongwen's lawyers in 2016,[110] the prosecution called expert psychiatrists to testify about Ongwen's mental health and development. Their evidence has been closely linked to Ongwen's past as a child soldier, with one expert stating that the Court should take into consideration the fact that Ongwen was abducted as a child and developed in a 'toxic' environment.[111] The expert stated that 'there are indications that Mr Ongwen beat all the odds just like a child who lives in a very adverse situation and thrives ... many things led to his resilience, and

---

[105] Ibid.: [48].
[106] Ibid.: [52] (original emphases).
[107] Jorgensen 2012.
[108] Drumbl 2016: 20; Natukunda 2018: 4; see also Denov in this volume
[109] See Ramos in this volume.
[110] ICC, *Prosecutor v Ongwen* 2016.
[111] International Justice Monitor 2018.

I am wondering whether this resilience should be punished'.[112] She went on to say, in response to a question about the impact of growing up in the LRA: 'I really do not want to make a general statement because I have seen children who have been in this kind of situation and that have had a gross impact on their mental health, and there are those who have coped.'[113]

Against this backdrop, commentators have pointed to the illogicality of drawing a line in the sand between actions that a child commits up to the stroke of midnight on his 18th birthday and anything that he does after that date.[114] Drumbl describes this as a 'bright chronological line' demarcating criminal responsibility, which highlights the unrealistic distinction between the 'child purposelessness [and the] adult purposefulness' that international criminal law ascribes to actors.[115] One of the authors of this chapter has considered at length the ways in which childhood is defined between societies and observed that meaning is stripped from the notion if it is defined only in terms of age.[116]

Such compromise and artificiality is an inevitable feature of any legal system. Leaving aside the impossible (though laudable) goal of dealing with every situation on a case-by-case basis that fully accounts for the specific circumstances and culpability of the child concerned, at some point, generalizations must be made. Those 'bright lines' aim to reflect the reality in most cases. While domestic jurisdictions tend to draw these lines to suggest that children accrue criminal responsibility somewhere between the ages of 10 and 16, it is inevitable that some children could be held criminally responsible for their actions before that age, while others should not be subjected to a criminal trial even after reaching the age of criminal responsibility.

The sheer scale of the child soldier problem and the various categories of children who fall within the umbrella of the term suggest that any compromise struck will always be less appropriately tailored than the approach taken within domestic jurisdictions. This is because broader brush strokes are required to accommodate the variation within the child soldiering problem and its features in different jurisdictions. Even accepting that, however, the line drawn by Article 26 is not appropriate. The compromise it strikes is unaligned with the approach taken by almost any domestic jurisdiction to the issue – it by no means represents the reconciliation of competing, justifiable approaches. Nor does it reflect the increasingly mainstream position that, in order to protect the fundamental rights of children, no person under 18 should be held criminally responsible for international crimes. Rather, it is based on the presumption that criminal responsibility will accrue at some age below 18, and instead of attempting to agree on the precise age, the age of 18 was chosen to sit above the disagreement.

It is desirable for a theoretically coherent position to be adopted at international law, particularly in light of the way in which the Rome Statute's jurisdictional exclusion configures advocacy efforts and, in turn, helps mould the international legal imagination. Gaps within the legal order are created by the failure to inquire into the theoretical justification

---

[112] Ibid.
[113] Ibid.
[114] Kennedy 2016; Freeland and Walther 2017: 42.
[115] Drumbl 2012: 92.
[116] Freeland 2008.

for rules. As we saw earlier, this has resulted in human rights groups adopting the Rome Statute as a signal of the legal response to the problem, and inferring from it that states, too, should not be prosecuting child soldiers. Yet Article 26 does not bar the prosecution of child soldiers in national courts,[117] and it is not clear whether the framers of the Rome Statute intended for domestic courts to prosecute children – as defined within their own laws – suspected of committing international crimes. Indeed, as observed above, at least for some international crimes there is an obligation on states to prosecute offenders, arguably including those below the age of 18.[118]

The danger of incorporating such foundational lapses into international law lies in the way in which these rules can be harnessed in support of political agendas. It is easy to imagine such ambiguities in the theoretical foundations of the prosecution of minors being identified and hijacked by advocates with a more damaging agenda. Laws resting on uncertain foundations become so malleable as to fail to protect those who need them the most – a phenomenon that is, sadly, observable today in the treatment of children suspected of terrorism offences.[119]

3.4 The Future

The endurance of international criminal law will be determined, at some level, by how it responds to complex legal and political challenges, including those discussed above. We believe that if international criminal law is to continue developing into a stable and relevant pillar of the international justice system, it needs to respond coherently and steadily to those challenges.

International criminal law offers a framework by which to understand the international order. It promises that no matter where a conflict occurs or how powerful the players involved, justice will be done and impunity not tolerated.

The negotiation of the Rome Statute was a landmark in the pursuit of these principles, and the ambitions of international lawyers for this field can be detected in its preamble:

> Affirming that the most serious crimes of concern to the international community as a whole must not go unpunished and that their effective prosecution must be ensured by taking measures at the national level and by enhancing international cooperation,
> Determined to put an end to impunity for the perpetrators of these crimes and thus to contribute to the prevention of such crimes.[120]

Undoubtedly, these outcomes could never have been achieved in one fell swoop. The politics of the international order and questions of resources and logistics mean that there will need to be an ongoing process of persuasion and acceptance of this order by states. That process is underway. But the aspiration of international criminal law – to become as fundamental to the international legal order as any domestic criminal justice system is

---

[117] Clarke and Triffterer 1999: 33.
[118] Art. 1, Genocide Convention.
[119] See Casey-Maslen in this volume.
[120] Preamble to the Rome Statute.

to a state – can be seen from its inception and should remain relevant to how we seek to develop it today.

4. CONCLUSION

Before attempting to identify the appropriate mechanisms and forums for dealing with child soldiers, the international community needs to answer two questions at the heart of the uncertainty surrounding the prosecution of children. Should international criminal law recognize a minimum age of criminal responsibility, and, if so, what should that age be?

As Happold observes, there are good reasons for regulating the minimum age of criminal responsibility for international crimes at the international level rather than leaving it to each state to prosecute child soldiers according to their own standards for criminal responsibility.[121] Most clearly, international crimes are of concern to the international community and often transcend national borders, so states' responses should be consistent. A defendant's culpability under international law should not hinge on venue.

Turning to the second question, the current policy push towards recognizing 18 as the minimum age of criminal responsibility for international crimes before international institutions, without any substantial contest about the merits of that position, needs to be approached with caution.[122] If acceptance of that standard was instead based on recognition of the fact that children who commit international crimes are likely, at some level, to themselves be victims, productive steps could be taken to recognize their experiences, and those of their victims, without resorting to a full trial before an international criminal court or tribunal. For example, diverting child perpetrators of atrocities into rehabilitation and reintegration programmes that operate with the predictability of criminal justice mechanisms would promote human rights norms more widely by recognizing, instead of overlooking, their experiences and actions.

The rules and principles of any system of law will be repeatedly tested and challenged, no matter how long-standing they are. That is the right of any accused person and the source of our comfort in the rule of law. It is important that, from the outset, international criminal law is capable of withstanding those challenges. Principled law making is fundamental to the longevity and continued relevance of international criminal justice and its effectiveness as a response to atrocities.

REFERENCED WORKS

Barrett, J.C. 2014. 'What a Difference a Day Makes: Young Perpetrators of Genocide in Rwanda' *University of Cambridge Faculty of Law Research Paper* 24/2014

Bergsmo, M. and Cheah, W.L. 2012. 'Towards Rational Thematic Prosecution and the Challenge of International Sex Crimes', in M. Bergsmo (ed.), *The Thematic Prosecution of International Sex Crimes* (Beijing: Torkel Opsahl Academic EPublisher) 2

Child Rights International Network 2008. 'Minimum Ages of Criminal Responsibility Around the World' [available at: https://www.crin.org/en/home/ages (accessed 16 November 2018)]

---

[121] Happold 2006: 4.
[122] See Rosen in this volume; Akello in this volume.

Clark, R. and Triffterer, O. 1999. 'Article 26: Exclusion of Jurisdiction over Persons under Eighteen', in O. Triffterer (ed.), *Commentary on the Rome Statute of the ICC: Observers' Notes, Article by Article* (Oxford: Hart Publishing) 494

Crane, D. 2008. 'Prosecuting Children in Times of Conflict: The West African Experience' 15 *Human Rights Brief* 3

CRC Committee [Committee on the Rights of the Child] 1995. 'Concluding Observations on the United Kingdom's Initial Report' (UN Doc. CRC/C/15/Add.34) (15 February)

CRC Committee 1996. 'Concluding Observations of the Committee on the Rights of the Child, Nigeria' (UN Doc. CRC/C/15/Add.61) (30 October)

Delgado, R. 1985. '"Rotten Social Background": Should the Criminal Law Recognize a Defense of Severe Environmental Deprivation' 3 *Law and Inequality* 9

Drumbl, M. 2012. *Reimagining Child Soldiers* (New York: Oxford University Press)

Drumbl, M. 2016. 'Victims Who Victimize: Transcending International Criminal Law's Binaries' *Washington & Lee Public Legal Studies Research Paper* 2

Dworkin, R. 1977. *Taking Rights Seriously* (Cambridge, MA: Harvard University Press)

Ea, M. and Sim, S. 2001. 'Victims and Perpetrators – The Testimony of Young Khmer Rouge Cadres at S-21' (Phnom Penh: Documentation Center of Cambodia)

Finn, P. 2010. 'Former Boy Soldier, Youngest Guantanamo Detainee, Heads Toward Military Tribunal', *Washington Post* (10 February)

Freeland, S. 2008. 'Mere Children or Weapons of War – Child Soldiers and International Law' 29 *University of La Verne Law Review* 19

Freeland, S. and Walther, P. 2017. 'Reimagining the Unimaginable? Reflections on Mark A. Drumbl's Vision of Child Soldiers' 11 *Criminal Law and Philosophy* 40

Goodman, R. and Jinks, D. 2005. 'International Law and State Socialisation: Conceptual, Empirical and Normative Challenges' 54 *Duke Law Journal* 983

Grossman, N. 2007. 'Rehabilitation or Revenge: Prosecuting Child Soldiers for Human Rights Violations' 38 *Georgetown Journal of International Law* 342

Happold, M. 2006 'The Age of Criminal Responsibility in International Criminal Law' [available at: http://ssrn.com/abstract=934567 (accessed 16 November 2018)]; final version in K. Arts and V. Popovski (eds) *International Criminal Accountability and Children's Rights* (The Hague: T.M.C. Asser Press)

Happold, M. 2008. 'Child Soldiers: Victims or Perpetrators?' 29 *University of La Verne Law Review* 56

Human Rights Watch 2001a. 'Congo: Don't Execute Child Soldiers – Four Children to be Put to Death' (2 May) [available at: https://www.hrw.org/news/2001/05/02/congo-dont-execute-child-soldiers (accessed 28 November 2018)]

Human Rights Watch 2001b. 'Congo Spares Child Soldiers' (31 May) [available at: https://www.hrw.org/news/2001/05/31/congo-spares-child-soldiers-0 (accessed 28 November 2018)]

Human Rights Watch 2009. 'Letter to Prime Minister Sheikh Hasina Re: International Crimes (Tribunals) Act' (8 July) [available at: https://www.hrw.org/news/2009/07/08/letter-prime-minister-sheikh-hasina-re-international-crimes-tribunals-act (accessed 28 November 2018)]

ICC, *Prosecutor v. Thomas Lubanga Dyilo* (Case No. ICC-01/04-01/06), Redacted Version of 'Decision on "Indirect Victims"' (8 April 2009)

ICC, *Prosecutor v. Dominic Ongwen* (Case No. ICC-02/04-01/15), Public Redacted Version of "Defence Request for a Stay of Proceedings and Examinations Pursuant to Rule 135 of the Rules of Procedure and Evidence" (5 December 2016)

International Justice Monitor 2018. 'Psychiatrist Says Ongwen's 'Resilience' Should be Taken into Account when ICC Considers Judgement' (13 April)

Isikoff, M. 2010. 'Landmark Gitmo Trial Puts White House in Tight Spot', *NBC News* (10 August)

Jorgensen, N. 2012. 'Child Soldiers and the Parameters of International Criminal Law' 11 *Chinese Journal of International Law* 657

Justice Health New South Wales 2009. 'NSW Young People in Custody Health Survey'

Kennedy, M. 2016 'Former Child Soldier Denies War Crimes in Trial at the International Criminal Court' *NPR* (6 December)

Lee, J. 2008 'Children as Terrorists: Wrong to Train, Wrong to Charge' *Jurist* [available at: https://www.jurist.org/commentary/2008/02/children-as-terrorists-wrong-to-train/ (accessed 19 November 2018)]

Machel, G. 2010. 'Foreword', in S. Parmar, M.J. Roseman, S. Siegrist and T. Sowa (eds), *Children and Transitional Justice: Truth-Telling, Accountability and Reconciliation* (Cambridge, MA: UNICEF; Harvard Law School)

Manirakiza, P. 2009. 'Les enfants face au système international de justice: à la recherche d'un modèle de justice pénale internationale pour les délinquants mineurs' 34 *Queens Law Journal* 719

Marmor, A. 1991. 'Coherence, Holism and Interpretation' 10 *Law and Philosophy* 383

Moreno-Ocampo, L. 2009. 'Opening Statement in Situation in the Democratic Republic of the Congo in the Case of *Prosecutor v Thomas Lubanga Dyilo*' (Case No. ICC-01/04-01/06)

Natukunda, C. 2018. 'Northern Uganda War Victims Face Stigma', *New Vision* (20 March)

Paoletti, S.H. 2008. 'Amicus Brief Filed by Sarah H. Paoletti on behalf of Canadian Parliamentarians and Law Professors, International Law Scholars with Specific Expertise in the Area of International Humanitarian Law, International Criminal Law and International Human Rights Law, and Foreign Legal Associations' in US Military Commission, *United States of America v. Omar Khadr* (18 January) [available at: https://www.law.utoronto.ca/documents/Mackin/khadr_Amicus%20Brief_080118.pdf (accessed 28 November 2018)]

President of the Security Council 2005. 'Statement in relation to children and armed conflict' (UN Doc. S/PRST/2005/8) (23 February)

Redress Trust 2006. 'Victims, Perpetrators or Heroes? Child Soldiers before the International Criminal Court' 1

Special Court for Sierra Leone 2002. 'Press Release: Special Court Prosecutor Says He Will Not Prosecute Children' (Public Affairs Office) (2 November)

Special Panel for Serious Crimes, East Timor, *Prosecutor v. 'X'* (Case No. 04/2002) Judgment (2 December 2002) [available at: https://www.ocf.berkeley.edu/~wcsc/wp-content/uploads/ET-Docs/CE-SPSC%20Final%20Decisions/2002/04-2002%20%20X%20%20Judgment.pdf]

T v. United Kingdom, No. 24724/94 and *V v. United Kingdom*, No. 24888/94, 30 EHRR 121 (2000)

UN Secretary-General 1993. 'Report pursuant to para 2 of SC Resolution No. 808' (UN Doc S/25704) (3 May)

UN Secretary-General 2000a. 'Report of the Secretary-General on the establishment of a Special Court for Sierra Leone' (UN Doc. S/2000/915) (4 October)

UN Secretary-General 2000b. 'Report of the Security Council mission to Sierra Leone 2000' (UN Doc. S/2000/992) (16 October)

UN Secretary-General 2001. 'Letter Dated Jan. 12 2001 from the Secretary-General addressed to the President of the Security Council' (UN Doc. S/2001/40) (12 January)

UNICEF Innocenti Research Centre 2010. 'Children and Truth Commissions' (prepared in cooperation with the International Centre for Transitional Justice)

16. Child soldiers in international courtrooms: unqualified perpetrators, erratic witnesses and irreparable victims?
*Barbora Holá and Thijs B. Bouwknegt**

International criminal trials are performative and didactic acts dealing with perpetrators and victims of international atrocity crimes. Offences perpetrated by and against child soldiers have repeatedly been litigated in both international and internationalized courtrooms. In this chapter, we focus on the Special Court for Sierra Leone (SCSL) and the International Criminal Court (ICC) and analyse trials in which child soldiers have appeared. We consider three specific dimensions: (1) child soldiers as perpetrators; (2) child soldiers as witnesses; and (3) child soldiers as victims. Under each category, we describe the applicable rules, discuss existing practices and identify core challenges. By doing so, we seek to provide an empirically grounded overview of encounters of child soldiers with international criminal justice, and further problematize the debate by posing critical questions and presenting facts, figures and experiences.

The ICC's very first trial against Thomas Lubanga Dyilo – a psychology graduate, politician and militia leader from the Democratic Republic of the Congo (DRC) – involved only charges of child soldier conscription, enlistment and use. Children therefore were central to the *raison d'être* of the case. However, this trial was not just *about* children. Youth also *featured* in the trial as live protagonists of traumatic experience, evidence and context. Casualties of their birthplace, they were caught up in yet another battle: the legal confrontation between defence and prosecution attorneys over case theory, legalities and evidence. Geographically and temporally distant from the crime scene in Ituri, alleged former child soldiers participated in the trial, testifying before three non-Congolese judges. Young adults at the time of the trial, they narrated stories about how political militants – including Lubanga – recruited, enlisted and used them in their armed movements.[1] As much as these underage combatants are 'tragic perpetrators and imperfect victims',[2] they are also complex trial participants. None of the child soldiers who the prosecution had relied on as being younger than 15 years old when recruited were in the end accepted by the judges as credible witnesses.

Although this trial was all about children, doing justice and seeing it done seemed a matter for grown-ups only. Last to speak for the prosecution was Benjamin Ferencz, the veteran Nuremberg prosecuting attorney. Ninety-two years old, he stepped into his own role as the wise, doting grandfather of international criminal justice. The otherwise

---

* The authors would like to thank Mao Xiao and Lisan Berk for research assistance.
[1] Namely the Union des Patriotes Congolais/Force Patriotique pour la Libération du Congo (UPC/FPLC).
[2] Drumbl 2016b.

austere trial chamber courteously listened to his 'personal observations' vis-à-vis the significance of the trial – even though these were substantially immaterial to the case. Across the courtroom, among the adult lawyers and legal assistants, sat the mature, middle-aged Lubanga. To his militia subordinates he was known as 'Papa Thomas'.[3] No children, however, were present for this elite-level and historic occasion. In fact, a rule was in place which stated that 'no [p]ersons under the age of 16 years may enter or be admitted to the public galleries of the Court whilst in session unless previously authorized by the appropriate Judicial Chamber'.[4]

In addition to *Lubanga*, the ICC has adjudicated a handful of other child soldier cases. In 2012 and 2014, Lubanga's rivals, Matthieu Ngudjolo Chui and Germain Katanga, were both acquitted of the charge of recruitment and use of child soldiers during the February 2003 attack on Bogoro village. In March 2018, the court closed evidentiary hearings in the case of Bosco Ntaganda, Lubanga's Deputy Chief of Staff. In addition to the child soldiering charges, Ntaganda faced accusations of rape and sexual slavery perpetrated by and against these child soldiers.[5] While Ntaganda had joined a rebel group (Rwandan Patriotic Front) in Uganda at the borderline age of 17,[6] it was Dominic Ongwen who became the ICC's true 'problem child'.[7] Separated from his parents and abducted at a young age, Ongwen grew up within the ranks of Uganda's Lord's Resistance Army (LRA) and is currently being tried for the crime that he once was a victim of.

The ICC is not the first international court to engage with child soldiering. Adjudicating a decade-long civil war, the SCSL had already addressed the phenomenon. Rooted in generational clashes and revolt by marginalized youth,[8] the Sierra Leone conflict became known for the abuses perpetrated by very young, often drugged, combatants in the rebel forces (Revolutionary United Front, or RUF), Civil Defence Forces (CDF) and military junta (Armed Forces Revolutionary Council, or AFRC). Setting legal precedents, the SCSL did not prosecute former child soldiers or litigate the crimes perpetrated by the 'Small Boys Units' (SBU) and 'Small Girls Units' (SGU). Instead, it put on trial their commanders: adult men. All of the SCSL's main cases included charges of child recruitment and use, and relied on evidence provided by former child soldiers.[9] Despite defence arguments that 15 was an 'arbitrary [age] in the African setting' and that youngsters were commonly part of the army, Alex Brima, Brima Kamara and Santigie Kanu became the first persons to be convicted by an internationalized court for conscripting, enlisting and using child soldiers.[10]

These various encounters of the international criminal courts with marginalized children from the 'African bush' were often inappropriate, uncomfortable and uneasy.[11]

---

[3] ICC, Lubanga Transcript (15 November 2006): 45.
[4] ICC, Rules of Decorum: 2.
[5] ICC, Ntaganda Confirmation of Charges 2014; ICC, Ntaganda Judgment on Appeal 2017.
[6] ICC, Ntaganda Transcript (14 June 2017): 49.
[7] Bouwknegt 2015.
[8] Peters 2011.
[9] The SCSL convicted nine defendants in four cases: the *AFRC*, the *CDF*, the *RUF* and the *Taylor* cases. Six defendants (Alex Brima, Brima Kamara, Santigie Kanu (AFRC); Issa Hassan Sesay, Morris Kallon (RUF); and Charles Taylor) were convicted of charges of recruitment and use of child soldiers by the Court.
[10] SCSL, AFRC Judgment 2007: [730].
[11] See also Kelsall 2009: 146–70.

In both international and internationalized courtrooms, child soldiers were approached as unqualified perpetrators, erratic witnesses and irreparable victims. A myriad of critical questions arises regarding the seemingly uneasy rapport between international criminal justice and child soldiers. To date, however, there are few empirically grounded explorations of these questions. This chapter is a first attempt to bridge the gap by offering an explorative analysis that connects legal principles, proceedings and courtroom dynamics.

1. CHILD SOLDIERS IN INTERNATIONAL COURTROOMS: UNQUALIFIED PERPETRATORS

> Because at that time the situation was very scared and we were ordered by Gabriel Kolo as our chefe of the village as acting also as a commander of the milisia Sakunar and I am young and afraid I didn't have a plan to kill him . . . – 'X'[12]

Prosecuting child soldiers for international crimes they have allegedly committed under the orders of adult commanders presents complex challenges. To our knowledge, only a few such individuals have been pursued by international or internationalized prosecutors. When it comes to minors, international criminal law remains abstruse regarding from what age tribunals and courts *should* start investigating, charging and prosecuting minors. Courts – with the exception of the ICC – *can* prosecute individuals who were younger than 18 when they were allegedly involved in atrocity.[13] In practice, however, prosecutors rarely choose to use this power.

International criminal tribunals and courts are often mandated to pursue those 'most responsible' for atrocity crimes. 'The most responsible' conventionally refers to a role played in crime or in an organization, irrespective of age. However, given the law's desire to impose clear categories onto what is often a complex and shifting reality, laws set thresholds of when accountability starts, or at least when courts may pursue individuals from a jurisdictional perspective. In terms of mass atrocity violence, the transition from being 'not responsible' – a compromised child with little capacity to act – to potentially the 'most responsible' – an adult with full choice and capacity to act – for the most inhumane acts is rather abrupt. From one day to the next, an individual can be transformed from a victim into a perpetrator. Thus, the boundaries between who international criminal justice wants to *protect* the most from international crimes and who international criminal justice seeks to *punish* the most is rather abrupt, artificial and adversarial.

At the International Military Tribunals in Nuremberg (IMT) and in Tokyo (IMTFE), all defendants were over 18 years old, representing the assumption that criminal responsibility comes with age.[14] With the advent of modern-day international criminal justice in the 1990s, the UN Security Council did not provide the ad hoc tribunals with any limits, rules or advice regarding the age of responsibility. Arguably, the drafters of the International Criminal Tribunal for the former Yugoslavia (ICTY) Statute saw no reason to mention age since the ICTY was to focus on deterring the adult leadership in the

---

[12] Cited in SPSC, X Judgment 2002: [59]. See also Kaushik and Freeland in this volume.
[13] Drumbl 2012: 126.
[14] This excludes the subsequent national military trials by the Allied Powers.

Balkans. Interestingly, the mixed State Court in Bosnia and Herzegovina (BiH) explicitly allows the prosecution of adolescents aged over 14 years at the time of the offence,[15] albeit with special rules regarding the treatment and punishment of juvenile offenders.[16]

Although young people were reported to be among the civilian killing squads in Rwanda, there was no age provision in the Statute of the International Criminal Tribunal for Rwanda (ICTR), which was more concerned with adjudicating high-level conspiracies to commit genocide.[17] Additionally, while the Khmer Rouge was known for its very young fighters, the Extraordinary Chambers in the Courts of Cambodia (ECCC) were set up to pursue only the 'Senior leaders of Democratic Kampuchea', and no other implicit or explicit reference was made to age in its Statute.[18] In contrast, the SCSL's Statute – adopted in 2002 – included an express reference to age, limiting the Court's personal jurisdiction to persons over 15 years when the crime occurred.[19] Moulded to capture the reality on the ground, the court also provided for a special penal regime regarding adolescent defendants between the ages of 15 and 18, who were to be:

> treated with dignity and a sense of worth, taking into account his or her young age and the desirability of promoting his or her rehabilitation, reintegration into and assumption of a constructive role in society, and in accordance with international human rights standards, in particular the rights of the child.[20]

In East Timor, and in response to the mass political violence in 1999 that involved children in all armed groups, the Special Panels for Serious Crimes (SPSC) in Dili had the lowest minimum age of criminal responsibility. This UN-sponsored jurisdiction allowed for the prosecution of 12-year-old individuals, while stipulating a specific legal regime for offenders under 16.[21]

While there is variation among the ad hoc and hybrid tribunals, at the treaty-based ICC, the Rome Statute excludes from the ICC's jurisdiction any person under the age of 18 at the time of the alleged crime.[22] Adopted in 1998, the Rome Statute does not codify a general principle of international law, nor does it proscribe the prosecution of minors by other courts and the statutes of later internationalized tribunals,[23] such as the special courts for Iraq (IHCC), Lebanon (STL), Chad (EAC), Kosovo (KSC) and the Central African Republic (SCC), which make no reference to age at all.[24]

---

[15] BiH Criminal Code, art. 1(11), 1(12); art. 10.
[16] Ibid., arts 75–105.
[17] We are cognizant of the fact that in the domestic courts of Rwanda, including the *Inkiko Gacaca*, adolescent children were prosecuted. Barrett 2014.
[18] ECCC Law.
[19] SCSL Statute, art. 7.
[20] SCSL Statute, art. 7; art. 19(1). Note that, despite this jurisdiction over minors, the first prosecutor of the SCSL declared that he would not prosecute children but rather those who had forced children to commit crimes.
[21] UNTAET Regulation 2001/25 and UNTAET Regulation No. 2000/30.
[22] Rome Statute, art. 26.
[23] For further discussion on the Statute's drafting history and the possible effects of this arbitrary threshold on ongoing and future prosecutions of international crimes, see Drumbl 2012: 119–22.
[24] Statute of the Iraqi High Special Tribunal; Statute of the Special Tribunal for Lebanon; EAC Accord; KSC Law; SCC Law.

Except within the ICC, minors can be prosecuted and tried in international courtrooms, yet only a few adolescent perpetrators have faced international judges.[25] In East Timor, 'X' was indicted for the extermination of 47 men in 1999 – a crime against humanity – when he was only 14. During the trial, in October 2002, 'X' pleaded guilty to the alternative charge, under Indonesian law, of murdering three 'young men' with a machete. The defence argued that 'X' had been forced by the 'chief of Militias' to commit the crime and was thus a 'victim rather than a perpetrator'. As 'X' had spent already 11 months and 21 days in pre-trial detention, the defence reasoned that he should therefore not be sentenced with further imprisonment.[26] And indeed, in determining the one-year sentence, which by then 'X' had already served, the Trial Chamber considered 'X''s age, his guilty plea, the fact he acted under superior orders and also that he had no prior convictions. While the boy was already back at school during the sentencing, the Chamber legitimized his (pre-)trial detention on the basis that 'not all minors of the age of the accused were involved in that campaign', the 'victims of the acts perpetrated by the accused were defenceless young men', and the crime was committed in a 'horrible manner'.[27]

In July 2010, in the internationalized State Court in Sarajevo, Elvir Jakupovic – a former member of the BiH Army during the Bosnian–Croat war – pleaded guilty to a war crime charge of murder he had committed just over two months after turning 17, which was a 'very young age', according to the court.[28] On 9 June 1993, Jakupovic had shot Slavko Bozic – a prisoner of war – in the head at point-blank range. He committed the murder immediately after discovering that one of his fellow combatants had just been killed by enemy forces. Jakupovic was convicted and sentenced to five years' imprisonment, the absolute minimum term under the applicable law. In sentencing, the judges mentioned Jakupovic's guilty plea, his remorse, his family situation (he had two minor children) at the time of the verdict, and his diminished mental capacity during the crime.[29] Taking into account these mitigating circumstances, as well as his cooperation with the prosecution, good behaviour and very young age when he committed the murder, the judges found the sentence 'fully adequate and suitable for the accomplishment of the purpose of sanctioning in the specific case'.[30]

'X''s and Jakupovic's cases do not neatly fit the legal binaries of childhood or adulthood, guilt or innocence, victim or perpetrator.[31] Looking beyond these rare cases, similar pressing questions arise when dealing with former child soldiers who continued or even aggravated their crimes into adulthood. Sometimes, these adults spent their formative years – childhood and adolescence – as fighters, knowing no better. They then go on to

---

[25] At the ICTY, Esad Landzo, a former prison guard at the infamous Celebici camp, was convicted of war crimes committed only two months after crossing the Rubicon threshold of adulthood: 18 years of age. ICTY, Judgment Celebici 1998.

[26] SPSC, X Judgment 2002: [54].

[27] Ibid.: [57, 61–2].

[28] The Court of Bosnia and Herzegovina, Jakupovic Verdict 2010.

[29] The judges in this case cited an expert psychological evaluation of the accused, which determined that 'at the time of the perpetration of the criminal offence the capacity of the accused to understand the significance of his act as well as ability to govern his actions was diminished although not significantly'. Court of Bosnia and Herzegovina, Jakupovic Verdict 2010: 10.

[30] Ibid.: 9.

[31] Drumbl 2016a: 42.

allegedly cause the same harm they have suffered themselves to others. Dominic Ongwen can be seen as the 'poster child' of this legal and moral conundrum.[32] On the one hand, it could be argued that any recognition of kidnapping or prior recruitment as a defence cannot overcome the gravity of the crimes such defendants allegedly perpetrated as adults. On the other hand, a case could be made for granting ex-child soldier defendants immunity from prosecution. In reality, however, the ICC's prosecution presented Ongwen as the embodiment of the LRA, charging him with 70 counts of war crimes and crimes against humanity. A middle-ground position could be that recruitment as a child and its effects on an individual's level of maturity and development is a mitigating factor when sentencing a convicted perpetrator.[33] At the SCSL, for example, Sesay and Kallon asked for mitigation of their sentences because they claimed to have been forcibly recruited as teenagers by the same armed force they later commanded.[34] Here, however, the judges cursorily dismissed the claims as 'irrelevant' and argued that 'forced recruitment cannot mitigate the crimes' later committed. They further stated that both had been in their late teens and could have 'chosen another path'.[35] Another option would be for judges to convict and release or, as in Sierra Leone, for prosecutors to leave the matter to parallel alternative justice mechanisms, such as the Truth and Reconciliation Commission (TRC). So far, however, international courts have yet to resolve and reconcile the law with the complex realities on the ground.

2. CHILD SOLDIERS IN INTERNATIONAL COURTROOMS: ERRATIC WITNESSES

> A. I was in Ituri. I had completed my studies in mechanics, then I repeated the first year of secondary school. An NGO which helps troubled children arrived and called the children. I went and my friends did too. They promised us clothing and lots of other things. They took down our addresses and our IDs. Then I went back home.
> Q. Thank you, Witness. Before this happened, did you go to any training camp?
> A. I didn't go. They taught me those things. They really deprived me . . . I couldn't follow my mind. I told myself that I would do what they wanted, but in coming here I told myself that I would say what I know to be the truth. – Witness Dieumerci[36]

Whereas child soldier perpetrators have rarely featured as defendants, (ex-)child soldiers have frequently figured as witnesses. At least 45 of them have provided testimonies in at least six trials before the SCSL and ICC.[37] Years after the events – when

---

[32] See Ramos in this volume for an in-depth analysis of the *Ongwen* case.
[33] Romero 2004; Seyfarth 2013; Ferelli et al. 2015: 641.
[34] SCSL, RUF Sentencing Judgment 2009: [69, 85].
[35] Ibid.: [220, 250].
[36] ICC, Lubanga Transcript (28 January 2009): 40.
[37] SCSL: *CDF, RUF, AFRC, Taylor*; ICC: *Lubanga, Katanga* and *Ngudjolo*. The numbers presented here come from finalized trials, in which proceedings have ended and judgment was rendered. In ongoing cases, such as *Ntaganda* and *Ongwen* at the ICC, however, a significant number of ex-child soldiers were called to testify. For example, in the *Ongwen* case, we have identified at least 29 prima facie ex-child soldier witnesses, who so far have testified in the trial on behalf of the prosecution.

they had already become young adults – trial lawyers would often elicit from these former child soldiers painful, complex, tucked-away memories of stolen childhoods in Sierra Leone and the DRC. Almost exclusively, these child soldiers have testified for the prosecution. However, these encounters with international courtrooms have proven to be uncomfortable. The credibility of these witnesses and the reliability of their testimonies have been questioned. Consequently, judges have regularly hesitated to rely on their evidence.

Although no clear definition of 'a child' exists in international criminal law, it is widely recognized that children require special protection in judicial proceedings.[38] At the SCSL, judges ordered that children as 'witnesses in Category B testify with the use of a closed-circuit television; the image appearing on the public's monitors being distorted' because 'vulnerable witnesses such as children have a high risk of re-traumatization and the possibility of stigmatization and rejection is real and high'.[39] At the ICC, the prosecutor is to 'respect interests and personal circumstances of victims and witnesses, including [their] age' during investigations and take into account 'the nature of the crime, in particular where it involves [. . .] violence against children'.[40] Likewise, the Court has to adopt 'appropriate measures to protect the safety, physical and psychological well-being, dignity and privacy of victims and witnesses'.[41] A child – acting as a victim or a witness – can thus give testimony *in camera* or even outside the courtroom.[42] Child witnesses may be assisted by a 'child-support person' and may be exempted from making a solemn undertaking.[43] Special measures can also be ordered to facilitate the testimony of traumatized witnesses or children[44] to possibly reduce re-traumatization.[45] Additionally, both the ICC and the SCSL have adopted specific policy guidelines relating to the treatment of child witnesses.[46] At the ICC, the Office of the Prosecutor (OTP) has also formulated a detailed strategy on its interaction with children,[47] as well as with adult witnesses who were victimized as children.[48]

So far, there has been a general lack of empirical research on day-to-day practices of investigations and handling of witnesses at the international criminal courts.[49] Whether and how international investigators, analysts and lawyers approach, select and question future witnesses, and assess and balance their capabilities and vulnerabilities in their daily business remains relatively unknown. According to SCSL monitors Sanin

---

[38] Malone 2015; Neal 2015.
[39] SCSL, RUF Decision 2004: [34].
[40] Rome Statute, art. 54(1)(b).
[41] Ibid., art. 68(1).
[42] Ibid., art. 68(2).
[43] Rule 17(3) ICC RPE. According to Rule 19 the Unit may specifically include persons with expertise in children, in particular traumatized children. Rule 66 ICC RPE.
[44] Rule 86 ICC RPE. See also discussion in Malone 2015: 613 regarding the ICC child protection regime and human rights law.
[45] For an analysis of a legal regime for child witnesses at the ICC see Beresford 2005.
[46] ICC OTP Policy on Children 2016; Neal 2015: 636–7; Malone 2015: 612; Sanin and Stirnemann 2006: 16.
[47] ICC OTP Policy on Children 2016: [22].
[48] Ibid.: [21].
[49] For a very recent exception: Babington-Ashaye et al. 2018.

and Stirnemann, a careful approach was taken in Sierra Leone; in order to potentially evade the re-traumatization of ex-child soldier witnesses during the early investigations, assistance from UNICEF and other unidentified child protection agencies was solicited.[50] These organizations even actively participated in selecting witnesses, identifying 'the most resilient children and those best-suited for testimony'.[51] Generally, the aim was to prevent investigators from interviewing vulnerable or special-risk children, such as street children, orphans or those without support structures.[52] However, Sanin and Stirnemann report that in some instances, 'investigators' quest for compelling or dramatic evidence seems to have trumped concerns about witnesses' psychological resiliency'.[53] For example:

> One such witness was homeless and living in the streets of Freetown when investigators found him. He passed through numerous demobilization programs, but settled nowhere. He claims to be a former RUF combatant, and all of his family is either missing or dead. The prosecution included him in its list of confirmed witnesses, despite the recommendation against approaching street children. This witness quickly proved to be unreliable, and ultimately the prosecution was forced to drop him. Shortly thereafter, he sold the flat and the furniture that WVS had rented for him and used the money to buy drugs. He was arrested in Guinea for possession and sale of drugs in November 2005. This boy returned to Freetown as a homeless drug addict, with no family or community to support him, but he continues to receive assistance from WVS.[54]

A special psychosocial support service was provided for child witnesses at the SCSL, and all child witnesses were treated as victim-witnesses. During trials, they were allowed to testify via video link from a separate room to minimize stress,[55] avoid confrontation with the accused and reduce intimidation by the formal setting of a courtroom, all of which could have a negative effect on the quality of a child's testimony.[56] Some child soldiers, however, expressed that they would have preferred to see the defendants in person and 'say it to their faces'.[57] Some reported that they enjoyed cross-examination because they saw it as their chance to prove they were telling the truth. Despite general beliefs as to their traumatization and vulnerability, some children apparently felt empowered through their live testimony. It is hard to establish what witnesses themselves feel about their courtroom experiences. Only in rare cases have protected witnesses come forward with their stories.

Across international courts, the majority of ex-child soldier witnesses testified before the SCSL. Their stories were gruesome and illustrative of what it was like to be a child soldier. As crime-base witnesses,[58] they seemingly had an impact on SCSL judges. In the

---

[50] Sanin and Stirnemann 2006: 19.
[51] Ibid.
[52] Ibid.: 20.
[53] Ibid.: 21.
[54] Ibid.: 21.
[55] Ibid.: 27.
[56] Ibid.: 28.
[57] Ibid.: 29.
[58] In general, one can distinguish three types of witnesses in international criminal proceedings: (i) crime-base, who provide evidence on criminal acts, victimization and direct perpetrators; (ii) linkage, who provide evidence on criminal organization and a link between an accused and a crime; and (iii) expert witnesses, who provide evidence based on their specific expertise related to, among others aspects, technical, cultural, contextual or forensic issues.

Charles Taylor trial, for instance, witness TF1-158 testified through video-link. On a screen, the chamber saw a young man with a scar:

> Q. Sir, you pointed to this part, something below your eye. What was done there? Explain that to us again?
> A. They pierced it and they put – they applied cocaine on it. They said that was for us to be brave and be bold so we will not fear anything.
> Q. Sir, what they applied to that, what did it look like?
> A. It was just like dust. Brown. Brown.
> Q. Thank you. How did you feel after that dust was put on?
> A. You know, it was as if – it was as if my head was off. I looked like a mad person. In fact, I even felt like so, like a mad person.[59]

The children's narratives were considered to be so gruesome that they were hardly questioned. A prime example of that modus operandi comes from the first witness to share with international judges his purported experience as a child soldier – witness 'TF1-199', who had claimed to be 18 when testifying. He told the chamber how he was recruited into an RUF's Small Boys Unit when he was 11, how he was trained to become a soldier, how he was shooting his machine gun, smoking marijuana and was forced to rape a young girl.[60] Although 'TF1-199' had given contradictory information during his interrogation – he had first told investigators he was 22, not 18 – and he is not explicitly mentioned as one of the child soldier witnesses in the judgment,[61] the judges repeatedly relied on his testimony to establish judicial facts: the existence of children in armed groups, but also other crimes committed by the RUF soldiers.[62]

At the ICC, however, the scenario was somewhat different. As an ad hoc Special Court, the SCSL could specialize in one particular geographical, temporal and cultural setting. In contrast, the ICC can investigate crimes against children perpetrated across the globe, in very different contexts. Moreover, different investigative teams may operate in various situations under very different circumstances. In the DRC, the work terrain was difficult and complex from the beginning. There was no field office, the violence was ongoing and the UN peacekeeping force's assistance was minimal. The 12 investigators were heavily restricted from visiting crime scenes and potential witnesses. Most of the investigative work was seconded, particularly to NGO staff, who acted as 'intermediaries' – individuals recruited by the ICC to liaise between investigators and potential witnesses. The very first witness questioned in The Hague during the Lubanga investigations was introduced 'through' an NGO, while, in the field, the intermediaries were selecting more witnesses, recording their statements and corroborating information. At the time, however, UN agencies reported that some individuals were falsely presenting themselves at demobilization centres as former child soldiers to be allowed into reintegration programmes.[63]

---

[59] SCSL, Taylor Transcript (21 October 2008): 18824–5.
[60] SCSL, RUF Transcript (20 and 27 July 2004). His testimony was also 'recycled' in the AFRC case, where, however, much of his evidence was not relied upon as it fell outside the scope of the prosecution case. SCSL, AFRC Transcript (6 October 2005).
[61] SCSL, RUF Judgment 2009: [579–94].
[62] Ibid.: [987, 1170, 1251,1252, 1620, 1621, 1623,1638, 1647].
[63] ICC, Lubanga Transcript (16 November 2010) (Testimony Bernard Levigne, the chief investigator).

Moreover, it soon became known throughout Bunia that 'threatened witnesses' might be relocated and some locals treated this as an opportunity to secure free housing. Overall, there was a sense of caution as to the reasons why witnesses came forward.[64]

In January 2009, at the start of the Lubanga trial, the OTP's case dramatically shattered when the prosecution called a former child soldier as its first witness. From a black office-like chair, a timid boy whispered that he had lied and had been coached by an NGO. After withdrawing his statement, the young man – dubbed 'witness 298' – remained nameless.[65] He returned two weeks later under the pseudonym 'Dieumerci' – 'thank god' in French. This time the judges put up a curtain in court to block any possible eye contact between Lubanga and the boy, allowing the witness 'simply to tell the story in [his] own words'. He then narrated in a clear and chronological way how Lubanga's men had kidnapped him.[66] Nine more former child soldiers came to The Hague to testify for the prosecution, mostly in private sessions.[67]

After the presentation of the prosecution evidence, the elephant in the room was the reliability of the evidence that was brought to sustain the charge that children were recruited and that they were indeed under 15. Lubanga's lawyers called a range of witnesses who testified that they had been coached by intermediaries to produce stories of victimhood. 'The intermediaries knew exactly what story needed to be told', the defence argued, accusing the intermediaries of 'recruiting children' and telling them 'what they had to say'.[68] When Judge Adrian Fulford read a summary of the judgment on 16 March 2012, he lamented the fact that '[a] series of witnesses have been called during this trial whose evidence, as a result of the essentially unsupervised actions of three of the principal intermediaries, cannot safely be relied on'.[69] The consequence of the OTP's 'lack of proper oversight of the intermediaries', he further explained, 'is that they were potentially able to take advantage of the witnesses they contacted'.[70] As a result, the nine alleged child soldiers who had testified for the prosecution and claimed to be under 15 when recruited were ultimately found unreliable.

International prosecutors often face a dilemma when it comes to child witnesses. These prosecutors want the children to attest to the atrocities they went through, and perhaps also give them an opportunity to assist the court, but there are concerns about practicability.[71] Deciding whether to call a child witness to testify is a balancing act that weighs a child's desire to share his or her story with the legal necessity for the child's testimony and whether that testimony could be safely presented in an admissible form.[72] Despite hesitations to call child witnesses to testify given the risk of their

---

[64] For analysis: Bouwknegt 2014.
[65] Second author's observations, ICC, 28 January 2009.
[66] Second author's observations, ICC, 10 February 2009.
[67] Only one ex-child soldier witness, who claimed to be 17 when he joined the UPC (P-038), was relied upon by the judges. ICC, Lubanga Judgment 2012: [480]; ICC, Lubanga Judgment 2012: [481]. Compare ICC, Lubanga Dissenting Opinion of Judge Odio-Benito 2012: [32]. All the others were considered not credible and not relied upon in judicial fact-finding.
[68] ICC, Lubanga Transcript (26 August 2011): 15; 10.
[69] ICC, Lubanga Judgment 2012: [482].
[70] Ibid.
[71] Swanson et al. 2015: 651.
[72] Ibid.

re-traumatization,[73] susceptibility to the influence of others,[74] and concerns regarding their reliability and credibility,[75] prosecutors did repeatedly rely on ex-child soldier witnesses to prove the charges of their recruitment and use.

Ex-child soldiers – as direct victims – are believed to offer unique first-hand evidence, which cannot be delivered by any third party. We were able to identify 45 ex-child soldier witnesses who testified in the trials against their former commanders at the SCSL and ICC. Most were men who testified that, as young boys, they were abducted, beaten and forced to witness atrocities – including against their own family members. They talked about how they were then trained to become soldiers, abused, mutilated and drugged, and also how they laboured for their commanders, served as bodyguards and spies, and were forced to carry heavy loads. They recounted how they served on the frontline and were compelled to commit crimes, including killings, rape and looting. Seven female ex-child soldiers also shared with international judges their stories of forced abductions, abuse, forced marriages, forced labour and sexual exploitation during their captivity in armed groups.[76] Despite forensic uncertainties about the real ages of many of these witnesses,[77] all these young adults provided court testimony about what being a child soldier was like for them. Table 16.1 summarizes basic statistics regarding the ex-child soldiers' witness testimonies[78] and judges' evaluation of this evidence.[79]

Overall, child soldiers as fact providers have often proven problematic to judges. Because 'an African child will rarely have been asked to talk about personal experiences or reveal autobiographical memories in detail to an adult listener; especially not to a stranger',[80] their children's courtroom stories were often uncontrolled, confusing and incoherent. The children often got lost in the translation of their complex and fallible memories into the demandingly precise logic of the positivist law and the judiciary. With respect to 32 ex-child soldier witnesses (71%), judges noted problems in their evidence, such as vagueness, exaggerations, contradictions or inconsistencies with their previous statements or with other evidence. These factors, in one way or another, influenced the assessment of the children's credibility as witnesses and the reliability of their evidence. In many instances, despite these problems, these testimonies were relied upon when it came to their personal experiences in captivity – their victimhood – but not in other aspects,

---

[73] Ex-child solder witnesses constituted just a small fraction (6.6%) of the total number of 675 witnesses, who testified in the *AFRC*, *CDF*, *RUF*, *Taylor*, *Lubanga*, and *Katanga* and *Ngudjolo* cases combined, as demonstrated in Table 16.1.

[74] Sanin and Stirnemann 2006: 14; see also ICC, Lubanga Judgment 2012: [178–484].

[75] As Sanin and Stirnemann 2006: 8–11 sum up, the concerns regarding children's ability to testify relate to their linguistic, cognitive, emotional and moral development, affecting the witness and the quality of his or her testimony. Cf. Beresford 2005: 739, however, who discusses selected research findings regarding the general capacity of children to recall accurate and relevant information.

[76] For a detailed analysis of the gendered narrative regarding experiences of boy and girl child soldiers that emerged from the SCSL cases, see Oosterveld in this volume.

[77] We discuss problems with age determinations in more detail in section 3.

[78] Note that there may have been other instances where witnesses, who could be characterized as (ex-)child soldiers, testified, such as in the *Foca* case at the ICTY. See ICTY, Foca Judgment 2001.

[79] Data is drawn from the judgments of finalized cases in which charges of recruiting child soldiers were adjudicated.

[80] ICC, Lubanga Report of Ms. Elisabeth Schauer: 37.

Table 16.1 Overview of (ex-)child soldier witnesses who have testified in international courtrooms

Court	Case	Total number of witnesses	No. of ex-child soldier witnesses*	Problems in their testimony	Credibility not discussed	Relied upon in judicial fact-finding?
SCSL	AFRC June 2007	148: 59 OTP 88 Defence 1 Chamber	5	5	0	3 testimonies considered problematic but mainly as their testimony did not fit the OTP case 2 relied upon for personal experiences in captivity; corroboration required for other aspects
SCSL	RUF March 2009	171: 86 OTP 85 Defence	6	5	1	1 considered unreliable (but used when corroborated) 4 relied upon for personal experiences in captivity despite many inconsistencies in their evidence; corroboration required when it came to facts related to accused
SCSL	CDF	119: 75 OTP 44 Defence	5	0	4	1 credibility not discussed and relied upon 4 credibility not discussed and relied upon 1 considered highly credible and largely reliable, pivotal for factual findings
SCSL	Taylor May 2012	115: 94 OTP 21 Defence	11	8	3	2 considered unreliable (1 relied upon only when corroborated) 6 relied upon despite inconsistencies or other problems 3 credibility not discussed and relied upon (1 unchallenged)
ICC	Lubanga March 2012	67: 36 OTP 24 Defence 3 Victims 4 Chamber	15	11	0	11 considered unreliable 4 considered in general reliable and credible
ICC	Ngudjolo & Katanga December 2012 March 2014	55: 24 OTP 27 Defence 2 Victims 2 Chamber	3	3	0	2 considered unreliable 1 considered not credible with respect to particular pieces of information; corroboration required when it came to facts related to accused; with other aspects, case-by-case assessment

Note: *We recorded all the witnesses we were able to identify, who during their testimonies (as discussed by the judges in a judgment) claimed to be under 18 when recruited into armed groups. The majority were called by the prosecution; the remainder by the defence, or victims' representatives at the ICC.

such as identification of the accused or command structures of armed forces.[81] Sixteen child soldier witnesses were considered unreliable and their evidence was not used in establishing facts,[82] or only where corroborated by other reliable evidence.[83]

On the face of it, the SCSL judges were more receptive than the ICC judges to accept evidence given by former child soldiers. Even while noting problems, the SCSL judges still relied on elements of their testimonies:

> Due to the fact that the events they attempt to recount took place largely during their childhood, their ability to recall such events is compounded by the passage of time. This means that such witnesses generally experienced difficulty in remembering specific details about such events, and various minor discrepancies are identifiable in their evidence. However, the Chamber has generally accepted the evidence of former child soldiers, especially as it relates to their own experiences.[84]

Frequently, judges have concluded that the 'witness was not shaken on cross-examination and therefore in spite of his youth at the time of events [found] that the witness was credible and reliable with regards to the details of captivity and his treatment in captivity'.[85] Other findings were that '[he] came across as a candid witness',[86] or that, because 'the events happened many years ago',[87] or the witness was very young 'at the time the offences were committed'[88] or 'when he was giving previous statements',[89] or was traumatized,[90] some details could have been forgotten.

Although they faced similar challenges, the ICC judges in the *Lubanga* case were less accommodating regarding ex-child soldiers' testimonies than their colleagues at the SCSL. All testimonies of former child soldiers who claimed to be under 15 when recruited were dismissed as unreliable. One possible reason is that Lubanga was charged solely with child soldiering, while defendants at the SCSL were charged with child soldiering amongst many other offences.[91] In The Hague, the child soldier witnesses and their evidence were therefore subjected to focused, detailed and rigorous scrutiny[92] –particularly by the

---

[81] See SCSL, AFRC Judgment (witness TF1-157) 2007: [1255]; SCSL, AFRC Judgment (witness TF1-158) 2007: [1258]; SCSL, RUF Judgment (witness TF1-141) 2009: [583]; SCSL, RUF Judgment (witness TF1-263) 2009: [587]; SCSL, RUF Judgment (witness TF1 117) 2009: [590]; SCSL, RUF Judgment (witness TF1-314) 2009: [594].

[82] Testimonies of 11 child soldier witnesses (nine called by the OTP and two called by Victims' Representatives) in the *Lubanga* case at the ICC were dismissed. SCSL, Taylor Judgment (witness Edna Bangura) 2012: [1053]. As were testimonies of witnesses P-279 and P-280 called by the OTP in the *Katanga* and *Ngudjolo* cases. ICC, Katanga Judgment: [292, 319].

[83] For example, SCSL, RUF Judgment (witness TF1-093) 2009: [603]; SCSL, Taylor Judgment (witness TF1-375) 2012: [311, 312].

[84] SCSL, RUF Judgment 2009: [579].

[85] SCSL, AFRC Judgment 2007: [1255, 1258].

[86] SCSL, RUF Judgment 2009: [583]; see also SCSL, Taylor Judgment 2012: [316].

[87] SCSL, AFRC Judgment 2007: [1087].

[88] SCSL, RUF Judgment 2009: [587]; see also SCSL, Taylor Judgment 2012: [1398, 1401, 1591].

[89] SCSL, Taylor Judgment 2012: [1564].

[90] SCSL, RUF Judgment 2009: [583].

[91] In the *RUF* case, the defendants faced a total of 18 charges, varying from terrorizing the civilian population to attacks against peacekeepers.

[92] ICC, Lubanga Judgment 2012: [426–82].

defence – which contested all ex-child soldiers' ages and adduced evidence that cast doubt on their narratives. More important, however, was the OTP's outsourcing of the investigations to questionable intermediaries, who manipulated and improperly influenced child soldier witnesses who subsequently openly admitted to lying to investigators.[93]

The *Lubanga* trial was unique, even at the ICC. In all other cases that featured ex-child soldiers as witnesses – such as *Katanga* – the accused faced a range of additional charges and the defence adopted different strategies.[94] Some have argued that the judges in the *Lubanga* case showed 'a sense of paternalism . . . possibly based on the assumption a child cannot tell a truthful and coherent story'.[95] This theory is far-fetched and ignores investigative faults as well as actual trial dynamics. The extent to which the 'typification of child soldiers as faultless passive victims lacking in capacity' has impaired assessments of the children's credibility remains an open question.[96] In any event, and as with any witness, (former) child soldiers are susceptible to various proximal and mediating factors affecting memory and recollection, ranging from trauma, lapse of time and cultural differences, to stress, undue influences or unfamiliarity with a trial setting. These may render their courtroom testimonies inaccurate, which often – when coupled with their youth – makes them erratic witnesses.

3. CHILD SOLDIERS IN INTERNATIONAL COURTROOMS: IRREPARABLE AND SYMBOLIC VICTIMS

> The victims and witnesses who will file through this court will not be always the best. They will often be confused, vague, and hesitant. They will have forgotten things. There are some things they will not be able to say; they will make mistakes on some details. We should remember that these are people who have suffered and who are still suffering and who are taking personal risks in taking part in this new experience of international criminal justice. They deserve passion, sympathy and respect.
> – Luc Walleyn (victims' lawyer)[97]

Ever since the 1990s, the focus of international criminal courts and tribunals on crimes committed against children has emerged progressively. At the ICC, the OTP claims to pay particular attention to crimes against children as one of its strategic goals.[98] Child soldiers in international courtrooms primarily emerge as victims in three senses: (1) legal, (2) participating/benefitting and (3) symbolic.

First, child soldiers are *legal* victims. Legally, the existence of child soldiers, their age, and their recruitment and use has to be proven beyond any reasonable doubt. Without

---

[93] ICC, Lubanga Judgment 2012: [426, 427].
[94] In *Katanga*, the defendant was acquitted of charges of child recruitment and use due to the absence of evidence regarding his direct involvement in the use of child soldiers. Evidence provided by child soldier witnesses, who appeared in the courtroom, was, however, also considered problematic. ICC, Katanga Judgment 2014: [1086–7].
[95] Swanson et al. 2015: 649.
[96] Drumbl 2014: 102.
[97] ICC, Lubanga Transcript (9 November 2006): 91–2.
[98] ICC, OTP Strategic Plan 2016–2018: [4]. The same focus was incorporated in the previous Strategic Plan 2012–2015.

child soldiers as legally recognized victims and, thus without evidence of a crime, it would be impossible to convict and punish their recruiters and commanders. Further, the harm caused to such legally recognized victims together with the impact of the crime are used to assess the gravity of the crime when sentencing.

Second, child soldiers are *participating/benefitting* victims. At the ICC, former child soldiers and their parents can actively participate in proceedings.[99] In court, however, victims – including child soldiers – are often reduced to anonymized numbers lacking real capacity to act. They are represented by legal representatives who claim to speak on behalf of huge groups of victims.[100] In practice, an individual victim's active participation remains an illusion: indeed, in the *Lubanga* proceedings, the defence criticized the lawyers of unidentified victims for 'representing ghosts'.[101] Remarkably, when some of these victims 'materialized', trying to personally exercise their right to participate during the trial and provide evidence, the legal victimhood of all those former child soldiers was successfully contested, their status as participating victims revoked, and they were excluded from the case.[102] Additionally, at the ICC, child soldiers are able to apply for and benefit from reparations ordered against their recruiters – both financial and symbolic – on an individual or collective basis.[103] Similar to sentencing, the harm they suffered is evaluated and quantified by judges to determine what and how much is needed to provide redress to the victims.

Third, child soldiers can also be seen as *symbolic* victims. Despite the complexities regarding their victim-perpetrator status, child soldiers in the international criminal imagination are primarily represented as ideal victims.[104] They are part and parcel of the abstract category of 'the Victim', which justifies the existence and practices of international criminal justice.[105] Child soldiers around the globe are also believed to

---

[99] The Rome Statute allows victims to actively participate in the proceedings where their personal interests are affected, and they can present their views and concerns personally or via legal representatives. See e.g. arts 15(3), 19(3), 68(3) of the Rome Statute and Rules 85, 89–93 of the ICC RPE. See also: Tibori-Szabo and Hirst 2017; Killean and Moffett 2017; Stahn 2015; Moffett 2015; Catani 2012; and many references in these works.

[100] In *Lubanga*, for example, 129 victims (34 female and 95 male victims mainly alleged former child soldiers, as well as some parents or relatives of former child soldiers and a school) were authorized to participate in the proceedings. The participating victims were divided in two groups, represented by two teams of legal representatives and four victims-witnesses were represented by the Office of Public Counsel for Victims. ICC, Lubanga Judgment 2012: [13–21]. See also Haslam and Edmunds 2017.

[101] ICC, Lubanga Transcript (3 November 2006): 25.

[102] ICC, Lubanga Judgment 2012: [484, 502]. In *Lubanga*, there were at least seven ex-child soldier participating victims, who faced the judges and testified in the courtroom (of these, five were also prosecution witnesses and two were called by their legal representatives). In this respect, the test applied to assess 'victimhood' of these victims was much more stringent compared to those who were authorized to participate only based on their individual applications. See ICC, Lubanga Judgment Dissenting Opinion of Judge Odio-Benito 2012: [22–35]; Lieflander 2012; Catani 2012: 916.

[103] The ICC can order a convicted offender to pay appropriate reparations to victims, including restitution, compensation and rehabilitation. Arts 75, 79 Rome Statute; Rules 94–8 ICC RPE. See also Moffett 2017; Stahn 2015; Navarro 2018.

[104] Drumbl 2012; Wijk 2013.

[105] Kendall and Nouwen 2013.

benefit from the symbolic, expressive value of international criminal trials and judgments. In theory, international criminal justice supporters believe their ideals of justice could present, expose and recognize the plight of child soldiers around the world, address their suffering, acknowledge the harms, and confirm and express the legal prohibition and moral reprehensibility of their recruitment and abuse. The symbolic value of condemning a single offender for the recruitment and use of child soldiers is believed to extend well beyond any individual case so as to reinforce global consciousness and the rule of law.[106]

All three layers of victimhood come with distinct challenges and questions. We will briefly outline the challenges and tensions of assessing the legal victimhood of (former) child soldiers in international courtrooms. As legal victims, child soldiers constitute evidence of the war crime of their recruitment and use. In this 'capacity', however, they must satisfy strict legal criteria. The law requires proof beyond any reasonable doubt that, at the time of the crime, child soldier victims were below the age of 15. In practice, especially at the ICC, this turned out to be a thorny exercise. The ICC's *Lubanga* case was hijacked by battles over the age of Lubanga's alleged child victims. Although the UPC's soldiers looked like children, their age remained at issue. To ICC prosecutors, the crime itself hardly required proving: it seemed clear, obvious. Lubanga's lawyers, however, entered into an adversarial discussion before the Bench in order to 'understand what in the prosecutor's evidence is close to the truth and what, on the contrary, is far removed from the truth'.[107] It did not help the prosecution that its first witness – Dieumerci, whom we briefly mentioned above – retracted his evidence and said that he was coached by an NGO to articulate an incriminating story in The Hague.[108]

Only two weeks into the trial, the prosecution walked the court through several videos taken in UPC training camps, some of those depicting young people dressed in military fatigues.[109] In appearance, these people could very well have been younger than 15, but their ages remained factually unclear. Two X-ray specialists were called to discuss the ages of some of the alleged child victims, but there was a lack of precision in their findings. Discussing the X-ray images taken from the nine former UPC child soldier victims appearing as prosecution witnesses, who claimed to be under 15 when recruited, radiologist Catherine Adamsbaum told the Chamber that age determination 'is not a totally exact science'.[110] This testimony was reinforced by her colleague, Caroline Rey-Salmon, a paediatrician and forensic doctor. She testified that the X-ray images were of relatively bad quality, only showed hard-to-interpret jawbones, and that their methodology could not always establish a person's precise age.[111] In the end, the legal victimhood of all nine child soldiers called by the prosecution was successfully contested and all were dismissed as evidence providers.

While the Trial Chamber was extremely critical of the prosecutor's case, it was convinced, based on the physical characteristics of the young people in video evidence and age estimates of soldiers provided by several lay witnesses (a journalist, two humanitarian

---

[106] Amann 2013: 432; Drumbl 2016a.
[107] ICC, Lubanga Transcript (28 January 2009): 6.
[108] Ibid.: 40–41.
[109] ICC, Lubanga Transcript (16–20 February 2009).
[110] ICC, Lubanga Transcript (12 May 2009): 80.
[111] ICC, Lubanga Transcript (13 May 2009): 26–9.

aid workers and six UPC insiders), that there were soldiers under the age of 15 in Lubanga's militia. Lubanga was subsequently convicted, but not because he had 'meant to' conscript, enlist and use boys and girls in his militia, but because he 'was aware that, in the ordinary course of events, this would occur'.[112] At the SCSL, the fact that children under the age of 15 had been used was in essence undisputed, attested to by many witnesses – including the ex-child soldiers themselves – reported by experts and documented in various reports of international organizations and NGOs. No defence lawyer in any of the four trials substantially and seriously questioned the age of the alleged child soldier victims, the fundamental element of the crime;[113] rather, they disputed the criminal responsibility of the defendant.

Once a defendant is convicted of the illegal recruitment and use of child soldiers, the next step is for the judge to mete out punishment. At the international criminal courts, the primary form of punishment is imprisonment.[114] None of the statutes of the international criminal courts and tribunals, however, contain sentence ranges for individual offences and consequently do not distinguish individual international crimes on the basis of their abstract gravity. All international crimes are considered inherently serious and it is for international judges to determine in each individual case the severity of the crime under consideration. There are various aspects to sentencing which could be discussed when it comes to sentencing child soldier recruiters at the international courts.[115] For the purposes of this chapter, we limit ourselves to a discussion of how sentences for crimes against child soldiers compare to sentencing practices with respect to other international crimes, and what harm inflicted upon child soldier victims has been considered legally relevant for sentence determinations.

In its 'Policy on Children', the ICC's OTP 'takes the position that crimes against or affecting children should be seen as particularly grave for the purpose of sentencing, given the specific rights and protection that children enjoy under international law'.[116] Similarly, if one reads all the international sentencing judgments of child recruiters, judges often refer to the crime as 'undoubtedly very serious'[117] or of 'exceptionally high' gravity.[118] At the SCSL, in cases where judges imposed sentences on a defendant per individual count,

---

[112] ICC, Lubanga, Judgment 2012; ICC. On appeal, the trial judgment was endorsed. All grounds of appeal were rejected. Only the Latvian judge dissented from the majority on fundamental grounds. If it had been up to Judge Anita Ušacka, Lubanga would not have been convicted at all. 'In my view the evidence relied upon by the Trial Chamber to convict Lubanga was not sufficient to reach the threshold of beyond any reasonable doubt', she explained. 'In practice they have applied a lower standard' because, according to Ušacka, 'the Trial Chamber was motivated more by the desire to create a record of events, rather than to determine the guilt of [the] individual to the standard applicable in criminal proceedings'. Lubanga Dissenting Opinion of Judge Ušacka 2014: 15, 16.
[113] See for example SCSL, Taylor, Judgment 2012: [1410, 1412–16, 1421, 1433–4, 1467, 1486, 1488, 1503, 1504, 1512]. The testimony of several witnesses was stated to be unchallenged by the defence and was, therefore, accepted by the Trial Chamber. See also SCSL, AFRC Judgment 2007: [1250–51].
[114] Art. 19 SCSL Statute; art. 77 Rome Statute.
[115] Drumbl 2014; Amman 2013; Hola 2016; Kurth 2013; Lieflander 2012.
[116] ICC, OTP Policy on Children 2016: [102].
[117] ICC, Lubanga Sentencing Judgment 2012: [37].
[118] SCSL, RUF Sentencing Judgment 2009: [187].

sentences for the crime of recruitment and use of child soldiers ranked among the most severe, compared to other crimes.[119]

At the ICC, however, the narrative of exceptional gravity seems to have fallen by the wayside when the suffering and plight of child soldiers described in the judgment was translated by the judges into the actual sentence. Lubanga received a total sentence of 14 years, with judges distinguishing three distinct offences: forced conscription (13 years' imprisonment), voluntary enlistment (12 years' imprisonment) and use of child soldiers (14 years' imprisonment).[120] To date, the ICC has passed four determinate sentences: nine years for Ahmed al Faqi Al Mahdi,[121] 12 years for Germain Katanga,[122] 14 years for Lubanga, and 18 years for Jean Pierre Bemba Gombo (crucially, in June 2018 Bemba was acquitted by the Appeals Chamber).[123] The average determinate sentence at the ICTY was 15.1 years, and at the ICTR the average was 22.9 years (neither court adjudicated any cases that explicitly included child soldiers). Thus, the most serious crimes of international concern do not seem to attract the most severe punishments.[124] More often than not, judges' narratives as to the extreme seriousness and atrocity of international crimes seems to get lost in the translation into sentence length. There is a clear retributive gap if the harms narrated by the judges in international judgments are evaluated against the severity of the punishments imposed on the offenders, and the *Lubanga* case does not seem to be an exception.

References to 'harm' are particularly prevalent in sentencing justifications, where child soldiers have been described as 'vulnerable victims' 'robbed of' their childhood, who 'had their innocence stolen' and are 'destroyed for life' requiring 'specific protection'.[125] Irreparable harms inflicted upon child soldiers are narrated by international judges to demonstrate the particular gravity of the crime of their recruitment. In contrast to the individualized focus during the Lubanga trial and the stringent assessment of the legal victimhood of those alleged child soldiers who testified, the assessment of harm and impact for the purposes of sentencing by the ICC judges seems to be at a very abstract level. The ICC judges relied primarily on the expert report that psychologist Elizabeth Schauer submitted and presented during the trial to evaluate the gravity of Lubanga's crimes. The gravity evaluation rested on the repetition of general claims included in the

---

[119] SCSL, RUF, Sentencing Judgment 2009. Sesay was convicted on 17 counts with sentences ranging from 20 to 52 years. The count of recruitment and use of child soldiers was punished with 50 years' imprisonment. Kallon was also convicted on 17 counts, with sentences ranging from 15 to 40 years; for the crime of recruitment and use of child soldiers, he was sentenced to 35 years. In the CDF case (SCSL, CDF, Sentencing Judgment 2007), Kondewa was convicted of recruitment of one child soldier and sentenced to seven years on this count. His sentences for the other crimes ranged from five to eight years. Kondewa's conviction on child soldiering charges was however quashed on appeal. In the *Taylor* and the *AFRC* cases, the SCSL judges imposed one global sentence with respect to all counts and, therefore, it is impossible to see how crimes of child recruitment and use, and other crimes committed against child soldiers, were assessed in sentence determinations.
[120] ICC, Lubanga Sentencing Judgment 2012: [98].
[121] ICC, Al Mahdi Judgment and Sentence 2016: [109].
[122] ICC, Katanga Sentencing Judgment 2014: [147].
[123] ICC, Bemba Sentencing Judgment 2016: [97].
[124] Bagaric and Morss 2001: 253; Drumbl 2007: 15; D'Ascoli 2011: 50; Hola 2012: 39.
[125] ICC, Lubanga Sentencing Judgment 2012: [37]; SCSL, AFRC Sentencing Judgment 2007: [34, 41, 74]; SCSL, Taylor Sentencing Judgment 2012: [75].

expert report regarding the long-lasting and debilitating effects of child soldiering, which potentially transfer across generations.[126] Judges highlighted that:

> [A] significant number of the children [interviewed by the expert] had developed ... post-traumatic stress disorder ... that tends to persist, possibly for the remainder of the individual's life.[127]
> ... A significant percentage of the former child soldiers ... had abused drugs or alcohol; they suffered from depression and dissociation; and some demonstrated suicidal behaviour.[128]

These children have, according to the expert, difficulties controlling their aggressive impulses and handling life without violence;[129] they do not 'demonstrate civilian life skills as they have difficulties socializing, they missed schooling, and as a result they are at a disadvantage, particularly as regards employment'.[130] Judges generalized and juxtaposed the detrimental effects of child soldiering reported by the expert to all unknown child soldier victims of Lubanga's crime,[131] irrespective of their individual histories, characters, age, gender and the nature of their recruitment – voluntary or forced. Judges reiterated that, even if children joined the armed forces voluntarily, it is not a valid defence, as children often joined the armed group 'as a matter of pure survival' given their upbringing in the context of chronic poverty and violence.[132] However, for the purposes of sentencing, the element of compulsion in the crime of conscription of child soldiers was considered relevant.[133] Lubanga received one additional year's imprisonment for the crime of conscripting child soldiers compared to the crime of enlisting.

The gravity of Lubanga's crimes was assessed not by looking at the harm caused to and the impact of child soldiering on these specific children, who were voluntarily or forcibly recruited into the UPC/FPLC, and on which Lubanga's conviction rested. Rather, the judges' assessment heavily relied on the expert report summarizing existing studies carried out with former child soldiers in various countries, including Uganda and the DRC, between 2004 and 2008.[134] The prosecution argued that certain elements of this particular case, such as harsh conditions and the brutal treatment of child soldiers, their particular vulnerability due to their very young age, and the sexual violence they were subjected to, should be accepted in aggravation of Lubanga's sentence.[135] Judges, referring primarily to legal technical grounds, nonetheless rejected these submissions.[136]

In contrast, the SCSL – for example, in the RUF judgment – offered a more compre-

---

[126] ICC, Lubanga Sentencing Judgment 2012: [40].
[127] Ibid.
[128] Ibid.: [41].
[129] Ibid.
[130] Ibid.: [42].
[131] The identities of Lubanga's victims, or even the number of victims, were never established in the trial; only the 'widespread character' of the practice was established, which was also noted by the judges in evaluating the gravity of Lubanga's crimes for the purposes of sentencing. ICC, Lubanga Sentencing Judgment 2012: [49, 50].
[132] Ibid.: [43].
[133] Ibid.: [37].
[134] Ibid.: [40].
[135] Ibid.: [57, 60, 61, 77].
[136] Ibid.: [9, 67, 74, 75, 78].

hensive and also case-related assessment of harms inflicted upon child soldiers. The judges reiterated some of the gruesome facts of child maltreatment established during the trial and the effects thereof. The gravity of the crime was assessed by looking at the scale and brutality of individual instances of child recruitment and use, including the fact that children were 'used' to perpetrate crimes themselves. Courts also considered the vulnerability of child victims and their exceptionally young age, their number, the degree of suffering, and the impact of the crimes on child soldiers themselves, their relatives and society at large.[137]

In both the SCSL and the ICC, the very serious, long-lasting, irreversible character of harm inflicted upon child soldiers by their recruiters and abusers was at the forefront of judges' considerations when it came to sentencing. A review of sentencing judgments of adult recruiters would lead to the conclusion that child soldiers' harm is irreparable and that victimhood is irreversible – it stays with them for life. The extent to which this framing will have a bearing on cases of former child soldier perpetrators, such as Ongwen, briefly discussed above, remains to be seen.

4. CONCLUSION

In what ways have child soldiers been featured in international courtrooms? Based on an examination of statutes, case law and courtroom experiences mainly before the SCSL and ICC, we have problematized, questioned and analysed international criminal law's reckoning with child soldiers as perpetrators, witnesses and victims. While international criminal justice claims to act in the best interests of these children, its operational outcomes are less than satisfactory.

How to approach child soldiers as perpetrators? International criminal law does not establish a minimum age of criminal responsibility. Practice, however, demonstrates that international prosecutors tend to shy away from prosecuting children and adolescents. This is because complex ethical and legal challenges arise when it comes to investigating, prosecuting, convicting and sentencing child soldiers for crimes committed as 'recruits' of adult commanders. On the International Day against the Use of Child Soldiers, Chief Prosecutor Bensouda stated that 'our children are our future. If we fail them, we have failed humanity itself.'[138] Her message was clear: 'The vector of the law must be effectively employed to confront the cycle of impunity for crimes against and affecting children ...'[139] However, when framing her highly emotive message about the victimhood of children, Bensouda – who is leading the prosecution team in the Ongwen case – seemed to ignore the significance of Ongwen's own victimhood. She remained silent to the fact that she was levelling serious charges – with no less than 70 counts of war crimes and crimes against humanity, including atrocities against children – *against* a former child soldier. The international legal and moral threshold that marks the transition from an angel into a devil, and from the future of humanity to someone most responsible for the most heinous crimes, remains ambiguous. Is that transitory moment just an 18th birthday? The ICC

---

[137] SCSL, RUF Sentencing Judgment 2009: [180–87].
[138] ICC, OTP Press Release 2018.
[139] Ibid.

has turned this theoretical conundrum into a real-time laboratory, attracting a wide range of commentary and reflection on responsibility, culpability or justiciability of individuals like Ongwen.[140]

What about child soldiers as witnesses in international courtrooms? (Former) child soldier witnesses could provide unique and valuable evidence concerning the crimes committed both by and against them. Yet, despite specific legal regimes designed to protect vulnerable witnesses such as these in the courtroom, former child soldiers proved to be capricious, uncontrollable and susceptible to manipulation. In some cases, they would recant their stories. Other times, they alleged they were 'recruited' by NGOs, and not by the particular defendant, and instructed to tell a false story. Questions as to their reliability, credibility, trauma and age began to undermine the very cases initiated to protect them. Whether they were called to provide crime-base related, linkage or victims' evidence, red flags were raised. In over 71 per cent of instances involving (ex-)child soldier witnesses, judges identified fundamental problems with their testimonies. There are countless conceivable reasons why (former) child soldier witnesses do not provide courts with the type of facts (i.e. judicial truth) that adult prosecutors, defence lawyers and judges seek from them.[141] As outlined above, such reasons include memory issues as well as unfamiliarity with the court setting. In the cases we reviewed, more often than not, former child soldier witnesses were considered to be erratic.

If child soldiers are problematic perpetrators and erratic witnesses in international courtrooms, how then should they be viewed as victims and recipients of justice? Their legal victimhood is tested and contested during trial. As legal victims, child soldiers must meet strictly defined legal criteria, and their age must be established as a fact beyond any reasonable doubt. They become objects of judicial fact-finding and adversarial trial proceedings. In this respect, ICC judges in particular proved to be uncompromising and exclusionary. All child soldier victims who claimed to be below 15 when recruited, and who shared personal stories of their victimization in the Lubanga trial, failed to meet the legal requirements. Their victimhood was denied. Judges relied on other witnesses' testimonies, scarce audio-visual evidence, and their own common sense to establish the basis for Lubanga's conviction. During sentencing however, the harm inflicted upon a child soldier, by default, was presented by international judges as very serious, long-lasting and irreparable. The child remains a victim for life, with his or her past experience and memories of atrocity continuing to inflict pain. Arguably, child soldiers' voices resonate most powerfully and effectively in the echoes of international criminal justice, where they present not as fragile and malleable figurants in adversarial adult courtrooms, but as indisputable and uncontested, symbolic ghost victims.

---

[140] See, for a discussion, the contributions to the online Justice in Conflict symposium 'The Dominic Ongwen Trial and the Prosecution of Child Soldiers' by Adam Branch, Ledio Cakaj, Danya Chaikel, Mark Drumbl, Rosebell Kagumire, Barrie Sander, Alex Whiting and Mark Kersten [available at: https://justiceinconflict.org/2016/04/11/the-dominic-ongwen-trial-and-the-prosecution-of-child-soldiers-a-jic-symposium/ (accessed 8 April 2018)]; Baines 2009.

[141] Combs 2011.

REFERENCED WORKS

Books, Articles, Reports and Legal Provisions

Amann, D.M. 2013. 'Children and the First Verdict of the International Criminal Court' 12 *Washington University Global Studies Law Review* 411

Babington-Ashaye, A., Comrie, A. and Adeniran, A. 2018. *International Criminal Investigations, Law and Practice* (The Hague: Eleven International Publishing)

Bagaric, M. and Morss, J. 2001. 'International Sentencing Law: In Search of a Justification and Coherent Framework' 6 *International Criminal Law Review* 191

Baines, E. 2009. 'Complex Political Perpetrators: Reflections on Dominic Ongwen' 47 *The Journal of Modern African Studies* 163

Barrett, J.C. 2014. 'What a Difference a Day Makes: Young Perpetrators of Genocide in Rwanda' *University of Cambridge Faculty of Law Research Paper* No. 24/2014

Beckmann Hamzei, H. 2015. *Child in the ICC Proceedings* (Cambridge: Intersentia)

Beresford, S. 2005. 'Child Witnesses and the International Criminal Justice. Does the International Criminal Court Protect the Most Vulnerable?' 3 *Journal of International Criminal Justice* 721

BiH, Criminal Code of Bosnia and Herzegovina (2003 CC BH) adopted by the Parliamentary Assembly of Bosnia and Herzegovina on 27 June 2003 and published in the Official Gazette 37/03, as amended by Law 8/10 (2003) (27 June 2003) [BiH Criminal Code]

Bouwknegt, T. 2014. 'How Did the DRC Become the ICC's Pandora's Box', *African Arguments* (5 March)

Bouwknegt, T. 2015. 'Born at the Time of the White Ant, Tried by the ICC', *African Arguments* (20 January)

Catani, L. 2012. 'Victims at the International Criminal Court: Lessons Learned from the Lubanga Case' 10 Journal of International Criminal Justice 905

Combs, N.A. 2011. *Fact-Finding without Facts: The Uncertain Evidentiary Foundations of International Criminal Convictions* (New York: Cambridge University Press)

D'Ascoli, S. 2011. *Sentencing in International Criminal Law: The UN Ad Hoc Tribunals and Future Perspectives for the ICC* (Oxford: Hart Publishing)

Drumbl, M. 2007. *Atrocity, Punishment and International Law* (New York: Cambridge University Press)

Drumbl, M. 2012. *Reimagining Child Soldiers in International Law and Policy* (Oxford: Oxford University Press)

Drumbl, M. 2014. 'The Effects of the Lubanga Case on Understanding and Preventing Child Soldiering' 15 *Yearbook of International Humanitarian Law* 87

Drumbl, M. 2016a. 'Victims Who Victimize: Transcending International Criminal Law's Binaries' *Washington & Lee Legal Studies Paper* No. 2016-2

Drumbl, M. 2016b. 'Kapo on Film: Tragic Perpetrators and Imperfect Victims' *Washington & Lee Public Legal Studies Research Paper Series*, Accepted Paper No. 2016-13

EAC, Accord entre le gouvernement de la République du Sénégal et l'Union Africaine sur la création de chambres africaines extraordinaires au sein des juridictions Sénégalaises, Dakar (22 August 2012) [EAC Accord]

Ferelli, A., Heath, E., Jang, E. and Takeuchi, C. 2015. 'Expert Workshop Session: Regulatory Framework' 43 *Georgia Journal of International and Comparative Law* 639

Haslam, E. and Edmunds, R. 2017. 'Whose Number Is It Anyway? Common Legal Representation, Consultations and the "Statistical Victim"' 15 *Journal of International Criminal Justice* 931

Hola, B. 2012. *International Sentencing: 'A Game of Russian Roulette' or Consistent Practice?* (Oisterwijk: Boxpress)

Hola, B. 2016. 'Special Court for Sierra Leone: RUF Sentencing Judgment – Commentary', in A. Klip and S. Freeland (eds), *Annotated Leading Cases of International Criminal Tribunals* (Antwerp: Intersentia) 414

ICC, OTP Policy on Children (November 2016) [available at: https://www.icc-cpi.int/iccdocs/otp/20161115_OTP_ICC_Policy-on-Children_Eng.PDF (accessed 5 October 2018)]

ICC, OTP Press Release: 'Statement of the Prosecutor of the International Criminal Court, Mrs. Fatou Bensouda, on the International Day against the Use of Child Soldiers' (12 February 2018)

ICC, OTP Strategic Plan 2012–2015 (11 October 2013) [available at: https://www.icc-cpi.int/iccdocs/otp/OTP-Strategic-Plan-2013.pdf (accessed 5 October 2018)]

ICC OTP Strategic Plan 2016–2018 (16 November 2015) [available at: https://www.icc-cpi.int/iccdocs/otp/EN-OTP_Strategic_Plan_2016-2018.pdf (accessed 5 October 2018)]

ICC Rules of Decorum, ICC-PIDS-RD-001-09_ENG [available at: https://www.icc-cpi.int/iccdocs/PIDS/publications/ICCRODEngLR.pdf (accessed 5 October 2018)]

ICC Rules of Procedures and Evidence (ICC-ASP/1/3 and Corr.1) Official Record of the Assembly of States Parties to the Rome Statute of the International Criminal Court, First Session. New York (3–10 September 2002) [ICC RPE]

IHCC, Law No. (10) 2005. Law of the Iraqi Higher Criminal Court, Al-Waqa'I Al-Iraqiya. Official Gazette of the Republic of Iraq, Vol. 47, No. 4006 (18 October 2005) [Statute of the Iraqi High Special Tribunal]

Kelsall, T. 2009. *Culture Under Cross-Examination. International Justice and the Special Court for Sierra Leone* (London: Cambridge University Press)

Kendall, S. and Nouwen, S. 2013. 'Representational Practices at the International Criminal Court: The Gap between Juridified and Abstract Victimhood' 76 *Law and Contemporary Problems* 235

Killean, R. and Moffett, L. 2017. 'Victim Legal Representation before the ICC and ECCC' 15 *Journal of International Criminal Justice* 713

KSC, Law No. 05/L-053 on Specialist Chambers and Specialist Prosecutor's Office, Republic of Kosovo (3 August 2015) [KSC Law]

Kurth, M. 2013. 'The Lubanga Case of the International Criminal Court: A Critical Analysis of the Trial Chamber's Findings on Issues of Active Use, Age, and Gravity' 5 *Goettingen Journal of International Law* 431

Lieflander, T.R. 2012. 'The Lubanga Judgment of the ICC: More than Just the First Step?' 1 *Cambridge Journal of International and Comparative Law* 191

Malone, L.A. 2015. 'Maturing Justice: Integrating the Convention of the Rights of the Child into the Judgments and Processes of the International Criminal Court' 43 *Georgia Journal of International and Comparative Law* 599

Moffett, L. 2015. 'Meaningful and Effective? Considering Victims' Interests Through Participation at the International Criminal Court' 26 *Criminal Law Forum* 255

Moffett, L. 2017. 'Reparations for Victims at the International Criminal Court: A New Way Forward?' 21 *The International Journal of Human Rights* 1204

Navarro, N.T. 2018. 'Collective Reparations and the Limitations of International Criminal Justice to Respond to Mass Atrocity' 18 *International Criminal Law Review* 67

Neal, K. 2015. 'Child Protection in Times of Conflict and Children and International Criminal Justice' 43 *Georgia Journal of International and Comparative Law* 629

Oosterveld, V. and Marlowe, A. 2007. 'Prosecutor v. Alex Tamba Brima, Brima Bazzy Kamara and Santigie Borbor Kanu; Prosecutor v. Moinina Fofana & Allieu Kondewa' 10 *The American Journal of International Law* 848

Peters, K. 2011. *War and the Crisis of Youth in Sierra Leone* (London: Cambridge University Press)

Romero, J.A. 2004. 'The Special Court for Sierra Leone and the Juvenile Child Soldier Dilemma' 2 *Northwestern Journal of International Human Rights* 1

Sanin, K and Stirnemann, A. 2006. 'Child Witnesses at the Special Court for Sierra Leone' (Berkeley: War Crimes Studies Center, University of California)

SCC, Loi Organique n° 15-003 Portant Création, Organisation et Fonctionnement de la Cour Pénale Spéciale, Journal Officiel de la Republique Centrafricaine Bangui (5 June 2015) [SCC Law]

Seyfarth, L. 2013. 'Child Soldiers to War Criminals: Trauma and the Case for Personal Mitigation' 14 *Chicago-Kent Journal of International and Comparative Law* 117

Stahn, C. 2015. 'Reparative Justice after the Lubanga Appeal Judgment: New Prospects for Expressivism and Participatory Justice or 'Juridified Victimhood' by Other Means?' 13 *Journal of International Criminal Justice* 801

Swanson, C., Devos, E., Ricke, C. and Shin, A. 2015. 'Expert Workshop Session: Child Witnesses: Testimony, Evidence, and Witness Protection' 43 *Georgia Journal of International and Comparative Law* 649

Tibori-Szabo, K. and Hirst, M. 2017. *Victim Participation in International Criminal Justice. Practitioner's Guide* (The Hague: Springer, Asser Press)

UN Transitional Administration in East Timor, Regulation No. 2000/30 on the Transitional Rules of Criminal Procedure, UNTAET/REG/2000/30, 25 September 2000.

UN Transitional Administration in East Timor, Regulation 2001/25 on the Amendment of UNTAET Regulation No. 2000/11 on the Organization of Courts in East Timor and UNTAET Regulation No. 2000/30 on the Transitional Rules of Criminal Procedure, UNTAET/REG/2001/25, 14 September 2001

Wijk van, J. 2013. 'Who Is the "Little Old Lady" of International Crimes? Nils Christie's Concept of the Ideal Victim Reinterpreted' 19 *International Review of Victimology* 159

Judicial Proceedings

Court of Bosnia and Herzegovina, Jakupovic, *Prosecutor v. Elvir Jakupovic* (Case No. X-KR-10/906)
- Verdict (20 August 2010)

ICC, Al Mahdi, *Prosecutor v. Ahmad Al Faqi Al Mahdi* (Case No. ICC-01/12-01/15-171)
- Judgment and Sentence (27 September 2016)

ICC, Bemba, *Prosecutor v. Jean-Pierre Bemba Gombo* (Case No. ICC-01/05-01/08-3399)
- Decision on Sentence pursuant to Article 76 of the Statute (21 June 2016)

ICC, Katanga, *Prosecutor v. Germain Katanga* (Case No. ICC-01/04-01/07)
- Judgment pursuant to Article 74 of the Statute (7 March 2014)
- Decision on Sentence pursuant to Article 76 of the Statute (23 May 2014)

ICC, Lubanga, *Prosecutor v. Thomas Lubanga Dyilo* (Case No. ICC-01/04-01/06)
- Judgment pursuant to Article 74 of the Statute (14 March 2012)
- Separate and Dissenting Opinion of Judge Odio-Benito (14 March 2012)
- Decision on Sentence pursuant to Article 76 of the Statute (10 July 2012)
- Judgment on the appeal of Mr Thomas Lubanga Dyilo against his conviction (1 December 2014)
- Dissenting Opinion of Judge Anita Ušacka, appended to Judgment on the appeal, ICC-01/04-01/06-3121-Anx2 (1 December 2014)
- Report of Ms. Elisabeth Schauer following the 6 February 2009 'Instructions to the Court's expert on child soldiers and trauma' (25 February 2009)
- Transcripts:
  3 November 2006
  9 November 2006
  15 November 2006
  28 January 2009
  16–20 February 2009
  12 May 2009
  13 May 2009
  16 November 2010
  26 August 2011

ICC, Ntaganda, *Prosecutor v. Bosco Ntaganda* (Case No. ICC-01/04-02/06)
- Decision on Confirmation of Charges (9 June 2014)
- Judgment on the appeal of Mr Ntaganda against the 'Second decision on the Defence's challenge to the jurisdiction of the Court in respect of Counts 6 and 9' (15 June 2017)
- Transcripts:
  14 June 2017

ICTY, Celebici, *Prosecutor v. Zejnil Delalic, Zdravko Muci, also known as 'PAVO', Hazim Delic, Esad Landzo also known as 'ZENGA'* (Case No. IT-96-21)
- Judgment (16 November 1998)

ICTY, Foca, *Prosecutor v. Kunarac, Kovac and Vukovic* (Case No. IT-96-23 & 23/1)
- Judgment (22 February 2001)

SCSL, AFRC, *Prosecutor v. Alex Tamba Brima, Ibrahim Bazzy Kamara and Santigie Borbor Kanu* (Case No. SCSL-04-16)
- Judgment (20 June 2007)
- Sentencing Judgment (19 July 2007)
- Transcripts:
  6 October 2005

SCSL, CDF, *Prosecutor v. Sam Hinga Norman, Moinina Fofana and Allieu Kondewa* (Case No. SCSL-04-14)
- Judgment (2 August 2007)
- Judgment on the sentencing of Moinina Fofana and Allieu Kondewa (9 October 2007)
- Decision on Prosecution Motion for Modification of Protective Measures of Protective Witnesses (8 June 2004)

SCSL, RUF, *Prosecutor v. Issa Hassan Sesay, Morris Kallon and Augustine Gbao* (Case No. SCSL-04-15)
- Indictments
- Kallon – Decision approving indictment and order for non-disclosure. SCSL-03-07-I-003 (7 March 2003) (made public pursuant to order of 14 March 2003)
- Sesay – Decision approving the indictment and order for non-disclosure. SCSL-03-05-I-003 (7 March 2003)
- Gbao – Decision approving the indictment. SCSL-03-09-PD-011 (16 April 2003)
- Judgment (25 February 2009)
- Sentencing Judgment (8 April 2009)
- Decision on Prosecution Motion for Modification of Protective Measures for Witnesses (5 July 2004)
- Transcripts:
  20 July 2004
  27 July 2004

SCSL, Taylor, *Prosecutor v. Charles Ghankay Taylor* (Case No. SCSL-03-01)
- Judgment (26 April 2012)
- Sentencing Judgment (30 May 2012)
- Transcripts:
  21 October 2008

SPSC, X, *Prosecutor v. 'X'* (Case No. 04/2002)
- Judgment (2 December 2002)

17. Dominic Ongwen on trial: problematizing definitional boundaries and exploring the possibilities of socialization
Carse Ramos

> Your Honours are faced with the gigantic task to determine a few unfamiliar questions. Firstly, whether the accused qualifies as a victim. If so, whether his victimhood ceased at any time during his captivity under the LRA. Did he, having been a victim kept under the keen watch of Joseph Kony and his spy network and scared of spiritualism, transcend into a perpetrator? And did the accused, abducted at the age of 9 and having spent nearly 27 years in the vicious grips of the LRA, become an adult in terms of mind transformation? And, more poignantly, Your Honours will have to decide whether the accused, like many of his peers, believed in Kony's spiritualism. Did he believe he was helpless under the spell of Kony's spiritualism? If he did, how did it impact on his mind or on his mental disposition? Did it leave him with the presence of mind to act independently as a reasonable man, even after attaining physical adulthood.[1]

In 2005, the International Criminal Court (ICC) issued an arrest warrant for five high-ranking officers in the Lord's Resistance Army (LRA): Joseph Kony, the rebel group's leader; Vincent Otti, Kony's chief deputy and second in command; Raska Lukwiya, the third-highest-ranking officer in the LRA; Okot Odhiambo, a senior leader who later took up Otti's post; and Dominic Ongwen, a high-level commander who was allegedly in charge of the Sinia Brigade, a unit within the LRA. In 2015, through a complex series of exchanges, Dominic Ongwen surrendered to forces in the Central African Republic, after which he was subsequently handed over to US troops and then the relevant parties in The Hague. Joseph Kony is still at large, and the three others have either been confirmed or are presumed to be dead.[2] Ongwen, for his part, is now on trial in The Hague at the ICC.

Ongwen faces 70 charges of crimes against humanity and war crimes – more than any defendant to date. In addition to holding this dubious distinction, his case also marks the first whereby an individual is being charged with the same crimes of which he was also a victim: Ongwen was himself conscripted into the LRA at age nine.[3]

A plethora of voices exist within Uganda and outside the country regarding what should be or should have been done in such a complex case. A number of contentious

---

[1] Krispus Ayena Odongo, one of Dominic Ongwen's lawyers, in the defence's opening statement on 18 September 2018. Edited slightly for flow. ICC, Ongwen Transcript (18 September 2018): 5.
[2] Raska Lukwiya was killed in 2006 while fighting Ugandan government forces. Okot Odhiambo's death was confirmed as having occurred in 2013. Vincent Otti's death has never been confirmed legally, but it is widely accepted that he was killed in 2007, allegedly by Odhiambo, at Kony's command. Many claim that Kony had become suspicious of Otti due to the latter's dealings in the Juba peace talks.
[3] Dominic Ongwen's age at the time of his conscription has variously been given as 9, 10 and 14.

questions arise. First: what sort of justice-seeking mechanism is appropriate in Ongwen's case: a formal court process, traditional mechanism, some combination of the two or amnesty? Second: what exactly should Ongwen be held accountable for if so established on the facts? Some argue that he should be held accountable for all atrocities he committed, or that were committed at his behest; others argue that he should not be held responsible for any; and still another, larger, contingent favour holding him accountable for crimes he committed as an 'adult' but not those committed as a 'child', though the temporal parameters of these two categories in this (and arguably any) case prove problematic at best. Third: if a trial process is to proceed – which is indeed the case – how, if at all, should Ongwen's previous experiences as a victim count in that process? What weight should they be given? Again, opinions fracture. Some observers argue that, following the logic that Ongwen should be held accountable only for crimes committed as an 'adult', his 'childhood' experiences are irrelevant. A second voice, one which I heard most frequently during my time in Uganda, contends that the fact of his being conscripted at such a young age as well as his subsequent experiences should mitigate his sentence if he is found guilty. A third opinion is that, given Ongwen's experiences as a child, he could scarcely be expected to appreciate the gravity of what he was doing; in legal terms, this third position posits that he did not have – and could not have had – the requisite *mens rea*. This chapter emerges largely from an exploration of this last position.

This chapter is primarily a theoretical undertaking that grapples with some of the questions above, but which is rooted in a decade of fieldwork both in Uganda and within court systems. I draw on interviews, informal conversations and observations from my time in Uganda and elsewhere to make some preliminary findings.[4] The variety of voices that I encountered come together to paint a rich and composite picture, which both mirrors and adds nuance to that portrayed through academic debates. The chapter begins with a brief discussion of two definitional and categorical quandaries presented by child soldiers more generally and the Ongwen case in particular, namely age delimiters and victim-perpetrators. It then places these complex constructs into the trial setting. The chapter considers how these constructs play out in the proceedings against Ongwen and, more specifically, in his defence. The chapter concludes with an exploration of the role that socialization processes might play and the importance of incorporating sociology as a related but alternative framework through which to better understand Ongwen's case.

1. AGE AS A MATTER OF LAW

According to Article 26 of the Rome Statute, 'The Court shall have no jurisdiction over any person who was under the age of 18 at the time of the alleged commission of a crime.'[5] This is a crucial jurisdictional limitation. The UN Convention on the Rights of the Child (CRC) defines a child as 'every human being below the age of 18 years unless, under the law applicable to the child, majority is attained earlier'.[6] While 18 is taken to be the age of

---

[4] These are not intended to be representative of or generalizable to a broader population.
[5] See also Kaushik and Freeland in this volume; Holá and Bouwknegt in this volume.
[6] CRC, art. 1.

majority, a separate category arises in many legal documents beginning at age 15. This has prompted some variability in the international legal sphere.[7] Under the Rome Statute, for example, the conscription, enlistment, or active use of children under age 15 in combat is a war crime. Many argue that this second age delimiter stresses the gravity of conscripting younger children and would, therefore, serve to deter the use of child soldiers. Others have a different, more cautionary perspective. The differentiation of criminal categorization between those conscripted before and after age 15, in essence, creates a three-year window in which, on the one hand, conscription is not a war crime and therefore has lower costs, and, on the other, conscripted individuals within this age bracket cannot be tried by the ICC. Proponents of this interpretation argue that this discrepancy effectively creates a subgroup of combatants who can commit atrocities with impunity, which would actually encourage their use in military campaigns. Julia McBride observes:

> The [Rome] Statute undoubtedly goes further than any international treaty has on this issue, expanding the prohibited conduct to include a wider variety of combat and non-combat roles. Unfortunately, it chose to stick with the age limit of fifteen years, not only creating the undesirable result whereby recruiters can recruit soldiers who are immune to ICC prosecution (those aged between fifteen and eighteen), but also perpetuating a lacuna in the human rights framework relating to child protection. The 'Straight-18' movement suffered a strong blow indeed when this controversial age limit was maintained.[8]

The wording in the Optional Protocol to the CRC (OPAC) raises similar questions. What does it mean to take 'direct part' versus indirect part in hostilities? This proves vague both legally and conceptually. Further, does the differentiation in allowable age cut-off between state and non-state forces make sense? While one could perhaps posit a more widely acceptable justification for state use of 15- to 17-year-olds, understanding of the obligations of non-state actors is murky at best, and enforcement close to impossible.[9]

When it comes to criminal accountability, there is even less clarity. As noted above, the Rome Statute expressly disclaims jurisdiction for any acts committed by an individual when he or she is under age 18. This aside, however, there is little guidance in international law as to whether and how to hold former child conscripts accountable for their actions. Provisions dealing with accountability are also rarely found in documents intended to end conflicts, with a few exceptions such as the Juba Agreement. Even in this case, however, no clear guidelines are given regarding child soldiers. Sonia Grover notes that the government of Uganda and the LRA stipulated in the Juba Agreement that all matters dealing with accountability were to be 'handled at the local level via formal and informal mechanisms, though in the latter case also, there was no specific mention of child soldiers or their status as victims and/or alleged perpetrators'.[10] She continues:

---

[7] Grover 2012; Nylund 2016; Rosen 2005; Singer 2005.
[8] McBride 2014: 78.
[9] An in-depth treatment of international legal provisions and norms relating to the use of children associated with armed forces or armed groups transcends the scope of this chapter. So, too, does a full examination of the developing and increasingly robust critical literature on these regulations and standards. Other authors, however, have engaged with these discussions more comprehensively. See, e.g.: Nylund 2016; Grover 2012; Drumbl 2012; Wessells 2006.
[10] Grover 2012: 32.

Most commonly and importantly, in addition, these peace agreements often include no statement as to: (1) what status 'child soldiers' who have committed conflict-related atrocities hold . . . and (2) whether these children will be criminally prosecuted or otherwise held accountable for atrocities they committed as child soldier members of armed groups or national forces engaged in systematic mass atrocity and/or genocide.[11]

This ambiguity regarding potential criminal accountability in terms of both age and status contributes to the perpetuation of the falsely dichotomous peace versus justice debate that has been ongoing in Uganda since the early 2000s, with the advent of the country's amnesty law and discourse surrounding trials. Individuals did not know what, if anything, they would be held accountable for if they surrendered or submitted themselves voluntarily to a disarmament, demobilization and reintegration programme. Rumours abounded. This was, at least in part, due to issues pertaining to this grey area between childhood and adulthood.

Whether the age delimiter is cast at 15 or 18, however, the issue still remains that bright line rules are problematic at best in that they rest on a number of assumptions about the content and parameters of childhood, adulthood, adolescence, and the spaces in between. Nearly everyone outside the court system with whom I spoke in my qualitative research thought an age-based cut-off was arbitrary. Individuals self-identifying as victims expressed dissatisfaction with using age as a litmus test for what could be prosecuted, not least because age and adulthood do not always correspond. Most also echoed the words of multiple interviewees, namely that *childhood and adulthood mean very different things when you are brought up amongst rebels*. Or, as Roméo Dallaire has asked, 'Is a child still a child when pressing the barrel of a gun to your chest?'[12] It is worth noting, however, that while I encountered significant opposition to and critique of the so-called Straight-18 position amongst many in Uganda, I found no agreement as to another metric to offer in terms of what a sensible or workable delineation might look like.

Most current collective perceptions of child soldiers frame the figure of the child soldier as an inherently shocking one, 'an unnatural conflation of two contradictory and incompatible terms'.[13] And, indeed, most advocacy and awareness-raising done around the issue of children in combat – in addition to much of our related social and legal ordering – exploits this conflation. Substantial academic work has been undertaken in this area and largely paints child soldiers as naïve victims either of their captors or of circumstances.[14] David Rosen argues that this is largely due to what he calls the humanitarian narrative that has dominated in recent decades, based on the core assumptions of (1) the changing nature of war; (2) child soldiers as innocent, 'pure' victims, and (3) the proliferation of small arms. Peter Singer discusses each of these elements in depth to posit that the use of children in combat – in its present form – is a strictly modern phenomenon.[15] While this rather flat conceptualization still largely dominates discourse, it has been critiqued in a small but growing body of scholarship.[16]

---

[11] Ibid.: 32–3.
[12] Dallaire 2011: 2.
[13] Rosen 2005.
[14] See e.g., Singer 2005 and Wessells 2006. For a survey of relevant literature, see Drumbl 2012 and Honwana 2007.
[15] Singer 2005.
[16] Drumbl 2012; Rosen 2005; Honwana 2007; Gates and Reich 2010.

Rosen has observed that: 'age and childhood are contested domains. Chronological age has no absolutely fixed meaning in either nature or culture. Like ethnicity, age categories such as "child", "youth", and "adult" are situationally defined within a larger system and cannot be understood without consideration of conditions and circumstances.'[17] In other words, age is a social construct, given meaning by the society into which it is embedded. When societies deploy age as a structural category, Rosen suggests that there is necessarily continual social and political tension about the implications of the boundary lines. Further, according to Rosen and a number of other critics, the Straight-18 position is based on a Western-informed fictional narrative about what childhood and adulthood are supposed to be. Rather than being context-specific, this narrative requires universality across both time and space, thereby invoking the myth that age categories mean the same thing historically and geospatially. This, Rosen argues, is simply not the case. He further observes that youth and war have historically gone hand-in-hand, arguing against the idea that our current collective shock at the figure of the child soldier is constant or even long-standing.[18]

Mark Drumbl, too, deconstructs many aspects of the assumptions underlying the humanitarian narrative offered by Singer and others, persuasively arguing against the overly simplistic tropes of the child soldier as either an entirely naïve and helpless figure or a vicious, bloodthirsty monster – a 'killing machine' in Ugandan parlance. Rather, he illustrates that all types of children join armed forces for any number of reasons, including on their own initiative, though choice may look very different across contexts.[19]

2. CATEGORICAL COMPLICATIONS: CHILD SOLDIERS AS VICTIMS AND PERPETRATORS

Over the course of my fieldwork, most discussions that I had with interviewees and others about Ongwen's accountability were less concerned with establishing specific age. Instead, by far the most frequent question I have heard – and one that I have heard time and again – over the past several years, as people attempt to navigate this thorny terrain is, *at what point did Ongwen become a killing machine?* The ideas behind framing the question in this way are multifaceted, speaking – at different times – to the soldier's loss of both humanity and innocence, and to the pervasiveness of indoctrination and commission of crimes. It also ties to another, more basic question – at what point did this individual cease to be a victim and become a perpetrator? Asking such a question, of course, implies belief that the individual does, in fact, move from one category to another. To be clear, when speaking of someone losing their status as a victim, I am not referring to instances in which this is done by choice through the process of reclaiming individual agency. There has been significant research done in this area, largely, though not exclusively, in the field of psychology. While no doubt important, this research speaks about a different process. In this case, we are not looking at an individual's own way of perceiving themselves; rather,

---

[17] Rosen 2005: 132.
[18] Ibid.: 4.
[19] Drumbl 2012.

the loss of victimhood described here is concerned with the loss of ascribed conceptual or legal status which grants access to certain spaces.

I have had conversations about the appropriate way to deal with Dominic Ongwen's case in a number of configurations with probably around 200 people, ranging from civil society representatives to lawyers to drivers to random people I met at community meetings and while travelling. Unsurprisingly, opinions vary widely, but the discussions themselves nearly all come back to this central question of pinpointing a moment or period where he transitioned from victim to perpetrator. Most of my interlocutors admitted feeling uncomfortable with assigning an age or marking a particular moment. When pressed, however, they did so. Some located the point at which Ongwen became 'a killing machine' at his eighteenth birthday (though again, most frequently with great reservation); others suggested that the transition occurred after achieving a certain rank within the LRA or receiving certain awards for his performance; still others suggested that the age of culpability should mirror the age at which one can consent to marry, because whatever had happened in his past, he was then 'a man'; still others suggested he became 'a man' long before he turned 18. The one group of individuals for whom this question was relatively unmuddied were legal representatives (whether affiliated with the ICC or domestic Ugandan courts) I met in Kampala, Gulu and Lira. This is, perhaps, unsurprising, as the Rome Statute, which forms the basis for the ICC's existence and operation, excludes the jurisdiction of the ICC over those aged under 18. This jurisdictional exclusion has subsequently been incorporated into Uganda's body of law through its 2010 ICC Act.[20]

Some of my interlocutors, for a variety of reasons, suggested that Ongwen never made this move from one category to the other. Many believed that what happened to him as a child was quite simply too traumatic for him to ever be held fully accountable for his actions; others characterize him as an ongoing victim of Joseph Kony's manipulation. For these individuals, Ongwen remains a victim, and, while he perpetrated heinous crimes, he never became a perpetrator as such. Using such a framing, the acts are separated from the identity. Ongwen arguably remains in the interstices between the two categories.

Ongwen presents a paradigmatic example of a complex victim – someone who, according to Erin Baines' formulation, was 'subjected to the same harms in which they are also complicit'.[21] The construction and treatment of the complex victim – in this case, the 'victim-perpetrator' – is at the heart of this interstitiality. Not all, however, agree that the concept of 'victim-perpetrator' is useful. Sonja Grover argues that not only is this an inappropriate framework into which to place former conscripts like Ongwen, but that the category itself is inherently contradictory and makes no sense as a legal designation. She writes:

> [T]he social science concept of 'victim-perpetrator' which has gained popular use in the context of the issue of child soldiers who have committed conflict-related atrocity as members of a murderous armed group is, from a legal perspective, as devoid of meaning as would be the

---

[20] International Criminal Court Act, 2010. *The Uganda Gazette* No. 39 Volume CIII dated 25th June 2010. Article 19(a) of the ICC Act, which deals with 'General Provisions of Criminal Law' states that 'the following provisions of the Statute apply, with any necessary modifications' and then lists several articles of the Rome Statute, including Article 26.

[21] Baines 2016: 6.

concept of a 'civilian-combatant' under IHL. One is either a civilian or a combatant under IHL; not both simultaneously... The concept of 'victim-perpetrator' simply sidesteps the issue of accountability by assigning it on the one hand and removing it entirely on the other, and is therefore not viable as a legal concept.[22]

In other words, according to Grover, Ongwen must be either a perpetrator – and thus fully accountable for his actions – or a victim, in which case he is not. Her point here is that 'victim' and 'perpetrator' spaces are entirely mutually exclusive, as they imply different mental states. One either has the requisite *mens rea* (perpetrator) or one does not (victim). Legally, Grover argues, this is a simple issue. Perhaps Grover is right in her characterization here, but only in terms of the limitations of the legal imagination. Law – at least formal justice-seeking processes – necessarily operates according to such binaries. In my own research, I have long considered the idea, while lawyers might like to think otherwise, that law is too blunt an instrument to effectively deal with the complexities of such cases. Formal courts, such as the ICC, are not nimble enough to operate and adjudicate in the liminal, or 'in-between', spaces that victim-perpetrators occupy. In their current form, legal mechanisms require clearer categories and simpler narratives. Child soldiers are doubly complex, because they are at once situated in the interstices between victim and perpetrator categories and are occupying both of these spaces simultaneously. Along these lines, Mark Drumbl further posits that individuals such as Ongwen may be non-justiciable, and eloquently observes that 'law could respect imperfect victims and tragic perpetrators by staying away from them'.[23]

However, the substance of the issues raised here extends beyond the strictly legal. In subsequent chapters of her book, Grover clearly advocates her position that Ongwen is in fact a 'continuing victim'. While I place her terminology into a different context here, it proves a useful framework through which to think about the interaction of socialization processes and criminal accountability and provides an alternative way to ask questions about Ongwen and those in similar situations.[24] Can victimhood be lost? Can Ongwen, or anyone else, cease being a victim? Can victim status be ceded? Or is this status 'continuing' regardless of what may later come to pass?

3. CHILD SOLDIERS ON TRIAL

> So who do you judge? The chubby 10-year-old boy who loved to tend to his garden – the one who got abducted? Or the murderer he is accused of becoming?[25]

Child soldiers came squarely to international attention in the context of Sierra Leone's civil war in the 1990s and early 2000s.[26] The recruitment and use of child soldiers largely formed the backbone of this conflict. Experiences of former conscripts, such as Ishmael

---

[22] Grover 2012: 254.
[23] Drumbl 2016: 245.
[24] Grover (2012) uses this term as part of an argument for understanding forced conscription as an act of genocide.
[25] Garsd and Crossan 2017.
[26] See also Oosterveld in this volume.

Beah, wound their way into popular culture.[27] The first ICC conviction for child conscription as a war crime[28] derives from significant jurisprudential advances in this area that had been effected by the Special Court for Sierra Leone (SCSL).

Much of the discourse in Sierra Leone mirrors that discussed throughout this chapter regarding Uganda. Are former conscripts victims? Are they perpetrators? Did they start as victims but become perpetrators, and if so, at what point did the transition occur? Or are they dually victims and perpetrators? The SCSL had jurisdiction to try individuals over the age of 15, unlike the ICC, but its first Chief Prosecutor, David Crane, opted not to prosecute former child soldiers at the SCSL. Crane was motivated by a number of considerations, the weightiest of which speak to the amount of responsibility borne by child combatants and the practicality of prosecution:

> The Prosecution decided early in developing a prosecutorial plan that no child between 15 and 18 had the sufficiently blameworthy state of mind to commit war crimes in a conflict setting. Aware of the clear legal standard highlighted in international humanitarian law, the intent in choosing not to prosecute was to rehabilitate and reintegrate this lost generation back into society. It would have been impractical to prosecute even particularly violent children because there were so many. Further, it was imperative that the prosecution seriously consider the clear intent of the UN Security Council and the drafters of the Statute creating the Court to prosecute those and only those who bore the greatest responsibility – those who aided and abetted; created and sustained the conflict; and planned, ordered, or directed the atrocities. No child did this in Sierra Leone.[29]

In the end, the issue of child soldiers was left to the corresponding Truth Commission.

Ongwen's trial, therefore, marks the first time a formerly abducted and conscripted individual will be adjudicated by an international court of law, and this presents a host of complications.[30] Should Ongwen's socialization into and growing up within the LRA mitigate his sentence or negate *mens rea* altogether? Opinions among those I interviewed in the civil society sector varied greatly, as did the opinions of those I observed in town hall meetings and with whom I randomly found myself engaged in conversation.

Some of my interlocutors felt that Ongwen neither could nor should be held accountable. There were several reasons given for this, ranging from the power of what many called indoctrination; the idea that he was forced to perform any atrocities that he may have committed; and that Ongwen himself was a victim. Whether indoctrinated or forced to commit the acts of which he is accused, such individuals claimed that Ongwen could not have had the requisite criminal intent. He either did not realize the gravity of what he was doing or had no choice. Other critics noted the unfair burden placed on Ongwen as

---

[27] Beah 2008.
[28] ICC, Lubanga Judgment (14 March 2012).
[29] Crane 2008: 15.
[30] Samuel Hinga Norman, who was prosecuted by the SCSL for forcibly conscripting children during the war, was also said to have to have been a former child soldier in the so-called Boys Platoon as part of the West African arm of the British Army. He was said to have been conscripted at 14. To this end, Ongwen is not technically the first former child soldier per the Straight-18 cut-off to be in front of an international tribunal. Norman's trial concluded in 2006; however, he died in 2007 prior to the verdict. It is, therefore, unclear whether or how his previous experiences would have been taken into account. McBride 2014: 92.

an effective 'representative' of the LRA, arguing that if anyone should be held singularly accountable, it must be Joseph Kony. Further, many argued that Uganda's amnesty process, of which Ongwen has been unable to avail himself, had worked and catalysed the demobilization of the LRA. These interlocutors disagreed with the proposition that Ongwen, who otherwise met the conditions in terms of his surrendering, and others of his purported rank, should be ineligible.[31] If, as one taxi driver told me, amnesty were to be extended to such high-ranking persons, more people would feel safe enough to 'come out of the bush'.[32] While over a decade has passed since the initially shaky ceasefire agreed in 2006 as part of the Juba peace talks, concern that fighting will resume still remains palpable.

Other voices are located at the opposite end of the spectrum. At this end, the tenor is that Ongwen was responsible for mass atrocities. He was not merely a simple foot soldier. Individuals propounding this position argue that amnesty was not designed for such cases. Otherwise, it would reinforce or perhaps even create a culture of impunity, something that many in the country are trying to overcome. Some went so far as to suggest that Ongwen should be held fully accountable for all crimes committed, although most adopted a qualified position, arguing that he was fully responsible for all crimes committed as an adult, in line with the ICC's cut-off age for jurisdiction. Even if, such voices argue, he himself was victimized as a child, by the time he reached adulthood, he knew or should have known better.

The most common point of view I encountered was that Ongwen should be tried and held accountable, but that the trauma he experienced as a child should come in to 'soften the blow' when he received his sentence. This would mean that the discussion would be displaced into the sentencing context as a mitigating factor. There was, of course, no agreement as to how exactly this should work or what the purported sentence should be, but the many people who expressed this opinion said that this would be the fairest approach. In this way, they said, Ongwen could be dealt with as a perpetrator, but his victimhood could be acknowledged in the process.

Both the ICC's Office of the Prosecutor (OTP) as well as the Office of Public Counsel for the Victims (OPCV) have acknowledged the complexity of Ongwen's case. In their opening statements, each respectively addressed the claims that Ongwen himself was a victim, with the OTP noting that many Ugandans might feel that the stories they were hearing from victims in the case could have been Ongwen's own. Indeed, Chief Prosecutor Fatou Bensouda observed, '[p]eople following the case against Dominic Ongwen may do so with mixed emotions. They will feel horror and revulsion at what he did but they will also feel sympathy'.[33] Nevertheless, the OTP maintains that Ongwen must be held accountable for the crimes with which he is charged, irrespective of his past, arguing that 'victimisation in the past is not a justification or an excuse to victimise others. Each human being must be taken to be endowed with moral responsibility for their actions'.[34] Similarly, Francisco Cox, who, together with Joseph Akwenyu Manoba represents 2,605

---

[31] Indeed, it has been widely noted that Ongwen himself surrendered on the assumption that he would receive amnesty.
[32] Fieldnotes, June 2016.
[33] ICC, Ongwen Transcript (6 December 2016): 36.
[34] Ibid.: 37.

of the victims participating in this case, noted that many victims believed Ongwen's conscription may had made him a victim as a child, but that his failure to escape and his continuing to commit atrocities as an adult rendered him responsible. To that end, Cox stated that the victims they represented in this case believed Ongwen must be held accountable.[35]

4. DEFENDING: DURESS AND DIFFICULTY

At the time of writing, both the ICC's OTP and OPCV have wrapped up their cases in the Ongwen proceedings, and the defence team has begun its case. Sources suggest that the defence plans to call 72 witnesses to speak to the circumstances under which Ongwen was living within the LRA and his actual or likely state of mind at various points.

At present, the particulars of the case that Ongwen's defence team will present are unfolding, but they have argued that Ongwen did not and could not have had requisite *mens rea*: namely, he was incapable of forming the necessary criminal intent. Under Article 31 of the Rome Statute, there are four acceptable enumerated grounds for excluding criminal responsibility. The defence team has indicated that they are raising a duress defence pursuant to Article 31(1)(d) of the Rome Statute. Additionally, emphasizing Ongwen's past victimization through his own experiences of being conscripted as a child, the defence team will also raise a mental disease defence under Article 31(1)(a), as well as an alibi defence regarding part of the charges.[36] The general public has not yet been informed of exactly how these grounds will be argued or who the witnesses will be, but mention has been made in both media interviews and in the defence opening statement about indoctrination, Ongwen's belief in Kony's spiritualism, and Stockholm syndrome.[37] At this point, it is unclear how much weight these defences will be given by the three judges.

Duress is defined in the Rome Statute as 'resulting from a threat of imminent death or of continuing or imminent serious bodily harm against that person or another person, and the person acts necessarily and reasonably to avoid this threat, provided that the person does not intend to cause a greater harm than the one sought to be avoided'.[38] The Rome Statute further elaborates that such a threat can come from another person or from circumstances beyond the control of the individual. In other words, this argument would suggest, Ongwen only acted because he was forced to, either explicitly by his superiors or implicitly through reasonable fear of what would happen if he disobeyed orders or tried to escape.

While points relating to all of the elements of duress have been raised, a great deal of attention has been placed on Ongwen's failure to escape.[39] Extensive discussion has arisen, both at trial and in Uganda, of the harsh punishments meted out to those who tried to

---

[35] ICC, Ongwen Transcript (7 December 2016): 63–5.
[36] Maliti 2018a.
[37] ICC, Ongwen Transcript (18 September 2018). See also Maliti 2018b.
[38] Rome Statute, art. 31(d).
[39] This is likely because the logistics and possibility of escape also dominate discussions on amnesty, which are inextricably linked with this case.

escape from Kony's control. There was wide belief that those caught attempting to escape would be killed. Whether or not this was always or even usually the case is both unknown and, to some extent, irrelevant. Rather, what matters is that this was a strong narrative that existed among LRA members. This is an issue that has already come up repeatedly at trial, and the defence team has indicated that this belief will form a critical backbone of its case. I also frequently heard this narrative within my own fieldwork, from former conscripts and others alike. Even with promises of amnesty, escaping was still a risky business. Further, many have noted that for LRA soldiers in positions of power, such as Dominic Ongwen, escape was made even more difficult by the increased level of scrutiny and surveillance placed on officers. This has already come up a number of times at trial.

Undoubtedly, a number of the witnesses for the defence will also speak to Ongwen's being forced to follow Kony's orders and his inability to leave. Interviews and outreach sessions with a number of representatives from the team suggest that the defence will probe the idea that not only did Ongwen fear for his life due to Kony's unpredictability but that he, like many of his fellow soldiers, also believed the latter to possess powerful magical powers.[40] Further, the team suggests that it will argue that not only had Ongwen heard rumours about the consequences of disobeying or deserting, but that he knew first-hand what Kony was capable of through the orders he gave in conjunction with Vincent Otti's death. Ongwen's lawyers have indicated that they will use the circumstances and purported impact of Otti's death as support for their duress claim.

If Ongwen's team of lawyers can establish a successful duress defence, then Ongwen will be acquitted. This, however, is likely to prove a tall feat. Both OTP and OPCV have already identified facts which would prove problematic for a duress defence: Kony's actual level of control over his men, the officers' discretion and the oft-repeated assertion that so many from the LRA manage to escape.

One particularly difficult challenge to Ongwen's defence came up repeatedly during my own research, namely that Ongwen did not simply follow orders – he excelled, outshining his peers. One former conscript I interviewed described Ongwen as an exceptionally talented soldier, a claim substantiated in reports, literature and in ICC testimony I observed. Ongwen was said to be always ready to carry out Kony's orders with precision and without hesitation – and that he was accordingly rewarded handsomely. It was precisely for this reason, according to this interlocutor, that Ongwen deserved to be on trial and sitting before the ICC. 'You know', he told me, 'the LRA soldiers were paid with men and wives. Dominic had many, many. Kony gave him many women and more soldiers.' Plus, Ongwen was able to grow his forces himself: 'That is why children were taken, you know. To have more and more people to command.'[41] While some soldiers were given or redistributed to Ongwen, my interviewee was of the view that Ongwen was quite capable of increasing his own numbers. For this, and for his unquestioning allegiance, Ongwen was repeatedly promoted and rewarded with yet more soldiers. In other words, Ongwen did not simply do what he felt he had to do to stay alive. He went above and beyond, taking pleasure in doing his job well. Even if the issue of childhood and adulthood were not so

---

[40] See e.g. Ogora 2018. This issue has also been raised repeatedly at trial. See also Barrett in this volume.
[41] Interview, 2017 (Soroti, Uganda).

problematic in this case, for my interviewee, Ongwen's culpability was clear. 'You do not excel so strongly out of fear of being killed', he insisted.[42] Rather, to use the phrase so often employed throughout Uganda, he had become a 'killing machine' and should be tried and punished accordingly.

Throughout the trial, testimony has been given that supports this depiction of Ongwen. Indeed, in early 2017, while I myself was sitting in the observation chamber, I heard recordings of Kony and Otti discussing a promotion for Ongwen (and others, including Kony himself) on the basis of his extraordinary abilities and dedication. And, of course, stories and reports such as this complicate the duress defence. After all, it is hard to make an argument that someone complied with orders due to fear of consequences, when that person went above and beyond what they were asked to do – or so the prosecution, victims' representatives and a number of other voices have argued.

This characterization of Ongwen has in turn been contested by his attorneys, however. In the defence's opening statement, lawyer Chief Charles Achaleke Taku highlighted that, by the time that Ongwen escaped from the bush, Ongwen's status had been reduced to the position of Private. Taku argued that this demotion challenges the idea of 'rapid promotion'.[43] If and how this will be further addressed by the defence team will be seen as the trial unfolds. However, for reasons argued in the final section of this chapter, the relationships between Ongwen's 'success' as a soldier and his victimhood status and culpabilities are not as straightforward as they seem at first glance.

5. RECONSIDERING ONGWEN AS A SOCIAL AND SOCIALIZED BEING

Mark Drumbl has noted that Ongwen provides a classic candidate for the 'rotten social background' (RSB) defence.[44] In the theory's original formulation, RSB was equated with severe economic deprivation. Richard Delgado asked whether, given the known strong relationships between severe socio-economic deprivation and criminal behaviour, coming from a rotten social background could serve as a defence for criminal activity.[45] If we stipulate that environmental adversity is a determining (if not causal) factor in the commission of crime, should that not then be taken into consideration as either an exculpatory or mitigating factor?[46] Extrapolating, and applying RSB theory to Ongwen's case, it could be argued that he is simply a product of his environment. However, this key idea can be conceptualized at a more fundamental level, and it is here that applying a sociological lens proves useful.

A key tenet of sociology is that of socialization, the processes through which we learn how to exist in social space as social beings. It is through socialization processes that we come to understand and internalize (or reject) the norms and values of the societies in

---

[42] Ibid. See also Akello in this volume. For a discussion of former LRA child soldiers as refugee applicants, see Rikhof in this volume.
[43] ICC, Ongwen Transcript (18 September 2018): 70.
[44] Drumbl 2016.
[45] Delgado 1985: 10.
[46] Ibid.

which we live. We learn how to interact with others in the social landscape and internalize not only how to perform any number of roles (such as that of girl, boy, child, mother, son, teacher, student, athlete, criminal, soldier, attorney and countless others) but how to perform them well. We know, usually from a quite young age, what it means to act like a 'good' child, boy, mother, and so on. As we get a bit older, we learn how to perform different roles well: student, teacher, employee, citizen and any number of others. The traits and values associated with 'good' performance are socially defined and attached to the particular societies, places and times in question, but as individuals grow up, they learn and internalize the rules and parameters set by their own situation. An individual, for example, may have a rebellious streak in adolescence, but they would have had to learn and internalize the rules in order to frequently break and react against them.

Socialization processes are also how we adapt to new environments. Moving from one country, town, job, school or peer group, for example, to another requires learning an entirely new set of cues, norms and social rules so that we can effectively interact with others and perform our roles well. These processes take place over the life course and are constant, iterative and progressive.

Social institutions or social units – such as the family, educational and religious institutions, the media and peer groups – facilitate socialization processes. For most, the first and primary social institution is the family. Through our families, we come to understand social norms and roles, develop value systems, and learn 'right' from 'wrong', both within in a given setting and as a moral concept. That is not to suggest that individuals learn a universal right and wrong from their families (and other social institutions), but rather that morality itself is socially and locally situated. That said, through the process of socialization, we often come to believe that our own values systems are or should be universal.

As social beings, we learn through interaction and observation. The former occurs chiefly through feedback – positive and negative reinforcement – either experiential or perceived. If a child grows up in a social unit that follows the axiom that children should be seen and not heard, he or she may be rewarded with praise or tacit approval for sitting quietly and politely in a public space and censured for playing loudly or engaging in other raucous behaviour. Through these responses, the child learns how to be 'good' according to parental and societal standards. Similarly, as part of the learning process we observe not only how others interact but also note the feedback that they receive. A younger child may observe that whenever an older sibling vocally disagrees with their parents, the sibling receives some sort of punishment. The younger sibling then learns to keep quiet in order to avoid punishment. Or, entering a new social environment, an individual may observe the way new peers greet one another and do the same. Finally, through the familial unit (and others), children also learn the social rules of their community or society. Children observe the way their parents interact with others and whether this interactional behaviour receives a positive or negative response. They also compare the behaviour of their parents to other adults in the context of this reward–punishment structure. In the film *Chocolat*, for example, the protagonist does not conform her behaviour to that of the small town to which she and her daughter, Anouk, have recently relocated and is the target of much disdain. At some point, upset and exasperated, Anouk asks 'Why can't you wear black shoes like the other mothers?' Here, the girl has not only learned that violating the town's social code has negative consequences but that, as is the case with the other mothers, following social convention is rewarded in a number of ways, including acceptance and access to social space. She herself craves this positive reinforcement.

We can see these same processes reflected in Ongwen's story. Conscripted at age nine, he would have gone through much of his socialization within the LRA. In addition to learning how to fight, obey and give orders, and any number of other skills that are required be a soldier and, more particularly, to be a soldier in this type of warfare, he also would have learned and internalized the norms and rules of the group – his community for what would be decades.[47] As many have pointed out, he would have gone through some of his initial value-setting at a younger age; however, following this line of reasoning, he would have, over time, adapted to these new norms.

Being conscripted at such a young age, the LRA would have taken the place of several of Ongwen's social units. It would have served as his peer group, school, workplace and family. Mention of this last aspect came up several times in a number of conversations I had in Uganda, particularly the ideas that fellow soldiers were brothers and sisters and that Kony, despite being widely feared, came to be viewed by many recruits as a father figure.[48]

Relatedly, Erving Goffman posited the idea of the total institution – a singular place in which all spheres of life take place under the same authority, in which an individual spends all of his or her time with roughly the same group of people, and in which all of an individual's time is tightly controlled and scheduled. These three factors come together, Goffman argued, 'as parts of a single overall rational plan purportedly designed to fulfil the official aims of the institution'.[49] Within the context of a total institution, resocialization processes occur, whereby individuals re-learn new ways of social being. Of relevance here, Goffman's framework explicitly contemplates military structures and carceral systems, in which nearly all aspects of an inmate's life are strictly regulated by a single authority figure or mechanism imposing formal and informal rules. The total institution is all encompassing and acts as a barrier to interaction with wider society. This framework can be readily applied to Ongwen's case, strengthening the impact that his growing up in such an environment would have had. Not only did the LRA serve as a primary unit of socialization, it served as *the only* unit though which Ongwen's socialization took place, through which he learned or re-learned norms, values and how to be part of society. Given that Ongwen was in the LRA for 20 years, should it then be surprising that he went on to be a 'good' soldier (if indeed he did) in such social world? As one civil society representative I interviewed noted:

> So, if you have been abducted and you have been indoctrinated into that system – some children like Dominic Ongwen were abducted as young as 7 years – and grow into that system, he does not know what is good. He only knows where you live you need to kill and to do this. And to come back and take these people to court, it would be almost double jeopardy, because when they were abducted their life was ruined and now when they come out you're taking them to court to answer for those charges. . . . But [in Uganda] a child of 7 years has an empty mind, and the things that you begin to put in the mind of that child that is what the child grows with and for

---

[47] For an account of growing up in the LRA and the impact this had on children's sense of identity, see Denov in this volume.
[48] See also Cakaj 2016.
[49] Goffman 1958: 45.

me Dominic grew up with that. Now, if the ICC was going to take care of those facts, nobody would be worried taking Dominic Ongwen to the ICC. But if ICC is saying for the crimes when he was young we forgive him, but when he turned adult those ones he did we won't forgive, then ICC is doing a disservice. The situation would have been different if Dominic at say at the age of 17, 18, even 20, he'd heard there's a rebel group called the LRA, and he said I have come here I am, I want you to recruit me. Then he is recruited then he started going into the ranks that would be a different case altogether. Nobody would say it is wrong. People would say, okay he chose to go there let him face the justice.[50]

There has been much talk about indoctrination, both inside and outside the courtroom. While indoctrination is found along the socialization spectrum, socialization is a broader concept that does not speak to any particular intent. Indoctrination implies the teaching of a specific doctrine or ideology. This, according to many observers, is indeed what the LRA does among those conscripted, but to focus solely on these interactions provides a much narrower and far less rich understanding of the complex layers of social ties that both bind Ongwen to the LRA and would have proven formative to his own social identity.

6. CONCLUSION

It is still too soon to know how these issues will be treated by all parties in the trial. However, their treatment in this case will set the standard going forward in important ways. In adjudicating cases like Ongwen's, courts are actually making decisions not only about the content of these various categorical designations discussed above (e.g., victim, perpetrator, child and adult), but also the socialization processes themselves: what constitutes legitimate social transmission and how catalytic this process is within a given context.

This is all the more interesting, complicated and crucial in the international forums, as such decisions will undoubtedly have a universalizing or flattening effect across vastly different landscapes, and risk further homogenizing what, for example, 'we' believe constitutes an appropriate delimiter for childhood and adulthood, what the content of these two categories should be, what is acknowledged as a legitimate way to learn how, for example, to be a child, adult, 'good' person and 'good' soldier, and how much weight this is to be given in the judicial process. Further consideration of these processes and their impact in the international criminal sphere, the outcomes and methods of their adjudication, and the related implications, also contribute to a richer understanding of whether and how victimhood is indeed seen to be 'continuing' and what that means. This chapter, in the end, posits that a more fruitful approach flows from taking sociological cues, namely by exploring the roles of socialization processes.

---

[50] Interview, 2016 (Gulu, Uganda).

REFERENCED WORKS

Books, Articles and Reports

Baines, E. 2016. *Buried in the Heart: Women, Complex Victimhood and the War in Northern Uganda* (Cambridge: Cambridge University Press)
Bakker, C. 2010. 'Prosecuting International Crimes Against Children: The Legal Framework' Innocenti Working Paper 2010-13 (Florence: UNICEF Innocent Research Centre)
Beah, I. 2008. *A Long Way Gone: Memoirs of a Boy Soldier* (New York: Sarah Crichton Books)
Cakaj, L. 2016. *When the Walking Defeats You: One Man's Journey as Joseph Kony's Bodyguard* (London: Zed Books)
Crane, D. 2008. 'Prosecuting Children in Times of Conflict: The West African Experience' 15 *Human Rights Brief* 11
Dallaire, R. 2011. *They Fight Like Soldiers, They Die Like Children* (London: Walker & Co.)
Delgado, R. 1985. 'Rotten Social Background: Should the Criminal Law Recognize a Defense of Severe Environmental Deprivation?' 3 *Law & Inequality: A Journal of Theory and Practice* 9
Drumbl, M. 2012. *Reimagining Child Soldiers* (Oxford: Oxford University Press)
Drumbl, M. 2016. 'Victims Who Victimise' 4 *London Review of International Law* 217
Garsd, J. and Crossan, A. 2017. 'How Do You Judge a Child Soldier?' *PRI's The World* (4 August)
Gates, S. and Reich, S. 2010. 'Introduction', in S. Gates and S. Reich (eds), *Child Soldiers in the Age of Fractured States* (Pittsburgh: University of Pittsburgh Press) 3
Goffman, E. 1958. 'Characteristics of Total Institutions' *Symposium on Preventive and Social Psychiatry* (Washington: Walter Reed Army Institute of Research) 43
Grover, S. 2012. *Child Soldier Victims of Genocidal Forcible Transfer: Exonerating Child Soldiers Charged with Grave Conflict-Related International Crimes* (Berlin; Heidelberg: Springer-Verlag)
Honwana, A. 2007. *Child Soldiers in Africa* (Philadelphia: University of Pennsylvania Press)
Maliti, T. 2018a. 'Defence Phase of Ongwen's Trial Begins This Week', *International Justice Monitor* (17 September)
Maliti, T. 2018b. 'Ongwen's Lawyers Ask Court to Dismiss All Charges Against Him', *International Justice Monitor* (19 September)
McBride, J. 2014. *The War Crime of Child Soldier Recruitment* (Amsterdam: Asser Press)
Nylund, B. 2016. *Child Soldiers and Transitional Justice: Protecting the Rights of Children Involved in Armed Conflicts* (Cambridge: Intersentia)
Ogora, L. 2018. 'Defence Counsel: Ongwen Followed Kony's Orders Because He Believed Kony Possessed Spiritual Powers', *International Justice Monitor* (3 September)
Rosen, D. 2005. *Armies of the Young: Child Soldiers in War and Terrorism* (New Brunswick, NJ: Rutgers University Press)
Singer, P. 2005. *Children at War* (New York: Pantheon Books)
Sloth-Nielsen, J. (ed.) 2008. *Children's Rights in Africa: A Legal Perspective* (Farnham, UK: Ashgate Publishing)
Wessells, M. 2006. *Child Soldiers: From Violence to Protection* (Cambridge: Harvard University Press)

Judicial Proceedings

ICC, Lubanga, *Prosecutor v. Thomas Lubanga Dyilo* (Case No. ICC-01/04-01/06)
– Judgment pursuant to Article 74 of the Statute (14 March 2012)
ICC, Ongwen, *Prosecutor v. Dominic Ongwen* (Case No. ICC-02/04-01/15)
– Transcripts:
  6 December 2016
  7 December 2016
  18 September 2018

18. Child soldiers and asylum – duality or dilemma?
Joseph Rikhof

Children who have been involved in armed conflict will not necessarily remain in their own countries. They often will leave in search of a better life either by themselves or accompanied by their families. While the majority of children travel to a neighbouring country or a country in the same region, it is certainly not uncommon to see these children take lengthy and perilous journeys, overland or by sea, to reach countries in Europe and North America as well as Australia and New Zealand. This phenomenon is not new. Every time in history that there has been a mass migration movement, children have constituted a major part of the exodus. From the upheavals after the First and Second World Wars, primarily within and from Europe, to similar events after the uprisings in Hungary in the 1950s and Czechoslovakia in the 1960s, to the refugees coming from Chile and South-East Asia in the 1970s, to the large-scale migration into Europe via the Mediterranean sea and overland voyages in the 2010s, to the plight of the Rohingya refugees arriving in Bangladesh most recently, children have been a very visible representation of these terrible events.

This chapter will examine the situation of children caught in the predicament of involuntary departure from their homes due to turmoil caused by war, precarious human rights situations or natural disasters from the perspective of refugee law. The countries mentioned in the previous paragraph all have in place laws and processes addressing the status of persons who want to seek asylum there, both in general as well as specifically for children. In this chapter, the emphasis in examining these domestic laws and processes will be on court decisions rendered in refugee cases – refugee law provides a fertile and consistent research environment since virtually all major aspects dealing with criminality in refugees eventually trace their way back to the 1951 Convention Relating to the Status of Refugees (Refugee Convention). In contrast, domestic immigration laws have many more permutations, thereby making it difficult to discern patterns and thus reach meaningful conclusions.[1]

The notion of a refugee should be placed in the larger context of international migration, which can be divided into two main categories: voluntary and involuntary migration. Voluntary migration connotes situations whereby people seek better circumstances for themselves without feeling compelled to leave their country. This usually occurs when people go to other countries for economic reasons or family reunion. Involuntary or forced migration refers to the movement of persons who are leaving an intolerable situation in their own country and seeking protection in another country. These concepts should be distinguished from the notion of irregular migration, which is migration that takes place outside state procedures established to manage the orderly flow of migrants into, through and out of their territories, and is often associated with migrant smuggling and human

---

[1] For an example of a comparative discussion in the immigration context, see Rikhof 2009.

trafficking. International legal efforts to counter these phenomena are contained in the Protocol to Prevent, Suppress and Punish Trafficking in Persons, Especially Women and Children, and the Protocol against the Smuggling of Migrants by Land, Sea and Air, which are part of the United Nations Convention against Transnational Organized Crime (Palermo Convention) and will not be discussed in this chapter.[2]

This chapter will provide an overview of the general precepts of refugee law, both in respect to adults and children. It will then proceed to discuss the approach taken in respect to children who have been involved in armed conflict. While these events comprise a very small number of the total cases processed, they are often high profile in nature. They are also exceedingly difficult from a humanitarian perspective as they present the same dilemma addressed in other chapters of this book,[3] namely the duality inherent in children involved in armed conflict. Such children are victims of crimes and inhuman circumstances, while simultaneously perpetuating the same type of misery visited upon others. This chapter will provide a comparative analysis of the practice in a number of countries addressing this duality while also attempting to tease out some conclusions.

1. CONTEMPORARY ASYLUM CONTEXT

The global asylum situation is grim. According to the United Nations High Commissioner for Refugees (UNHCR), in 2015 there were 65.6 million people displaced in the world, meaning they were forced from their homes. Of this number, 22.5 million were refugees and 10 million were stateless. Most of these people are living in refugee camps administered by the UNHCR in conjunction with the states to which these persons have fled. More than half of the refugees are under the age of 18.[4] Of these child refugees, in 2015–16 over 300,000 were unaccompanied or separated from their families, which is a five-fold increase from the period 2010–11.[5] Almost all of these instances occurred at the US–Mexican border or in Europe.[6]

2. OVERVIEW OF BASIC REFUGEE LAW CONCEPTS

Refugee law is based on two pillars. First, an asylum seeker who fulfils the requirements of being a refugee will be granted asylum. Second, a person who receives this status cannot be removed from the country which has granted asylum to the country against which asylum was claimed – this is called protection against refoulement. Upon receiving refugee status, a person is entitled to basic rights according to the Refugee Convention, such as

---

[2] For a discussion of irregular migration, see Rikhof 2012: 10–11.
[3] See for example Akello; Denov; Hanson and Molima; Ramos, all in this volume.
[4] UNHCR 2017b; for more details see UNHCR 2017a.
[5] UNICEF 2017a: 4
[6] Ibid.; see also UNICEF 2017b and UN Human Rights Council 2017: 6–10; for more details regarding the US–Mexican border, see UNHCR 2014; for more details regarding the European situation, see UK House of Lords 2016.

the right of association (Article 15), employment (Articles 17–19), housing (Article 21), education (Article 22), social security (Article 24) and freedom of movement (Article 26).

In order to receive refugee status, a person has to show that (s)he has a 'well-founded fear of being persecuted for reasons of race, religion, nationality, membership of a particular social group or political opinion, is outside the country of his nationality and is unable or, owing to such fear, is unwilling to avail himself of the protection of that country ...'.[7] Such an assessment is based on both past and future fear of persecution. Because this concept of persecution was framed immediately after the Second World War and not all issues arising out of situations of turmoil causing refugee movements are covered by the Refugee Convention, new concepts such as complementary, temporary and subsidiary protection have emerged at the global, national and regional levels to fill the gap between new realities and the existing Convention's legal regime.[8]

Similarly, the notion of refoulement has also undergone changes over the last decades. While the Refugee Convention contains exceptions[9] for the application of this concept, and as a result allows for the expulsion of persons who have been granted refugee status, the protection against refoulement is based on the same grounds as contained in the definition of refugee, namely persecution. To avoid situations whereby a person could be expelled who might be exposed to other human rights abuses or who falls outside the groups mentioned in this provision, regional and national legislative instruments supplement the concepts of the Refugee Convention. This is done by either providing a different form of protection, such as subsidiary protection, at the front end of the refugee process or by expanding the reasons for prohibiting refoulement at the back end. These expanded forms of protection have been borrowed from other human rights instruments[10] and typically include protection against killing, torture or other cruel, inhuman or degrading treatment or punishment.[11]

While the Refugee Convention, regional refugee treaties and national legislation primarily regulate aspects relating to obtaining refugee status and their associated rights, they do contain exceptions to these general tenets. For example, in certain circumstances refugee status will be denied, can be revoked or will not impede the removal of a refugee from a country of refuge.[12] This chapter will only discuss exceptions related to criminality, of which the one employed at the front end of the process called exclusion is the most important.[13] The exclusion clause in the Refugee Convention, which has been incorporated by all countries which have ratified it,[14] reads as follows:

---

[7] Refugee Convention, art. 1A(2).
[8] For details see Rikhof 2012: 14–17.
[9] They can be found in arts 32(1) and 33(2) of the Refugee Convention; the exceptions are in connection to the commission of very serious criminal offences or on grounds of national security or public order, usually when occurring in the country of refuge; for a detailed study of these exceptions see Rikhof 2012: 379–458.
[10] See the International Covenant on Civil and Political Rights (ICCPR); the Convention against Torture (CAT); and the International Convention for the Protection of all Persons from Enforced Disappearance. At the regional level, see the European Convention on Human Rights (ECHR).
[11] See Rikhof 2012: 17–21.
[12] For more details see Rikhof 2012: 21–6.
[13] With respect to criminality at the back-end, see Rikhof 2012: 22–6.
[14] All countries which will be discussed later in this chapter have ratified the Convention with

The provisions of this Convention shall not apply to any person with respect to whom there are serious reasons for considering that:
(a) he has committed a crime against peace, a war crime, or a crime against humanity, as defined in the international instruments drawn up to make provision in respect of such crimes;
(b) he has committed a serious non-political crime outside the country of refuge prior to his admission to that country as a refugee;
(c) he has been guilty of acts contrary to the purposes and principles of the United Nations.[15]

There has been much academic and jurisprudential debate about the relationship between the process of assessing the refugee claim (inclusion) and the application of the exclusion clause. The majority of countries discussed in this chapter favour an approach whereby exclusion, if applicable, is assessed first, and when established, inclusion will not be considered or balanced against exclusion.[16]

3. REFUGEE PROCEDURES FOR CHILDREN

Given the fact that children, especially unaccompanied children, are particularly vulnerable[17] when entering national refugee systems, the UNHCR has devised guidelines to assist and improve the decision-making processing with respect to these children. The main principles are the following:

- unaccompanied children should not be denied access to the territory of a country of refuge;
- they should be identified as such at the first possible instance when arriving on such territory;
- they should be registered through professionally conducted interviews to establish effective documentation;
- an experienced guardian or advisor should be appointed as soon as possible;
- they should always have access to asylum procedures;
- they are entitled to special care and protection;
- they should not be detained;
- their asylum applications should be given priority and processed as expeditiously as possible;
- if they are granted asylum, a durable solution based on local integration or third country resettlement should be found;

---

the exception of the United States; for more information about the regime in the US see Rikhof 2012: 177–80 and 255–6.

[15] Refugee Convention, art. 1F.

[16] See Rikhof 2012: 114–22. The UNHCR has maintained the opposite position both in general terms (UNHCR 2003a: 7; UNHCR 2003b: 27–8) and for children (UNHCR 2009: [62]).

[17] For more details regarding the unique types of persecution children face as well as how the four victim groups can apply to them, see UNHCR 2009: 6–19.

- if they are not granted asylum, an assessment of the solution that is in the best interests of the child should follow as soon as practicable.[18]

4. CHILD SOLDIERS IN REFUGEE PROCEEDINGS

The situation of child soldiers has been examined both at the inclusion and exclusion[19] stages in a number of countries. The notion of refoulement has also been taken into account at times. Most general aspects of refugee processing that are used in proceedings involving adults also apply to children. However, the proceedings can have disproportionate consequences for the latter group of refugee claimants. One such issue is the standard of proof and the type of evidence which can be adduced, especially in exclusion. The standard of proof set out in Article 1F of the Refugee Convention is 'serious reasons for considering that' a person has committed a 1F crime. While there have been some discrepancies in the interpretation of the meaning of this phrase, there has been agreement in the jurisprudence that this standard of proof is below the criminal standard of beyond reasonable grounds and might even be below the civil standard of balance of probabilities.[20] Along the same lines, the type of evidence required for both inclusion and exclusion is more relaxed than in criminal or civil cases. For example, the Canadian Immigration and Refugee Protection Act indicates that a decision maker 'is not bound by any legal or technical rules of evidence'.[21] This means that the evidence adduced is usually the testimony of the claimant, taken together with human rights reports regarding the situation in the country against which asylum is claimed. Given the fact that the testimony of the claimant is elevated to an essential part of the proceedings, credibility is always of crucial importance.

The last point of importance specifically in exclusion proceedings is the fact that over 95 per cent of 1F crimes amount only to indirect involvement due to the expansive reading of the word 'committed' in Articles 1F(a) and (b). The highest courts in the UK, New Zealand and Canada recently sought a more direct connection with international criminal law than had been the case in earlier jurisprudence. However, this notion of complicity can still be applied to a large spectrum of situations.[22] As a result, defences, especially the defence of duress, have been raised in a number of cases involving child soldiers.

In spite of the relative ease by which persons can be excluded from obtaining refugee status, the number of adults who have been excluded during refugee processes in Europe,

---

[18] UNHCR 1997; this was repeated in UNHCR 2009: 25–8; for details of about the implementation of the guidelines in Europe, see UNHCR/Council of Europe 2014 and the European Union Agency for Fundamental Rights 2016.

[19] There is a substantial amount of literature on the issue of exclusion of children. See Bond and Krech 2016; Dankoff 2011; Drumbl 2012: 131–2; Everett 2009; Grover 2008; Lonegan 2011; Maystre 2014; Rikhof 2012: 291–4; Rossi 2013; White 2010.

[20] Rikhof 2012: 109–13; Holvoet 2014.

[21] Immigration and Refugee Protection Act (IRPA), s 170(g), 173(c) and 175(1)(b).

[22] For the jurisprudence regarding complicity until 2012, see Rikhof 2012: 210–74; for an analysis of the three recent cases, see Rikhof 2015: 565–76.

North America, Australia and New Zealand is very small, ranging from 0.1 per cent to 0.4 per cent.[23] While there is no empirical evidence with respect to children, it is likely that the number is even lower.

4.1 Exclusion Proceedings

The issue of children in exclusion proceedings has been one of concern to the UNHCR and has been addressed twice in its guidelines: once in 2003 in a general guideline regarding exclusion[24] and once in 2009 in special guidelines with respect to children.[25]

The most important elements in the 2009 guideline deal with the mental capacity of children when committing crimes and says the following:

i. When determining individual responsibility for excludable acts, the issue of whether or not a child has the necessary mental state (or *mens rea*), that is, whether or not the child acted with the requisite intent and knowledge to be held individually responsible for an excludable act, is a central factor in the exclusion analysis. This assessment needs to consider elements such as the child's emotional, mental and intellectual development. It is important to determine whether the child was sufficiently mature to understand the nature and consequences of his/her conduct and, thus, to commit, or participate in, the commission of the crime. Grounds for the absence of the *mens rea* include, for example, severe mental disabilities, involuntary intoxication, or immaturity.

ii. If mental capacity is established, other grounds for rejecting individual responsibility need to be examined, notably whether the child acted under duress, coercion, or in defence of self or others. Such factors are of particular relevance when assessing claims made by former child soldiers. Additional factors to consider may include: the age at which the child became involved in the armed forces or group; the reasons for which s/he joined and left the armed forces or group; the length of time s/he was a member; the consequences of refusal to join the group; any forced use of drugs, alcohol or medication; the level of education and understanding of the events in question; and the trauma, abuse or ill-treatment suffered.[26]

On the national level, only the Netherlands has put in place special guidelines with respect to child soldiers in exclusion proceedings in its Aliens Manual of 2003, which instructs decision makers not to consider exclusion for child soldiers under the age of 15 years. For child soldiers between 15 and 18 years of age, each case must be considered on its own facts, but a number of circumstances need to be taken into consideration, namely the age at the moment of joining an organization; whether entering the organization was forcible or voluntary;[27] the consequences of refusing to join; events affecting the child's free will upon joining; the duration of employment as a child soldier; the possibility of early disassociation from the organization and/or from personal participation in crimes; the forced use of drugs and/or medication; and promotions for 'good work'.

When considering refusal to become a child soldier, the Manual makes it clear that it should be taken into account whether the minor could reasonably be expected to resist

---

[23] Rikhof 2012: 369, footnote 1413.
[24] UNHCR 2003b: 34.
[25] UNHCR 2009: 22–4.
[26] Ibid.: [64].
[27] For an interesting discussion on a regional approach to the issue of voluntariness, see Odongo in this volume who discusses the African regional system.

the pressure placed upon him or her. Events affecting the will are related to traumatic events. Lastly, the Manual explains that some factors can be considered as moving along a continuum. For example, joining an organization before the age of 15 will be seen in a more positive light than joining at a later age.[28]

Several courts have interpreted these guidelines. Four district courts overruled the assessments of the decision makers with respect to child soldiers on procedural grounds because it was not apparent that the age of the claimants had been taken into consideration.[29] Additionally, from a substantive perspective, a number of other decisions indicate that young persons under the age of 18 who were forcibly recruited into the armed forces and indirectly involved in the commission of international crimes should be excluded. The first such case involved a person who worked for UNITA (one of the three anti-colonial rebel groups) in Angola between the ages of 15 and 17.[30] The court excluded the person on the basis that, as head of logistics, he was sufficiently connected to the crimes committed by the organization to fall within parameters of complicity. In two other cases, one person working for the RUF in Sierra Leone and another for UNITA, the court rejected the defences of duress and acting under the influence of drugs because the criteria for these defences were not established. In the RUF case, the court also made credibility determinations, believing that the person could have refused to engage in rapes and arson, and could have left the camp where he was stationed given the camp's lax security.[31] Lack of credibility also led to a finding of exclusion in the UNITA case.[32]

In a further case, the court excluded a soldier who had been working for the Ugandan army from a young age. Although the court only assessed his involvement from the age of 15, the child had the choice of extracting himself from the army but had not done so.[33] The court reached a similar result regarding a person who voluntarily joined the PKK in Turkey at the age of 15, was complicit in terrorist activities and stayed on for another ten years.[34]

On the other hand, in another case, an appellate court reversed the decision maker's exclusion finding with respect to a person who carried out a number of serious criminal acts while a member of the RUF. The considerations in this case included the fact that the person had been voluntarily recruited at 15 years old, an age close to the legislative prohibition; the fact that the decision maker had interpreted the factor 'events affecting the free will upon joining' too narrowly by requiring a lack of *mens rea* while the legislative intent was to account for severe traumatization as a result of recruitment with very serious violence; and the fact that the person was under constant threat to carry out such

---

[28] Rikhof 2012: 291–2.
[29] Rb (Rechtbank) The Hague, Awb 02/50465, 4 December 2003 for Sierra Leone; Rb, The Hague, Awb 02/89347, 13 February 2004 for Turkey; Rb, The Hague, Awb 05/51473, 25 January 2007 for Afghanistan; Rb, The Hague, AWB 04/23019, 17 February 2005 for Sri Lanka.
[30] AbRS (Raad van State, Afdeling Bestuursrechtspraak, or Council of State, Administrative Jurisdiction Division, for appeals from the district courts), May 2006, 200601236/1.
[31] Rb, The Hague, Awb 02/3824, 7 October 2003.
[32] Rb, The Hague, Awb 03/52062, 22 December 2004.
[33] Rb, The Hague, Awb 04/20056, 24 February 2005.
[34] Rb, The Hague, Awb 12/39626, 25 April 2014.

criminal acts and that refusal to do so resulted in the killing or mistreatment of others in the same position.[35]

In Canada there has been some jurisprudence regarding the liability of children for international offences. In the *Saridag* case the court decided that asylum could be denied to a member of a terrorist organization in Turkey, while between 11 and 13 years old, as long as it could be established that the person 'had knowledge of some of the acts of violence'.[36] In the *Ramirez* case the court excluded a child soldier who voluntarily enlisted in the Salvadoran army for a period of two years at the age of 15 out of revenge for atrocities committed against close family members by insurgents. As a member of the army he participated in over 100 engagements and was present during the torture and killing of many prisoners; he was excluded on this basis. The court rejected his motive as well as his duress defence as he did not meet the proportionality requirement.[37] Furthermore, in the *Penate* case, the court excluded Penate, who joined the Salvadoran army in 1978 when he was 13 years old, because he remained in the army until 1988, gradually rose to the rank of sergeant and continued to participate in combat missions, planning and carrying out the attacks.[38] Similarly, the court excluded a child who was forcibly recruited into the Salvadoran army at age 15 in the *Gracias-Luna* case. He was appointed to be the interrogator for his army unit after five months' training; conducted eight interrogations in four months; and, after the initial interrogation, passed the guerrilla suspects to a specialized army unit called S2 for further interrogation and torture.[39]

While these Canadian cases mention age in passing to conclude that a young person can be held responsible for international offences, this issue has only been analysed in detail by the Federal Court of Appeal in Canada in the *Poshteh* case. This involved a person who participated in distributing propaganda on behalf of the Mujahedin-e-Khalq (MEK) in Iran for a two-year period, for which he was given a deportation order under Canadian immigration legislation for being a member of a terrorist organization. He was between 16 and 18 years old at the time. The court dismissed the appeal against the deportation order and made the following comments regarding age and responsibility:

> While a finding of membership in a terrorist organization may be possible for a minor of any age, it would be highly unusual for there to be a finding of membership in the case of a young child, say, under the age of twelve. . . . matters such as knowledge or mental capacity are the types of considerations to be taken into account in deciding whether a determination of membership in a terrorist organization in the case of a minor is to be different than in the case of an adult.[40]

There have been two early decisions by tribunals in Australia with respect to child soldiers, both members of the RUF in Sierra Leone. Both personally killed and tortured civilians, and both claimed that it had been caused by duress and forced drug ingestion. In the first case, the claimant's narrative was not found to be credible with respect to these defences.[41]

---

[35] Rb, The Hague, Awb 04/22429, 4 April 2005.
[36] *Saridag v. Canada* (Minister of Employment and Immigration) [1994] IMM-5691-93.
[37] *Ramirez v. Canada* (Minister of Employment and Immigration) [1992] 2 F.C. 306.
[38] *Penate v. Canada* (Minister if Employment and Immigration) [1994] F.C. 79.
[39] *Gracias-Luna v. Canada* (Minister of Citizenship and Immigration) [1995] F.C.J. No. 812.
[40] *Poshteh v. Canada* (Minister of Citizenship and Immigration) 2005 FCA 85.
[41] N96/12254 [1997] RRTA (Refugee Review Tribunal of Australia) 492.

In the second case, the elements of duress were not present because the claimant did not receive specific orders to kill or abuse people. Furthermore, he also had the choice not to carry out these crimes without necessarily attracting censure.[42]

In France the refugee tribunal has recognized that child soldiers should be given special considerations because of their age. For instance, a person was not excluded from the refugee process after being forcibly recruited by the FARC in Colombia at a young age. He was in a particularly vulnerable situation, was only marginally involved by carrying out surveillance against his neighbourhood on behalf of the FARC and disassociated himself from the organization whose methods he did not support.[43]

In another case, a child soldier was forcibly recruited by the RUF in Sierra Leone after several members of his family were killed by this rebel force. He participated in attacks against civilians and pillaged under threats against his life but left the RUF two months after joining. As a result, he was not excluded from the refugee process.[44] The refugee tribunal reached the same conclusion in a similar situation for a member of the National Congress for the Defence of the People (CNDP) in the Democratic Republic of the Congo.[45]

In Belgium, a minor was not excluded after the LTTE in Sri Lanka forcibly recruited him at the age of 13. He stayed with this organization for seven years and became the bodyguard for a senior officer involved in reconnaissance missions against the Sri Lankan army. The refugee tribunal determined that he would face persecution if returned to Sri Lanka. He was not excluded based on several factors: his recruitment at a young age; the limited duration of his involvement as an adult; and the fact that his involvement either did not amount to war crimes (as it was allowed under international humanitarian law) or was not significant enough to be considered complicity.[46]

In the United States a child soldier involved in persecution in Sierra Leone was not entitled to asylum status primarily because his defence of duress was rejected on principle.[47]

Lastly, a tribunal in Luxembourg excluded a child soldier who had committed war crimes in Liberia. On the other hand, a Denmark tribunal did not exclude a LTTE soldier because of his age, rank and lack of knowledge with respect to attacks on civilian targets.[48]

4.2 Non-Exclusion Proceedings

The UNHCR explains how children in general can be subject to persecution while belonging to one of the four groups mentioned in the Refugee Convention. Child soldiers are brought up briefly in the context of social group and are discussed as follows:

---

[42] N1998/532 and Minister for Immigration and Multicultural Affairs [1999] AATA (Administrative Appeal Tribunal of Australia) 116.
[43] CRR (Commission des Recours des Réfugiés), 459358, V. [26 May 2005]. For details of child soldier recruitment and use in the armed groups/criminal bands in Colombia, see Jiménez in this volume.
[44] CRR, 448119, C. [28 January 2005].
[45] CNDA or Cour Nationale du Droit d'Asil, 10004872, Mr. N. [20 December 2010].
[46] RvV (Raad voor Vreemdelingenbetwistingen or Aliens Litigation Council), 115005 [3 December 2013].
[47] Bah v. Ashcroft, 341 F.3d 348, 351 (5th Circuit, 2003); for a background see Rikhof 2012: 284–5.
[48] Rikhof 2012: 123.

> Where children are singled out as a target group for **recruitment or use by an armed force or group**, they may form a particular social group due to the innate and unchangeable nature of their age as well as the fact that they are perceived as a group by the society in which they live.[49]

At the national level, there have been a number of cases in Belgium, Denmark, the Netherlands and the UK where an asylum claimant asserted future persecution based on the fear that he might be recruited as a child soldier upon return to the country of origin. All these claims were rejected as being too speculative to amount to persecution with the exception of one case in Denmark in 2017. These cases are not included in this chapter as the discussion here centres on actual child soldiers.

An Australian federal court addressed persecution at the national level in a case involving a female child soldier from Nepal. She was abducted by Maoists at 13 years of age and forced to join the Maoist Party, remaining forcibly involved with the Maoists for seven years until her departure for Australia in 2010. She applied for asylum on the basis of her alleged fear of physical and mental harm from the Maoists if she returned to Nepal by reason of her disassociation from the Maoist Party, and by society and the other side for her prior association with the Maoists. The court denied her claim because Maoists had not visited her family home searching for her since her departure, country information reports indicated that political violence was decreasing in Nepal, she no longer wished to be involved with the Maoists and she was previously only involved because she was forced to join them as a child.[50]

Belgium refused asylum to a person who had been abducted as a child soldier by a rebel group in Sierra Leone in 1996 and was involved in criminal activities for ten years. The Aliens Litigation Council denied asylum in part because it was found not plausible that she would still face persecution after a period of ten years of absence, during which time there had been a successful integration campaign in Sierra Leone for ex-child soldiers.[51] Similarly, Australia denied asylum to a child soldier who was recruited by the LTTE in Sri Lanka in 2002 in a case dealing with persecution.[52] A UK judgment also denied asylum during a refoulement proceeding, again involving a former child soldier from Sierra Leone who suffered from PTSD.[53] In a Canadian deportation case where an immigration tribunal needed to balance the humanitarian considerations against the criminal behaviour of a former child soldier from Sierra Leone, the tribunal decided that the hardship this person would face upon return as a result of his PTSD and lack of support did not outweigh his well-entrenched criminal lifestyle in Canada and thus the risk he posed to the safety and security of Canada.[54]

Another UK decision assessed the case of a child soldier from Liberia who was

---

[49] UNHCR 2009: [52, iii] (original emphasis).
[50] *SZTPM v. Minister for Immigration and Border Protection* [2015] FCA 813.
[51] RvV (Raad voor Vreemdelingenbetwistingen or Aliens Litigation Council), 191949 [13 September 2017]; see also along the same lines for another child soldier from Sierra Leone, RvV, 189654 [11 July 2017].
[52] 1212854 [2012] RRTA (Refugee Review Tribunal of Australia) 1118 [13 November 2012].
[53] [2017] UKAITUR (Asylum and Immigration Chamber, Upper Tribunal) AA104442014, 24 October 2017.
[54] *Jalloh v. Canada* (Minister of Public Safety and Emergency Preparedness), IAD, [2015] VB2-02130.

forcibly recruited and witnessed and participated in atrocities. Before the rebels took him, members of his family were killed, and his house was burned down. After being taken, he suffered ill-treatment at the hands of the rebels. As a result, he too suffered from PTSD. His asylum claim was rejected for two reasons: first the person's subjective fear of persecution was not well founded in view of the change in circumstances in Liberia since his departure; second, the category of mentally ill people is too broad to fit within the social group as set out in the Refugee Convention definition. Additionally, his claim for refoulement was rejected on grounds of human rights considerations because he did not meet the threshold to show that removal to Liberia would cause possible deterioration of his mental health, even considering the adverse consequences, such as homelessness and destitution.[55]

In contrast, another deportation proceeding appeal in the UK involving a child soldier from Sierra Leone found that the original decision was unreasonable as there was evidence that the person would be 'likely to suffer a profound mental collapse, possibly amounting in effect to a destruction of their personality'.[56]

In a US case, the LRA in Uganda abducted a person at the age of 15. He was forced to perform manual labour, fight against Ugandan government soldiers and carry stolen food and animals to the LRA camp after attacks on civilian villages. The LRA would punish escape attempts with death. The appellate court held that the claim for asylum should be granted for two reasons: first, he would face persecution upon return by the LRA (although not the Ugandan government); and, second, he belonged to the fairly narrow social group of 'former child soldiers who have escaped from the LRA'.[57]

Similarly, the US granted asylum to a former child soldier, who was forcibly recruited by the NPFL in Liberia at the age of 14. He participated in the killing of women and children under the threat of death, after having been tortured and while under the influence of drugs and alcohol. The US granted asylum because he would likely be killed or tortured upon return due to the general political turmoil at the time.[58]

France granted asylum to a person who was forcibly recruited in Angola by the People's Movement for the Liberation of Angola (MPLA) at the age of 11. He faced physical violence and malnutrition while also carrying out mine clearing operations for five years. France granted asylum because his treatment was of exceptional gravity and caused serious psychological consequences, which amounted to persecution. Additionally, Angola was unlikely to provide sufficient state protection from further persecution considering the government's structure. The FLEC-FAC (Front for the Liberation of the Enclave of Cabinda – Armed Forces of Cabinda), which fought the MPLA during the civil war, possessed significant power. As an aside, an important factor in this decision was the fact that the recruitment of children under the age of 15 is prohibited under international humanitarian law and is a war crime in the Rome Statute.[59]

Sometimes, an asylum case is rejected because the person lacked general credibility to

---

[55] [2014] UKAITUR IA045922012.
[56] [2017] UKAITUR RP001312016.
[57] *Lukwago v. Ashcroft*, 329 F.3d 157 (3d Circuit, 2003).
[58] *Sackie v. Ashcroft*, 270 F.Supp. 2d 596 (E.D. Pa. 2003).
[59] CNDA, 10016657, M.J [2011].

support such a claim, including the narrative of being a child soldier[60] or with respect to the specific claim that (s)he was a child soldier in the first place.[61]

5. POST-EXCLUSION ISSUES

As indicated above, when persons, including children, cannot be removed because of the risk of death, torture, cruel, inhuman or degrading treatment or punishment, but they do not satisfy the requirements to obtain refugee status under the Refugee Convention, they are given subsidiary protection status. Since there is an expectation that removal can occur when the human rights situation in the country of removal improves, the benefits of this subsidiary protection status are not the same as with refugee status. Like refugees they are allowed to stay in the country of refuge, but the rights associated with subsidiary status tend to be fewer. While the substantive rights, such as the right to education, medical care and employment, are generally the same, the right to remain in the country of refuge is subject to greater conditions. This is usually expressed by granting a permit to stay in the country for a limited time period.

This applies generally to all persons with subsidiary status, but such rights are further restricted for persons with a criminal background. For example, exclusion and exceptions to the non-refoulement provisions may be applied to persons applying for subsidiary status. In such situations, only a suspension on removal until the situation in the country of removal improves is granted, although in some countries this minimal right applies to all persons with subsidiary protection status.

However, the assumption that a situation in a country with serious human rights violations will improve will not always be correct, certainly often not in the short term. For that reason, countries have sought other solutions to deal with the conundrum of having very serious criminal refugees on their territory, whose deportation is prohibited by human right obligations and who are usually not entitled, because of their criminality, to a regular type of immigration status.[62] The most common devices developed in the countries of interest in this chapter are criminal prosecution of criminal refugees;[63] extradition to their country of origin;[64] long-term detention;[65] and humanitarian solutions.[66] None of these approaches have been fully satisfactory to date.[67]

The Netherlands is the only country that has given specific attention to long-term residents with a 1F exclusion background by introducing legislation with a so-called durability and proportionality test. If a person can fulfil both parts of this test, then (s)he

---

[60] See *Mayombo v. Canada* (Minister of Citizenship and Immigration), 2004 FC 1378, [2004] for a situation in the DRC.
[61] See in the US, *Kporlor v. Holder*, 597 F.3d 222 (4th Circuit, 2010) for a situation in Liberia.
[62] Rikhof 2012: 459–60.
[63] Ibid.: 460–1; Rikhof 2017.
[64] Rikhof 2012: 469–73; Gilbert 2017; Giuffré 2017; Irving 2017.
[65] Rikhof 2012: 473–7; Juss 2017; Koutsouraki 2017.
[66] Rikhof 2012: 477–9; Bolhuis et al. 2017; Bond 2017; Doğar 2017; Peyronnet 2017; Singer 2017.
[67] Rikhof 2012: 481–3.

would be entitled to have his or her status regularized by obtaining a temporary residency permit. The test requires that:

- the person has found himself for a lengthy period of time in a situation where (s)he cannot be deported because of human rights concerns;
- there is no prospect of change in this situation in the near future;
- the person cannot be removed;
- departure to a third country in spite of sufficient efforts by the person concerned has proven to be impossible;
- the person is in an exceptional situation in the Netherlands.

The government interprets a lengthy period to be more than ten years from the date of the initial claim to refugee status, which has been deemed to be reasonable by the judiciary.[68] With respect to an assessment of proportionality, the judiciary generally gives the government a great deal of deference. Because of the high standard of this test, there have been very few instances where a person has been given legal permission to stay in the Netherlands.[69] There have been no instances of jurisprudence where these factors have been applied to children.

States vary in dealing with the problem of persons who have been excluded but cannot be removed. Some apply enforcement procedures, such as detention, while others apply humanitarian solutions, such as granting limited immigration status. A recent policy brief following a two-year research project examining this problem of persons who are undesirable but unreturnable (UBUs) made a number of observations regarding policy responses. With respect to the option of extradition or transfer to international criminal institutions, the main obstacle was that those institutions prosecute only a limited number of individuals, generally those considered to be the 'most responsible' or having direct involvement. Extradition to other states may be impracticable because extradition is often blocked due to human rights or fair trial concerns, which cannot always be resolved by relying on diplomatic assurances. Similarly, domestic prosecution would not be applicable to a great number of excluded persons given that such prosecutions are 'extremely resource-intensive and complex because of the nature of the alleged crimes and the context in which they allegedly took place'.[70]

Outside the criminal approach, some states are willing to provide temporary residence permits through existing (Germany) or specifically tailored schemes (Denmark, Norway and the UK) to accommodate such persons. Others (Belgium and the Netherlands) do not provide any temporary residence permit, which means UBUs are considered undocumented migrants and cannot work, lease accommodation or receive health care. Lastly, although this is not an ideal situation, some countries use detention as a means to deal with UBUs. Indefinite detention is not permitted in European and North American countries: UBUs can only be detained temporarily in cases where a fast return or removal

---

[68] Ibid.: 480.
[69] Ibid.: 479–81.
[70] Refugee Law Initiative and Center for International Criminal Justice 2016: 4.

constitutes 'a realistic option'. Australia, on the other hand, has a broader approach with respect to detention, which often causes much longer immigration incarceration.[71]

In terms of solutions, the same policy brief indicated in general with respect to UBUs that, because of the lack of a coherent policy response, guidance should be provided to states. The first steps would include measures that would 'limit the number of allegedly criminal migrants ending up in legal limbo' by either reducing the number of persons considered to be 'undesirables' or by increasing the number of those who are returned or removed.[72] The policy brief recognized that in spite of such measures, there will remain a number of UBUs whose legal status continues to be uncertain. For this group, the policy brief suggested a balancing test whereby a state's interests in prolonging the 'status of undesirability', such as the level of an acute security threat, the seriousness of the alleged crimes, and the level of responsibility of the individual, would be weighed against the UBU's interests of being removed from the category of 'undesirable', especially in relation to the social, psychological and physical impact of the protracted situation of uncertainty.[73]

It should be noted that neither the Dutch policy nor the policy brief specifically addressed the situation of child soldiers, and it would not be unreasonable to expect that some of the aspects in the abovementioned document would result in more favourable outcomes for children.

6. CONCLUSION

Before examining trends in the jurisprudence with respect to child soldiers in the asylum context, it is useful to provide some statistical background. This chapter has looked at 36 cases dealing with child soldiers: 25 in the area of exclusion and 11 addressing issues of non-exclusion. The asylum claimants who were the subject of these proceedings came from a dozen countries on four continents: Europe (Turkey), Latin America (Colombia and El Salvador), Asia (Afghanistan, Iran, Nepal and Sri Lanka) and Africa (Angola, DRC, Liberia, Sierra Leone and Uganda). The nine countries which assessed these claims in both specialized refugee tribunals or in regular courts were the Netherlands (ten exclusion cases), Canada (five exclusion and two non-exclusion cases), France (four exclusion and one non-exclusion decisions), the US (one exclusion and three non-exclusion judgments), Australia (two of each), the UK (three non-exclusion cases), Belgium (one of each), Denmark (one exclusion case) and Luxembourg (one exclusion case). This number can be expected to rise, especially in countries such as Germany, the Netherlands and Sweden, which have had a large influx of asylum seekers in the last two years and which have put in place rigorous processes to assess both legitimate refugee claims and persons who might have been involved in criminal activities before arriving in Europe.

When examining trends in both the inclusion and exclusion areas of asylum processing, it should be pointed out that there does not appear to be a great deal of cooperation

---

[71] Ibid: 5; see also Rikhof 2012: 483–4.
[72] Refugee Law Initiative and Center for International Criminal Justice 2016: 5.
[73] Ibid.

between countries in terms of sharing or being aware of each other's national jurisprudence in exclusion or inclusion in general, let alone with respect to child soldiers.[74]

In terms of trends with respect to non-exclusion jurisprudence, there is some variation both in determining whether child soldiers can fit within the concept of persecution and in how far the notion of refoulement can be applied to them. Two aspects in relation to persecution have been addressed. First, whether child soldiers could fall within the category of social group – the only one of the four groups relevant to them. A UK tribunal viewed the category of mentally ill people, which child soldiers frequently fall within due to having PTSD as result of the deprivations suffered, as too broad to be included within the concept of social group. On the other hand, a US case did find that child soldiers could be considered within that group as long as the group was defined along narrower lines than just child soldiers. In this case the social group was defined as former child soldiers who had escaped from the LRA in Uganda. A description somewhere between those extremes could find acceptance by not limiting the group by a geographical boundary, but by following the example of the UNHCR. In its 2009 guidelines regarding children, the UNHCR defined the social group as a group targeted for recruitment or use by an armed force or group, which resembles the definition of the war crime of child recruitment in the Rome Statute.[75]

The second aspect on the persecution side relates to the rejection of a number of asylum claims where it was seen as implausible that a child soldier would face any substantial harm as a result of the passage of time after involvement in an armed group, especially if there had been attempts to reintegrate former child soldiers into society. Tribunals reached this conclusion for former child soldiers from Sierra Leone in Belgium and the UK, from Sri Lanka in Australia and from Liberia in the UK. Another Australian case reached the same conclusion for a female child soldier from Nepal because her family was not subject to harassment and political violence had decreased since her departure. On the other hand, future persecution was present if there was clear evidence that the child soldier would be killed or tortured upon return as indicated in the US with respect to Liberia. It is noteworthy that in this US case the time lapse between the child soldier being part of an armed group and his return was shorter than in the cases above of Liberia, Sri Lanka, Nepal and Sierra Leone. It appears that the longer it takes for the asylum claim of a child soldier to be processed, the more the chances of asylum diminish, unless the country of origin is still in severe turmoil. The above-mentioned US case, which was decided during a refoulement proceeding, makes it clear that human rights concerns upon removal outweigh the criminal past of the child soldier. For example, if the removal would result in killing or torture, an absolute ban is placed on such removal no matter how badly the child soldier acted in the past.

However, if the human rights concerns are less severe, countries balance the criminal past and the type of persecution the person will face. In this context, suffering from

---

[74] Only in February 2017 a European exclusion network was launched under the auspices of the European Asylum Support Organization (EASO) to strengthen practical cooperation with respect to exclusion. See EASO 2017, 'EASO Exclusion Network'.

[75] Rome Statute, art. 8.2(e)(vii). This is the definition for war crimes committed in non-international armed conflicts. The equivalent for international armed conflicts, art. 8.2(b)(xxvi), does not refer to armed groups.

PTSD is not a guarantee that this balance will favour the child soldier, as can be seen in the Canadian case involving a person from Sierra Leone and in the UK case involving a person from Liberia. However, if the PTSD is extreme, asylum may be granted, as happened in France with a person from Angola and in the UK for a person from Sierra Leone.

With respect to exclusion, age has played an important role in countries such as the Netherlands, France, Denmark and Belgium. In the Netherlands, legislation makes it clear that children who were under the age of 15 should not be excluded. In France, a young age was relevant in a case involving a child soldier from Colombia. In Belgium, a person from Sri Lanka was not excluded as a result of his age, the short duration in the armed group and his nominal involvement in criminal acts. These same three factors led to the same result in France for child soldiers from Colombia and the DRC; in Denmark for a person from Liberia; and in the Netherlands for a person from Sierra Leone. In this last case, having PTSD and being under constant threat were factors to be considered as well. However, if a person was able to easily leave the organization, as was found in the Netherlands in respect to a person from Uganda, or if the person continued to work for the organization for a lengthy time period after the age of 15, as was the case again in the Netherlands for a person from Turkey, exclusion will follow.

Common law countries such as Australia, Canada and the US will determine each case on its own merits regardless of age, as was done for situations arising out of Sierra Leone, El Salvador, Iran and Turkey. Given the fact that child soldiers in exclusion proceedings were often directly involved in criminal acts (unlike the majority of cases involving adults where the allegations are based on indirect involvement) but were usually also under the influence of drugs or alcohol or were acting under duress, these defences, especially that of duress, have played an important role in exclusion proceedings. The results have been mixed. In some cases, as in Australia, the duress argument was found not to be credible for a case originating in Sierra Leone. This was also the case in the Netherlands for cases originating in Sierra Leone and Angola. In addition, the US rejected a duress defence on principle in respect of a child soldier from Sierra Leone. The defence of duress was similarly rejected by the Netherlands as not meeting the required criteria in cases arising out of Angola and Sierra Leone; Australia for a person from Sierra Leone; and Canada for a child soldier from El Salvador. In conclusion, unless a child soldier is under, or close, to 15 years old, left the armed unit fairly quickly or can raise the defence of duress with credibility, the chances of exclusion are fairly high.[76]

The result is that a high percentage of child soldiers will end up in the post-exclusion dilemma described above. The solution offered to deal with such so-called UBUs, namely a better balancing between humanitarian solutions and acknowledging that these child soldiers have committed serious criminal offences, should be better calibrated to account for the special vulnerability of these children and the circumstances that they often acted under ongoing severe stress or duress and they frequently also still suffer from PTSD. The result should make their path to a permanent immigrant status easier than is the case for adults.

---

[76] Bond and Krech 2016: 572–3 refers to solutions put forward by commentators to alleviate this problem.

REFERENCED WORKS

Bolhuis, M., Battjes, H. and Van Wijk, J. 2017. 'Undesirable but Unreturnable Migrants in the Netherlands' 36 *Refugee Survey Quarterly* 61

Bond, J. 2017. 'Unwanted but Unremovable: Canada's Treatment of "Criminal" Migrants Who Cannot Be Removed' 36 *Refugee Survey Quarterly* 168

Bond, J. and Krech, M. 2016. 'Excluding the Most Vulnerable: Application of Article 1F(a) of the Refugee Convention to Child Solders' 20 *International Journal of Human Rights* 567

Dankoff, J. 2011. 'Advocating Duress and Infancy Exceptions to the Persecutor Bar to Asylum for Former Child Soldiers' 31 *Children's Legal Rights Journal* 43

Doğar, D. 2017. 'Against All Odds: Turkey's Response to "Undesirable but Unreturnable" Asylum-Seekers' 36 Refugee Survey Quarterly 107

Drumbl, M. 2012. *Reimagining Child Soldiers in International Law and Policy* (Oxford: Oxford University Press)

EASO [European Asylum Support Office] 2017. 'Newsletter March 2017' (March) [available at: https://www.easo.europa.eu/news-events/easo-newsletter/subscribe-our-newsletter/easo-newsletter-march-2017 (accessed 18 July 2018)]

European Union Agency for Fundamental Rights 2016. 'Current Migration Situation in the EU: Separated Children' (December)

Everett, J.C. 2009. 'The Battle Continues: Fighting for a More Child-Sensitive Approach to Asylum for Child Soldiers' 21 *Florida Journal of International Law* 286

Gilbert, G. 2017. 'Undesirable but Unreturnable: Extradition and Other Forms of Rendition' 15 *Journal of International Criminal Justice* 55

Giuffré, M. 2017. 'Deportation with Assurances and Human Rights: The Case of Persons Suspected or Convicted of Serious Crimes' 15 *Journal of International Criminal Justice* 75

Grover, S. 2008. '"Child Soldiers" as "Non-Combatants": The Inapplicability of the Refugee Convention Exclusion Clause' 12 *International Journal of Human Rights* 53

Holvoet, M. 2014. 'Harmonizing Exclusion under the Refugee Convention by Reference to the Evidentiary Standards of International Criminal Law' 12 *Journal of International Criminal Justice* 1039

Irving, E. 2017. 'When International Justice Concludes: Undesirable but Unreturnable Individuals in the Context of the International Criminal Court' 15 *Journal of International Criminal Justice* 115

Juss, S. 2017. 'Detention and Delusion in Australia's Kafkaesque Refugee Law' 36 *Refugee Survey Quarterly* 146

Koutsouraki, E. 2017. 'The Indefinite Detention of Undesirable and Unreturnable Third-Country Nationals in Greece' 36 *Refugee Survey Quarterly* 85

Lonegan, B. 2011. 'Sinners or Saints: Child Soldiers and the Persecutor's Bar to Asylum after Ngusie v. Holder' 31 *Boston College Third World Law Journal* 71

Maystre, M. 2014. 'The Interaction between International Refugee Law and International Criminal Law with Respect to Child Soldiers' 12 *Journal of International Criminal Justice* 975

Peyronnet, C. 2017. 'Undesirable and Unreturnable Migrants under French Law: Between Legal Uncertainty and Legal Limbo' 36 *Refugee Survey Quarterly* 35

Refugee Law Initiative and Center for International Criminal Justice, 'Policy Brief. Undesirable and Unreturnable? Policy Challenges around Excluded Asylum-Seekers and Migrants Suspected of Serious Criminality but who Cannot Be Removed' (CICJ, 2016) [available at: https://cicj.org/events/undesirable-and-unreturnable/ (accessed 18 July 2018)]

Rikhof, J. 2009. 'War Criminals Not Welcome: How Common Law Countries Approach the Phenomenon of International Crimes in the Immigration and Refugee Context' 21 *International Journal of Refugee Law* 453

Rikhof, J. 2012. *The Criminal Refugee: The Treatment of Asylum Seekers with a Criminal Background in International and Domestic Law* (Dordrecht, NL: Republic of Letters Publishing)

Rikhof, J. 2015. 'International Criminal Law and Refugee Law: Lessons Learned?', in C. Jalloh and A. Marong (eds), *Promoting Accountability for Gross Human Rights Violations in Africa under International Law: Essays in Honour of Prosecutor Hassan Bubacar Jallow* (Leiden, NL: Martinus Nijhoff Brill) 552

Rikhof, J. 2017. 'Prosecuting Asylum Seekers Who Cannot be Removed: A Feasible Solution?' 15 *Journal of International Criminal Justice* 97

Rossi, E. 2013. 'A Special Track for Former Child Soldiers: Enacting a Child Soldier Visa as an Alternative to Asylum Protection' 31 *Berkeley Journal of International Law* 392

Singer, S. 2017. '"Undesirable and Unreturnable" in the United Kingdom' 36 *Refugee Survey Quarterly* 9

UK House of Lords 2016. 'European Union Committee. 2nd Report of Session 2016–17. Children in Crisis: Unaccompanied Migrant Children in the EU' (HL Paper 34) (26 July)

UN Human Rights Council 2017. 'Global Issue of Unaccompanied Migrant Children and Human Rights' (UN Doc. A/HRC/36/51) (24 July)

UNHCR [United Nations High Commissioner for Refugees] 1997. 'Guidelines on Policies and Procedures in Dealing with Unaccompanied Children Seeking Asylum' (February)

UNHCR 2003a. 'Guidelines on International Protection: Application of the Exclusion Clauses: Article 1F of the 1951 Convention relating to the Status of Refugees' (HCR/GIP/03/05) (4 September)

UNHCR 2003b. 'Background Note on the Application of the Exclusion Clauses: Article 1F of the 1951 Convention relating to the Status of Refugees' (4 September)

UNHCR 2009. 'Guidelines on International Protection No. 8: Child Asylum Claims under Articles 1(A)2 and 1(F) of the 1951 Convention and/or 1967 Protocol relating to the Status of Refugees' (22 December)

UNHCR 2014. 'Children on the Run: Unaccompanied Children Leaving Central America and Mexico and the need for International Protection'

UNHCR 2017a. 'Statistical Yearbook 2015, 15th edition'

UNHCR 2017b, 'Statistical Yearbook 2015, 15th edition: Figures at a Glance' [available at: http://www.unhcr.org/figures-at-a-glance.html (accessed 18 July 2018)]

UNHCR/Council of Europe 2014. 'Unaccompanied and Separated Asylum-Seeking and Refugee Children Turning Eighteen: What to Celebrate? Field Research on European State Practice regarding Transition to Adulthood of Unaccompanied and Separated Asylum-seeking and Refugee Children' (March)

UNICEF 2017a. 'A Child Is a Child. Protecting Children on the Move from Violence, Abuse and Exploitation. Executive Summary'

UNICEF 2017b. 'Ad Hoc Committee on Refugees and Stateless Persons. A Deadly Journey for Children: The Central Mediterranean Migration Route'

White, K. 2010. 'A Chance for Redemption: Revising the "Persecutor Bar" and "Material Support Bar" in the Case of Child Soldiers' 43 *Vanderbilt Journal of Transnational Law* 191

PART IV

AFTERWORLD(S)/ AFTERWARDS: TRANSITIONAL JUSTICE AND BEYOND

19. Navigating the mystical: child soldiers and reintegration rituals in northern Uganda
Jastine C. Barrett

The argument has been advanced by scholars and activists alike that indigenous forms of justice and reconciliation practices should play some role in post-conflict societies. In particular, it has been suggested that indigenous mechanisms may assist with the reintegration of former child soldiers. Abducted child soldiers, sometimes forced to commit atrocities, can be perceived simultaneously as victims and perpetrators. Arguably, indigenous mechanisms may be better placed than formal state-organized or internationally sponsored mechanisms to address such complex identities.

This chapter draws on existing literature and semi-structured qualitative interviews with current and former staff members of organizations that worked with former child soldiers in northern Uganda to examine the use of indigenous rituals or ceremonies in reintegration processes. By reintegration, I mean a reciprocal process in which a child soldier is reintroduced to civilian life and is accepted by his or her family and community. The chapter begins with a brief background section to contextualize the use of indigenous mechanisms. It then turns to consider the role of such mechanisms in transitional justice and reconciliation in a broad sense before specifically examining the position of indigenous mechanisms in Ugandan law and policy. I then provide a picture of the main reintegration rituals utilized in the Acholi sub-region of Uganda, highlighting their mystical or spiritual elements and linking this to the importance of the spirit world in Acholi cosmology. It is not the aim of this chapter to evaluate the Acholi approach to justice or examine empirically the extent to which local approaches to reintegration were appropriate or successful in addressing the child soldier issue. However, this chapter draws some basic conclusions from existing literature on the potential role for localized mechanisms. The chapter also explores the approach of local and international actors to the return of child soldiers from captivity in the Lord's Resistance Army (LRA), focusing on their perception of local approaches to reintegration. It ends by examining the United Nations Children's Fund's (UNICEF) perspective on indigenous mechanisms, which, as the lead international agency for children, provided support to many of the actors operating in northern Uganda. My aim is to elucidate whether indigenous mechanisms were seen by organizations as compatible with their institutional ethos, be that founded on religious principles and/or child rights.

1. CHILDREN RETURNING FROM LRA CAPTIVITY

A conflict between the LRA and the Ugandan government (under President Yoweri Museveni) raged for more than two decades in northern Uganda from the mid-1980s. This conflict primarily affected the population in the Acholi sub-region, but also touched upon neighbouring areas. During this time, up to around 90 per cent of the population was displaced, often forcibly into internally displaced persons' (IDP) camps.[1] In addition to fighting Museveni's National Resistance Movement, the LRA, led by Joseph Kony – a self-proclaimed prophet – aimed to create a new Acholi society and set about spiritually cleansing or purifying the Acholi of corruption and immorality. It thus targeted the civilian population. A key strategy included the abduction of local people, children in particular, to initiate them into the LRA's way of life, produce a new pure generation of Acholi (through the birth of children to abducted women and girls) and use them as fighters. Between 30,000 and 60,000 children and young people were abducted over the years to join the LRA's ranks.[2] Some estimates suggest that abducted children accounted for more than 80 per cent of LRA soldiers.[3] A number of the abducted were compelled to commit atrocities against civilians, and some were forced to kill or maim members of their own family and community as part of the initiation into the LRA.

Throughout the conflict, the return of children who had been associated with the LRA through escape, rescue[4] or (occasionally) release was largely spontaneous. The number of child returnees peaked in the early to mid-2000s, coinciding with a massive military offensive (Operation Iron Fist) by the Ugandan army (UPDF) against the LRA.[5] The military offensive, which targeted LRA bases in southern Sudan, resulted in the LRA returning to northern Uganda and abducting children on a much larger scale than previously, albeit often for short-term use after which they were released.[6] Children were initially returned to IDP camps until a cessation of hostilities in August 2006 led to the population gradually relocating to their villages and towns, following which many children returned to their place of origin. The official procedure for reintegrating child returnees involved taking them to Child Protection Units run by the UPDF and then sending them to reception centres, which assisted children in their rehabilitation and return to society. During this process, the children could also apply for amnesty. However, many children (especially those abducted for a short period of time) did not go through the formal reception process but returned directly home.[7]

Studies on the perception of child returnees found that almost all were welcomed by their family and also revealed a high level of acceptance by communities.[8] Nonetheless

---

[1] For more detail on the conflict and its effects on the population, see Allen 2006; Finnström 2008; Akello in this volume.

[2] Baines 2010: 409. Figures for the number of abductees vary considerably given the lack of systematic reporting, differences in defining abduction and over-reporting: see Allen 2006: 60–64 and 112–13.

[3] See World Vision 2004: 5, 11 and 18; Annan et al. 2006: 59; cf. Allen and Schomerus 2006: 19–22; Allen 2006: 63–4.

[4] The issue of 'rescue' was contentious. Mads Oyen, a UNICEF Uganda child protection officer from 2002 to 2004, commented that a child in the LRA who survived a military action would be labelled as 'rescued' by the UPDF, whilst a child who was killed was an 'LRA fighter' (interview, 16 July 2017).

[5] Pham et al. 2007: 14. Confirmed by Cornelius Williams, UNICEF Uganda 2004–2009, currently UNICEF Global Chief of Child Protection, interview, 16 August 2017; Oyen, interview, 16 July 2017.

[6] Oyen, interview, 16 July 2017.

[7] See Annan et al. 2006: 63–5; Maina 2010: 169; cf. Veale and Stavrou 2003: 36, stating that most former abductees went through a reception centre.

[8] Annan et al. 2006: 66; Atri and Cusimano 2012: 16.

these same studies revealed some residual negativity: in one study, more than 25 per cent of returnees commented that they had received insults from, or were feared by, community members.[9] Another report indicated that 66 per cent of respondents felt that community members were still angry at the children, 53 per cent felt that community members still feared the children and 35 per cent reported that children continued to be insulted.[10] The feeling of local communities towards these individuals is clearly highly complex and ambivalent. To some degree, the children are seen as victims, respondents in one study arguing that 'formerly abducted children were also victims of this brutal war and had been forced through abductions and excessive indoctrination to carry out violent acts'.[11] Yet at the same time there remains some reluctance to accept these children. Stigmatization, resentment and, in some cases, rejection of child returnees appear to be linked to a number of factors, including knowledge that the young people committed specific atrocities against family or community members and/or participated in the abduction of other children who have not yet returned, or suspicion that they killed innocent civilians given the time spent with the LRA. These factors can lead to a desire for justice as well as fear that returnees are a source of spiritual danger. Indeed, Maina reports that some victims of child soldiers 'wished for nothing less than retributive justice', it being hard to accept the narrative of victimhood in respect of these children.[12] In another study, whilst only 13 per cent of respondents believed that children should be punished for war-related crimes, and 31 per cent believed that children were to blame for their actions, a large majority (88%) considered that children should apologize,[13] thus underlining the complexity of feelings towards these children who could be labelled 'victim-perpetrators'.

In Uganda, most low-level perpetrators will not face criminal prosecution for various reasons: they are so great in number; they 'rarely reach the threshold of responsibility considered worthy of trial';[14] and, in the case of children, some may even be below Uganda's minimum age of criminal responsibility (12 years old). Of course, this assumes that there is a criminal justice response at all: those who qualify for amnesty are immune from prosecution. In addition to issues relating to accountability for atrocities, the majority of Acholi people believe in the phenomenon of *cen* or vengeance of the spirit world. This belief in the spirit world has a significant influence on the Acholi conceptualization and perception of justice and reconciliation.[15] Acholi cosmology will be addressed in more detail below but, in short, there is a belief that *cen* is sent by the spirit world when wrongdoing has been committed against the dead. Former abductees may thus be seen, or indeed see themselves, as spiritually polluted and thus a source of misfortune and illness. For these individuals, there has to be some way of facilitating their acceptance by the community.

---

[9] Annan et al. 2006: 66; see also Allen and Schomerus 2006: 9.
[10] Atri and Cusimano 2012: 16 and 28.
[11] Maina 2010: 198.
[12] Ibid.: 203.
[13] Atri and Cusimano 2012: 2, 4, 42 and 44.
[14] Baines 2010: 412.
[15] Baines 2005: 72.

2. THE PLACE OF INDIGENOUS MECHANISMS IN TRANSITIONAL JUSTICE AND RECONCILIATION

Huyse speaks of the rise of two models in transitional justice: the first is top-down, 'formal and rational-legalistic' and controlled by national or international institutions, with an emphasis on prosecution, courtrooms and judges; the second is generally informal, 'ritualistic-communal', community-led and involves the use of local mechanisms. He adds: 'The north Ugandan rite of stepping on the egg, exercised to reintegrate former child soldiers, is a striking demonstration of this [second] type of approach.'[16]

The potential for indigenous mechanisms to contribute to transitional justice has been recognized at the international level. In his 2004 'Report on the Rule of Law and Transitional Justice in Conflict and Post-Conflict Societies', Kofi Annan noted the 'often vital role' that such mechanisms play in dispute settlement and the administration of justice.[17] A report from the previous year referred to the effectiveness of traditional 'cleansing' ceremonies, such as in Mozambique, in facilitating the reintegration of children.[18]

From a child-rights perspective, the Convention on the Rights of the Child provides for the use of alternatives to criminal proceedings (Article 40(3)(b)) and also for measures to promote the physical and psychological recovery and social reintegration of child victims of armed conflicts (Article 39),[19] albeit it is silent on what such measures might include. Indigenous mechanisms have been explicitly identified by child rights instruments as potentially helpful in the context of justice and in the reintegration process. The UN Common Approach to Justice for Children states that programming on justice for children must build on 'informal and traditional justice systems' provided these comply with human rights standards.[20] And the non-binding Paris Principles specifically contain reference to cultural reintegration practices, providing: 'In some communities, children are viewed and view themselves as carrying bad spirits from their experiences with armed forces or armed groups. Appropriate cultural practices, as long as they are not harmful to children, can be essential to a child's reintegration and should be supported.'[21] This is not to say that other, perhaps more 'Western', approaches are eschewed: the Paris Principles also promote the use of psychosocial support. They suggest that a 'combination of traditional approaches and opportunities for supportive conversations' can be beneficial for most children.[22] There is thus recognition, at least on paper, of the role that traditional mechanisms[23] can play.

Some of the literature, both activist and academic, that addresses the use of indigenous mechanisms supports this perspective on the complementary use of indigenous and

---

[16] Huyse 2008: 5.
[17] UN Security Council 2004: [36].
[18] UN Secretary-General 2003: [65].
[19] The Optional Protocol on the Involvement of Children in Armed Conflict contains a similar provision (art. 6(3)) on recovery and reintegration in respect of children who are demobilized or otherwise released.
[20] UN 2008: Guiding Principle 8.
[21] Principle 7.53.
[22] Principle 7.75.5. For a critique of practical application of the Paris Principles in northern Uganda, see Akello in this volume.
[23] I use 'traditional' and 'indigenous' interchangeably to avoid repetition but prefer the latter as these mechanisms are not static in time or space.

'Western' approaches in justice and reintegration. Amnesty International notes the important role that traditional mechanisms can play in reintegrating abducted persons, including children, but stresses that these mechanisms should supplement rather than replace criminal justice procedures.[24] Marques, writing on reintegration in Mozambique, argues that traditional healing rites (often purification rituals) can assist in dealing with the psychological and emotional concerns of the child soldier but also can restore group identity and facilitate the child becoming an active member of society, whilst Western approaches often fail in this regard. She asserts: 'It is essential that humanitarian organizations operating in this field recognize such roles and work side by side with the traditional healers and the whole community.'[25] Marques acknowledges also, however, the validity of Western methods, noting that many community members felt that psychological support, education and vocational training may be necessary in addition to the traditional rituals. For Honwana, localized rituals are 'a fundamental condition for individual and collective healing and protection' as well as 'important means of conflict resolution, reconciliation, and social reintegration of war-affected persons'.[26] In Mozambique and Angola, purification ceremonies were used not only to 'exorcize' harmful spirits but also to acknowledge atrocities committed and absolve the child from sin and guilt.[27]

Some commentators propose that traditional rituals could be used as an 'alternative' form of accountability to criminal justice for child soldiers. Huyse suggests that formal criminal justice may not be 'capable of the subtlety' needed to deal with the ambiguity of a 'victim-perpetrator' such as a child soldier who has been forcibly abducted and forced to commit atrocities. He adds: 'A combination of palavers, the African way of prolonging discussions, and ritual events creates in principle more opportunities for exploring issues of accountability, innocence and guilt that are integral to the legacy of violent conflict.'[28] Such forms of accountability could 'not only ... confront child soldiers with their deeds but also ... allow their appropriate reintegration into communities and society at large'.[29] Local mechanisms may thus be useful for dealing with victim-turned-perpetrators or 'intimate enemies' who have to come together after mass violence.[30]

Studies on demobilization, disarmament and reintegration (DDR) have also highlighted the contribution that can be made through the incorporation of 'traditional reconciliatory rituals', such as cleansing ceremonies, into the reintegration process. Such ceremonies are believed to 'address both the psychosocial needs of child soldiers in terms of acceptance and fears of community members'.[31] Rituals and traditional cleansing have been part of DDR programmes for child soldiers since 2001 in various African countries and have been deployed to restore social harmony following conflict.[32]

---

[24] Amnesty International 2008: 19.
[25] Marques 2001: 25.
[26] Honwana 2006: 106.
[27] Ibid.: 110.
[28] Huyse 2008: 15. See also Allen and Macdonald 2013: 12–13.
[29] Derluyn et al. 2015: 6 and 8. (The authors refer to *mato oput* as an example, but do not discuss it in any detail.)
[30] Baines 2010: 412.
[31] Babatunde 2014: 381–2.
[32] Ibid.: 382. Mozambique and Angola are mentioned above; in Sierra Leone child ex-combatants went through a 'cooling the heart' ceremony upon their return home.

Specifically in the Ugandan context, the government has officially endorsed the use of traditional justice and reconciliation mechanisms. The Amnesty Act 2000 (Section 9(c)) provides that a function of the Amnesty Commission is to 'consider and promote appropriate reconciliation mechanisms in affected areas'. This has been interpreted to include traditional ceremonies, in addition to other religious and secular mechanisms. Traditional institutions are perceived as playing a 'vital complementary role'.[33] This was followed by an Agreement on Accountability and Reconciliation between the government and the LRA in June 2007 (together with its Annexure of 19 February 2008),[34] which provides for the use of both formal and informal justice mechanisms for conflict resolution and reconciliation. It stipulates that traditional mechanisms (including the Acholi *mato oput* – see below) 'shall be promoted, with necessary modifications, as a central part of the framework for accountability and reconciliation'.[35] In respect of children, the parties agree to '[e]nsure that children are not subjected to criminal justice proceedings, but may participate, as appropriate, in reconciliation processes'.[36] The Annexure requires the government to examine traditional practices to identify the most appropriate roles for such mechanisms, considering in particular 'the role and impact of the processes on women and children'.[37] It further provides that no one shall be compelled to participate in any traditional ritual.[38]

Despite this explicit acknowledgment of the role of traditional mechanisms by the Ugandan government and at the international level, Ochen finds 'little interface' between local reintegration and reconciliation approaches and international or even national efforts, and 'a lack of global and national recognition for such a rich body of indigenous knowledge'.[39] Further, he asserts that, although some scholars have recognized the 'critical role' such mechanisms can play in the reintegration of child returnees, their role has largely been neglected 'both within academic and policy debate'.[40] In this volume, both Wessells and Akello refer to the lack of attention on the part of humanitarian agencies paid to *cen* and thus to indigenous means of tackling it. Earlier research by Allen and Schomerus, however, identified a turn towards, and promotion of, traditional and religious healing at the local and international civil society level from the late 1990s onwards. They identified a foregrounding by NGOs of an Acholi culture of 'forgiveness', the view being that Acholi understandings of justice were based on reconciliation and reintegration rather than revenge: local justice could thus constitute a 'viable alternative' to criminal justice measures.[41] Indeed, Huyse refers to the tendency of Western NGOs (and academ-

---

[33] Baines 2005: 44.
[34] See Amnesty International 2008: Appendices, for the full text of the Agreement and Annexure. This Agreement (one of six constituting the Final Peace Agreement) was signed during the Juba peace talks, but the Final Peace Agreement was never signed.
[35] Art. 3.1. Similar wording is provided in paragraph 19 of the Annexure.
[36] Art. 12(iv).
[37] Paragraph 20.
[38] Paragraph 22.
[39] Ochen 2014: 249.
[40] Ibid.: 248.
[41] Allen and Schomerus 2006: 17. They take issue with this view of Acholi justice, arguing that misinterpretation of the Acholi language could have led to a conceptual misunderstanding of various Acholi notions; see also Allen 2008: 47–8.

ics) to 'romanticize' tradition.[42] In this chapter, I aim to shed light on how international and domestic actors interacted with, and perceived, indigenous mechanisms, and thus respond, to some degree, to the seemingly divergent interpretations by commentators. First, however, I will provide an overview of the main indigenous mechanisms and briefly consider the extent to which these mechanisms were used in practice for children returning from LRA captivity.

3. ACHOLI INDIGENOUS MECHANISMS – SPIRITUALISM AND SYMBOLISM

3.1 Acholi Cosmology

The Acholi people maintain sophisticated animist beliefs which mould their conceptualization of justice, forgiveness and reconciliation. The majority of Acholi believe in the existence of *jok* (*jogi*: plural), an ancestral spirit linked to a specific geographical area and a particular clan or chiefdom that provides protection and assistance and would generally not send 'unjustified punishment'. There are, however, also free *jogi*, which are not connected to any particular area and that are 'prone to possess people and could be used not only to heal but to cause harm'.[43] Baines explains that, with displacement and the 'moral decay' brought about by the conflict (exacerbated by the inability to properly bury the dead), the number of free *jogi* has increased, bringing misfortune to the Acholi.[44]

Cen is a type of free *jok* and is a 'vengeful spirit of persons who either died badly (murder, neglect) or were treated badly in death (failure to give a proper burial or treating a corpse without respect)'.[45] Allen and Schomerus describe *cen* as a kind of spiritual pollution, affecting those who have performed violent acts, or who have witnessed them, or those who have been in contact with death.[46] It is believed that *cen* is sent by the spirit world when wrongdoing has been committed against the dead and that it can be contracted by someone who killed personally or even simply encountered a dead body or passed through an area where killings had taken place. *Cen* can move from one person to another and can thus pollute the family or wider community of the afflicted person. There is therefore the fear of 'catching' *cen* from another.

Cen can take various forms: for the individual 'haunted' by the evil spirit, it can manifest itself as nightmares, visions, insomnia, flashbacks and memories of the individual's actions and can lead to mental illness 'until the wrong is made right';[47] for the community, it can cause illness, death and misfortune. The influence of *cen* can constitute a barrier to reintegration into the community, particularly where the symptoms of *cen* are evident to others. Not only are those who are perceived to have *cen* ostracized: given the fear of pollution from *cen*, both the afflicted person and their extended clan are isolated. It is

---

[42] Huyse 2008: 8.
[43] Harlacher et al. 2006: 46.
[44] Baines 2010: 418.
[45] Ibid.: 420.
[46] Allen and Schomerus 2006: 11.
[47] Akello et al. 2006: 237.

therefore in the interest both of clan members to cleanse the person to improve social relations,[48] and the afflicted person who will continue to be troubled by *cen* until cleansed.

To rid the afflicted person of *cen*, a ritual or ceremony is performed, which in most cases involves sacrificing an animal to 'chase away "bad spirits" to the setting sun'.[49] Baines comments that community reconciliation usually meshes with Acholi cosmological beliefs, the Acholi 'invok[ing] the spirit world to help right wrongs committed by them against others, or by others against them'.[50] Where there have been large-scale atrocities, the local population may call for cleansing rituals to be conducted to 'appease the spirit world' and restore the moral order: even where there are political or legal responses to these atrocities, 'this spiritual dimension still demands resolution'.[51]

The need to address this spiritual concern (even if only in respect of a minority of returnees) was evident from a 'Survey for War Affected Youth' (SWAY) conducted in 2006 on behalf of UNICEF. This found: 'The Acholi cosmology and spiritual world is central to understanding and aiding adversely psychologically-affected youth.'[52] It noted that 5 per cent of the almost 750 youths who participated in the survey (most of whom had been abducted) stated that they had been haunted by *cen*. These suffered various symptoms of distress, the acuteness appearing to be linked to the degree of violence perpetrated or experienced. One-third of these reported that they saw traditional rituals or visiting a witchdoctor as a way of removing *cen*, and another third responded that they believed that prayers or becoming a born-again Christian would heal them of spiritual pollution.[53]

This final cited finding of the SWAY survey brings to light an added dimension of Acholi beliefs: religion. Baines found that most of the Acholi she interviewed for her research in 2005 believed in *cen*, it being primarily born-again Christians and Muslims who were sceptical of or opposed to these cultural beliefs.[54] The majority of Acholi are Christian, yet they continue to be rooted in traditional practice and beliefs, such that the latter 'permeate and shape the interpretation of Christian teachings' and 'Christian teachings were incorporated into the indigenous cosmology'.[55] There is thus a very complex, syncretic relationship between traditional Acholi beliefs and Christianity, a point that will be revisited when considering the approach of local and international actors to indigenous practices.

A further factor to bear in mind is that the LRA itself is strongly imbued with spiritual values and uses spiritual rituals in the initiation of new recruits, to prepare troops for battle and also after battle for purification purposes. As Allen and Schomerus explain, Kony 'effectively harnessed widely recognized and feared spiritual forces', with many recruits believing that he could 'see into their minds'.[56] Rituals are not simply an 'expression of

---

[48] Baines 2010: 423.
[49] Baines 2005: 13.
[50] Baines 2010: 413.
[51] Ibid.: 422.
[52] Annan et al. 2006: iv.
[53] Ibid: 17–19. Note, however, that the data collected by this survey found no significant difference between those who had gone through ceremonies and those who had not.
[54] Baines 2005: 72.
[55] Harlacher et al. 2006: 50.
[56] Allen and Schomerus 2006: 16.

beliefs'; they also 'shape or create beliefs', and the reiteration of rituals can very much influence what people, in particular children, believe to be true.[57] This has led some commentators to perceive the use of indigenous reintegration mechanisms as 'pitched against the rituals of Kony', suggesting that 'the battle is not just for the "hearts and minds" of the Acholi, but also for the soul'.[58] One implication is that indigenous mechanisms might be useful for reintegrating LRA combatants, although some organizations (such as World Vision – see below) would argue the very opposite. Rituals were used by the LRA both to indoctrinate and to intimidate children and the wider population. Allen, writing in 2005, commented that whilst Kony was allegedly no longer possessed at that time, the spiritual significance of the LRA endured, 'continuing to instil both fear and respect for his powers'.[59] Kony's claim to have spiritual powers and the belief in and fear of these powers by abducted children and the targeted populations have significant consequences for the reintegration of former LRA child soldiers.

3.2 The Mechanisms

There are various indigenous ceremonies and rituals that are utilized by the Acholi people which historically were not used to address atrocities and large-scale violence, but rather to deal with disputes within the family or clan or between clans. My aim in this section is to outline the key characteristics of those cited frequently in existing literature on justice and reconciliation in northern Uganda and which appear to have been used (to a greater or lesser degree) to deal with children returning from LRA captivity. Note, however, that most studies have indicated that 'traditional' ceremonies have been modified, the greatest adaptation perhaps being the use of collective rather than individual ceremonies, often taking place in IDP camps rather than at the home of the returnee.[60] The mechanisms have been promoted in particular by traditional leaders through the *Ker Kwaro Acholi*, a traditional cultural institution in northern Uganda.

A number of ceremonies and rituals aim at welcoming and cleansing returnees, whilst others are conducted to prevent or resolve conflicts. Perhaps the most cited of the latter is *mato oput* (drinking the bitter root). Despite its frequent reference, however, *mato oput* (as properly understood) appears to have been used only marginally for the reintegration of returnees (see below). Based on discussions with participants in this research, and as confirmed by other researchers[61] the phrase and concept of *mato oput* has often been used generically to refer to *every* type of reconciliation ritual, ceremony or process that has taken place in the Acholi sub-region. Additionally, rituals have frequently been 'mislabelled' and confused with other rituals.[62] It is worth noting also the manifold variations between clans of *mato oput* as well as other ceremonies or rituals. As a result, what

---

[57] Ibid.
[58] Bradbury 1999: 20.
[59] Allen 2006: 42–3.
[60] There has been much discussion of the reinvention of 'traditional' justice mechanisms as well as criticism of international donor support for the formalization of Acholi traditional justice. Branch 2014: 608.
[61] See e.g. Acirokop 2009: 10; Harlacher et al. 2006: 79.
[62] See e.g. Harlacher et al. 2006: 69.

comes next is an attempt to draw out the main features of the different mechanisms, whilst acknowledging that this may not be what each clan recognizes as being intrinsic to the particular ceremony or ritual as practised amongst its members.

The first ceremony that may be performed for a returnee is the 'stepping on the egg' ceremony or *nyono tong gweno*. This is used to welcome someone home after an extended absence and is usually performed by the family or clan on the path leading to the returnee's home. There have, however, been collective ceremonies performed by the *Ker Kwaro Acholi* in IDP camps and town centres,[63] although many Acholi elders recommend the ceremony be repeated at the family level, together with other elements of cleansing.[64] Similarly, a returnee who goes home directly (rather than passing through a reception centre) and thus walks straight into the homestead is often required by the elders to go through the process.[65]

The fairly brief ceremony involves the returnee stepping on a raw egg, which has been placed next to a twig from the *opobo* tree and a *layibi* (a stick used to open the granary). In addition to serving as a 'gesture of welcome and commitment . . . to begin living together in harmony again',[66] the ceremony aims to cleanse the returnee of any evil spirits that might have been contracted whilst in captivity and that thus risk contaminating the community. The egg symbolizes innocence and purity, and breaking the eggshell represents breaking the child's links with the LRA or also breaking the barrier between the child and his/her community.[67] The *opobo* twig is slippery and thus symbolizes cleansing, and the *layibi* is used to indicate that the child will share food again with the community. After the ceremony is performed, the child is 'forgiven and cleansed'.[68] As confirmed by a Ugandan NGO staff member, stepping on the egg did not require any truth-telling by the child: indeed, it could be used to cleanse a person of evil spirits contracted simply by walking through a contaminated area or being near a dead body.[69] The ceremony is not a dispute settlement mechanism but may be seen as a precursor to *mato oput* (see below).[70] Further, where a person has contracted *cen* through killing, a more elaborate ritual (such as *moyo kom*, *ryemo jok* or *kwero merok* – see below) may be required to cleanse the returnee: the stepping on the egg ceremony would be inadequate.[71]

The stepping on the egg ceremony is often combined with the *lwoko pik wang* or 'washing away the tears' ceremony (sometimes referred to collectively as *moyo kom*, although this can also be a distinct cleansing ritual). Symbolically washing away the tears that the family shed in mourning the child whilst also washing away the thought of death and any 'attendant bad omen' aims to restore the relationship.[72] Additionally, the family may sprinkle the child with water as a blessing or pour water on the roof of the home so

---

[63] Baines 2005: 44. Also confirmed by NGO staff member A, interview, 24 August 2017.
[64] Latigo 2008: 106; Harlacher et al. 2006: 69–70.
[65] Interview with NGO staff member B, 11 April 2018.
[66] Harlacher et al. 2006: 66.
[67] Akello et al. 2009: 198.
[68] Ibid.
[69] Interview with NGO staff member A, 24 August 2017.
[70] Hovil and Quinn 2005: 24.
[71] Harlacher et al. 2006: 66.
[72] Ibid.: 71; see also Baines 2005: 28.

that it drips onto the child when he or she enters and leaves and, where resources allow, slaughter a goat.[73]

Practices of *moyo kom* (or *yubu kum*)[74] vary considerably but common elements may include the elders blessing the returnee and appealing to ancestors for their blessing, and the slaughtering of a goat. The aim of this more complex ceremony is to cleanse the returnee of evil spirits, and it is believed that this can be achieved either by placing some parts of the goat's body (usually its intestines) on the person to be cleansed or by dragging the speared goat across a compound to ward off the evil spirit.[75]

Another complex cleansing ceremony is *kwero merok*. This ceremony, traditionally used for fighters returning from war against an enemy rather than intra-clan killings, has been used in northern Uganda for returnees who have killed within their clan where they suffer from extreme psychological distress, although this use has been controversial.[76] The ritual, lasting a few days, varies depending on whether the person killed was female or male, but common elements involve cleansing the ancestral shrine, singing specific songs related to the killing, spearing a goat, putting out the fire used to roast the meat with bare feet, cleansing at a termite mound (the offender being pulled across the mound) and chewing a bitter herb.[77] The ceremony, more elaborate than 'stepping on the egg' is considered necessary for those severely afflicted by *cen*.

Where it appears that a person continues to be haunted by *cen* despite having undergone one or more of the cleansing rituals outlined above, an *ajwaka* (spirit medium or witchdoctor) may be requested to perform the *ryemo jok* ritual. This involves the *ajwaka* consulting the possessing 'free' spirit to discover what measures are necessary for it to leave the possessed person. The process usually includes sacrificing a goat or chicken, the spirit being gifted the animal or being transferred into the animal, and may involve the animal being thrown into the area where the evil spirit resides.[78]

As noted above, the most-cited reconciliation mechanism is *mato oput* (drinking the bitter root), which is described by Baines as 'both a process and ritual ceremony to restore relationships between clans in the case of intentional murder or an accidental killing'.[79] The traditional form of *mato oput*, used for individual killings as opposed to mass atrocities, would often take many years to complete. The process involves separating the relevant clans for a 'cooling off period', mediating to find the 'truth' and payment of compensation (*culo kwor*), before the perpetrator and victim are brought together in a ceremony in a 'quest for harmony', which marks the end of the dispute.[80]

The ceremony usually begins by the representatives of each party engaging in a mock fight, beating a *layibi* (granary stick) held by the elders ('beating of the stick'), after which the offender's clan acknowledges responsibility for the wrong committed and confirms its readiness to pay the compensation. The offender's clan provides a sheep and the victim's

---

[73] Harlacher et al. 2006: 71–2.
[74] Baines 2005: 28.
[75] See Harlacher et al. 2006: 97–9; Ochen 2014: 245; Latigo 2008: 106.
[76] Acirokop 2009: 9; Harlacher et al. 2006: 100.
[77] Harlacher et al. 2006: 101–7.
[78] Ibid.: 109–12; Baines 2005: 28.
[79] Baines 2005: 54.
[80] Ibid.: 54–5.

clan produces a goat, both of which are cut into two halves across the stomach, the blood being collected in a bowl. The front half of the sheep and goat are exchanged, and the blood of the animals is mixed together in a bowl with the pounded root of the *oput*, or 'bitter root', which represents bitterness or ill-feeling between people and the loss of life. The parties then drink together from the bowl in pairs to signify unity.[81] The livers of the animals are roasted, the meat being mixed together before being eaten by the parties' representatives. The rest of the meat is then cooked, whilst the compensation is paid. All the food is then eaten by the participants. This is followed by each clan 'hosting' the other in a hut assigned to them in a neutral village, after which the ceremony is concluded, and the clans are then reconciled. A further, final element – although now largely historical – is the birth of a new life with the same name as the deceased, which completes the cycle of life and death.

Central to the process are the offender's voluntary confession to, and apology for, the crime, a collective assumption of responsibility by the offender's clan for the offender's action and the clan's readiness to pay compensation (each household being required to make a contribution). It thus 'embraces collective guilt as well as individual guilt'[82] and can 'serve as a form of accountability and a tool for generating acknowledgement and long-term reconciliation'.[83]

In addition to being a conflict resolution mechanism, *mato oput* is also used to address a spiritual concern. Latigo talks of a 'supernatural barrier' between the clans which results in the clans no longer interacting with each other – this barrier is only removed after the killing is 'atoned for and a religious rite of reconciliation has been performed, to cleanse the taint'.[84] Failure on the part of the perpetrator to confess would thus result in misfortune, illness or death brought about by the *cen* of the deceased. Harlacher et al. comment that this belief has frequently provided 'strong motivation' for the perpetrator to initiate the process, particularly if he or she has suffered from illness or nightmares that could be linked to *cen*. They add: 'Whether or not the killer believes in the traditional interpretation of *cen*, escaping the social consequences of this still widely held belief is often difficult, as he might easily be accused of being the cause of diseases and misfortune befalling the family.'[85]

3.3 The Use of Indigenous Mechanisms for LRA Returnees

The extent to which indigenous ceremonies and rituals have been used in reintegrating formerly abducted children is difficult to determine, not least because such mechanisms are by their very nature localized and family- or community-led. There have been a number of surveys and studies in this area, which allow for some basic conclusions to be drawn on the incidence of these indigenous mechanisms (as well as religious ceremonies), but the findings and statistics vary considerably. Additionally, not all studies focus solely on children; many include adults who were also abducted by the LRA. And, of course, many of those abducted as children would, by the time of their return (and by the time

---

[81] Acirokop 2009: 12.
[82] Latigo 2008: 108.
[83] Acirokop 2009: 268.
[84] Latigo 2008: 103.
[85] Harlacher et al. 2006: 80–81.

of the survey), have reached adulthood. Given the number of children that constituted the LRA forces, however, it can be assumed that many, if not a majority, would have been children at the time of their abduction.

Research undertaken by Allen and Schomerus revealed that 29 per cent of respondents had taken part in a religious or traditional ritual.[86] A study conducted for the World Bank found that 27.1 per cent of returnees participated in one traditional ceremony, with 14.2 per cent participating in more than one. The figures for participation in religious ceremonies were slightly higher, with 28.9 per cent participating once in a religious ceremony and 19.7 per cent participating more than once.[87] Other studies put the numbers much higher. Allen found that almost all of the 200 returnees interviewed for his study had participated in a healing ritual (religious or indigenous),[88] and Latigo reported that 'almost all the LRA returnees' (estimated at over 12,000) had participated in the stepping on the egg ceremony, often in collective ceremonies conducted by the *Ker Kwaro Acholi*.[89]

Indeed, the stepping on the egg ceremony appears to be the most frequently used of all the ceremonies, possibly because of its brevity, simplicity and the affordability of the resources required (egg, *opobo* twig, granary stick).[90] According to an NGO staff member I interviewed, most children had to step on an egg, 'families always insisting' on this before a child entered the house.[91] She added that there were other rituals, such as those requiring a goat, but these were used less frequently as communities had been 'largely wiped' of these resources. Baines found that just over 50 per cent of returnees had gone through a family-level stepping on the egg ceremony. Another 31 per cent of returnees additionally underwent other rituals (including cleansing the body and washing away the tears rituals).[92] Of these, 16 per cent participated in further rituals involving the slaughter of a goat.[93] The SWAY study found a higher number of cleansing ceremonies involving animal sacrifice, reporting that just under half of surveyed formerly abducted youth had been involved in such ceremonies.[94] And, as indicated earlier and explored below, *kwero merok* was used, to some degree, for LRA returnees.

It would appear, however, that *mato oput*, despite attracting a lot of publicity, was used to a much lesser degree. Latigo refers to 54 *mato oput* ceremonies performed between 2004 and 2006.[95] Afako refers to a group *mato oput* ceremony being held in November 2001 in Pajule for returnees from LRA captivity (their age is not noted) and to another ceremony in Gulu district, noting that further ceremonies were planned in other parts of the region. Afako distinguishes clearly between these *mato oput* ceremonies and individual cleansing rituals that also occurred.[96] And a 2005 report by IRIN recounts the experience

---

[86] Allen and Schomerus 2006: 18.
[87] Finn et al. 2012: 86. (The study included child and adult respondents from groups including, but not exclusively, the LRA.)
[88] Allen 2006: 164.
[89] Latigo 2008: 106.
[90] Harlacher et al. 2006: 69.
[91] Interview with NGO staff member A, 24 August 2017.
[92] Baines 2005: 39.
[93] Ibid.
[94] Annan et al. 2006: 17.
[95] Latigo 2008: 105.
[96] Afako 2002: 4.

of a former girl soldier who had passed through a reception centre and received amnesty before being returned to the Labuje IDP camp in Kitgum:

> At Labuje, she was taken through 'mato oput', a traditional Acholi justice ritual in which she accepted responsibility for her crimes and her family made reparations to the families of those she had harmed during her time [as part] of the rebellion. Afterwards, she was reintegrated into her community.[97]

However, Baines, whose research was also conducted in 2005, found that, whilst there was evidence of traditional cleansing ceremonies being used in camps, there was no documented evidence of *mato oput* being used for formerly abducted persons.[98] Similarly, Allen did not encounter any *mato oput* ceremonies being performed to reintegrate LRA returnees, noting that those that had been performed involved general killings as opposed to those committed in the course of the conflict.[99] Rather, ceremonies performed for LRA returnees, whilst sometimes labelled *mato oput*, were in fact often the stepping on the egg ritual. Harlacher et al. also note that *mato oput* was 'relatively rare . . . especially in the reintegration of former LRA combatants'.[100] They cite poverty as a possible reason for this but also suggest that a lack of knowledge of, and belief in, the spirit world might have led to a decline in its use. Interestingly, in a more recent study by Atri and Cusimano, 81.5 per cent of respondents indicated that children who committed crimes should undergo *mato oput*.[101] Yet they also found limited use of the mechanism. They suggest that this could be due to popular conceptions, as opposed to experienced knowledge, of the process, 'assenting respondents voic[ing] an understanding of *Mato Oput* that referred more to the *concept* of reconciliation than to the actual *practice*'.[102]

In general, studies reported the positive influence that participating in indigenous ceremonies and rituals (or in some cases religious practices) could have on the returnee, but also the broader community. For some returnees, undergoing a ceremony could have a positive psychological effect, bringing an end to nightmares and other symptoms of *cen*. Harlacher et al. recount the positive experience of a returnee abducted as a child and kept in LRA captivity for four years. Returning to his community, the returnee suffered extreme psychological disturbances as a result of having been forced to commit atrocities. It was only after going through the *kwero merok* ritual (having already received psychosocial rehabilitation and religious support from evangelical 'born again' Christians which had not worked) that he experienced positive change and was able to reintegrate into his community.[103] Baines similarly reported that rituals could be an 'important form of therapy and healing', but considered that understanding the significance of the traditional ritual was important: 81 per cent of returnees who fully understood the cultural significance felt a positive change, compared with just 20 per cent of those who lacked

---

[97] IRIN 2005a.
[98] Baines 2005: 69.
[99] Allen 2006: 165.
[100] Harlacher et al. 2006: 90.
[101] Atri and Cusimano 2012: 57.
[102] Ibid.: 58 (original emphasis).
[103] Harlacher et al. 2006: 152–4.

cultural knowledge.[104] Indeed, for some returnees, rituals were 'largely irrelevant'.[105] A former NGO staff member recalled asking one female returnee if she felt cleansed following a ceremony involving animal sacrifice. She responded that she had gone through the ritual 'just because [the family] wanted it'; she did not feel any different.[106] Still others refused to participate in rituals, 'explaining that they had not perpetrated violence and therefore did not want to be implicated by the rituals'.[107]

Even where the returnee him or herself did not believe in the ritual or indeed in the existence of *cen*, participation could facilitate acceptance by the family and community and thus social reintegration. For some communities, absent any formal criminal justice response, indigenous mechanisms, in particular *mato oput*, were seen as the only way of obtaining justice.[108] Indeed, many considered it essential that returnees undergo cleansing to propitiate spirits and cleanse the returnee of spiritual pollution. Where a returnee had undergone a ceremony, family and community members noted improved behaviour and considered that the ceremony facilitated reintegration into the wider community rather than just family.[109] Harlacher et al. assert that the stepping on the egg and washing away the tears ceremonies that were used in IDP camps 'proved to be instrumental' in facilitating the reintegration of LRA returnees.[110]

Nonetheless, even after participating in a ceremony, some returnees felt that they were still not truly accepted by the community. For example, the former girl soldier who went through *mato oput* in Labuje IDP camp referenced above said that 'most people' had not fully accepted or forgiven her, 'still think[ing] of her as a killer' and resenting her for money received pursuant to the amnesty process;[111] other former combatants reported that the community's forgiveness was superficial.[112] For an NGO staff member, the 'ritual has nothing to do with whether people welcomed you or not';[113] what was important was the community's perception of what the child had done in captivity. If a community believed that a child had been very active in committing atrocities, a ritual or ceremony would not eliminate the stigma surrounding that child. For some victims, indigenous mechanisms and rituals can 'never heal the wounds caused by the LRA': for these, retributive justice is the only appropriate response.[114] Further, *cen* is not the only impediment to reintegration: some women (often children themselves when abducted), who return from the 'bush' with children fathered by an LRA member, face rejection given the additional burden they place on their families. And for children born of that union, their identity of having been raised in the LRA may cloud the community's view such that they are never accepted.[115]

---

[104] Baines 2005: 40–41.
[105] Allen and Schomerus 2006: 11.
[106] Interview with NGO staff member A, 24 August 2017.
[107] Annan et al. 2009: 660.
[108] IRIN 2008.
[109] Baines 2005: 45–6.
[110] Harlacher et al. 2006: 64–5.
[111] IRIN 2005a. The former girl soldier also continued to suffer from nightmares.
[112] IRIN 2005b.
[113] Interview with NGO staff member A, 24 August 2017.
[114] IRIN 2008.
[115] Interviews with NGO staff member A, 24 August 2017 and NGO staff member B, 11 April 2018. See also Denov in this volume; Shanahan and Veale in this volume.

As evinced above, not all LRA returnees went through indigenous ceremonies. Reasons for this might include, as already mentioned, a lack of desire to participate on the part of the returnee him or herself or lack of knowledge of the ceremonies. Many commentators observe that traditional practices have fallen out of use, particularly given the displacement of communities during the war and its deleterious effect on the social fabric, noting that young people are not familiar with the practices and thus question their relevance and value.[116]

Poverty, and thus the inability to obtain the resources necessary for the performance of the ceremony (including for example the payment of compensation in *mato oput*), is another reason. As regards *mato oput*, not knowing the identity of the victims can also be a hurdle. And finally, religious beliefs may lead to a returnee and/or the family rejecting indigenous practices. As will be recalled, the vast majority of Acholi are Christian, with a smaller number being Muslim. In many cases, religious ceremonies and prayers were used in conjunction with indigenous ceremonies – religious beliefs and Acholi cultural practices deemed to be compatible by many.[117] However, for some, in particular 'born-again' Christians, indigenous practices were considered satanic;[118] an NGO staff member commented that Pentecostal Christian families would 'insist on prayers only'.[119] Indeed, there are reports that some religious reception centres instructed returnees not to accept traditional ceremonies on this basis, an issue that will be explored in more detail below.

4. INTERNATIONAL ACTORS, LOCAL ACTORS AND REINTEGRATION RITUALS

Referring to interventions by international actors including UNICEF in Africa, Green and Honwana assert that the focus has been on the development and use of psychosocial therapy that centres on the individual and thus 'ignores local beliefs in the role that ancestral and malevolent spiritual forces play in the causation and healing of the affliction'.[120] They argue that this individualistic approach can undermine the involvement of the family and wider community in the process. As will be recalled, Ochen similarly found that international, but also national, efforts paid little attention to indigenous knowledge,[121] whilst Allen and Schomerus identified a turn towards such knowledge by international and local civil society.

In this section, I aim to shed light on international and local actors' perceptions of indigenous ceremonies and rituals. I focus on GUSCO (Gulu Support the Children Organization – a local actor) and World Vision (an international actor) operating in Gulu, both of which had reception centres that received high numbers of former child soldiers[122] and thus played a key role in reintegrating these children. I also explore in greater detail

---

[116] See e.g. Allen 2006: 165–6; Latigo 2008: 109.
[117] See e.g. Hovil and Quinn 2005: 25; Allen 2006: 135–7.
[118] Baines 2005: 40; Latigo 2008: 109.
[119] Interview with NGO staff member A, 24 August 2017.
[120] Green and Honwana 1999: 2.
[121] See also Akello in his volume; Wessells in this volume.
[122] See Pham et al. 2007.

UNICEF's approach to the reintegration of child soldiers – as the leading international agency for children and also given that it provided support to both World Vision and GUSCO (as well as other organizations). Whilst these organizations may not have been directly involved in organizing indigenous ceremonies, their approach nonetheless influenced methods used to reintegrate children. My aim here is to draw out whether the policy of these organizations was supportive of the use of rituals, or whether they were sceptical of, or even opposed to, their use.

4.1 GUSCO and World Vision Reception Centres

Reception centres, which were established throughout the Acholi sub-region, provided short-term care, including psychosocial support or 'counselling', for formerly abducted children (and in some cases adults) and sought to prepare them for reintegration. What distinguishes the two reception centres discussed below is their approach to counselling but also their view of indigenous processes. A psychosocial needs assessment from 1998 reported that reception centres sometimes referred children to 'traditional healers' for cleansing rituals where counselling had failed, or where the child and family had strong beliefs in traditional healing.[123] Only some reception centres embraced this approach.

GUSCO, a community-based programme established in 1994, received support from various international organizations including UNICEF and Save the Children. Its programming relating to formerly abducted children was two-pronged: reception centre-based rehabilitation and community-based reintegration. In 2010, GUSCO reported that more than 8,900 children and young women had been reintegrated into their communities after receiving assistance from the organization.[124]

At its reception centre for formerly abducted children in Gulu (formally opened in 1997), GUSCO provided medical treatment, material support and basic skills training as well as group and individual counselling. Allen and Schomerus describe GUSCO's group counselling as being more 'open-ended' than that at other centres, with sessions taking place under a tree and addressing general concerns.[125] Specific issues, including issues arising from life in captivity, would be discussed during individual counselling sessions. GUSCO also undertook family tracing and community sensitization in which it would provide information on child rights but also explain to the community that the children had been abducted and forced to commit atrocities against their will.[126] It further arranged social activities, such as sports and traditional dances, to which children from local communities would be invited; the aim being to increase contact and thus assist reintegration.

GUSCO's approach, to individual counselling at least, was secular, drawing on Western psychosocial methods. Yet it blended this with Acholi culture when it came to reintegration. GUSCO believed that rituals performed by traditional chiefs could assist in restoring social relations ruptured by crimes, in particular homicides, and could also

---

[123] Barton and Mutiti 1998: 63.
[124] GUSCO 2010a: 7.
[125] Allen and Schomerus 2006: 51–2.
[126] Interview with NGO staff member B, 11 April 2018.

foster individual and collective healing.[127] GUSCO's Programme Director affirmed that GUSCO was 'open to traditional beliefs' and would offer help, such as money for a goat, to families and communities dealing with the spiritual possession of children.[128] Indeed, an NGO staff member informed me that GUSCO had a budget that specifically supported traditional ceremonies.[129]

Akello et al. report that in 2004, GUSCO 'cleansed' 400 returnees in a collective stepping on the egg ceremony in northern Uganda.[130] GUSCO's annual report of 2010 refers to the reunification of children with their families following family tracing, and notes that 'traditional welcome ceremonies were organised for the children on arrival'.[131] It appears that most children who passed through the GUSCO reception centre took part in a traditional ceremony. A former GUSCO staff member who was responsible for taking children from the GUSCO centre to their community recalled that, in most cases, the family would be waiting at the entrance to the homestead with a branch and an egg, ready to perform the ceremony.[132]

In contrast to GUSCO's emphasis on local healing rites, the approach of World Vision (an international Christian humanitarian organization) to reintegration and counselling 'has its roots in Christian ideas about confession and repentance of sins, and healing by forgiveness and seeking refuge with God'.[133] Its Children of War Rehabilitation Centre began operating in Gulu in 1995 and more than 14,000 children had passed through the centre by 2013.[134] In addition to providing health care, material support and vocational training, World Vision provided counselling to formerly abducted children. This took the form of group discussions on topics such as reconciliation and forgiveness or peace, or individual sessions, in which children could talk about their experiences of abduction and captivity. Religion and prayer were the foundational blocks for World Vision's approach, prayers being an important part of the daily activities.[135] Children were told that they were not at fault for being abducted and forced to commit atrocities and were encouraged to forget these acts and forgive those who forced them to carry them out. Akello et al. draw out the Christian values and psychotherapeutic concepts that underpinned World Vision's intervention, highlighting two main themes. First, that it was considered essential for the child to repent and be forgiven, which was facilitated through therapeutic counselling. Second, the emphasis was on the child's innocence and vulnerability, which relates to Western ideas of vulnerable children.[136] After a stay at the centre, which varied considerably in length,[137] efforts were made to reintegrate the children into their communities through family tracing and sensitization.

---

[127] GUSCO 2010a: 31–2.
[128] Cited in Mawson 2004: 137.
[129] Interview with NGO staff member A, 24 August 2017.
[130] Akello et al. 2009: 197.
[131] GUSCO 2010b: 9.
[132] Interview with NGO staff member B, 11 April 2018.
[133] Akello et al. 2006: 230. See also Akello in this volume for greater detail on World Vision's activities and the emphasis on being 'saved'.
[134] Nabanoba 2013.
[135] Akello et al. 2006: 232; Nabanoba 2013.
[136] Akello et al. 2006: 233–4.
[137] Ibid.: 233, noting that when many children were freed, the maximum length of stay was three weeks; Nabanoba (2013) notes that one returnee spent three years at the centre.

A World Vision report from 2004 recommended that reintegration activities for children, including former child soldiers, include sensitization and reconciliation 'using appropriate cultural tools', but did not go into any greater detail as to what such 'cultural tools' might include.[138] These 'tools from local culture' were referenced as being used by communities and children to 'achieve forgiveness for deeds that the children have committed, which allows them to be accepted again'.[139] However, despite this acknowledgement of 'local culture', it appears that World Vision largely rejected, or at the very least disregarded, the use of indigenous ceremonies and rituals.

Allen and Schomerus note that, whilst GUSCO encouraged returnees to participate in indigenous ceremonies, 'the institutional attitude at Christian reception centers, such as World Vision, is less positive'.[140] They reference a World Vision staff member explaining that some returnees, in particular children 'are upset by the violence in sacrificial ceremonies, and dislike the ritual ablutions because they remind them of the healing rites that were performed by the LRA in the bush'.[141]

Various studies have suggested that World Vision expressly instructed children not to participate in cultural rituals. Baines reports that some returnees were 'warned' that participating in the stepping on the egg ceremony would lead to them being abducted again, with others told that 'cultural activities were satanic'.[142] Acirokop found that some children had been informed by reception staff not to participate in cultural rituals on the basis that it would not benefit them (one boy saying that he would take part in a ceremony if it were not 'ungodly'); instead, they were told to 'pray and forgive and forget what happened to them while in the "bush"'.[143] According to research by Maina, many children who passed through religion-based reception centres were instructed that God had forgiven them for their actions whilst in captivity, resulting in returnees refusing to comply with community demands for them to participate in traditional rituals.[144] She adds:

> Many of the returnees who go through the World Vision reception centre argue that this would conflict with their new found faith. . . . These conflicts over belief systems and rituals continue to create a social and psychological rift and conflict between some of the returnees and their communities. The choice over what to believe as an answer to getting rid of 'Cen' has profound psychological implications on formerly abducted children and their recipient families.[145]

Conflict between the returning child and his or her family given this rejection of indigenous beliefs has been identified by other commentators. One girl interviewed by Acirokop reported that her family was insisting that she participate in the rituals, whilst she had been taught at the reception centre that she should not. Acirokop commented

---

[138] World Vision 2004: 45.
[139] Ibid.: 18.
[140] Allen and Schomerus 2006: 18.
[141] Ibid.
[142] Baines 2005: 43. Baines is critical of this approach, believing that 'false' information about cultural ceremonies was being provided that was 'undermining and threatening to cultural beliefs'.
[143] Acirokop 2009: 26.
[144] Maina 2010: 223.
[145] Ibid.: 223–4.

that the girl was 'torn apart by this alleged contradiction between traditional practices and her religious belief'.[146]

It must be noted, however, that World Vision's approach does not run counter to the perspectives of all Acholi. As Ochen notes: 'Acholi society has undergone a cultural revolution and . . . not all people within the community fully subscribe to these cultural rituals and practices, with some sections of the population preferring stronger Christian and Western psychiatric/psychological practices to address personal psycho-emotional and reintegration issues.'[147] For some former abductees, their stay in the World Vision centre was extremely positive: the counselling taught them about child rights and collective forgiveness and helped with their reintegration into their community.[148] Further, for many, prayer was considered 'one of the best things' about their stay in the reception centre.[149]

As is evident from the above, the approach of GUSCO and World Vision differed. GUSCO adopted a secular counselling model and its approach to reintegration was 'a lot more embedded in culture and in traditional approaches', when compared to World Vision and other organizations.[150] World Vision's whole programme was very much grounded in Christian teaching. Further, some commentators have noted a difference in emphasis: according to Veale and Stavrou, World Vision 'works intensively with children . . . for a number of months before supporting their reintegration' whereas GUSCO, whilst having a centre, tends to 'move children to communities and identify themselves as a community-based programme'.[151] Leila Pakkala, who was in Uganda during the early years of the reception centres, reflected that, at that time, children who were being supported by World Vision seemed to have 'a lot more structured support' whilst at the centre, but 'the follow up was not necessarily as structured and that was one of our concerns'.[152] GUSCO, in contrast, had 'less-developed capacities in terms of the approaches to counselling and support but there seemed to be more rigorous follow up' after children returned to their communities.[153]

4.2 UNICEF and Reintegration Rituals

In northern Uganda, UNICEF worked on 'the process of release, reception and reintegration' of child returnees in collaboration with various state and civil society institutions.[154] To give just one example of its role, UNICEF supported the reunification of 2,639 child returnees between 2006 and 2009.[155] A key element of UNICEF's work in this area was the support provided to reception centres for formerly

---

[146] Acirokop 2009: 26.
[147] Ochen 2014: 246.
[148] See Veale and Stavrou 2003: 40.
[149] Allen and Schomerus 2006: 51.
[150] Interview with Leila Pakkala, a UNICEF Uganda child protection and advocacy adviser from 1996 to 1998, 8 March 2018.
[151] Veale and Stavrou 2003: 37 (they found that children spent on average four to six weeks at GUSCO); cf. Pham et al 2007: 36 (who found that the average stay at GUSCO was four months).
[152] Interview, 8 March 2018.
[153] Ibid.
[154] UNICEF 2006.
[155] UNICEF Uganda 2010: [15].

abducted children. These included those located in Gulu and run by GUSCO and World Vision.[156]

During the 1990s and early 2000s (before Operation Iron Fist), when relatively few children were returning from captivity, UNICEF's attention as regards reintegration was directed more at counselling, in particular the support of community-based volunteer counsellors.[157] The former UNICEF Representative for Uganda from 1993 to 1997 commented that UNICEF was 'just learning' about, but was very interested in, indigenous ceremonies at that time.[158] Indigenous ceremonies were being used to reconcile communities – and seemingly with some success – but were not to any large degree being used for former LRA combatants. UNICEF was 'positive to community traditions' and was thus open to the idea of the use of indigenous ceremonies, provided they were not harmful for children.[159] Leila Pakkala, who was a child protection and advocacy adviser for UNICEF Uganda from 1996 to 1998, told me that 'traditional mechanisms were not coming out as the primary approach, or even perceived as happening in an extensive way' at that time.[160] That said, a psychosocial needs assessment conducted in 1998 had confirmed the salience of cultural institutions in northern Uganda (although it had also referenced the difficulties of applying traditional interventions to war-related violence).[161] Pakkala, referring to this assessment, recalled that the research team had the sense that 'the communities saw quite a strong value in their traditional mechanisms and they saw it as part of the journey in healing their communities'.[162] By the early 2000s, some UNICEF staff members had witnessed indigenous ceremonies, but were not involved in any material way. Mads Oyen, a UNICEF Uganda child protection officer from 2002 to 2004 recalled attending a large collective stepping on the egg ceremony involving around 30 young returnees and commented that 'there was a lot of that; that was used throughout'.[163] In his opinion, UNICEF did not 'have any views one way or another on these things'.

More recent UNICEF reports explicitly reference traditional cleansing ceremonies that were used in the reintegration of child returnees, and UNICEF's perception appears broadly positive. From a review of UNICEF's own reports as well as those by the local organizations it supported, and as corroborated by participants in this research, UNICEF – as an international actor – did not directly organize indigenous ceremonies, but rather worked through local actors. An evaluation of UNICEF's programmes in Kitgum reported that 216 children associated with the LRA had been reunited with their families between 2006 and 2008 and affirmed that interventions had been effective 'particularly in adapting strategies to the local culture, including traditional cleansing ceremonies'.[164] In its 2013 annual report, UNICEF's child protection programmes were cited as providing reintegration support to child returnees, including psychosocial

---

[156] UNICEF Uganda 2004a and 2004b.
[157] Confirmed by Oyen, interview, 16 July 2017 and Pakkala, interview, 8 March 2018.
[158] Kathleen Cravero, interview, 25 October 2017.
[159] Ibid.
[160] Interview, 8 March 2018.
[161] Barton and Mutiti 1998: 51.
[162] Interview, 8 March 2018.
[163] Interview, 16 July 2017.
[164] Carnegie 2008: 23.

support, and it was noted that 37 children 'benefitted' from participation in traditional cleansing rituals.[165] A media report by UNICEF Uganda, which referred to UNICEF's work with an NGO in Kitgum, relates the story of a woman abducted as a child into the LRA who underwent a cleansing ceremony. This included stepping on the egg and also animal sacrifice, which aimed to 'officially welcome her back in the village, cleanse her of the past misfortune, reconcile her with the communities and bless her family'.[166] The report refers to the acceptance of the woman following this ceremony and notes that the woman's behaviour and also symptoms improved. It concludes by emphasizing UNICEF Uganda's support for this project.

However, there were concerns about this approach to reintegration. Cornelius Williams, the head of UNICEF's Kitgum office from 2004 to 2006 and then Chief of Child Protection in Uganda from 2006 to 2009, referred to discussions that took place when assessing the use of indigenous ceremonies, including *mato oput*. He noted that there were concerns over a child 'implicating' him or herself where the ceremony included acknowledgement of wrongdoing. This would be of concern both for children over the age of criminal responsibility as well as those below that age who cannot be held criminally responsible. However, 'if it achieved the aim of social harmony and it facilitated the reintegration of the child into his or her community, then we felt it was in the best interests of the child'.[167] For him, the amnesty process raised more concerns than indigenous ceremonies when it came to self-incrimination and issues of accountability.[168] In any event, as discussed earlier, it seems that most former child soldiers participated in the stepping on the egg ceremony, which did not require a full acknowledgement of acts committed, rather than *mato oput*.

Other concerns from a child rights perspective related to the issue of consent. Many of those I interviewed were unclear as to whether children had been consulted about their participation in a particular ceremony. Pakkala, who stressed that she had not witnessed any ceremonies first-hand, had the sense that participation in anything that was 'dubbed as a traditional justice mechanism or linked to religion' was a requirement on the child rather than the result of consultation.[169] Williams, who was present when ceremonies were performed, questioned whether any consent would have been informed and further commented that it was an 'adult process determined by the elders'.[170] However, he recognized the challenges of seeking consent in such a difficult context. For him, the right to be heard, guaranteed under Article 12 of the CRC is a hallmark of a rights approach and as such should be integrated into UNICEF's programmatic approach.[171] Yet there was a tension between that right and the best interests of the child, enshrined in Article 3 of the Convention. In the Uganda case, it appears that the best interests of the child prevailed.

In a publication on children affected by armed conflict, UNICEF referred to a number of best practices that inform its policy and programming on the demobilization and

---

[165] UNICEF Uganda 2013: 21.
[166] Garofalo and Aturia (undated).
[167] Interview, 16 August 2017.
[168] This was also raised as an issue by NGO staff member A, interview, 24 August 2017.
[169] Interview, 8 March 2018.
[170] Interview, 16 August 2017.
[171] Ibid.

reintegration of children. One such practice was involving children in the process, including 'healing or forgiveness rituals' when appropriate.[172] The publication does not refer to UNICEF's work in northern Uganda but does refer to support provided in Angola, where cleansing ceremonies were used to liberate children from 'the spirits of war'.[173] In relation to dealing with children in post-conflict situations, UNICEF states:

> In several countries, UNICEF explores and supports, whenever possible and appropriate, the involvement of more traditional justice mechanisms where traditional leaders and local communities but also the families and children concerned play an active part. These mechanisms, if compliant with all human rights principles, have proven to be sound alternatives for dealing with young people in conflict with the law and also in post-conflict situations.[174]

My interviews with UNICEF staff members were consistent with this narrative, with most appearing pragmatic in their approach to reintegration interventions. Taking a holistic approach to the reintegration of former child soldiers, indigenous approaches were perceived as being potentially useful, provided they were consistent with child rights, in particular the best interests of the child. Pakkala commented:

> It's important to make sure that whatever traditional mechanisms are used are not resulting in either a psychological or physical effect on children, and the minimum child protection considerations are taken into account in any community ritual. You have FGM [Female Genital Mutilation] being seen in some places as a traditional practice and we would see that in absolute contradiction to the principles of child rights, and from a health-related point of view, we would see that as contrary to child rights. The key principle of any traditional or cultural ceremony has to be that it cannot and should not be in contradiction with child rights and child protection considerations which are enshrined in the Convention.[175]

A distinction is thus drawn between social norms and harmful traditional practices. Ibrahim Sesay, the UNICEF Focal Point for child recruitment, release and reintegration in New York referred to the need to assess whether a ceremony has any negative consequences: 'key is upholding local values without infringing on the rights of children, families and the community'.[176] He further highlighted the importance of working with the community: there is a need for UNICEF to work with community structures and institutions and 'build on assets and value systems that already exist'.[177]

5. CONCLUSION

According to Akello et al., both types of reintegration programmes (based on Christian values or traditional ceremonies) have had limited success in Uganda: of 300 children 'reintegrated' in 2004–2005, not one was found three months later in the community

---

[172] UNICEF 2002: 36.
[173] Ibid.: 38.
[174] Ibid.: 121.
[175] Interview, 8 March 2018.
[176] Interview, 10 August 2017.
[177] Ibid.

in which they had been reintegrated.[178] I did not set out to evaluate the effectiveness of indigenous mechanisms in reintegrating former child soldiers and nor do I claim to do so here. However, I can offer some very broad conclusions as to the use of indigenous mechanisms. Perhaps the first important point is that indigenous mechanisms seem to be perceived as both a form of justice and cleansing, but there has been considerable confusion over what ceremonies or rituals were performed: *mato oput* has frequently been used as a 'catch-all' term for all types of rituals, which makes it difficult to determine how frequently the different rituals were utilized and would also render an evaluation of their effectiveness extremely difficult. Reports on the number of returnees who participated in ceremonies vary significantly, and often do not specify the type of ritual used.

As indicated briefly above, indigenous ceremonies seem to have been effective in some cases, but failed in others, particularly where accountability was at issue. The stepping on the egg ceremony – used most frequently – cannot really be said to serve an accountability function, albeit that it could be perceived as a form of socio-cultural justice if it results in reconciliation. There is no requirement to discuss, and thus acknowledge responsibility for, acts committed. There is also no requirement to make any form of reparation or pay compensation. It is thus perhaps most appropriate as a means of social reintegration where the family and community are more concerned about spiritual pollution than accountability: for example, where the child has committed crimes outside the community or has contracted *cen* as a result of passing through polluted areas. Additionally, it appears to have been beneficial where the child believes him or herself to be possessed. *Mato oput*, which, although widely proclaimed, appears in practice to have been used to a lesser extent than the stepping on the egg ceremony, gets closer to addressing accountability issues, in that it includes acknowledgement of wrongdoing and the payment of compensation. Nonetheless, some accounts from former child soldiers in the literature suggest that *mato oput* did not fully assist with their reintegration: for some community members, retributive justice would be the only acceptable response. In summary, indigenous mechanisms seem at the very least to offer a contribution to spiritual rehabilitation and reconciliation and can perhaps best be seen as a complementary instrument in the transitional justice toolbox.

As regards the approach of local and international actors to indigenous forms of justice and reconciliation, as perhaps might have been expected, GUSCO, a local organization, was much more in tune with local traditions than World Vision, an international organization. GUSCO appears to have fully embraced the use of indigenous ceremonies (primarily stepping on the egg) and identified itself as a community-based organization. World Vision, whilst acknowledging 'cultural tools' in its reports, reportedly instructed, or at least encouraged, children not to partake in indigenous rituals. The use of such rituals ran counter to its institutional ethos, founded on religious principles. The time and space limits of this research did not allow me to explore the work of other organizations working on reintegration issues in northern Uganda. However, I am aware that Caritas, a faith-based organization that also ran a reception centre in northern Uganda, did support the use of 'traditional Acholi practices' in assisting reconciliation and reintegration.[179] It

---

[178] Akello et al. 2009: 188; Akello in this volume.
[179] Caritas Gulu Archdiocese.

would thus be interesting to compare and contrast the approaches of Caritas (Catholic) and World Vision (evangelical) in further research.

As the lead agency for children, UNICEF provided support to both GUSCO and World Vision. I have outlined above its broadly supportive view of indigenous reintegration mechanisms. There were concerns regarding consent and participation rights as well as the right not to incriminate oneself. However, provided there was no negative physical or psychological impact, the use of indigenous ceremonies was considered to be in the best interests of the child if such ceremonies facilitated reintegration. Although not discussed above, UNICEF was also supportive of religious approaches to rehabilitation and reintegration. A media report that covered UNICEF's work with an NGO in Kitgum noted that 'the community decides on the best way to reintegrate the women and the children, which could be a traditional ceremony or a religious ritual with the best interest of the child at heart on what she/he is comfortable with'.[180] As Leila Pakkala stressed to me, there is a need to look at and learn from different approaches.[181] In Uganda, my research suggests that UNICEF was open to all approaches provided that they did not conflict with child rights, in particular the key principle of the best interests of the child. Working with communities to promote local approaches may, in many circumstances, be the best starting point.

REFERENCED WORKS

Acirokop, P. 2009. 'Addressing the Potential and Limits of the "Mato Oput" Process as a Basis for Accountability, Justice and Reconciliation for Children in Northern Uganda (Draft)' (UNICEF) [available at: https://www.unicef-irc.org/knowledge-pages/Children-and-Transitional-Justice-Conference--27-29-April-2009/592 (accessed 28 November 2018)]

Afako, B. 2002. 'Reconciliation and Justice: "Mato Oput" and the Amnesty Act' in L. Okello, *Protracted Conflict, Elusive Peace: Initiatives to End the Violence in Northern Uganda* (London; Conciliation Resources) 64 [available at: http://www.c-r.org/accord-article/reconciliation-and-justice-%E2%80%98mato-oput%E2%80%99-and-amnesty-act-2002 (accessed 28 November 2018)]

Akello, G., Richters, A. and Reis, R. 2006. 'Reintegration of Former Child Soldiers in Northern Uganda: Coming to Terms with Children's Agency and Accountability' 4 *Intervention* 229

Akello, G., Richters, A. and Reis, R. 2009. 'Coming to Terms with Accountability: Why the Reintegration of Former Child Soldiers in Northern Uganda Fails' in P. Gobodo-Madikizela and C. Van Der Merwe (eds), *Memory, Narrative and Forgiveness: Perspectives on the Unfinished Journeys of the Past* (Newcastle upon Tyne: Cambridge Scholars Publishing) 188

Allen, T. 2006. *Trial Justice: The International Criminal Court and the Lord's Resistance Army* (London; New York: Zed Books)

Allen, T. 2008. 'Ritual (Ab)Use? Problems with Traditional Justice in Northern Uganda' in N. Waddell and P. Clark (eds), *Courting Conflict? Justice, Peace and the ICC in Africa* (London: Royal African Society)

Allen, T. and Macdonald, A. 2013. 'Post-Conflict Traditional Justice: A Critical Overview', JSRP Paper 3 (London: Justice and Security Research Programme, LSE)

Allen, T. and Schomerus, M. 2006. 'A Hard Homecoming: Lessons Learned from the Reception Center Process in Northern Uganda: An Independent Study' (Washington, DC: Management Systems International)

Amnesty International 2008. 'Uganda: Agreement and Annex on Accountability and Reconciliation Falls Short of a Comprehensive Plan to End Impunity' (AI Index: ARF 59/001/2008) (March)

Annan, J., Blattman, C. and Horton, R. 2006. 'The State of Youth and Youth Protection in Northern Uganda: Findings from the Survey for War-Affected Youth' (Kampala: UNICEF) (September)

Annan, J., Brier, M. and Aryemo, F. 2009. 'From "Rebel" to "Returnee": Daily Life and Reintegration for Young Soldiers in Northern Uganda' 24 *Journal of Adolescent Research* 639

---

[180] Garofalo and Aturia (undated).
[181] Interview, 8 March 2018.

Atri, S. and Cusimano, S. 2012. 'Perceptions of Children Involved in War and Transitional Justice in Northern Uganda' (Toronto: University of Toronto) (March)

Babatunde, A.O. 2014. 'Harnessing Traditional Practices for Use in the Reintegration of Child Soldiers in Africa: Examples from Liberia and Burundi' 12 *Intervention* 379

Baines, E. 2005. 'Roco Wat I Acoli: Restoring Relationships in Acholi-Land: Traditional Approaches to Reintegration and Justice' (Liu Institute for Global Issues) (September)

Baines, E. 2010. 'Spirits and Social Reconstruction after Mass Violence: Rethinking Transitional Justice' 109 *African Affairs* 409

Barton, T. and Mutiti, A. 1998. 'NUPSNA: Northern Uganda Psycho-Social Needs Assessment for UNICEF-Uganda and the Core Team for Psycho-Social Programmes in Northern Uganda' (Kampala: UNICEF)

Bradbury, M. 1999. 'An Overview of Initiatives for Peace in Acholi, Northern Uganda' (CDA Collaborative Learning Project) (October)

Branch, A. 2014. 'The Violence of Peace: Ethnojustice in Northern Uganda' 45 *Development and Change* 608

Caritas Gulu Archdiocese, 'Building Peace – the Social Service Program' [available at: https://sites.google.com/a/caritasgulu.org/www/our-work/social-services (accessed 10 July 2018)]

Carnegie, R. 2008. 'Final Review of UNICEF-Supported Programmes for Children Affected by Conflict in Kitgum, Northern Uganda' (Hunter Foundation)

Derluyn, I., Vandenhole, W., Parmentier, S. and Mels, C. 2015. 'Victims and/or Perpetrators? Towards an Interdisciplinary Dialogue on Child Soldiers' 15 *BMC International Health and Human Rights* 28

Finn, A., Jefferson, C., Vusia, S. and Yiga, D. 2012. 'Uganda Demobilization and Reintegration Project: Beneficiary Assessment' (Washington: The World Bank)

Finnström, S. 2008. *Living with Bad Surroundings* (Durham, NC and London: Duke University Press)

Garofalo, M. and Aturia, P.S. (undated). 'UNICEF Uganda – Media Centre – UNICEF Helps Reconstruct Lost Hope and Future for Child Mothers and Children Born in Captivity' [available at: https://www.unicef.org/uganda/media_17158.html (accessed 28 November 2018)]

Green, E. and Honwana, A. 1999 'Indigenous Healing of War-Affected Children in Africa', IK Notes No. 10 (World Bank) (July)

GUSCO 2010a. 'Reintegration of Returnees, Ex-Combatants and Other War-Affected Persons in the Communities of Gulu and Amuru Districts, Northern Uganda – Research Report' (January)

GUSCO 2010b. 'Annual Report – Strengthening Child Protection Systems in Gulu and Amuru Districts'

Harlacher, T., Okot, F.X., Obonyo, C.A., Balthazard, M. and Atkinson, R. 2006. *Traditional Ways of Coping in Acholi: Cultural Provisions for Reconciliation and Healing from War* (Kampala: Caritas)

Honwana, A. 2006. *Child Soldiers in Africa* (Philadelphia: University of Pennsylvania Press)

Hovil, L. and Quinn, J. 2005. 'Peace First, Justice Later: Traditional Justice in Northern Uganda', Refugee Law Project Working Paper No. 17 (July)

Human Rights Watch 2003. 'Stolen Children: Abduction and Recruitment in Northern Uganda' (Vol 15, No. 7 (A))

Huyse, L. 2008. 'Introduction: Tradition-Based Approaches in Peacemaking, Transitional Justice and Reconciliation Policies', in L. Huyse and M. Salter (eds), *Traditional Justice and Reconciliation after Violent Conflict: Learning from African Experiences* (Stockholm: International Idea)

IRIN [Integrated Regional Information Networks] 2005a. 'Uganda: Forgiveness as an Instrument of Peace' (9 June)

IRIN 2005b. 'Uganda: Traditional Ritual Heals Communities Torn Apart by War' (9 June)

IRIN 2008. 'Uganda: Tribal Justice Takes Root' (10 November)

Latigo, J.O. 2008. 'Northern Uganda: Tradition-Based Practices in the Acholi Region', in L. Huyse and M. Salter (eds), *Traditional Justice and Reconciliation after Violent Conflict: Learning from African Experiences* (Stockholm: International Idea)

Maina, G. 2010. 'An Analytical Study of the Reintegration Experience of the Formerly Abducted Children in Gulu, Northern Uganda: A Human Security Perspective' (PhD Thesis, University of Bradford)

Marques, F.N. 2001. 'Rehabilitation and Reintegration of the Former Child Soldiers in Mozambique' (Maxwell School of Citizenship and Public Affairs) (March)

Mawson, A. 2004. 'Children, Impunity and Justice: Some Dilemmas from Northern Uganda', in J. Boyden and J. de Berry (eds), *Children and Youth on the Front Line: Ethnography, Armed Conflict and Displacement* (New York and Oxford: Berghahn Books)

Nabanoba, S. 2013. 'Marred by War, Redeemed by Love' *World Vision International* (17 May) [available at: https://www.wvi.org/uganda/article/marred-war-redeemed-love (accessed 28 November 2018)]

Ochen, E.A. 2014. 'Traditional Acholi Mechanisms for Reintegrating Ugandan Child Abductees' 37 *Anthropology Southern Africa* 239

Pain, D. 1997. 'The Bending of Spears: Producing Consensus for Peace and Development in Northern Uganda' (London: International Alert and Kacoke Madit)

Pham, P., Vinck, P. and Stover, E. 2007. 'Abducted: The Lord's Resistance Army and Forced Conscription in Northern Uganda' (Berkeley-Tulane Initiative on Vulnerable Persons) (June)

UN 2008. 'UN Common Approach to Justice for Children' (March)
UN Secretary-General 2003. 'Report of the Secretary-General on Children and Armed Conflict' (UN Doc. A/58/546-S/2003/1053) (10 November)
UN Security Council 2004. 'Report of the Secretary-General on the Rule of Law and Transitional Justice in Conflict and Post-Conflict Societies' (UN Doc. S/2004/616) (23 August)
UNICEF 2002. *Children Affected by Armed Conflict: UNICEF Actions* (UNICEF)
UNICEF 2006. 'Statement of UNICEF Executive Director Ann M. Veneman on Uganda' (29 August) [available at: https://www.unicef.org/media/media_35475.html (accessed 28 November 2018)]
UNICEF Uganda 2004a. 'A Chance to Return to Normal Life: Former Child Soldiers Return Home in Northern Uganda' (17 May) [available at: https://www.unicef.org/infobycountry/uganda_return_normal.html (accessed 28 November 2018]
UNICEF Uganda 2004b. '47 Children, Formerly Abducted by LRA, Come Back Home' (27 August) [available at: https://www.unicef.org/media/media_23404.html (accessed 28 November 2018)]
UNICEF Uganda 2010. 'Uganda Country Programme Document 2010–2014'
UNICEF Uganda 2013. 'Annual Report 2013'
Veale, A. and Stavrou, A. 2003. 'Violence, Reconciliation and Identity: The Reintegration of Lord's Resistance Army Child Abductees in Northern Uganda' (Institute for Security Studies)
World Vision 2004. 'Pawns of Politics – Children, Conflict and Peace in Northern Uganda' (Washington)

20. Child agency and resistance to discourses within the Paris Principles in rehabilitation and reintegration processes of former child soldiers in northern Uganda

*Grace Akello**

During the prolonged civil war in northern Uganda, up to 1.7 million people were displaced from their livelihoods, settled in overcrowded protected villages, and exposed to disease and suffering. The Lord's Resistance Army's (LRA) tactic of abducting and conscripting children into armed rebellion as child soldiers and sex slaves galvanized international media attention. The Ugandan government regularly attacked the LRA armed group and rescued some of the child combatants at the war front. Other abducted children escaped from captivity. While certain children settled back into their communities without rehabilitation, many national and international emergency agencies, including the United Nations Children's Fund (UNICEF), implemented rehabilitation and reintegration programmes for former child soldiers. The main framework for their activities was the 2007 Paris Principles and Guidelines on Children Associated with Armed Forces or Armed Groups. These Principles, I argue, present child soldiers as immature and innocent victims. When the communities into which returnees are reintegrated view them in a different light, these Principles urge that these communities be sensitized about the returnees' innocence. During my ethnographic study, I observed how local and international emergency aid agencies organized workshops for different stakeholders and war-affected people to promote awareness about the innocence of rescued LRA child and adult fighters prior to their reintegration. One of the unintended consequences of this approach was silencing victims of war violence who would have preferred disclosure, reparation and compensation. Many people after all were exposed to extreme events carried out by child fighters. I analyse experiences of some of the children abducted by the LRA in northern Uganda who were subsequently resettled into their communities in line with the Paris Principles. I identify lessons learnt and propose ways in which this framework, which is increasingly seen as soft law and a best practice, could be modified to better guide comprehensive rehabilitation and reintegration processes of former child soldiers.

Children experience significant behavioural changes when they are forcibly recruited as fighters, live in complex emergencies and in war zones and are kept in captivity for years. These difficult experiences interface with and reconstitute their development. This was the case in northern Uganda with regard to the children who were abducted by the Lord's Resistance Army (LRA). These children were trained to live in militaristic ways and forced to kill civilians (including on occasion even their own siblings). They lived

---

* This chapter is adapted from but expands upon and updates an earlier publication by the same author: Akello 2015. Tables 20.1 and 20.2 herein are drawn from this earlier publication.

Rehabilitation and reintegration processes in northern Uganda 437

under extreme stress. They witnessed many events such as gunfire exchange, war violence and abduction of other children. They were exposed to injuries, diseases and murders. The LRA also taught the abducted children how to live in harsh conditions through looting property and engaging in acts of war violence which some former child soldiers recalled as tantamount to 'kill to live or be killed'. Some former child soldiers discussed incidences of yearning to kill people – as a matter of habit.

When the abducted children were rescued by the Uganda People's Forces or escaped from these iniquitous living conditions to reintegrate with their families, they were changed people with changed behaviour. They had learnt different ways of living. Whatever their starting point, they left the war as fundamentally different individuals from what they were like when they had entered the war.

The Paris Principles on Children Associated with Armed Forces or Armed Groups guided national and international aid organizations in the process of reintegrating these children with their families and communities. My experiences with these guidelines suggest that their implementation neglects the changed status and behaviour of former child soldiers, thereby leading to a failure to address their needs and those of the war-affected communities. Many examples abound. For instance, in Akello, Richters and Reis, we show how money donated to one returnee at the time of reintegration was typically used in underproductive ways.[1] Apiyo, a former child soldier, revealed how people in the community pretended to work closely with her, advising her and sometimes borrowing the money she had been given during reintegration processes.[2] However, as noted 'when the money got finished, people became so hostile to her, calling her names, like "Child of Kony", that she did not know where to start to ask for her money back'.[3]

In general, the reintegration process yielded limited success. I interviewed a coordinator of Save the Children in Uganda (which funded and monitored reintegration processes) who mentioned that over three hundred former child soldiers left their communities within three months of reintegration. The crux of the problem, I argue, is that former child soldiers constructed by international and national organizations as innocent children were simply not seen as such by the community. In informal settings, these children freely discussed their experiences in carrying out various war atrocities including abducting other children. Another local indicator through which former child soldiers were judged is the idea that some of them were frequently disturbed by cen – the revengeful spirits – of people they had killed. Neither of these realities were adequately expiated by reintegration processes rooted in the Paris Principles.

This chapter begins by casting light on the setting and providing background information about northern Uganda and how the phenomenon of former child soldiers came into being. I then set out the different sections of the Paris Principles germane to the rehabilitation processes of the former child soldiers. In my analysis I will suggest that the Paris Principles guided the process of rehabilitating and reintegrating former child soldiers while silencing victims of war violence. One of the unseen consequences, however, was that, due to the discourse in the Paris Principles, former child soldiers faced community

---

[1] Akello et al. 2006: 232–4.
[2] All names used in this chapter are pseudonyms to protect participants' anonymity.
[3] Akello et al. 2006: 234.

stigmatization and alienation: they were not welcomed as traumatized and innocent children. In my experience, community members who had encountered war atrocities perpetrated by former child soldiers were uncomfortable with the propagated narratives of faultlessness and passivity.

1. THE SETTING

The war in northern Uganda started in 1986 when General Tito Okello's regime was ousted from power by the National Resistance Movement (NRM) led by Yoweri Museveni who later became President of Uganda. Alice Lakwena initially led a rebel group, the Holy Spirit Movement, which fought against the National Resistance Army (NRA), the armed wing of the NRM. Alice Lakwena promoted spiritism and superstition among fighters.[4] However, the NRM defeated her group in Jinja, about 34 kilometres from Uganda's political capital Kampala. The remnants of Alice Lakwena's army regrouped as the LRA in the late 1980s under the leadership of Joseph Kony. The LRA was comprised mostly of Acholi people living in the northern Uganda districts of Amuru, Agago, Gulu, Kitgum, Nwoya and Pader. The LRA thrived in northern Uganda from the late 1980s until the early 1990s in part due to support from the Acholi people. The ruling party's brutal violence inflicted on the civilian population during regular raids (e.g. Operation North) stoked antipathy among the general population. Many civilians had been exposed to brutalities by both the NRA (renamed the Uganda People's Defence Forces (UPDF)) and LRA rebel fighters. A Justice and Reconciliation Project Field Report (2013) titled 'The Beasts of Burcoro: Recounting Atrocities by the NRA's 22nd Battalion in Burcoro Village in April 1991' suggested the following: 'Operation North was characterised by a broader militarisation of the conflict and the overwhelming use of heavy-handed tactics against civilians, including arbitrary arrests, torture, extrajudicial killings, sexual violence and abduction.'[5]

The insecurity triggered by war compelled people to leave their homesteads and settle in camps (also called protected villages). The mass loss of lives, displacement and subsequent resettlement in congested camps led to the breakdown of the Acholi social fabric. The displaced population was exposed to infectious diseases, sometimes breaking out as epidemics, and to war crimes. Previously self-reliant communities became reduced to war-affected people living in camps and waiting for food handouts and emergency aid services. This situation lasted for about 20 years.[6] As of 2007, LRA fighters fled to the Democratic Republic of Congo and Central African Republic. The LRA has been greatly weakened.

The LRA's pattern of abducting children and forcing their conscription into armed rebellion as child soldiers and sex slaves garnered significant global attention. UNICEF estimated in 2004 that the LRA abducted about 27,000 children aged between 7 and 17 years.[7] Some authors have documented the stories of Aboke girls abducted in northern

---

[4] Allen 2006: 23–30.
[5] Justice and Reconciliation Project 2013: 5.
[6] Ibid.: 1; Akello et al. 2010: 213–20; Akello et al. 2008: 186–210.
[7] UNICEF 2004: 21.

Uganda, the social impact of war, the effect of war on the physical and psychological wellbeing of children, and what Sverker Finnström describes as living in bad surroundings.[8]

Acholi children were exposed to multiple atrocities and hard labour. Their training involved forced killings, abduction of other children, attacking civilian camps, and being obliged to walk long distances while carrying heavy luggage. Some of the children witnessed their siblings collapsing and dying from backbreaking exhaustion, deaths through drowning and brutal murders. As a consequence of witnessing and participating in these horrific acts, some previously innocent children turned into ruthless fighters.[9]

One former child soldier described his experience – an experience that I find is largely indicative of the experiences of others:

> From the day I was abducted by those people, there was too much suffering. That day I was coming from school and going home when we met a group of LRA soldiers. When I reached the point where they were ordering me to obey everything they commanded, they immediately told me to lie down. Many other people who followed me using the same path were immediately told to lie flat on their stomachs. We were taken to a very far village I had never even heard about. While there, there was strict training of the children to become soldiers. The commander used threats and violence in training. Children were trained to be spies. They were told to climb trees, and to protect commanders by sleeping on trees. In case they saw anything the children had to immediately jump down. Some children even broke their legs in the process. Any child who showed any rebellious behaviour would be punished severely. Both boys and girls had to act as security and were trained in the same way. Girls also had other roles like cooking for all the soldiers and making fires for commanders. That is how some of them became wives.
>
> There were parades during the dry seasons. The lines of children had to be straight. The commander would determine the straightness by firing shots aimed at close range. Injured children were left without any help. When one dies, the expectation was to step over them. Children would be instructed that there was no need to attend. I regret most of the killings we carried out. This has caused a condition in my health till today. I see scary images of killing and the people I participated in killing. Although I went through counselling, and also did many traditional ceremonies, I still see these things they call *cen*.[10]

As will be discussed in further detail below, narratives from adults who had been abducted from displaced persons' camps by child fighters and who eventually managed to escape are replete with statements depicting many child soldiers as cruel and merciless fighters. One adult said: 'It was very dangerous to be abducted by a child-led LRA group, since these children practised the most brutal forms of violence without any reflection.'[11]

The NRA routinely attacked LRA groups. Sometimes the NRA rescued child fighters at the warfront. Many LRA child combatants, moreover, escaped from captivity and settled back within their communities. Although statistical data about the undocumented returnees is difficult to come by, during interviews I undertook with local leaders in one village, a counsellor discussed how the presence of young men who had escaped from the LRA after many years of training to become fighters became a security threat to the

---

[8] Finnström 2003: 4–38.
[9] Akello 2015: 1038.
[10] Interview with 17-year-old rescued former child soldier at the point of rehabilitation at the World Vision Centre for Formerly Abducted Children.
[11] Interview with one returnee adult who was abducted in Kitgum Matidi by a known child soldier.

villagers. According to this counsellor, the returnees often migrated to urban areas in the morning hours where they spent most of their time gambling, only to come back late in the night – often heavily inebriated. Many returnees, it was mentioned, neither wanted to engage in economic activities nor rebuild their families.

2. REHABILITATION PROCESSES FOR FORMER CHILD SOLDIERS

In some communities, opinions were divided even within families about how to deal with returnee children. Reintegration challenges for the children began immediately upon their repatriation. For example, in Gulu town, local media and loud-speaker announcements were aired for the children's families. These announcements called on these families to identify and shelter the abducted children. Instead of taking these rescued children home, however, many people deliberately avoided Gulu town streets when these children were lined up there for identification. Some people made negative comments to rescued children because of the atrocities they were believed to have committed and others expressed fear of cen- revengeful spirits – which such returnee children might have picked up during their captivity.[12] It is also important to note that some former child soldiers resisted rehabilitation attempts.

Retaining rescued (and experienced) child fighters for prolonged periods of time in the barracks proved expensive for the UPDF. This prompted the UPDF to recruit some of the experienced child fighters back into active armed combat. The UPDF did so despite the unlawfulness of child recruitment under both national and international law. In these tragic instances, the rescued former child soldiers were mostly deployed in spying, accessing information and identifying LRA bases. That said, these re-recruited children were not in the majority, meaning that most returnees needed to be rehabilitated and reintegrated within their communities, including in situations where the former child soldiers had inflicted atrocities within those communities and villages.

3. POLICY CONTEXT

Many humanitarian agencies which focused on the reintegration of former child soldiers adopted the Paris Principles. They did so as a 'best practice', so to speak, interpreting the Paris Principles in the way they are intended to be interpreted, namely, as a manual or guideline. Table 20.1 identifies key sections of the Paris Principles that proved particularly salient to official reintegration practices.

Table 20.1 demonstrates that international soft law and policy depict former child soldiers as traumatized, innocent, immature, and as victims of violence. When it comes to truth-seeking and reconciliation mechanisms, children should be treated equally (and only it seems) 'as victims or as witnesses' (as opposed to also as actors or perpetrators), and their participation in such mechanisms must be voluntary and in no way a precondition for the receipt of any services or support (Paris Principles 8.15 and 8.16).

---

[12] See Akello 2015: 1038. See also Barrett in this volume.

Table 20.1 Paris Principles: legal provisions for the rehabilitation and reintegration of former child soldiers

Incidences involving former child soldiers	Paris Principles provision
Rehabilitation	Paris Principle 1.5 affirms that the Paris Principles 'tak[e] a child rights-based approach to the problem of children associated with armed forces or armed groups, [and] underscore the humanitarian imperative to seek the unconditional release of children from armed forces or armed groups at all times'.
When a former child soldier commits crimes	Principle 3.6 urges that 'children who are accused of crimes under international law allegedly committed while they were associated with armed forces or armed groups should be considered primarily as victims of offences against international law; not only as perpetrators'. Wherever possible, Principle 3.7 mandates alternatives to judicial proceedings. Principle 3.8 emphasizes that 'where truth-seeking and reconciliation mechanisms are established, children's . . . participation must be voluntary and by informed consent by both the child and her or his parent or guardian where appropriate and possible'.
Where former child soldiers are stigmatized, there is a provision to sensitize the community about their innocence	Principle 7.39 mentions stigma, return and reintegration and notes that 'Children are frequently perceived initially as troublemakers prone to aggressive behaviour or criminal activities. The preparation of communities and on-going support to communities needs to address these perceptions and to help communities understand that the children are primarily victims.' Principle 7.42 advances risk assessments 'where it is likely that children will be feared, become targets of hostility for having been in enemy groups or be ostracised or neglected'. In these cases, Principle 7.42 recommends that 'intensive community sensitisation' be 'undertaken before children return'.
Cultural reintegration practices	Principle 7.53 provides: 'In some communities, children are viewed and view themselves as carrying bad spirits from their experiences with armed forces or armed groups. Appropriate cultural practices, as long as they are not harmful to children, can be essential to a child's reintegration and should be supported.'
Justice for former child soldiers	Principle 8.11 states that 'children associated with armed forces or armed groups who return to communities without undergoing any judicial or other proceedings should be closely monitored to ensure that they are not treated as scapegoats or subjected to any processes or mechanisms that contravene their rights'.

In northern Uganda, returnees were perfunctorily reintegrated into communities without participation in transitional justice processes for their acts during wartime. Whilst the Paris Principles do recognize the potential of cultural practices in the reintegration of former child soldiers, it is my experience that interventions by humanitarian agencies did not sufficiently take account of traditional mechanisms.[13] As a general norm, transitional

---

[13] One such traditional practice was reported by Girling 1960: 50 (underscoring the importance

justice mechanisms are invoked to expiate the resentment of the community towards suspected atrocity perpetrators and deliver a sense of justice. Yet this was not the case in northern Uganda, where the norm instead was to sensitize members of the community to overcome their bad feelings without any sense of reciprocal obligations on the part of returnees. In this regard, the reintegration of child soldiers suspected of involvement in atrocities deviated from norms of accountability and justice.

Prior to the reinsertion of returnee children, families, teachers, health care providers and the Uganda Police were sensitized to accept and assist former child soldiers to re-join civilian life. Sensitization sessions were conducted as seminars. These ranged from one day in duration to two weeks of training. At these gatherings, national and international organizations concerned with the rehabilitation and reintegration of former child soldiers invited particular stakeholders to specific hotels or training centres. In a one-week sensitization workshop for primary school teachers in August 2004 which I attended, Norwegian Refugee Council workers told teachers about the presence of former child soldiers in their schools, how they were traumatized, and characteristics of traumatized innocent children which include being hyperactive, sometimes withdrawn and easily frightened and jittery especially when they heard the sound of gunshots. In another sensitization seminar for counsellors in rehabilitation centres for former child soldiers, a group of experts invited by Save the Children discussed how former child soldiers must be viewed as innocent victims of a senseless war. The former child soldiers needed all the unconditional support they could get to resume a normal civilian life.

4. METHODOLOGY

This section sets out the methodology I followed. I report some case studies and criminal incidents involving rehabilitated former child soldiers which I observed during my ethnographic study. I analyse these findings while problematizing the 'child innocence' discourse which is the main operational undercurrent within the Paris Principles and I subsequently examine how this undercurrent influenced returnees' rehabilitation and reintegration processes.

4.1 Study Site

I conducted a 12-month-long ethnographic study in Gulu District, northern Uganda, in 2004–2005. Gulu district was, at that time, safer than neighbouring districts and, as a result, many people from Kitgum and Pader relocated to displaced persons camps in Gulu, joining Gulu residents who had left their communities due to war. In addition, in subsequent years (including as recently as 2018), I have regularly conducted interviews with community members about their perceptions of former child soldiers. Prior to the declaration of northern Uganda as a conflict-free zone in 2007, various humanitarian aid

---

of the Acholi perpetrator leaving that locality until anger cooled down, prior to resettling – and seeking repentance); see also Barrett in this volume for a discussion of local and international actors' perceptions of indigenous mechanisms; Wessells in this volume.

agencies operated there, including UNICEF, World Vision and Gulu Save the Children Organisation (GUSCO). Save the Children in Uganda specifically focused on *Acholi traditional ways* of rehabilitating and reintegrating former child soldiers. Acholi traditional ways are particularly distinct from the World Vision Centre for Formerly Abducted Children (WVCFAC) approach since they supported methods such as stepping on an egg and drinking bitter roots during rehabilitation.

Other stakeholders, including the Uganda Police, Uganda Prisons, the District Court and the Psychiatric Clinic at Gulu Regional Referral Hospital participated in reintegration processes. The objective of the study was to examine children's illness experiences and quests for therapy during wartime. One category of children with whom I frequently interacted were former child soldiers.

Children who participated in this study were returnees aged 9 to 16 years who had passed through the WVCFAC. Apart from a few exceptions,[14] WVCFAC only welcomed former child soldiers who were less than 18 years of age at the time of rescue. Some child participants lived in night commuter shelters and attended displaced primary schools; some former child soldiers were recruited from Pentecostal churches which conducted deliverance services from *cen* (haunting evil spirits).[15] Another group of former child soldiers who were interviewed during this ethnographic study had been arrested for ordinary crimes committed following their exit from the armed conflict or were formerly rehabilitated at WVCFAC but still exhibited militaristic behaviour many months after reintegration. These children were presented to the Psychiatric Clinic for assessment by the Police's Child Protection unit with an aim of finding the link between the presenting complaint and their past traumatic experiences.

4.2 Methods

Qualitative techniques of data collection were employed. These included in-depth interviews and participant observation, especially in the WVCFAC where I conducted regular interviews and emically participated in group counselling sessions. I also distributed basic necessities in the rehabilitation centre to child soldiers who were bed-ridden due to serious gunshot wounds and were undergoing rehabilitative treatment at the WVCFAC. Additionally, I interviewed pregnant girls to find out about their experiences before and after rescue.

4.3 Ethical Considerations

This study was approved by the Uganda National Council for Science and Technology (UNCST). In addition, permission was sought from the Resident District Commissioner,

---

[14] I observed some former LRA commanders and their wives living in separate huts within the WVCFAC. The Coordinator mentioned that it was a directive from the barracks that they will be rehabilitated as a family within the WVCFAC.

[15] Some former child soldiers, after being rehabilitated at WVCFAC, were reintegrated into communities. For some, the rehabilitation process only lasted two or three weeks. Some rehabilitated former child soldiers were recruited at churches, where they reintegrated. Because the context in which I conducted my study was still unsafe, some recently returned former child soldiers joined other children to commute to the night commuter shelter at night for their own safety.

managers of night commuter shelters, coordinators of emergency aid institutions which targeted war affected children, head teachers in primary schools where displaced children attended, the District Education Officer, and the District Health Officer. I also sought permission from children who participated in this study. They offered verbal consent. All names used in this paper are pseudonyms in order to protect the anonymity of the respondents. I assume professional responsibility for the consent and process.

4.4 Data Analysis

I followed a grounded theory approach in examining and analysing my research findings. In grounded theory, researchers do not frame their observations within existing anthropological theoretical frameworks as they collect data. Instead, they reflect on their data, examine recurring themes and interrogate the respondents' narratives. During fieldwork I wrote detailed notes. I recorded my discussions with respondents with a digital recorder where possible and where permission had been granted by the respondents. From the field notes, the following thematic categories were identified: (1) children narrating extreme events to which they were subjected during their captivity; (2) children's experiences with rehabilitation and reintegration at the centres; and (3) children's points of view and experiences as perpetrators of war crimes and atrocities.

My analysis suggests that the assumptive discourse proposed by the Paris Principles about wartime children departed from children's own narratives. Although the Paris Principles provided a framework for the reintegration of returnees, this framework did not adequately address the needs of both children and the victims and indeed other stakeholders of war atrocities in northern Uganda. The Paris Principles authenticated a simplistic approach of passivity and purposelessness that did not prove operationally effective, in my estimation, nor reflective of the experiences and self-perceptions of the former child soldiers.

5. FINDINGS: RESCUED CHILD FIGHTERS AT A REHABILITATION CENTRE

Judith Herman[16] and Derek Summerfield[17] offer extensive analyses of trauma as a concept commonly evoked for people who have experienced extreme events and violence. This discourse was visible in northern Uganda right from the time the state army made radio announcements suggesting a successful attack by the UPDF on the LRA. The state army frequently highlighted the idea of rescuing innocent children used as pawns by the LRA for battle. I attended some handover ceremonies at Gulu airfield and the WVCFAC where senior commanders paraded rescued child fighters and adults who were captured during gunfire exchange with the LRA. Many civilians, researchers, journalists and NGO representatives were present to witness the handover ceremony. During these ceremonies, high-ranking army officers and other district officials would

---

[16] Herman 1997.
[17] Summerfield 1999: 1449–62.

take turns to condemn the senseless war in which innocent children were used to fight. The rescued children were repeatedly cast as innocent children. The rehabilitating institutions received the rescued innocent children. Some of the severely injured children were taken to Lacor hospital for free treatment. Some were acutely malnourished, with signs of having lived under poor hygiene conditions. They wore torn clothes. These children were immediately taken to the rehabilitation centre where they proceeded through basic hygiene practices and were given clean clothes and properly fed. Rescued pregnant girls were examined by a centre midwife and received medical counselling. In addition, these girls were enrolled in Lacor hospital for close monitoring of their high-risk pregnancies until they gave birth. Some children with minor or severe gunshot wounds were admitted to the WVCFAC for treatment and counselling. As a researcher at the WVCFAC, I was sometimes assigned the task of distributing washing soap and other detergents to many former child fighters injured during gun fire exchanges with the UPDF.

Following medical treatment, the focus was on psychosocial care. Counsellors at the WVCFAC assured the rescued children of their innocence. Both individual and group counselling sessions were convened. During individual counselling sessions, a counsellor interviewed a rescued child about his or her abduction process, where s/he lived prior to their abduction, whether s/he knew about his or her parents' whereabouts. Each session would end with advice for the innocent child to forgive their captors who did not know what they were doing – another peculiar form of silencing. Any alternative discussions about former child soldiers' experiences were systematically marginalized. No attempt was made to inquire into the likelihood that the child may have committed atrocities. In Akello, Richters and Reis we give examples of former child soldiers who discussed freely how they engaged in war violence. For instance, one told us how he had killed a boy from Kitgum, another shared how he had ordered the killing of one of his counsellor's uncles, and a father had sent away his returnee son after his son had disclosed that he had killed his uncle.[18] When the counsellor uncontrollably broke down in tears while calling the innocent child a killer, she was isolated and advised never to interact with that particular innocent traumatized child. The same discourse of traumatized innocent child could be seen in group counselling sessions.

At WVCFAC, following a Christian approach of counselling, a pastor or counsellor would address about 200 rescued children as a group. The pastor told the rescued children about God's love and forgiveness. The children also were told to forgive their captors so that they could start living a normal life. A group counselling session would end with inviting rescued children to get 'saved'. Getting 'saved' meant that the rehabilitated child became born again. Having heard the Good News of Jesus Christ and His saving power, the child was led through a prayer to accept Jesus as the Lord and Saviour of their life. The child was also led through a prayer of repentance and then pledged to live a new life as a Christian.

Children who listened to God's word and became 'saved' were deemed successfully rehabilitated and a reintegration session would be organized within two to three weeks. Prior to their reinsertion in the community, counsellors collected sufficient information to enable them to engage in contact tracing, a process through which a counsellor would

---

[18] Akello et al. 2006: 235, 243–4.

visit the family or village of the respective former child soldier and sensitize them about the importance of helping the returnee.

6. REINTEGRATION OF FORMER CHILD SOLDIERS

I attended a reintegration session in Pagak camp. Pagak is a camp where the LRA conducted a massacre and burned huts in 2005. Acholi people in this camp knew that some of the LRA perpetrators were child soldiers – just like the one who was brought back by World Vision. At this session, a World Vision counsellor addressed the parents and war-affected people as follows:

> Today is yet another great day for the people of Pagak, and in particular the parents of Okumu. Okumu was lost at the early age of eleven years, but today, seven years later, God has returned him back to us. The LRA wanted to destroy his life by forcing him to fight a senseless war, but it was God's plan to save his life. During his counselling at the trauma centre, Okumu listened to the word of God and he became saved. The meaning is that he has become a new person. All his sins were forgiven by God. As we bring him back to live with you here in Pagak, I suggest that people of Pagak will work together to help him relive a normal life.

This handover ceremony triggered mixed reactions. Okumu's parents were grateful to World Vision for returning their child, yet Okumu's father also expressed fear about living with a child who had been trained by the LRA fighters for many years. At the time of departure, Okumu was given a hoe, a mattress, some bedding and 300,000 shillings (about €88). Other community members, who were not allowed to make any comments, joined in the celebrations. This case captures the standard procedure employed by World Vision for the reintegration of former child soldiers.

My encounters with these processes lead me to express concern that the Paris Principles, as implemented, tended to deprioritize, and even dismiss, the experiences of war-affected people, in particular, people affected by atrocities committed by former child soldiers. Various former child soldiers who had committed war crimes within their communities and who were then reintegrated were brought to the psychiatric clinic for assessment by the Police's Child Protection Unit. Regrettably, most of these children exhibited delinquent behaviour subsequent to their reintegration.

Atim, abducted at the age of 16, presents as a second case study. Here is her account from her interview with me:

> I knew some of the boys who abducted us from Kitgum Matidi, even though it was at night when we were abducted. They camouflaged as soldiers and carried various ammunitions, some of which I had never seen. At the time of abduction, together with three of my neighbours we were among the children snatched away from our parents' homes. I never saw my neighbours' children again. After we were abducted, we were made to carry heavy loads and ordered to travel towards South Sudan. During this difficult journey, made at night, some weak children collapsed to their deaths under the heavy weights they were made to carry. Some boys who attempted to escape were shot. One fighter made one of the children kill the other as a warning act to all children who wanted to escape.
>
> It was common for captors to make captives kill those closest to them, for instance, a brother made to kill his sister or a brother was set against a brother or best friend.
>
> After I was rescued by UPDF I was sent to World Vision rehabilitation centre. Although at

first, neighbours were calm and friendly, sometimes I was forced to act violently. One neighbour I attacked and fought with frequently called my child whom I returned with from the bush 'Kony's child'. My child also declined to attend school because of children's constant derogatory remarks made about his links with Kony and that he should go back to the bush.

Neighbours often make negative comments when counsellors from the World Vision visit saying I was being rewarded for the crimes committed. My life within this community is unbearable because each time I would hear such comments, I would fight and I did not spare even children, kin or teachers. Although I requested World Vision to relocate me somewhere within the municipality, I was told that the program had no such budget.

That is how I decided to escape from my village and settle here in Limu without telling the counsellors.

In the case study above, we see how acts of brutality whilst the child was held captive ultimately instilled fear in child abductees. Subsequently, they acted impulsively without any reflection. In effect innocent children were turned into fighters and into individuals who only knew how to live in a militaristic way. Adult returnees reflected on the brutality of armed child fighters. During interviews, one returnee woman described her ordeal:

Children who abducted us from Kitgum Matidi camp were too young, some of whom were fit to be my grandchildren. However, their behaviour was so brutal and violent, that we sometimes thought it was better to be abducted by adult LRA rebels. One night, as I tried to find a way of easing my pain, the moment one armed child saw me get up, he immediately pulled the trigger which shot my right arm, without even inquiring about my motive.

In another situation, a child soldier who led an attack in his own camp in Kitgum Matidi declined to be reintegrated with his family. Instead he preferred to be resettled in Gulu town. Although counsellors visited his family in Kitgum Matidi to sensitize them to the impending reintegration of an innocent child who was made to participate in a senseless war, people who had been affected by the various atrocities he perpetrated in Kitgum Matidi rejected the discourse. On the day of sensitization and family tracing (gathering information to enable counsellors identify the returnee's family and place of origin), the World Vision counsellors were shown a child who was shot during the abductions led by that former child soldier. Although the child survived, he was disabled. Parents inquired about how it was possible that the child who led the attacks was currently viewed as an innocent child.

In many instances too, the local concept of distress – *cen* – was evoked each time a former child soldier was reintegrated into the community. Among the Acholi people, it is believed that haunting spirits of people killed would seek revenge through continual disturbance of the perpetrator of the crime.[19] In one focus group discussion, school-age children discussed how children who were forced to kill were not disturbed by *cen* since the responsibility always lies with the commander. But when returnee children discussed or showed signs of being disturbed by *cen*, the interpretation was that they had committed many crimes including killing people on their own volition during their captivity. In one interview, one returnee indicated that even the various cleansing ceremonies that had been conducted for him yielded no signs of recovery from such torment by *cen* which continues to haunt him.

---

[19] See also Barrett in this volume, who discusses the phenomenon of *cen* as well as the use of cleansing ceremonies.

During my ethnographic study, as summarized in Table 20.2, I witnessed up to 70 child-soldier-related crime scenes, some of which involved recidivism where a previously 'exonerated' child soldier committed another crime. The main reason why the police and prison wardens brought an incarcerated child soldier for assessment at the Psychiatric Unit was to ascertain the link between past trauma and the current presenting criminal complaint. These subsequently committed crimes were ordinary infractions, not crimes against humanity or war crimes committed during conflict. It was contended that the incarcerated former child soldier could have engaged in criminal activities due to their trauma. Although for all cases observed the senior psychiatrist did not find a link between past trauma and current presenting crime, it was common knowledge that if the senior psychiatrist confirmed that there indeed were such a link, the former child soldier would be released immediately – thereby exonerated once again of any crime. Conflicting viewpoints arose from different stakeholders. For example, parents of the incarcerated former child soldiers were happy with the diagnosis of trauma, while the victims felt that they were denied justice. The senior psychiatrist sometimes tactfully avoided confirming a trauma diagnosis in order to draw the attention of the different stakeholders to daily realities of post-reinsertion crime, recidivism, and the need for justice by communities exposed to extreme events by the LRA and some former child soldiers. Table 20.2 explores these realities of recidivism further.

Mark Drumbl examines the consequences of depicting former child soldiers as faultless, passive victims of war.[20] Whilst he suggests that criminal sanctions against former child soldiers in the aftermath of conflict for conflict-related atrocities are best avoided, he nonetheless argues that the lack of transitional justice initiatives hinders reintegration efforts. I agree but would go even further to suggest that avoiding criminal sanctions for their atrocities creates an atmosphere of impunity for the former child soldiers, thereby leading to their alienation and stigmatization and, in some cases, recidivism.

7. DISCUSSION

While many children in northern Uganda were abducted and forced to commit war crimes, evidence also points to scenarios where they acted independently in directing and committing war atrocities. When reintegrated former child soldiers discussed their experiences freely, in some instances these conversations contradicted the 'innocent victim' narrative and suggested their active engagement in carrying out war atrocities. National and international aid organizations therefore ought to engage in a critical examination of the Paris Principles and the extent to which they provide a comprehensive legal framework to guide the rehabilitation and reintegration processes. Further research is required to systematically document the children's perspectives, assess their involvement in the context of war and examine the impact thereof on them and their communities.[21] The tension here is between finding ways of ensuring the children are accountable in some way for

---

[20] Drumbl 2012: 7.
[21] See also Shanahan and Veale in this volume, who emphasize the importance of taking account of former child soldiers' perspectives and coping strategies in reintegration programmes.

Table 20.2 Summary of cases observed involving former child soldiers who were presented to the senior psychiatrist for assessment[†]

Year/month of crime	Age range	Nature of crime	Frequency	Cumulative frequency
2004				
August	13–18	Theft, defilement, habitual fights	4	4
October	15–20	Violence and fights over property, theft, burglary	5	9
November	14–30	(1 repeat) Theft, rape, assault and one neighbour reported that his cattle had disappeared, which he attributed to the former child soldier	4 (1 repeat)	13
December	18–30	Defilement, rape, theft, violent attack/assault	4	17
2005				
July	16–19	Theft and habitual fights with neighbours, severe assault of a neighbour	4 (1 female)	21
August	15–19	Rape, defilement, theft, aggressive behaviour	8	29
September	16–25	Destruction of property, severe assault and rape within the displaced persons camp	6	35
October	14–25	Theft, defilement, burglary	6	41
November	17–25	Threats of violence, severe assault, attack of camp security personnel	7 (1 repeat)	48
December	13–26	Fights with neighbours, defilement, theft	10 (2 repeat arrests)	58
2006				
January	14–28	Theft, burnt down neighbour's hut, severe assault, threats at knifepoint	12 (1 repeat arrest)	70
Total				**70**

Note: † Part of this data was presented in Akello 2015: 1038 in analysing the participation of the Uganda Police and the psychiatrist in promoting the reintegration processes of former child soldiers.

the crimes their communities perceived them to be responsible for, and the need for these children to go through comprehensive rehabilitation and reintegration processes that respect their rights and acknowledge the war crimes that have been perpetrated against them. In the end, I argue for a perspective that derives from a view that victims indeed can victimize, and victimizers indeed can be victims. The persecuted may themselves persecute. The Paris Principles, by eschewing these painful and nuanced realities, thereby, in my estimation, fall short of being as effective as they otherwise could be if they engaged more confidently with these nuances.

I believe there is interpretive room within this process to achieve better results. Stakeholders should recognize that abducted children were forced to commit crimes *and* that there are instances where they acted independently. Doing so would limit the children-as-innocents discourse and prompt all stakeholders to finesse the operational content of the Paris Principles. Such a move would generate a framework in which the needs of both the children and the other war-affected people could be better respected. Rescued children who disclose that they believe that there are crimes which they committed in their own right could thereby be encouraged to actively participate in reconciliation processes and community service. In essence, the former combatants may be held accountable with less of a focus on punishment and more of a focus on recognition of the past and a commitment to moving forward in a way that is mindful of all stakeholders during the prolonged civil war.

Furthermore, the fact that the children's behaviour changes drastically during captivity needs to be taken into consideration. Many authors suggest that children who grow up in the context of war and violence are likely to exhibit violent behaviour themselves.[22] Table 20.2 shows that many incarcerated returnees did subsequently commit acts of violence including assault, defilement, rape and burglary.

8. CONCLUSIONS, IMPLICATIONS AND RECOMMENDATIONS

The legal framing of former child soldiers in the Paris Principles as innocent and traumatized victims influences both their rehabilitation and reintegration. When former child soldiers are rehabilitated as innocent and traumatized victims, their changed behaviour is unacknowledged and receives insufficient attention. Many community members were directly or indirectly exposed to war violence sometimes perpetrated by the former child soldiers. Even after reintegration, community members were exposed to everyday violence and delinquent behaviour exhibited by some former child soldiers. Whereas there were mechanisms to deal with crimes committed by former child soldiers when they returned to live in their communities, such as stepping on an egg, drinking bitter root and cleansing with animal blood – which were also on occasion promoted by national and international organizations[23] – evidence suggests a contradiction between community needs and what is provided for in this international legal framework.

At times, community members viewed returnees as having been rewarded for the crimes they had committed. Hence the former child soldiers experienced rejection and stigmatization in the community which was not pleased with the reintegration approach taken: namely, to *sensitize* them to help former child soldiers resume a normal life.

In view of the lessons learnt above, I propose the following points in revisiting the Paris Principles with the aim of designing a framework which will take into account the needs of both former child soldiers and communities exposed to acts of violence during war.

1. A legal framework needs to take into account both the vulnerability of former child soldiers and their changed behaviour as a result of being used as agents in executing various war atrocities. This framework should also acknowledge that victims of war violence do not make a clear distinction between acts of violence committed by a child and any other acts of violence. Therefore, it is prudent to design a framework which takes community perspectives into account. It is legally important to consider the age of the offender, whilst also acknowledging that those who have had violence

---

[22] Akello 2015: 1038; Akello et al. 2006: 229–43; Muldoon and Wilson 2001: 112–24; Udwin 1993: 115–27; Cairns 1996: 11.
[23] On this, see Barrett in this volume.

perpetrated against them by children also require recognition and justice (such as through reparation of some kind).
2. There are major limitations to the process of didactically 'sensitizing' the community. Such sensitizations may be more grudging than genuine.
3. Policy-makers and human rights activists ought to pursue a diversification of remedies, including even greater attention to traditional mechanisms. In addition, remedies could include community service activities like cleaning the town and participating in agricultural activities for people affected by war.
4. Policy-makers and activists ought to recognize a more nuanced view of the victim/victimizer binary as actually being positions on a continuum. Such a move could better address the needs of former child soldiers, including abductees, to deal with their innate sense of responsibility – as exhibited in the troubling experience of *cen*. Doing so may facilitate a sense of remorse for these actions by the children and may also promote an active search for forgiveness and reconciliation by the communities, which in turn may enable individual or group responsibility for acts of violence committed by the LRA.

REFERENCED WORKS

Akello, G. 2015. 'The Impact of the Paris Principles on the Reintegration Processes of Former Child Soldiers in Northern Uganda' 3 *Annals of Psychiatry and Mental Health* 1038

Akello, G., Richters, A. and Reis, R. 2006. 'Reintegration of Former Child Soldiers in Northern Uganda: Coming to Terms with Children's Agency and Accountability' 4 *Intervention* 229

Akello, G., Richters, A. and Reis, R. 2008. 'Coming to Terms with Accountability: Why the Reintegration of Former Child Soldiers in Northern Uganda Fails', in P. Gobodo-Madikizela and C. van der Merwe (eds), *Memory, Narrative and Forgiveness: Perspectives on the Unfinished Journeys of the Past* (Cambridge: Cambridge University Press) 186

Akello, G., Richters, A. and Reis, R. 2010. 'Silencing Distressed Children in the Context of War: An Analysis of its Causes and Health Consequences' 71 *Social Science & Medicine* 213

Allen, T. 2006. *Trial Justice: The International Criminal Court and the Lord's Resistance Army* (London: Zed Books)

Cairns, E. 1996. *Children and Political Violence* (Oxford: Blackwell)

Drumbl, M. 2012. *Reimagining Child Soldiers in International Law and Policy* (New York; Oxford: Oxford University Press)

Finnström, S. 2003. *Living with Bad Surroundings: War and Existential Uncertainty in Acholiland, Northern Uganda* (Uppsala: Uppsala Studies in Cultural Anthropology)

Girling, F.K. 1960. *The Acholi of Uganda* (London: Her Majesty's Stationery Office)

Herman, J. 1997. *Trauma and Recovery: The Aftermath of Violence – From Domestic Abuse to Political Terror* (New York: Basic Books)

Justice and Reconciliation Project 2013. 'The Beasts of Burcoro: Recounting Atrocities by the NRA's 22nd Battalion in Burcoro Village in April 1991' (July)

Muldoon, O. and Wilson, K. 2001. 'Ideological Commitment, Experience of Conflict and Adjustment in Northern Irish Adolescents' 17 *Medicine, Conflict and Survival* 112

Summerfield, D. 1999. 'A Critique of Seven Assumptions Behind Psychological Trauma Programmes in War-Affected Areas' 48 *Social Science and Medicine* 1449

Udwin, O.1993. 'Children's Reactions to Traumatic Events' 34 *Journal of Child Psychology and Psychiatry* 115

UNICEF 2004. 'Comprehensive Education Assessment in Eight Conflict Affected Districts' (Kampala: UNICEF) (on file with author)

21. Children associated with Boko Haram: disassociation, protection, accountability and reintegration
Stuart Casey-Maslen

Disarmament, demobilization and reintegration (DDR) activities are crucial components of both the initial stabilization of war-torn societies as well as their long-term development. Disarmament is the collection, documentation, control and disposal of small arms, ammunition, explosives, and light and heavy weapons of fighters.[1] Demobilization is the formal and controlled discharge of active fighters from armed forces or other armed groups.[2] Reintegration is the process by which former fighters acquire civilian status and gain sustainable employment and income. Reintegration, the United Nations affirms, is 'essentially a social and economic process with an open time frame, primarily taking place in communities at the local level. It is part of the general development of a country and a national responsibility, and often necessitates long-term external assistance.'[3] In this chapter, I explore approaches taken towards children associated with Boko Haram and argue that disengagement and disassociation are replacing disarmament and demobilization, and that reconciliation is an additional element that needs to be factored in. I also argue that interventions must include robust protection and accountability measures.

Boko Haram has recruited and used both boys and girls widely in their grim campaign of brutality in the Lake Chad Basin: as fighters, suicide bombers, cooks, wives and sexual slaves. The popular name for the group translates as 'Western education is harmful', while the full title is Jama'atu Ahlis Sunna Lidda'awati wal-Jihad – 'People Committed to the Prophet's Teachings for Propagation and Jihad'. Since 2015, the group has also been known as the Islamic State in West Africa. For the purposes of this chapter though, I will retain the name Boko Haram.

This chapter discusses four fundamental issues related to children associated with Boko Haram: their protection; the space for DDRR (Disengagement, Disassociation, Reintegration and Reconciliation); accountability for war crimes children associated with Boko Haram may have committed; and desirable measures of reintegration – not only within Nigeria but also in its conflicted neighbours. Throughout, considerable reference is made to the 2007 Paris Principles in light of their emergence as enshrining 'best practices'

---

[1] UN IDDRS 2014: 2.
[2] Ibid. The UN explains that the first stage of demobilization may extend from the processing of individual fighters in temporary centres to the massing of troops in camps designated for this purpose (cantonment sites, encampments, assembly areas or barracks). The second stage of demobilization encompasses the support package provided to the demobilized, which is called reinsertion.
[3] Ibid.

of sorts. First, though, some conceptual background to DDR is warranted, followed by an overview of the conflicts in which Boko Haram has been implicated.

1. DDR: SURVEY AND DEVELOPMENTS

The blueprint for DDR interventions has evolved over time, passing through a series of iterations, variously described as 'generations' or 'waves'. Robert Muggah and Chris O'Donnell, for example, in a thoughtful article from 2015 entitled 'Next Generation Disarmament, Demobilization and Reintegration', recalled that no fewer than 60 separate DDR initiatives had been fielded around the world since the late 1980s.[4]

Muggah and O'Donnell describe the first wave of DDR interventions as those intended to help bring to an end numerous protracted non-international armed conflicts across Latin America and southern Africa. The basis for these interventions was a cookie-cutter approach that involved common cantonment and demobilization of commanders and rank-and-file fighters 'with the goal of breaking their command and control'.[5] Often receiving key support from the United Nations, DDR programmes in El Salvador, Guatemala, Mozambique, Namibia and South Africa sought to retrain and reintegrate into communities many of the former fighters while allowing some to join newly formed 'unified' armed forces. According to Muggah and O'Donnell: 'While far from perfect, DDR processes were surprisingly orderly and carried out with military-like precision.'[6] In all of these conflicts, children played a role (albeit a fairly minor one).

Experiences and lessons learned from this first 'wave' of DDR would be the basis for the 2006 UN Integrated DDR Standards (IDDRS), which are now spread across 25 modules and three sub-modules.[7] These Standards, which are currently being subjected to thorough revision, serve as a set of policies, guidelines and procedures for the planning, implementation and evaluation of DDR programmes. Their aim has been to bring consistency to the 'fragmented' UN approach to DDR, while seeking to ensure that the process of removing weapons from the hands of fighters, taking the fighters out of military structures, and then helping them to integrate socially and economically back into society, enables them to become 'active participants in the peace process'.[8] This is an ambitious agenda.

The issue of children and DDR is considered in a specific module (5.30) in the IDDRS. Therein it is stated that 'child DDR is not the same as that for adults. Rather, it is a specific process with its own requirements, several of which are fundamentally different from adult demobilization programmes.'[9] At the same time, the IDDRS caution that: 'There is no simple formula for the DDR of children that can be routinely applied in all circumstances, so each programme needs to be context-specific and developed and managed in order to

---

[4] Muggah and O'Donnell 2015.
[5] Ibid.
[6] Ibid.
[7] UN IDDRS 2018.
[8] UN IDDRS 2014: 2.
[9] UN IDDRS 2006b: 1.

be sustainable.'[10] The challenge, the Standards observe, 'is to encourage girls and boys to benefit from DDR programmes while avoiding any damaging effects'.[11]

In fact, operational practice has largely been to exclude children (at least those under 15 years of age) from more formal DDR processes. Instead, the focus has been placed on ensuring that those released from armed forces and armed groups after advocacy and negotiation are tracked swiftly into mainstream rehabilitation and reintegration programmes akin to those aimed at other conflict-affected children. This option is partially recognized in the Optional Protocol to the 1989 Convention on the Rights of the Child (CRC) on the involvement of children in armed conflict, which provides that: 'States Parties shall take all feasible measures to ensure that persons within their jurisdiction recruited or used in hostilities contrary to the present Protocol are demobilized *or otherwise released from service.*'[12]

While this approach has a certain logic – and attraction – it can also create frustration, particularly among older children. Thus, a separate IDDRS module (5.20) specifically considers youth and DDR, which includes children from the age of 15 (and adults up to the age of 24). As the module recognizes, youth 'fall between the legal categories of child and adult, and their needs are not necessarily well served by programmes designed for mature adults or very young children'.[13]

Warning of the dangers of failure for the success of a fragile peace, the module calls for DDR programmes to 'analyse and deal with the reasons why young people join armed forces and groups', with a view to providing 'the type of DDR assistance that would make them feel secure'.[14] A further challenge is the need to coordinate youth DDR programmes with those for children and adults 'in order to deal with the particular needs of this "in-between" group and make sure that people who started out as child soldiers but are now over 18 receive proper support'.[15] But while the module is relatively strong on analysis and theory, it offers remarkably little in terms of programming.

A second generation of DDR began to emerge in the 2000s, while the IDDRS were already being completed. This new, more sophisticated approach saw adaptation occurring 'in line with the evolution of global peace, security and development agendas'.[16] The features of this new generation reflected a broadening of focus from 'a narrow preoccupation' with the demobilization and reintegration of former fighters to the far more expansive – and expensive – goals of building the conditions for sustainable peace.[17] These second wave DDR programmes, especially common following conflicts in the Balkans, South-East Asia, and West and Central Africa, were expected to 'contain and reduce multiple forms of violence, while also neutralizing spoilers, building bridges with communities, and contributing to legacy public goods'.[18] The agenda for DDR was becoming even more ambitious.

---

[10] Ibid.: 2.
[11] Ibid.: 8.
[12] Art. 6(3) (emphasis added).
[13] UN IDDRS 2006a: 1.
[14] Ibid.: 3.
[15] Ibid.: 4.
[16] Muggah and O'Donnell 2015.
[17] Muggah 2005.
[18] Muggah and O'Donnell 2015.

Employing first-generation approaches to DDR in more complex scenarios, as was initially attempted following the 2004 crisis in Haiti for instance, proved a failure. The methods tailored for former warring factions were 'ill-suited to urban armed gangs with ties to political elites and organised crime'.[19] A new community-oriented model was therefore developed to try to address gangs, who, in form, behaviour and motivation, were distinct from the military units that had hitherto been the typical focus of DDR programmes around the world.[20] But one linkage to the first generation remained consistent: DDR was still a post-conflict (or at least post-generalized violence) endeavour.

This strict demarcation between war and peace was never likely to hold firm. Thus, so-called third-generation DDR, which has taken root since the 2010s, is implemented during ongoing armed conflict, with a view to promoting – or even forcing – peace. Muggah and O'Donnell give the example of the Democratic Republic of Congo (DRC), where some 20,000 members of the Forces Démocratiques de Libération du Rwanda (FDLR) were sent back to Rwanda between 2000 and 2010 (including many children), leaving some 2,000 FDLR fighters who continued to 'ravage' the east of the DRC. With respect to these hard-core elements 'a new kind of forceful DDR was initiated in the context of "robust peacekeeping" operations in 2012'.[21]

Arguably, this experience marked a shift in the direction of DDR, which had evolved from post-conflict programming by consent, implemented with a view to *building* peace, to a new, more coercive form of programming that was implemented during armed conflict with the aim of *achieving* peace (or at least a peace of sorts). In the Central African Republic, Libya, Mali, the Niger Delta and Yemen, DDR was being 'reconceived' in the shape of 'dynamic political processes' instead of 'stand-alone or one-off enterprises'. Therein, this new way of working was 'connected in complex ways to peace negotiations and robust peace operations, justice and security sector reform, and peace- and state-building'.[22]

But this is not the end of the story, only a new beginning. In an era increasingly pockmarked by terrorism and counterterrorism, I believe we are now looking at a fourth generation of programming. In what may become the new normal, disengagement and disassociation are beginning to replace disarmament and demobilization. Nowhere is this more starkly illustrated than in the Lake Chad Basin. Traditional DDR, in any of its three former generations, is simply an inadequate conceptualization of the scope of action needed to address children and adults associated with Boko Haram in its ongoing conflicts across four countries in West Africa. To incite sustained defections from the group, broader *DDRR interventions* (by which I mean Disengagement, Disassociation, Reintegration and Reconciliation) will have to be intertwined with robust protection and accountability policies and practices across the north-east of Nigeria (whence the group originated) as well as the Federal Republic's three impacted neighbours on its northern borders: Cameroon, Chad and Niger.

---

[19] Muggah et al. 2009: 206–25.
[20] Muggah and O'Donnell 2015.
[21] Ibid. (citing UN Security Council 2014b).
[22] Muggah and O'Donnell 2015.

2. BACKGROUND TO THE CONFLICTS WITH BOKO HARAM

The conflict with Boko Haram erupted after what was reportedly an extrajudicial execution by the Nigerian police of the group's spiritual leader, Muslim cleric Mohammed Yusuf, in 2009. Yusuf had formed the group in 2002 in Maiduguri, the capital of Borno state in north-east Nigeria, establishing a mosque and an Islamic school to which many poor Muslim families from across Nigeria as well as neighbouring countries sent their children.[23] The group came to prominence, first sub-regionally and then nationally, following a series of armed attacks on police stations and other government buildings.[24] It subsequently further extended its operations into Cameroon, Chad and Niger.

After Yusuf's death the Nigerian army declared the group finished, but under new leadership Boko Haram broadened and deepened its attacks across the north of Nigeria, leading to the declaration in May 2013 by the government in Abuja of a state of emergency in the region's three states: Adamawa, Borno and Yobe. The group also attacked the UN headquarters in the capital itself in 2011. In April 2014, Boko Haram further drew international condemnation – and widespread media attention – when it abducted more than 200 schoolgirls from Chibok town in Borno state, announcing that they would be treated as slaves and married off as the spoils of war. In August 2014, Boko Haram's then unchallenged leader, Abubakar Mohammed Shekau, declared a caliphate in areas under the group's control, with the town of Gwoza as its seat of power.[25] A split occurred in 2017, leading to two Boko Haram factions operating in the Lake Chad Basin: one under Ahubakar Mohammed Shekau; the other led by Abu Musab Al-Barnawi.[26]

Boko Haram has been identified at the international level as a terrorist group and subject to sanctions. In May 2014, the UN Security Council's Al-Qaida Sanctions Committee approved the addition of Boko Haram to its list of individuals and entities subject to targeted financial sanctions and an arms embargo, as set out in Security Council Resolution 2083.[27] As a result of the listing by the Sanctions Committee, any individual or entity that provides financial or material support to Boko Haram, including by providing arms or recruits, is itself eligible to be added to the Al-Qaida Sanctions List and subject to the sanctions measures.[28] In a statement released in November 2012, Abubakar Shekau had expressed the group's solidarity with al-Qaida affiliates in Afghanistan, Iraq, North Africa, Somalia and Yemen. He also encouraged violent extremists across Africa and other areas to continue engaging in terrorist attacks.[29] Abubakar Shekau himself is listed as an international terrorist.[30]

---

[23] BBC 2016b.
[24] See, e.g., Ford 2014: 2; Smith 2014.
[25] BBC 2016b.
[26] See, e.g., Reuters 2017.
[27] UN Security Council Resolution 2083 (2012), adopted by the Security Council by consensus at its 6890th meeting on 17 December 2012: [1].
[28] UN Security Council 2014a.
[29] See Security Council Committee pursuant to Resolutions 1267 (1999), 1989 (2011) and 2253 (2015) concerning ISIL (Da'esh), Al-Qaida and associated individuals, groups, undertakings and entities, UN Security Council 2014c.
[30] 'The List established and maintained pursuant to Security Council Res. 1267/1989/2253.'

Boko Haram had already been designated by the United States (US) Department of State in November 2013 as a Foreign Terrorist Organization[31] and a Specially Designated Global Terrorist. At the beginning of December 2015, the US Department of the Treasury announced the designation of two senior Boko Haram leaders, Mohammed Nur and Mustapha Chad, as terrorists, pursuant to Executive Order 13224. Mohammed Nur, formerly Boko Haram's third in command, was said to have helped organize the 26 August 2011 suicide attack on the UN headquarters in Abuja. Mustapha Chad is reported to have spearheaded a 2013 Boko Haram offensive to take over Maiduguri.[32] In February 2018, the US Department of the Treasury added Shekau's challenger, Abu Musab Al-Barnawi, the head of the rival Boko Haram faction, to its sanctions list for global terrorists.[33]

On 3 June 2014, following the decision by the United Nations, the European Union (EU) announced it too had imposed sanctions on Boko Haram as an al-Qaida-linked terrorist group.[34] The decision subjects the organization as well as any individuals or entities that support it financially or materially to sanctions, including an arms embargo, asset freeze and a travel ban.[35]

Sustained military action by the Nigerian armed forces, as well as by its Cameroonian, Chadian and Nigerien counterparts in a Multi-National Joint Task Force as the conflict spread over Nigeria's northern borders, has pushed Boko Haram back on the defensive, forcing it to yield territory it effectively controlled. In so doing, though, the military campaign inflicted clearly excessive civilian casualties, adding to the plethora of war crimes and crimes against humanity committed by Boko Haram, and pushed more recruits into the arms of the group. The action of, especially, the Nigerian armed forces was accompanied by widespread allegations of abuses, including summary and arbitrary executions.[36]

In addition, in the course of government-run operations, many men, women and children were detained by the various security forces enrolled in the campaigns. In particular, detainees relating to the conflict in Nigeria's north-east comprise a wide range of individuals, some of whom remain dedicated to pursuing acts of terrorism, others were forced recruits or opportunists that took up arms but may regret doing so, while still others are civilians trapped by the fighting and swept up in the Nigerian military's operations. Among the many detainees are a significant number of boys and girls of whom some are perpetrators of atrocities, while the remainder are not. All of these children, though, can be viewed to some degree as victims of the conflict. The same situation, albeit on a smaller scale, exists in the other countries affected by Boko Haram's rampage across West Africa.

---

[31] See US Department of State 2018.
[32] US Department of the Treasury 2015. As a result of the designation, all assets of the two men that were under the jurisdiction of the United States or in the control of US persons were frozen, and US persons were generally prohibited from engaging in transactions with them.
[33] Vanguard 2018.
[34] AFP/PTI 2014.
[35] Benari 2014.
[36] See, e.g., Amnesty International 2016/2017; Nossiter 2015. See also Bakary 2017. In June 2017, it was reported that the United States and the United Kingdom had revoked or refused visas for certain military figures implicated in human rights violations. Campbell 2017.

3. THE PROTECTION OF CHILDREN ASSOCIATED WITH BOKO HARAM

It is clear that children have been affected by the conflicts with Boko Haram in part due to a failure of protection. First and foremost, this is visible in the failure by the respective governments to prevent widespread recruitment or abduction of children by Boko Haram. Once enrolled into the group's ranks, the treatment of fighters is almost relentlessly brutal, and is accompanied by the widespread rape of girls who are largely treated as sexual slaves. Thus, in December 2017, it was reported that 'at least 7,000 women and girls have endured Boko Haram's sexual violence'.[37] In turn, Boko Haram fighters, including children, are instructed and prompted to murder and torture, leading to the group being considered as the deadliest terrorist group in the world in 2015.[38]

Among other methods of warfare and terror, Boko Haram has continued to use children as fighters, including those under the age of 15. Some have been employed as suicide bombers, a practice that seems to be intensifying. Indeed, information reviewed by the Office of the Prosecutor of the International Criminal Court (ICC) in 2017 indicated a sharp increase in the use of boys and girls in suicide attacks in the first eight months of the year.[39] According to the UN Children's Fund (UNICEF), between January and August 2017, 83 children were used as 'human bombs', of whom 55 were girls, most often under 15, and 27 were boys; one of the most perverse victims was a baby strapped to a girl suicide bomber.[40] By the end of the year, the number of child suicide attacks in Nigeria and Cameroon had grown to envelop a total of at least 135 children: 'almost five times the number in 2016'.[41]

But besides the atrocities against children perpetrated by Boko Haram, the Nigerian security forces have also failed to respect their duties to protect children. Since 2011, Nigerian Security Forces have reportedly arrested at least 20,000 people, mostly young men in Adamawa, Borno and Yobe states.[42] According to the Office of the Prosecutor of the ICC, more than 7,000 men, women and children may have died in military detention in March 2011 through June 2015 from illness, poor conditions, overcrowding, torture, ill-treatment and extrajudicial execution.[43] The Office's report on its preliminary examination in 2015 noted allegations of 'mass arrests of boys and young men suspected of being Boko Haram members or supporters, followed by large-scale abuses, including summary executions and torture'.[44] In addition, it is claimed that a number of Nigerian soldiers and others operating as de facto agents of the state have raped victims of the conflict: dozens of cases of rape or other forms of sexual violence and exploitation were reported in seven camps in Borno state in 2016, carried out by guards, camp officials, security officers and members of civilian vigilante groups.[45]

---

[37] Searcey 2017.
[38] Institute for Economics and Peace 2015: 2.
[39] ICC OTP 2017: 47, [211].
[40] See, e.g., Aziz 2017.
[41] Tih 2017.
[42] ICC OTP 2017: 47, [212].
[43] ICC OTP 2015: 48, [210]. See also Human Rights Watch 2013: [8].
[44] ICC OTP 2015: 48, [211].
[45] Searcey 2017.

With these issues in mind, in April 2016, the UN Secretary-General welcomed the establishment of a human rights desk at army headquarters tasked to investigate human rights violations committed by the military. He encouraged the inclusion of dedicated child protection capacity to investigate grave violations committed against children. Further, expressing his concern over the number of children recruited and used by the Civilian Joint Task Force (CJTF, a militia spontaneously created locally in Borno state to combat Boko Haram), he called on the government to take swift action to prevent further cases.[46] In September 2017, the UN Special Representative of the Secretary-General for Children and Armed Conflict, Virginia Gamba, and UNICEF in Nigeria welcomed the signing by the CJTF in Maiduguri of an action plan, developed in collaboration with the Nigerian authorities, to end and prevent the recruitment and use of children.[47]

The responsibility of the government aside, the taint of association with Boko Haram is hard to remove from a child and an adult – whether or not it is merited on the facts. Sadly, on this core issue of the protection of children associated with an armed group and who are subsequently released or captured or who manage to escape, in light of today's realities in West Africa the 2007 Paris Principles do not seem fit for purpose. As they justly recall, all children are entitled to protection and care under a broad range of international, regional and national instruments,[48] but they go on to address the specific 'Protection of children who have been associated with armed forces or armed groups' in just two paragraphs, one of which recalls general human rights principles, while the other focuses on children born to girls during their time amid armed forces or armed groups.[49]

Furthermore, the thorny issue of detention (not just treatment but also the legal basis for prolonged pre-trial incarceration) scarcely merits a reference, while neither terrorism nor violent extremism is even mentioned in the 44-page document. In Niger, both UNICEF and the UN Office on Drugs and Crime (UNODC) have been working to ensure that children are treated differently from adults, in accordance with international standards on the rights of children.[50] As of February 2017, 61 children were said to be detained in the juvenile section of Niamey prison while 23 others whose age was unknown were in Kollo prison.[51] One media report from June 2017 recorded that in Niamey, a young boy who escaped from Boko Haram (after his village was raided and he was forced to carry supplies for Boko Haram for one day and then let go) had been languishing in prison for two years.[52] There are also dozens of children, including babies, some newborn, in the defector's camp at Goudoumaria.[53]

Another gap in the Principles applies to the principle of *non-refoulement*, an issue of importance in West Africa since foreign fighters (from the region) number highly among Boko Haram's ranks in Chad, Cameroon and Niger. For states parties to the 1966 International Covenant on Civil and Political Rights (among which are Chad, Cameroon,

---

[46] UN Secretary-General 2016: 32, [195].
[47] UN Special Representative of the Secretary-General for Children and Armed Conflict 2017.
[48] Paris Principle 3.0. See also Akello in this volume.
[49] Principles 7.6–7.7.
[50] UNODC 2017: 22.
[51] Cluster Protection Niger 2017: 1.
[52] Felbab-Brown 2017.
[53] Cluster Protection Niger 2017: 7 (citing Paris Principle 3.6).

Niger and Nigeria), for instance, the obligation in Article 2 that they 'respect and ensure the Covenant rights for all persons in their territory and all persons under their control entails an obligation not to extradite, deport, expel or otherwise remove a person from their territory, where there are substantial grounds for believing that there is a real risk of irreparable harm'.[54] The 2002 Robben Island Guidelines are also explicit, stipulating that 'States should ensure no one is expelled or extradited to a country where he or she is at risk of being subjected to torture.'[55]

These international and regional human rights standards mean that in any circumstances, including after they have either served a prison sentence or completed a de-radicalization process, foreign nationals may not be deported or extradited to another state (or its jurisdiction) where there are substantial grounds for believing they will be subjected to ill-treatment. But both children and adults are believed to have been deported from each of the four countries of the Lake Chad Basin, without adequate consideration of their particular circumstances, or the fate that potentially awaits them.

Based on the experience with respect to Boko Haram, these various concerns need to be urgently addressed. There has been precious little evidence of the UN's Rights Up Front initiative[56] being implemented in the Lake Chad Basin: UN entities have largely failed to speak out against abuse in relation to both detention and deportation issues. In other respects, however, and despite the lacunae in the Paris Principles, some concrete action is underway in affected countries. In December 2017, following months of work by the authorities supported by the International Organization for Migration (IOM), Nigeria made explicit pledges to address some of the concerns raised by the conflict with Boko Haram. At a dedicated workshop and subsequent high-level conference, the government affirmed that in 'all aspects' of its DDRR programme, Nigeria 'will comply with international human rights and humanitarian law. All terrorist suspects will be treated humanely at all times.'[57]

The government also agreed to further improve the conditions of detention for terrorist suspects 'in order to meet international standards'. A specific commitment was made with respect to children, many of whom were being housed in overcrowded and unsanitary military barracks in Maiduguri. According to the communiqué of the conference: 'Appropriate facilities will be identified or established to house children suspected

---

[54] Human Rights Committee 2004: [12]. Such envisaged harm is that prohibited by arts 6 and 7 of the Covenant, namely arbitrary deprivation of life, torture or other inhumane treatment. See also Human Rights Committee 1992: [9]: 'States parties must not expose individuals to the danger of torture or cruel, inhuman or degrading treatment or punishment upon return to another country by way of their extradition, expulsion or refoulement.'

[55] Guideline 15.

[56] As the UN recalls, the initiative 'aims to realize a cultural change within the UN system, so all staff and UN entities conduct their work with an awareness of their wider responsibility to support the UN Charter and overall UN mandates. It encourages staff to take a principled stance and to act with moral courage to prevent serious and large-scale violations, and pledges Headquarters support for those who do so. It also seeks operational change, and change in UN engagement with Member States.' See, e.g., United Nations Information Centre in Canberra, 'United Nations Human Rights Up Front Initiative', 28 September 2016, at: https://un.org.au/2016/09/28/united-nations-human-rights-up-front-initiative/.

[57] Abuja, High-Level Conference 2017.

or convicted of terrorist offences.'[58] In the Plan of Action annexed to the communiqué the authorities undertook to review the now outdated 1962 Borstal Act, which concerns all child offenders, and to review and adopt a policy on the prosecution of child terrorist suspects. More generally, it was agreed that community renewal programmes will 'focus on the needs and concerns of victims'. Support, it is promised, 'will be provided for citizenship and leadership programmes for youth'.

4. THE SPACE FOR A DDRR PROGRAMME?

Nigeria has explicitly and deliberately made space for a DDRR programme, understanding that not everyone should be – or indeed realistically can be – successfully prosecuted and incarcerated. At the end of March 2017, the UN Security Council unanimously adopted Resolution 2349, in which it urged Lake Chad Basin governments to implement consistent policies to promote defections from Boko Haram, to de-radicalize and reintegrate those who had already defected, and to ensure there was no impunity for those responsible for terrorist attacks.[59] De-radicalization (or, in less politically charged language, disengagement and disassociation) seeks to persuade former adherents to eschew indiscriminate violence in pursuit of religious aims. When done well, it enables the targets to think critically about the choices they make; when done badly, it may do little more than replace one form of brainwashing with another.

According to the non-binding 2005 Madrid Guiding Principles,[60] UN member states are called on to consider appropriate administrative measures and/or rehabilitation and reintegration programmes as alternatives to prosecution in appropriate cases. 'Such measures should be used in a manner compliant with applicable international human rights law and national legislation and should be subject to effective review', according to the Security Council's Counter-Terrorism Committee Executive Directorate (CTED).[61] The 2012 Rome Memorandum and its 2016 Addendum[62] further recommend actions that a state should take in addressing violent extremism, although these instruments are similarly not legally binding.[63]

Some relevant policy and programmatic initiatives are being prepared in Nigeria's neighbours, albeit a little sporadically, but many have focused on reinforcing judicial sanctions for Boko Haram associates, including children, leaving little or no space for DDRR. In Niger, for instance, trials conducted *in camera* of around 1,000 suspected Boko Haram fighters began in early 2017 on charges of criminal conspiracy for terrorism. The defendants were Malians, Nigerians and Nigeriens. Niger's Attorney-General told

---

[58] Ibid.
[59] UN Security Council Resolution 2349 (2017), adopted by the Security Council by consensus at its 7911th meeting on 31 March 2017: 7–8, [31].
[60] CTED 2015: 19, Guiding Principle 31.
[61] CTED 2017: 53.
[62] GCTF 2016.
[63] In particular, the 2016 Addendum offers specific guidance regarding the need to review and potentially update a state's legal framework. Ibid.: 2.

the press that convictions and acquittals of terrorist suspects had already occurred with sentences of between three and nine years' imprisonment for the convicted.[64]

As of mid-January 2018, 200 individuals were reported to have been convicted of terrorist offences in Niamey in Niger, and a further 500 released (many due to lack of probative evidence). It is not known if this includes any children. Following requests from communities in Diffa region, trials of Boko Haram associates were due to occur in the town of Diffa instead of Niamey in early February 2018, facilitating witness testimony.[65] This plan was postponed *sine die* following Boko Haram attacks in the Diffa region in late January 2018. Instead, trials recommenced in Niamey in early February 2018.[66]

Back in December 2016, however, following an initiative by the Governor of Diffa region (and despite the sworn commitment of the Ministry of Justice to pursue prosecutions), the Nigerien Minister of the Interior made a surprise announcement that repentant Boko Haram associates would be given the opportunity to hand themselves in to the authorities and accept a de-radicalization programme rather than be prosecuted.[67] This amounts to an effective amnesty for crimes, including those who had killed in the course of their affiliation to Boko Haram. Some of these acts amount to war crimes and some even to crimes against humanity.[68] Arguably, therefore, a blanket amnesty that includes a promise not to prosecute those suspected of war crimes does not comply with international human rights law, the law of armed conflict, or international criminal law.[69]

Meanwhile, in Cameroon, the 2014 Anti-Terrorism Law[70] prescribes the mandatory death penalty for any person who commits, or threatens to commit, an act likely to cause death, injury, or material damage where there is intent to intimidate the public or disrupt the functioning of public services.[71] In early 2016, Cameroon sentenced 89 Boko Haram fighters to death[72] and many trials have taken place since then.[73] Currently, very little space appears to be available for DDRR in Cameroon, which has implications for how children are treated. The apparent determination to prosecute and convict all adult Boko Haram associates is likely to further exacerbate overcrowding in Cameroon's prisons without

---

[64] AFP 2017.
[65] This was an important recommendation from the local communities and other stakeholders. See, e.g., International Symposium on Youth Deradicalisation and the Reinsertion of Repentants from Boko Haram Movement 2017: 84.
[66] Radio Anfani 2018.
[67] Brackley 2017.
[68] See, e.g., France 2 TV 2017.
[69] Cluster Protection Niger 2017: 5. See also OHCHR 2009; Paris Principle 8.5 ('States should ensure that perpetrators of violence against children associated with armed forces or armed groups, including sexual violence against girls are prosecuted, either through national legislation or through the International Criminal Court.').
[70] Law No. 2014/028 on the Suppression of Acts of Terrorism 2014 (Cameroon).
[71] Ibid.: Section 2(1). Section 16 of the Law, however, stipulates that prosecution 'shall be waived' for any person who, after agreeing with another to commit an act of terrorism, reports the plan to a public official; uses 'all means' to help prevent the commission of the offence; and helps to identify his or her co-offenders or accomplices.
[72] BBC 2016a.
[73] Despite requiring the pronouncement of the death penalty for many offences, Cameroon is an 'abolitionist' state, meaning that there is a de facto moratorium on the execution of the death sentence.

encouraging low-level or ancillary Boko Haram associates to defect and thereby further weaken the group.

Chad has similarly taken a repressive approach to its threat from Boko Haram. In early August 2015, following a series of attacks, Chad adopted a new anti-terrorism law.[74] As in Cameroon, the mandatory death penalty is imposed on any person who commits, finances, recruits or trains people to participate in acts of terrorism.[75] The law reintroduced the death penalty just six months after the government had proposed a new version of the 1967 Penal Code that would have abolished it. The penalty for lesser terrorist offences is life imprisonment.[76]

5. THE ACCOUNTABILITY OF CHILD BOKO HARAM ASSOCIATES

The situation is more nuanced with respect to the responsibility of children under international criminal law than it is for adults. It is certainly not irrelevant that the ICC does not prosecute anyone who was under the age of 18 years when he or she was alleged to have committed any international crime potentially falling within the Court's jurisdiction.[77] Thus, the Paris Principles affirm that children accused of international crimes 'allegedly committed while they were associated with armed forces or armed groups should be considered primarily as victims of offences against international law; not only as perpetrators'.[78] Further, children associated with armed forces or groups 'should not be prosecuted or punished or threatened with prosecution or punishment solely for their membership of those forces or groups'.[79] But as the UN Secretary-General has observed, in UN member states' responses to violent extremism, 'children are often systematically treated as security threats rather than as victims, and are administratively detained or prosecuted for their alleged association'.[80]

The Paris Principles call for children accused of international crimes to be treated 'in accordance with international law in a framework of restorative justice and social rehabilitation, consistent with international law which offers children special protection through numerous agreements and principles'.[81] In this respect, the binding provisions of the CRC, applicable to all children who come into conflict with the law, are particularly relevant. These include the use of diversion rather than criminal proceedings, the use of alternatives to detention (which should be used only as a measure of last resort), and the

---

[74] Law 034/PR/2015 (Chad), adopted on 5 August 2015. The text of the law is available in French in FIACAT 2016: Annex 2.
[75] Law 034/PR/2015, arts 14–17 and 25.
[76] Ibid., art. 24.
[77] According to art. 26 of the Rome Statute (Exclusion of jurisdiction over persons under eighteen): 'The Court shall have no jurisdiction over any person who was under the age of 18 at the time of the alleged commission of a crime.' See also Kaushik and Freeland in this volume; Ramos in this volume.
[78] Principle 3.6.
[79] Principle 8.7.
[80] UN Secretary-General 2016: 4, [16].
[81] Principle 3.6.

overarching obligation to act in the best interests of the child. In a similar vein, the UN Secretary-General affirms that:

> Depriving children of liberty following their separation [from an armed group] is contrary not only to the best interests of the child, but also to the best interests of society as a whole. This approach further complicates efforts to reintegrate children, given that it separates them from their families and can also lead to the creation of community grievances.[82]

And as experience has found with respect to child members of gangs in Western nations, suppression (for example, policing, legislation, incarceration) has been found to be largely ineffective.

The IDDRS module on children and DDR, however, takes a seemingly contradictory position on prosecution.[83] On the one hand, it asserts that former child soldiers are victims of criminal policies for which adults are responsible, stipulating, without caveat, that children 'shall not be prosecuted or detained for . . . criminal acts committed while associated with armed forces or groups'. It then claims, citing Article 37 of the CRC, that the detention of a child 'shall be used only as a measure of last resort and for the shortest appropriate period of time', recalling that 'international child rights and juvenile justice standards require that alternatives to normal judicial proceedings in criminal courts should be applied, providing that human rights and legal safeguards are fully respected'.[84] In revising this module, these provisions merit particular attention to assure a greater coherence and consistency. Moreover and in contrast, in the module on youth and DDR, the issue of criminal responsibility is not even mentioned. This also needs to be addressed.

But how does one promote accountability while not stigmatizing and further victimizing children? An approach that regards anyone under 18 purely as a 'victim' is not the way to go.[85] Accountability can take many forms, but blanket immunity and universal forgiveness is not the way to a justice-led peace. Even for younger children, it is still necessary to help them to understand and accept that what they did was wrong even though no criminal liability should be pursued. It does not suffice that they denounce Boko Haram and its methods and aims. Yet this is what has happened in some countries. In January 2018, for instance, the Nigerian army announced it had released 244 Boko Haram suspects (including 19 teenagers and 51 children) on the basis that when they had been screened, they had denounced the group.[86]

In a study for UNICEF, published in 2017, community-level respondents in north-east Nigeria generally believed that children associated with Boko Haram should face some form of justice. However, three schools of thought were reported. The first held that anyone who has been associated at any time with the group must be held fully accountable for his/her actions, irrespective of age or sex. The second believed that those who joined willingly and were the core members should be held responsible, while those who were

---

[82] UN Secretary-General 2016: 4, [16].
[83] UN IDDRS 2006b: 9, [5.8].
[84] Ibid.
[85] See also Wessells in this volume.
[86] Associated Press 2018.

forced to join should not be held accountable and should be pardoned. The third school of thought argued that accountability should depend on the seriousness of the offence.[87]

In stark contrast, in Cameroon, a Protocol elaborated between UNICEF and the authorities (though not yet signed by the government at the time of writing) foresees the 'immediate' handover to the Ministry of Social Affairs of any child detained in the course of counterterrorism operations by the Cameroonian security forces. No prosecution can be envisaged in any circumstances. So, as worded currently, the Protocol effectively institutes an amnesty for any child Boko Haram associate irrespective of the acts he or she has committed, including those that may rise to the level of war crimes and crimes against humanity. This does not appear to comply with the state's international legal obligations and may not be in the child's best interests: no other measures are foreseen. This approach to child Boko Haram associates, however, was the clear decision of the Cameroonian government.

As the Paris Principles justly assert, of course, children associated with armed groups are 'not only' to be treated as perpetrators. However, I would suggest that some form of accountability may be appropriate, not least to assist with the reintegration of children into their communities. One possible approach is that adopted in Niger, where traditional ceremonies known as '*Ardia*' are organized at community level to facilitate the safe return and reintegration of older repentant children who were formerly associated with Boko Haram following their release.[88] More research is needed into traditional accountability and reinsertion mechanisms across the Lake Chad Basin, whether these are focused on adults or children.

6. THE REINTEGRATION OF CHILDREN FORMERLY ASSOCIATED WITH BOKO HARAM

'Effective reintegration of children formerly associated with groups perpetrating violent extremism should be a priority', the UN Secretary-General recalls.[89] The older the child, though, the tougher the challenge is likely to be. It is obvious that young children used primarily as lookouts will not demand the same approach as teenagers who have killed, tortured, or raped during their time in Boko Haram.

But little reintegration has taken place in the Lake Chad Basin so far. In the report published by UNICEF in 2017, respondents from north-east Nigeria demonstrated a very low level of community awareness of any services that existed, either run by governments or non-governmental organizations, to support de-radicalization and reintegration programmes for children associated with armed groups.[90] As the report cautions, failure to provide effective programming 'will not only impact the individual children but may also

---

[87] UNICEF/Nigeria Stability and Reconciliation Programme 2017: 4. See also Barrett in this volume for an account of community perspectives towards the accountability of child soldiers in northern Uganda.
[88] See, e.g., International Symposium on Youth Deradicalisation and the Reinsertion of Repentants from Boko Haram Movement 2017: 84.
[89] UN Secretary-General 2016: 4, [16].
[90] UNICEF/Nigeria Stability and Reconciliation Programme 2017: 4, 7.

lead to criminality and future radicalization of the next generation of disaffected youth'.[91] The authors of the report recommended that reintegration be approached through 'whole community strategies', where economic empowerment, education and skills acquisition programmes, and the like, 'not only target those associated with armed groups but benefit communities as a whole'. This would 'mitigate further resentment' against Boko Haram associates, who may otherwise be seen as being 'rewarded for their participation'.[92]

Lessons could also perhaps be drawn from programmes adopted to address child gang members in the United States (where most join between the ages of 12 and 15).[93] These have demonstrated that a multidisciplinary intervention is most likely to be successful. A five-pronged approach is recommended by the Office of Juvenile Justice and Delinquency Prevention (OJJDP)'s 'Comprehensive Anti-Gang Initiative'. This involves community mobilization, the provision of opportunities, social intervention, suppression, and organizational change and development. 'Thus, a range of services and sanctions is required, often in some interactive way.'[94] What is clear is that single-faceted approaches (e.g. those focused solely on prevention, intervention or suppression) have been found to be ineffective. Nonetheless, it remains 'important that youth understand that they will face consequences if they do not follow [the] rules, laws, conditions, or reasonable expectations' of a rehabilitation and reintegration project.[95]

Transposing these lessons to the Lake Chad Basin is, though, fraught. For one thing, multidisciplinary interventions are, of course, resource intensive, both in human and financial terms. For another, the conflict is ongoing. Each report of the death of Boko Haram, not least on a number of occasions from Nigeria's president,[96] has turned out to be premature. Attacks against both military objectives and civilians and civilian objects have persisted across the four countries. In mid-January 2018, for instance, a suspected Boko Haram attack against a village near Lake Chad in Niger near the Nigerian border killed at least four soldiers and wounded eight others; the militants also stole ten armoured vehicles in the attack.[97]

With ongoing violence comes continued insecurity – constraining many civilians within displaced and refugee camps; impeding, if not frustrating reconstruction; and negating hopes of meaningful reintegration. Children can receive education and teenagers can also benefit from vocational training, but boredom and lack of opportunity can lead inexorably to fresh recruitment. In fact, what is perhaps most remarkable about the situation is how little is being done to promote the reintegration of former child soldiers and sexual slaves in the Lake Chad Basin.

Programmatically, there is a need for innovative action given the nature and scale of the problem; the classical remedies seem markedly inadequate. In this regard, the research

---

[91] Ibid.: 7.
[92] Ibid.: 42.
[93] OJJDP 2018.
[94] See OJJDP 2009: 4–7.
[95] Ibid.
[96] On 24 December 2015, for example, President Muhammadu Buhari announced that Boko Haram had been 'technically' defeated. See, e.g., BBC 2015.
[97] Aksar 2018.

report for UNICEF on Nigeria, cited above, recommended that a special office be created under the Ministry for Reconstruction, Rehabilitation and Resettlement to tackle, rehabilitate and reintegrate the children associated with armed groups.[98] In my view, this is a step in the right direction.

7. CONCLUSION

One of the remarkable aspects of the Lake Chad Basin is the difference in approach across the countries affected by Boko Haram's many acts of terror. The treatment of child Boko Haram associates is a clear instance of this. Cameroon wants every child to get a free pass from prosecution, no matter what crimes have been committed. In contrast, in Niger a representative from one UN agency told the author that every member of Boko Haram should go before the courts and be judged. Neither approach is a solution. Older children need some form of DDRR, tailored and backed up by community development. Younger children need more classic rehabilitation and reintegration support. But every child needs to understand the nature of his or her acts and why they were wrong. There must be age-appropriate accountability for all, even if the formal juvenile justice approach should be reserved only for the most serious offenders.

By early 2018, in the Lake Chad Basin a DDRR programme was only truly operational in Nigeria. And this, despite the fact that Boko Haram's insurgency was already in its tenth year. The UN needs to do far more to support the four affected countries to coordinate approaches and exchange lessons learned. It also needs to respect its own pledges under the Rights Up Front initiative, to call out abuses by the authorities when they occur. Studies have consistently indicated abuses by the security forces as the biggest factor in promoting Boko Haram recruitment.

In addition to promoting consistent approaches to child Boko Haram associates across the region, UNICEF should consider coordinating a careful revision of the Paris Principles to ensure that the protection of children associated with armed groups is addressed seriously. This should include the need to address children in detention, especially as suspects for terrorist offences. In tandem, the IDDRS modules on both children and youth need to be made consistent with the renewed Principles. It is planned to elaborate a new IDDRS module specific to counterterrorism. These issues will similarly arise in that context.

REFERENCED WORKS

Abuja, High-Level Conference 2017. 'Integrating DDRR into the PCVE Policy and National Action Plan: Communiqué' (9 December)

AFP 2017. 'Niger: discrets procès d'un millier de militants de Boko Haram' (10 March) [available at: https://www.rtbf.be/info/monde/detail_niger-discrets-proces-d-un-millier-de-militants-de-boko-haram?id=9550874 (accessed 7 August 2018)]

AFP/PTI 2014. 'EU Adds Nigeria's Boko Haram to Blacklisted Terror Groups' (Brussels, 3 June)

---

[98] UNICEF/Nigeria Stability and Reconciliation Programme 2017: 42.

Aksar, M. 2018. 'Suspected Boko Haram Attack in Niger Kills at least Four Soldiers', *Reuters* (18 January) [available at: https://www.reuters.com/article/us-nigeria-security/suspected-boko-haram-attack-in-niger-kills-at-least-four-soldiers-idUSKBN1F726X (accessed 7 August 2018)]

Amnesty International 2016/2017. 'Nigeria 2016/2017' [available at: https://www.amnesty.org/en/countries/africa/nigeria/report-nigeria/ (accessed 30 August 2017)]

Associated Press 2018. 'Nigeria Army Releases 244 Boko Haram Suspects', *Voice of America* (16 January) [available at: https://www.voanews.com/a/nigeria-releases-boko-haram-suspects/4210186.html (accessed 10 April 2018)]

Aziz, S. 2017. 'UNICEF: Boko Haram Use of Child Bombers Soars', *Al Jazeera* (22 August) [available at: http://www.aljazeera.com/news/2017/08/unicef-boko-haram-child-bombers-soars-170822160541719.html (last accessed 10 April 2018)]

Bakary, I.T. 2017. 'Cameroon: War Against Boko Haram – Government Refutes Amnesty International Torture Allegations', *All Africa* (24 July) [available at: http://allafrica.com/stories/201707240633.html (accessed 10 April 2018)]

BBC 2015. 'Nigeria Boko Haram: Militants "Technically Defeated" – Buhari' (24 December) [available at: http://www.bbc.com/news/world-africa-35173618 (accessed 10 April 2018)]

BBC 2016a. 'Cameroon Sentences 89 Boko Haram Fighters to Death' (17 March) [available at: http://www.bbc.com/news/world-africa-35831432 (accessed 10 April 2018)]

BBC 2016b. 'Who Are Nigeria's Boko Haram Islamist Group?' (24 November) [available at: http://www.bbc.com/news/world-africa-13809501 (accessed 10 April 2018)]

Benari, E. 2014. 'EU Imposes Sanctions on Boko Haram', *Arutz Sheva* (3 June) [available at: http://www.israelnationalnews.com/News/News.aspx/181329 (accessed 7 August 2018)]

Brackley, E. 2017. 'West Africa: The Region in Niger Quietly Piloting a Boko Haram Amnesty', *All Africa* (20 April) [available at: http://allafrica.com/stories/201704220068.html (accessed 10 April 2018)]

Campbell, J. 2017. 'U.S. and UK Revoke Visas for Nigerian Officers Connected to Human Rights Abuses', *CFR Blog* (27 June) [available at: https://www.cfr.org/blog/us-and-uk-revoke-visas-nigerian-officers-connected-human-rights-abuses (accessed 10 April 2018)]

Cluster Protection Niger 2017. 'Redditions de combattants ex-Boko Haram au Niger: Eléments d'un positionnement commun de l'Equipe Humanitaire Pays (EHP)' (17 February)

CTED [UN Security Council Counter-Terrorism Committee Executive Directorate] 2015. 'Madrid Guiding Principles on Stemming the Flow of Foreign Terrorist Fighters' (UN Doc. S/2015/939) (23 December)

CTED 2017. 'Technical Guide to the Implementation of Security Council Resolution 1373 (2001) and Other Relevant Resolutions' (UN Doc. S/2017/716) (21 August)

Felbab-Brown, V. 2017. 'Under the Hot Sahel Sun: "Post"-Boko Haram Challenges in Niger and Nigeria', *Brookings* (8 June) [available at: https://www.brookings.edu/blog/order-from-chaos/2017/06/08/under-the-hot-sahel-sun-post-boko-haram-challenges-in-niger-and-nigeria (accessed 10 April 2018)]

FIACAT [International Federation of Action by Christians for the Abolition of Torture] 2016. 'FIACAT's Contribution to the Consultation for the Report of the High Commissioner on "Terrorism and Human Rights"' (Law 034/PR/2015) (adopted 5 August 2015) [available at: https://goo.gl/1vjMBm (accessed 10 April 2018)]

Ford, J. 2014. 'The Origins of Boko Haram', *The National Interest* (6 June) [available at: http://nationalinterest.org/feature/the-origins-boko-haram-10609?page=2 (accessed 10 April 2018)]

France 2 TV 2017. 'Niger: un centre de déradicalisation pour les repentis de Boko Haram' (16 December) [available at: https://www.francetvinfo.fr/monde/afrique/boko-haram/niger-un-centre-de-deradicalisation-pour-les-repentis-de-boko-haram_2516943.htm (accessed 10 April 2018)]

GCTF [Global Counterterrorism Forum] 2016. 'Addendum to Rome Memo on Good Practices for Rehabilitation and Reintegration of Violent Extremist Offenders' [available at: https://www.thegctf.org/Portals/1/Documents/Toolkit-documents/English-Addendum-to-the-Rome-Memorandum-on-Legal-Frameworks.pdf (accessed 10 April 2018)]

Human Rights Committee 1992. 'General Comment No. 20: Article 7 (Prohibition of Torture, or Other Cruel, Inhuman or Degrading Treatment or Punishment)' (10 March)

Human Rights Committee 2004. 'General Comment No. 31: Nature of the General Legal Obligation on States Parties to the Covenant' (UN Doc. CCPR/C/21/Rev.1/Add.13, 2004) (29 March)

Human Rights Watch 2013. 'Nigeria: Boko Haram Abducts Women, Recruits Children' (29 November)

ICC OTP [Office of the Prosecutor of the ICC] 2015. 'Report on Preliminary Examination Activities 2015: Nigeria' 44–51 (12 November)

ICC OTP 2017. 'Report on Preliminary Examination Activities: Nigeria' 46–50 (4 December)

Institute for Economics and Peace 2015. 'World Terrorism Index 2015' [available at: http://economicsandpeace.org/wp-content/uploads/2015/11/Global-Terrorism-Index-2015.pdf (accessed 10 April 2018)]

International Symposium on Youth Deradicalisation and the Reinsertion of Repentants from Boko Haram Movement 2017. 'General Report' (Diffa, 15–17 May)

Muggah, R. 2005. 'No Magic Bullet: A Critical Perspective on Disarmament, Demobilization and Reintegration (DDR) and Weapons Reduction in Post-Conflict Contexts' 94 *The Commonwealth Journal of International Affairs* 239

Muggah, R., Molloy, D. and Halty, M. 2009. '(Dis)integrating DDR in Sudan and Haiti? Practitioners' Views to Overcoming Integration Inertia', in R. Muggah (ed.), *Security and Post-Conflict Reconstruction: Dealing with Fighters in the Aftermath of War* (Routledge: London) 206

Muggah, R. and O'Donnell, C. 2015. 'Next Generation Disarmament, Demobilization and Reintegration' 4 *Stability: International Journal of Security and Development* Article 30

Nossiter, A. 2015. 'Abuses by Nigeria's Military Found to Be Rampant in War Against Boko Haram', *New York Times* (3 June) [available at: https://www.nytimes.com/2015/06/04/world/africa/abuses-nigeria-military-boko-haram-war-report.html (accessed 10 April 2018)]

OHCHR [Office of the United Nations High Commissioner for Human Rights] 2009. 'Rule-of-Law Tools for Post-Conflict States: Amnesties'

OJJDP [Office of Juvenile Justice and Delinquency Prevention] 2009. 'Chapter 2: The OJJDP Comprehensive Gang Model' Implementation Manual [available at: https://www.nationalgangcenter.gov/Content/Documents/Implementation-Manual/Implementation-Manual-Chapter-2.pdf (accessed 10 April 2018)]

OJJDP 2018. 'Comprehensive Anti-Gang Initiative' [available at: https://www.ojjdp.gov/programs/antigang/ (accessed 29 January 2018)]

Radio Anfani 2018. 'Niger Court Specialized in Fight Against Terrorism Poised to Open Trials of Suspects' (2 February)

Reuters 2017. 'Boko Haram Split Creates Two Deadly Forces', *Voice of America* (4 August) [available at: https://www.voanews.com/a/boko-haram-split-two-deadly-forces/3970425.html (accessed 10 April 2018)]

Searcey, D. 2017. 'They Fled Boko Haram, Only to Be Raped by Nigeria's Security Forces' *New York Times* (8 December) [available at: https://www.nytimes.com/2017/12/08/world/africa/boko-haram-nigeria-security-forces-rape.htm (accessed 10 April 2018)]

Smith, M. 2014. 'Factsheet: Explaining Nigeria's Boko Haram and its Violent Insurgency' (Africa Check) (last updated 31 July 2017) [available at: https://africacheck.org/factsheets/factsheet-explaining-nigerias-boko-haram-and-its-violent-insurgency/ (accessed 10 April 2018)]

Tih, F.N. 2017. 'Boko Haram "Forced" 135 Children into Suicide Bombings', *Anadolu Agency* (28 December) [available at: http://aa.com.tr/en/africa/boko-haram-forced-135-children-into-suicide-bombings-/1017196 (accessed 10 April 2018)]

UN 'Human Rights Up Front' Initiative 2015 (December)

UNICEF/Nigeria Stability and Reconciliation Programme 2017. 'Perceptions and Experiences of Children Associated with Armed Groups in North-East Nigeria' (Research Report) [available at: http://www.nsrp-nigeria.org/wp-content/uploads/2017/03/Research-Report-Children-Associated-with-Armed-Groups.pdf (accessed 10 April 2018)]

UN IDDRS [Integrated DDR Standards] 2006a. Module 5.20, 'Youth and DDR' [available at: http://unddr.org/uploads/documents/IDDRS%205.20%20Youth%20and%20DDR.pdf (accessed 10 April 2018)]

UN IDDRS 2006b. Module 5.30, 'Children and DDR' [available at: http://unddr.org/uploads/documents/IDDRS%205.30%20Children%20and%20DDR.pdf (accessed 10 April 2018)]

UN IDDRS 2014. Modules 1.10, 'Introduction to the IDDRS' [available at: http://unddr.org/uploads/documents/IDDRS_1_10_Rev_2014.pdf (accessed 10 April 2018)]

UN IDDRS 2018. IDDRS Framework [available at: http://www.unddr.org/iddrs-framework.aspx (accessed 10 April 2018)]

UNODC [United Nations Office on Drugs and Crime] 2017. 'Résultats et activités. Programme Sahel: Rapport d'activité Juin 2017' (June)

UN Secretary-General 2016. 'Children and Armed Conflict. Report of the Secretary-General' (UN Doc. A/70/836–S/2016/360) (20 April)

UN Security Council 2014a. 'Security Council Al-Qaida Sanctions Committee Adds Boko Haram to its Sanctions List' (Press Release) (UN Doc. SC/11410) (22 May)

UN Security Council 2014b. 'Report of the Secretary-General on the United Nations Organization Stabilization Mission in the Democratic Republic of the Congo' (UN Doc. S/2014/450) (30 June)

UN Security Council 2014c. 'Jama'atu Ahlis-Sunna Lidda'awati Wal-Jihad (Boko Haram)', *Narrative Summaries of Reasons for Listing* (QDe.138) (9 September) [available at: https://www.un.org/sc/suborg/en/sanctions/1267/aq_sanctions_list/summaries/entity/jama%27atu-ahlis-sunna-lidda%27awati-wal-jihad-%28boko (accessed 10 April 2018)]

UN Special Representative of the Secretary-General for Children and Armed Conflict 2017. 'Civilian Joint Task Force in Northeast Nigeria Signs Action Plan to End Recruitment of Children' (15 September) [available at: https://childrenandarmedconflict.un.org/children-not-soldiers-nigeria-action-plan/ (accessed 10 April 2018)]

US Department of State 2018. 'Foreign Terrorist Organizations' [available at: https://www.state.gov/j/ct/rls/other/des/123085.htm (accessed 10 April 2018)]
US Department of the Treasury 2015. 'Treasury Sanctions Senior Boko Haram Leaders' *Press Center* (1 December)
Vanguard 2018. 'US Adds Nigeria's Abu Musab Al-Barnawi to Global Terrorism List' (27 February) [available at: https://www.vanguardngr.com/2018/02/947617/ (accessed 10 April 2018)]

22. Do no harm: how reintegration programmes for former child soldiers can cause unintended harm
Michael G. Wessells

In different war-torn countries worldwide, children (defined under international law as people under 18 years of age) are exploited as child soldiers performing diverse roles such as combatants, sex slaves, porters, cooks, spies and bodyguards, among others.[1] Broadly, reintegration programmes are organized by governments, UN actors and international NGOs as a means of enabling the integration or reintegration of former child soldiers into civilian life. These programmes vary according to the context, but typically include components such as family reunification, mental health and psychosocial support, education, livelihood training, and community mobilization and support.[2]

A diversity of positive motivations underlies reintegration programmes for former child soldiers. As outlined in the Paris Principles – the main global technical guidelines on the reintegration of former child soldiers – reintegration programmes aim to ensure the rights of former child soldiers[3] to resources such as psychosocial support and education and also aim to protect children against further abuses and re-recruitment. This reintegration and rights-oriented approach, however, exists alongside another motivation behind reintegration programmes that is often backed by greater funding and inter-governmental support, namely, to help stabilize fragile, post-conflict societies and create space for development and peace. Disarmament, demobilization and reintegration (DDR) programmes often seek to stand down opposing armies, restructure security forces, and enable former combatants to find a place in civilian life.[4] Destabilization and militarization of the post-conflict environment could occur if significant numbers of children continued to support rebel groups or carried and used weapons for purposes such as meeting their basic needs through crime.

Despite the positive motivations behind reintegration programmes for former child soldiers, significant questions arise in regard to their design, implementation and effectiveness. Amidst the chaos and fluidity of war zones and post-conflict settings, it can be difficult to make causal determinations regarding the effectiveness of particular reintegration components or modalities. Overall, there is a weak evidence base regarding reintegration programmes for former child soldiers.[5] Some research has reported that former child soldiers who went home on their own (so called self-demobilizers) have achieved outcomes as positive as those who had gone through formal reintegration

---

[1] Wessells 2006.
[2] Wessells 2006; Wessells 2009a.
[3] The Paris Principles uses the term 'children associated with armed forces or armed groups' (CAAFAG), yet the less cumbersome term 'child soldiers' is used here.
[4] UN 2006. See also Casey-Maslen; Jiménez; and Vastapuu, all in this volume.
[5] Betancourt and Williams 2008; Wessells 2006.

programmes.[6] However, these studies are frequently difficult to interpret since there may have been differences between the children who self-demobilized and those who chose to enter reintegration programmes. Also, there may have been differences in the levels of non-formal supports provided by inter alia families, community members, and religious groups.

Furthermore, significant ethical questions arise in regard to reintegration programmes for former child soldiers. Good intentions aside, all humanitarian programmes may have a mixture of intended and unintended outcomes.[7] Although some unintended outcomes may be positive, others could be negative and violate the humanitarian imperative 'do no harm'. For the most part, ethical attention has been focused on issues such as confidentiality and avoiding the use of exploitative photographs that could endanger former child soldiers and their families. Also urgently needed, however, is discourse about the wider ethical issues associated with reintegration programmes for former child soldiers.

The purpose of this chapter is to analyse ethical issues associated with reintegration programming. This chapter aims to move these issues from the margins and into the heart of critical discourse. The intent is neither to disparage nor discourage reintegration programming, but rather to help strengthen it by identifying key do no harm issues and also practical strategies for managing and preventing such externalities. The spirit of this chapter is that we learn as much from our mistakes as we do from our successes. Practitioners need to adopt a self-critical stance, demonstrate willingness to document and discuss openly the negative, unintended consequences of programmatic activities, and incorporate the lessons learned to adjust current reintegration programmes as well as strengthen the design and implementation of future programmes.

Of necessity, this chapter relies extensively on case studies and the author's experience as a practitioner. Because scant literature exists regarding the ethical aspects of reintegration programmes, an essential first step is to identify various issues using cases from different countries. For ease of exposition, this chapter identifies and analyses three categories of do no harm issues: (1) discrimination; (2) the imposition of outsider approaches; and (3) the increase in child protection issues. Each of these concerns has arisen or been exacerbated through various reintegration programmes for former child soldiers.

1. DISCRIMINATION

The post-conflict environments in which most reintegration programmes are conducted attest to a need to support social unity and inclusivity. However, reintegration programmes may unintentionally promote social divisions by discriminating against particular groups of war-affected children. This section examines how discrimination frequently arises in regard to children who have not been recruited and former girl soldiers. It also points out how reintegration programmes often discriminate against children by minimizing their voices and agency in the design and implementation of the reintegration programmes.

---

[6] Humphries and Weinstein 2007.
[7] Anderson 1999; Slim 2015; Wessells 2009b.

1.1 Excessive Targeting of Former Child Soldiers

Many reintegration programmes for children focus mostly on supporting former child soldiers because they are presumed to be the most vulnerable children. For example, during the war in northern Uganda, children who escaped from the Lord's Resistance Army (LRA) or who had been captured by the Ugandan army often went to reception centres where they received psychosocial care, food, safety, health and hygiene supports.[8] Following family tracing, they returned to their families and communities, where volunteers worked to support their social acceptance and integration.

To be sure, there was good justification for supporting formerly abducted children. Known for its brutality, mass killing of civilians and mutilations, the LRA subjected children to immense danger and mistreatment.[9] The LRA abducted children at gunpoint and sometimes forced the children to kill members of their own family or community.[10] If a child attempted to escape, the LRA required the other abducted children to beat the escapee to death or suffer the same fate themselves. Girls were frequently given to males as 'wives', and many became mothers inside the LRA as a result of the forced sex. Exposed to massive violence,[11] significant numbers of formerly abducted children developed mental health problems such as post-traumatic stress disorder (PTSD) and depression.[12] Some developed a cultural affliction – *cen* – wherein the spirits of those who had been killed attached themselves to and possessed the formerly abducted children.[13] Formerly abducted children also had significant health problems, as many had untreated wounds and had suffered poor nutrition and hygiene.[14]

By excessively targeting formerly abducted children, this approach discriminated against children who had not been abducted by the LRA but who themselves were highly vulnerable and had many unmet needs. During the war, civilians in northern Uganda, including children, were subjected to repeated attacks, coupled with killings and looting that resulted in extensive losses of family and friends, homes, farms, and means of livelihood such as animals. Unable to protect the civilian population, the Ugandan government moved civilians into camps for internally displaced people (IDPs). Shortly after 2000, some 1.8 million people lived in the IDP camps. These camps were infamous for their squalor, overcrowding and difficult living conditions.[15] The camps did not protect people from LRA attacks, and the camps themselves were awash in crime and sexual exploitation and violence.[16] Many civilian children suffered hunger and malnutrition, lacked access to basic health services,[17] and were unable to participate in quality education.[18] Further, these civilian children suffered high levels of exposure to traumatic events and, as a result,

---

[8] Allen and Schomerus 2006.
[9] Amone-P'Olak 2004; Amone-P'Olak 2005; Amone-P'Olak 2009; Baines 2017.
[10] Annan et al. 2006; Human Rights Watch 2003.
[11] Amone-P'Olak et al. 2013; Annan et al. 2006.
[12] Amone-P'Olak et al. 2013; Moscardino et al. 2012; Okello et al. 2014; Vinck et al. 2007.
[13] See also Barrett in this volume.
[14] Amone-P'Olak 2009; Akello 2010.
[15] Dolan 2009.
[16] Ibid.
[17] Akello 2017.
[18] Akello 2010; Dolan 2009.

significant numbers of them also developed mental health problems such as PTSD and depression.[19] Within the general population, nearly 14 per cent of war-affected children were afflicted by cen.[20] From a humanitarian standpoint, the singling out of former child soldiers for support, coupled with the denial of supports to other vulnerable children, was discriminatory.

This kind of discrimination frequently engenders reverse discrimination against the former child soldiers. In rural areas of Sierra Leone, many former child soldiers had been part of the rebel group, the Revolutionary United Front (RUF). The RUF was infamous for attacking civilians and amputating people's arms as a means of terrorizing the population. Following the establishment of a ceasefire, the reintegration programmes for children provided them with psychosocial and livelihood supports and sent them home wearing new shoes and t-shirts. However, former child soldiers in Sierra Leone reported that this nice clothing made them targets of discrimination since local people lacked such items.[21] Not only were locals jealous, but they saw the supports as a way of rewarding the people who had attacked them. In neighbouring Liberia, local people referred to the supports for former child soldiers as 'blood money'. In both countries, former child soldiers spoke of how this reverse discrimination angered people, worsened their situation, and dimmed their chances of being accepted into civilian society.

The problem of reverse discrimination against former child soldiers receiving reintegration supports is also aggravated by the individualization of any such support. Most contemporary armed conflicts occur in collectivist societies. In collectivist societies, the good of the group is of paramount importance, and takes precedence over individual well-being.[22] People pride themselves on being members of their families, clans, or ethnic identity groups, but they do not conceptualize individual rights as having central importance. To call attention to one's own suffering and need of support in collectivist settings violates social norms and heightens one's risk of ostracism at a moment when stigma already poses a formidable obstacle to reintegration.[23]

One way to prevent discrimination is to avoid the excessive targeting of former child soldiers by providing supports for a mixture of the latter and other vulnerable children. This mixed approach is appropriately enshrined in the Paris Principles. However, this approach comes with its own complications. For one, there is a paucity of evidence regarding which mixtures are effective. In addition, this more comprehensive approach raises thorny questions such as who decides which children are most vulnerable? Often, 'outside' child protection workers decide which children are most vulnerable, yet local people may hold different views on delicate matters of vulnerability and precarity.

In my experience, it can be useful to listen and learn first from local people, and to engage directly with marginalized children such as children with disabilities. This type of approach can help to uncover the lived experiences of children who are positioned in different ways and to avoid facile assumptions that former child soldiers are among the

---

[19] Moscardino et al. 2012; Pfeiffer and Elbert 2011; Roberts et al. 2008.
[20] Neuner et al. 2012.
[21] Wessells 2006.
[22] Triandis 2001.
[23] Betancourt et al. 2010.

most vulnerable children. In essence, this approach uses a social justice lens to help avoid the discrimination that comes from focusing only on former child soldiers.

1.2 Gender Discrimination

The reoccurrence of privileging boys over girls is an egregious form of discrimination in reintegration programmes.[24] In Sierra Leone, for example, reintegration supports were intended for boys and girls equally, but in practice, the children were required to pass a 'weapons test' in order to receive aid. This eligibility test required the child to strip down, reassemble and fire an AK-47. This test discriminated against large numbers of girls who had not been combatants but who had served roles such as porters, spies, cooks and sex slaves. It also discriminated against some boys who had been part of the Civilian Defence Forces and had fought with more basic weapons such as pangas (machetes).

A related problem is that the supports for formerly recruited girls and women tended to reflect the broader gender stereotypes and national and global patterns of gender discrimination. In Sierra Leone, formerly recruited boys received training on how to do 'man's' labour such as bricklaying or carpentry; whereas girls received training in more 'womanly' occupations such as sewing and tailoring. Discussing an NGO-run reintegration programme, one young woman who had been a commander in Sierra Leone asked, 'What makes them think I'm going to go back and sit quietly behind a sewing machine, when I was a *commander* who made life and death decisions?'[25]

The civil war in Mozambique revealed the problems of forcing former girl soldiers back into secondary roles backed by demeaning stereotypes of women. Between 1977 and 1992, the ruling Front for the Liberation of Mozambique (FRELIMO), which had helped to achieve independence from Portuguese colonial rule, sought to establish a socialist state. Opposing FRELIMO were the forces of the Mozambican National Resistance (RENAMO), which received support from anti-communist regimes in Rhodesia and South Africa. FRELIMO recruited significant numbers of young women and indoctrinated them in anti-colonial ideology that viewed women's emancipation as part of the anti-colonial campaign and a project of creating the 'new socialist woman'.[26]

Girls who became part of Female Detachments internalized the liberationist ideology and embraced narratives of heroic youth fighting for the end of all kinds of exploitation. While the young women were being used by FRELIMO, on the one hand, they also leveraged this situation to advance their own personal project of creating new gender roles in which they were equal to men and respected actors within society, on the other.[27] Following the end of the war, however, young women experienced frustration and feelings of abandonment associated with FRELIMO's decreased commitment to gender equity. In addition, they were angered by expectations that they assume their 'normal'

---

[24] Brett and Specht 2004; McKay and Mazurana 2004; Verhey 2001; Wessells 2006; Wessells 2010. See also Vastapuu in this volume.
[25] See also Oosterveld in this volume who discusses the gendered construction of girls in Sierra Leone's armed groups.
[26] West 2004.
[27] Ibid.

roles including subservience to men.[28] This example serves as a poignant reminder that reintegration programmes need to pay careful attention to issues of gender equity and to the wider forces of gender discrimination that permeate many societies.

In general, reintegration supports tend to be developed with boys or men in mind. As a result, the reintegration supports frequently fail to take into account the gendered nature of girls' and boys' war experiences and their equally gendered perceptions about what they need the most. In many situations of child recruitment, girls are subjected to extensive sexual violence inside the armed group.[29] The girls themselves carry a heavy burden of stigma because they are seen as having violated customary norms of marriage and are frequently seen as 'promiscuous' or even to blame for having been raped or sexually exploited.[30] Sexual violence also occurs against boys inside some armed forces and groups.[31] However, the global scale of this violence is far less than that against girls. Reintegration programmes typically do not take adequate steps to address this extensive sexual violence, which leaves strong, potentially life-long, psychological scars. Nor do they make the reduction of stigma a top priority, possibly because the stigma is usually less for boys and men. For former girl soldiers, however, stigma is typically one of the greatest sources of distress,[32] and it often endures well beyond the period of reintegration programming.[33] By not addressing sexual violence and its distinctive stigma directly, reintegration programmes quietly discriminate against girls and women.[34]

Nowhere is the problem of unintended discrimination more visible than in regard to young mothers whose child or children had been conceived or born while the girls were inside the armed group.[35] Children who were born inside the LRA during the conflict in northern Uganda were doubly stigmatized as being 'illegitimate' and born to a 'rebel' father. A key point overlooked in reintegration programming was that the young mothers defined their own needs and well-being in relational terms that featured their motherhood. Formerly recruited young mothers said that, more than anything, they wanted to be good mothers, and family and community members watched the young mothers carefully to see whether they treated their children well. Unfortunately, the reintegration supports did not adequately recognize the girls' motherhood or support their effective mothering.

2. THE IMPOSITION OF OUTSIDER APPROACHES

Like humanitarian programmes in general, reintegration programmes are typically designed by outside 'experts', who adhere to international standards that may reflect

---

[28] Ibid.
[29] McKay and Mazurana 2004; Wessells 2006.
[30] Baines 2007.
[31] Allen and Vlassenroot 2010; Wessells 2006.
[32] Betancourt et al. 2010; Wessells 2006.
[33] Tonheim 2012; Tonheim 2014.
[34] Sexual violence also occurs against boys inside some armed forces and groups. However, the global scale of this violence is far less than that against girls.
[35] Akello 2013; Apio 2008; Denov and Lakor 2017; McKay et al. 2011. See also Denov in this volume.

outsider values. Typically, such programmes are implemented in a context of enormous power asymmetries between outside agencies (Governmental, UN or NGO) and local people. Usually, local people are consulted but have no significant power to make decisions regarding the exogenously inspired reintegration programming. Not infrequently, local people are relegated to the status of beneficiaries. The inadvertent harm triggered by these impositional approaches may be seen in regard to children's participation rights, mental health and psychosocial supports, and the relative inattention to local justice processes that hold former child soldiers accountable for their actions.

2.1 Children's Participation Rights

The UN Convention on the Rights of the Child (CRC), and also its regional counterparts such as the African Charter on the Rights and Welfare of the Child,[36] call consistently for the protection and achievement of children's participation rights. For example, Article 12 of the CRC provides that children have the right to participate in making decisions that relate to their lives and to influence decisions taken within the family, the school or the community that pertain to their well-being. Unfortunately, in the international humanitarian system, the participation of children is best described as 'participation light'. In the field of child protection, for example, children are often 'consulted' about a problem or invited to participate in an adult-led process, but they seldom have any real power to help guide or make decisions. Some analysts[37] see this situation as reflecting adult fears of sharing power with sometimes unruly adolescents. Pressed by donors and managers to achieve quick results on a certain scale, practitioner agencies often worry that deeper participation will take too much time. In addition, many societies are gerontocentric and have the attitude that 'children are to be seen but not heard'.

Most reintegration programmes quietly trample children's participation rights and achieve only low levels of child participation. The reintegration planners – invariably adults – work in a rapid, top-down approach in which experts conceive, design, implement and evaluate reintegration programmes and processes. Most programme developers do not take time to learn deeply from – or really listen to – formerly recruited girls and boys of different ages, what their needs are, and what would help them the most.[38] Where participation occurs, it tends to be tokenistic and in the order of inviting the children in a Reception Centre to organize themselves to keep the Centre clean. Although such activities are useful, they are far from a fully participatory process in which the children have meaningful voice and roles, not to mention a significant influence on decisions.

The violation of children's participation rights in reintegration programmes is ethically unacceptable because one of the most firmly entrenched principles of children's programming is that programmes should support children's rights and, equally, via the do no harm imperative, avoid undermining children's rights.[39] The violation of children's participation

---

[36] For a detailed and insightful discussion of the African Charter and its monitoring Committee, see Odongo in this volume.
[37] E.g., Boyden 2003.
[38] Lenz 2017; Wessells 2006.
[39] Child Protection Working Group 2012.

rights is also highly concerning on a practical level. To be effective and achieve sustainable results, reintegration programmes need to address children's actual needs, but these are often identified by adult 'experts' who have given scant attention to children's views. Yet children, rather than adults, are in the best position to identify what their needs and situations are. Reintegration programmes ought to be guided by an understanding of the lived experiences of formerly recruited or associated girls and boys rather than by adult experts' assumptions. By taking time to learn separately from girls and boys, reintegration programmes stand a better chance of helping to meet the gendered needs of formerly recruited girls and boys, respectively.

Further, reintegration programmes should make it a high priority to strengthen the agency of former child soldiers. It is now widely recognized that child soldiers are not passive robots, but make decisions and cope with their environment, even in situations in which they had been abducted into armed groups. Having witnessed killings, fought, or made life and death decisions, it can be frustrating and humiliating for former child soldiers to enter a reintegration programme that is infantilizing and treats them as if they were passive beneficiaries. Psychologically, former child soldiers benefit from the affirmation and strengthening of their sense of agency and self-efficacy, which in turn forms an integral part of their healing, and is essential for fostering hope and well-being.[40] In addition, when former child soldiers participate actively and help to guide decisions about their reintegration, they use their formidable creativity, energy and understanding of the local context to support the reintegration process. Since they take ownership for the process, they are more likely to pour themselves into the work and take some measure of responsibility for its success. To take responsibility for making the transition from military to civilian life is itself an important part of the process of reintegration.

There are various ways in which reintegration programmes can become more supportive of the participation rights of former child soldiers. At the beginning of the process, the assessment of the children's situation and needs should be highly participatory and designed to elicit the children's lived experiences and ideas about how to enable the transition into civilian life. The design of the programme should draw systematically on the voices and views of children, with careful attention given to issues of gender, age, religion, and other pertinent issues. This could be accomplished by having democratically selected girls and boys give inputs on the design process, promote youth involvement in the implementation process, and help with the programme evaluation. As NGOs and other actors implement the reintegration programmes, they should, whenever it is appropriate, use participatory methods such as participatory action research wherein groups of young people themselves decide on their key needs, decide or aid in deciding how to address them, and then work with others to implement community action to support reintegration.[41] In such approaches, it would be key to engage not only former child soldiers but also other vulnerable children in the community.

---

[40] Bandura 1977; Bandura 1982; Hobfoll et al. 2007; Wessells 2006; Wessells 2009b.
[41] McKay et al. 2011.

2.2 Mental Health and Psychosocial Supports

Mental health and psychosocial supports are much needed. Former child soldiers frequently face significant stigma, have suffered multiple losses, and, as explained earlier, significant numbers develop mental disorders such as PTSD or depression. In addition to stigma, former child soldiers often experience a diversity of everyday stressors, including: displacement, family separation, lack of education, severe poverty, HIV and AIDS, sexual violence, trafficking and re-recruitment, among many others. These everyday distresses can cause enormous suffering, and their effects frequently mediate the development of disorders such as PTSD.[42] In particular, children who are exposed to horrendous events are more likely to develop PTSD if they also experience high levels of everyday distress.

In every war zone I have worked in, a cottage industry develops around presumably traumatized children, and disproportionate funding is often allocated for their treatment. This raises two related ethical issues, the first of which involves the labelling of children as having PTSD or as needing specialized support. Such labelling can exacerbate stigma. Far from improving children's well-being, this labelling contributes to their suffering and social isolation. In the worst cases, children are labelled prematurely, before the passage of several months that is required before one can legitimately determine that a particular child suffers from PTSD.

The bigger problem is that the neo-colonial imposition of outsider categories such as PTSD and major depressive disorder draws considerable attention to these challenges, thereby encouraging the use of treatment modalities that specifically aim to address them. This is not entirely a bad thing since these maladies are present in many different societies and clearly warrant attention. However, the singular or excessive attention to these presumably universal disorders simultaneously marginalizes local categories regarding mental health and psychosocial problems. Each culture has its own culturally constructed ideas about disorders; these beliefs have significant impact on the well-being of former child soldiers and other people even if they do not fit into the diagnostic categories that have been constructed primarily by Western psychiatrists and psychologists and codified into standardized schemes such as the International Statistical Classification of Diseases and Related Health Problems (ICD-10) or the Diagnostic and Statistical Manual of Mental Disorders (DSM-5). When local categories of distress are marginalized, harm is caused by too little attention being given to what former child soldiers may see as one of their main problems.

A case in point is the reintegration work in northern Uganda, which focused mostly on Reception Centres, which, as explained above, provided a transitional space and a mixture of health and psychosocial supports.[43] The international agencies that oversaw most of the Reception Centres or who had trained the national groups and people who staffed them had a strong focus on trauma and PTSD rather than on locally constructed maladies. However, the former child soldiers who came from Acholiland sometimes identified *cen* as one of their biggest problems and sources of distress. According to the local beliefs of most Acholi people, *cen* are the angry spirits of people who have been killed, and who

---

[42] Miller and Rasmussen 2010; Amone P'Olak et al. 2013.
[43] Allen and Schomerus 2006.

haunt either the people who did the killing or others who had been around dead bodies in the bush.[44] *Cen* evoke powerful feelings of fear since they are believed to be able to cause problems such as illness or death.

In contrast to the Western focus on individual maladies, *cen* is seen as a collective affliction since the vengeful spirits can attach to and attack other people. A former child soldier who has *cen* is extremely fearful because the *cen* can harm him or can also possess him, causing him to act in irrational ways or attack other people. Similarly, other people fear a former child soldier who has *cen*, thereby creating an obstacle to reintegration. For the most part, international agencies neither recognized nor tried to help address the problem of *cen*.[45]

People who suffer as a result of *cen* can potentially be helped by having a traditional healer conduct an appropriate ritual that is believed to cleanse the person of *cen*.[46] Unfortunately, NGOs or governments that are eager to address problems such as trauma and depression may pay little attention to *cen* or to local, sustainable treatments such as traditional rituals. Alternately, they may actively seek to deter the use of such treatments. In one Reception Centre that I visited, Christian NGO workers refused on ideological and religious grounds to recognize the importance of *cen* and told former child soldiers who had asked for a cleansing ritual to pray instead.[47]

Similar beliefs about angry spirits and the importance of cleansing rituals are also visible in other parts of sub-Saharan Africa. In Angola, which was ravaged by war for over 40 years, I worked with a talented Angolan team that, on the advice of a Western consultant, had focused on ameliorating trauma through Western methods such as talking and working through one's feelings. As young people began to be demobilized from the opposition group (the National Union for the Total Independence of Angola (UNITA)), the leader of the Angolan psychosocial programme – Carlinda Monteiro – encountered a 14-year-old former boy soldier, who reported having nightmares and being unable to sleep. Rather than assuming that these were symptoms of trauma, however, Carlinda asked the boy why he was unable sleep. He replied that the spirit of the man he had killed came to him during the night and asked, 'Why did you do this to me?' The boy stated that where he lived, angry spirits could harm him and also cause bad things such as illness and death or crop failures for family and community members. Asked what could help him, he replied that he needed a traditional healer who would conduct a cleansing ritual that would appease the angry spirit and restore harmony between the living and the ancestors. Monteiro and her team subsequently included traditional cleansing rituals as part of a number of holistic supports for former child soldiers' reintegration.[48] Case studies conducted as part of this work indicated that following the carrying out of a traditional cleansing, the person who had been cleansed was warned that talking about their war experiences could invite back the angry spirits.[49] In this situation, a well-intentioned Western counsellor could cause unintended harm by asking a former child soldier to discuss his or her war experiences.

The problem of the imposition of outsider approaches is systemic and has multiple

---

[44] Baines 2005; Baines 2007.
[45] See also Barrett in this volume.
[46] Baines 2005; Schultz and Weisaeth 2015.
[47] See also Akello in this volume; Barrett in this volume.
[48] Honwana 2006; Wessells and Monteiro 2004.
[49] Wessells and Monteiro 2004.

causes at different levels. Individually, these approaches are grounded in neo-colonial attitudes that assert the supremacy of Western approaches and also in attitudes that demonize local cultures or relegate them to such low priorities that workers take little time to learn about them and the potential resources they offer. Also, significant personal gains such as career advancement and self-affirmation follow from being the 'expert' who analyses the local problem of former child soldiers and then decides which interventions are needed to support their reintegration. Because donors and the humanitarian system demand quick results using 'proven' interventions, agencies feel pressure to use top-down approaches that enable rapid action, as well as employing a 'one size fits all approach' that is short on listening, adapting one's approach to the local context and, ultimately, sustainability. Institutionally, particular agencies pride themselves on what they have accomplished, leaving scant opportunities for the accomplishments and potentially more sustainable results that could be achieved through local action.

Addressing this situation requires a systemic approach that recognizes the importance of local culture and affords greater power to local views and action. Individually, humanitarian workers can promote ethical practice through developing strong habits of self-reflection in which they critically interrogate the power dynamics of the humanitarian work and their own positioning within it, their own motives for engaging in humanitarian work, their views of local people and culture, and how their views and actions can cause unintended harm.[50] Also, through listening systematically and engaging in deeper ways with local actors, they can more fully identify the problems of former child soldiers as they are understood in the local context. Similarly, the humanitarian agencies can create spaces in which local people and outside actors discuss how it could be possible to blend local and outside supports in ways that make sense and seem advantageous to local people. Through a willingness to share greater power, agencies can also create spaces in which local actors themselves plan and take action to enable the reintegration of former child soldiers. To encourage donors to support this more flexible, sustainable approach that puts greater power in the hands of local people, humanitarian agencies can collect evidence and conduct pilot studies that document the value of local practices. At the inter-agency level, there can be collective commitment to fulfilling the Grand Bargain,[51] which calls for more participatory approaches and the restructuring of humanitarian financing in ways that provide significantly more funding for local actors and efforts. As local actors become more prominent in guiding humanitarian efforts, they will likely use more contextually appropriate approaches, including ones that make use of local cultural resources.

In operationalizing this approach, however, it is important to critically interrogate assumptions and views regarding local culture. Calls to build upon local cultural resources may themselves cause unintended harm if they encourage romanticized images of local culture that fail to recognize that some cultural practices are harmful to children. For example, families in many developing countries tend to support early child marriage[52] as a means of protecting their daughters from sexual abuse, keeping them marriageable, and protecting family honour. From a standpoint of human rights, it would be wholly

---

[50] Wessells 2009b and Columbia Group for Children in Adversity (forthcoming).
[51] Australian Aid et al. 2016.
[52] UNICEF 2018.

inappropriate for external agencies or inside groups to promote forced early marriage as a family- or community-led means of protecting girls. Throughout the grounded processes of learning and community-guided action discussed above, it is crucial to identify and avoid any harmful cultural practices.

2.3 Lack of Accountability Processes

The problems associated with the imposition of outsider approaches are also visible in regard to the tendency of international actors and agencies to view former child soldiers as passive victims and to avoid processes of holding former child soldiers accountable for their actions.[53] In essence, international actors frequently impose an approach that frees former child soldiers of any accountability for harms they may have perpetrated. While it is beyond the scope of this paper to consider the extensive debate about whether former child soldiers ought to be held legally accountable for their actions, from a grounded perspective the reality is that many communities see former child soldiers as having harmed the community and as needing to give back to the community or to do something to repair the wrongs they have committed.[54]

A poignant example comes from personal experience in Sierra Leone following the signing of a ceasefire in 2002, when I talked with a Paramount Chief in Koinadugu District about the war. As the discussion turned to children, I asked whether any children had been associated with armed groups or forces. Interrupting me, he clapped his hands, and pronounced 'Bring forward a child ex-combatant.' Minutes later, villagers returned with a 17-year-old boy who had been with the rebel group, the RUF, making me feel anxious that my question would only add to the boy's stigma or invite reprisal attacks against him.

In fact, my concerns were ill founded, as the boy and the community had gone through a months-long process that had enabled him to be restored as a full member of the village. When the boy had returned to his village (on his own, without NGO support), the Chief, elders and community people had used a traditional practice to enable the boy's social acceptance and reintegration. First, the boy's family had petitioned the Chief for an audience with their son. Having agreed to meet with the boy, the Chief learned from others as much as possible about the boy's war experiences and what he had done. Next, the Chief met with the boy, who laid face down on the ground, holding the Chief's ankle in a posture of extreme submission. As the boy told what had happened and what he had done, the Chief listened carefully to see whether the boy told the full truth and showed remorse. Since the boy had caused harm to the village and regretted his actions, the Chief indicated that the boy issue a public apology, do community work that made amends for the harm he had caused, and receive moral tutelage from a respected elder. Over a period of months, the boy followed the Chief's ruling, and with remarkable effects. Indeed, the villagers, including peers and elders, confirmed that he had given back for the wrongs he had done and was now fully accepted by the community, who no longer feared him or wanted to exact vengeance against him.

It should be noted, however, that efforts to promote accountability could also be imposed

---

[53] Drumbl 2012.
[54] Akello et al. 2006; Drumbl 2012; Kiyala 2015; UNICEF and SRSG 2009.

and cause unintended harm by marginalizing or weakening local processes of restorative justice. In northern Uganda, such concerns were expressed in regard to the effort of the International Criminal Court (ICC) to prosecute top commanders of the LRA.[55] More than a few practitioners had concerns that the ICC process would impose a legal, retributive justice approach, and marginalize the local Acholi means of restorative justice. There were other concerns as well, not least of which was that President Museveni was using the case against the LRA as a means of distracting attention away from the significant harms which government forces (Ugandan People's Defence Force (UPDF)) had inflicted upon children and other civilians. Subsequently, these concerns have diminished, owing in part to the realization that traditional Acholi means of justice had difficulty handling the unique, mass injustices associated with the LRA rampage.[56] Also, the ICC has attempted to take a more locally sensitive, culturally grounded approach in its current trial of Dominic Ongwen, one of the top former LRA commanders.[57] For example, the ICC prosecution team has called not only Ugandan survivors but also Ugandan and other expert witnesses who can speak from first-hand experience and understand the local culture and context. This serves as a reminder that restorative justice is not a one-size-fits-all solution in regard to accountability. A key step in ending the recruitment, abuse and exploitation of children as soldiers is to use legal channels to end the impunity of commanders who recruit children.

The problem of imposing an approach of non-accountability regarding former child soldiers could be reduced by taking an empirical orientation. In particular, reintegration actors should conduct an assessment of whether an accountability process is seen locally as being central for the former child soldiers' reintegration and whether appropriate local restorative justice processes exist that could be activated and used to help in this regard. If the need for an accountability process is high, then agencies could encourage or support the use of the local restorative justice process as part of comprehensive reintegration supports. If, however, no indigenous restorative justice processes are available or appropriate, one could explore the applicability of processes such as restorative justice peace circles, which Kiyala[58] has found to be highly effective in the DRC context and which can be tailored to fit different contexts. This multi-step approach could help to correct the well-intended but, in some contexts, discernibly false, view that former child soldiers are best regarded as innocents. In using this approach, critical reflection is of paramount importance and can help to reduce romanticized views of local justice processes or of international processes such as those of the ICC.

3. RAISED EXPECTATIONS

Frequently, reintegration supports have the unintended consequence of inflating local expectations to unrealistic levels. For example, reintegration programmes have often provided former child soldiers with skills training as a means of boosting their chances of

---

[55] Allen 2005.
[56] Allen 2010; Baines 2007; Baines 2017.
[57] For an analysis of Ongwen's trial, see Ramos in this volume.
[58] Kiyala 2015; Kiyala 2018.

employment afterwards. In practice, though, the expected jobs typically do not materialize since specific programmes do little to develop the wider markets that are needed to enable sustainable job creation.[59] In extreme cases, such as one NGO reintegration project that I visited in northern Uganda, nearly 100 children were trained as bicycle mechanics in a village that could not possibly have supported more than three or four bicycle mechanics. Even more than matters of inefficiency and poor use of funding, this situation induces harm by generating frustration and feelings of having been misled. A child who enters such a programme cannot help but feel that his or her chances of employment will increase and in a chronically impoverished environment, employment is seen as the pathway towards earning money, supporting one's family and having a positive future. When these expectations are unmet, it can trigger frustration, increase the child's vulnerability, and dim hopes for the future.

The problem of raised expectations is closely interconnected with donors' short funding cycles. Most practitioners view the reintegration of former child soldiers as a multi-year, extended process.[60] Yet, in reality, funding to support children's reintegration is notoriously short-term and fickle. Quite often, reintegration support lasts one or two years only, and, in a financial equivalent of the 'CNN effect' the funding typically dries up as other conflicts capture international attention. In practice, this can result in temporarily helping former child soldiers to do things such as get an education or receive psychosocial support in a matter of a year or so. But when the funding has ended, the supports typically end with it, leaving the children feeling frustrated and abandoned at a time when they need support and hope for the future.

Broadly, there are two ways of managing and preventing this situation. One is to organize multi-year funding for reintegration programming from the outset. If large government donors tend to give the shorter grants that can exacerbate the problem of raised expectations, NGOs could use a strategy of mingling funds from public and private donors, since the latter frequently offer longer-term support.

A second strategy is to design and implement the reintegration supports in a manner that builds sustainability. Quite often, NGOs work in a top-down manner in which the NGO conducts an assessment, designs the reintegration programme, decides how to implement it, monitors it, and makes improvements as it moves along. In this approach, the NGO holds the power, and although the community members may partner with the NGO, they do not make key decisions. With the NGO in the role of provider and leader, local people take a back seat and tend to become dependent on the NGO. Indeed, the local people tend to see the work as 'an NGO programme' rather than their own process and a way of fulfilling their collective responsibility to their children. Taking little ownership for it, the reintegration programme has low sustainability. The supports tend to fall apart once the external funding ends.

As an alternative to this approach, NGOs and other actors should promote grassroots action and take a community-led approach that puts the power in the hands of the community.[61] In a community-led approach, local people would lead the learning about the situation of former child soldiers, decide which community actions could help to support

---

[59] Brett and Specht 2004.
[60] See Paris Principles; Wessells 2006.
[61] Columbia Group for Children in Adversity (forthcoming); Wessells 2015.

their reintegration and implement those actions. NGOs would play a facilitative support role. Because this bottom-up approach is community owned, it tends to be more sustainable following the end of external funding. Also, it favours a relational approach that features community acceptance of former child soldiers and offers the greatest likelihood for reintegration.[62] Although much remains to be learned about community-led processes in regard to reintegration, community leadership could help to avoid the problems of individualism and of taking a one-size-fits-all approach.

4. INCREASED RISKS TO FORMER CHILD SOLDIERS

Although reintegration programmes for former child soldiers can do much good, they may also unintentionally aggravate threats facing former child soldiers. This section examines risks associated with labelling, re-recruitment and making reintegration efforts subservient to anti-terrorism agendas.[63]

4.1 Labelling

In communicating with donors who support reintegration programmes, agencies frequently use labels such as 'child soldiers' or, following the Paris Principles, 'children associated with armed forces or armed groups'. At ground level, however, such labels can worsen the situation of the children whom the agency had intended to support. A label such as 'former child soldier' essentializes a child by defining her or him in terms of a particular set of negative experiences. More than a few former child soldiers have asked me, 'Why should I be called a "former child soldier" when I'm a human being?' As this question indicates, reductive labels can drain a child's sense of dignity and humanity at the time when that child most needs support and the affirmation of her dignity.

Perhaps even more concerning is the way in which labels such as 'former child soldier' can increase stigma and social isolation. Children who enter a reintegration programme are more likely to be labelled as 'former child soldiers' even if they had been held with an armed group against their will for only one or a few days. Many children avoid reintegration programmes as a means of reducing the chances that they will be seen as formerly recruited children and stigmatized accordingly. For example, during the war in Angola, child protection workers thought for some years that only boys had been recruited by UNITA, the opposition group. Years after the end of the war in 2002, however, research indicated that thousands of girls had been recruited and had served roles such as porter, 'soldier's wife' and cook.[64] Girls' and women's fears of being stigmatized were so strong that they had deliberately concealed the fact that they had been girl soldiers. In such a context, it would have been inappropriate to set up a reintegration programme and to channel formerly recruited girls through it. In a similar vein, harm can be caused to girls

---

[62] Derluyn et al. 2013; Vindevogel 2017.
[63] See also Casey-Maslen in this volume; Bloom in this volume.
[64] Wessells 2010.

(or boys) by requiring that all former child soldiers go through a formal reintegration programme.

Furthermore, a label such as 'former child soldier' can single out particular children and invite bad behaviour by some people at community level. If, for example, a girl mother enters her community bearing the label 'former child soldier', people who are bitter over how the community had suffered as a result of attacks might denigrate her by calling her 'rebel girl' and calling her child 'rebel child'. By inducing stigma, these labels cause enormous psychosocial distress, particularly in a collectivist context in which people define their well-being in terms of the quality of their relationships with others. Also, the use of negative labels such as 'rebel girl' or 'rebel boy' can remind people of what the rebel group had done, igniting anger among local people over the losses and horrors they had endured. Use of these labels can encourage peers to harass a girl who, being a 'rebel girl', is seen as being sexually promiscuous and also a 'bad' girl. Similarly, it can lead peers to pick a fight with a former boy soldier who is viewed as having been part of the rebel group that had attacked the village.

Worse yet, the derisive labels can help to target individual children for potentially lethal reprisal attacks. In northern Sierra Leone, for example, the label 'former child soldier' reportedly led some community members to 'become hot' and to want to harm or kill the child as a way of getting revenge for the bad things they had done. Fortunately, cooler heads usually prevailed and dissuaded such reprisal attacks.

Both professionals and the media may use negative labels that detract from children's dignity and well-being. It is not uncommon for analysts and reporters to speak of former child soldiers as a 'Lost Generation', which implies that former child soldiers are damaged goods and, ultimately, a burden on society. Similarly, psychologists who are concerned about mental health issues may apply diagnostic labels such as PTSD, which may imply to local people that former child soldiers are crazy, thereby stigmatizing them further. Legal professionals as well as practitioners may use labels such as 'victim' to absolve former child soldiers of any responsibility for the bad things they had done while they were with an armed force or group. Unfortunately, calling former child soldiers 'victims' can add to their sense of helplessness at the very moment when they need to have a sense of agency and self-efficacy, which is central to healing and well-being.[65]

Perhaps the best means of avoiding the problems associated with labelling is to reflect critically on how we, as analysts or practitioners, may deploy labels that are well-intentioned but could cause unintended harm in particular settings. Also, we can use dialogue with former child soldiers to learn from them how they see particular terms and the impact of using particular terminology. This critical awareness and dialogue can help us to take a humanizing approach in discussing former child soldiers and to use non-stigmatizing descriptors, recognizing that there are no 'one size fits all' terms that will universally avoid stigmatization. At the end of the day, we have to be keenly attentive to the local context.

---

[65] Bandura 1977; Bandura 1982.

4.2 Re-Recruitment

Reintegration programmes frequently focus so strongly on enabling former child soldiers to return home to their families and communities that they overlook or downplay the significant risk that former child soldiers will be re-recruited. In Sri Lanka, for example, the Liberation Tigers of Tamil Elan (LTTE) used a quota method of requiring each household to turn over a child. As a result, returned former child soldiers in Sri Lanka on occasion decided to present themselves for enlistment in order to save their siblings from the ordeal of child soldiering.[66] When this happens, reintegration programmes become something of a band-aid or a revolving door, as children repeat cycles of soldiering followed by participation in a reintegration programme.

The causes of re-recruitment are best seen in an ecological perspective.[67] At the individual level, a child who had formerly been abducted by a particular armed group may decide during the reintegration phase to join an opposing group or force as a means of getting revenge for the way in which he or she had been mistreated. Also, individual children may decide that their best chances for achieving security or income lie with membership of an armed group, so they may re-join a national group or even become mercenaries and join armed struggles in other countries. At the family level, too, ongoing pressures to support the family can lead former child soldiers to join an armed force or group as a means of sending money home and helping to meet basic needs. If the conflict is seen by one side as a liberation struggle in which entire families and communities participate, a former child soldier who has returned home could be encouraged or pressured by family and community members to take up the armed struggle again. A highly unfortunate dynamic is that, if former child soldiers are stigmatized when they return to their community, they may decide that civilian life is not for them and return either to the armed group they had been with or to another group. Reintegration programmes can contribute to this dynamic by compounding former child soldiers' stigmatization and doubts that they can fit into civilian life.

To break this cycle and prevent re-recruitment, reintegration programmes should be comprehensive and include strong child protection components, with an abiding emphasis on prevention. Effective preventive work also requires an ecological approach that operates at multiple levels. Families need to emphasize the importance of staying in school and the dangers associated with joining armed forces or groups. At community level, there needs to be monitoring of possible recruiting activities and steps to avoid them by, for example, not having armed forces or groups in or near schools. At the macro-level, there need to be processes or mechanisms that hold child recruiters accountable for their actions. Accountability processes could include a mixture of restorative and retributive approaches, with the mix being tailored to each particular context. The important thing is to take the view that prevention is an ethical imperative, as it is objectionable to take the response-only approach of waiting for children to be (re-)recruited and then picking up the pieces afterwards.

---

[66] Human Rights Watch 2004.
[67] Wessells 2002.

4.3 The Securitization of Reintegration Programming

Globally, concerns about terrorism have evoked widespread public concern and also outright hysteria. If the world was shocked by images of beheadings by the Islamic State (IS), it has been horrified by the extensive recruitment and brainwashing of children with the intent to exploit them as the next generation of suicide bombers, beheaders and terrorists.[68] Political leaders in different countries, including the US, have used fears of 'terrorism' and 'violent extremism' to usher in harsher security measures[69] and immigration policies that are racist and make a mockery of child rights.[70]

The rising fears of 'terrorism' and 'violent extremism' and the associated new security and immigration policies are having a host of negative effects on efforts to reintegrate former child soldiers. One of the most pernicious effects is that security often takes precedence over reintegration. In practice, a country may seek to provide reintegration supports for former child soldiers. But if the children are depicted as 'terrorists', there is often a retreat from children's rights to doing 'whatever it takes' to protect national security. A recent case in point was that of Omar Khadr, a Canadian citizen who was recruited by his father into Al Qaeda.[71] Khadr reportedly threw a grenade at age 15 that killed a US medic in the armed conflict in Afghanistan.[72] Khadr was detained and mistreated at Guantanamo Bay. Plans were drawn up for his reintegration in Canada, where a moderate imam and non-extremist family members were willing to work with him. However, fears about security undermined the reintegration plans. Khadr remained at Guantanamo Bay for ten years. The Supreme Court of Canada ruled that his constitutional right had been violated, but refused to order his repatriation, which was left to the executive branch of government (which at the time had no interest in repatriating him). In 2017, the newly elected Canadian government (under Justin Trudeau) awarded him a cash settlement of $10.5 million. Nevertheless, casting aside the plans for his reintegration violated his rights and amounted to a most unfortunate outcome. The CRC (Article 39) clearly provides that an individual such as Khadr is entitled to psychological support and recovery. It is doubtful that any meaningful recovery is possible in situations that are viewed primarily as urgent issues of national security. This kind of framing frequently justifies detaining suspects militarily outside the scope of civilian law, tramples civil rights, and creates conditions tragically conducive to the use of torture and cruel, inhuman and degrading treatment.

Securitization can be a problem even in cases in which there is a reintegration process. Overall, the securitization concerns tend to pull reintegration programmes away from their humanitarian and human rights roots. Imagine, for example, what might happen if a hardened group of IS teenagers were captured. It is not difficult to imagine that during a reintegration programme, security personnel might question the teenagers in the hopes of obtaining actionable security information. In this manner, the reintegration process

---

[68] For accounts of children recruited by IS and by Boko Haram, see Bloom and Casey-Maslen respectively in this volume.
[69] O'Neil and Van Broeckoven 2017.
[70] For discussion of child rights in the refugee and asylum context, see Rikhof in this volume.
[71] For a detailed review of the Khadr case, see Rosen in this volume.
[72] For an account of child soldiers in Afghanistan, see Van Engeland in this volume.

could be used as a 'front' for a security process. Even if torture and abuse were not part of this process, this would amount to a subversion of the reintegration process, and an exploitation of the former child soldiers in ways that could subsequently get them killed. Further, if the former IS teenagers returned to civilian life, they would likely carry the extreme stigma of 'terrorist' with them and continue to be targets for people who want to kill terrorists or, alternately, for IS members who saw them as having divulged information or as now being significant security risks.

Although the securitization of reintegration processes can cause significant harm, no easy paths or means of addressing these concerns exist. Necessary steps include the development of policies and measures that protect the rights of former child soldiers, processes of humanization that help former child soldiers to be seen as actual persons rather than as terrorists or bloodthirsty killers, policies that prevent the use of torture and the abuse of detained children, and public education that helps to inoculate citizens against public hysteria and the fear tactics of political leaders.

5. CONCLUSION

The diversity and magnitude of these do no harm issues indicate the need for more concerted attention to ethical imperatives in efforts to reintegrate former child soldiers. Together, these issues suggest that it is not enough for reintegration programmes to be called successful because they have achieved their expected positive outcomes. Attention must also be paid to any unintended outcomes as well, particularly to negative outcomes. In keeping with the ethical principles of beneficence and non-maleficence, reintegration programmes must simultaneously achieve a mixture of relatively high levels of positive outcomes for children and a relatively low level of harmful outcomes for children.

These diverse ethical issues serve as poignant reminders that reintegration work requires keen ethical sensitivities, and a clear eye for the way in which programmes may cause unintended harm to children. They suggest that reintegration practitioners need to maintain a stance of critical reflexivity in their work and engage in ongoing dialogue and co-learning in regard to ethical issues and how to manage and prevent them. Perhaps most important, they must have a strong commitment to adapt and change course as they learn about unintended consequences for children. Until now, there has been a general reluctance to document do no harm issues in reintegration work, most likely due to concerns over loss of image, funding, or both. This approach, too, needs to change.

REFERENCED WORKS

Akello, G. 2010. *Wartime Children's Suffering and Quests for Therapy in Northern Uganda (African Studies Collection, No. 25)* (Leiden: African Studies Centre)

Akello, G. 2013. 'Experiences of Forced Mothers in Northern Uganda: The Legacy of War' 11 *Intervention* 149

Akello, G. 2017. 'Health Care Services to War-Affected Children in Northern Uganda: Accounting for Discrepancies Between Interventions and Children's Needs', in M. Denov and B. Akesson (eds), *Children Affected by Armed Conflict: Theory, Method, and Practice* (New York: Columbia University Press) 233

Akello, G., Richters, A. and Reis, R. 2006. 'Reintegration of Former Child Soldiers in Northern Uganda: Coming to Terms with Children's Agency and Accountability' 4 *Intervention* 229

Allen, T. 2005. *War and Justice in Northern Uganda: An Assessment of the International Criminal Court's Intervention* (London: London School of Economics)

Allen, T. 2010. 'Bitter Roots: The "Invention" of Acholi Traditional Justice', in T. Allen and K. Vlassenroot (eds), *The Lord's Resistance Army: Myth and Reality* (London: Zed Books) 1

Allen, T. and Schomerus, M. 2006. *A Hard Homecoming: Lessons Learned from the Reception Center Process on Effective Interventions for Former 'Abductees' in Northern Uganda*. An independent report commissioned by USAID and UNICEF (Washington, DC: Management Systems International)

Allen, T. and Vlassenroot, K. 2010. 'Introduction', in T. Allen and K. Vlassenroot (eds), *The Lord's Resistance Army: Myth and Reality* (London: Zed Books) 242

Amone-P'Olak, K. 2004. 'A Study of the Psychological State of Former Abducted Children at Gulu World Vision Trauma Centre' 14 *Torture* 24

Amone-P'Olak, K. 2005. 'Psychological Impact of War and Sexual Abuse on Adolescent Girls in Northern Uganda' 3 *Intervention* 33

Amone-P'Olak, K. 2009. 'Torture Against Children in Rebel Captivity in Northern Uganda: Physical and Psychological Effects and Implications for Clinical Practice' 19 *Torture* 102

Amone-P'Olak, K., Jones, P.G., Abbott, R., Meiser-Stedman, R., Ovuga, E. and Croudace, T.J. 2013. 'Cohort Profile: Mental Health Following Extreme Trauma in a Northern Ugandan Cohort of War-Affected Youth Study (The WAYS) Study' 2 *SpringerPlus* 300.

Anderson, M. 1999. *Do No Harm: How Aid Can Support Peace – or War* (Boulder, CO: Lynne Rienner)

Annan, J., Blattman, C. and Horton, R. 2006. *The State of Youth and Youth Protection in Northern Uganda: Findings from the Survey for War Affected Youth* (Kampala: UNICEF)

Apio, E. 2008. *Bearing the Burden of Blame – The Children Born of the Lord's Resistance Army, Northern Uganda* (London: Coalition to Stop the Use of Child Soldiers)

Australian Aid, Belgian Development Cooperation, Government of Canada, German Humanitarian Assistance et al. 2016. *The Grand Bargain – A Shared Commitment to Better Serve People in Need* (Istanbul, Turkey)

Baines, E. 2005. 'Roco Wat I Acholi/Restoring Relationships in Acholi-Land: Traditional Approaches to Justice and Reconciliation', Gulu: Conflict and Development Programme (Liu Institute for Global Issues, Gulu District NGO Forum and Ker Kwaro Acholi)

Baines, E. 2007. 'The Haunting of Alice: Local Approaches to Justice and Reconciliation in Northern Uganda' 1 *The International Journal of Transitional Justice* 91

Baines, E. 2017. *Buried in the Heart: Women, Complex Victimhood and the War in Northern Uganda* (New York: Cambridge University Press)

Bandura, A. 1977. 'Self-Efficacy: Toward a Unifying Theory of Behavioral Change' 84 *Psychological Review* 191

Bandura, A. 1982. 'Self-Efficacy Mechanism in Human Agency' 37 *American Psychologist* 122

Betancourt, T.S., Agnew-Blais, J., Gilman, S.E., Williams, D.R. and Ellis, B.H. 2010. 'Past Horrors, Present Struggles: The Role of Stigma in the Association Between War Experiences and Psychosocial Adjustment Among Former Child Soldiers in Sierra Leone' 70 *Social Science & Medicine* 17

Betancourt, T. and Williams, T. 2008. 'Building an Evidence Base on Mental Health Interventions for Children Affected by Armed Conflict' 6 *Intervention* 39

Boyden, J. 2003. 'The Moral Development of Child Soldiers' 9 *Peace and Conflict: Journal of Peace Psychology* 343.

Brett, R. and Specht, I. 2004. *Young Soldiers* (Boulder, CO: Lynne Rienner)

Child Protection Working Group 2012. *Minimum Standards for Child Protection in Humanitarian Action* (Geneva: Author)

Columbia Group for Children in Adversity (forthcoming). *Supporting Community-Led Child Protection Processes: A Guide and Toolkit for Reflective Practice* (New York: Author)

Denov, M. and Lakor, A.A. 2017. 'When War Is Better than Peace: The Post-Conflict Realities of Children Born of Wartime Rape in Northern Uganda' 65 *Child Abuse & Neglect* 255

Derluyn, I., Vindevogel, S. and De Haene, L. 2013. 'Towards a Relational Understanding of the Reintegration and Rehabilitation Processes of Former Child Soldiers' 22 *Journal of Aggression, Maltreatment & Trauma* 869

Dolan, C. 2009. *Social Torture: The Case of Northern Uganda 1986–2006* (New York: Berghahn)

Drumbl, M. 2012. *Reimagining Child Soldiers in International Law and Policy* (Oxford: Oxford University Press)

Hobfoll, S.E, Watson, P., Bell, C.C., Bryant, R.A., Brymer, M.J., Friedman, M.J., Friedman, M., Gersons, B.P.R., de Jong, J.T.V.M., Layne, C.M., Maguen, S., Neria, Y., Norwood, A.E., Pynoos, R.S, Reissman, D., Ruzek, J.I., Shalev, A.Y., Solomon, Z., Steinberg, A.M. and Ursano, R.J. 2007. 'Five Essential Elements of Immediate and Mid-Term Mass Trauma Intervention: Empirical Evidence' 70 *Psychiatry* 283

Honwana, A. 2006. *Child Soldiers in Africa* (Philadelphia: University of Pennsylvania Press)

Human Rights Watch 2003. *Stolen Children: Abduction and Recruitment in Northern Uganda* (New York: Author)

Human Rights Watch 2004. *Living in Fear* (New York: Author)

Humphries, M. and Weinstein, J.M. 2007. 'Demobilization and Reintegration' 51 *Journal of Conflict Resolution* 531

Kiyala, J.C.K. 2015. 'Challenges of Reintegrating Self-Demobilised Child Soldiers in North Kivu Province: Prospects for Accountability and Reconciliation Via Restorative Justice Peacemaking Circles' 19 *Human Rights Review* 99

Kiyala, J.C.K. 2018. *Child Soldiers and Restorative Justice* (New York: Springer)

Lenz, J. 2017. 'Armed with Resilience: Tapping into the Experiences and Survival Skills of Formerly Abducted Girl Child Soldiers in Northern Uganda', in M. Denov and B. Akesson (eds), *Children Affected by Armed Conflict: Theory, Method, and Practice* (New York: Columbia University Press) 112

McKay, S. and Mazurana, D. 2004. *Where Are the Girls?* (Montreal: International Centre for Human Rights and Democratic Development)

McKay, S., Veale, A., Worthen, M. and Wessells, M. 2011. 'Building Meaningful Participation in Reintegration Among War-Affected Young Mothers in Liberia, Sierra Leone and Northern Uganda' 9 *Intervention* 108

Miller, K. and Rasmussen, A. 2010. 'War Exposure, Daily Stressors, and Mental Health in Conflict and Post-Conflict Settings: Bridging the Divide Between Trauma-Focused and Psychosocial Frameworks' 70 *Social Science & Medicine* 7

Moscardino, U., Scrimin, S., Cadei, F. and Altoe, G. 2012. 'Mental Health Among Former Child Soldiers and Never-Abducted Children in Northern Uganda' *The Scientific World Journal*

Neuner, F., Pfeiffer, A., Schauer-Kaiser, E., Odenwald, M., Elbert, T. and Ertl, V. 2012. 'Haunted by Ghosts: Prevalence, Predictors and Outcomes of Spirit Possession Experiences Among Former Child Soldiers and War-Affected Civilians in Northern Uganda' 75 *Social Science & Medicine* 548

Okello, J., De Schryver, M., Muisi, S., Broekaert, E. and Derluyn, I. 2014. 'Differential Roles of Childhood Adversities and Stressful War Experiences in the Development of Mental Health Symptoms in Post-War Adolescents in Northern Uganda' 14 *BMC Psychiatry* 260

O'Neil, S. and Van Broeckhoven, K. (eds) 2017. *Cradled by Conflict: Child Involvement with Armed Groups in Contemporary Conflict* (New York: United Nations University)

Pfeiffer, A. and Elbert, T. 2011. 'PTSD, Depression and Anxiety Among Former Abductees in Northern Uganda' 5 *Conflict and Health* 14

Roberts, B., Ocaka, K.F., Browne, J., Oyok, T. and Sondorp, E. 2008. 'Factors Associated with Post-Traumatic Stress Disorder and Depression Among Internally Displaced Persons in Northern Uganda' 8 *BMC Psychiatry* 38

Schultz, J.H. and Weisaeth, L. 2015. 'The Power of Rituals in Dealing with Traumatic Stress Symptoms: Cleansing Rituals for Former Child Soldiers in Northern Uganda' 18 *Mental Health, Religion, & Culture* 822

Slim, H. 2015. *Humanitarian Ethics: A Guide to the Morality of Aid in War and Disaster* (New York: Oxford University Press)

Tonheim, M. 2012. '"Who Will Comfort Me?" Stigmatization of Girls Formerly Associated with Armed Forces and Groups in Eastern Congo' 12 *The International Journal of Human Rights* 278

Tonheim, M. 2014. 'Genuine Social Inclusion or Superficial Co-Existence?' 18 *The International Journal of Human Rights* 634

Triandis H. 2001. 'Individualism and Collectivism', in D. Matsumoto (ed.), *The Handbook of Culture and Psychology* (New York: Oxford University Press) 35

UN 2006. *Integrated DDR Standards* (New York: United Nations Disarmament, Demobilization and Reintegration Resource Centre)

UNICEF 2018. *New Global Estimates of Child Marriage* (New York: Author)

UNICEF and SRSG [United Nations Office of the Special Representative of the Secretary-General for Children and Armed Conflict] 2009. 'Machel Study 10-year Strategic Review: Children and Conflict in a Changing World' (New York: Author)

Verhey, B. 2001. *Child Soldiers: Preventing, Demobilizing and Reintegrating*, Africa Region Working Paper Series no. 23 (Washington, DC: World Bank)

Vinck, P., Pham, P.N., Stover, E. and Weinstein, H.M. 2007. 'Exposure to War Crimes and Implications for Peace Building in Northern Uganda' 298 *JAMA* 543

Vindevogel, S. 2017. 'Resilience in the Context of War: A Critical Analysis of Contemporary Conceptions and Interventions to Promote Resilience Among War-Affected Children and Their Surroundings' 23 *Peace and Conflict: Journal of Peace Psychology* 76

Wessells, M. 2002. 'Recruitment of Children as Soldiers in sub-Saharan Africa: An Ecological Analysis', in L. Mjoset and S. Van Holde (eds), *The Comparative Study of Conscription in the Armed Forces (Comparative Social Research, Vol. 20)* (Amsterdam: Elsevier) 237

Wessells, M. 2006. *Child Soldiers: From Violence to Protection* (Cambridge, MA: Harvard University Press)

Wessells, M. 2009a. 'Supporting the Mental Health and Psychosocial Well-Being of Former Child Soldiers' 48 *Journal of the American Academy of Child and Adolescent Psychiatry* 587

Wessells, M. 2009b. 'Do No Harm: Toward Contextually Appropriate Psychosocial Support in International Emergencies' 64 *American Psychologist* 842

Wessells, M. 2010. 'The Recruitment and Use of Girls in Armed Forces and Armed Groups in Angola: Implications for Ethical Research and Reintegration', in S. Gates and S. Reich (eds), *Child Soldiers in the Age of Fractured States* (Pittsburgh: University of Pittsburgh Press) 183

Wessells, M. 2015. 'Bottom-Up Approaches to Strengthening Child Protection Systems: Placing Children, Families, and Communities at the Center' 43 *Child Abuse & Neglect: The International Journal* 8

Wessells, M.G. and Monteiro, C. 2004. 'Healing the Wounds Following Protracted Conflict in Angola: A Community-Based Approach to Assisting War-Affected Children', in U.P. Gielen, J. Fish and J.G. Draguns (eds), *Handbook of Culture, Therapy, and Healing* (Mahwah, NJ: Erlbaum) 321

West, H. 2004. 'Girls with Guns: Narrating the Experience of War of FRELIMO's "Female Detachment"', in J. Boyden and J. de Berry (eds), *Children and Youth on the Front Line* (New York; Oxford: Berghahn Books) 105

23. How to find the 'hidden' girl soldier? Two sets of suggestions arising from Liberia
Leena Vastapuu

> [W]e must ask girls to tell their own stories of war, its impact on them, and ask for potential solutions rather than assume the right to speak for them.[1]

If calculating the exact number of child soldiers in general is a challenging task, estimating the number of girl soldiers in particular is nothing short of impossible. Currently, we simply do not have enough reliable data to undertake this kind of calculation.[2] Sometimes rough estimations such as 'between one-tenth and one-third of all child soldiers'[3] have been made, yet how these numbers are derived is rarely disclosed. At other times, numbers are drawn from Disarmament, Demobilization and Reintegration (DDR) programmes' participant lists. This approach is certainly misleading since it is well known that most female soldiers, especially in African conflicts, do not participate in these programmes if specific efforts are not made to encourage their participation.[4] Therefore, to obtain a comprehensive understanding of the phenomenon of girl soldiering, and thus better equip ourselves to respond to the needs of girl soldiers/veterans in DDR programmes and beyond, an acute need arises for more empirical data from a variety of warscapes around the world. The major challenge with this task is that girl soldiers/veterans are often difficult to find.[5]

In this autoethnographic chapter, I describe some of the challenges and successes which I have encountered in my own research project with former girl soldiers in Liberia between 2012 and 2014. Whilst each conflict environment is context-specific and thus has distinct internal conflict and gender dynamics,[6] I maintain that some generalizations can be drawn from this particular case study. The motivation for writing the piece is a practical one: My aim is to produce the kind of chapter I would have once yearned to read myself, preferably before embarking for Liberia for the very first time.

After first setting the scene, the chapter is divided into two main sections. The first part is targeted primarily at researchers who aim to undertake empirical fieldwork on the ground. Relying strongly on my personal research journals and autobiographical notes from Liberia, I critically reflect on the successes and challenges of the approach I took in this research project. In addition, I discuss the 'do no harm' principle, with the overall aim of debunking the myth of a 'super-human researcher'.[7] The second main section of

---

[1] Nordstrom 1998: 87.
[2] See Rosen in this volume.
[3] Fox 2004: 465.
[4] Coulter et al. 2008: 20.
[5] Nordstrom 1997: 37–8.
[6] Eriksson Baaz and Stern 2014: 161; and Vastapuu 2018.
[7] Marshall 2011.

the chapter is directed mainly at DDR officers undertaking very challenging screening interviews with child soldiers on the ground. In addition, this second main section might prove useful to anyone wishing to create a holistic understanding of the actual number of girls, women, boys and men in any fighting faction. Before moving forward to the first main section of the chapter, a few general remarks on Liberia's civil wars, girl soldiers, DDR programmes and the research data informing this article have to be made.

1. SETTING THE SCENE

1.1 Liberia in War

Liberia's first civil war began on 24 December 1989 when Charles Taylor led between 100 and 200 fighters to Nimba County from Côte d'Ivoire. Taylor's multi-ethnic force, called the National Patriotic Front of Liberia (NPFL), had the goal of deposing President Samuel Doe, who acted also as the commander-in-chief of the Armed Forces of Liberia (AFL). Taylor's forces grew at an astounding rate, such that within a few months he had over 20,000 soldiers under his command.[8] Before the Abuja II Accord (a treaty that marked the end of the first civil war of Liberia) was finally signed in August 1996, at least 13 peace agreements had been negotiated, but failed to end the conflict. In addition to the AFL and NPFL, there were several smaller fighting factions taking part in the hostilities, of which the most notorious were the Independent National Patriotic Front of Liberia (INPFL) and the United Liberation Movement of Liberia (ULIMO), which later split into two groups: ULIMO-J and ULIMO-K. After the first civil war of Liberia, not only the country but also the wider Mano river region were in chaos, and tens of thousands of Liberians had lost their lives.[9]

Between 1997 and 2000 a period of relative peace held fast in Liberia. Charles Taylor had won the 1997 elections, with his National Patriotic Party gaining over 75 per cent of the vote, and had finally managed to fulfil his dream of becoming the president.[10] Taylor was, however, unwilling to integrate former enemy soldiers into the AFL which was now under his command, and the government under his leadership suffered from instability. In the meantime, a new faction called Liberians United for Reconciliation and Democracy (LURD) was forming behind the scenes with the goal of deposing Taylor.

The second civil war of Liberia began in the early 2000s at the border with Guinea when LURD attacked AFL. In 2002, a faction called the Movement for Democracy in Liberia (MODEL) came onto the scene, also with the aim of overthrowing the government. Taylor, who had been weakened by UN sanctions, was incapable of fighting a two-front war against forces that had significant support from outside powers. He was therefore forced to participate in peace talks organized in Ghana in June 2003.[11] In August, ECOWAS launched its Nigerian-led mission in Liberia (ECOMIL), with support from

---

[8] Moran 2006: 16.
[9] Bøås 2005: 82.
[10] Kieh 2008: 156.
[11] Bøås 2005.

the United Nations Mission in Liberia (UNMIL). Charles Taylor handed over the presidency and left the country the same month, and the Comprehensive Peace Agreement (CPA) was signed on 18 August 2003. The National Transitional Government of Liberia (NTGL) began its duties the following October.

Child soldiering was a characteristic feature in both Liberian civil wars, and at least 38,500 child soldiers participated in warfare duties. It has been estimated that around 10 per cent of Liberia's child soldiers were girls,[12] although my research data suggest the number to be as high as 40 per cent. It must therefore again be emphasized that there are currently no reliable data on the number of girl soldiers in the country. In Liberia, a reference point has often been taken from the participant lists of DDR programmes implemented after the wars. This perspective is inherently flawed since most of Liberia's female soldiers did not take part in these programmes – according to my data only around 14 per cent of female soldiers went successfully through the whole process in the country.[13] In addition, it is often forgotten that the term 'girl soldier' does not only refer to young women carrying guns but also to girls who have been acting in supporting roles, for example as cooks, spies, carriers or sexual servants. When estimating the percentage of female soldiers, it is an easy trap to take account only of the frontline fighters and not the 'invisible' supporting units that run the daily routines for the troops.[14]

1.2 Introduction to DDR

In light of the composition of modern DDR programmes, we can identify a major turning point in world politics. After the end of the Cold War, the UN Security Council requested Boutros-Boutros-Ghali, the newly elected Secretary-General, to prepare an analysis of how to strengthen the UN's capacities in the areas of peace-making and peacekeeping.[15] The resulting report entitled 'An Agenda for Peace'[16] is often understood as the 'genesis of the DDR process' as we know it today.[17] The basic idea of any DDR programme is to support the reintegration of former soldiers (back) into civilian life through a step-by-step approach. According to the UN:

> DDR lays the groundwork for safeguarding and sustaining the communities in which these individuals can live as law-abiding citizens, while building national capacity for long-term peace, security and development. It is important to note that DDR alone cannot resolve conflict or prevent violence; it can, however, help establish a secure environment so that other elements of a recovery and peace-building strategy can proceed.[18]

Disarmament is a rather straightforward process where arms, ammunition and other weaponry are collected and documented in a period of a few hours or days.[19] *Demobilization*

---

[12] Achvarina and Reich: 2006.
[13] See also Basini 2013.
[14] See also Vastapuu 2018.
[15] UNSC 1992: 3.
[16] UN 1992.
[17] E.g. Knight 2008: 25.
[18] IDDRS 2006 [module 1.10, 2].
[19] See Casey-Maslen in this volume.

means the discharge of soldiers from armed forces typically to assembly areas or cantonment sites where former soldiers are provided with different benefits ranging from small support packages to direct cash transfers. This second step of demobilization is sometimes referred to as reinsertion and can entail various support measures, including, but not limited to, medical care, clothing, educational programmes and food aid. Demobilization is a longer process than disarmament since its aim is to disband former soldiers and begin the process of turning them into civilians. Demobilization can take up to one year, depending on the programme. *Reintegration*, in turn, is the most challenging part of any DDR programme. The aim of this process is to reintegrate former soldiers into civilian networks at the community level and on a sustainable basis. This process is highly demanding and takes several years. The challenges are legion, of which one is the need to consider not only the individual soldier but also the wider societal context into which the veteran is supposed to reintegrate.[20]

What is often ignored in the academic literature on DDR is the tremendous effect of the screening process on the success or failure of any DDR programme. According to the UN's Integrated Disarmament, Demobilization and Reintegration Standards,[21] the main responsibility for deciding who can enter a DDR programme is assigned to military personnel. Even though the military side is supported by civilian personnel, and there should always be a list of the specific eligibility criteria on which the screening process is based, the emphasis on military know-how has inevitable consequences for the programme's outcomes.[22] This challenge and its consequences are further discussed in the second main section of this chapter.

1.3 Why Girls Get Left Behind in DDR: What Do We Know?

As Dyan Mazurana and Linda Eckerbom Cole remark, although 'there have been important advances in how DDR programmes are designed and implemented, the invisibility and marginalization of women and girls within DDR processes continue'.[23] Mazurana and Eckerbom Cole have identified several reasons for this failure that can be traced back as far as the peace negotiation stage.[24] Firstly, girls and women in general – and those in particular who have detailed knowledge on gender composition in different fighting forces – are rarely invited to the negotiating table. As a result, the eligibility criteria for entering the programme might be set too high and thus favour male combatants. Where the entry criteria allow for the participation of soldiers without serviceable weapons or particular rounds of ammunition, an effective and well-functioning communication strategy that reaches communities is very difficult to implement in war-devastated environments. In practice, information about the

---

[20] UN 2006a; Knight and Özerdem 2004; Özerdem 2012; see also Casey-Maslen in this volume. Sometimes additional letters such as R for Rehabilitation are added to the abbreviation DDR in Liberia (thus the programmes implemented after the civil wars are commonly referred to as DDRR). For the sake of clarity, however, I will use the abbreviation DDR throughout the chapter.
[21] IDDRS 2006 [module 4.10, 9–12].
[22] Ibid.
[23] Mazurana and Eckerbom Cole 2013: 194.
[24] Ibid.: 202–6, 212.

DDR programmes is often channelled through (male) commanders and other senior members of the fighting forces – a process that tends to privilege male combatants over girls and women. Related to communication challenges, male commanders are typically asked to provide lists of soldiers within their respective forces; lists that also tend to favour boys and men. In addition, the attitudes of DDR officers themselves might be militarized and gendered, resulting in priority being placed on taming the 'main security threat', that is, young (idle) men.[25] And finally, even if all the previous obstacles are conquered and girl and women soldiers are aware of their right to sign up to the programme, they might prefer not to do so for practical and/or personal reasons. Practical reasons include the distance to the disarmament site, family obligations and caretaking responsibilities, as well as the need to feed their families. Among personal reasons, the fear of stigmatization on a communal level or within the family is typically referenced. For these multiple reasons the 'self-demobilization' of girls and women regularly occurs.[26] The tendency of female soldiers to 'self-demobilize' as well as 'self-reintegrate' is a remarkable feature that should be carefully considered at all the stages of a DDR programme.

In Liberia, a DDR programme was planned and implemented following both civil wars. Even though it was explicitly stated in both programmes that the specific needs of children and women would be taken into account at all stages, the results were poor in both instances.[27] All in all, it can be surmised that DDR programmes in Liberia following both civil wars were highly militarized and gendered from the start, with the consequence being the wide exclusion of women and girl soldiers from all stages.[28] The neglect of girl and women soldiers in Liberia is especially disheartening since the United Nations Mission in Liberia (UNMIL) was the first peacekeeping mission ever with an explicit mandate to mainstream[29] United Nations Security Council Resolution (UNSCR) 1325.[30] Furthermore, although several evaluations and reports highlighted the need to make adjustments to the second DDR programme,[31] the recommendations were largely ignored, and girl and women soldiers were left to fend for themselves.[32]

1.4 General Remarks on the Research Data

The research data that this chapter draws from were collected between 2012 and 2014 in Liberia primarily using a method I name the auto-photographic research approach. This belongs to the wider selection of participant-generated image methods that have gained

---

[25] Jennings 2009; Kays 2005.
[26] E.g. Mazurana et al. 2002; Shepler 2002; Shepler 2014; Brett and Specht 2004; McKay and Mazurana 2004; Coulter 2009; Basini 2013; Vastapuu 2018.
[27] Vastapuu 2018: 95–9.
[28] Ibid.: 109–12.
[29] Njoki Wamai 2011: 53; Basini 2013: 71.
[30] UN Security Council Resolution 1325 was approved unanimously on 31 October 2000. The resolution stresses the importance of adopting a gender perspective assessing all stages of the conflict and its aftermath. Since Resolution 1325 was adopted, six complementary Security Council Resolutions have been adopted.
[31] E.g. Bernard et al. 2003: [94]; Bugnion et al. 2006; UN 2006b [7, note 23].
[32] Vastapuu 2018: 85–114.

popularity in recent years, especially in the fields of visual sociology and anthropology.[33] In practice, I conducted 133 informative interviews with former girl soldiers in the towns of Monrovia, Kakata, Gbarnga and Ganta. At this interview stage, I wanted to map out basic information about the roles and experiences of the interviewees during the civil wars and their aftermath. I analysed these data using the NVivo programme. I then selected 25 key interviewees and provided them with a camera each that I had previously gathered from my home country as donations. After explaining the purpose of this process and gaining (oral) informed consent, I asked the key interviewees to photograph their current lives under the themes of 'my current realities' and 'my aspirations/dreams for the future'. This rather laborious process resulted in thousands of pictures and highly fascinating photo elicitation interviews.[34] In these interviews, the printed photos were placed one by one in front of the interviewee who then explained why she had wanted to capture that specific photograph and what meaning she derived from it. As a small courtesy, each interviewee was given the camera she had used in the process.

In addition to these data, I had several discussions with former boy and men soldiers, community elders and local youth. Furthermore, I also organized group discussions with local journalists (one group); prostitutes (three groups) and a village meeting in the close proximity of Gbarnga. All the interview data were transcribed and analysed with the NVivo programme.

2. FINDING THE GIRL SOLDIER AS A RESEARCHER: AUTOBIOGRAPHICAL REMARKS

Up to this point, the present chapter has dealt with issues of which I had a rough knowledge myself before heading to Liberia for the first time in 2012. I had tried to read as much as possible on the wars and their aftermath; I also had discussions with several scholars who had conducted fieldwork in, and thus had an in-depth knowledge of, the country; additionally, I contacted possible reference persons in the NGO sector and beyond. Furthermore, I had managed to gather a rather impressive number of donated cameras from friendly individuals around Finland. Despite all these preparations, however, I felt a fair amount of anxiety during the weeks and days prior to my departure to Monrovia.

2.1 Embarking for Liberia for the Very First Time

> Whoa, I'm soon on my way. Within the next 25 minutes, I will board the plane to Frankfurt with the destination Brussels, from where I'll take another plane to Monrovia . . . It was such a hustle with getting all the paperwork done at the customs at the airport, owing to the cameras I currently have in my luggage. But now I should have everything – the correct papers, the correct stamps, the correct signatures from the Uni. At this moment, I feel bizarrely calm and balanced. Maybe because there is nothing else to do than to get into the plane and go. The situation was quite different only a few days ago, though . . . I guess my anxieties with this trip have had a lot to do with all the horrible stories that I have read and seen on-line, the torture, rape, atrocities, all that. About how we can all become monsters when the situation is 'favourable'. But I know that

---

[33] Balomenou and Garrod 2015.
[34] Harper 2002; Balomenou and Garrod 2015.

there is another side with all this, too. There is always the boring and beloved everyday life, the foundation for everything valuable and good. That is what I'm heading to Liberia to search for. And, if lucky, maybe I'll hear a few stories about the lives of former girl soldiers during the war and its aftermath. If only I'm lucky. (29 August 2012, excerpt from personal research journal)[35]

It seems that there is never enough time to prepare oneself for a trip to a far-away destination, but this seemed to be especially true whilst I was getting ready to go to Liberia for the very first time. In practice this meant, for instance: contacting the ethics board to gain research approval; obtaining official documents (with stamps!) and the travel visa; exchanging endless messages and phone calls with 'anyone who knows anything' about the country; having vaccinations and obtaining anti-malarial medication; arranging insurance and finding accommodation, with poor phone reception and an even worse understanding of Liberian English; the need to sort out everything at home while being away; endless background reading; and of course monetary issues. Regarding money, I was advised to carry with me everything in cash that I anticipated needing within the planned two months – and so I acquired a proper money belt stacked with USD $100 bills in it and felt ridiculous. My first advice? Schedule enough time for sorting out everything – and add at least two weeks to the amount of time that you feel is 'surely enough'.

2.2 Settling In

I spent the first night in Monrovia in a pre-booked traveller's home and met my future flatmate as well as research assistant, Glorious, in these premises early the next morning. I had received her contact details from a fellow researcher, who had not only provided me with very valuable practical tips prior to my departure, but also asked around for a trustworthy young woman in Monrovia for me to share a flat with. And so, after many phone calls over the previous months, Glorious now stood in front of me; she seemed a bit shy and terribly young, but nonetheless someone with whom I instantly felt comfortable.

After a few hours, it became evident that the neighbourhood where Glorious lived was far from luxurious. In pouring rain, we had run with my heavy luggage into a shabby quarter, balanced on slippery duckboards surrounded by murky water with all imaginable trash in it, greeted curious neighbours, marched through mud puddles, and finally found ourselves in our temporary home with bottles of local beer placed in our hands immediately after entering the house. Although located in a shanty town, the house was still luxurious in comparison with some other residential buildings in the area: it had concrete walls and an iron door, a small porch as well as a TV set, and, most importantly, an inside (= secure) toilet. There was no running water nor electricity, but I was told that every day enough water and coal would be purchased for our daily needs and, on occasion, some petrol would be bought and the small generator turned on for the TV. The mobile phone and laptop could be charged in commercial 'charging booths' one could find everywhere, some fresh bread and instant coffee was available in the nearby kiosk in the morning hours, and we could immediately go to buy a mosquito net from the pharmacy next door.

I would be taken care of, I was assured, and hurried into the master bedroom that would

---

[35] Translations (Finnish–English) by the author.

be mine for now, 'no question about it'. The monthly rent was US$50 – precisely the same amount I had paid for my previous night at the guest house – and with a small daily fee, I could also have a daily Liberian meal prepared by Glorious or the owner of the house. The owner herself turned out to be a brisk and strong woman in her late 30s, armoured with a very thick Liberian accent and a raspy laugh. In addition to these women, there were also two young boys sharing the house with us: relatives of the owner, I was told, who would help us with the housekeeping duties and have a chance to go to school in return. I felt extremely privileged and happy, at least according to my research journal.

Although I could not return to this same house during my next field research periods[36] due to some security worries on the one hand (two 'immigration officers' began constantly asking for my passport apparently looking for bribes), and relationship disputes within the family on the other hand, I still have very warm feelings whenever I think about this first 'home' of mine in Liberia.

2.3 Finding the Girl Soldier? Or Rather, the Other Way Around?

After about a week, I had managed to meet every person with whom I had been in contact already by email prior to my departure. Everyone turned out to be extremely nice and helpful, but my main goal of finding former girl soldiers had not thus far been achieved as a result of these encounters. Furthermore, although my understanding of Liberian English had somewhat improved, the owner of the house still had difficulties in understanding what I wanted to say to her. Therefore, I asked if Glorious would be available for a temporary job as a research assistant – a position she gladly approved. We made a good team from the start: it became evident that Glorious was very talented socially as well as emotionally, and she patiently explained to me all kinds of cultural customs and practical tips that I would need in my everyday life in Monrovia. I learnt, for instance, how to wave my hand the right way for getting around the town with public cars or motorbikes, how to wash laundry by hand in the yard without making myself look completely ridiculous, and how to flush the toilet without wasting a whole bucket of water in the process. During the evenings, we usually sat on the porch and 'lectured' (discussed) about everything with local youth who entered the house on a regular basis. Later, I learnt that the youth were in fact lured to the porch not only by the opportunity to lecture, but also by 'eggnog' – a cannabis-spiced drink the owner prepared and sold under the counter to earn some extra income. As the neighbourhood soon proved to be very risky with armed robberies and street violence regularly occurring, the owner had in this manner created a very clever security network to safeguard the house. The local youth, some of whom were quite possibly involved in the attacks themselves, were on her side, anytime.

It was in this house where I first got to know some former child soldiers. From the start, I had been relatively open about my 'agenda' in Liberia, and thus rumours had started to circulate. Apparently, I had been observed for a while to see what I was made of before some of the more curious young veterans began to approach me themselves. I made it very clear to everyone that I had nothing to give except for the occasional meal or

---

[36] For the purposes of this project, I undertook three separate field research trips to four counties in Liberia between 2012 and 2014. In total, I gathered research data for just over five months.

drink as well as explaining in detail what my research was all about. Thus, the snowball began to roll. The majority of my research participants from Monrovia were found in this manner. In addition, I organized a small group of interviewees through the contacts of an NGO employee, and a Monrovia-based reverend provided some valuable contacts for 'setting the ball rolling' in the rest of the research spots. Therefore, quite surprisingly, it was actually I who was found by the interviewees, and not the other way around. Being aware of both the dangers of 'victimcy talk'[37] – where interviewees deliberately present themselves as victims in order to gain expected benefits – and possible research and/or NGO fatigue,[38] I was more than happy about this turn of events.[39]

2.4 Some Practical Lessons on the Do No Harm Principle[40]

The ambiguities and challenges of the obligation to do no harm in war-devastated environments are well debated both in the humanitarian field as well as in academia.[41] Prior my departure, I had read and discussed extensively what the do no harm principle would likely mean in practice on the ground in Liberia, yet I soon came to learn that my pre-readings had not quite prepared me for the situations I was about to encounter in my everyday life. In this section, I present some of the practical lessons drawn mainly from my research journals. Let us, however, begin with a methodological discussion.

There are valid reasons why one cannot find any photographs in this chapter, despite the chosen research methods. Already in November 2012, it began to occur to me what problems published photographs might cause in practical terms for the research interviewees themselves, even after an extended period of time. My personal wake-up call was a phone call coming from Monrovia from an interviewee called Juliet. She sounded anxious and agitated while urging me to 'tell the BBC' to remove her picture from the Internet.[42] Juliet had just discovered that a close-up photograph of her holding an AK-47 was online, and her face was easily recognisable through the screen of a computer. According to Juliet, the photograph was taken during the second Liberian civil war from a helicopter that had suddenly appeared above her. As quickly as the helicopter had arrived, it disappeared, and Juliet had already forgotten the whole incident. But now, after discovering her face in this picture, everything came back to her once more. Juliet was extremely worried that the picture might prevent her from travelling abroad, and about the stigma that it might still cause her and her children, some nine years after the war had ended. I promised Juliet that I would see what I could do and call her back as soon as possible. Before long, however, it became evident that my abilities were very limited in this matter since the photograph had already spread all over the Internet, and was on people's personal websites, news sites

---

[37] Utas 2005.
[38] Basini 2013: 96–7.
[39] It is highly interesting and somewhat worrying that in several studies on child or youth soldiers in Liberia the same NGO (NEPI) has acted as the link between researchers and research participants.
[40] See also Wessells in this volume.
[41] E.g. Anderson 1999; Wessells 2009.
[42] 'The BBC' is an umbrella term used in Liberia for the international media, so the reference to this broadcasting company did not mean that 'the BBC' had actually published the picture.

and blogs. Juliet and I thus concluded that it would be better to simply leave the matter be and just hope that the photograph would also one day be quietly forgotten.

Therefore, I decided early on to be extremely cautious about publishing any pictures of the research participants. While giving interviews to media, I also made it very clear *why* it was not an option to use one of the stock photos of girl soldiers provided by several international photo agencies. All the journalists empathetically agreed. This did not prevent a few professionals from breaking their promises, however, and despite my well-meaning yet undeniably naïve intentions, I found myself a few times to be a part of the problem rather than the solution.

First two lessons on do no harm:

- Even if a photograph of a (girl) child soldier/veteran could seem harmless today, it might not be so tomorrow.
- When communicating with journalists, do not trust oral promises but always have all the details in a written form.

The second set of lessons came from a surprising direction: myself. Even though my PhD supervisor had wisely urged me to book a debriefing appointment with a psychologist prior to my departure to Liberia, and I had read about the emotional whirlwind that this kind of a topic might launch in a researcher,[43] I was still ill-prepared and likely vicariously traumatized. I had also underestimated the need to have enough time to rest and recover, especially in times of sickness, as the below excerpt aptly demonstrates:

> Today's interview was a disaster. Antoinette and Vivienne, both former frontline fighters, came to the photo interview with well over 200 pictures taken with their digital cameras. The women seemed highly excited and enthusiastic as they climbed up the stairs to the quiet restaurant in central Monrovia. However, both I and Glorious quietly felt disappointed that they had not failed us. That they were as trustworthy as they had always been; on time, sharp and ready to answer all the questions we might have. Firstly, I had both malaria and typhoid fever. In addition, Glorious was also taking heavy drugs for her almost conquered typhoid and was constantly falling asleep. We felt exhausted, tired and powerless. As I later listened to our recordings, I couldn't help but laugh. I should not have done it, I know, but the interview seemed to have taken place rather in the TV series *Smack the Pony*[44] than in an academic setting. For example, when Antoinette was explaining that she had taken the photograph at hand to explain the current drug business with former child combatants, my answer was: 'Okay, let's take the next picture then'. Also recorded is my anxious comment to Glorious during the interview: 'Hey G, you just cannot sleep during the interview – you're working now woman!' It was evident that we were in no shape to conduct the interview but nonetheless tried to act as heroines. And that was, of course, pure idiocy. (26 March 2013, excerpt from personal research journal)

Indeed, a time of sickness is by no means ideal for an important research interview. In addition, just before meeting Antoinette and Vivienne, I had been discussing with Glorious ('G') the serious matter concerning her current living environment. During the previous night armed robbers had entered her neighbour's house, shot a person and

---

[43] Marshall 2011; Davies and Spencer 2010; Thomson et al. 2013.
[44] *Smack the Pony* was a British comedy show where three women comedians perform sketches dealing with daily life. The show ran between 1999 and 2003 on Channel 4.

wounded two others. The quarter's unofficial 'security guards' had caught one of the robbers, killed him and thrown his body into the river. Later, when the police came to the quarter, none of the residents confessed to having known the person who had killed the robber. When the police left, the 'security guards' were celebrated as heroes, since nobody seemed to trust the police anymore. Because of these events, Glorious had slept only a few hours during the previous night. She was extremely worried about the safety of her daughter and herself because there was currently no iron door in their house – a security guarantee she hoped soon to invest in. I was also extremely worried about their safety, but at the same time very relieved that I had not been living in Glorious' house, as was originally planned. If I had been there, I reasoned, our house would have certainly been one of the most obvious targets in the slum since no other white persons lived there.

In this way, as a researcher who was seeking to be as close to her interviewees as possible, I would not only have put myself in danger but also Glorious and her daughter. I felt very guilty that I had not considered this aspect before. The lessons on do no harm:

- Remember that you are quite likely to get sick. Do not try to be a superhero researcher and work whilst ill: it not only makes your recovery slower but can also produce very poor research data.
- Do not work during the weekends. Or at least have two days off every week. Although you might not feel it yourself, you need to rest and recover as well.
- Through your presence only, you might inadvertently put people in danger. Always discuss this possibility with trusted locals when choosing a place to stay.

Indeed, during my second field research period in 2013, the harsh realities of the war and its aftermath began to emerge in some interview situations. Looking back now, I am certain that both Glorious and I were vicariously traumatized by some of these encounters, even though we certainly did not realize it and would have never admitted it at the time. Luckily, we both had the chance – and even the need – to use plenty of time after each interview to discuss and reflect upon the interviews of that day. However, and quite likely also because of my failure as a supervisor to book enough time for R&R, sometimes too much was too much as we will soon come to learn.

My first encounter with Teta took place in a small room in a Monrovian slum, a room that had cardboard walls and was owned by a shopkeeper living in the same zinc house. The shopkeeper allowed idle youth to spend time in that room; sometimes they bought liquor or other commodities from him, and at other times he just liked to have them around to provide some company. In addition, by allowing these youngsters to stay in his shop, he created a small-scale security network and a resource base should he one day need some services. I was astounded by Teta's beauty once she sat down in front of me the first time in that room and asked me what right I had to interfere in her life with all my questions. It took some time, and numerous encounters, to gain Teta's trust, but in the end, she agreed to take a camera and photograph her daily activities and future aspirations. Through these pictures, it became evident that Teta was a drug seller who saw either prostitution work or drug selling as her only livelihood options. She had been in jail numerous times, she lived in a tarpaulin house that was almost collapsing, and most of her family members had either abandoned her or were dead. Initially, Teta had ended up on the street because of her beauty: during the years preceding the war her aunt had started to make money from Teta by selling her sexual services to those who wanted them. Teta decided therefore to run away. She first ended up on the street and then undertook combat service support duties from 15 years of age onwards once the second Liberian civil war broke out.[45] Teta's pictures were extremely revealing about the realities of street life. She had, for example, taken detailed photographs of the users of different kinds of narcotics and later gave detailed accounts of how those drugs were consumed, what their costs were and what effects they had. In many of the pictures, former child soldiers, today's adult veterans, were completely high on drugs, leaning on the walls with empty eyes. She expressed worry when the picture of her house was in front of us since the rainy season was about to arrive and its tarpaulin walls were likely to collapse once the heavy rains hit. In addition, however, there were also pictures of joy and laughter, revealing the support networks these women possessed. Teta was, for example, smiling very warmly when we looked at pictures of her 'street sisters' or 'street brothers': her street family that provided protection or shelter in times of need.

Once, I met Teta while she was still in the process of taking photographs. She was worried about the fact that her right hand was completely swollen and had two deep cuts in it. Because of this injury she was unable to take any pictures. She explained that the reason for her condition was that her current boyfriend had beaten her severely for some trivial reason. While Teta was explaining all these issues, I suddenly realized that I felt emotionally numb. Evidently, I empathized with her current struggles and felt that she and her street sisters truly needed some help. I also knew that for many slum dwellers occasional violence at home would still be a better alternative than having to live 'without protection' by themselves. But, for the first time during this research process, I did not somehow seem to 'share' this woman's pain, and I found this concerning. Was my psyche starting to break down? A rendezvous in yet another Monrovian shantytown the following week further increased my anxieties.

With only a few exceptions, each of the 25 women in the group participating in the auto-photographic study were former girl soldiers who were now engaged in prostitution. Their stories were filled with violence, abuse and despair. Many were on drugs at the time of our encounter and told their stories with anger or tears in their eyes. Three of the women wanted to share with me their experiences of cooking human flesh, including the types of 'soups' they had prepared either from the behinds of 'long-butt women' or from enemies' internal organs. Their stories were absolutely horrific and appalling, but I felt absolutely nothing – nothing at all. Moreover, in the recordings of these discussions one can hear that the more terrifying the story was, the calmer my voice became. In my field notes I consider the reasons behind this lack of emotion and express some concern about the matter. After many pages of other random thoughts, I wrote: 'During the last few days I have been extremely tired. Really, really tired. I guess a test for parasites would not be a bad idea.' I had thus reasoned that the cause for my tiredness would most likely be found in parasites or other outside intruders, rather than my experiences over the previous few months. I was evidently suffering from a type of 'superhuman researcher syndrome', where one of the symptoms was that I believed that my psyche was capable of absorbing almost anything. Indeed, if I felt tired, it was because of something or someone else, not because of myself.

---

[45] Vastapuu 2018.

Later, when I discussed the matter with a professional psychologist, she indicated two different and possibly overlapping explanations for my lack of emotions on this occasion. Firstly, she suggested that it was rather likely that my psyche had been operating on a self-regulating mode. When something becomes too much for a person to bear, the unconscious parts of the mind are activated and begin to protect the conscious mind. Secondly, she explained that this could also be due to a certain amount of professional development – maybe I was able to distance myself from the interviewees and not take their struggles on my own shoulders. Be that as it may (although I strongly believe the first scenario to be true), I had learnt a few important lessons through these incidents:

- If the emotional spectrum of a researcher or a member of her team changes suddenly, that is a sign of something, and that something should always be given some thought.
- If possible, have an immediate debriefing after each interview. As a minimum, write regularly in your research journal and reflect as openly as possible about the status of your own emotional well-being. If available, use the services of a professional psychologist after returning home.
- The do no harm principle applies also to the researcher herself and the whole research team, and not only to research participants.

3. THE CHALLENGING TASK OF A DDR PRACTITIONER

Many DDR practitioners – most of whom come from a military background – possess their own understanding of what constitutes a soldier, an understanding that is often heavily gendered.[46] Similar types of gendered attitudes are also present in the NGO sector, however, and even when gender analyses are undertaken, their real purpose might not be fully grasped.[47] It is therefore essential to be as precise and detailed as possible in any gender 'toolbox' targeted at DDR practitioners. Unfortunately, this is not currently the case, as is presented below.

In this second main section of the chapter, I critically examine the current Integrated DDR Standards (IDDRS) created by the UN's Inter-Agency Working Group (IAWG) on Disarmament, Demobilization and Reintegration, focusing specifically on gender. At the time of writing, the IDDRS are being revised but, as the process is still ongoing, I have to base my analysis here on the current document published in 2006. The IDDRS[48] itself is 777 pages long, and even the Operational Guide to the Integrated Disarmament, Demobilization and Reintegration Standards is 317 pages long. The paradox is that the aim of the latter is to 'help users find their way through the IDDRS document by briefly explaining the key guidance contained in each IDDRS module'.[49]

The IDDRS and the complementary Operational Guide are without a doubt the most

---

[46] Mazurana and Eckerbom Cole 2013: 212.
[47] Kays 2005.
[48] IDDRS 2006.
[49] IDDRS Operational Guide 2014 [13].

important guiding documents ('best practices') in today's DDR programmes. They have an impact on both the actual country-specific DDR programmes as well as on their practical implementation. As explained in the IDDRS Operational Guide,[50] the IDDRS were developed because:

> the UN continued to lack a common strategic framework to carry out and support DDR programmes. Each new DDR initiative had to be developed almost from scratch, relying mostly on the knowledge and experience of DDR programme staff, who often turned to the several reports, studies and works on DDR issues prepared by the UN, donor agencies, international and national nongovernmental organizations (NGOs), and research institutes. However, guidance could be only inferred, was not always clear and often became difficult to translate into practice.
>
> As a result, DDR was carried out in a fractured way; lacked adequate coordination among the UN peacekeeping mission, agencies, programmes and funds; and was compromised by poor planning and support. A consensus has therefore emerged among the UN and DDR stakeholders about the need to improve the Organization's[51] performance in this area.

In the ensuing sections, I argue that, in its current form, there are several contradictory guidelines in different parts of the IDDRS documents that leave a considerable amount of interpretative power to the individual DDR practitioner. It is precisely here in this interpretative vacuum where personal and organizational attitudes on gender, militarism and warfare may have an influence on the typically highly demanding decisions the individual officer undertakes in her/his daily work.

3.1 Contradictions on Gender-Related Activities in the Current IDDRS Document

Module 5.10 of the IDDRS document is entitled Women, Gender and DDR.[52] In the introduction to this module, it is stated that although women typically take on several roles in conflicts, ranging from support work to periods of fighting, those women who have already returned to their communities at the time of the commencement of DDR should *not* be encouraged to participate in the DDR programme.[53] It is explained that the reason for this is that 'the resources allocated for DDR are limited' and that it 'is therefore appropriate, in the reconstruction period, to focus resources on women and men who are still active fighters and potential spoilers'.[54] However, on the following page of the same document it is emphasized that the previously utilized narrow definition of a combatant has left many women out of the process and that this is why, from now on, the principles of non-discrimination and gender equality should be applied at all times in UN-supported DDR processes.[55] Thus, *at the same time*, and astonishingly, in the following pages two guidelines are in obvious contradiction: one cannot simultaneously both concentrate solely on active fighters – 'active' itself excludes non-active and self-demobilized soldiers

---

[50] Ibid.: [13–14].
[51] It is unclear what is exactly meant by 'Organization' in this context, although presumably it is the UN.
[52] IDDRS 2006 (in the whole document, pages 522–561). To avoid confusion, however, I will refer to the document in its printed form, with page numbers beginning from 1 in each separate module.
[53] Ibid. [module 5.10, 2–3].
[54] Ibid.
[55] Ibid.: [4, see also 10].

whereas 'fighters' excludes all the other categories of soldiers, such as combat service support staff – and practise the principles of non-discrimination and gender equality. What causes further confusion is that in the same section[56] it is emphasized that *former* (that is non-active) combatants, *supporters* and *dependants* (thus not only fighters) should be encouraged to join the programme through various information campaigns. In addition, the DDR staff are advised to approach female community members and enquire about the 'self-reintegrated' female soldiers in order to encourage them to participate in the DDR process.[57] Thus to encourage or not to encourage: the decision depends on how the document is interpreted and/or what sections are being referred to.

Another example of a contradiction in the module can be found in the pages dealing with demobilization. As is explained earlier in the IDDRS document,[58] 'shall' is meant as a sign of an obligatory requirement, whereas 'should' refers to a preferred but not obligatory requirement. When considering this terminology, as well as the previously mentioned requirement to practise non-discrimination at all stages of any DDR programme, the need to ensure that 'DDR programme participants *shall* include those [typically females] who play support functions essential for the maintenance and cohesion of armed groups and forces'[59] is perfectly reasonable. However, and again on the following page, a list of what *should* (not shall) be done for ensuring gender equity in DDR processes is provided. The 'should list' includes, for example, adequate financing and other resources for gender-related activities, the hiring of gender experts and advisers, as well as gender mainstreaming and sensitization among all staff members. The contradiction here is in the language: it is simply not possible to ensure/encourage the participation of female supporters if the allocation for adequate resources to undertake this work is in practice voluntary.

3.2 Consulting 'Women's Organizations' = Adequate Representation of Women Is Ensured?

Throughout module 5.10, the need to consult 'women's groups' in different phases of DDR processes is emphasized. The definition and areas of expertise that these groups should possess, however, are left open and vague; it almost seems that any (local) women's group is fit for this purpose, provided it is comprised of women. We may ask, on the one hand, why a random women's organization should have any knowledge of female participation in the given conflict? Or, on the other hand, why should a women's organization have any incentive for promoting the participation of female soldiers if their members are not among its interest groups in the first place? Indeed, previous studies have effectively revealed that there are various social hierarchies between (and within) women's organizations that compete for funding and other resources.[60] Naturally, if there is a women's organization that is particularly focused on promoting the needs of girl and women soldiers, this type of organization should indeed be consulted. However, very

---

[56] Ibid.: [15].
[57] Ibid.: [18].
[58] Ibid.: [17].
[59] Ibid.: [module 5, 10, 11, emphasis mine].
[60] See Poster 1995; Markowitz & Tice 2002; Strolovitch 2006; Debusscher and Martin de Almagro 2016.

careful consideration should be practised when consulting any organization outside its areas of expertise.

Instead of the current emphasis on women's organizations, former soldiers and commanders themselves (both female and male) should play a vital role when trying to find the 'hidden' girl and women soldiers.

3.3   What Then? Who Should Be Consulted and Why?

The module Women, Gender and DDR of the IDDRS does not recognize the existence of female commanders.[61] Instead, when commanders are mentioned in the module[62] they are understood as implicitly male, who quite likely may try to exclude girl and women soldiers from the DDR process altogether, for example by not providing the correct figures or by removing the guns from the hands of female fighters prior the commencement of the DDR process. In this manner, the gender section of the IDDRS is indeed gendered itself: it is not mentioned anywhere in the module that commanders may also be girls and women,[63] and that consultations with female commanders themselves are of utmost importance if the aim is to try to trace the 'hidden' girl and women soldiers in the given conflict site.

Furthermore, a few simple questions targeted at *all* DDR programme candidates in the screening phase of the process would significantly assist in estimating the actual number of girls and boys, women and men in each faction. In addition to asking about the rank of the interviewee and her/his superiors, one should always inquire about the support work undertaken in the given fighting faction. The following questions should be asked, as a minimum:

- Who cooked in your faction?
- Who washed your clothes?
- Who carried all the necessary equipment (ammunition, everyday essentials, food)?
- Did you have a girlfriend/boyfriend in the forces? If yes, what were her/his duties in the forces?
- When I ask about the number of soldiers in your forces, do you also include the cooks, cleaners, carriers etc.? How about girlfriends or boyfriends?

No armed faction can function without combat service support (CSS) work. For example, in the US military alone, only 15 to 20 per cent of the military personnel participate in combat activities; the large majority perform CSS tasks.[64] In the civil wars of Liberia, most combat service support providers were girls and women, with the tasks ranging from cleaning and washing services to cooking and carrying; from nursing and spying responsibilities to caretaking duties. The sexual abuse of CSS personnel regularly occurred.[65] Without detailed and reliable statistics, that are rarely available in the context of the global

---

[61] See also Aijazi, Amony and Baines in this volume; Denov in this volume.
[62] IDDRS 2006 [module 5.10, 9,10, 15, 16, 18].
[63] E.g. Thompson 1982; Vastapuu 2018.
[64] Mazurana and Eckerbom Cole 2013: 20.
[65] Vastapuu 2018: 53–6.

South, the exact number of these personnel and their gender composition can only be determined by posing specific questions about CSS staff to *all* programme candidates.

4. CONCLUSION

Dyan Mazurana perceptively notes that 'when we see an NSAG [non-state armed group] whose public face is completely male and we cannot easily "find" the women and girls that we know must in some ways be supporting them, we should immediately become curious'.[66] In this chapter, I have unfolded my own struggles and successes in finding the 'hidden' girl soldiers – today's women veterans – from Liberia, as well as providing a set of suggestions on how to address the given challenge both as a researcher and a DDR practitioner. I have argued that the current IDDRS document is both contradictory and confusing in its approach on gender and suggested a few basic questions that should always be asked in the screening interviews, regardless of the candidate's sex or age.

If nothing else, any forthcoming IDDRS document, as well as operational guide, should deliver what it claims to do, that is 'give DDR practitioners the opportunity to make informed decisions based on a clear, flexible and in-depth body of guidance across the range of DDR activities'.[67] We all – researchers, humanitarian workers, politicians, citizens – owe that, not only to DDR practitioners on the ground, but especially to all those girl soldiers and veterans who have been ignored both in the policy world as well as in academia, for far too long already.

REFERENCED WORKS

Achvarina, V. and Reich, S.F. 2006. 'No Place to Hide: Refugees, Displaced Persons, and the Recruitment of Child Soldiers' 31 *International Security* 127

Anderson, M.B. 1999. *Do No Harm: How Aid Can Support Peace – Or War* (Boulder, CO: Lynne Rienner Publishers)

Balomenou, N. and Garrod, B. 2015. 'A Review of Participant-Generated Image Methods in the Social Sciences' 10 *Journal of Mixed Methods Research* 335

Basini, H. 2013. *An Imperfect Reality: Gender Mainstreaming and Disarmament, Demobilisation, Rehabilitation and Reintegration (DDRR) in Liberia* (Doctoral dissertation, University of Limerick)

Bernard, B., Brewer, B., Dharmapuri, S., Dobor, E., Hansen, A. and Nelson, S. 2003. 'Assessment of the Situation of Women and Children Combatants in the Liberian Post-Conflict Period and Recommendations for Successful Integration: A Report prepared for USAID Washington: Development Alternatives, Inc.' (December)

Bøås, M. 2005. 'The Liberian Civil War: New War/Old War?' 19 *Global Society: Journal of Interdisciplinary International Relations* 73

Brett, R. and Specht, I. 2004. *Young Soldiers: Why They Choose to Fight* (Boulder, CO; London: Lynne Rienner Publishers)

Bugnion, C., Lafrenière, L., Gbaydee Doe, S., Tefferi, H. and Garlo, C. 2006. 'External Mid-Term Evaluation Report of the Disarmament, Demobilisation, Rehabilitation and Reintegration Programme in Liberia: Final Report' (2 October)

Coulter, C. 2009. *Bush Wives and Girl Soldiers: Women's Lives through War and Peace in Sierra Leone* (Ithaca: Cornell University Press)

---

[66] Mazurana 2013: 162.
[67] IDDRS 2006 [module 1.10, 3].

Coulter, C., Persson, M. and Utas, M. 2008. *Young Female Fighters in African Wars: Conflict and its Consequences* (Uppsala: The Nordic Africa Institute)

Davies, J. and Spencer, D. 2010. *Emotions in the Field: The Psychology and Anthropology of Fieldwork Experience* (Stanford: Stanford University Press)

Debusscher, P. and Martin de Almagro, M. 2016. 'Post-Conflict Women's Movements in Turmoil: The Challenges of Success in Liberia in the 2005-Aftermath' 54 *The Journal of Modern African Studies* 293

Eriksson Baaz, M. and Stern, M. 2014. 'The Gendered Subject of Violence in African Conflicts', in J.J. Hentz (ed.), *Routledge Handbook of African Security* (New York: Routledge) 157

Fox, M.-J. 2004. 'Girl Soldiers: Human Security and Gendered Insecurity' 35 *Security Dialogue* 465

Harper, D. 2002. 'Talking about Pictures: A Case for Photo Elicitation', 17 *Visual Studies* 13

IDDRS [The Integrated Disarmament, Demobilization and Reintegration Standards] 2006. United Nations Disarmament, Demobilization and Reintegration Resource Centre [available at: http://unddr.org/iddrs-framework.aspx (accessed 15 April 2018)]

IDDRS Operational Guide 2014 [available at: http://unddr.org/uploads/documents/Operational%20Guide.pdf (accessed 15 April 2018)]

Jennings, K.M. 2009. 'The Political Economy of DDR in Liberia: A Gendered Critique' 9 *Conflict, Security & Development* 475

Kays, L. 2005. 'Why We Cannot Find the Hidden Girl Soldier: A Study of Professional Attitudes Towards Gender Analysis in International Conflict and Development Work' 6 *Conflict, Security & Development* 1

Kieh, G.K. 2008. *The First Liberian Civil War: The Crises of Underdevelopment* (New York; Oxford: Peter Lang)

Knight, M. and Özerdem, A. 2004. 'Guns, Camps and Cash: Disarmament, Demobilization and Reinsertion of Former Combatants in Transitions from War to Peace' 41 *Journal of Peace Research* 499

Knight, W.A. 2008. 'Disarmament, Demobilization, and Reintegration and Post-Conflict Peacebuilding in Africa: An Overview' 1 *African Security* 24

MacKenzie, M. 2010. 'Securitization and De-Securitization: Female Soldiers and the Reconstruction of Women in Post-Conflict Sierra Leone', in L. Sjoberg (ed.), *Gender and International Security: Feminist Perspectives* [Kindle eBook] (London; New York: Routledge) 151

Markowitz, L. and Tice, K.W. 2002. 'Paradoxes of Professionalization: Parallel Dilemmas in Women's Organizations in the Americas' 16 *Gender & Society* 941

Marshall, S. 2011. 'Super-Human Researchers in Feminist International Relations' Narratives', in C. Sylvester (ed.), 'The Forum: Emotion and the Feminist IR Researcher' 13 *International Studies Review* 688

Mazurana, D. 2013. 'Women, Girls, and Non-State Armed Opposition Groups', in C. Cohn (ed.), *Women and Wars* (Cambridge: Polity Press) 146

Mazurana, D. and Eckerbom Cole, L. 2013. 'Women, Girls, and Disarmament, Demobilization and Reintegration (DDR)', in C. Cohn (ed.), *Women and Wars* (Cambridge: Polity Press) 194

Mazurana, D., McKay, S., Carlson, K. and Kasper, J. 2002. 'Girls in Fighting Forces and Groups: Their Recruitment, Participation, Demobilization, and Reintegration' 8 *Peace & Conflict* 97

McKay, S. and Mazurana, D.E. 2004. *Where Are the Girls? Girls in Fighting Forces in Northern Uganda, Sierra Leone and Mozambique: Their Lives During and After War* (Montreal: Rights & Democracy)

Moran, M.H. 2006. *Liberia: The Violence of Democracy* (Philadelphia: University of Pennsylvania Press)

Njoki Wamai, E. 2011. 'Security Council Resolution 1325 Implementation in Liberia: Dilemmas and Challenges', in F. Olonisakin, K. Barnes and E. Ikpe (eds), *Women, Peace and Security: Translating Policy into Practice* (New York: Routledge) 52

Nordstrom, C. 1997. *A Different Kind of War Story* (Philadelphia: University of Pennsylvania Press)

Nordstrom, C. 1998. 'Girls Behind the (Front) Lines', in L.A. Lorentzen and J. Turpin (eds), *The Women and War Reader* (New York & London: New York University Press) 80

Özerdem, A. 2012. 'A Re-Conceptualisation of Ex-Combatant Reintegration: "Social Reintegration" Approach' 12 *Conflict, Security & Development* 51

Poster, W.R. 1995. 'The Challenges and Promises of Class and Racial Diversity in the Women's Movement: A Study of Two Women's Organizations' 9 *Gender & Society* 659

Shepler, S. 2002. 'Les Filles-Soldats: Trajectoires d'Après-Guerre en Sierra Leone' 88 *Politique Africaine* 49

Shepler, S. 2014. *Childhood Deployed: Remaking Child Soldiers in Sierra Leone* (New York: New York University Press)

Strolovitch, D.Z. 2006. 'Do Interest Groups Represent the Disadvantaged? Advocacy at the Intersections of Race, Class, and Gender' 68 *Journal of Politics* 894

Thompson, C.B. 1982. 'Women in the National Liberation Struggle in Zimbabwe: An Interview of Naomi Nhiwatiwa' 5 *Women's Studies International Forum* 247

Thomson, S., Ansoms, A. and Murison, J. (eds). 2013. *Emotional and Ethical Challenges for Field Research in Africa: The Story Behind the Findings* (Basingstoke & New York: Palgrave Macmillan)

UN 1992. 'An Agenda for Peace: Preventive Diplomacy, Peacemaking and Peace-Keeping: Report of the Secretary-General' (UN Doc. A/47/277) (17 June)

UN 2006a. 'Disarmament, Demobilization and Reintegration: Report of the Secretary-General' (UN Doc. A/60/705) (6 March)

UN 2006b. 'Internal Audit Report: UNMIL DDRR Programme. OIOS Audit No. AP2005/626/07' (UN Doc. E/ICEF/2005/P/L.5) (25 January)

UNSC [United Nations Security Council] 1992. 'Note by the President of the Security Council' (UN Doc. S/23500) (31 January)

Utas, M. 2005. 'Victimcy, Girlfriending, Soldiering: Tactic Agency in a Young Woman's Social Navigation of the Liberian War Zone' 78 *Anthropological Quarterly* 403

Vaha, M. and Vastapuu, L. 2018. '"My Heart was Already Cooked": Girl Soldiers and Situated Moral Agencies' 31 *Cambridge Review of International Affairs* 223

Vastapuu, L. 2018. *Liberia's Women Veterans: War, Roles and Reintegration*, illustrated by Emmi Nieminen (London: Zed Books)

Wessells, M. 2009. 'Do No Harm: Toward Contextually Appropriate Psychosocial Support in International Emergencies' 64 *American Psychologist* 842

PART V
EPILOGUE

Beyond 'the child soldier': from a recognition of complexity to an ethics of engagement
Nesam McMillan

> To the real question, How does it feel to be a problem? I answer seldom a word.
> (W.E.B. Du Bois) [1]

The 'problem' of 'the child soldier' is a touchstone of our contemporary time. It names an impassioned concern with the exploitation and victimization of children in situations of armed conflict by more powerful state and non-state actors – a concern which is understood to reflect a global humanitarian sentiment that has emerged in response to the grave violence and injustice that occurs in the world. Influential international actors and institutions frame child soldiering as 'one of the most deplorable developments in recent years' and a 'crime against humanity', cautioning that '[e]mpathy alone with the suffering of boys and girls in times of conflict is not enough. We must act.'[2] The problem of child soldiering thus justifies a variety of humanitarian campaigns, international justice initiatives and political interventions designed to end the practice. In the name of preventing and redressing the scourge of child soldiering, individuals, communities and organizations come together to denounce this practice and respond to its effects. And at the heart of many of these collaborations and campaigns lies an image of the vulnerable (often African) child compelling protection and care. This is an image that can appear as transparent as it is problematic; an unquestionable depiction of injustice that seems to demand a certain reaction.

This is the work of *problematization*. Problematization refers to the socially, legally, politically, culturally and historically located processes whereby a particular issue or concern emerges on the social and legal scene. It is the giving of form to something which previously did not exist as such, in particular ways. Problematization refers to 'the totality of discursive or non-discursive practices that introduces something into the play of true and false and constitutes it as an object for thought (whether in the form of moral reflection, scientific knowledge, political analysis)'.[3] Here then, problematization refers to the way in which the complex array of contexts and experiences that have been described so carefully in the preceding pages come to be understood as parts of a whole, as different perspectives on 'the problem of the child soldier'.[4] And it is from this understanding and articulation of a shared problem that potential solutions can then be crafted – solutions which are always delimited to the terms and truths upon which the initial problematization

---

[1] Du Bois 2008: 9. This quote was brought to my attention through the excellent work of Hussein Mohamud.
[2] These quotes are taken, in order, from UNICEF 1996: 14; Child Soldiers Initiative; Bensouda 2018.
[3] Foucault 1988: 258.
[4] See Foucault 1984: 389.

is based. An attention to problematization, therefore, separates an acknowledgement of the reality of children's participation in conflict from the current, somewhat cohesive and consistent, way of understanding (and indeed pathologizing) this participation, its nature, causes and potential solutions.

Yet, a key contribution of the chapters throughout this *Research Handbook* is how they powerfully reveal that there is not *one* new and urgent problem of 'the child soldier'. There are many problems, complex layers of inequality and exploitation and different forms of responsibility and accountability that are implicated in the participation of children in warfare throughout time and space. In each of the contexts discussed, the involvement of children in armed conflict takes different forms, it emerges from a unique constellation of enabling and coercive environmental contexts, and the individuals and communities most directly affected negotiate such experiences in a range of ways. It is in this way that this *Research Handbook* exceeds its stated goal to 'render the invisible visible', going further to draw out the irreconcilable complexities that characterize the nature, use and socio-legal significance of the involvement of children in armed conflict. The collective story the preceding chapters weave – of growing up amongst armed conflict and structural inequality and of negotiating its difficult aftermath – is undoubtedly powerful and deeply moving. But it takes the reader well beyond the comfort of a singular, definable problem demanding redress to a much more difficult and unsettling consideration of the pervasive force of militarization throughout time and space, the prevalence of physical, economic and other structural violence across the world and the potentially negative effects of dominant, internationalized responses to child soldiering. Children involved in armed conflict emerge as resilient, but they also appear as potential subjects of justice and accountability. Traditional conceptualizations of responsibility and the oppositional distinction between victims and perpetrators are unsettled and it becomes possible to more clearly make out the overlaps, tensions and continuities between experiences of victimhood and perpetration in conflict settings. The contributions here maintain a commitment to responding to the injustices experienced by children and young people in conflict, whilst also engaging deeply and thoughtfully with questions of accountability, resilience and survival that transcend current legal frameworks.

On the other hand, however, this *Research Handbook*, like all contemporary attempts to grapple with the existence and involvement of children in armed conflict, is framed by the prevailing concept of 'the child soldier'. The notion of 'the child soldier' functions as a common problem through which the diverse situations and issues discussed in this book can be intelligibly read together as parts of a whole. It is thus in this way that the extant problem of 'the child soldier' facilitates dialogue and collaboration, often directed towards better understanding and responding to the injustices experienced (and indeed perpetrated) by children. But then it is also the same 'child soldier' frame that occludes, silences and fails to account for nuance and complexity. In its current instantiation, the problem of 'the child soldier' is culturally particular, often based on a concern with the exploitation of African children in African contexts, with little acknowledgement of the prevalence of children's involvement in armed violence across the world. It is historically specific, connected to a distinct shift in the nineteenth century to seeing children as inherently good but underdeveloped people, deserving of protection and care.[5] There is

---

[5] See Rosen in this *Handbook*; see also Malkki 2010: 61–2.

an urgency that currently characterizes the problem of child soldiering, its recognition and redress, an urgency which belies the continued use of children in military forces throughout time and also demands its own investigation.[6]

Perhaps most problematically, though, there is also a silencing inherent in the contemporary problematization of child soldiering, which is predominantly a field of discourse and practice that speaks for or on behalf of its always vulnerable subject. The notion of 'the child soldier' is one that is authored, described and defined by those in positions of institutional, political, social and legal power – prosecutors of international criminal tribunals, Hollywood actors, international political representatives and academics and policy-makers. Contemporary global attention to the problem of 'the child soldier' in this way forms part of a broader history of campaigns for children's rights that advocate for the child without being substantively grounded in their participation.[7] It is thus here that Du Bois' words used to open this epilogue resonate most strongly (*'To the real question, How does it feel to be a problem? I answer seldom a word'*). Du Bois was writing of a different type of problematization, namely the racist and discriminatory construction in the United States of America of African Americans as a social problem. He uses these words, though, to frame a discussion of the 'double consciousness' this produces for African Americans who, in their day-to-day lives, experience a 'sense of always looking at one's self through the eyes of others'.[8] It is in this sense that there is a danger that the more one dominant idea of 'the child soldier' develops without being directly shaped by the experiences, needs and wishes of those children actually involved in armed conflict (in their diversity and multiplicity), the more these very children may endure a similar 'double consciousness', whereby they must see and understand themselves through a pre-established lens that references their experience but may also depart substantially from it.

Thus, to recall Abu-Lughod's important work on the contemporary constitution of the 'honour crime' as a pressing social issue, when confronted with an instance of problematization it is always important to ask what 'political work' is being achieved?[9] What institutions and regulatory frameworks are being given social, legal and political power, what interventions are being legitimated, and what responses are presented as natural? Indeed, the preceding chapters chart an insightful picture of the numerous institutions that have assumed leadership roles in responding to the problem of child soldiering, from international institutions (such as the United Nations and international legal bodies) to international and national non-governmental organizations (involved in reintegration and rehabilitation) to nation states themselves. Their involvement is particularly deserving of interrogation given a theme that cuts across many chapters of this volume of the frequent disconnect between externally designed and administered programmes and the specific contexts and peoples to whom they are applied. And to the extent that the children and communities most affected by the participation of children and young people in armed conflict are not integrally involved with the naming, understanding and responding to

---

[6] See Mertens and Pardy (2017: 963) who problematize the current urgency surrounding the issue of sexual violence in the Congo.
[7] Pupavac 2001: 99.
[8] Du Bois 2008: 11.
[9] Abu-Lughod 2011: 26, see also 40–44.

'the problem' of child soldiering in their community, there remain serious questions to be asked.

The point of such a claim is not to downplay the salience of the experiences of exploitation and injustice described in the previous chapters, but to begin to think about how to continue to engage – in the spirit of this volume – in a project of thinking otherwise, responding differently and collaborating in new ways. Just as Abu-Lughod asks whether one can 'acknowledge the seriousness of violence against women without contributing to this stigmatization of particular communities?',[10] it might be possible to ask whether one can acknowledge the significance and ethical import of the participation of children in armed conflict without silencing, occluding and dehistoricizing. Is it possible to hold on to the complexity, nuance, discontinuities and productive parallels charted throughout the chapters in this important edited collection, whilst also engaging reflexively and collaboratively with the stories and experiences of those young people who participate in armed conflict in our own countries and elsewhere and the need to offer some form of response?

Indeed, there may even be new affective potentialities sparked by 'the child soldier' frame itself. Dominant frameworks regarding 'the child soldier' do not just shape how this problem is known and understood. Frames, as Butler has shown, also have affective and emotional consequences, shaping and regulating how it is possible to *feel* about and *connect* with certain experiences of suffering.[11] And it is clear that current frameworks for understanding 'the child soldier' invite and even compel affective relations, entreating people and communities from elsewhere to both know *and care* about the experiences of child soldiers, in African contexts in particular.

That is to say, whilst dominant constructions of the vulnerable and exploited child have been implicated in the continual exclusion of children from discussions and decisions that concern them, they also promote rather than stymie affective connections. The image of the child – the suffering child, the vulnerable child – is a powerful one. It galvanizes people and serves to build coalitions. Sometimes these relations may be based on stereotypes that valorize children, which may need their own interrogation. In particular, it is important to remain attentive to whether and how they connect external people with real, complex, agentic and resilient children with unique stories and histories. But, as is evident from the contemporary social, political and legal interest in the problem of 'child soldiering', the construction of children as particularly special and privileged members of global and local communities is productive, connecting people throughout the world and raising the possibility of new affective connections and cross-cultural collaborations.

So, what else might come of the contemporary power of the image of the child soldier and its problematization?

An emphasis on the unjustified use and participation of children in conflict, for example, has arguably functioned to bring the violent destructiveness of war into sharp relief. The brutality of warfare, the prioritization of corporate and governmental interests over human life and the exploitation by those in power of those who are power-less may be more easily made out and appreciated as unjustifiable when children are involved. The problematization of child soldiers may also make it easier to *feel* outrage and a

---

[10] Ibid.: 18.
[11] Butler 2009: Introduction.

sense of injustice at broader situations of economic and political exploitation that can be otherwise normalized as inevitable, or at least difficult to change. It might also compel the development of justice measures which depart from the prevailing legal model of individualistic retributivism towards a greater appreciation of the communal and contextual dynamics of conflict.

And these possibilities might be extended further. Could the participation, resilience and agency of children in times of conflict precipitate a fuller conception of 'the child' more generally that recognizes the ability of children to speak and be knowledgeable on both the issues that affect them and key social and political issues in the world? And might these new directions lead, as is the concern of many contributors to this volume, to more substantive and ethical responses to the victimization and other experiences of children (of all genders and sexualities) who participate in warfare in various roles? More expansively, could the vulnerable child soldier frame inspire a reflection on the continuities between the participation of children in war and their offending in other contexts, perhaps leading to a greater recognition of the limits on the agency of children in national criminal justice systems (which in many Western countries currently adopt a hard 'law and order' approach to youth offending)? Or might the growing recognition of children's qualified agency and resilience in situations of armed conflict facilitate a broader acknowledgement of the strength and capability of all victims, a perspective often missing from dominant discourses about the victim of international and national crime?

To be sure, the affective potentialities of the contemporary notion of 'the child soldier' are compromised and shaped by the limits of dominant frameworks (their cultural bias, ahistorical nature and distance from experience 'on the ground', in particular). But this is where the contributions in this *Research Handbook* offer a crucial supplement to prevailing frames – engaging with the dominant problem of 'the child soldier' and yet also demonstrating the context-specific nature of the participation of children in warfare, its relation to structural violence and the complex social, cultural, historical and political dynamics that surround both. When brought into conversation with the prevailing problem of 'the child soldier', they move discussion beyond a straightforward problematization of the child in conflict, compelling a more serious and sustained engagement with the intersecting political, economic and social inequalities that are imbricated in it.

Of course, the question of what else might flow from the current problematization of 'the child soldier' is more an invitation to consider than a question to be answered. And it is not one that should be prioritized over the imperative of a more careful and sustained engagement with the actual lives and perspectives of those individuals who ostensibly constitute the focus of the current attention on child soldiers, namely children themselves. Indeed, perhaps the most significant intervention of this edited collection is the way in which it draws the reader back to the concrete and the lived, connecting broader discourses on child soldiers with the experiences and insights of children themselves. As such, the purpose of this concluding reflection is not to inaugurate another global programme undertaken in the name of individuals and peoples who are not able to effectively speak or be heard in dominant international discourse. Rather it is to connect the rich empirical and case-specific analyses offered here with the question of problematization; to ask where both – together – might lead? For a reflection on what is known, how it is known and how that leads to particular solutions is not antithetical to the ethical imperative to respond adequately to the harms experienced by children. Rather it is, in part, through such processes of interrogation that it might become possible to think and act differently and change the status quo.

REFERENCED WORKS

Abu-Lughod, L. 2011. 'Seductions of the "Honor Crime"' 22 *Differences: A Journal of Feminist Cultural Studies* 17

Bensouda F. 2018. 'Statement of the Prosecutor of the International Criminal Court, Mrs Fatou Bensouda, on the International Day against the use of Child Soldiers' [available at: https://www.icc-cpi.int/Pages/item.aspx?name=180212-otp-stat (accessed 5 November 2018)]

Butler, J. 2009. *Frames of War: When is Life Grievable?* (London: Verso)

Child Soldiers Initiative. *What We Do* [available at: https://www.childsoldiers.org/what-we-do/ (accessed 5 November 2018)]

Du Bois, W.E.B. 2008. *The Souls of Black Folk* (EBook, Project Gutenberg)

Foucault, M. 1984. 'Polemics, Politics, and Problematizations', in P. Rabinow (ed.), *The Foucault Reader* (New York: Pantheon Books) 381

Foucault, M. 1988. 'The Concern for Truth', in L.D. Kritzman (ed.), *Michel Foucault: Politics, Philosophy, Culture: Interviews and Other Writings 1977–1984* (New York; London: Routledge) 255

Malkki, L. 2010. 'Children, Humanity, and the Infantilization of Peace', in I. Feldman and M. Ticktin (eds), *In the Name of Humanity: The Government of Threat and Care* (Durham: Duke University Press) 58

Mertens, C. and Pardy, M. 2017. '"Sexurity" and its Effects in Eastern Democratic Republic of Congo' 38 *Third World Quarterly* 956

Mohamud, H. *Being Made Black in Australia: The Role of Race in the Making of a Nation* (PhD Thesis, University of Melbourne).

Pupavac, V. 2001. 'Misanthropy Without Borders: The International Children's Rights Regime' 25 *Disasters* 95

UNICEF 1996. *The State of the World's Children* (Oxford and New York: Oxford University Press)

Index

accountability 44, 319
  CDI definition 311
  children associated with armed groups
    288–9, 463, 465, 482–3, 514
    Boko Haram 464–5
    in Paris Principles 463
  criminal liability for economic crimes 320, 321–2
    corporate criminal liability 320
    implicating children 321
    pillage 320
  exclusion of child soldiers from framework of 342
  gap 300, 322, 342
  local governance dynamics affecting 319
  mechanisms *see* accountability mechanisms
  of severely traumatized persons 379
  of under-18s 376–7
    15–17-year-olds 376
    no clear guidelines 376, 377
    problem of bright-line rules 377
  for unlawful recruitment 160, 292, 317–19
accountability mechanisms 298
  anti-impunity efforts 299
  DRC sanctions committee 313–14
  effectiveness 311, 314
    delisting of Congolese army 314–16
    in DRC 316–17
    insufficient 319
    judicial efforts 317–19
    lack of cohesion 321
    sanctions 316
  indigenous/traditional mechanisms 413–14, 419–20, 432
  national action plans 313
  policy recommendations 293, 299
  rewarding DRC for lowering rates of child recruitment by FARDC 298
  UN listing mechanism 312–13
  UN Monitoring Reporting Mechanism (MRM) 312
adaptability 47, 48
Afghanistan 175–6
  'Afghan War Diary' 176
  bacha bazi 186, 187–8
    instrumentalization of, during conflict 187, 188
  children
    agency of *see* agency
    demobilized 185
    early socialization of 190–91
    involuntary recruitment 175
  communities/security actors relationship 180
  decades-long conflict in 176–8
  deliberate targeting of civilians 177
  Dilawar 166
  impact of decades-long conflict 178–81
    abusive use of authority 188
    constraint of agency 183, 185, 188
    endemic violence in 176–7
    pervasion of culture by conflict 187
    power vacuum 179
    pushing of children into roles characterized by suffering 186
    surge in criminality 180
    transformation of males into societal objects 186
    wide distribution of firearms 180
  Mohamad Jawad 166–7
  Mullah Habibullah 166
  multiplicity of actors 176, 177
    Al Haqqani network 177
    al-Qaeda *see* al-Qaeda
    Hezb-e Islami 177, 178
    ISIS *see* ISIS
    Islamic Movement of Uzbekistan 177
    militias 180
    Taleban *see* Taleban
  as narco state 177
  narrative of adulthood 189–90
  party to UN CRC 175
  Parwan Province 177–8
  presidential decree criminalizing recruitment of child soldiers (2015) 184
  recruitment
    avoiding 184–5, 188
    children offered by family 183, 184
    children's lack of agency in 188
    economic and social incentives 183
    by insurgent forces 182, 183, 184
    by state forces 182, 183
African Children's Charter (1990) 10, 19, 280, 295, 477
  Article 2 280, 288
  Article 5 288
  Article 11 287–8

Article 14 288
Article 16 288
Article 22 280, 284–5, 287
Article 23 285–6
Article 25 285, 286
Article 42 290, 291
Article 43 286, 298
Article 45 289, 290
CRC comparison 280
definition of child 280
minimum recruitment age 34
  high threshold 281
  significance of 282–4
  straight-18 prohibition 280–82
monitoring body *see* African Committee of Experts
most countries not compliant with 294
normative framework 295
preamble 37
special protection for children 285
  continuing during times of conflict 286
  extended to children deprived of family environment 286
  extended to internally displaced children 286
state party obligation on recruitment of under-18s 280
uniqueness of 281–2
African Committee of Experts 282
  adjudication of Uganda case 287
    background 287
    complaints 287–8
    findings 288
    follow-up on implementation 289
    gradual progress following 288–9
    substantive recommendations 288, 289
  call to mainstream rights-based approach to children's rights 294–5
  on children's potential commitment to armed struggle 283
  developing enforcement framework 289
  fact-finding missions 290–91
    Central African Republic 290, 291
    South Sudan 290, 291
  legally binding decisions 288
  mandate
    adjudication 286–7
    cooperation with other institutions regarding children's rights 287, 293
    investigation 286, 290
    state report examination 286
  on state obligations on children's direct participation in hostilities 282–3
  state progress reports 293–5
    paucity of relevant information in 294

Tanzania 294
Uganda 293–4
study on the impact of conflicts and crisis on children in Africa 293
UN counterpart 286
age
  appropriate accountability 23
  of criminal responsibility *see* criminal responsibility
  as social construct 378
  as structural category 378
  of unlawful recruitment *see* recruitment
  voting 8
agency 44, 113, 122–3, 127, 185, 436, 517
  of Afghan children 186–91
    and abuse of authority by community elders 188
    and asylum 187
    cultural/traditional influences on 183, 185, 186
    culturally lacking 187, 191
    lack of in recruitment process 188
    lost in a trade-off between actors 186
    no return home after avoiding recruitment 188
    objectivization v empowerment 189
    and protectors' role in recruitment 186
    resilience as 187
    at time of recruitment 186
  Afghanistan conflict challenging concept of as universally shared value 192
  being adult not equated with empowerment 191
  binding contingencies negating 189
  children as victims deprived of 185, 187
  context shaping 188–9
  definition 274
  delimited, bounded and confined 191
  denial of 111, 122, 284
  exercised on external environment 274
  intent 188
  and intersectionality 189
  Paris Principles ignoring 436
  recognition of 123
  and reconciliation 449–50
  of survival decisions 191
  tactical 191
al-Qaeda
  Birds of Paradise 56
  Boko Haram affiliation 456
  in Iraq (AQI) 211
  /ISIS difference in attitude to women on front line 211
  Youth of Heaven 56

Index   521

armed conflict
  changing nature of 52, 69
  defining 55
  and girls 54
  impact on children 53–4
    invisible 53
    significant harmful threat 53–4
  prolonged conflicts proliferating 53
armed groups
  Abu Sayyaf 220
  Al Aqsa Martyrs 211
  al-Nusra Front 199
  al-Shabaab 4, 196
  Bangsa Moro Islamic Freedom Fighters 220
  child fighters in
    as distinguished from child soldiers 196
    numbers unknown 199
    underreporting of 197
  exploitation of children 195–6
    advantages of 199
    psychological breaks 202
  FLEC-FAC 400
  Free Syrian Army 199
  gender and role differentiation 211–12
  Hamas 204
  Hezbollah 204
  Imarat Kavkaz 211
  IRA 211
    gender equality in 212
  Jama'atu Ahlis Sunna Lidda'awati wal-Jihad see Boko Haram
  Kurdish People's Protection Units 199
  Maute group 221
  Moro Islamic Liberation Front 201
  MPLA 400
  PFLP 208, 211
  recruitment 200–201
    drug and alcohol use during 201–2
    perpetrating acts of extreme violence as part of 202
  Red Brigades 204, 211
  Revolutionary United Front 201
  Sinn Fein 204
  Tamil Tigers see Sri Lanka
  training 207–8
  UNITA 396
  use of education system for recruitment 206–7
  women in 211
  see also individual groups and countries
asylum 21, 390–91, 403
  assessment of claims 403
    no international cooperation on 403–4
  child soldiers 404, 405
  denial of claim 399–400, 401

  age in 405
  Australia 399
  Belgium 399
  Canada 399
  UK 399–400
  USA 400
  global situation 391
  granting
    France 400
    UK 400
    USA 400
  historicity of 390
  seekers 186
  see also refugee law
autoethnography
  auto-photographic research 497–8
  Liberian study 498–505
    do no harm principle see do no harm issues
    vicarious traumatization 503

BACRIM 52, 57, 61–2
  characterization of 61–3, 64
    consequences for child protection 65–6
    as criminal bands 65
    as parties to armed conflict 65
  child recruitment 60
  child recruits 52
    and CODA certification 68
    Constitutional Court recognition as victims 68, 70
    criminal law applied to 61
    included in Victims Unit Registry 69
    no reparation for 68, 69
  composition of 60
  defining 61, 62
  FARCRIM 60
  implications of defining as illegal armed group 62–3, 64
  legal uncertainties for children involved in 67
  Los Rastrojos 60
  as neoparamilitary groups 62
  as threat to human rights 62
  as threat to public order 62
  types of 60
Beah, Ishmael 379–80
  A Long Way Gone (2007) 9, 28
  adaptability 47
  childhood memories 49
  drug use 33
  education 42–3
  exiting childhood 32–3
  father figure 41
  forced recruitment 40
  impossibility of erasing one's past 46–7

indoctrination 33
lure of power 43
orphaned by soldiers 40
rap music 32
rehabilitation 35
repatriation 41–2
resilience 48, 49
status of children in times of conflict 43
Boko Haram 452
  Abu Musab Al-Barnawi 457
  Abubakar Mohammed Shekau 456
  attack on UN headquarters 456
  bay'ah 212
  child abduction 456
  child recruitment 452
  children associated with
    accountability 463–5
    amnesty 465
    detention of 459, 460–61
    differing approaches to 467
    failure to protect 458–9
    and principle of non-refoulement 459–60
    reintegration 465–7
    stigmatization 459
  conflict history 456
  crimes against humanity 457
  defectors' camp 459
  denunciation of 464
  extension of operations 456
  Islamic State in West Africa 452
  Mohammed Nur 457
  Mohammed Yusuf 456
  Multi-National Joint Task Force against 457
  Mustapha Chad 457
  ongoing violence 466
  rise to prominence 456
  sanctions
    EU 457
    UN 456
  sexual violence against women and girls 458
  solidarity with al-Qaeda affiliates 456
  US designation as terrorist group 457
  use of children as suicide bombers 458
  use of female suicide bombers 212, 458
  war crimes 457
  as world's deadliest terrorist group 458
  see also Lake Chad Basin; Nigeria
boy soldiers
  age of recruitment 80
  branding of 78
  recruitment by coercion 77
  recruitment patterns 76, 77, 151–5
  routinely given drugs/alcohol 78, 80, 88
  service in active conflict 76
  sexual abuse by 80
  sexual abuse of 80
  use as guards 79
  use as servants 79
  use as spies 78
  violence against 76, 77, 78
  violence committed by 77, 79, 88
  see also individual countries
British military recruitment 6, 132–33
  advertisements 140–41
  against UNICEF recommendations 133–4
  Be the Best campaign 141
  child recruitment policy
    aimed at increasing numbers of infantry 136
    challenges to 135
    as exploitation 143
    and full and informed consent 135
    legal situation of recruits 135–6
    and mental health 136
    minimum service 136
    parental consent requirement 135
    under-18s 132–3
    weak foundations of 136–7, 145
  child soldier culture 137–40, 145
    Armed Forces Day 138
    cadet programmes in state schools 137–8
    challenging 142–6
    commissioning of military toys 139–40
    everyday normalization 139
    normalization of recruitment of under-18s 137
    school visits 137
    targeting children on social media 139, 140
  child soldiers 133
    exemption from Education and Skills Act 136
    increased risks 136
  counter-recruitment activities 142–3, 146
    #MakeIt18 campaign 144–5
    Action Man: Battlefield Casualties 143–4
    activist groups 143
    direct lobbying 143
    dissemination of information 142–3
    legal challenges 143
  cultural forms of militarization 133, 134
  decline in voluntary recruitment 134–5
  Digital Strategy 140
  direct 137
  indirect 137, 138–9
    Armed Forces Covenant 138
    development of academies and schools run by ex-military personnel 137
    growing number of military charities 138

increase in military presence in public
    spaces 138
  Military to Mentors programme 137
  Troops to Teachers initiative 137
 minimum age 133
  raising 145
 minimum service policy 136
 myths of 133, 136
 This Is Belonging campaign 132, 133,
    140–42
  criticism of 141
  giving sanitized representation of military
    service 142
  glossing over inequalities in the army
    142
  as 'lads on tour' representation of military
    life 141
  media used 140
  playing on psychological weakness of the
    young 141–2
  portraying army as safe place 141
  video adverts 141
 see also historical patterns of recruitment

Cambodia 24, 219
 ECCC *see* international courts and tribunals
 Khmer Rouge 24
Canada
 exclusion proceedings 397
 Immigration and Refugee Protection Act
    394
 Omar Khadr 166, 168–70, 488
 rules of engagement for encounters with
    child soldiers 120
Cape Town Principles 240
Central African Republic 279
 African Committee of Experts' fact-finding
    mission 290, 292
  recommendations 292
  report 292
 child soldiers in 292
 ratification of African Children's Charter
    292
 special tribunal for conflict-related crimes
    (SCC) 292, 353
child
 definition 10, 133, 189
  in Afghanistan 189–90
  African Charter 280
  CRC 375
  international community 189
  Paris Principles 133
  UN 224
 shift in discursive age of 160
 universal 162

child labour 20
 in DRC *see* Democratic Republic of the
    Congo
 as generally neglected field of interest 301
 as highly publicized concern 301
 international 'Worst Forms' of 10, 54, 304,
    307
child perpetrators 325–6, 334
 background as complete defence 338–9
 Dominic Ongwen *see* Ongwen, Dominic
 prosecution 334
  decline of in domestic cases 336
  decline of in international crime 335–6
  in domestic jurisdictions 335
  domestic/international differences 339,
    345
  dominant view in international law
    334–5
  ICTR not indicting 335
  ICTY not indicting 335
  only in exceptional circumstances 337
  recommendations on 342
  SCSL approach 335, 342–3
 as victims by default 339
 victims' experiences 343–4
 see also individual countries
child prostitution 188
 bacha bazi 187–8
child rights
 advocacy 112
 conceptual framework 114–15
 emancipatory impulse 8
 interpretation 114
 as living rights 113
 in the military 121
 as modern concept 162
 no consensus on 113
 participation 113
 protective impulse 8, 111, 112–13
 realized through engagement in military
    121–2
 recruitment to armed groups as violation
    of 54
 social justice 113–14
 translation of 114
child soldiering
 agency in 17
 framing of 513, 514–15
  affective potentialities 516–17
 gendered nature of 15, 74
 global phenomenon 5–6, 279
 historical 17, 36
 minimum age 115
 resilience of phenomenon 283
 responsibility for 9–11

child soldiers
  age range 161–2
  as celebrities 28, 40
  challenging stereotype 134
  as complex trial participants 350
  as constructed in literature see literary narrative
  as contradictory and incompatible term 162–3, 377
  as creation of their environment 223
  defining 4, 5, 240
  as distinct from child fighters 196
  effects of legal categorization 14–15
  empirical description/humanitarian advocacy gap 163–4
  essentialized image of as problematic 171
  as existing in liminal space between child and soldier 258
  exposure to atrocities 439
  gendered division of labour 84
  girls see girl soldiers
  historical amnesia about 150
  historicity of 2, 240
    see also historical patterns of recruitment
  hostilities
    active use in as war crime 120
    minimum age for participation in 119, 120
    prohibition on participation in 119
  humanitarian narrative of 377
  identity see identity
  infantilization of 5, 170
  as inherently shocking concept 377
  international prosecution of 339
  isolation of 208
  justice for 343
  loss of humanity and innocence 378
  in modern Britain see British military recruitment
  as more obedient 89
  as more reliable in combat 89
  myths regarding 134
    pathologizing poorer countries 134
  as new technology 279
  numbers of 160, 224, 279
  as oxymoron 35 36
  pervasiveness of indoctrination 378
  politicization of concept 171
  post-puberty 190, 191–2
  problematization of 513–14, 517–18
    and outrage 516–17
    political work in 515–16
    silencing inherent in 515
  prosecuting 11, 70, 330–31, 332, 346, 352, 369
  protectionism rhetoric/lived reality gap 170

  reality of 1–2
  reimagining 112
  responsibility of 11–13
  self-conceptions 16
  shifting rhetoric on 162–4, 221
    mobilization of public sentiment 162
  simplified image of 1
  spectrum of 191
  as tragic perpetrators and imperfect victims 350
  training see training
  as victims 341–3
    of criminal adult abuse 183
    dangerously simplified view 341
    ICC approach 341, 342
    legally 363–4, 365–6
    loss of status 378–9
    participating/benefitting 363, 364
    SCSL approach 342
    symbolically 364–5
    two-dimensionality of approach 341
  see also individual countries
child witnesses 20–21
childhood
  /adulthood bright line distinction 162, 345
  age-based understanding of 106–7
  loss of 48
  modern concept of 150
  no golden age depiction of 190
  rethinking
    incorporation into law 155
    increasingly idealized 155
    as middle-class process 155
    nineteenth-century beginnings 155
    reality in America 155
  as state of vulnerability 2–3
children
  affected by armed conflict see children affected by armed conflict
  agency 123, 127
    see also agency
  behavioural changes as result of forced recruitment 436–7
  best interests of 9
  changing attitudes towards 1
  criminal responsibility of 110
  gullibility of 39
  key determinants of developmental outcomes 246
  malleability of 37
  militarization 54, 134
  no subjective right to join military 121, 126–7
  protectionist view 111, 122, 128
  right to leave military 121

self-judgment 44
status of
  in Haiti 57
  in times of conflict 43
victimhood 111, 185, 187
  in times of war 43
vulnerability of 54, 171
children affected by armed conflict (CAC) 279, 298
  abuse of 165–70
    FBI involvement 167
  accountability mechanisms for 298, 311
    see also accountability mechanisms
  born in captivity see children born in captivity
  born of conflict-related sexual violence see children born of rape
  detention 7, 165–6
  as having independent response to experienced violence 123
  helping prolong conflict 219
  pernicious nature of violations against 298
  shortcomings of agenda on 298, 309
  as survivors 187
  switching identities 245
  as targets of armed groups 53
  UN CAC agenda 311–12
    inadequacy of protections 9
  as useful tools 54
children born in captivity 242
  bush family 246
  family relationships 246
    confusion and ambivalence over 248–9
    fathers 247–9
    mothers 249–50
  family structures 246–7
  home 243
    the bush as 244, 255
    loss of 245
  largely neglected in global politics 254
  not having symbolic resources 266–7
  notion of place 243–4
    and identity 244–5
  perceptions of 251
  reintegration 252
  unique perspective of 245
  wartime/post-conflict life comparison 251–2
  'war was better than peace' 251, 255
  see also children born of rape
children born of rape 240–42, 254–5
  largely neglected in global politics 254
  in LRA 241–2
    belonging to their fathers 247
    bond with mother 249–50
  complexity of mother–child relationship 250
  family 255
  fatherly love 248
    as highly valued 247
  post-conflict marginalization 242, 250
    by family 250
  post-conflict stigmatization 242, 250, 251
    by community 250–51
  post-conflict violence against 242
  unique reality of 241, 254, 255
  see also children born in captivity
citizenship
  children's 126–7
  citizen–soldier tradition 126
  conferring rights related to the military 125, 126
  free citizen concept 126
citizenship rights
  and joining the military 124, 125, 126
  based on individual freedom 126
  France 124
  South Africa 125
  UK 124
  USA 124–5
  voting 124
Colombia
  Amnesty International reports on 58, 60
  Autodefensas Unidas de Colombia (AUC) 62
  bandas criminales (BACRIM) see BACRIM
  child recruitment 57, 59
    paramilitary/guerilla differences 59
  Children and Adolescence Code Art (175) 66
  children returning direct to home communities 67
  Coalition to Stop the Use of Girls Boys and Youths in the Armed Conflict in Colombia (Coalico) 66
  CODA 68
    certification 68–9
    uncertainty about what constitutes illegal armed group 69
  Colombian Family Welfare Institute (ICBF) 61
  Constitutional Court Judgment C-069 (2016) 68
  Criminal Code 65
  Decree 128 of 2003 68
  demobilization 67–8
  difficulties applying IHL in 63
  emergence of new illegal armed groups 59
  forced disappearances 58
  Hercules Task Force 61
  human rights violations 57–8

ICBF programme for demobilized children 66
  broad concept of recruitment 66
  failures of 67
  refusal of entry into 66
  reintegration 66–7
illegal armed groups 62–3
  government recognition of 69
Integral System of Truth Justice Reparation and Non-Repetition 58
internal armed conflict 57
  2016 Report of the UNSG 60
  ceasefire 58
  parties to 58
  peace agreement 57, 58, 59
internally displaced persons 57
Juvenile Criminal Responsibility System 66
  criminal proceedings against children 66–7
Law 418 of 1997 68
Law 1448 (2011) (Victims and Land Restitution) 65, 69
  no reparation for child BACRIM members 68
Law 1908, Article 2 61
M-19 59
National Liberation Army (ELN) 59
National Victims Unit 57
need to bring BACRIM under legal control 70
need to strengthen child recruitment prevention policy 70
paramilitary groups
  demobilization 59
  government tolerance of 59
Popular Liberation Army (EPL) 59
Popular Revolutionary Anti-Terrorist Army (ERPAC) 64
prosecutorial discretion 66
reintegration 70
reparations 68, 70
Revolutionary Armed Forces (FARC-EP) 52, 58
  agreement to not recruit children 58–9
  demobilization 61
  motivations for joining 210
  sexual violence 57–8, 59
  summary executions 58
  threats to peace 60
United Self-Defense Forces of Colombia (AUC) 60
communities/security actors relationship 180
conflict minerals
  in DRC 301, 302, 304
  International Tin Supply Chain Initiative (iTSCi) 304

OECD
  Due Diligence Guidance on 304–5
  guide to identifying worst forms of child labour in supply chains 305
  traceability initiatives 304
  focus on buyers and economic dimensions 305
conscription 1, 10, 44, 55, 76, 83, 96, 118–19, 126, 150, 156–9, 240, 281, 350, 367–8, 376, 381, 383, 438
Convention Relating to the Status of Refugees (1951) *see* Refugee Convention
CRC 25 477
  /African Charter on the Rights and Welfare of the Child comparison 280
  age of criminal responsibility 327
  Article 1 133
  Article 3 8–9
  Article 12 112, 430, 477
  Article 29 121
  Article 37 464
  Article 38 10, 115, 119, 133, 281–2
  Article 39 285, 412, 488
  Article 40 12, 327, 412
  binding provisions 463–4
  Committee on the Rights of the Child 67
  as contested 113–14
  definition of child 34, 133, 375
  minimum recruitment age 34
  Optional Protocol on the Involvement of Children in Armed Conflict *see* OPAC
  preamble 37
  reintegration provisions 412
crime against humanity 21, 44, 344
  child soldiering as 513
  forced marriage as 11, 15, 342
  mass murder as 354
  rape and sexual slavery as 83
crimes committed by child soldiers *see* child perpetrators
criminal law
  benefitting from literary accounts 45–6
  binary absolutes in 45
criminal proceedings 66, 343
  due process 12
  punishment 12
  sanctions 12
criminal responsibility 46
  15–18-year-olds 376
  actus reus 325
  age 18 standard 336–8, 345
  as bright chronological line 345
  as dominant view in international law 334, 337
  emerging consensus 338, 340

incoherence 340–41
  mitigating sentences of child offenders 338
  as problematic 340
  push towards 340
  shaky foundations of 337
of children 20, 325–6
  see also child perpetrators
  uncertainty in international jurisprudence 325
mens rea 325, 383
  of children 325, 337, 339
minimum age 325, 326
  differing 12
  domestic jurisdictions 328
  ECCC 332
  ECtHR 328–9
  ICTR 331
  ICTY 331
  international courts and tribunals 330
  in international instruments 326–7
  no definitive 333
  Rome Statute 330–31
  SCSL 332–3
  UN Committee on the Rights of the Child 12, 340
  UN Special Panels for Serious Crimes in East Timor 331–2
  for war crimes 334
need for theoretically coherent position on 345–6
/recruitment age conflation 334
see also child perpetrators

Dallaire Romeo 164, 377
  Child Soldier's Initiative 202
data-driven analysis 150–51
  historical patterns of recruitment 151–5
    see also historical patterns of recruitment
  key elements 151
  modern child soldiers *see* child soldiers
  national conscription 157–8
  recruitment by non-state actors 161
  rethinking childhood 155–6
    see also childhood
DDR 452, 471
  activities crucial to stabilization of war-torn societies 452
  best practices
    DDRR 452
    de-radicalization 461–2
    interventions 455
  demobilization 21, 452, 495–6
    self- 471–2, 497
  disarmament 22, 452, 495

entry criteria
  excluding females 496
  favouring males 496
first wave 453–4
  failure of 455
fourth-generation 455
  disengagement and disassociation replacing disarmament and demobilization 455
  as post-conflict endeavour 455
programmes as militarized and gendered 497
reintegration *see* reintegration
second wave 454–5
  agenda 454–5
  aims 454, 455
  broadening focus 454
  community-oriented model 455
shift in direction 455
strict demarcation between war and peace 455
third-generation
  implemented during ongoing conflict 455
  robust peacekeeping 455
UN IDDRS 453–4
  aim of 453
  as best practice 505–6
  challenges 454
  and children 454
  consultation of 'women's organizations' 507–8
  contradiction on gender-related activities 506–7
  focus 454
  not recognizing women commanders 508
  Operational Guide 505, 506
  operational practice 454
  position on prosecution of children 464
  on youth 454, 464
decommissioning 17, 46
Democratic Republic of the Congo *see* DRC
desensitization 18, 47, 205, 223
detention of child combatants
  abuse during 165–70
    Church Report on 166–7
    FBI involvement 167
    pattern of 166, 167
    sleep deprivation 167–8
    techniques of 167
    threats of sexual violence 169
    by US military 166
  Canadian policy 165
  coerced confessions 166, 169–70
  criminalization of combatants 165
  punitive sentences 170
  subverting Geneva Conventions 165–6

treatment as adults 167
without evidence 168–9
disarmament, demobilization and reintegration *see* DDR
disengagement 220, 228, 229
   certificates of 234
   'moral' 205
   PTSD following 229
displacement 245, 291, 391, 436
   camps 410, 439, 442, 473
   external 279
   internal 30, 57, 95, 178, 228, 286
do no harm issues 23–4, 471–2, 489
   discrimination in reintegration programmes 472
      gender-based 475–6
      targeting former child soldiers 473–5
      unintended 476
   imposition of outside approaches 476–7
      challenging 481–2
      children's participation rights 477–8
      exacerbating stigmatization 479
      lack of accountability 482–3
      marginalizing local categories of distress 479–80
      mental health 479–80
      as systemic and neo-colonial 481
   inadvertent harm to others 503
   inadvertent self-harm 502–4
   raised expectations 483–5
      counter-balancing 484–5
      generating frustration and resentment 484
   risks to former child soldiers 485
      labelling 485–6
      re-recruitment 487
      securitization of reintegration programmes 488–9
   short-term funding 484
   sustainability 484
   use of photographs 501–5
Dongala, Emmanuel
   childhood memories 49
   children recruiting children 31–2
   dual nature of child soldiers 35
   education 42
   fall from innocence 34
   growing-up prematurely 30–31
   Johnny Mad Dog (2005) 28, 29, 48, 49–50
   lure of power 43
   recruitment tactics 39
   resilience 48, 49–50
   status of children in times of conflict 43
   violence rendering unrecognizable 33

DRC
   Armed Forces Revolutionary Council (AFRC) 351
   artisanal mining 302
      armed group interference in 303
      ban on 304
      as conflict driver 302
      gold *see* gold mining in DRC
      illegal taxation of 309–10
      proportion of population working in 302
      sexual violence 307
      as source of armed group funding 302
      as source of illicit personal profit 303
   child labour 300, 303, 304
      drivers of 307
      endemic in artisanal mining 299, 301, 305
      forced 307–8
      in gold mining 306–8
   child labour case study 298, 305
      methodology 299–300
   child recruitment 219
   conflict dynamics 300
      child labour *see* DRC, child labour
      cycles of armed conflict 298, 300
   'conflict' minerals
      as conflict driver 301, 302
      international boycott on 304
      international efforts to mitigate impact of 304
   Court of Military Order prosecution of children 336
   economic crime
      as conflict driver 298, 300–304
      mitigating measures 304–5
   economic weight of extractive industry 301–2
   effectiveness of accountability mechanisms in 299, 314, 316–17
      delisting of army 314–16
      judicial 317–19
      sanctions 316
   FARDC 110
      criminal responsibility of children leaving 110–12
      involvement in illicit exploitation of natural resources 303
      UN delisting 314–16
   First Congo War 118–19
   gender-based violence against children as underreported 308
   gold mining *see* gold mining in DRC
   long-standing violations against children in 299
   minimum age for recruitment 110, 127
   non-state armed groups

Alliance of Democratic Forces for the
    Liberation of Congo 118–19
  Congolese Liberation Movement 303
  Democratic Forces for the Liberation of
    Rwanda 305, 455
  Mai Mai Yakutumba 305, 306
  Mayi Mayi Sheka 319
  Rally for Congolese Democracy 302,
    303
  peace agreement (2003) 303
  ratification of OPAC 111
  ratification of UN CRC 10–11
  Second Congo War 302
  signatory to ILO Convention (182) 307
  UN Stabilization Mission to 322

East Timor
  Special Panels for Serious Crimes 331–2
    age of criminal responsibility 353
    Transitional Rules of Criminal Procedure
      331
    trial of 'X' 354
education
  role in child development 42
  as victim of war 42
environmental adversity as determining factor
    in criminal behaviour 385
ethics
  of observation 24
  practitioner 23–4
European Convention on Human Rights
  Article 3 329
European Court of Human Rights 328–9
  T v the United Kingdom 329
  V v the United Kingdom 329

family
  failure of 41
  grounded in positive affiliation 38
  importance of 41–2
forced marriage 11, 15, 99–102, 105, 342
  male experience of in LRA 100, 101, 102
  release from after childbirth 100
France
  Civil Code, Article 21-14-1 124
  Foreign Legion 6, 117, 119, 124
'Free Children From War' conference (2007)
    338

Geneva Conventions
  Additional Protocol I 119, 285, 334
    conflating age of recruitment with age of
      criminal responsibility 334
  Additional Protocol II, Art 4(3)(c) 119
  Common Article 3

  not applying to al-Qaeda 166
  not applying to Taliban 166
  Fourth 285
  prohibition of recruitment and use of
    children under 15 281
  special protection for children 285
girl soldiers
  abduction 82
  branding of 84
  combat service support work 508
    as servants 79, 82, 85
  hidden 2, 24, 493–4, 508, 509
  in DDR 496–7
  need for questions targeting 508–9
  no IDDRS recognition of women as
    commanders 508
  multifaceted roles of 82
  post-conflict ostracization and
    stigmatization 90
  recruitment patterns in Sierra Leone 82
  sexual abuse of 80, 81, 82, 83–4, 85
  training 82
  violence against 82
  violence committed by 82, 83
gold mining in DRC 305
  armed group involvement 308–11
    direct 308, 309
    exclusive control 309
    FARDC 305, 308–9
    indirect 308, 309–10
  child labour 306–8
    boys 306–7
    FARDC exploitation 308, 310–11
    girls 307
  conflict-free certification 305
  forced labour 307, 309
  funding armed conflict 306
  prevalence in eastern DRC armed conflict
    305–6
Gulu district case study 442
  community perception of returnees 450
  data analysis 444
  ethics 443–4
  innocent child discourse 444–5
    community sensitization 425
    forgiveness in 445, 446
    marginalizing alternative discourse 445,
      446, 448
    rehabilitation 445–6
  medical treatment 445
  methodology 443
  psychosocial care 445, 449
  recommendations 450–51
  reintegration 446–8
    challenges 446–7, 450

handover ceremonies 446
recidivism 446, 448
refusal of 447
study site 442–3

Haiti
armed groups in 56–7
child recruitment in 56
demobilizing children in 57
UN Stabilization Mission (MINUSTAH) 56
historical patterns of recruitment
American Civil War 153–5
age at first enlistment 154, 156
Battle of New Market (1864) 154
conscription 156
Enrollment Act (1863) 156
General War Order No (1) 156
parental consent 156
teenagers 154
Union forces 153–4
American Revolutionary Army 151–3
10th Virginia Regiment 153
age distribution of groups 152
age range of soldiers 152–3
Connecticut regiments 152
Daniel Granger 153
focus of recruitment 152
leaders 152
Maryland line 152
NY 2nd Regiment 152
Pennsylvania Line 152, 153
Peter Francisco 153
Rhode Island Regiments 152
continuance by non-state actors 161
World War I 157–8
national conscription 157–8
National Registration Act (UK) (1915) 157
Selective Service Act (US) (1917) 157
underage enlistment 158, 159
humanitarian rhetoric explaining away lethality of children 170

ICC 11, 25, 28, 54, 120, 281, 350
Ahmed al Faqi Al Mahdi 367
Bosco Ntaganda trial 351
on conscription 55, 150
determinate sentences 367
deterrence potential of 318
Germain Katanga 351, 367
Jean Pierre Bemba Gombo 367
Lubanga case *see Prosecutor v Thomas Lubanga Dyilo*
mandate to investigate crimes against children globally 358
Matthieu Ngudjolo Chui acquittal 351
minimum recruitment age 34, 281
no jurisdiction over under 18s 375
Office of Public Counsel for the Victims 382
Ongwen case *see Prosecutor v Dominic Ongwen*
OTP
lack of supervision of intermediaries in *Lubanga* case 359
particular focus of 363
Policy on Children 366
Rome Statute
Article 8(2) 55, 160
Article 26 330, 337, 338, 346, 375
Article 31 383
children's criminal responsibility 330–31, 353
provision for victims 343
identity
child soldiers
discontinuity of experience 258, 259
multiple identities 258
self-construction 258–9
split rebel/civilian 258
children affected by conflict 259
impunity 111–12, 300, 319, 376, 382, 448, 483
anti- 298, 299
cycle of 369
high risk of 64
innocent child discourse creating atmosphere of 448
International Committee of the Red Cross on domestic implementation of IHL 111–12
international courts and tribunals
Central African Republic (SCC) 353
Chad (EAC) 353
child soldiers as perpetrators 369–70, 378
see also child perpetrators
child soldiers as victims 363–9, 370, 378
challenges of 365–6
legal 363–4
participating/benefitting 363, 364
symbolic 363, 364–5
child soldiers as witnesses 355, 361, 370
almost exclusively for prosecution 356
caution over 358–9, 362–3
credibility of 359, 360, 361–2
direct victim accounts 360
practicability concerns 359–60
psychological support for 357
reliability of 359, 360, 361–2
special protection of 356
standards for treatment of 356–7
testimony 357–8, 359, 362

complex challenges of 352
    criminal responsibility *see* criminal responsibility
difficulties dealing with former child soldiers 351–2
Extraordinary Chambers in the Courts of Cambodia (ECCC)
    age of criminal responsibility 332
    focus of 353
ICC *see* ICC
International Criminal Tribunal for Rwanda (ICTR) 25
    no age provision in Statute 353
International Criminal Tribunal for the Former Yugoslavia (ICTY)
    focus 352–3
    no age provision in Statute 352
    Tadic Interlocutory Appeal 55
International Military Tribunal in Nuremberg (IMT) 352
International Military Tribunal in Tokyo (IMTFE) 352
Iraq (IHCC) 353
Kosovo (KSC) 353
Lebanon 353
mandate to prosecute 'the most responsible' for atrocity crimes 352
prosecution of minors 354
    Dominic Ongwen 355
    Elvir Jakupovic 354
    not using power of 352
    who commit crimes as adults 354–5
    'X' 354
SCSL *see* Special Court for Sierra Leone
sentencing 366–7, 369
    and element of compulsion 368
    justification 367–8
    retributive gap in 367
International Covenant on Civil and Political Rights 459
    Article 2 460
    Article 14(4) 332
International Criminal Court *see* ICC
international criminal law 10–11
    aspiration of 346–7
    blind spots 55
international humanitarian law 10
    blind spots 55
    challenges to application of 52, 55, 57
    children as terrorists 56
    combatant/civilian distinction in 56
    proportionality principle 56
    regarding recruitment and deployment of child soldiers 120
    and use of children in terrorist attacks 56

ISIS 175
    adult use of drugs and alcohol 202
    affiliates 212
    Al Khansaa Brigade 212
    branding as utopian state 202
    co-option of DDR programmes 213
    Cubs of the Caliphate 196, 199, 207
        /child soldiers differentiation 202
        funneling children into 203
        male only 207
        and propaganda 203
        sense of camaraderie among 207
        specialized tasks 208–9
        training 207
    de facto authority over Syrian schools 206
    demobilization of child fighters 213
    emigrants to 202–3
    exploitation of children 195, 197
        as executioners 198–9
        expendable/useful distinction 200
        no use of drugs or alcohol 202
        in propaganda 198, 200, 203
        as recruiters 209
        as spies 207
        as suicide bombers 195, 208–9
        training 198, 209
        from young age 204
    forced recruitment 183
    gender differentiation 211
        hyper-segregation 212
    indoctrination 204, 206, 209
    kill houses 198
    loss of territorial control 197
    martyrdom cult 183
    Muhammad Mossalam 198
    payment of children 205
    recruitment 197, 199–203
        abducted children 199
        children born overseas 199, 200, 203
        children born to emigrant parents 201
        children born to local fighters 199, 200
        as differing from other groups 200–203
        direct appeals to young people 203
        of girls/women 203
        grooming process 199–200
        illusion of voluntariness 209–11
        as long-term strategy 213
        orphaned and abandoned children 199
        in schools 206–7
        'voluntary' 183, 199
    Ryan Essid 198
    socialization 204–5
        desensitization to violence 205
    training camps 205
        bleak life in 207

use of social media 197
women in use of 211
Islam
   jihad 230, 232, 234, 235
      cool 209
   Qur'anic teaching 232
   Ummat Al-Islamiyah 230
Islamic State of Iraq and Syria *see* ISIS

justice
   indigenous and traditional 22, 412–15, 430
   social 113–14
   transitional *see* transitional justice

Kafka, Franz 2–3
Kourouma, Ahmadou
   adapting to new realities 47
   Allah Is Not Obliged (2000) 28
      Captain Kid 35
   childhood memories 49
   child-soldier transformation 31
   disintegration of family 38–39
   education 42
   father figure 41
   funeral orations 40–41, 42, 44
   lure of power 43

Lake Chad Basin 23, 455
   Cameroon
      amnesty for child detainees 465
      Anti-Terrorism Law (2014) 462
      death sentence for Boko Haram fighters 462
      no use of DDRR 462–3
   Chad 463
   continuing insecurity in region 466
   differing approaches to terrorist actions across 467
   Niger 461
      amnesty 462
      Ardia ceremonies 465
      convictions for terrorist offences 462
      de-radicalization programme 462
   Nigeria *see* Nigeria
   non-application of non-refoulement principle in 459–60
   see also Boko Haram; DDR
liberation struggles /terrorism distinction 56
Liberia 493
   Abuja II Accord 494
   Armed Forces of Liberia 494
   auto-photographic research approach 497–8
      see also autoethnography
   Charles Taylor *see* Taylor, Charles
   child soldiering in 495
   Comprehensive Peace Agreement 495
   DDR in 495–6
      girls left behind in 496–7
   ECOMIL in 494–5
   first civil war 494
   Independent National Patriotic Front of Liberia 494
   Liberians United for Reconciliation and Democracy 210, 494
      women in 212
   Movement for Democracy in Liberia 210, 494
   National Patriotic Front of Liberia 494
   National Transitional Government 495
   second civil war 494–5
   UN Mission in 495
   United Liberation Movement of Liberia 494
literary narrative 14, 28–9
   A Long Way Gone see Beah, Ishmael
   Allah Is Not Obliged see Kourouma, Ahmadou
   benefitting criminal law 45–6
   Chris Abani, *Song for Night* (2007) 28
   Couo-Zotti Florent, *Charly en geurre* (1998) 28
   Dayo Olopade Dayo, *The Bright Continent* (2014) 38
   dual nature of child soldiers 35–6
   film
      Kim Nguyen, *War Witch* (2012) 28 41
      Neil Abramson, *Soldier Child* (1998) 28
      Sorious Samura, *Return to Freetown* (2002) 28
   God of War game 30
   Hannah Arendt, *The Crisis in Education* (1954) 37
   Johnny Mad Dog see Dongala, Emmanuel
   Joseph Plumb Martin, *Private Yankee Doodle* 153
   Ken Saro-Wiwa, *Sozaboy* (1985) 28
   recruitment 41
   WEB Du Bois, *Souls of Black Folk* 47–48
   William Golding, *Lord of the Flies* 33–34
living rights 16, 112, 113–15, 127
Lord's Resistance Army 24, 44, 409–11, 436
   aims 410
   bases in Sudan 98
   child abduction and forced recruitment 438–9
   children born in *see* children born in captivity
   consensual affairs 103
   female power in 102–4
      coercive sexual relations with boys 102, 103, 106

girls in 241
Joseph Kony 98, 241, 410
  see also Kony, Joseph
male sexual violence against boys 104–5
nepotism in 101
organized around military–familial unit 98
rape
  children born of 241–2
    see also children born of rape
  by lower ranks 99
receiving aid from Sudanese government 98
retreats to Sudan (1993; 2008) 98, 410
return to Uganda (2003) 98, 410
sexual governance 98–9
  affairs forbidden 99, 100
  consequences of breaking rules 106
  distribution of young girls 100
  forced marriage 99–102
  involvement of Joseph Kony in 99, 100
  permission to marry 100
  rape forbidden 99
  rationales for 100–101
  by ruling elite 101
  sex only within marriage 99, 101
  see also forced marriage
sexual violence in 107
'socialization' of abducted children 98–9
state of coercion in 99, 101
ting tings 100
use of spiritual rituals 416–17
Lubanga, Thomas 11, 281, 341
  ICC conviction 317
    deterrence value of 317
  scope of crimes 341
  victimizing children 341

Machel Report 1, 53, 186, 311, 337
Madrid Guiding Principles (2005) 461
migration
  involuntary/forced 390
    see also asylum; refugees
  irregular 390–91
  voluntary 390
military service representation/reality gap 132
moral responsibility 44, 46, 382
motherhood 250, 476
Mozambique
  FRELIMO 475–6
  RENAMO 475

neo-colonialism 23, 479, 481
Netherlands
  Aliens Manual 395–6
  exclusion proceedings 396

NGOs
  Amnesty International 60, 301, 413
  Child Soldiers International 28, 36, 117, 135, 164, 195–6
  Coalition to Stop the Use of Child Soldiers 117, 119
  Coalition to Stop the Use of Child Soldiers in Paraguay 116
  Conflict Dynamics International 311, 314
  Gulu Support the Children Organization 424, 425–8
  Human Rights Watch 64, 205, 283
  International Crisis Group 60, 64
  Rebuild Hope for Africa 317
  War Child 28
  World Vision 424, 425–8
Nigeria
  action plan to end and prevent child recruitment 459
  armed conflict in 456
  Boko Haram see Boko Haram
  Civilian Joint Task Force recruiting children 459
  DDRR programme 460
    de-radicalization 461–2
    see also DDR
  detention of terrorist suspects 460–61
  state forces
    allegations of sexual violence 458
    failure to protect children 458
  state of emergency 456

Ongwen, Dominic 12, 21, 44–5
  as both victim and perpetrator 46, 344–5, 379
  as candidate for RSB (rotten social background) defence 385
  challenging questions
    accountability 381, 382–3
    regarding treatment of 374–5
    sentencing 382
    at what point did he become a killing machine? 378
    at what point did he cease to be a victim? 378
    whether scapegoat for Joseph Kony 381–2
  as complex political victim 45
  duress defence 383–4
  ICC trial see Prosecutor v Dominic Ongwen
  indoctrination 383
  LRA abduction 351
  as mass murderer 382
  mental health 344, 383
  as not having requisite mens rea 383
  not simply following orders 384–5

socialization within LRA 387
Stockholm syndrome 383
OPAC 9, 28, 150–51, 281
   Article 1 9, 115
   Article 2 9, 115
   Article 3 9, 54–5, 116, 117, 118, 119, 121
   Article 4 10, 115, 118
   Article 8 116
   on child recruitment 54–5, 115, 116
   interpretation of 'take part in hostilities' 376
   on voluntary recruitment 116, 281

Paris Principles 3–4, 436
   'children associated with armed forces and armed groups' 4, 240
   cultural reintegration practices 412
   see also reintegration
   definition of child 133
   guiding reintegration organizations 437
   innocent child discourse 436, 440, 441, 442
      and accountability 448–9
      as silencing victims 437–8
      need for critical examination 448
   neglecting changed status of returnees 437
   non-refoulement gap 459
   as not fit for purpose in West Africa 459
   provisions for reintegration and rehabilitation 441
   reintegration organizations' adoption of 440
parties to conflict, legal determination of 63, 64
Philippines 217–18
   Abu Sayyaf 220
   anting-anting culture 225
   Autonomous Region of Muslim Mindanao 217
   Bangsa Moro Islamic Freedom Fighters 220
   case study
      conceptual framework 222–3
      methodology 222
      objective 221
      scope and limitations 223–4
      significance 222
   Catholic Relief Services 229
   child soldiers 217, 218
      auxiliary roles 227, 228, 229, 232, 233
      factors influencing disengagement 233–4
      factors influencing engagement 224–31
      female 233
      fighting 227, 228, 233
      indoctrination 232, 233
      madrasah education 234–6
      relatives not opposing enlistment 230
      remuneration 226
      shift in motivation 225
      training 231–2
   child warrior as engrained cultural phenomenon 220
   Comprehensive Agreement on Bangsa Moro 236
   declaration of martial law 225
   disengagement 228, 229, 231
      demobilization 234
      as result of motivational shift 234
      temporary 233–4
   Framework Agreement on Bangsa Moro (2012) 236
   freedom fighters 227
   historical conflict 217, 218, 220, 236
      Moro resistance to American occupation 226
      Moro resistance to Spanish occupation 217–18, 220
   Institute of Peace and Development in Mindanao 229
   internally displaced persons 228
   Lanao provinces pro-ISIS/other Muslims distinction 234
   madrasah (*madaris*)
      definition 234
      developmental/formal 235
      institutionalization 235
      integrated/pilot 235
      lack of government supervision 235
      as platform for ideological propagation 236
      radicalization in 235, 236
      teaching jihad as Islamic obligation 226, 229–30
      traditional/weekend 235
   madrasah education 234–6
      following foreign curricula 235
      history 235
      major factor in recruitment 221, 222, 226
      as parallel system of education 237
   Maute group 221, 231
      allegiance to ISIS 221
      cash for war approach 234
      Dawlah 232
      defeat of 234
   Mindanao
      Autonomous Region of Muslim Mindanao 236
      Barracudas 225
      as belonging to Muslims 226, 229
      Blackshirts 225
      Ilaga group 225
      insurgency as part of community life 233

Mindanao Crisis 225
Muslim/Mindanao Independence
   Movement 225
recruitment of child soldiers 225–6
Moro Islamic Liberation Front 220
   Bangsa Moro Armed Force 234
   child soldiers in 224
   demobilization 237
   disengaging child soldiers 220, 234
   female child soldiers 233
   origins 225
   peace agreement 225
   terror tactics 223
   UNICEF action plan 224
Moro National Liberation Front 220
   origins 225
   peace agreement 225
   terror tactics 223
Muslim Mindanao Autonomy Act No. (279) 234
recommendations
   autonomy in southern provinces 237
   education 237
   peace-building process 236–7
   reintegration of former child soldiers 238
recruitment
   through cash inducement 232
   growing up in armed group 226, 227
   indoctrination 223
   induction of children into militant groups 223
   through *madaris* 227, 234
   by parents 226
   radicalization in religious boarding schools 224
   shift in 225–6
   of under-18s 224
   voluntary 227
Republic Act No. 11054/Bangsa Moro Organic Law 237
Republic Act No. (6734) 236
Treaty of Paris (1898) ceding to USA 226
unresolved armed conflict in 224
   potential for *ridu* 231
   siege of Marawi 218, 220, 221
place
   as activity 243–4
   identity 244–5
   as meaning 244
   as physical setting 243
political action
   as privilege of adulthood 122
   youth activism 16, 122, 144
political violence 122
   compliance approach 122–3

difference approach 122, 123
manipulation approach 122
post-colonial Africa 279–80
   Burundi 210
   African Charter on the Rights and Welfare of the Child (1990) *see* African Children's Charter
   African Committee of Experts on the Rights and Welfare of the Child *see* African Committee of Experts
   African Union/Organization of African Unity 280
      proposed Pan-African legal instrument to combat child soldiering 280
   Angola 279
   CAR *see* Central African Republic
   Congo *see* Democratic Republic of the Congo
   Mozambique 279
   Somalia 279
   South Sudan *see* South Sudan
   Sudan 279
      civil war 98
      prosecution of children 336
   Uganda *see* Uganda
   use of child soldiers 279
post-conflict marginalization 242, 250
Prosecutor v Dominic Ongwen 344–5, 351, 355, 374, 388
   accountability 382–3
   challenges of 375, 381–2
   charges 374
   complexity of case 382
   defence 383–5
   duress 383–4
Prosecutor v Thomas Lubanga Dyilo
   child soldiers as only victims 343–4
   child soldiers not deemed credible witnesses 350, 359, 362–3
   conviction 283, 317
   exclusion of under-16s from court 351
   indirect victims 344
   not recognizing victims of child soldiers' actions 343
   reparations judgment 342
   sentence 367
   sentencing 368
   thematic prosecution 341, 343, 362
   uniqueness of 363

reconciliation 22, 412
   cultural mechanisms 414
      traditional rituals 413
   see also reintegration; transitional justice

recruitment 5
  abduction 8
  accountability for unlawful 160, 292, 317–19
  Australia 134
  by being born into armed groups 8, 18–19
  and belonging 16
  Burma 219
  Cambodia 24, 219
  Canada 6
  commonalities in 197–8
  conscientious objectors 126
  conscription 8, 55, 150, 158–9
    British in WWI 158–9
    effect on child recruitment 159
    US in WWI 159
  in diaspora communities 195–6
  enlistment *see* voluntary recruitment
  forced by family 184
  France 6
  Germany 6–7
    under-18s 132
  in Great Lakes region of Africa 202
  of Hazara children 188
  historical patterns of *see* historical patterns of recruitment
  increasing 224
  intensified and systematic 219
  international standards 54
    best practice 9
    conscription 55
    lack of clarity on 55
  lure of power 43
  mass warfare as curtailment of recruiting child soldiers 159
  minimum age 34, 115, 240
    customary international law 281
    enforcement problem 283–4
  Myanmar 6
  by non-state actors 161
  OPAC safeguards on 116
  radicalization through schools 224
  re-recruitment 487
  of rescued child soldiers into state armed forces 440
  role of peers in 210, 217
  routine use of alcohol and drugs 201–2
  Sri Lanka 24
  straight-18 approach 35, 115, 133
    reluctance to adopt 37
  UK 6, 132
    see also British military recruitment
  unlawful 10, 11
  USA 6
    under-18s 132
  voluntary *see* voluntary recruitment

Refugee Convention 390
  Article 1F 394
  basic rights under 391–2
  exclusion clause 392–3
refugee law 391–3
  Aliens Manual (Netherlands) 395–6
  child soldiers 394–5, 403
    as particular social group 398–9, 404
  children's procedures 393–4
  criminal prosecution of criminal refugees 401
  denial of status 392
  enforcement procedures 402
  evidence needed 394
  exclusion numbers 394–5
  exclusion proceedings 394, 395
    Australia 397–8
    Belgium 398
    Canada 397
    child soldiers 395, 396–7
    children in 395
    Denmark 398
    duress defence 405
    France 398
    issue of age in 405
    Luxembourg 398
    Netherlands 396
    USA 398
  expanded forms of protection 392
  Immigration and Refugee Protection Act (Canada) 394
  limited immigration status 402
  non-exclusion proceedings 398–401
  persecution 399, 404
  refoulement 392
  Refugee Convention 1F exclusion 401–2
  refugee status 392, 401
    /subsidiary protection status differences 401
  standard of proof 394
  subsidiary protection status 401
    limited permit to stay 401
    persons with criminal background 401
  undesirable but unreturnable persons 402–3, 404–5
    child soldiers as 405
    detention 402–3
    domestic prosecution 402
    international prosecution 402
    policy brief 402, 403
    temporary residency permit 402
    as undocumented migrants 402
  see also asylum
rehabilitation

and religious conversion 445
resilience as necessary condition of 48
see also Gulu district case study;
  reintegration
reintegration 19, 22, 23, 253, 258–9, 273–4,
  409, 452, 496
  Acholi ceremonies
    kwero merok 419, 422
    lwoko pik wang 418–19
    mato oput 417–18, 419–20, 421–2, 424, 432
    moyo kom/yubu kum 418, 419
    nyono tong gweno 412, 418
    ryemo jok 419
  after LRA captivity 409–11, 420–24
    Child Protection Units 410
    children born in captivity 423
    perception of child returnees 410–11
  challenges 440, 446–7
    fear of *cen* 440, 447
  of children associated with Boko Haram
      465–7
    in Chad Basin 465–6
    as priority 465
    transposition of US multidisciplinary
      intervention approach 466
  cultural 409, 412, 432–3
    Angola 480
    cen as barrier to (Uganda) 423
    as essential to children 412
    facilitating acceptance 423
    little local/international interface 414
    numbers engaging in 420–21
    purification rituals 413
    reconciliatory rituals 413
    traditional healing rites 413
  definition 409
  disarmament demobilization and *see* DDR
  Gulu district case study *see* Gulu district
      case study
  GUSCO reception centres 425–8
    community sensitization 425
    counselling 425
    family tracing 425
    use of traditional ceremonies 425–6
  individualistic approach ignoring indigenous
      knowledge 424
  key mediators 259
  positive motivations behind 471
  programmes
    differing approaches 428
    effectiveness 471–2
    ethics 472
    gendered 476
    ignoring children's participation rights
      477–8

limited success of 431–2, 437
risk of securitization 488–9
unintentionally promoting social division
    472–3
psychosocial support 412
refusal of 447
self- 497
superficial community forgiveness 423
symbolic resources and *see* symbolic
    resources
undocumented returnees 439–40
UNICEF 428–31
  best practices 430–31
  child rights perspective on 430, 431
  concerns over indigenous ceremonies 430
  counselling 429
  supporting other NGOs 428–9, 433
  and use of indigenous ceremonies 429–30
World Vision reception centres 426–8
  Children of War Rehabilitation Centre
      426
  community sensitization 426
  family tracing 426
  opposition to indigenous ceremonies 427
  positive aspects 428
  religion and prayer as foundation of work
      426
  use of Western psychotherapeutic
      methods 426
see also reconciliation; transitional justice
resettlement 168, 393, 436, 438, 447
resilience 47, 49–50, 345, 514
  and black survival of slavery in America
      47–8
  memory as foundation of 48–9
  as necessary condition of rehabilitation 48
  suffering closely related to 270
rules of engagement 164–5
  Canadian Armed Forces Joint Doctrine
      Note 2017-01 Child Soldiers 164–5
  detention of child combatants 165
  firing on child combatants 164–5
Rwanda
  age of criminal responsibility 335
  genocide 164
  recruitment 219
  re-education centres 335
  Rwandan Patriotic Army 118
  Rwandan Patriotic Front 118, 351
  UNAMIR 164

sensitization 22–3, 422
  community 425
sexual violence
  against boys *see* sexual violence against boys

against girls *see* sexual violence against girls
  avoiding conceptual trap 96–7
  discourses focusing on women and girls 95
  dual form of 95
  forced marriage *see* forced marriage
  gendered and age-based assumption about 96
  insufficient language on 96
  perpetrators as victims 107
  problematic framework 100, 105
  relational approach to 97, 100, 105
  underreporting of 96
sexual violence against boys 15–16
  discourses silent on 95, 106, 107
  in Lord's Resistance Army 102–4, 104–5, 107
  male commanders in LRA 104–5
  as social taboo 95
    heteronormative ideals of manhood and masculinity 106
sexual violence against girls 80, 81, 82, 83–4, 85
  as bush wives 82
  forced marriage 85
  pregnancy 82, 83
Sierra Leone
  Armed Forces Revolutionary Council 74, 76, 81
    girl soldiers recruited 81
  boy soldiers 71
    Small Boys Units 76, 78, 351
    see also boy soldiers
  Civil Defence Forces/*Kamajors* 74, 86, 87
    Avondo society 88
    Bondo society 88
    breakdown of prohibitions 86
    child recruitment 86, 87, 89
    female initiates 89, 90
    motivations for joining 209
    popular support for 90
    rapid enlargement 86
    Small Hunters 89
  gender difference in age of abduction 77
  gendered targeting of children 81
  girl soldiers 81
    Small Girls Units 77, 84, 351
    see also girl soldiers
  internal armed conflict 74
  recruitment 219
  Revolutionary United Front 74, 201–2
    boy soldiers recruited 76
    gendered role development 211–12
    girl soldiers recruited 81
  Special Court for *see* Special Court for Sierra Leone
  training of child soldiers 77–8
    length of 77
  Truth and Reconciliation Commission 92, 355, 381
  use of forced marriage 80–81
  West Side Boys 164
socialization 385–7
  and adaptability 386
  learning process 386
  positive reinforcement 386, 387
  social institutions facilitating 386
South Africa
  Truth and Reconciliation Commission 123
  Youth Day 125
South Sudan 279
  African Committee of Experts' fact-finding mission 290, 291–2
    recommendations 291–2
    report 291
  Child Rights Act (2008) 291–2
  commitment to demobilization of under-18s 291
  commitment to ending recruitment of under-18s 291
  special tribunal to investigate conflict-related human rights abuses 292
Special Court for Sierra Leone 10, 350
  AFRC trial 74
  age of criminal responsibility 332–3
  Alex Brima conviction 351
  Brima Kamara conviction 351
  CDF trial 74
  Charles Taylor trial 75, 84
    child witness testimonies 358
  child witnesses 356, 357, 362
  gendered construction of boys 91
    invisibility of sexual abuse against boys 80
    potential victim status of boys forced to commit rape not discussed 80–81
    visibility of sexual violence by boys 80
  gendered construction of girls 91, 92
    in AFRC and RUF
    emphasis on sexual violence against as civilians 83
    little testimony on experience as soldiers 83, 86
    sexual violence/standard recruitment distinguished 83, 90
  invisibilities based on gender in CDF trial 89
    absence of the stories of girls 89–90
    all male testimony 89
    directly-recruited boy soldiers 91
    exclusion of all evidence of sexual and gender-based violence 90–91
    not distinguishing forced/voluntary enlistment into CDF 87

not prosecuting former child soldiers 351, 381
prosecution of 15–18-year-olds 335
prosecution of war crimes
  child recruitment and use as soldiers 74, 87, 351
  convictions 74–5
  rape and sexual violence 83
  RUF trial 74
  sentencing 368–9
Santigie Kanu conviction 351
sentencing 366–7
special penal provisions regarding adolescents 353
Statute 281
  age provisions 353
  Article 4(c) 160, 342
  Article 7 333
surfacing gendered experience of children 75, 83, 92
  obscuring sexual and gender-based violence against girl soldiers 83
task of 74
testimonies 75, 91
  Akiatu Tholley 82–3
  Edna Bangura 84
  Komba Sumana 79
  Witness TF1-026 84–5
  Witness TF1-143 78, 79, 81
  Witness TF1-157 76
  Witness TF1-158 76–7
  Witness TF2-002 88–9
  Witness TF2-021 88
  Witness TF2-140 87–8, 91
  Witness TFI-199 358
Sri Lanka
  Liberation Tigers of Tamil Eelam (LTTE) see Sri Lanka, Tamil Tigers
  Sinhala security forces targeting children 219
  Tamil Tigers 24, 201, 211
    motivations for joining 210
    recruitment 219
    training 208
state responsibility 10, 36–8
  failure of 41
  for safety of children 37
survival 31, 38, 47, 86, 90, 186, 191, 219, 368, 514
symbolic resources
  Acholi concept of 'piny maber' 275
  children born in captivity not having 266–7
  contributing to understanding of agency 274
  definition 260
  external 260
  formerly abducted young women's use of 265–6
  to cultivate resilience in their children 272–3
  imaginings of the future 267, 275
  to mediate sense of self 265
  memories of home 266, 274
  psychological distantiation 266
  as psychosocial trauma interventions 275
  riddle telling 273
  rituals 270–72
  songs and storytelling 268–9
  supporting one-another 269–70
  use of prayer 267–8, 274–5
intra-personal 259
maintaining sense of continuity 267
PAR study
  design 261
  materials 263
  methodology 263–4
  participants 261–5
relational 259–60
rituals 270
  cleansing 270–71
  symbolic acts of discontinuity 271–2
use of 260–61
  cultural element 260
world-making 269
Syrian Observatory for Human Rights 199, 204

Talal al-Zahrani, Yasser 166
Taleban 175, 176, 178
  Afghanistan Islamic Emirate 177
    Rules and Regulations 189–90
  /community relations 180, 185
    and establishing legitimacy 185
    martyrdom and honour discourse 183
    no united approach to 180–81
    using local feuds to establish authority 180
    using local resentment against authorities 180
    using local resentment against foreign troops 180
  controlling faction 185
  counter-offensive 176
  increasing area of control 180
  motivations for joining 210
  narrative of adulthood 189–90
  recruitment 178–9
    avoiding 179
    as endemic 179
    impact of rivalry with other groups 179
    at schools and mosques 179
    through tribal agreements 184
    of workers for illegal mines 179

recruitment of child soldiers 181–3
  as fighting asset 183–4
  as force enablers 184
  forced 182
  forced by family 184
  in Pakistan 182
  as permanent 181
  recent surge in 181
  relying on children's lack of agency 188
  targeted 182
  voluntary 183
  vulnerable children 182, 183
 shadow provincial governments 178
 Wasil Ahmad 181–2
technofetishism 139–40
terrorism
 characteristics predisposing towards 223
 children implicated in 17–18, 55–6, 164
 lack of clear definition 56
 /liberation attacks distinction 56
 martyrdom
  thatkodai brigades 201
 suicide bombers 195–6
  median age of 196
  training 196
  women and girls 212
 see also individual groups
Timor-Leste 118
 Armed Forces for the National Liberation of East Timor 118
 exclusion of child soldiers from peace process 123
torture, admissions made under not admissible in court 168
total institution (Erving Goffman's) 387
training 198, 207–8, 209
  combat 232
  firearms 231
  first aid 231
  girl soldiers 82
  physical 231
transitional justice 12–13, 412
 art and drama therapy 13
 ceremonial rituals 13
 community service 13
 formal 412
 indigenous mechanisms 412
  Acholi 416
   see also Uganda, Acholi cosmology
  as alternative form of accountability 413
  as complementary to criminal justice procedures 413
  effectiveness of 412
  as especially helpful for children 412
  lack of use of 442–3
  little local/international interface 414
  positive influence of 422–3
  potential contribution 412
  refusal to participate 423
  use of for former child soldiers 420–21
 rebuilding trust 13
 truth commissions 12
 see also reintegration
translation of norms 114

Uganda 96–8
 accepting the Straight-18 prohibition rule 284
 Acholi ceremonial 417–20
  mato oput as spiritual cleansing 420
  mato oput embracing collective as well as individual guilt 420
  see also reintegration
 Acholi cosmology 415–17
  cen 415–16, 439
  central to understanding and aiding adversely psychologically-affected youth 416
  cleansing rituals 416
  jok (jogi) 415
  spiritual pollution 416
  syncretic relationship with Christianity 416
 Alice Lakwena 98, 99, 438
 Amnesty Act (2000) 414
 Amnesty Commission 414
 amnesty process 382
 coup-d'etat in 98
 Holy Spirit Mobile Forces 98, 438
 ICC Act (2010) 379
 Ker Kwaro Acholi 417, 418, 421
 Lord's Resistance Army *see* Lord's Resistance Army
 LRA Agreement on Accountability and Reconciliation (2007) 414
 minimal government assistance for child victims of conflict 252–3
 National Resistance Army (NRA) 98, 438
  acts of terror 98
 National Resistance Movement 438
 northern Uganda war 98
  displaced population 438
  history 438
  Operation Iron Fist 98, 410
  peace talks 98, 414
  protected villages 438
 recommendations on children born within LRA
  access to education 253
  access to land 253

access to vocational training 253
protective laws 254
sentitization at all levels 253–4
reintegration 410–11
and Acholi culture of forgiveness 414
amnesty for all formerly abducted persons 252
and concept of *cen* 411, 414, 419
GUSCO reception centre 425–8
processes as deviating from accountability and justice norms 442
Reception Centre focus 479
sensitization 442
use of traditional mechanisms 414
World Vision Reception Centre 425–8
Tambo 110, 127
conviction for desertion 110, 111
Ugandan People's Defence Forces 98
Child Protection Units 410
Women's Advocacy Network 97
UK
appropriation of poppy symbolism 139
Education and Skills Act 136
military recruitment *see* British military recruitment
UN
Assistance Mission for Rwanda (UNAMIR) 164
Beijing Rules age of criminal responsibility 327
Children's Fund *see* UNICEF
Committee on the Rights of the Child 12, 113, 115, 339–40
minimum age of criminal responsibility 327
Common Approach to Justice for Children 412
Convention against Transnational Organized Crime (Palermo Convention) 391
Convention on the Rights of the Child *see* CRC
Group of Experts 312, 314
Integrated DDR Standards (IDDRS) 23, 453
see also DDR
list of armed groups recruiting child soldiers delisting mechanism 314–16, 321
Rights Up Front initiative 460
sanctions 316, 494
Sanctions Committee 456
list 456, 457
Secretary-General on Children and Armed Conflict 6, 57
Secretary General's list of countries recruiting children 289

Security Council
Counter-Terrorism Committee Executive Directorate 461
on de-listed parties 64
Resolution 2068 (2012) 63–4
resolutions 1
Special Representative for Children and Armed Conflict 1, 6, 28, 57
Special Representative on Violence Against Children 57
Stabilization Mission in Haiti (MINUSTAH) 56
Stabilization Mission to the DRC 322
Working Group on Children and Armed Conflict 321–2
UNICEF 1, 409, 425
advocating Straight-18 ban 281
Survey for War Affected Youth 416
Universal Declaration of Human Rights (1948) 126
USA
Constitution 125
debate over right to military service 125
District of Columbia v Heller 125
Dodd Frank Act (2010) sec (1502) 304
military recruitment *see* historical patterns of recruitment; recruitment, USA
Office of Juvenile Justice and Delinquency Prevention 466
US Institute of Peace 179
war on terror 170

Vancouver Principles on Peacekeeping and the Prevention of the Recruitment and Use of Child Soldiers 4
victim
complex 45, 379
child soldiers 380
continuing 380
victimhood, whether can be lost 380
victimization 383
victim-perpetrator 44, 409
accountability 379
see also accountability
Dominic Ongwen 46, 378–9
see also ICC; Ongwen, Dominic
and duress 383–4
as inherently contradictory concept 379–80
point of transition 379
prosecution of 57
Vienna Convention on the Law of Treaties, Article 31 117
violence
normalization of 77, 137

political *see* political violence
sexual *see* sexual violence
voluntary recruitment 6, 8
  by armed groups 118
    in DRC 118–19
    in Rwanda 118
    straight-18 approach 118
    in Timor-Leste 118
    where group has supplanted national army 118, 119
  of children 150
  in China 116–17, 119
  competing approaches to 117
  and death of caregivers 200–201
  illusion of 209–11
    when no alternative 209
  minimum age 115–16, 127
    arguments in favour of low 117
    asymmetries in 119
    attempts to raise 116
    double standards of 127
    nations having low 116–17
    under OPAC 10, 115–16, 120
  motivations for 8, 18, 210–11
  protection 209–10
  safeguards 120–21
  UK State Party report (2007) relating to 118
  of under-18s 150

war
  all children being victims of 43
  as disruptor of societal and personal development 30
  modern Western experience of 171–2
  as shortcut to adulthood 33
war crimes 344
  age of responsibility in 334
  mens rea of children 337
  under Rome Statute 55, 375
  use of children under 15 in armed conflict 28, 54, 55, 376